# THE HISTORY OF THE IRISH FAMINE

# THE HISTORY OF THE IRISH FAMINE

*Edited by*
*Christine Kinealy, Gerard Moran*
*and Jason King*

Volume I

The Great Irish Famine

*Edited by Christine Kinealy*

LONDON AND NEW YORK

First published 2019
by Routledge
2 Park Square, Milton Park, Abingdon, Oxon OX14 4RN

and by Routledge
711 Third Avenue, New York, NY 10017

*Routledge is an imprint of the Taylor & Francis Group, an informa business*

© 2019 selection and editorial matter, Christine Kinealy, Gerard Moran and Jason King; individual owners retain copyright in their own material.

The right of Christine Kinealy, Gerard Moran and Jason King to be identified as the authors of the editorial material, and of the authors for their individual chapters, has been asserted in accordance with sections 77 and 78 of the Copyright, Designs and Patents Act 1988.

All rights reserved. No part of this book may be reprinted or reproduced or utilised in any form or by any electronic, mechanical, or other means, now known or hereafter invented, including photocopying and recording, or in any information storage or retrieval system, without permission in writing from the publishers.

*Trademark notice*: Product or corporate names may be trademarks or registered trademarks, and are used only for identification and explanation without intent to infringe.

*British Library Cataloguing-in-Publication Data*
A catalogue record for this book is available from the British Library

*Library of Congress Cataloging-in-Publication Data*
A catalog record for this book has been requested

ISBN: 978-1-138-20077-7 (set)
ISBN: 978-1-138-20087-6 (volume I)
eISBN: 978-1-315-51389-8 (set)
eISBN: 978-1-315-51381-2 (volume I)

Typeset in Times New Roman
by Apex CoVantage, LLC

# CONTENTS

*Chronology of the Great Famine, 1845 to 1852*  viii

The Great Famine revisited: general introduction  1

**PART I**
**Poverty and perspectives: Ireland before 1845**  61

1 George Nicholls Esq., *Poor Laws – Ireland. Three reports by George Nicholls, Esq., to her Majesty's principal Secretary of State for the Home Department* (British Parliamentary Papers, 1836–1838)  63

2 Lydia Jane Fisher, *Letters from the Kingdom of Kerry in the year 1845*. Letter VIII (1847)  119

3 Reports of Messrs. Kane, Lindley and Playfair, Commissioners, *On the potatoe [sic] disease* (1845)  127

**PART II**
**The potato blight examined**  147

4 Reports of the Mansion House Committee on the potato disease in 1845 (1846)  149

5 Alfred Smee, *On the cause of the potato disease: Aphis vastator* (1846, 1847 and 1878)  160

## PART III
### Appeals, prays and philanthropy — **169**

6 Dr John Edgar, *An appeal in Belfast for the people of Connaught* (October 1846) — 171

7 The Queen's Letter for Ireland (January 1847) and consequent parliamentary questions — 183

8 Bishop Hughes, *A lecture on the antecedent causes of the Irish Famine in 1847* (New York, March 1847) — 189

## PART IV
### Visitors to Ireland — **207**

9 Elihu Burritt, *A journal of a visit of three days to Skibbereen, and its neighbourhood* (February 1847) — 209

10 William Bennett, *Six weeks in Ireland* (March and April 1847) — 221

## PART V
### Official response and reaction — **301**

11 Isaac Butt, *A voice for Ireland, the Famine in the land. What has been done and what is to be done* (1847) — 303

12 Charles E. Trevelyan, *The Irish crisis: being a narrative of the measures for the relief of the distress caused by the Great Irish Famine of 1846–7* (January 1848) — 370

## PART VI
### Reflections and regrets — **455**

13 W. R. Wilde, *Irish popular superstitions* (1852) — 457

14 S. Reynolds Hole, *A little tour in Ireland by an Oxonian*, Chapter V (1859) — 466

15 John Mitchel, *The last conquest of Ireland, perhaps*. Chapter xxiv (1861) — 472

**PART VII**
**A poetic ending** **487**

16  George Francis Train, *Three cheers for the Famine* (1872)   489

   *Bibliography* 493
   *Keywords* 499

# CHRONOLOGY OF THE GREAT FAMINE, 1845 TO 1852

## 1845

| | |
|---|---|
| February | The Devon Commission on land-holding in Ireland submitted its report. |
| August | A new disease, increasingly referred to as blight, was damaging potato crops in parts of mainland Europe and appeared to be spreading westwards. It was first recorded in Ireland at the Botanic Gardens in Dublin on 20 August. |
| September | The blight was sighted in many parts of Ireland, although its appearance was patchy. The diseased potatoes were inedible. |
| October | The British Prime Minister, Sir Robert Peel, summoned an emergency meeting of the Cabinet. He also appointed a Scientific Commission to inquire into the cause of the disease and find a remedy. It was unsuccessful. |
| November | The Cabinet debated and divided on the issue of repealing the Corn Laws, which would bring down the price of grain. |
| | It was decided to import Indian Corn secretly from the U.S. for sale and free distribution to the poor the following spring. |
| | Potato shortages were causing food prices to rise. Workhouses were allowed to provide alternatives to potatoes to the inmates. |
| | A Temporary Relief Commission met in Dublin to oversee local relief efforts. |
| December | The Irish Board of Works was asked to assist in providing relief by organizing employment for the destitute on public works schemes. |
| | Peel offered his resignation after failing to persuade his Cabinet to repeal the Corn Laws, but Lord John Russell was unable to form a government. |

## 1846

| | |
|---|---|
| January | Disease was spreading in Ireland, especially dysentery, fever and diarrhea, caused by eating rotten potatoes or uncooked grain. |
| March | A Fever Act established a temporary Board of Health in Dublin. |
| June | Sir Robert Peel resigned as Prime Minister, having lost the support of his party over the repeal of the Corn Laws. |
| July | Lord John Russell and his Whig Party formed a new, minority government. |
| | The Treasury supervised the closing of Peel's public works schemes. |
| | Reports of the reappearance of the potato blight were increasing. |
| August | A new, harsher system of public works was introduced, with wages more tightly regulated. |
| September | The potato disease returned and spread rapidly, destroying more of the crop than in the previous year. |
| November | Deaths from famine were being recorded, although no official list of mortality was ever kept. |
| December | The small town of Skibbereen in County Cork achieved international notoriety for the scale of disease and death occurring there daily. |

By the end of the year, one-third of a million people were employed on public works for government-imposed low wages. More than half of the workhouses in Ireland were full, but outdoor relief was illegal under the terms of the 1838 Poor Law.

## 1847

| | |
|---|---|
| January | Despite delays and problems in opening the public works schemes, more than 600,000 people were employed on them for a minimal wage. |

A number of private individuals formed committees to help the Irish poor. The largest charitable organization was the British Relief Association, which had its headquarters in London.

Parliament reconvened and changes in government relief were announced: the public works were to be phased out and government soup kitchens were to be opened.

The first Queen's Letter was issued.

# CHRONOLOGY OF THE GREAT FAMINE, 1845 TO 1852

|  |  |
|---|---|
|  | Publication in the *Nation* of the poem 'The Famine Year' by Speranza, the pen-name of Jane Elgee. It was a searing indictment of the British government's policies in Ireland.<br>(28th) Temporary Relief Act introduced. |
| February | (4th) Lord George Bentinck introduced a Railway Bill into parliament. It was defeated. |
|  | The *Illustrated London News* commissioned Cork-born artist James Mahony to visit Skibbereen in west Cork 'with the object of ascertaining the accuracy of the frightful statements received from the West, and of placing them in unexaggerated fidelity before our readers'. |
| March | (20th) The Treasury implemented a 20 per cent reduction on those employed on the public works, with further reductions to follow. |
|  | (24th) A national day of fast and humiliation, called for by the Queen, was observed throughout the UK. |
|  | (25th) Pope Pius IX issued a Papal Encyclical on behalf of the Famine. |
| April | (5th) Soyer's model soup kitchen was opened in Dublin. |
| May | Government soup kitchens opened throughout the country, but with some delays and reports of poor quality soup. |
| June | (8th) New Poor Law legislation was enacted, including 'An Act to make further Provision for the Relief of the destitute Poor in Ireland' (10 Vic., c. 31). As a result, responsibility for both 'ordinary' and 'extraordinary' relief was to transfer to the Poor Law following the closing of the soup kitchens. |
| July | More than three million people were being fed daily in the government soup kitchens. |
|  | Although the new potato harvest was relatively blight-free, the crop was small. |
| August | Soup kitchens were closed down. The Poor Law Amendment Acts transferred the responsibility for all relief to the workhouse system. They provided for more workhouses to be built and for a restricted form of outdoor relief to be permitted. |
| November | Major Denis Mahon, a landowner in Strokestown, County Roscommon, was shot dead. He had attempted to clear his estate by arranging for the emigration of large numbers of his tenants to Quebec: |

one-third of them perished. He also instigated large-scale evictions. Mahon's assassination caused international outrage.

December　The change to Poor Law relief had not only failed to save lives, but had contributed to an increase in evictions and emigration. An estimated 220,000 people left Ireland in 1847. Of this number, 100,000 had arrived at the Quarantine Station in Grosse Île in British North America (Canada). The majority were Irish and suffering from malnutrition and disease.

## 1848

February　Approximately 200,000 people were receiving relief in the workhouses; almost 500,000 were receiving outdoor relief.

April　More than 600,000 people were receiving outdoor relief. Evictions and emigration were also increasing, but no central records were kept.

(22nd) The Treason Felony Act was introduced making it an offense to 'compass, imagine, invent, devise, or intend' any act that would hurt the monarch.

Charles Trevelyan, Permanent Secretary at the Treasury, and officious overseer of all Famine relief since 1845, was knighted for his services. He was also awarded a salary bonus.

May　John Mitchel was sentenced to fourteen years' transportation.

June　More than 200 female orphans, who had been inmates of the workhouses, sailed for Australia. Hundreds more followed.

July　Potato blight was spotted in parts of the west; much of the north east was reporting healthy crops.

(22nd) – Suspension of Habeas Corpus, in response to growing nationalist unrest.

(29th) – A nationalist group known as Young Ireland led a small, unsuccessful rebellion against British rule. The leaders were found guilty of treason and sentenced to death, which was later commuted.

August　The first Encumbered Estates Act was passed to facilitate the sale of land that was heavily mortgaged.

November　Many of the poorest Poor Law workhouses were in debt, but as many as 3,000 people were applying for relief daily.

| | Count Paul de Strzelecki, agent for the British Relief Association, was knighted for his services to Ireland. He refused to accept any payment for his work. |
|---|---|
| December | Cholera appeared in some parts of Ireland, adding to the already high death toll from disease. An estimated 180,000 emigrated in 1848. |

## 1849

| | |
|---|---|
| February | To assist the struggling Poor Law, the British government made a grant of £50,000 available. |
| March | The Irish Church Missions was founded by a number of Anglican evangelicals to consolidate efforts to convert poor Catholics to Protestantism. The Missions were receiving approximately £26,000 a year from England to support its proselytizing work. |
| April | The recent government grant was exhausted and the Poor Law Commissioners were without funds. |
| June | A new Irish tax, the Rate in Aid of 6d. in the pound, to be levied on each Poor Law Union, was introduced. |
| | Death of James Clarence Mangan (b. 1803) of cholera, exacerbated by alcoholism and malnutrition. His poems included 'Dark Rosaleen'. |
| July | Almost 800,000 people were in receipt of outdoor relief. |
| | A second Encumbered Estates Act was passed. |
| August | Queen Victoria and her family visited the east of Ireland. Overall, they were warmly received. |
| | Some blight was evident, but mostly in the west. |
| December | Artist James Mahony returned to the west of Ireland, this time to County Clare, where evictions and mortality were increasing. His images resulted in the *Illustrated London News* series on the 'Condition of Ireland'. |
| | The government announced that a second Rate in Aid tax would be introduced in 1850. |
| | During this year, the number of evicted families totaled almost 17,000, while an estimated 220,000 emigrated. |

## 1850

| | |
|---|---|
| February | Following complaints about the orphan girls being sent to Australia, an enquiry was held. |
| May | More than one million people were receiving both workhouse and outdoor relief. |
| August | There were only limited instances of blight on the potato crop, mostly in the south west of the country.<br>Approximately 210,000 people emigrated. |

## 1851

| | |
|---|---|
| March | The census was taken. It recorded that the Irish population had fallen from 8,175,124 people in 1841, to 6,552,385. |
| June | Dr Hill and Dr Hughes sent to County Clare to examine mortality in the local workhouses. |
| August | The potato crop was largely blight-free.<br>An estimated 250,000 had emigrated during the year. |

## 1852

Although the Great Hunger was widely considered to be 'over', levels of eviction and emigration remained high.

## Legacies

### 1861

The population had fallen to 5,798,967.

# THE GREAT FAMINE REVISITED
## General introduction

*Malone:* Me father died of starvation in Ireland in the Black '47. Maybe you've heard of it.
*Violet:* The Famine?
*Malone:* No, the starvation. When a country is full o' food, and exporting it, there can be no famine.
(George Bernard Shaw, *Man and Superman*, 1903)

During a century that was filled with food shortages and famines both in Ireland and in other parts of the British Empire, the Great Famine stands out as exceptional in terms of its impact and longevity. In a world where poverty and hunger are endemic, it remains relevant, while the deep scars that it created have still not disappeared. Given the enormity of the event and its geographic and temporal impact, it is strange that there was so much silence surrounding the Famine in the decades that followed.[1] The place of Famine – or its absence – in nineteenth and early twentieth century literature has engaged a number of cultural critics, most notably Terry Eagleton, Seamus Deane and Declan Kiberd. For Deane, the Literary Revival at the end of the nineteenth century achieved 'the remarkable feat of ignoring the Famine and rerouting the claim for cultural exceptionalism through legend rather than through history'.[2] Others, including Robert Smart and Matthew Schultz, have argued that the Famine, in fact, haunted Irish writers in the decades that followed. Smart suggests that it was Irish gothic literature, rather than the Revival, that preserved the memory of the tragedy.[3] Schultz explores these 'rhetorical hauntings' through a range of post-colonial Irish novels, from James Joyce to Sebastian Barry.[4] Recent research has shown that the writings of the diaspora frequently addressed this topic, even if the references were sometimes oblique.[5] However, just as few historians addressed the topic directly, the same can be said of Irish novelists. A largely forgotten exception was Mildred Derby's gothic account, aptly named *The Hunger*, published in 1910.[6] Liam O'Flaherty's 1937 *Famine* received far more attention, he being an established author whose works included *The Informer*.[7] Woodham-Smith's 1962 publication *The Great Hunger* influenced more creative writing on the Famine, notably in the fields of poetry and children's literature.[8]

Since 1995, the 150th anniversary of the first appearance of the potato blight in Ireland, there has been an explosion of interest in the topic of the Great Hunger. This focus is evidenced by an outpouring of scholarly books and articles, multiple conferences and summer schools, international memorials and artwork, new heritage centres and museums, as well as commemorative poetry and music, including even an opera, which celebrates the role played by Asenath Nicholson.[9] There is also a growing amount of literature aimed at young adults, ranging from pop-up stories to a graphic novel, which was also published in Irish.[10] Irish humanitarian organizations that advocate for global social justice have forcefully pointed to the parallels between the Great Famine in Ireland and hunger and starvation in the world today.[11] This public display of interest is in stark contrast to the relatively muted response prior to the anniversary, with few public memorials and only a handful of major studies having been published. In fact, professional historians came late to the table in terms of writing about the Great Famine.

The first major account of the tragedy was written by a Catholic priest, Canon John O'Rourke,[12] in 1874.[13] Despite being a Famine survivor – he had been a student in Maynooth at the time of the tragedy – little of what he wrote was personal. As part of his research, though, he sent query sheets to other survivors. Inevitably perhaps, because of his calling, O'Rourke viewed the Famine as an attack on the Catholic faith.[14] He made this point even more forcefully in his later book *The Battle of the Faith in Ireland* (1887) in which he claimed, 'the famine of 1847 and the years which immediately followed, have, there can be no doubt, won for untold numbers the martyr's crown'.[15] O'Rourke's book was well received in both Ireland and North America. The *Freeman's Journal* averring:

> We heartily congratulate the Rev. Mr. O'Rourke on the manner in which he has performed a labour requiring not merely assiduity and research, but also the nicest judgment and an especial skill in the grouping as well as the generalization of fact and incident. But these qualities are the very highest necessary to the writing of such a book as this, which is not only history, but, for literary treatment, most difficult and delicate history. It is rarely that the ability to employ graceful, yet muscular, language, a capital power of topical concentration, and a liberal and accurate knowledge of all the elements which had informed or influenced the matter discussed, are possessed by the same writer.[16]

The more conservative *Irish Times* was similarly fulsome in its praise:

> No element of the subject is neglected, and its political aspect is rendered full justice. The sufferings of the peasantry in the South and West are delineated with a graphic pen, and the misunderstandings and mismanagement which so largely served to thwart the intentions of the well-wishers of Ireland are skilfully traced to their source.[17]

On the other side of the Atlantic, the *Irish American* opined:

> To write the history of that terrible time – to depict the wretchedness of the people – to show that they were dying in their own beautiful country because the potato failed, while their lives could have been spared if they had seized the food that had been sent out of the country in ship-loads, or if the Government had insisted that this food should be distributed among a people whose ordinary food had been swept out of existence in one fatal night – this is a great task the Rev. John O'Rourke has set himself. He has performed it well, and the country should heartily thank him. He has done good work – he has served his native land.[18]

The influential, and conservative, London paper the *Spectator* was more measured. While agreeing with some of O'Rourke's conclusions, it simultaneously pointed to 'unfair notes of partisanship' in the author's interpretation.[19]

When O'Rourke died in 1887, among his many achievements, he was praised for his Famine publication:

> Many have treated of this latter subject, but Canon O'Rourke is the only author who has given a connected account of the Famine, one of the most terrible inflictions a country ever underwent, and one that has revolutionised the social slate.[20]

Two decades after O'Rourke, W. P. O'Brien,[21] also a Famine survivor, wrote another impersonal account.[22] O'Brien, a retired government official, had commenced work in 1847 under Burgoyne's Relief Committee and had later served as a Poor Law Inspector in some of the poorest unions, including Clare, Kerry and Leitrim.[23] He took a providentialist view of the tragedy.[24] Perhaps this was not surprising given that he relied heavily on the writings of Charles Trevelyan, a fellow civil servant. Both men had been recognized for their public service. Trevelyan had been knighted in 1848, while O'Brien had been made a Companion of Bath in the Queen's Birthday Honours List in 1892. At that stage, he was serving on the Prison Board in Ireland.[25] O'Brien explained his approach in his publication thus:

> [N]ever having contemplated such a task as the writing of the volume, and consequently not having kept notes or records such as would be likely to be useful for such a purpose, yet the episode being regarded with much general interest, and only a comparatively few people of the present day having any clear or definite conception of the actual facts of the case, and that an authentic detail of them by one who was there would be a welcome addition to the present limited stock of information possessed upon the subject.[26]

Five hundred copies were printed.[27] The release of the book coincided with another poor harvest in the west of Ireland and an impending famine, which the nationalist politician William O'Brien predicted would be the worst since the Great Famine.[28]

William Patrick O'Brien's book did not receive the same attention as O'Rourke's in the Irish press.[29] However, its pro-government sympathies received a mixed response. One regional Irish newspaper, the *Leinster Express*,[30] praised the publication both for its detail and for rebutting some of the nationalist interpretations of the Famine, claiming:

> The volume is remarkable for the enormous amount of statistical information it contains, and also for its lucidity, accuracy, and unbiased manner of placing facts before the reader. Its study will dissipate many of the delusions prevalent since the date of the late Mr Butt's article in the 'Dublin University Magazine' in 1848—'The Famine in the Land'—down to the latest vapourings of irresponsible scribblers. We commend to the notice of public financiers three important factors in their calculations frequently overlooked, *viz.*, the placing of the expense to the Imperial Exchequer of the constabulary, the cost of the maintenance of Irish prisons, and the remission of £240,000 yearly incurred by local bodies for the relief of distressed districts. The immense sums contributed by parliament to the famine funds also deserve particular notice, and the tributes paid to the many self-sacrificing persons who worked in the cause of charity and relief are well deserved.[31]

The nationalist *Freeman's Journal* was more measured in welcoming the volume, pointing out that 'it was a matter of regret that a writer with the exceptional knowledge of Mr W. P. O'Brien did not from his own experience and, in his own words, more fully describe the terrible scenes and the important transactions that he actually saw or took part in'. While acknowledging that the book was written 'with an open and honest mind, free from any intentional prejudice', it also pointed out that:

> the work is that of a trained Civil Servant who, while it is admitted that he was discharging his duties with zeal and ability, does not seem to have questioned, even in after life, the wisdom of the measures that he was engaged in helping to administer. It would not be sufficient for a student of the history of the Famine to read Mr O'Brien's book only in order to gain a full knowledge of the causes of the famine and the remedies that were adopted.

Included in their list of additional readings was O'Rourke's volume, which they recommended should be 'carefully read', as should, they suggested, John Mitchel's 'vigorous cut and thrust' *Last Conquest of Ireland (Perhaps)*.[32] Interestingly, the reviewer further suggested that the government accounts should be looked at, including those penned by George Nicholls and Trevelyan, while cautioning:

> But all these official accounts, with their statistics, cut and dry facts, and their highly respectable and unemotional verbiage, requires to be vivified by the burning words of John Pitt Kennedy, the Rev. John O'Rourke, and last but not least, John Mitchel.[33]

The conservative British newspaper the *Spectator*, in a brief review focused on the amount of money that had been expended by the British government throughout the Famine, concluded by stating, 'Mr. O'Brien is conspicuously just in his estimate of the policy pursued'.[34]

Both of these early accounts focused primarily on Skibbereen and the west of the country – a pattern that persisted in many subsequent accounts, which tended to ignore the impact of the Famine on both the north east of the country and on Protestants in general. Also, these books and their reception preempted some of the later divisions within Famine historiography, between a nationalist interpretation and a more sympathetic approach to the problems faced by the British government. For the fifty years that followed, however, little of scholarly interest was written on the Famine.[35]

In post-Partition Ireland, historians on both sides of the border sought to make their discipline both more professional and more scientific, thus allowing themselves to write 'objective' history.[36] According to historian Mary Daly:

> The revolution in Irish historical scholarship in the 1930s, which led to the formation in Belfast in February 1936 of the Ulster Society for Irish Historical Studies; the Dublin-based Irish Historical Society in November 1936, and the journal Irish Historical Studies, which appeared as a joint publication of the two societies in 1938, was forged at the Institute of Historical Research. At this time, Irish history was characterized by strong ideological commitments and passions – 700 years of English mis-rule, a determination to trace the origins of Irish nationalism back to pre-Christian times, or alternatively to showing how Anglo-Norman settlement and British rule had civilized the lawless Irish, or indeed that Ulster was indeed a place apart and had been since the time of Cuchulainn. These young scholars were determined to transform Irish history into a scientific discipline based on careful examination of the sources; with an emphasis on value-free history.[37]

This new generation of Irish historians showed little interest in applying this methodology to a study of the Famine.

Other developments, initiated by politicians, were taking place that were to have a longer-term impact in preserving the memory of the Famine. In 1935, largely due to the patronage of the *Taoiseach*, Éamon de Valera, the Irish Folklore

Commission (*Coimisiún Béaloideasa Éireann*) was established as a State Institute, which was attached to University College, Dublin, but operated under the Department of Education. It made use of questionnaires as a means of collecting and preserving the folklore of Ireland. Séamus Ó Duilearga (Delargy), the first Director, regarded the Famine as 'the greatest disaster that ever befell the Irish people'. Moreover, it had contributed to a decline of interest in folklore. Ó Duilearga singled out William Wilde, oculist, Census Commissioner and antiquarian, for preserving these memories in his 1852 book *Irish Popular Superstitions*, in which he had also included a pioneering questionnaire.[38] One of the Commission's first projects was a Schools' Collection Scheme, an all-Ireland voluntary project carried out in 1937 and 1938 by schoolchildren aged between 11 and 14 that had the ambitious task of 'rescuing from oblivion the traditions . . . of the historic Irish nation'.[39] It included memories of the Famine. This was followed up by a questionnaire in 1945, entitled 'The Great Famine of 1845–1852'. The dates chosen are interesting, suggesting that the crisis was of seven years' duration. While there were no survivors by this stage, many of the contributors had first-hand recollections of those who were. The 4,650 hand-written pages of information were given to Roger J. McHugh, a literary critic,[40] who used them as the basis for his chapter in the volume commissioned by de Valera.[41]

The anniversary of the Famine was marked in a number of other ways. In March 1945, a new play, *The Black Stranger* by Gerard Healy, was premiered at the Gate Theatre in Dublin.[42] It had opened in the Opera House in Cork two weeks earlier.[43] The Dublin opening night was attended by many government and ex-government ministers.[44] The work had been specially commissioned to mark the centenary.[45] However, staging this topic was clearly challenging, and Healy's inclusion of themes such as prostitution and a dog gnawing at the head of a once beautiful young woman proved to be difficult for the Irish audience to watch.[46] Moreover, as one critic observed, 'To measure up a play in three fairly short acts of two and a half hours' duration against the titanic stature of the famine years is a task that calls for a daring and able dramatist'.[47] The night was remarkable for another reason as it marked the first appearance of the newly formed Players' Theatre in Dublin, and they received a 'tumultuous welcome'.[48] The play was published in 1950,[49] but it largely disappeared from view in subsequent years, with the exception of six performances in the Peacock Theatre in Dublin in October 1973, as well as runs by the Gaelic Park Players in Chicago and the Gaelic Players in Connecticut, both in 1996.[50]

In 1946, the Irish government commissioned an exhibition to commemorate the centenary of Young Ireland, while showcasing key moments in Ireland's history.[51] The exhibition was held in the National College of Art on Kildare St, Dublin, and included the works of forty-eight living Irish artists.[52] In total, of the eighty-seven pieces displayed, nine were representations of the Famine, the catalogue explaining the interest as:

> The social and political results of the famine in Ireland in 1845–47, the state of misery and the starvation to which the people were reduced

while it ran its course and the mass emigration which followed it make the catastrophe and event of major significance in Irish history.[53]

The title of these paintings is indicative of the lack of consensus in naming the tragedy: *Famine, Gorta, An Ghorta, Connemara Cottages Abandoned during the Famine, Bliahain na Gorta, Famine, Ocras, 1850, The Emigrant* and *Decorative Design*. At the close of the exhibition, the government purchased sixteen of the works, including *Bliadhain na Gorta*, by Padraig Woods (£55), *Famine*, by Muriel Brandt (£150) and *Evictions*, by George F. Campbell (£55).[54] Apart from these initiatives, the centenary of the Great Hunger passed relatively quietly, overshadowed by the celebrations, and turmoil, which accompanied the ending of the Second World War. Significantly, no public or national monuments to commemorate the centenary were commissioned.[55] Moreover, the centenary passed without a major reappraisal by historians or other academics, although, in 1945, John Mitchel's strident *Jail Journal* was reissued.[56]

Two years later, on the anniversary of 'Black '47', however, Rev Timothy O'Herlihy, a Venetian priest, who had taught at both St Patrick's College in Dublin and the Irish College in Paris, published a now largely forgotten 88-page pamphlet entitled *The Famine 1845–47: A Survey of Its Ravages and Causes*.[57] While suggesting that the government had failed to make sufficient provision for the Irish people, it explained their response on the grounds that they did not want to 'disturb the balance of trade'. Mirroring O'Rourke's earlier interpretation, O'Herlihy suggested that 'The Famine was more than the rot of the potato crop; it was almost the rot of the body and soul of the nation'.[58] He cautioned against minimizing the suffering of the population both during that time and in the preceding centuries.[59] His appeal fore-shadowed that which would be made by Brendan Bradshaw forty years later. *The Famine* was reviewed in a number of newspapers, to a mixed reception.[60] While some reviewers, such as in the *Tuam Herald*, felt his treatment of the British government was even-handed, the *Irish Examiner* was less persuaded by his conclusions, averring, 'Father O'Herlihy details a multitude of facts and is inclined to accept the popular and obvious explanation – bad government, worse landlordism, as solely responsible for the catastrophe. But there were many contributory causes, some of which were remote and not as easily discerned at the time'.[61] Whatever the merits or otherwise of O'Herlihy's book, it failed to make a lasting mark on Famine historiography.

The need for a scholarly publication to be written on the Famine to mark the 100th anniversary was an aspiration of the *Taoiseach*, de Valera. Despite the offer of an attractive subvention, Irish historians were reluctant to take on this project. It eventually fell to two Dublin-based historians to edit a collection of essays. A public announcement concerning this project was made in April 1945 by Thomas Derrig, the Minister for Education,[62] who informed the *Dáil*:

> The Irish Committee of Historical Sciences were making arrangements to publish a history of the Great Famine. It would be a comprehensive history dealing with all aspects of the Famine, economic and political.

The history would be under the joint editorship of Professor R. Dudley Edwards and T.W. Moody and a specially selected group of research workers would be responsible for the various sections. It was estimated that the total cost of the work would be about £1,500.[63]

In the interim period since the last major publications on the Famine, the *Irish Historical Studies*, influenced by the Institute of Historical Research in London, had been created (in 1938), which promised a more professional and objective approach to the writing of history. Also, as the new Free State, soon to be Republic, sought to establish its identity, academic historians promised to remove some of 'myths' of the nationalist writing of history. As a consequence, scholarship became a 'self-conscious reaction against an earlier nationalist tradition of historical interpretation'.[64] Later, this general approach would be referred to under the umbrella of 'revisionism'.

At this stage, Edwards and Moody, founders of *Irish Historical Studies*, were the most influential historians in Ireland, committed to making their discipline more professional and less politically charged, that is, value-free. In 1946, however, Moody withdrew his involvement and was replaced by T. D. Williams, who specialized in German and diplomatic history.[65] In the intervening period, one important, and sometimes overlooked, initiative had been commenced by the editors. Acting under the auspices of the Irish Folklore Commission, in 1945 a questionnaire on the Famine had been distributed and:

> The questionnaire proper resulted in more than 900 pages of material being collected. However, it was decided to augment this material by sending a more detailed questionnaire along with special copybooks to the full-time collectors and certain other people. This resulted in approximately a further 3,750 pages of material being collected.[66]

The centenary of the first appearance of potato blight in Ireland coincided with another subsistence crisis. The ending of the Second World War had signaled the return of mass starvation to Europe, with an estimated eighty million people facing the prospect of famine in the winter of 1945 to 1946.[67] De Valera pledged that his government would assist, by sending food, clothing, blankets and cookers.[68] Ireland's own tragic history was never far from view, one newspaper reminding its readers: 'Memories of famine still linger in Ireland to an extent that should make us sympathetic to the cry of its victims in any part of the world. It is small help that a country such as Ireland, with its limited area and diminished population, can render. What little is possible should be done and wholeheartedly and ungrudgingly'.[69] Similar sentiments were expressed in the *Dáil*, with Joseph Blowick, the TD for south Mayo, pointing out that even though it was 100 years ago 'they still remembered with gratitude the aid they received from various countries at that time'.[70] Regardless of Ireland's generosity to other countries, the decade after 1945 was marked by food shortages, a fuel famine and a housing crisis, especially in the west, while tuberculosis and other infectious diseases were increasing.[71] At this stage also, Ireland was undergoing another mass emigration of its people – the largest exodus since the Famine.[72] The remittances from emigrants, however, were depended upon to help buoy up the economy.[73] Moreover, the country had the lowest marriage rate in Europe, a fact that also alarmed politicians, with de Valera admitting he was 'gravely worried by the whole outlook'.[74] The parallels with 100 years earlier were clear although the context was different and emigrants were overwhelmingly choosing to settle in Britain, not North America, the destination of so many Famine emigrants. At the end of 1947, as the food shortages remained and the economy continued to decline, the government was chastised:

> It is strange with what apathy the government continues to ignore the fact that the government of this country is going to be caught in a rapidly approaching food crisis. Indeed, if correct and energetic steps are not quickly taken, the nation may be involved in a catastrophic failure to obtain the necessities of life, as disastrous in its permanent effects as the Famine of a hundred years ago.[75]

The memory of the Great Famine, it seemed, had cast a long shadow that independence could not dispel.

The publication envisioned by de Valera to mark the centenary of the Famine did not appear in 1945 as he had hoped. In fact, it did not appear until long after the anniversary had passed and the final product was about half the length of what had been commissioned. *The Great Famine: Studies in Irish History*, edited by Edwards and Williams, was published in 1956.[76] It was an uneven book, which, as its title suggested, comprised a number of individual studies rather than a complete overview of the event. It contained seven chapters, all penned by male writers, but none were written by the editors. Overall, the publication provided a cautious and sanitized view of the tragedy. In the 'Introduction', which was ghost written by a student, the editors set the tone for what followed by stating that they did not want to discuss contentious issues such as mortality and culpability.[77] The limitations of the approach were acknowledged privately by Dudley Edwards who believed there was a danger of it being regarded as 'dehydrated history'.[78] Ironically, for a book that sought to avoid controversy or excite passions, its value and contribution continue to be argued over by historians. A number of prominent non-historians also entered the fray, with novelist Colm Tóibín, who 'studied with a few of the people involved in the project', accusing them of post-colonial insecurity:

> It was clear from their bearing, the timbre of their voices and their general interest in source material that their time in British universities had been very important for them, that they were happier reading *Hansard* than going through lists of the names of people who died on coffin ships. It was equally clear that they would never have edited a book about the

Famine had they not been commissioned to do so. If they did not come from a class which was largely spared the Famine and land clearance, then they certainly aspired to it.[79]

While *The Great Famine* was praised by the academic community, popular response to it was more muted.[80] Moreover, de Valera was privately disappointed in the final outcome.[81] However, as this book was published, another book on the topic was in the process of being researched, and the response to this Famine publication would be far from muted.

Cecil Woodham-Smith began researching the Famine in 1953, although she claimed that she 'had had the story in her head for far longer than that'.[82] At this stage, she had published two critically acclaimed, and commercially successful, narrative histories – on Florence Nightingale and the Crimean War. Woodham-Smith was an independent writer who was not attached to any university – in fact, when Woodham-Smith had attended Oxford University from 1914 to 1917, women were not even allowed to graduate. She had been born in Wales, but claimed Irish heritage through her Fitzgerald father. As a student and later in life, she publicly associated herself with a number of liberal causes, including a united Ireland, the ending of capital punishment and the de-criminalization of homosexuality. Woodham-Smith's interest in the Famine evolved out of her earlier work on the Crimean War and the notorious Lord Lucan. She was aware of the work being published in Ireland. In a rare review written by Woodham-Smith,[83] she praised *The Great Famine* for its 'justice and generosity' although she also noted its 'sober scholarship'.[84] In turn, Dudley Edwards, who knew of her project and her previous work, privately admitted that Woodham-Smith's research possessed the 'ability to be on fire'.[85]

*The Great Hunger* was based on meticulous research carried out in libraries, record offices and private collections in Ireland, Britain, the U.S. and Canada over a period of ten years. Towards the end of the process, she was mentored by R. B. (Robert Brendan) McDowell, a history lecturer in Trinity College in Dublin, who had been a contributor to *The Great Famine*. McDowell was originally from Belfast and was a Unionist and a member of the British Conservative Party, who expressed little patience with what he regarded as 'the fatuity of extreme nationalism'.[86] Woodham-Smith regarded his politics as 'perfect' in giving balance to her interpretation.[87]

*The Great Hunger* was launched in November 1962, initially in London and, a few days later, in Dublin. Among the forty guests who attended the Dublin party were Professor Delargy of the Folklore Commission, Professor Dudley Edwards and his wife, R. B. McDowell, K. B. Nowlan, and Lord and Lady Wicklow.[88] While in Ireland, the author undertook a long interview with the *Irish Independent*, from her penthouse suite in the Gresham Hotel. The title of the article was a quote from Woodham-Smith, 'Never call me a Novelist,' the journalist explaining:

> Not a novelist but a historian, Mrs. Woodham-Smith nevertheless brings the drama of created characters to her real-life record, imbuing the facts

objectively collated with an unmistakably subjective compassion and sympathy.

It is this conjunction of intellectual detachment and sensitive understanding of humanity which gives to her books the excitement of the novel which she so flatly repudiates.[89]

The publication of *The Great Hunger* was widely welcomed and praised in the press in Ireland, Britain and North America. Sales were buoyant and by June 1963 more than 80,000 copies had been sold and plans were being made for French, Swedish and German translations. The book was fifth in the U.S. Non-Fiction list, and still climbing.[90] Already, a paperback version of *The Great Hunger* was being produced. By April 1964, more than 150,000 copies had been sold.[91] In comparison, in its first two years of publication, *The Great Famine* had not sold its 2,000-print run.[92] Regardless of its popular appeal, some members of the Irish academic community were less positive in their response and a small number chose to insult Woodham-Smith in ways that were as ungracious as they were inaccurate. One review by the Irish historian, F. S. L. Lyons, which appeared eighteen months after publication, was particularly barbed:

> To the serious historian, *The great famine* is the touchstone by which *The great hunger* must be judged. Mrs Woodham-Smith is herself aware of this and acknowledges her debt in her preface ... but the appearance of this second study in a field where so much distinguished work has already been done, raises two questions for the critic. First, given the existence of *The great famine* was *The great hunger* really necessary? And second, if it was necessary, wherein lies Mrs Woodham-Smith's distinctive contribution?

Although Lyons paid tribute to Woodham-Smith's skills as a writer and a researcher, it was followed by an *ad hominem* attack on her ability as a historian:

> Why then does one come from it – as in the end one does – with a sense of dissatisfaction, almost of disappointment? The answer, I think, may be that Mrs Woodham-Smith's narrative runs too smoothly, it is limpid as a pool is limpid – it lacks depth. Or perhaps one should put it another way and say that it lacks self-awareness, that lurking nagging uneasiness – which is the hall-mark of the true historian – that, however prolific his sources, there are still problems to be solved and much that remains untold. That is what one means, presumably, by the necessary humility of the scholar. I do not, I confess, see very much of that humility here.[93]

Perhaps, then, it was no coincidence that in the final-year History examination in University College, Dublin, in 1963, history students encountered as the essay topic the dismissive proposition, 'The Great Hunger is a great novel'.[94] More than twenty years after the book had been published, both it and its author bothered the new generation of revisionist historians as much as it had bothered the earlier generation. Consequently, Roy Foster, in a 1986 polemic entitled 'We Are All Revisionists Now', referred to the now dead Woodham-Smith as a 'zealous convert'.[95] The description was as inappropriate as it was gratuitous.[96] Equally inaccurate was novelist Colm Tóibín's 1998 disparaging characterization of Woodham-Smith, 'Her tone is English to the core, a cross between Margaret Thatcher and A. S. Byatt [Antonia Susan Duffy]; she knows the difference between right and wrong (a matter which is still hotly debated in Ireland), and she knows a bad man when she sees one'.[97] Such a statement revealed more about the prejudices of its writer than about Woodham-Smith or her research. Significantly, decades after *The Great Hunger* was first published, it was still continuing to outsell other books on Irish history, leading Cormac Ó Gráda to suggest that there was 'undoubtedly an element of sour grapes in the Irish historians' reaction'.[98] Elizabeth Malcolm has also identified layers of sexism by a largely male body of historians and others, who resented Woodham-Smith's gender, her alleged Englishness and her amateur status.[99] Recent appraisals have been more balanced in recognizing the contribution of Woodham-Smith to Famine historiography.

Regardless of the power and popularity of Woodham-Smith's book, Famine scholarship remained dominated by the 'revisionist' orthodoxy. The onset of the civil rights agitation in the north of the country in the mid-1960s, which evolved into a long and violent conflict, added a further layer of complexity and self-censorship to the way in which academics chose to engage with painful aspects of Ireland's colonial past.[100] An important challenge to this denial of critical moments in Irish history – including the Great Famine – was offered by Brendan Bradshaw in 1989.[101] He believed that 'Irish historiography took a wrong turn in the 1930s' and in the intervening decades, much had been lost in scholarship due to the domination of the revisionist approach and its illusion of objectivity. Moreover, in the effort to remove nationalist 'myths', the importance of conquest, colonization and conflict to the Irish experience had also been written out of the history. Bradshaw made a powerful case for the necessity 'to restore Irish historical experience in a way that was both sympathetic and highly scholarly'.[102] In response, a number of academics accused Bradshaw of 'concocting a conspiracy theory'.[103] Nonetheless, his views did resonate with some, including non-historians. Cultural critic Seamus Deane, in a series of lectures given in Oxford in 1995, rejected the writing of Irish history that was self-consciously anti-myth and anti-nationalist, evident in books such as *The Great Famine*. His criticisms were pointed: 'revisionism remains happily ensconced not only in ignorance of its own theory but the more happily so because it regards such ignorance as the badge of its peculiar notion of professionalism'. The timing of his words was significant as a new generation of historians was emerging who were also challenging the revisionist orthodoxy in regard to the Famine.[104] In the longer-term, Bradshaw's views have proved to be more in keeping with the approach and tone of recent historiography.

The sesquicentenary of the Irish Famine coincided with a number of developments that favoured a reappraisal of Ireland's history in general, and the Famine in particular. The start of an economic boom, which became known as the Celtic Tiger, was combined with a renewed international interest in Irish culture; this was show-cased by *Riverdance*, but mirrored by the achievements of Seamus Heaney, who, in 1995, was awarded the Nobel Prize in Literature. In the same year, the rock band U2 were named Best Group at the 1995 MTV Europe Music Awards.[105] It seemed that 150 years later, the post-Famine maxim, 'Music, poetry and dancing died', had finally been reversed.[106] Political developments paralleled the cultural ones. A cease-fire by the Irish Republican Army in 1994 provided an important step towards the Peace Process, codified in the 1998 Good Friday Agreement.[107] Combined, these developments produced a climate that was conducive to re-examining even unpalatable aspects of Ireland's past, and doing so with a renewed confidence in the future.

Since 1995, much has been published and many monuments and other forms of memorialization have appeared that remember the Great Famine. Moreover, just as the Irish diaspora has had a global reach, so too has the memory of this tragedy, and the desire to honour it. At the core of this process is the large amount of scholarship that has emerged which underpins and makes possible the various commemorations. Significantly, the topic is increasingly being examined from multiple disciplinary perspectives, not simply by historians, but by economists, sociologists, musicologists, art historians, geographers, poets, nutritionists and scientists. In regard to the latter, recent breakthroughs in DNA sequencing have led to a better understanding of the genome of the tuber crop potato, and its resistance to disease.[108] Similarly, pioneering research, most notably by Oonagh Walsh, has revealed the epigenetics of famine, not simply on the victims, but on the descendants of survivors.[109] Meanwhile, Jonny Geber, by using a multi-disciplinary approach, but with a special focus on bioarchaeology, has examined nearly 1,000 skeletons of impoverished workhouse inmates to learn more about their lives, and their deaths.[110] Additionally, the examination of the regional and local dimensions of the Famine has resulted in a re-evaluation of the tragedy at the national level. As the research demonstrates, no part of Ireland escaped from the devastation of these years, while the impact and consequences of the suffering were felt by all communities, from the Catholic cottiers in Skibbereen to the Presbyterian mill-workers in east Belfast.[111] Moreover, pioneering work by Ciarán Ó Murchadha, Ciaran Reilly and Gerard MacAtasney, in particular, has demonstrated how a close reading of local sources, including eyewitness accounts, can result in an outcome that is both empathetic and scholarly.[112] Scholarly and popular interest in the Famine also moved closer together, as was demonstrated when the 728-page *Atlas of the Great Irish Famine* was named Best Irish Published Book of the Year in 2012.[113] More than two decades after the sesquicentenary, interest in the tragedy has shown no sign of diminishing, with a profusion of ways of remembering and commemorating it.

Despite the outflow of research and writing since 1995, certain areas still remain relatively unexplored, with research on women, children, Protestants, merchants and other local elites remaining greatly under-represented. Further local and comparative studies will provide further insights and afford more nuanced perspectives. Despite the vast amount of research since 1995, there still remains no consensus on when the Famine commenced or when it ended, although, unlike in some earlier accounts, nobody would simply limit the suffering to the year 1847. But when does a famine become a famine? If excess mortality and population loss are the measure, then it began in the autumn of 1846, but it persisted long after the blight disappeared from the country, in 1852. A further question that has no easy answer is how should the tragedy be named? The famine of 1740–1741, which may have been as lethal in terms of mortality, is widely remembered as *Bliain an Áir*, or the 'Year of Slaughter'.[114] There is no similar consensus for naming the later famine. As the Great Famine was unfolding, it was more frequently referred to by officials in London in what would now be regarded as euphemisms – calamity, dearth, destitution, distress, misery, etc. Within Ireland, it is generally referred to as the 'Great Famine', which distinguishes it from earlier and later periods of famine and food shortages. The nearest Irish language equivalent to this is *An Gorta Mór*. Since 2008, the government of the Republic has held an annual commemoration known as National Famine Commemoration Day (*Lá Cuimhneacháin Náisiúnta an Ghorta Mhóir*). The crisis of the 1840s was later referred to as the 'black famine'.[115] Those who lived through the tragedy (or indeed other subsistence crises) would refer to it as *an droch shaol*, roughly translated as 'the bad years' or 'the bad times'. More forcefully, Michael Davitt, himself a Famine survivor, writing in 1904 referred to it as 'the holocaust of humanity', a word now appropriated to describe another man-made human tragedy of the twentieth century.[116] The popular historian P. S. O'Hegarty, in his *History of Ireland under the Union* (1952), similarly rejected the word 'famine', preferring to use the more evocative term 'the Great Starvation'.[117] While Woodham-Smith was not the first to use the appellation 'the Great Hunger', her book did popularize its use.[118] Only months after its publication, the Highland clearances were being referred to as 'Scotland's Great Hunger'.[119] Since the sesquicentenary commemorations, the use of the word 'famine' has been questioned, usually on the grounds that large amounts of food continued to be produced in Ireland, although mostly for export.[120] Consequently, an increasing number of people, especially in Irish America, now prefer to use the phrase 'the Great Hunger', or its translation, also *An Gorta Mór*. Whatever designation is preferred, the Great Famine is one of the greatest tragedies of the nineteenth century, rendered even more tragic in that it was not inevitable.

If the Great Famine was not inevitable, what factors made the impact of the potato blight so deadly? The opening months of 1845 in the United Kingdom provided no indication of the storm that would be unleashed as the year closed. Queen Victoria was on the throne and Sir Robert Peel headed a Conservative government, elected in 1841 with a large majority. Railway mania in Britain showed no signs of diminishing, although its too rapid and unregulated expansion was to contribute to a credit crash two years later. One of the biggest domestic scandals occurred in the Andover workhouse in Hampshire in England, where the inmates were so starved that they had eaten the animal bones that they were supposed to be crushing for fertilizer.[121] It was a grim insight into the way the poor were being treated under the new system of revised Poor Laws.

Ireland at the commencement of 1845 was relatively quiet. 'The Royal Commission on the state of the law and practice relating to occupation of land in Ireland', also known as the Devon Commission, submitted its report in February, after a two-year enquiry. It was one of the most extensive investigations into Irish land-holding ever held, based on the evidence of more than 1,000 witnesses and containing 100 appendices.[122] The Commissioners recommended various reforms including the consolidation of property, although suggesting that tenants should receive some protections, including being assisted to emigrate. They also urged that landlord and tenant relations should be improved as a basis for making other improvements, but recognized that many landowners were deeply in debt.[123] But if hopes were raised by the report, they were to be disappointed as land reforms did not follow, although the approaching crisis was to have a major impact on the way that land was owned and occupied. Politically, the Repeal movement was in trouble. Daniel O'Connell, now aged 70, weakened by the Clontarf debacle in 1843 and increasingly estranged from Young Ireland, was in poor health. However, he joined forces with the Catholic hierarchy to oppose the introduction of legislation for non-denominational colleges – the Godless colleges, as critics, including O'Connell, called them. Around the same time, the government made an enhanced grant to Maynooth Seminary. Both actions allowed for all denominations to see the impending famine through a providential prism.

On 20 August 1845, Dr David Moore, curator at the Botanical Gardens in Dublin, noticed a disease on potato crops. Within days, newspapers were reporting its appearance elsewhere, including an urgent editorial in the prestigious *Gardeners' Chronicle* by Dr John Lindley referring to the mysterious disease as a 'murrain'.[124] The destruction of the potato crop in Ireland in 1845 did not come as a complete surprise to either horticulturists or government officials as the disease had been damaging crops in North America in 1843 and had been observed in Europe for a number of months.[125] Consequently, it reached Ireland relatively late in the season, which reduced the level of destruction. Also, the high yield of the crops in 1845 provided an additional buffer.

Prime Minister Peel was no stranger to famine or to Ireland, having served in Dublin Castle from 1812 to 1818. He had, however, taken back to England with him a suspicion of Irish embellishment, believing, 'there is such a tendency to exaggeration and inaccuracy in Irish reports that a delay in acting on them is always desirable'.[126] To ensure accurate accounting on the spread of the disease, in October Peel appointed a Scientific Commission headed by an Englishman, with the dual purpose of finding the cause of the potato disease and finding a palliative for it. They were unsuccessful on both counts. Ironically also, the Commissioners inadvertently exaggerated the extent of the crop lost, estimating it to be in the region of 50 per cent. Their findings alarmed Peel who admitted privately that he found the reports of 'the men of science . . . very alarming'.[127] Both the Mansion House Committee and the Irish Constabulary carried out their own surveys of the extent of the potato loss, which revealed that the counties that had experienced the highest losses were Armagh, Clare, Kilkenny, Louth, Monaghan and Waterford.[128] The fact that the losses were less severe in the poorest western counties also helped to mitigate the impact of the blight in the first year of shortages. While the amorphous way in which the blight appeared meant there was little consensus on its magnitude, in total less than 40 per cent of the crop was lost. Other countries in Europe may have suffered a higher percentage loss of their potato crop in 1845, but their populations did not have same level of dependence as the Irish population.

Numerous theories were put forward about the best way of countering the disease and utilizing damaged potatoes, including by the government's own Scientific Commission. Some attributed its spread to atmospheric factors solely, while remedies for preserving the seed potatoes ranged from soaking in a saline solution to sprinkling with either sulfuric or hydrochloric acid. These suggestions demonstrated how little people, even leading scientists, understood about the nature of the blight. The government Commissioners made a number of suggestions regarding the storage and usage of potatoes. However, potatoes that were already diseased could not be saved. Essentially the type of potatoes grown in Ireland, especially the ubiquitous lumper variety, had no defence against this new form of blight. Nothing proved efficacious in stopping it. The bafflement caused by the potato disease continued for many more decades. Although an antidote (copper sulphate) was discovered in the 1880s, it was not until 2013 that the pathogen that caused *phytophthora infestans* was identified.[129]

In addition to establishing a Scientific Commission, Peel introduced a number of other measures which were both cautious and traditional. In November, he established a Temporary Relief Commission, based in Dublin, which was to operate in parallel to, but distinct from, the Poor Law. The main function of the Relief Commission was to oversee the work of locally established committees which, in turn, were to provide food and establish a limited system of public works for the poor. Money raised by the local committees received a matching grant from the government. Concurrently, the government secretly arranged for £100,000 of Indian Corn (maize) to be purchased in America. This food was put under the control of the Army Commissariat. Peel also set up locally funded public work schemes which, at their peak, employed around 140,000 people, representing in the region of 700,000 family members.[130]

A number of relief measures were proposed, but rejected. The Viceroy, Lord Heytesbury, suggested that the Irish ports be 'opened' to facilitate the faster and cheaper import of corn products. Both the Prime Minister and his Home Secretary, Sir James Graham, rejected this on the grounds that to do so would give Ireland preferential treatment.[131] Opening the Irish ports was also suggested by the Dublin

Mansion House Committee, which had sought a meeting with the Lord Lieutenant to propose a package of relief measures. However, they were treated 'curtly' and their proposals disregarded.[132] Similar demands made by the local authorities in Derry, Cork and Belfast were also rejected.[133] Interestingly, such demands were not confined to Ireland. The Town Council of Sheffield had adopted a memorial to the Queen praying for the opening of the ports, 'adding to it a strong expression of sympathy for the present condition of Ireland and Scotland'.[134]

A further suggestion made by the Mansion House Committee was that the use of grain in distilleries should be temporarily banned. The town of Belfast also memorialized the government asking for a suspension of distillation by grain.[135] This suggestion was forwarded by Heytesbury to Peel, with him pointing out that 'this is demanded on all sides'.[136] This measure was a traditional response to subsistence crises by governments throughout Europe, including in Ireland. During the 1766 famine, Irish distillers themselves had initiated this ban.[137] A further suggestion that was made more forcefully as the Famine progressed was for the ports to be closed to allow food to remain in Ireland. Again, there were precedents for such a measure. In December 1767, for example, the Irish Privy Council had issued a proclamation banning the export of grains.[138] In 1782, the Lord Lieutenant, believing that it was 'patently absurd to export grain which was needed at home', approved a proclamation that banned the export of corn, potatoes and flour, and their byproducts.[139] Historian James Kelly believed that a recourse to such measures helped ensure that excess mortality was kept low, leading some historians to identify a 'gap in famines' in the late eighteenth century.[140] These measures were carried out during the time when Ireland had its own parliament in Dublin. Such interventionist measures, however, were disliked by the Westminster governments of the 1840s. Even though almost all of the 130 workhouses were open and providing relief, it was decided to keep the newly introduced Poor Law separate from the special relief measures, rather than extend its provisions. The Home Secretary justified this approach on the grounds that, 'As the evil is likely to be temporary, it [is] better to meet the emergency by extraordinary means, rather than introduce a mischievous system of administration into Ireland'.[141]

Overall, Peel's interventions had proved effective and few, if any, had died of starvation during the first year of food shortages. But they were too little and too late, leading people to sell or pawn what few resources they had, and thus leaving them vulnerable in subsequent years of shortages. They also paved the way for what was to come as the crisis deepened. From the outset, the food shortages were viewed as an opportunity to effect changes in Irish society. To this end, Sir Randolph Routh, who was in charge of the Temporary Relief Commission, opined:

> The little industry called for to rear the potato, and its prolific growth, leave the people to indolence and all kinds of vice, which habitual labour and a higher order of food would prevent. I think it very probable that we may derive much advantage from this present calamity.[142]

Significantly also, a civil servant from the Treasury was given a prominent position in overseeing the distribution of relief. His name was Charles Trevelyan.

The first appearance of the potato disease coincided with the presence of the London *Times* 'special commissioner' who was travelling around the country. He was unsympathetic to the people and to their leader, Daniel O'Connell. In one of the few reports where he mentioned the blight, he castigated the poor for observing All Saints' Day with a holiday while the crops were rotting, him mistakenly suggesting that the potatoes could be saved if the people made more effort.[143] Reluctance to come to the assistance of the Irish poor was also in evidence. Even though nobody could foresee that blight would return in varying degrees for a further six years, already some parts of the British press were openly stating that Ireland should not be allowed to depend on English resources.[144] The *News of the World* summed this up by saying, 'it is not fitting that Ireland should become a beggar to England'.[145] Such sentiments not only made a mockery of the Union but were a fore-shadow of the response to the subsequent failures of the potato.

An unforeseen consequence of the blight was that it precipitated the downfall of the British Prime Minister. In June 1846, Sir Robert Peel used the food shortages in Ireland to dismantle the protective tariff on corn imported into the United Kingdom.[146] The repeal of the Corn Laws did not have the support of many within his own Conservative Party, who regarded it as a betrayal of the landed interest in Britain. Consequently, he was forced to resign as Prime Minister. His action split the Conservatives into two factions: the Peelites and the Protectionists. The latter were led by Lord George Bentinck, assisted by Benjamin Disraeli.[147] Peel was replaced as Prime Minister by Lord John Russell, leader of the Whig Party – a party generally regarded as being more sympathetic to Ireland. However, Russell came to power as head of a minority government, with no General Election planned until the summer of 1847. This meant that, at a time of crisis in Ireland, British politics were in disarray. Divisions were also taking place in Irish politics. The Repeal Party, which had agitated for a parliament in Dublin, was in turmoil, with a major split occurring in the summer of 1846 between Young and Old Ireland.[148]

One of the first acts by the new Whig government was the closure of Peel's relief works on 21 July 1846, the overseeing of which was carried out by the Treasury. At this stage, sightings of blight were being recorded in the country. The reappearance of the blight in July 1846, far earlier in the season and therefore even more damaging in its impact, was to prove lethal to people whose meagre resources and reserves had been depleted to cope with the first year of shortages. It transformed the temporary food shortages into a major subsistence crisis. The second potato blight resulted in the destruction of more than 90 per cent of the crop. Apart from the enormity of the loss, the cumulative effect of a second year of shortages left the poor with few resources, either physically or materially. Faced with this woeful situation, the widespread expectation was that the new Whig government would intervene to compensate for the shortages. This hope appeared to be realized when the new Premier, Lord John Russell, informed the

House of Commons on 17 August 1846 that he would employ the 'whole credit of the Treasury . . . to avert famine and maintain the people of Ireland'.[149] In retrospect, it was a hollow promise.

In the second year of shortages, continuity was provided in that the Treasury was again to oversee the new relief measures. Charles Trevelyan, the principal civil servant at the Treasury, was given a primary role in administering assistance to Ireland. Unfortunately for the Irish poor, Trevelyan allied himself with a 'moralist' group within British politics who viewed the food shortages in providentialist terms.[150] Simply put, they suggested that the food shortages and consequent famine were God's will. Moreover, Trevelyan's strident manner and dogmatic approach were disliked by others involved in the relief operations.[151] Nonetheless, he had a number of powerful allies. The new Whig Chancellor of the Exchequer, Sir Charles Wood, shared Trevelyan's providentialist view of the Famine and, together, they were able to ensure a stringent and minimalist approach to the giving of relief. As a consequence, the lives of many Irish poor had become dependent on one civil servant in London, and the machinations of a weak and divided government at Westminster.

The second potato failure combined with a number of factors that made the situation far more serious than in the previous year. In 1846, there was a poor corn harvest, not only in Ireland, but throughout Europe. Despite the large shortfall in food production, the new Whig government decided not to intervene in the marketplace, but to leave food supply to market forces, as even Peel's limited interventions in the previous year had angered merchants and proponents of free trade. Nonetheless, the government agreed to import a small amount of Indian Corn into the country, but it was stored in government depots, until Trevelyan decreed that it should be made available and then only sold at market prices.[152] Food exports were to remain unregulated. Ireland at this stage was a major supplier of corn to Britain, supplying enough to feed approximately two million people. British people were also massive consumers of other Irish foodstuffs, notably bacon, eggs, butter and fish.[153] Large amounts of alcohol were exported, including porter and whiskey, which were both made from grain.[154] Several members of the new Whig government regarded the relief measures of the previous year as having been too generous and suggested that Irish reports of suffering had been embellished. Consequently, demands from nationalists and others, including the political economist Isaac Butt, for the Irish ports to be temporarily closed were ignored. Cattle exports even increased as the poor sold what little resources they had left.[155] The unregulated continuation of these exports led one Belfast newspaper to suggest that if food supplies were left in Ireland there would be no shortages:

> The harvest was sufficiently abundant to give food for beast and man. The famine – if there be a famine – is man-made. We have malted and distilled the famine. That fact must never be forgotten – unless we would lose the lessons that this judgement should teach.[156]

Moreover, both Irish and British merchants were showing more interest in using the food shortages as a way of maximizing their profits, rather than in getting food to the poor and the starving. Lord Bessborough, a leading Whig politician and Lord Lieutenant in Ireland, privately expressed his frustrations to the Prime Minister, informing him that the merchants had done 'as little as they could' to bring food to Ireland, adding:

> I know all the difficulties that arise when you begin to interfere with trade, but it is difficult to persuade a starving population that one class should be allowed to make a fifty per cent profit by the sale of provisions, while they are dying in want of these.[157]

The poor harvests combined with an industrial downswing. In Britain, this was exacerbated by a credit crisis, which was partly due to the preceding railway mania. The industrial recession was particularly severe in the north of England and in the north of Ireland. In Belfast, at the end of 1846 the flax-spinning mills placed their workers on 'short time', on account of the depression in trade. This move affected an estimated 10,850 people, who lost £1,620 from their collective earnings.[158] At the beginning of November, the Mayor of Belfast was petitioned to convene a meeting for the purpose of establishing a General Soup Kitchen 'to alleviate the recent existing distress'.[159] He agreed and a large meeting was held in the town on 17 November. It was attended by local businessmen and a number of clerics, including Dr John Edgar, who was then in the process of establishing the Belfast Ladies' Committee on behalf of the poor in Connaught.[160]

Regardless of the greater need for relief and the fact that the people had already undergone one year of privations, the Whig government decided that public works, based on hard physical labour, were to be the main means of providing relief in the second year of food shortages. There were a number of changes from the way in which they had operated in the previous year, which made them little suited to the needs of a hungry and weak people. As far as possible, the daily rate of pay was based on output, which disadvantaged people who were already debilitated. The works undertaken – usually roads or walls built in out-of-the-way places – were to serve no function, except to act as a test of destitution. No individual landowners were to benefit from the works undertaken, which was a disincentive to support them, especially as much of the cost would be a local charge. Moreover, regardless of widespread distress, the public works proved slow to become operative, largely due to their cumbersome bureaucracy, which caused further hardship. The average time lapse from public works being requested to receiving Treasury sanction was six to eight weeks.[161] When they did commence, the hard physical labour – 12 hours a day, six days a week – drained what few resources the workers had left. The advent of a particularly severe winter, with snow falling into April 1847, increased the misery of enforced labour out of doors. The severe weather inevitably led to a suspension of many public works, leading the Board of Works to issue provisional regulations during periods of 'forced idleness'. The amended system was:

1. On such occasions, the labourers are to attend at roll-call in the morning; and all who attend will, if it be impossible to set them to work then, be entered on the pay-list for half a day's daily pay.
2. If the weather be fine, they will be expected to commence work immediately: if at or before nine o'clock, they will be paid for the whole day; if at or after twelve o'clock, for as many hours as they may be entitled to between that and half a day. If they don't come to work as soon as the day is fine, they will receive no pay. In order to guard against abuse, the inspecting-officers or engineers will be careful that this system of relief is never resorted to when there is any work to be performed, in breaking stones, scraping snow off the roads, etc.[162]

Deliberately low wages also contributed to the starvation gap as food prices soared. In the words of one observer, the public works were guilty of 'slow murder'.[163]

Even as the works got underway, they proved inadequate for the demands being placed on them. One consequence was that the workhouses started to fill: as early as November, for example, the Sligo Union stopped making further admissions.[164] The large number of workhouse inmates put pressure on local ratepayers, especially in areas where they were being called upon to finance other forms of relief. Inversely, therefore, the poorest areas were paying the highest amounts of taxation. By the end of the year, many workhouses were full and not able to admit any more people, while outdoor relief remained illegal. To ease the situation, Sir Randolph Routh, the Commissioner in charge of relief in Ireland, pleaded with Trevelyan to allow the supplies in the government food depots to be released onto the market. Trevelyan refused, having decided that the depots would not open until 28 December. In a terse and telling note to Routh, Trevelyan informed him, 'If we make the prices lower, I repeat for the HUNDRETH time, that the whole country will come upon us'.[165] Ireland was to be left to invisible market forces, but the visible consequences were the deaths that were occurring daily.

An early report of the death from starvation of a man employed on the works near Skibbereen provided a foreboding of things to come in the district:

> An inquest has been held at Skibbereen, on the body of the man M'Kennedy, who was alleged to have died of starvation, although at the time there were a fortnight's wages owing to him from the Government . . . On the day of his death, Saturday the 24th October, the steward, a very kind-hearted man of the name of Donovan, gave him a piece of bread; and in the act of putting it to his mouth he sank and died. The two physicians swore that such an instance of starvation they never before met with. He was so attenuated from want of food, that all the

fatty substance of the system was totally absorbed and gone. Nothing in the stomach and intestines but a piece of raw undigested cabbage-stalk; which was produced, and the remnants of some other raw vegetable matter. A verdict was returned, 'That the said Denis M'Kennedy, on the 24th day of October in the year aforesaid, at Caheragh Road in the county aforesaid, died of starvation, owing to the gross negligence of the Board of Works'.[166]

Concurrently with deaths from starvation being reported in Ireland, a number of British newspapers were highlighting the perceived lawlessness of the Irish poor:

The increased pressure of distress in Ireland is marked by a corresponding growth of disturbance. The provincial papers record many acts of turbulence. In Limerick, four hundred labourers paraded the streets with spades, shovels, and hammers, as emblematic of their destitution, and plundered two bread-carts; the meal-dealers and bakers demanded protection of the Magistrates, and the military were called out. The people, however, dispersed. A meeting of Magistrates was immediately held, and a memorial adopted to the Lord-Lieutenant, representing that the wages fixed by Government – 2d. less than the current rate in any district – were inadequate to support existence.[167]

A number of Irish commentators did not blame the people for committing crimes, but the relief policies being pursued by the government. Lord Monteagle, an Anglo-Irish landowner and Whig politician who had served as Chancellor of the Exchequer from 1835 to 1839, was worried that politicians and civil servants in London did not understand the scope of the suffering in Ireland.[168] He privately wrote to Trevelyan at the beginning of October 1846 outlining his concerns. Trevelyan's response was typically dismissive:

I must beg of you to dismiss all doubt from your mind of the magnitude of the existing calamity and its danger not being fully known and appreciated in Downing Street. The government establishments are strained to the utmost to alleviate this great calamity and avert this danger, as far as it is in the power of government to do so; and in the whole course of my public service I never witnessed such entire self-devotion and such hearty and cordial cooperation on the part of officers belonging to different departments.[169]

Lord Cloncurry, a prominent member of the Mansion House Committee, chaired a meeting of landowners and Irish MPs held at the end of 1847 over a number of days in Rotunda in Dublin, asking for more assistance for Ireland.[170] In his 1849 memoir, he included a rare reference to the existence of cannibalism, writing that the hunger was so severe that 'mothers ate their own children amidst 16,000,000 tons of grain which a paternal government allowed its starving people to look upon, but not to touch'.[171] He believed that the Irish poor had been 'a sacrifice to mercantile avarice'.[172]

Isaac Butt, political economist and then a supporter of the Conservative Party, criticized the government for its relief policies and its failure to meet in the months following the second appearance of the potato blight. Parliament had been prorogued on 28 August 1846, on 4 August and again on 12 August, after which it did not meet again until 19 January 1847, by which time it was – as Butt recognized – too late as thousands of people in Ireland were weak or dead.[173] William Smith O'Brien, the leader of the Young Ireland movement and also a member of the British government, regarded the failure of the government to meet in the final months of 1846 as deliberate. His explanation of the delay was that it was 'thought more prudent, by a Government which cannot command a majority in Parliament, to avoid the risk of losing their places'. He also blamed the weak leadership of the Prime Minister:

> Little as I am disposed to place confidence in the kindly feelings of the British Legislature towards Ireland, I yet cannot believe that all the leading statesmen of the empire would have adopted, on the approach of famine, the same tone of philosophical calmness with which Lord John Russell promulgates the abstract doctrines of political economy as a substitute for energetic action.[174]

Butt and O'Brien, arguing from opposing political perspectives, came to the same critical conclusions of the policies of the Whig government.

Within some sections of the press, there was disillusionment with the new government and doubts about its ability to survive. The *Spectator*, while recognizing that the failure of parliament to meet was 'advantageous to the present Administration', noted that the decision had also caused 'many a pang of hunger, not a few deaths by actual starvation, a great waste of labour, and much social disorganization'.[175] The *Kerry Evening Post*, reporting that famine 'is staking through the length and breadth of this land', also quoted from the London *Morning Herald*, which had predicted that the Whigs' adherence to political economy meant that they would not survive in power beyond Christmas 1846.[176] Sadly for Ireland, this prediction was not correct as, possibly as a reflection of the divided Conservative opposition, the Whigs won the General Election in 1847 and remained in office until 1852.

The British parliament finally reconvened on 19 January 1847.[177] At this stage, excess mortality was being reported in the press in Britain and Ireland daily. One Anglican religious journal cast aside traditional religious divisions to ask how such suffering could occur in a Christian land. They concluded:

> With all allowance for exaggeration in one place and imposture in another, of this there can be no doubt, that the poor in parts of this country are

suffering most dreadfully. It is a horrible thing to be said in a Christian country, where, taking the whole, there is, we believe, no positive lack of food, *that Christian people are dying of hunger*.[178]

The Queen's Speech, to mark the commencement of a new parliamentary session, made immediate reference to the 'dearth of provisions which prevails in Ireland and in parts of Scotland'. She then went on to state that, in relation to Ireland,

> the loss of the usual food of the people has been the cause of severe sufferings, of disease, and of greatly increased mortality among the poorer Classes. Outrages have become more frequent, chiefly directed against property; and the transit of provisions has been rendered unsafe in some parts of the country.[179]

Two days after parliament met, Russell introduced a bill for a suspension of the duties upon foreign corn and for a temporary suspension of the navigation laws.[180] During the debate, Russell pointed out that there had been a suspension on a number of previous occasions including in 1756, 1766, 1791 and 1800.[181] Both measures were intended to facilitate more food being brought into Ireland, as the onset of winter (and a particularly harsh one) meant that at this time, many ports in the northern hemisphere were now closed.[182] Shortly after this, the government announced other changes that would be introduced, including the closure of the public works and, from August, a transfer of both ordinary and extraordinary relief to the Poor Law. In the interim period, between the public works closing and an extended Poor Law being available, government soup kitchens were to be established in the country.

The 1847 parliamentary session was historic for one other reason – it marked O'Connell's final speech in Westminster. O'Connell had sat in parliament since his historic election in 1830 and, during these years, he had been a thorn in the side of various governments, especially the Conservatives. O'Connell had used his brilliant oratory skills, knowledge of the law and irrepressible energy to effect change, and his humanitarian gaze had spread beyond the people of Ireland to argue for the rights of Jews, Aborigines, Maoris and slaves.[183] O'Connell's final speech in the House of Commons was made on behalf of his starving countrymen. He chastised his fellow parliamentarians on the grounds that he:

> did not think they understood the miseries – the accumulation of miseries – under which the people were at present suffering. It had been estimated that 5,000 adults and 10,000 children had already perished from famine; and that 25 per cent of the whole population would perish unless the House should afford effective relief. They would perish of famine and disease unless the House did something speedy and efficacious – not doled out in small sums – not in private and individual subscriptions, but by some great act of national generosity, calculated upon a broad and

liberal scale. If this course were not pursued, Parliament was responsible for the loss of 25 per cent of the population of Ireland.

He concluded his impassioned speech by stating that his beloved country:

> was in their hands – in their power. If they did not save her, she could not save herself. He solemnly called on them to recollect that he predicted with the sincerest conviction, that one-fourth of her population would perish unless Parliament came to their relief.[184]

However, it was the appearance of the Liberator, rather than his spoken words, which most troubled those who listened to his speech. O'Connell was aged 72 and suffering from a degenerative brain disease. A final wish of the fading man was to meet the Pope in Rome. O'Connell died on 15 May 1847 in Genoa. He never made it to Rome. At the time of his death, a new system of relief was being established throughout Ireland. The public works had been closed and a network of soup kitchens was being established. The sharp rise in mortality in the spring of 1847 told its own story of government failure.

As the Famine progressed in Ireland, the response of formal religion was mixed, with no denomination having a coherent answer to the food shortages. An exception was the Society of Friends which not only used their international network to obtain relief, but utilized their own members to distribute it.[185] By doing so, these men, many of whom were only in their 20s, put their lives at risk – with as many as twenty Quakers dying of exhaustion or famine-related diseases.[186] Similarly to other philanthropic bodies, by the beginning of 1848, donations had dried up and their resources were depleted, so they withdrew from giving direct relief.[187] However, as the Poor Law struggled to cope with its new responsibilities, mortality showed no signs of diminishing, Trevelyan made a secret proposition to the Quakers. He offered to give them £100 from Treasury funds if they would resume their operations. The Quakers refused, responding that the distress was so severe that it required the resources of the government to alleviate it.[188]

While no other religious bodies had the same coordinated response as the Society of Friends, or left behind such a complete record of their activities, individual priests and clerics from the other churches put their lives at considerable risk to assist the poor. The wives and daughters of Anglican ministers were also active in providing aid and often served on ladies' relief committees, many of which received their funding from the Quakers. In 1847 alone, an estimated thirty Anglican priests died from famine-related diseases.[189] The responses of the Protestant churches, however, were tainted by the memory of proselytism, using the hunger of the people to win converts. Although relatively rare and highly localized, there were instances of what was referred to as 'souperism'. The Belfast Ladies' Committee for Connaught, for example, which consisted primarily of Episcopalians and Presbyterians, initially provided relief without recourse to religion but, in 1848, they openly declared that its mission was to promote 'industrial Scriptural education'.[190] The vast majority of private relief, however, was given without recourse to converting the recipients. This was true of the largest relief organization, the British Relief Association, which was largely the initiative of a wealthy British Jew, Lionel de Rothschild. Through their agent in Ireland, the indefatigable Paul de Strzelecki, relief was distributed in a way that was both practical and compassionate.[191]

At the end of 1846, the small town of Skibbereen achieved a bleak notoriety as a place of suffering and starvation, destitution and death. A number of public appeals were made on behalf of the poor of the town, one of the first being made by an anonymous lady who in mid-December 1846 placed an advertisement in the *Freeman's Journal* requesting 'aid in trifling sums'. She divided the £10 that she raised between the local Protestant and the Catholic clergymen.[192] Skibbereen also became the focus of a number of curious, philanthropic and artistic visitors. They included the young Lord Dufferin, a student from Oxford University, Elihu Burritt, an American humanitarian, and James Mahony, Cork-born artist for the *Illustrated London News*. Many of these visitors left eyewitness accounts which were published as famine continued to decimate the population. For the most part, the accounts were sympathetic to the starving Irish and they helped to attract international donations. The proceeds of Dufferin's pamphlet (which cost 1 shilling) were donated to Skibbereen, together with the money raised amongst his fellow students upon his return to university. Dufferin also made a personal, and anonymous, donation of £1,000. What commenced as a student jaunt, therefore, ended as a serious errand of mercy, with Dufferin's interventions being recalled favourably in Ireland, 100 years later.[193] Before travelling to Ireland Burritt, together with James L. L. F. Warren,[194] had suggested to Lord John Russell that the government pay the shipping costs of relief coming from the United States. Two days later, Charles Trevelyan of the Treasury responded in the affirmative, saying that 'the Lords will be prepared to pay the freight of any provisions or clothing which benevolent persons in the United States may send to Ireland or the distressed districts in Scotland'.[195] Burritt's arrival in Cork City was noted by a small number of Irish newspapers:

> 'He this day' says the [Cork] *Reporter* 'starts for Skibbereen, Bantry and the western districts, in order to have personal proof of the horrible spectacles which that distressed locality presents, and for the purpose of taking such steps as he may deem necessary for the distribution of relief to be forwarded. It is his intention to visit Cork again, in a few days, on his way to Limerick and Dublin, but his stay will not be prolonged'.[196]

In the event, Burritt cut his stay in Skibbereen short when he became ill, leaving the town, while 'a deep sense of gratitude pervaded my heart that I had escaped being prostrated by fever in that pest house'. On 28 February 1847, he sailed by steamer from Cork to Dublin. Before leaving Ireland, he wrote an appeal to the people of New England to help the starving Irish. He concluded by saying, 'I have spent nearly a $100 and a month's hard labor in trying to bring relief to the perishing in this land. I shall return to England with some sense of satisfaction that I have not withheld my mite to mitigate this mass of misery'.[197] Burritt's final view of Ireland was also filled with sadness as he witnessed emigrants leaving their families behind: 'and when the steamer's last bell rung, the wail of lamentation arose like the voice of many waters. Never had I witnessed, not even at the bed of death, such agonizing expressions of affection'.[198]

William Bennett, an English Quaker, travelled to Ireland in early 1847 to distribute seeds. He had been only a few days in the country when he witnessed his first corpse lying on a public road, him assuming the death had been caused by starvation. Such scenes were undoubtedly shocking on first view, but soon became commonplace, although no less disturbing.[199] During his first few days in Belfast, he encountered snow. Unfortunately, other parts of the country were also experiencing snow falls and frosty weather.[200] The elderly Quaker William Forster, who was at that time travelling in Counties Mayo and Donegal, accompanied by his son and son's friend, the young James Hack Tuke, encountered similar inhospitable weather. Tuke described their journey as, 'Miserable accommodation, bad food, the exposure suffered in the course of long journeys on outside cars in snow and rain, were all borne without a murmur, in spite of delicacy of health'. At one point, 'when the horses could no longer drag our car through the snow, we had to walk along the mountain'. When Forster became too ill to travel, 'his difficulty of breathing made it needful to lay him down at times on his back in the snow to recover strength'. Nonetheless the three men persisted on their mission. In Tuke's memoir, written when he himself was an old man, he wrote:

I have often thought in looking back how strange and remarkable it was that, among the many experienced men of his time in England, one man alone, and he advanced in years and in poor health, should have so strongly felt the burden of this misery as to be impelled to devote many months of that terrible season to the task of organising local relief committees for the relief of the starving multitudes in the west of Ireland.[201]

These freezing weather conditions were apparent elsewhere in Europe, with even the more southerly countries reporting heavy snow falls into spring.[202] For those poor Irish, however, who were employed on the public works, shoeless and without warm clothing, the impact of such ungenial weather was horrendous. In regard to agriculture also, the extended period of snowfall and frost (more than was usual in Ireland) hampered the spring planting of crops.[203] The need for clothing and bedding, especially during the freezing and prolonged winter of 1846 to 1847, was overlooked by the British government. Instead, women and the Society of Friends were at the forefront of filling this deficit. One such organization, which was based in London, was the British Ladies' Clothing Association for Ireland and Scotland. These Quaker women appealed for donations to be made on the grounds that 'needful clothing for the wretched sufferers now seems to be absolutely called for, and presents a claim in equal importance to that of food'. They explained it was required 'either for health or decency'. By June 1847, the Committee had raised £5,700, £2,000 of which had been given to them by the British Relief Association.[204] Contributions in clothing, materials or bedding were collected on their behalf by Abraham Taw, a Quaker merchant, who personally travelled to Ireland in spring 1847 to distribute them.[205]

While the Quakers responded to the shortages in Ireland in numerous practical ways, the hierarchies of the main churches responded to the food shortages in Ireland in more traditional ways. Following the recurring appearance of blight, the Anglican Bishops in England responded to the second potato failure by calling for a day of fast and prayer on behalf of Ireland. Friday, 20 November 1846, was chosen as a day of humiliation to be observed all over the United Kingdom. On that day, divine service was performed in the churches, in accordance with the instructions prescribed in the circular of the Lord Primate.[206] At the beginning of 1847, a similar call was repeated by Queen Victoria, the head of the Anglican Church, who announced that on 24 March 1847, a national day of fast and humiliation would be kept throughout the United Kingdom.[207] The power of prayer, as a means of alleviating suffering, was foregrounded by some of the English press:

> We dare not to inquire what may be the dealing of the All-Wise with us on the present occasion, but we should be sinfully ungrateful to forget what followed the similar act of national humiliation upon occasion of the cholera pestilence: England humbled herself, and the plague was stayed from the very day of the fast,—a day made gloriously memorable in the religious history of this country by more than half a million of persons having partaken of the holy sacrament in the London churches alone. The disease rapidly declined in this country, while it continued its ravages over nearly the whole of the rest of Europe. For more than seventeen hundred years such acts of national humiliation, under great and unusual afflictions, have been the usage of the Christian Church; and it would be difficult to point out an instance in which they have not been followed by a manifest abatement of the Divine anger.[208]

On the actual day, many businesses and factories closed down and large numbers of people, including the Queen and her family, attended religious services. In acknowledgement of the day, the Catholic Church in Britain called for a special prayer to be said, as did the Reverend Dr Adler, Chief Rabbi of the Jews in the United Kingdom.[209] While Queen Victoria was the public instigator of the day of humiliation, she did so on behalf of her ministers. Privately, she rejected a providential interpretation of the Famine believing that it presented an almost 'blasphemous view' of a God whom she believed to be loving, not punitive. Further, the Queen expected that the day of humiliation would be 'disapproved by all enlightened people as a very absurd thing of bygone days'.[210] What the day did reveal was 'the extent to which a Christian – and more particularly a Protestant evangelical – world-view permeated early Victorian British society'.[211] A Queen's Letter issued in January, together with the day of humiliation, raised more than £17,000. However, as famine and the need for relief saw no signs of declining, in May, the *Irish Ecclesiastical Record* posed the question, 'is this enough?' They believed that more prayer was necessary, answering their own question:

> We think not. The chastisement, so far from being lightened, is daily assuming more threatening features; the condition of the country seems to cry loudly to the Church for her prayers. For our own part, we do not think that in this respect her duty, either to the people or to God, will be fulfilled until she has appointed a stated day of public prayer and humiliation, to recur at least once in the month, to be continued as long as God is pleased to continue the visitation under which the people are now suffering.[212]

Around the same time that the Queen was leading the call for prayers on behalf of the Irish poor, Pope Pius IX was intervening in a number of ways to assist Ireland, which ranged from gifting a donation of 100 Roman crowns to issuing an encyclical calling for the international Catholic community to pray for Ireland and to make their own donations. The encyclical *Praedecessores Nostros* was issued on 25 March. The calling for an encyclical for such a purpose was unprecedented and reflected Pius's close relationship with a number of Irish priests and his admiration for Daniel O'Connell. Dr Paul Cullen, who was then based in Rome, privately informed Archbishop Murray in Dublin that the situation in Ireland had made the Pontiff 'very sad'.[213] In later correspondence, he added, 'His Holiness is not happy with the slowness of the [British] parliament to deal with the situation'.[214]

As various churches were calling for prayers on behalf of Ireland, a new system of relief was being established in Ireland. At the beginning of 1847, the government had announced that the public works were to be brought to an end. Instead, a series of relief measures were to be introduced that would lead to the Poor Law becoming responsible for all relief in Ireland at the end of summer. In the intervening months, a Temporary Relief Act would operate, under which government soup kitchens would be opened. The scheme was to be overseen by Relief Commissioners, based in Dublin and appointed by the Lord Lieutenant.[215] Even after the closure of public works had been announced, the numbers employed on them continued to increase. During the week ending 27 February 1847, 708,228 persons were employed on public works but this had grown to 734,000 by early March.[216] This meant that approximately two million people were either directly or indirectly dependent on this form of relief. The Treasury, anxious to bring this expensive project to an end, announced on 20 March that there would be a minimum 20 per cent reduction in the number of people employed, to be swiftly followed by further reductions. Part of the government's rationale for the peremptory discharge of so many was that they wanted people to return to their regular agricultural pursuits:

> The matter has now become of so grave and critical a nature, that if the number of persons employed on the relief works is not reduced in time to remove all obstacles to the usual amount of labour being employed in preparing the land for the next harvest, evils must ensue, which, while they would be painfully felt throughout the whole kingdom, would in Ireland produce calamities greater even than those which have been hitherto experienced.[217]

The decision to close the public works before soup kitchens had been set up ignored the fact that dozens of letters had been sent to the Treasury in the early months of 1847, by officials providing relief, outlining the starving condition of the poor, even of those employed on the works. A British Relief Association agent reported on 1 May 1847 that the poor in Arklow 'do not look so well as they did when I was here last; many of the old people as well as the young are dropping off; they have generally a paler and more sunken appearance, and more cases of swollen ankles'.[218] Increasingly, decisions being made in London bore no relation to the eyewitness testimony of officials working in Ireland or to the accounts of death from starvation or famine-related diseases that appeared in the press daily.

The closure of the public works at a time when many soup kitchens remained inoperative meant that there was a hiatus in the provision of government relief. The decision was condemned throughout Ireland. The Grand Jury in County Kerry described the Treasury's decision as equivalent to signing a 'death warrant' on the poor of Ireland, while the *Nation* newspaper categorized the action as 'murderous absurdity that would lead to even more deaths from starvation'.[219] In the absence of official relief, it was left to private resources to fill the starvation gap. For Count Strzelecki of the British Relief Association, the impact of the sudden closure of the public works was to increase demands made on charitable resources. Throughout April, he doubled the grants that he was making available to local Poor Law officials.[220] In the absence of government relief, therefore, private charity was the only buffer between life and death. The Society of Friends, which had been active in providing relief since the end of 1846, were pessimistic, believing that even when the government soup kitchens opened, their involvement would still prove to be necessary:

> From the present aspect of things around us, we cannot venture to anticipate an early termination or even diminution of our labours, but must rather contemplate increasing claims for help for several months to come, in consequence of the continued impoverishment of those classes bordering on the wholly destitute, whose means of support are abridged by the failure of employment, arising from the non-consumption to so large an extent of the ordinary products of their industry.[221]

The Temporary Relief Act, also known as the Soup Kitchen Act, which provided for the establishment of soup kitchens and the distribution of cooked food to the poor, was a new departure for the British government. The Act's introduction caught the imagination of a French society chef, Alexis Soyer, who lived in London.[222] By 1847, Soyer had already achieved celebrity status, not only for the recipes he served up to the rich and powerful, but also for his pioneering ergonomic use of kitchen space and his interest in devising nutritious recipes for the poor.[223] In 1847, desiring to alleviate poverty in London, he had opened a soup kitchen in Leicester Square, at which he fed between 200 and 300 people each day. Prince Albert had attended to taste the soup. Around the same time, Soyer had written a number of letters to the press about the Famine in Ireland.[224] Soyer initially travelled to Dublin sponsored by private subscriptions, but his services were retained by the British government. His aim was to create both soup recipes and a custom-designed soup kitchen, to help ensure that the relief would be provided in the most efficient and economical way possible. On 5 April 1847, Soyer's 'model' soup kitchen was opened in Dublin, amidst great fanfare. To mark the opening, the Viceroy, Lord Bessborough, was present but was so ill that he had to remain in his carriage. However, he did not escape the tasting, as Soyer hand-carried a portion of the soup to him. The other dignitaries who attended the grand opening, perhaps inevitably, pronounced the soup to be 'delicious'.[225]

The way in which the poor received their daily ration of soup was tightly regimented. The kitchen, in fact, was a large tent, which was located outside the Royal Barracks in Dublin.[226] Paupers queued up outside until a group was brought into a narrow passage. A bell then told that group when they could enter the food tent. Inside the eating area, there were long tables, each with bowls and spoons, attached to the tables with chains. A prayer was said before eating commenced. A quarter of a gallon of soup was provided to each person, and a further quarter pound of bread was given to be eaten after they left the tent. The whole process, from entering to leaving the tent, was to take only six minutes.[227] For those who had no other source of food, Soyer's soup would be their only means of survival until the new harvest. By July 1847, more than three million people were receiving free daily rations of food from the soup kitchens that covered the country, making it the largest relief scheme ever mounted in Ireland. While mortality rates did slow down during the summer, the health of many of the poor remained fragile. Asenath Nicholson, an American philanthropist and abolitionist, who was travelling through Connaught in the summer of 1847, was dismayed by the scenes she witnessed on a regular basis, writing: 'I could scarcely believe that these creatures were my fellow-beings. Never had I seen slaves so degraded'.[228] While most of the poor who died in 1847 did so without rite or ritual to mark their passing, one death in Ireland attracted much attention. On 16 May, the day after O'Connell had passed away in Italy, Lord Bessborough died. According to one English newspaper:

> After lingering many days in a state of hopeless exhaustion, Lord Bessborough has at length sunk under his malady. He died on Sunday night;

being up to the last moment in possession of his faculties. He dictated a letter to Lord John Russell on the state of the country only two or three days before; being then quite aware of the approach of death. He took leave of the several members of his family about an hour before his decease. The usual notification of the event was made to the Mayor of Dublin; and on Monday the tolling of the bells and firing of minute-guns proclaimed it to the citizens . . . As a tribute of respect to the memory of the deceased Viceroy, the Repeal Association adjourned on Monday without doing any business.[229]

The same paper announced that Lord Clarendon had been appointed the new Lord Lieutenant and Governor-General of Ireland.[230] Privately, Clarendon likened this appointment as akin to being thrown into an Irish bog, and he arrived with a vision for Ireland that included a determination to end dependency on government assistance.[231] He regarded the impending transfer to the Poor Law as an important step in this process, which would also bring longer-term benefits to Ireland, claiming:

In the next two years there will be a grand struggle, and the government of Ireland will be a painful, thankless task, but I am convinced that the failure of the potatoes and the establishment of the Poor Law will eventually be the salvation of the country.[232]

He too appeared to have little sympathy for the Irish poor. He explained to Russell in regard to the plundering of food supplies in Ireland, 'It is difficult to tax the industrious paupers of England for the support of such ruffians'.[233] Overall, though, he was pleased at how tranquil the country was, admitting that, 'if it were not for the harassing duty of escorting provisions, the troops would have little to do'.[234] Regardless of Clarendon's initial optimism, and his belief that the worst of the Famine was over, a number of factors worried him. He was concerned that the closure of the soup kitchens in August and the transfer of all relief to the Poor Law would cause some initial hardships. To ease the transition, he asked the Treasury – in effect, Charles Trevelyan – to allow Edward Twisleton, the Poor Law Commissioner, 'flexible powers to provide food and money'.[235] His request was refused. Moreover, in September 1847, the Treasury was continuing to resist demands for further expenditure in Ireland, even though it was clear that the newly amended Poor Law was foundering.[236]

The Whig Party's handling of the Famine was criticized by a number of British politicians, including George Bentinck, Benjamin Disraeli and George Poulett Scrope,[237] all of whom believed that alternative responses were possible. Bentinck, who was the leader of the Protectionist section of the Conservative Party, criticized the public works on the grounds that if employment was provided, the outcome should be beneficial to Ireland. In a long, detailed speech, he explained to the House of Commons the benefits of building railways, as opposed to useless roads, in Ireland. Bentinck completed his speech by speaking in defence of the patience of the starving Irish poor:

> I have heard it said, at different times, that there is a danger of an outbreak in Ireland. We have heard this story a thousand times repeated, and as often refuted, 'that the starving peasantry of Ireland are purchasing arms with which to commence an outbreak in that country.' Sir, I do not believe one word of any such representation. I can only express my great surprise, that with a people starving by thousands – with such accounts as we have read during the last two days – of ten dead bodies out of eleven found lying unburied in one cabin; of seven putrid corpses in another; of dogs and swine quarrelling over and fighting for the dead carcasses of Christians; of the poor, consigned coffinless to their graves, and denied the decencies of Christian burial, that the price of the coffin saved might prolong, for a few days, the sufferings of the dying – I, Sir, for one, look with amazement at the patience of the Irish people. I see it not in my own country; we see it not in France. We have heard of seven villages in France burned by the peasantry in the course of last autumn; and, seeing this, I think, with regard to the Irish people, we ought to look with admiration on the patience they have displayed. Talk of discontent – talk of sedition – talk of outbreaks – let me, I say, which I will do if this Bill is allowed to pass, fill the starving bellies of the Irish peasantry with good beef and good mutton – with good wheaten bread and good strong beer; and their pockets with English gold, wherewithal to purchase for themselves the blankets and broad cloths of Yorkshire and of Wiltshire, and the fustians of Manchester; and, for their wives and their daughters the printed cottons of Stockport; and may be the ribbons of Coventry; and I, the Saxon, with my head will answer for the loyalty and the honour of the Irish people. Yes. Sir, I, the Saxon, will lead them through their wants fulfilled, their wishes gratified, their warm sympathies and grateful hearts not to sever, but to cement, the union with England. Sir, I have now done; and it only remains for me to thank the House, with my whole heart for the unmerited kindness, patience, and indulgence with which they have for the hundredth time listened to me. I move, Sir – That leave be given to bring in a Bill for the prompt and profitable Employment of the People, by the encouragement of Railroads in Ireland.[238]

Bentinck's Railway Bill won mixed support in Ireland. Butt agreed that relief work should be of some use, rather than simply acting as a test of need. O'Connell was more equivocal. At the weekly meeting of the Repeal Association, held on 15 February, a letter was read from O'Connell as he was too ill to attend in person. Regarding the Railway Bill, he expressed only a qualified approval:

> It has, however, one overwhelming recommendation: it would give some employment and some wages to the starving people. These advantages

are greatly exaggerated; still there are advantages not to be overlooked in such a season of direful calamity as this. This is the principle upon which I act – Lord George proposes to employ sixteen millions sterling in Ireland; if I saw anybody who was disposed to give more, I should reject Lord George, and take the larger sum; but when I cannot see anybody offering so much, with the people dying in thousands about us, I cannot afford to reject his proposal.[239]

The Railway Bill did not pass through the House of Commons. The vote of the Irish members demonstrated their ambivalence: thirty-nine in favour, thirty-one against and thirty-five not present.[240] Henry Grattan, an Irish MP, responded to this defeat by suggesting, 'the Lord Lieutenant has no power and Downing Street has no heart'.[241] Following rejection of his idea, Bentinck regretted the fact that politicians were in such thrall to the pronouncements of political economists:

> The British government, reined, curbed and ridden by political economists, stands alone in its unnatural, unwise, impolitic and disastrous resolves, rather to grant lavishly for useless and unproductive works and for Soyer's Soup Kitchens, than to make loans on a private and efficient scale and on ample security, and to stimulate private enterprise.[242]

Bentinck and his colleague Disraeli also made repeated requests that the government keep a record of deaths in Ireland.[243] Russell continually suggested that such accounting was not possible, which led Bentinck to suggest that the government did not want the level of mortality to be made public.[244] In response to the government's suggestions that collecting such data would be too difficult, Disraeli pointed out

> that if returns were moved for of the quantities of pigs and poultry consumed within a given time, there would not be the least objection raised to any such return. Now there was, however, a remarkable and unprecedented mortality afflicting the sister kingdom, and the difficulties placed in the way of obtaining an exact statement of the deaths appeared to be insuperable.[245]

Chastising those who opposed more relief and better records to be kept, Bentinck warned:

> The time will come when we shall know what the amount of the mortality is, and though you Gentlemen may groan, and wish to conceal the truth, yet the truth shall and will be known; the time will come when the public, and the world itself, will be able to estimate at its proper value your management of the affairs of Ireland.[246]

Regardless of his lack of success, Bentinck's interventions were welcomed in Ireland. The Mayor of Cork City thanked him on behalf of the Irish people for his 'practical effort to relieve the distress of this country'. Bentinck responded, 'the warm-hearted thanks I daily receive from the Irish people, I am a hundred-fold repaid for my feeble and, alas, I fear, futile efforts to serve the Irish nation'.[247] Bentinck died in September 1848, aged only 46. On the centenary of his death, he was still remembered in Ireland as the man who tried to save the country from famine.[248]

After August 1847, the Irish Poor Law was made responsible for all relief in Ireland.[249] This move in effect meant that Irish taxation, through the mechanism of the poor rates, was to finance all relief. The amended Poor Law of 1847 was a major departure from the 1838 legislation as it permitted the granting of relief outside the workhouse, subject to a number of restrictions. It also provided for an additional thirty-three unions to be created and workhouses to be built. Edward Turner Boyd Twisleton, an Englishman, was appointed Chief Commissioner, working with the Chief and Under Secretaries to the Lord Lieutenant to manage this new enterprise.[250]

As the summer of 1847 came to a close, the government was hopeful of a good harvest with early reports suggesting little evidence of blight on the potato crop and an 'unusually abundant' corn harvest. However, it was also recognized that the plantation of potatoes had been very limited.[251] Although the area under potato cultivation was much smaller than usual, the large corn crop provided some hope that there would be enough food for all those who had survived until that time.[252] Encouraged by this news, the British government suggested that the Irish Famine was over. This announcement effectively marked the end of most of the fund-raising activities that had taken place over the previous year, while it consolidated all relief provision under one system. The government further announced that if any more relief was required, it had to come from Irish, not British, taxation. This change-over was facilitated by the introduction of the Poor Law Extension Act, under which both permanent and extraordinary relief were to be consolidated. Twistleton, the newly appointed Chief Commissioner, was to oversee this ambitious endeavour, assisted by the administration in Dublin Castle.[253] To make a relief system that had been designed to support 100,000 people, now responsible for more than one million, entailed a number of major changes. Significantly, the new act provided for thirty-three additional workhouses to be built and, for the first time, for relief to be provided outside of the workhouses.[254] Local poor rates were to finance all of this relief. By this time, private charity had largely dried up and so the poor, now facing a third year of shortages, were dependent on the new Poor Law to survive. Clearly, despite the optimism of officials in London, the Famine was not over and, in 1848, more than one million people turned to the Poor Law, and its minimal form of relief, for survival. From the perspective of the government, however, the transfer of relief to the Poor Law meant that Irish taxpayers were now solely responsible for financing Irish relief.

Despite widespread poverty, a new stringency was evident in collecting the poor rates. Property was increasingly seized, and to enforce payment, the military augmented the constabulary. At the end of the year, it was reported in the press, 'Large bodies of military are concentrating in the disorderly districts in Ireland: several regiments on horse and foot are mentioned as being in motion for that purpose'.[255] In addition to paying for the newly extended Poor Law, the local rates were also responsible for paying off the loans for earlier relief schemes. The burden for financing both the Soup Kitchen Act and the amended Poor Law fell primarily on owners and occupiers of land, but particularly on landlords who owned estates containing many small occupiers.[256] The large number of absentee landlords in many of the poorest districts exacerbated the difficulties of providing relief and of collecting the local taxes necessary to fund it. The negligence of absentee landowners was lamented by the Quakers, amongst others, and, as the following report shows, it had a basis in reality:

> At a meeting of a Relief Committee, recently held in Queen's County, it came out that the annual properties of absentees from the district was 25,578*l*., and their subscriptions 208*l*.; but while the annual properties of the residents were only 4,550*l*., their subscriptions amounted to 459*l*.[257]

The response of landowners who were resident varied greatly. Newspapers in County Mayo, for example, praised the actions of individual landowners, in particular the many interventions by Lord Sligo and his family.[258] By 1848, however, there were evictions on the Westport Estate, although Lord Sligo claimed that he did so only out of economic necessity, and with careful selection.[259] In contrast, Sir Roger Palmer, who owned estates in the nearby Belmullet, achieved a grim notoriety for the heartless way in which his tenants were evicted, leading a local newspaper to describe him as 'monstrous'.[260] Undoubtedly, as the Famine progressed and the fiscal burden on occupiers of land increased, even benign landlords came under financial pressure. One outcome was large-scale evictions, which meant that homelessness, combined with hunger, became a major source of mortality after 1847. If some landlords behaved badly, they were not the only group to take advantage of the vulnerability of the poor. Food contractors and merchants sometimes exploited the situation. In Ballinrobe, for example, the Poor Law Inspector Dr Dempster re-weighed the food that was being sold to the local people by local merchants. He found that in many cases the amount fell short of the amount being paid for – sometimes by almost 4 pounds. The inspector suggested that this practice was widespread and that all merchants involved should be 'indicted for fraud'.[261] No action appears to have been taken as the same inspector was still reporting on similar incidents in the months that followed.[262] These events reveal that even when relief was being given, the circumstances of the poorest and most vulnerable members of society were fraught with difficulties as societal ties and social contracts broke down.

The transfer to Poor Law relief placed a heavy burden on people whose resources were much diminished. In recognition of this difficulty, the twenty-two poorest Poor Law Unions were officially designated 'distressed' and they were to be offered minimal support from the Treasury. A controversial aspect of the new legislation was the 'Quarter-Acre Clause', which deemed that anybody who occupied more than this amount of land was not eligible to receive government relief. Consequently, smallholders who had held onto their land during the previous two years of shortages were now forced to vacate it if they wanted to avail themselves of Poor Law relief. John O'Rourke, an early historian of the Famine, claimed:

> A more complete engine for the slaughter and degradation of a people was never designed. The previous clause offered facilities for emigrating to those who would give up their land; the quarter-acre clause compelled them to give it up or die of hunger.[263]

This Clause, however, was also part of the desire to re-structure land-holding and Irish society. In a letter to Prime Minister Russell, dated 20 May 1848, Lord Palmerston, an Irish landowner and a member of the government, explained the motivation for such harsh requirements thus:

> It is useless to describe the truth that any great improvement in the social system in Ireland must be founded on an extensive change in the present state of agrarian occupation, and that this change implies a long, continued and systematic ejectment of small holders and squatting cottiers.[264]

This harsh new requirement was a reminder that rather than simply save lives, a purpose of the government was to bring about social change in Ireland. This measure contributed to the large-scale abandonment of small properties after 1847, which added greatly to the dislocation and despair of the poorer classes.

Other changes were taking place in land occupancy as a result of the relief policies introduced by the British government. After August 1847, much of the financial burden for financing the amended Poor Law fell on landowners. While a number used the nonpayment of rent as an excuse to implement large-scale evictions and thus consolidate their estates, others struggled to meet the heavy financial burdens placed on them. For a number of policymakers in London, Irish landowners were just as much a barrier to economic progress as the potato growers at the other end of the social scale.[265] To clear Ireland of indebted proprietors, in 1848 and 1849, the Encumbered Estates Acts were passed, which forced landowners who were in debt and unable to meet their financial obligations to sell their properties. Overall, a social revolution was being imposed upon the Irish landscape and on Irish society, irrespective of the high human cost.

At the end of 1847, although food supplies were more plentiful than they had been in the preceding year, the people were still without the means to purchase them. Even more worrying, the amended Poor Law – now the only relief provided by the government – was inoperative in some of the poorest areas, leading the Quakers to warn that 'in many districts the provisions of the poor law, under which all destitute persons are entitled to maintenance, are very imperfectly carried out'.[266] Asenath Nicholson also noted the adverse changes in the Irish workhouses since the commencement of the food shortages:

> Before the famine they were many of them quite interesting objects for a stranger to visit, generally kept clean, not crowded and the food sufficient. But when the famine advanced, when funds decreased, when the doors were besieged by imploring applicants, who wanted a place to die so that they might be buried in a coffin, they were little else than charnel houses, while the living, shivering skeletons that squatted upon the floors, or stood with arms folded against the wall, half-clad, with hair uncombed, hands and face unwashed, added a horror if not a terror to the sight.[267]

By the end of 1847, when it was clear that neither the relative absence of blight nor the introduction of the extended Poor Law was keeping people alive in Ireland, John O'Connell, Daniel's son and political successor, made a personal appeal to both the monarch and the government. Appealing for more aid for Ireland, he requested that 'these and every other constitutional means of making what is not unlike a death struggle, should be instantly universally adopted'. In a direct appeal to the Queen, he added, 'Assuredly, our beloved Queen will not reject the prayer thus made. She will not refuse to listen to her faithful, her ever loyal Irish subjects. Her woman's heart will be moved by the appalling tale of our miseries, and she will instruct her Ministers to call on Parliament to relieve them'.[268] As the new year dawned, the looked-for assistance did not arrive.

Sympathy for the Irish poor, however, was no doubt diminished by continued reports of Irish lawlessness. By end of 1847, British newspapers were recording an increase in assassinations in Ireland, the most high profile of which was the murder of Major Mahon in Strokestown. The government, showing its determination to protect other landowners from a similar end, offered a reward of £100 for the discovery of his murderers.[269] Reporting on the reception of the Irish people to such news, the Dublin correspondent for the *Morning Chronicle* posed the question,

> Will Parliament act promptly and effectively, and give a deathblow to these brutalizing sights? I have an average opportunity of knowing the state of feeling in the minds of the people, and with confidence I can assure you, that the amount of joy depicted on their countenances when one of these sickening announcements takes place is not equalled by a Christmas merrymaking.[270]

The early months of 1848 brought little respite from suffering for the poor, with a higher number of applications for Poor Law relief occurring in February than in January.[271] The distress was exacerbated by the spread of disease, especially typhus fever, and by the inclement weather. Regardless, Trevelyan, in an effort to cut costs, suggested that they reduce the payments made to surgeons who tended to the poor to 5 shillings a day. When the surgeons, whose numbers had been depleted tending to so many diseased people, resisted, Trevelyan instead proposed 'to employ all the disposable surgeons in the navy to take their place, and to join with them detachments of sappers and miners to bury the dead'.[272] In 1848, Count Strzelecki of the British Relief Association reported that the condition of the poor in parts of Connacht and Munster was worse than in the previous two years. He estimated that 99,000 holders of land had been evicted and were homeless. Many of them did not want to take shelter in the workhouse due to the policy of 'domestic separation', that is, the forcible separation of family members within these institutions. Instead, they applied for outdoor relief, even though they had no homes.[273] Strzelecki, who had been in Ireland since January 1847 and had witnessed much suffering, recorded on 12 March 1848, 'The Inspectors of Ballina and Belmullet write to me that, notwithstanding all their efforts, this district is a disgrace to any civilized country'.[274] Clearly, in 1848 the Famine was far from over.

However, as the misery of Ireland continued with little respite, in London a number of people were being recompensed and honoured for their part in providing relief. In August and September 1847, as the extended Poor Law was coming into operation, a number of leading relief officials received financial bonuses for their work over the previous two years. These men included Colonel Harry Jones of the Board of Works, Major John Burgoyne of the Relief Commission and Charles Trevelyan of the Treasury.[275] Trevelyan's was the most generous, him being awarded £2,500 tax free, which was equivalent to his annual salary. This was given in acknowledgement of his 'extraordinary labours during that trying time'.[276] It was not until almost one year later that the proprietary of making such an award was debated in the House of Commons. One Irish MP in particular, Colonel Dunne,[277] questioned the generosity towards the civil servant for merely 'overlooking Irish supplies of oatmeal and potatoes', pointing out that Soyer had received no recompense for the work that he had carried out.[278] At this point, Trevelyan offered to return his bonus, although there is no evidence that he did so.[279] However, Trevelyan was honoured in another way. In April 1848, both he and Routh received the Order of the Bath for their services in Ireland. During the same ceremony, George Nicholls received the Second Class Honour for his services to the Poor Law.[280] Six months following Trevelyan's knighthood, Strzelecki was similarly honoured, the *Morning Chronicle* pointing out that his recognition was made 'somewhat tardily'. The paper also made a pointed comparison between how Trevelyan, 'one of their own paid servants', had been rewarded, compared with Strzelecki, who had refused any payment for his work in Ireland, and, moreover, was being given only a Third Class Honour, for reasons that had not been specified.[281] The contrast between the two men was stark, while the distance between the British government and the poor in Ireland had never seemed as great.

Blight reappeared on the potato crop of 1848, although other food produced was healthy. Nonetheless, a fourth year of shortages, combined with widespread disease and extensive evictions, put pressure on the already strained resources of the Poor Law. Unlike two years earlier, however, there was little charitable money to prop up the government's relief measures.

Reluctantly, in February 1849, the government made available a small grant of £50,000 to assist the poorest districts in Ireland. At the same time, they made it clear that no further public money would be given to Ireland. In the succeeding months, however, the distress in parts of unions in Connacht and Munster proved to be even more severe than in 1847. The suffering was exacerbated by homelessness. John MacHale, the Catholic Archbishop of Tuam, reported that while the crops promised to be abundant, large-scale evictions meant the poor had no access to that food:

> ... the demolition of their houses, and the dispersion of their families, and the hunger and nakedness of the desolate little children left without a roof to shelter them, as harrowing to the Christian feelings as any that even the cruel annals of these latter years could supply ... as if the external ordinances of the Christian law should have been superseded by the capricious enactments of landlord legislators.[282]

The government in London could have been in no doubt about the situation, with even the unsympathetic *Times* reporting on the continuing misery:

> While hundreds of thousands were deprived of food and health by the failure of the potato crop, about 90,000 holders of land had lost their hearths by evictions and voluntary surrender and become houseless, some taking refuge in the workhouses – others took outdoor relief – in a state of emaciation, sickness and nudity hardly credible.[283]

Moreover, in April 1849, the Lord Lieutenant of Ireland, Lord Clarendon, had privately expressed his concerns to the Prime Minister about the failure to regulate evictions: 'I do not think there is another legislature in Europe that would disregard such suffering as now exists in the west of Ireland, or coldly persist in a policy of extermination'.[284] The emotional appeal of the government's chief representative in Ireland made no difference, as no more money was to be forthcoming from the British Treasury.

The government's solution to the crisis was to impose a further tax on the already stretched resources of the Poor Law. At the beginning of 1849, it was announced that a new tax, known as the 'Rate in Aid', of 6d. in the pound, was to be levied on every Poor Law Union, for redistribution to the poorest ones. It was an unpopular measure in Ireland. It also showed that, despite the existence of the Act of Union, and at the time of unquestionable need, the Irish people were to be left to their own resources. This point was made in the House of Commons by William Sharman Crawford who argued, 'The present case was an extraordinary one – it was a case of famine; and as such it ought to be provided for, not by the poor-laws, but out of the imperial exchequer'.[285] Such appeals fell on deaf ears with only thirty-four people voting against the bill in the House of Commons. However, Edward Twisleton, the Poor Law Commissioner, who had been increasingly frustrated by the callousness shown to the Irish poor, resigned in protest at the introduction of this tax. Privately, Clarendon sympathized with Twisleton's decision, explaining to Russell:

> He thinks that the destitution here is so horrible and the indifference of the House of Commons to it is so manifest, that he is an unfit agent of a policy that must be one of extermination.[286]

In the two years that Twisleton had been in charge of the extended Poor Law in Ireland, he had had many clashes with Trevelyan. Following his resignation, in a number of public statements, he made his frustration clear. Before he left office, Twisleton informed Trevelyan that as the Poor Law officials had been repeatedly denied all their requests for assistance, he considered him and his colleagues to be 'absolved from any responsibility on account of deaths which may take place in consequence of those privations'.[287] More poignantly, he informed a public enquiry on the Poor Laws that many of the deaths in the poorest unions could have been prevented 'by the advance of a few hundred pounds'.[288] It was a chilling and damning admission.

In June 1849, at the same time as the Rate in Aid tax was being implemented, a number of British politicians, supported by the Queen, raised a private subscription for the Irish poor. In total, it amounted to £6,400.[289] The money was entrusted to Count Strzelecki. When he arrived in the west of the country, he was dismayed by what he found as 'the distress of these ill-fated districts presented in June a character of suffering greatly exceeded in severity than that which I witnessed in the fatal winter of 1846–47'.[290] From late June to early September, Strzelecki travelled almost 3,000 miles, giving relief to those whom the Poor Law did not reach.[291]

In summer 1849, as the Rate in Aid was being implemented, there were 200,000 inmates in the workhouses, 770,000 people were receiving outdoor relief and 25,000 were in workhouse infirmaries. The reports from the western districts made harrowing reading, with even people in receipt of outdoor relief being described as 'crowding together and crouching under heaps of rotten straw of their unroofed cabins, under bridges, burrowing on the roadside, or in the ditches of the cold and wet bogs'.[292] Moreover, the absence of people, birds and animals was having an impact. According to Hugh Dorian, a school teacher in Donegal, 'in a very short time there was nothing but silence, a mournful silence in the villages'.[293] As 1849 came to a close, it was announced that a second Rate in Aid tax would be introduced in 1850. Clearly, the poorest districts in Ireland required external assistance, but just as clearly, the government was not willing to provide any more financial support.

While no further money was to be provided from London, a distraction was offered in the person of Queen Victoria. At the beginning of August 1849, accompanied by Prince Albert and four of their children, she visited Ireland for the first time. Originally, it had been scheduled for 1846, but it had been postponed due to the appearance of blight. Her short, carefully choreographed visit was confined to the east coast. Also, rather than travel overland, the royal party travelled by yacht, from Cork to Dublin, and from Dublin to Belfast. She went inland on only one occasion, when she visited Carton Estate, near Maynooth, on 11 August. Wearing a dress trimmed with Limerick Lace, she travelled there in an open barouche, along the banks of the Liffey. Thousands of people, included large numbers of what was referred to as 'the Irish peasantry', lined the route.[294] When Victoria reached Maynooth, the students of the Seminary dressed in their college regalia cheered as she passed. Thousands of other people had come to the town by train, carriage or on foot. Shortly after arriving, the royal party and about forty guests, overwhelmingly drawn from the Anglo-Irish gentry, sat down to 'partake of a magnificent dejeuner'. While they ate, about 160 people were given refreshments 'of the most varied and costly kind' in tents erected in the grounds of the estate. After viewing the gardens, the guests were shown 'a real Irish jig, which was danced to the music of an Irish piper by a number of the Duke's tenants and their wives and daughters'. The press reported that the Queen 'laughed most heartily at the performers and the royal party seemed to be highly pleased with them'. Shortly afterwards, the royal party left for Dublin, and that evening they sailed for Belfast where, the following day, she spent a few hours only before departing for Scotland.[295]

Victoria expressed delight with her reception in Ireland, writing to her Uncle Leopold, the King of Belgium, 'Everything here has gone beautifully since we arrived in Ireland and our entrance to Dublin was really a magnificent thing . . . Our visit to Cork was very successful . . . the enthusiasm is immense'.[296] However, behind the gaiety and conspicuous consumption, there was some dissent. Some members of the Catholic Church hierarchy refused to meet the Queen,[297] and a ditty was sung surreptitiously:

> Arise ye dead of Skibbereen
> And come to Cork to see the Queen.[298]

Although on a prison hulk, thousands of miles away, unrepentant nationalist John Mitchel attributed the seeming warmth of the welcome to the natural kindness of the Irish people and vigilant policing by Dublin Castle.[299] Nonetheless, a façade of a country that was free from famine, and a population who were happy subjects, had been presented to the wider public. Meanwhile, mortality in parts of the west was continuing to rise.

In the 1849 harvest, the potato blight was mostly confined to Counties Clare, Kerry, Limerick and Tipperary. The London *Times* took this as a positive sign that the Famine was over:

> Can it be there is a good time coming? . . . a feeling of hopefulness is beginning to spring up, while the sense of utter despondency which seemed to have overpowered all classes is gradually giving way to a more healthy course of action; in the perhaps (over sanguine) belief that the crisis has passed and there is still sufficient stamina in the country to recover from the shock of a three year famine.[300]

The paper's optimism was misplaced. As the year closed, the workhouses remained full, while the number of people surviving on the Poor Law in Counties Kerry and Clare was even higher than in the previous year. Within County Clare, the small town of Kilrush achieved a grim notoriety that equaled that of Skibbereen two years earlier, its fame based on the callousness of its local landowners, Colonel Vandeleur and Marcus Keane, and the continuation of high levels of excess mortality. The *Illustrated London News*, which had helped to expose the suffering of the poor in west Cork in 1847, sent the artist James Mahony to the area. Just as powerful as his images was the text that accompanied them:

> Kilrush, which gives its name to a Poor-law union, will be celebrated in the history of pauperism. With Clifden, Westport, Skibbereen, and other places, it forms one of the battle-fields of Ireland, in which property, under the guidance of legislation, has fought with poverty . . . The board agreed yesterday to petition the Poor-law Commissioners on the state of the Union, and said that the guardians would not be morally responsible for the deaths that may occur through starvation . . . The present condition of the Irish, we have no hesitation in saying, has been brought on by ignorant and vicious legislation.[301]

Despite receiving media attention, the situation in Kilrush and other nearby unions continued to deteriorate. In June 1851, the government appointed two Dublin doctors to visit the area and report on the continuing high levels of mortality.[302] Their report showed that conditions in the workhouses were detrimental to the health of the inmates. Following its publication, the new Poor Law Commissioner, Alfred Power, pleaded with Trevelyan to release more funds to the union.[303]

Although there was some evidence of blight on the potato crops of 1850 and 1851, it was increasingly becoming limited to districts in the west of the country. It was not until 1852 that the blight fully disappeared from Ireland. The 1851 census, which was not published until 1854, revealed that from a combination of deaths, emigration and averted births, the population had fallen by more than 25 per cent – the amount predicted by O'Connell. What made the tragedy more lamentable was the fact that, since 1800, Ireland had been part of the United Kingdom, which was at the center of the vast, powerful and resource-rich British Empire. Unfortunately, the resources of that Empire had not been deployed to mitigate the sufferings of the poor in Ireland.

The impact of seven years of food shortages continued to resonate well beyond 1852, and far beyond the shores of Ireland. Even after good harvests had returned to the country, the Irish population continued to fall. In 1841, the population of Ireland had been in excess of eight million; by 1901, it had fallen to a little more than four million. At the beginning of the twenty-first century, it still remained smaller than it had been in 1845. Using this simple demographic measure, it is possible to see that Ireland never recovered from the tragedy of the Great Famine. However, beyond the loss of population, much more was lost in those dark years, losses that are more difficult to quantify or to describe. Just as visitors and others noted the silence that accompanied the Famine years as people, dogs, frogs, birds, pigs and fowl disappeared from the landscape, so too was post-Famine Ireland a country possessing many silences and spaces. As Kerby Miller has pointed out, 'An entire generation virtually disappeared from the land; only one out of three Irishmen born about 1831 died at home of old age'.[304] The loss of the Irish language was inevitable given that so many of the dead were native Irish speakers. Moreover, post-Famine emigrants, who overwhelmingly moved to English-speaking countries, understood the merit of speaking the dominant language.

Being an observer of the unfolding crisis in Ireland must have taken a toll. William Bennett, an English Quaker, was aware that what he had witnessed would disturb him long after he had left the country, admitting, 'The scenes of human misery and degradation we witnessed still haunt my imagination, with the vividness and power of some horrid and tyrannous delusion, rather than the features of a sober reality'.[305] Bennett spent only six weeks in Ireland, so how did people who witnessed these scenes for six years process them? Recent research by Oonagh Walsh on epigenetics has pointed to the longer-term, transgenerational legacy of food shortages and trauma, with mental illness being one possible consequence.[306] While the wider cultural loss is harder to quantify or define, Máire Ní Grianna, descended from a Famine survivor from County Donegal, articulated the sense of bereavement: 'Poetry, music and dancing died . . . The Famine killed everything'.[307]

By any standard of suffering, the Great Famine remains extraordinary in terms of its immediate death toll and the longer-term demographic decline. Given the resources of the British government in the 1840s, a question remains of how a famine of such magnitude could have taken place at the centre of the richest and most integrated empire in the world. This raises the question of what it meant to be part of a United Kingdom at a time of suffering and need. What did it mean to be a British colony?[308] Clearly, the Union which had created a 'united' kingdom was a sham. Moreover, while the British government took administrative responsibility for what was happening in Ireland, increasingly it denied any financial or fiscal responsibility. This disconnect proved lethal to the Irish poor. The documents that follow show the Famine from a number of perspectives that are a testament both to human compassion and to inhuman callousness.

## A note on the documents

The Great Famine of the 1840s is sometimes compared with the famine of the early 1740s, in terms of its lethalness. One major difference, however, is the amount of written information available for the later tragedy, especially by the British government, it being bookended by the census returns of 1841 and 1851, and the subject of thousands of pages of official printed reports in the form of Blue Books, while many of the key players left copious amounts of correspondence.[309] Much of this writing is from the cold, clinical hand of a civil servant or government official. Unfortunately, in this as in other famines, those who suffered most left no account of their experiences. However, despite the devastation, disease and death within Ireland after 1845, visitors continued to travel to the country and to record what they saw. Consequently, in addition to the dry bombastic reports of government officials, there are numerous eyewitness accounts of what was happening from diverse perspectives.

The sheer volume of writing before, during and following the Famine makes a selection of the most significant documents difficult to make or to prioritize. Moreover, interest in the tragedy was international, with fund-raising projects established as far apart as Calcutta in India and Boston in America in 1845.[310] Understanding how the poor, more specifically, the Irish poor, were regarded by those who legislated on their behalf provides the starting point of this collection. In the first document, Irish poverty and its relief are seen through the eyes of English Poor Law Commissioner George Nicholls. The debates that led to the introduction of the Irish Poor Law in 1838 make the decisions that were taken in the British parliament after 1845 easier to understand. Ireland attracted many overseas political and social commentators in the early nineteenth century, who often published their experiences. Lydia Fisher is unusual, not simply because of her gender, but also because she lived in Ireland, and wrote about her holiday in County Kerry in the summer of 1845. Her letters offer no suggestion of the disaster about to unfold in Ireland.

The appearance of a new form of disease on the potato crop was the immediate trigger for the Famine. While the disease was not unique to Ireland, no other country had such high dependence on this tuber. The origins and erratic proliferation of the blight baffled horticulturalists and scientists alike. The three documents included show the response to the potato blight from very different perspectives.

News of the reappearance of blight in 1846, quickly followed by reports of large-scale mortality, attracted a number of visitors to Ireland, their motives ranging from that of Lord Dufferin, looking to make his spring vacation from Oxford University interesting, to Asenath Nicholson, eccentric and forthright American

Abolitionist and Bible Protestant anxious to help the poor, to the multiple young Quakers who came to assist in giving relief by the most direct method possible. With the artwork of Cork-born illustrator James Mahony, commissioned by a London newspaper to travel to the south west of Ireland, we have an example of the artist as witness. Moreover, Mahony accompanied his illustrations with words – he penned two articles for the *Illustrated London News* in 1846 to 1847, and seven in 1849 to 1850.[311] Unusually, he also attempted to give a voice to the poor people whom he met. As a consequence, the Famine was observed and recorded by sympathetic individuals, who witnessed deaths on a daily basis.[312] The pamphlet, books and press articles written by these three observers have, for reasons of space, not been included in the document section, but their sympathetic testimonies remain compelling.

The published account of Elihu Burritt has been included in this volume. Like Nicholson, Burritt was American and an Abolitionist, and he was also a skillful self-promoter, who had come to Europe in 1846 to advance his own causes of Peace and the transatlantic Penny Post. Events in Ireland had led him to travel there, 'to fathom the cause, extent and cure of its misery'.[313] Similarly to other visitors, he chose to visit the area that was perceived to be the epicentre of the suffering, Skibbereen. What his pamphlet does not reveal is that after only two days in Skibbereen, he awoke feeling feverish and his clothes were 'saturated with nauseating effluvia of the cabins', and so he decided to cut his stay short.[314] Burritt's experiences are a reminder of the considerable risks faced by those who engaged in giving relief to the Irish poor.

The impact of private charity is difficult to quantify or evaluate partly due to its amorphous nature, but also because of the sheer number of people who made donations to Ireland. As the reasons for giving varied greatly or remain unknown, it is also difficult to draw conclusions about motivations. Documents that relate to three diverse individuals involved in fund-raising have been included: Reverend John Edgar of Belfast, Queen Victoria based in London and Tyrone-born Bishop John Hughes in New York. Their appeals, from a Presbyterian, an Anglican and a Catholic perspective respectively, indicate the importance of religion in private charity, while raising the spectre of proselytism. However, private relief during the Famine was overwhelmingly provided with no attempt to win converts. In the vanguard of this philanthropic movement was the British Relief Association and the Society of Friends, their paths crossing quite literally as their agents traversed Ireland, providing relief in a manner that was more practical, more immediate and more compassionate than that provided by the government. Many of these visitors wrote of their experiences and provide powerful testimony of the suffering and the patience of the Irish poor. Only the account of William Bennett, an English Quaker, has been included in this volume, but a fuller picture of the role of the Quakers is available in their 1852 publication *Transactions of the Central Relief Committee of the Society of Friends*. Poignantly, the latter volume concludes with the reflection that they had failed in their mission.

The humility of these caregivers is in strong contrast to the hubris of Charles Trevelyan. As the leading civil servant at the Treasury, he was a key figure in managing the various relief measures introduced by both the Peel and the Russell governments. His account, *The Irish Crisis*, is that of a bureaucrat who was based in London, far removed from the scenes of suffering, yet fully informed of the impact of the food shortages and the relief policies. Trevelyan's article placed the Famine in its longer historical context and provides a useful summation of the relief measures during the two years following the first appearance of blight. It also provided a blueprint for future polices – making it clear that the government no longer considered the Famine to be a British responsibility.[315] The writing is precise, cold and detached, reflecting the character of the man who not only controlled the purse strings, but micromanaged the way in which government relief was provided. In light of recent attempts to either rehabilitate Trevelyan as a hard-working civil servant who had considerable sympathy and affection for Ireland, or alternatively to demonize him as guilty of genocide, this document bears revisiting.[316]

Two men, both born in Ulster, both Protestant, both trained in Law, and only two years apart in age, were radicalized by the Famine, each regarding the government's relief policies as inappropriate and misguided. However, Isaac Butt and John Mitchel argued from different ends of the political spectrum, Butt as a Conservative Orangeman, Mitchel as the radical face of Young Ireland. Both men spoke out against the policies of the government; in the case of Mitchel, it led to him being found guilty of treason and sentenced to fourteen years' transportation. Butt's more measured response, *A Voice for Ireland: The Famine in the Land*, was nevertheless a damning indictment of British relief measures.

Two men who loved Ireland, its history, its culture and its landscape, but who viewed it through different political prisms, reflected on the impact of the Famine on their beloved country. William Wilde, as Census Commissioner in both 1841 and 1851, had a unique insight into the impact of the food shortages and relief policies. John Mitchel, writing from his exile in Bermuda, Tasmania and America, continued to be ever-present as a commentator on the tragedy. The anger that he had manifested in 1848 towards the oppressors of his people showed little signs of diminishing with age or distance. These two men were bound together in a further way. In 1851, Wilde had married the nationalist poet Speranza, who had been a colleague of Mitchel on the *Nation* newspaper.[317]

Regardless of the devastation of the Famine years and the dislocation that followed, Ireland continued to attract visitors and was increasingly depicted as a tourist destination. In fact, 'between 1845 and 1923, more than 569 travel narratives and tourist guides were published addressing Ireland'.[318] The penultimate document is by one of those visitors, Samuel Hole, an English Anglican minister who visited Ireland in 1859. His tone is whimsical and affectionate, him and his companion being charmed by what they beheld. A more somber note is introduced through a conversation with a servant who recalls the tragic years. Overall, Hole was more sympathetic and hopeful for Ireland than Thomas Carlyle and Harriet Martineau, two better known political commentators who had visited in 1849 and 1852 respectively. This volume concludes with a poem written by an American politician which was based on a quote by an English politician. It provides a reminder that the memory and the legacy of the Famine was, in the words of Matthew Schultz, 'a non-present presence' that haunted people on both sides of the Atlantic.[319]

The documents in this volume tell a sad tale. A common theme of the eyewitness accounts was that no language had the power to convey the awfulness of what they were observing. Despite these limitations, the following documents help to explain the complexity and the tragedy of the Great Famine. However, despite the millions of words written about the Famine, and the ever-increasing availability of artwork and memorials, it many ways the suffering of the victims will always remain elusive and unfathomable.

This volume, 'Attenuated Apparitions of Humanity: The Great Famine in Ireland', which opens the series, is concerned with the Great Famine, arguably one of the greatest tragedies in Irish history. The subsequent volumes demonstrate, through different lenses, how far-reaching the impact of the Famine was largely as a result of the mass emigration that accompanied it, and persisted long after good harvests had returned to Ireland. Volume II, 'Irish Famine Migration Narratives: Eyewitness Testimonies', by Jason King, provides the primary sources and first-hand accounts of the Irish Famine migration of 1847–1848, written from the perspectives of the emigrants themselves and their caregivers in Canada and the United States. Volume III, ' "Fallen Leaves of Humanity": Famines in Ireland Before and After the Great Famine', by Christine Kinealy and Gerard Moran, places the Great Famine in its longer context. There were many famines and subsistence crises before 1845 and after 1852, but they have been overshadowed by the cataclysm that took place in the mid-nineteenth century. The final volume, 'The Exodus: Emigration and the Great Famine', by Gerard Moran, explores the complexity of the process of emigration, both as escape and as exile. It also shows how the emigrants were perceived and received in the places they chose as their new homes. Collectively, these volumes allow a reassessment of the impact of famine and emigration in Irish history, while allowing a fresh engagement with those who experienced them.

Christine Kinealy

## Notes

1 Niall O Cioséin, 'Was there "silence" about the famine?', *Irish Studies Review*, 13 (Winter 1995–1996), pp. 7–10.
2 Seamus Deane, *Strange Country: Modernity and Nationhood in Irish Writing Since 1790* (Oxford: Clarendon Press, 1997), p. 51.
3 Robert Smart, *Black Roads: The Famine in Irish Literature* (Hamden, CT and Cork: Quinnipiac University Press and Cork University Press, 2015).

4 Matthew Schultz, *Haunted Histories: The Rhetoric of Ideology in Postcolonial Irish Fiction* (Manchester: Manchester University Press, 2014).
5 Marguérite Corporaal, *Relocated Memories: The Great Famine in Irish and Diaspora Fiction, 1846–1870* (Syracuse, NY: Syracuse University Press, 2016).
6 Andrew Merry, *The Hunger, Being the Realities of the Famine Years in Ireland 1845 to 1849* (London: Andrew Melrose, 1910).
7 *The Informer* had been made into a Hollywood film by John Ford in 1935.
8 For example, Seamus Heaney in 'For the Commander of the "Eliza"' quotes from Woodham-Smith; Karen McNamara, 'It was a life-changing book', in George Cusack and Sarah Goss (eds), *Hungry Words, Images of Famine in the Irish Canon* (Dublin: Irish Academic Press, 2006), traces Woodham-Smith's impact on the children's literature of the Famine.
9 Donnacha Dennehy, *The Hunger*, an opera (New York: G. Schirmer Inc, 2014). This opera is based on Asenath Nicholson's experiences during the Famine.
10 Christine Kinealy and John Walsh, *The Bad Times: An Droch Shaol* (Hamden, CT: Quinnipiac University Press, 2015; Dublin: Coiscéim, 2016).
11 One of the first activists to make the link was Don Mullan who, at the time of the sesquicentenary, was working for 'Concern' (Dublin), an international humanitarian organization. See Don Mullan, *A Glimmer of Light – Great Hunger Commemorative Events in Ireland and Around the World* (Dublin: Concern Worldwide, 1995).
12 John O'Rourke (1810?–1887) was ordained in Maynooth Seminary in 1849. He was buried in Laragh Bryan cemetery in Maynooth.
13 It was published in Dublin by McGlashan and Gill, and was 584 pages in length and cost 8 shillings.
14 Christian Noack, Lindsay Janssen and Vincent Comerford (eds), *Holodomor and Gorta Mór: Histories, Memories and Representations of Famine in Ukraine and Ireland* (London: Anthem Press, 2012), p. 53.
15 Canon John O'Rourke, *The Battle of the Faith in Ireland* (Dublin: J. Duffy, 1887), p. 553.
16 'The history of the Great Irish Famine of 1847', *Freeman's Journal*, 18 December 1874.
17 'Just published', *Irish Times*, reprinted in *Freeman's Journal*, 28 January 1875.
18 Ibid., *Irish America*.
19 Quoted in Christophe Gillissen, 'Charles Trevelyan, John Mitchel et l'historiographie de la Grande Famine [Charles Trevelyan, John Mitchel and the historiography of the Great Famine]', *La grande famine en irlande, 1845–1851*, XIX.2 (2014), pp. 195–212; 'Ireland', *The Spectator*, 20 May 1876.
20 'The late very Rev. Canon O'Rourke', *Freeman's Journal*, 20 July 1887.
21 William Patrick O'Brien (1824–1898). A Catholic, he attended the elite Downside School in Somerset in England. His obituary appeared in the *Downshire Review* of 1889 (Somerset: Downside Abbey, 1898, vol. 18), p. 115. An obituary also appeared in the *Irish Times* of 11 April 1898. He died in Tudor House/Hall in Monkstown in Dublin, which was later the home of Tim Pat Coogan, the journalist.
22 William Patrick O'Brien, *The Great Famine in Ireland and a Retrospect of the Fifty Years 1845–95, With a Sketch of the Present Condition and Future Prospects of the Congested Districts* (London: Downey, 1896).
23 A Poor Law Union was an administrative unit upon which the locally charged poor rates were based. The 1838 legislation provided for Ireland to be divided into 130 unions, each with its own workhouse. This was changed by the 1847 legislation.
24 Noack *et al.*, *Holodomor and Gorta Mór*, pp. 53–54.
25 'Birthday honours', *London Gazette*, 24 May 1892.
26 Quoted in 'The Great Irish Famine', *Leinster Express*, 6 June 1896.

27 'Downey and Company's newest books', *Freeman's Journal*, 27 November, 1896. The book cost 10s and 6d.
28 'Mr William O'Brien on the harvest', *Southern Star*, 25 September 1897.
29 It was favourably reviewed in the *Lancet*, J. Onwhyn, 'The Great Famine' (1896), p. 1025 and in the *Ulster Journal of Archaeology* (Belfast: Marcus Ward and Co., 1896, vol. 2), p. 282.
30 The *Leinster Express* had been established in 1831. It was published in Maryborough (Portlaoise) in Queen's County (County Laois).
31 'The Great Irish Famine', *Leinster Express*, 6 June 1896.
32 'The Great Irish Famine: The record of an official eye-witness', *Freeman's Journal*, 6 June 1896.
33 Ibid.
34 'The Great Famine: A retrospect of fifty years', *The Spectator*, 30 January 1897.
35 An exception was George O'Brien, *An Economic History of Ireland From the Union to the Famine* (London: Longmans, Green & Co., 1921), which tended to use the same sources as the two earlier volumes.
36 T. W. Moody, one of the founding fathers of Irish revisionism, made a case for this approach in Theodore W. Moody, 'Irish history and Irish mythology', *Hermathena*, 124 (1978), pp. 1–24, University of Dublin.
37 Mary Daly, 'David Beers Quinn and Ireland', *The Hakluyt*, http://www.hakluyt.com/hak-soc-tributes-daly.htm, accessed 20 January 2017.
38 Seamus Delargy, 'The recording', *Irish Independent*, 27 September 1938.
39 Seán Ó Súilleabháin, *Irish folklore and tradition* (Dublin: Educational Company of Ireland Limited, 1942), p. 3, quoted in The Schools' Folklore scheme, www.clarelibrary.ie/eolas/coclare/history/schools_folklore/footnotes.htm#5, accessed 4 February 2017.
40 Roger Joseph McHugh (1908–1987) was a professor of Anglo-Irish literature at University College, Dublin. He was also a playwright and, after 1954, an independent member of *Seanad Éireann*.
41 Questionnaire: Irish Famine (1845–1852), https://digital.ucd.ie/view/ivrla:20162, accessed 20 April 2017.
42 Gerard Healy (1918–1963) was an actor and playwright. Between 1949 and 1951, he made a number of acclaimed drama-documentaries on behalf of Noel Browne, the Minister for Health.
43 Abbey Theatre Archives, www.abbeytheatre.ie/archives/play_detail/10215, accessed 1 March 2017.
44 T. W., 'Famine play at the gate', *Irish Press*, 7 March 1945.
45 Barry Cassin, *I Never Had a Proper Job: A Life in the Theatre* (Dublin: Liberties Press, 2014).
46 For the challenges of staging the famine and an examination of the paucity of plays see Elisabeth Angel-Perez and Alexandra Poulain (eds), *Hunger on the Stage* (Cambridge: Cambridge Scholars, 2009), p. 142.
47 'Famine play at the gate.'
48 Ibid.
49 Gerard Healy, *The Black Stranger: A Play in Three Acts* (Dublin: James Duffy, 1950). The book was only 53 pages in length.
50 Abbey Theatre Archives, www.abbeytheatre.ie/archives/play_detail/10215, and http://gaelicparkplayers.org/the-black-stranger-spring-1996/, and 'The Seanachie', 1996, http://digitalcommons.sacredheart.edu/cgi/viewcontent.cgi?article=1022&context=shanachie, all accessed 1 March 2017.
51 'Purchases by government', *Irish Examiner*, 31 August 1946.
52 The accompanying catalogue was called *Thomas Davis and the Young Ireland Movement Centenary: Exhibition of Pictures of Irish Historical Interest* (Dublin: Alexander Thom, 1946).

53 Ibid., p. 9.
54 'Historical pictures purchased', *Irish Independent*, 31 August 1946.
55 Emily Mark-FitzGerald, *Commemorating the Irish Famine: Memory and the Monument* (Oxford: Oxford University Press, 2015), pp. 58–61.
56 'Book reviews', *Munster Express*, 7 September 1945.
57 Timothy O'Herlihy, *The Famine, 1845–47: A Survey of Its Ravages and Causes* (Dublin: St Peter's Phibsboro, 1947). O'Herlihy had been born in Inniscarra in County Cork. He entered O'Hallows College to train for the priesthood in 1930, when aged only 15. For a number of years, he worked in St Patrick's College in Drumcondra. For many years also, he was editor of *The Golden Hour*, the official publication of the Eucharistic League in Ireland. He died in 1956. See *All Hallows Annual* (Dublin: Browne and Nolan, 1957/1958), pp. 98–99.
58 Quoted in 'Reviews: Short history of the Famine', *Tuam Herald*, 1 February 1947.
59 O'Herlihy, *The Famine*, p. 5.
60 'The crazy things of the Famine years', *Irish Independent*, 8 February 1947; *The Irish Press* on 6 March 1947 described it as 'an excellent little book [that] could hardly be bettered'. A less than favourable review did appear in the *Kilkenny People*, 12 July 1947, which accused the book of not being coherently written and containing many mistakes, while seeing its greatest strength lying in the 'sincerity' of the author.
61 'Black forty seven', *Irish Examiner*, 5 July 1947.
62 Thomas Derrig (1897–1956) had been born in Mayo. He participated in the 1916 Rising, the War of Independence and the Civil War, in the latter, on the de Valera/republican side. He served as Minister for Education during de Valera's first government, from 1832 to 1839, and held this position again from 1943 to 1948.
63 'History of Famine – £1,500', *Evening Herald*, 27 April 1945.
64 Brendan Bradshaw, 'Nationalism and historical scholarship in Ireland', *Irish Historical Studies*, xxvi (November 1989), pp. 329–351.
65 At the time the book was published, Robert (Robin) Dudley Edwards (1909–1988) and Theodore William Moody (1907–1984), together with David Quinn (1909–2002), dominated the writing of history in Ireland in the mid-twentieth century. They had all been trained at the Institute of Historical Research in London and were committed to writing 'value-free history'. Thomas Desmond Williams (1921–1987) had studied at Peterhouse in Cambridge, under the guidance of Herbert Butterfield. He specialized in German history. During the Second World War he had worked for the British Foreign Office as a member of British Intelligence. The editors, Edwards and Williams, both taught at University College, Dublin, when *The Great Famine* was published.
66 Michael Briody *et al.*, 'The commission's collectors and collections', *Studia Fennica, Finnish Literature Society*, 17 (2016), p. 285.
67 De Valera pledged that Ireland would do all it could to help. 'Letters, city allotments', *Irish Press*, 21 July 1945.
68 'Irish foodstuffs for Europe', *Evening Herald*, 18 May 1945; '£3,000 scheme to aid Europe', *Irish Independent*, 19 May 1945.
69 'Grow more food', *Westmeath Examiner*, 23 February 1946.
70 'Irish foodstuffs for Europe', *Evening Herald*, 18 May 1945.
71 'Price control blamed for egg shortages', *Sunday Independent*, 16 November 1847; ibid., 'Millions would be needed for Connemara's housing'.
72 Emigration was frequently discussed by all parties after the SWW. The comparison with the Famine was a frequent reference point. The high levels of emigration were debated during the General Election campaigns of 1948 and 1956. Emigration had risen from 3,000 in 1946 to 40,000 in 1950, with no more recent figures being available. See 'Fine Gael: General election quiz', *Nenagh Guardian*, 31 January 1948; 'Mr. de Valera replies to the *Taoiseach*', *Irish Independent*, 29 February 1956.

73 'Forecasts confirmed', *Sunday Independent*, 16 November 1847.
74 'Crisis level', *Strabane Chronicle*, 8 September 1951.
75 'Two dangers facing the country', *Kerryman*, 22 November 1947.
76 R. D. Edwards and T. D. Moody, *The Great Famine: Studies in Irish History* (Dublin: Browne and Nolan, 1956).
77 The Introduction was written by Kevin Nowlan.
78 Cormac Ó Gráda, 'Making history in the Ireland of the 1940s and 1950s: The saga of the Great Famine', *The Irish Review*, 12 (Spring/Summer 1992), pp. 87–107, 101, 107.
79 Colm Tóibin, 'The Irish Famine', in Colm Tóibín and Diarmaid Ferriter (eds), *The Irish Famine: A Documentary* (London: Profile Books, 1999), p. 9.
80 F. S. Lyons, who subsequently was highly critical of *The Great Hunger*, was overwhelmingly positive in his review, F. S. L. Lyons, 'Review', *Irish Times*, 21 January 1957.
81 See Ó Gráda, 'Making history'.
82 *Irish Independent*, 25 January 1963.
83 When asked to write a review she had declined, responding, 'I don't, in fact, much enjoy reviewing, perhaps because I have no gift or facility and hate finding fault', Woodham-Smith to *Time and Tide*, 6 March 1961 in Box 16, File 4, Woodham Smith Papers, Boston University.
84 Woodham-Smith, 'The harvest was death', *The New York Times*, 4 August 1957.
85 Ó Gráda, *Making History*, pp. 101, 107.
86 'Colourful historian of Ireland and stalwart of Trinity College Dublin: R.B. McDowell Obituary,' *Guardian*, 14 September 2011. McDowell was a supporter of the British Conservative Party and helped to bring leading Conservative politicians including Enoch Powell and Keith Joseph to TCD, R. B. McDowell, *McDowell on McDowell: A Memoir* (Dublin: Lilliput Press, 2012), pp. 162, 98–100.
87 Woodham-Smith to Jamie Hamilton, 5 December 1961, Hamish Hamilton Archive: DM1352, University of Bristol.
88 *Irish Independent*, 2 November 1962.
89 Ibid., 'Never call me a novelist,' 23 November 1962.
90 *Irish Independent*, 1 June 1963.
91 Ibid.
92 In comparison, *The Great Famine*, in its first two years of publication, had not sold its 2,000 print run, see Cormac Ó Gráda, 'Introduction' to Edwards and Williams, *The Great Famine: Studies in Irish History* (Dublin: Lilliput Press, 1994).
93 Review by F. S. L. Lyons, 'Reviews and Short Notices. The Great Hunger in Ireland', *Irish Historical Studies* (1964–1965), pp. 77–78.
94 James S. Donnelly Jr, 'The Great Famine and its interpreters, old and new', *History Ireland*, 1.3 (Autumn 1993), pp. 27–33.
95 Roy Foster's article appeared in the first issue of *The Irish Review*. It was entitled 'We are all revisionists now', 1 (1986), pp. 1–5.
96 For more on Cecil Woodham-Smith see Christine Kinealy, 'Never call me a novelist', in C. Kinealy, J. King and Ciarán Reilly (eds), *Women and the Great Hunger* (Cork: Cork University Press, 2017).
97 Tóibín, 'The Irish Famine', p. 29.
98 Ó Gráda, *Making History*, p. 97.
99 Elizabeth Malcolm, 'On fire: The Great Hunger: Ireland 1845–1849', *New Hibernian Review*, 12.4 (Winter 2008), pp. 143–148.
100 See Christine Kinealy, *A Death-Dealing Famine: The Great Hunger in Ireland* (London: Pluto Press, 1997), pp. 1–15.
101 Brendan Bradshaw (1937–) had been born in Limerick. He was both a priest and a historian. He was Fellow of St John's College, Cambridge, England, 1973–1975.

102 'A man with a mission: Interview with Brendan Bradshaw', *History Ireland*, 1.1 (1993), pp. 52–55.
103 Ibid.
104 Donnelly, 'The Great Famine and its interpreters', pp. 27–33; Christine Kinealy, *This Great Calamity: The Irish Famine 1845–52* (Dublin: Gill and Macmillan, 1994).
105 *Riverdance* was first performed in the 1994 Eurovision Song Content, which was held in Dublin, http://riverdance.com/blog/2014/04/29/the-night-riverdance-was-introduced-to-the-world; 'The Nobel Prize in Literature', https://www.nobelprize.org/nobel_prizes/literature/laureates/1995/; 'U2 at MTV Awards', https://www.atu2.com/news/u2-at-the-1995-mtv-europe-music-awards.html, all accessed 10 December 2016.
106 This was a quote from Máire Ní Grianna of Rannafast in Co. Donegal, quoted in S. Deane (ed.), *The Field Day Anthology of Irish Writing* (Derry: Field Day, 1991), pp. 203–204.
107 Christine Kinealy, *War and Peace: Ireland Since 1960* (London: Reaktion Books, 2011).
108 'Scientists sequence potato', DNA, 19 July 2011, http://www.dw.com/en/scientists-sequence-potato-dna/a-15250320, accessed 4 February 2017.
109 Oonagh Walsh, 'Nature and nurture: The Great Famine and epigenetic change in Ireland', in Kinealy et al., *Women and Great Hunger*.
110 Jonny Geber, *Victims of Ireland's Great Famine: The Bioarchaeology of Mass Burials at Kilkenny Union Workhouse* (Gainesville, FL: University Press of Florida, 2015).
111 See, for example, Christine Kinealy and Gerard MacAtasney, *The Forgotten Famine: Poverty, Hunger and Sectarianism in Belfast, 1840–1850* (London: Pluto Press, 2000).
112 Ciarán Ó Murchadha, *Figures in a Famine Landscape* (London: Bloomsbury Press, 2016); Ciaran Reilly, *Strokestown and the Great Irish Famine* (Dublin: Irish Academic Press, 2014).
113 John Crowley, William J. Smyth and Michael Murphy (eds), *Atlas of the Great Irish Famine* (Cork: Cork University Press, 2012).
114 David Dickson, *Artic Ireland: The Extraordinary Story of the Great Frost and Forgotten Famine of 1740–41* (Belfast: White Row Press, 1997).
115 The term 'black famine' was used a number of times in the 1940s: 'Fine Gael: General election quiz', *Nenagh Guardian*, 31 January 1948; 'Melancholy exception', *Sunday Independent*, 23 February 1947.
116 Michael Davitt, *The Fall of Feudalism; or, the Story of the Land League Revolution* (London: Harper and Brothers, 1904), p. 50.
117 'Cecil O'Hanlon reviews a history of Ireland under the union', *Irish Press*, 27 March 1952.
118 The publication of Kavanagh's poem 'The Great Hunger' in 1942 does not appear to have increased the usage of this phrase in Ireland. A trawl of digitized Irish newspapers (so neither scientific nor comprehensive, but indicative) reveals that an early use of the phrase 'the Great Hunger' in relation to the Famine first appears in 1946, 'Fungus started the Famine', *Irish Press*, 23 August 1946. The term appears again in Irish newspapers in an article about female religious orders in Skibbereen during the Famine, 'Nuns', *Irish Examiner*, 25 May 1960.
119 'Scotland's Great Hunger', *Irish Independent*, 26 October 1963.
120 Christine Kinealy, 'Food supply and trade', in Christine Kinealy, *The Great Irish Famine: Impact, Ideology and Rebellion* (Basingstoke: Palgrave Macmillan, 2002), pp. 90–116.
121 Ian Anstruther, *The Scandal of the Andover Workhouse* (London: Geoffrey Bles, 1973).

122 Digest of Evidence taken before Her Majesty's *Commissioners of Inquiry Into the State of the Law and Practice in Respect to the Occupation of Land in Ireland* (Dublin: Alexander Thom, 1848).
123 Ibid., pp. 13–14.
124 'Murrain' was an archaic word for an infectious disease that could affect cattle. It was probably derived from the Middle English word 'moreine', meaning death. The origins of the word 'blight' are obscure, it possibly deriving from the Old English word 'blæce, blæcðu', meaning a scrofulous skin condition.
125 Frederick Bravender, *The Potato Disease and How to Prevent It* (London: Farm Journal Office, 1880), p. 25.
126 Sir Robert Peel to the Duke of Wellington, 21 October 1845, 'Report for the commissioners of inquiry into matters connected with the failure of the potato crop', *British Parliamentary Papers* (BPP), 1846 [33], xxxvii, p. 223.
127 Peel to Sir Henry Hardinge (marked secret), 16 December 1845, in C. S. Parker, *Sir Robert Peel From His Private Letters* (London: John Murray, 1899), p. 280.
128 See 'Analysis of potato crop lost in 1845–1846', in Kinealy, *This Great Calamity*, pp. 360–362.
129 'Scientists finally pinpoint the pathogen that caused the Irish Potato Famine', *The Smithsonian*, 21 May 2013, www.smithsonianmag.com/science-nature/scientists-finally-pinpoint-the-pathogen-that-caused-the-irish-potato-famine-71084770/, accessed 28 May 2013.
130 'Correspondence Explanatory of the Measures adopted by Her Majesty's government for the relief of distress arising from the potato crop in Ireland', *BPP*, 1846, xxxvii.
131 Lord Heytesbury to Peel, 17 October 1845, in Lord Mahon and E. Cardwell, *Memoirs of the Right Honorable Sir Robert Peel* (London: John Murray, 1857), p. 125; ibid., Sir James Graham to Peel, 19 October 1845, pp. 126–127.
132 'Mansion House Committee', *Freeman's Journal*, 4 November 1845.
133 *Belfast Vindicator*, 1 November 1845.
134 'The town council', *Spectator*, 17 October 1846.
135 'Public benevolence of Belfast', *Belfast News-Letter*, 5 January 1847.
136 Lord Lieutenant to Peel, 27 October 1845, in Mahon, *Memoirs*, p. 138.
137 'Monthly chronologer for Ireland', in *The Gentleman's and London Magazine: Or Monthly Chronologer* (Dublin: John Exshaw, 1766, vol. xxxvi), p. 651.
138 *Dublin Gazette*, 29 December 1767.
139 See James Kelly, 'Scarcity and poor relief in eighteenth-century Ireland: The subsistence crisis of 1782–4', *Irish Historical Studies*, 28.109 (May 1992), pp. 38–62, 44.
140 Ibid.; David Dickson, 'A gap in Famines, a useful myth', in Margaret Crawford (ed.), *Famine. The Irish Experience 900 to 1900. Subsistence Crises and Famines in Ireland* (Edinburgh: John MacDonald, 1989), pp. 96–111.
141 Sir James Graham in House of Commons answering a question from Charles Sharman Crawford, 11 February 1846, quoted in *The Economist*, 14 February 1846 and the *Belfast News-Letter*, 17 February 1846.
142 Sir Randolph Routh to Charles Trevelyan, 1 April 1846, 'Correspondence explanatory of the measures adopted by Her Majesty's Government for the relief of distress arising from the failure of the potato crop in Ireland', *BPP*, 1846, xxxvii.
143 *Times*, 7 November 1845.
144 *Times*, 6 November 1845.
145 *News of the World*, 16 November 1845.
146 Geraint Parry, Hillel Steiner and Andrew Marrison (eds), *Freedom and Trade: Free Trade and Its Reception, 1815–1960* (London: Routledge, 1996), p. 50.
147 William George Bentinck (1802–1848), referred to as Lord George, was a Conservative politician who, with Disraeli, worked to end Peel's Premiership in 1846. He

became leader of the Protectionist faction, but resigned in early 1848, shortly before his death, probably from a heart attack. Benjamin Disraeli (1804–1881) was a Christianized Jew. He and Bentinck both spoke out in favour of Jewish Emancipation in 1847 (a cause that had been supported by O'Connell) but by doing so, they lost the support of many in the Protectionist Party. Disraeli would later serve as Prime Minister.

148 Christine Kinealy, *Repeal and Revolution: 1848 in Ireland* (Manchester: Manchester University Press, 2009).
149 Lord John Russell, *Hansard*, 17 August 1846, lxxxcviii, cc. 772–778.
150 This point is made in Peter Gray, *Famine, Land and Politics: British Government and Irish Society, 1843–1850* (Dublin: Irish Academic Press, 1999).
151 Kinealy, *A Death-Dealing Famine*, p. 138.
152 Trevelyan to Randolph Routh, Chief Secretary's Office Papers, National Archives, Dublin, 0.1957, 12 January 1847.
153 For example, Ireland exported an estimated ninety million eggs each year to Britain. See Roger Scola, *Feeding the Victorian City: The Food Supply of Manchester, 1770–1870* (Manchester: Manchester University Press, 1992); Kinealy, *The Great Irish Famine*, pp. 90–116.
154 'Report of the House of Lords to consider extending the functions of the Constabulary to suppress illicit distilling', *BPP*, 1854, x, pp. 448–459.
155 'Account of the number of cattle exported from Ireland to Great Britain, 1846–49', *BPP*, 1850, lii, p. 423; 'Exports of grain from Ireland', *Hansard*, xciii, 30 June 1847, pp. 1057–1059.
156 *Banner of Ulster*, 21 April 1846.
157 Bessborough, Dublin Castle, to Russell, Russell Papers, National Archives of England, 30 22 16A, 23 January 1847.
158 'Ireland', *Spectator*, 14 November 1846.
159 'To John Kane Esq, Mayor', *Belfast News-Letter*, 13 October 1846.
160 Soup Kitchens in Belfast', *Belfast News-Letter*, 20 November 1846.
161 'Return of number and description of works applied for, recommended and sanctioned in each district in Ireland for the year 1846', *BPP*, 1847, pp. 764, 1.
162 'Ireland', *Spectator*, 26 December 1846.
163 Hugh Dorian, Breandán Mac Suibhne and David Dickson, *The Outer Edge of Ulster: A Memoir of Social Life in Nineteenth-Century Donegal* (Notre Dame, IN: University of Notre Dame Press, 2001), p. 34.
164 *Nation*, 27 November 1846.
165 Trevelyan to Randolph Routh, Chief Secretary's Office Papers, National Archives, Dublin, 0.1957, 12 January 1847.
166 'Ireland', reprinted in the *Spectator*, 14 November 1846.
167 *Spectator*, 19 September 1846.
168 Thomas Spring Rice, 1st Baron Monteagle of Brandon (1790–1866), was a progressive landlord who, despite his Whig politics, was opposed to the policies of Russell's government.
169 C. E. Trevelyan to Lord Monteagle, 9 October 1846, Monteagle Papers, National Library of Ireland (NLI), 1846, MS. 13, 397/1.
170 Those who attended the meeting included John Mitchel, Samuel Ferguson and William Sharman Crawford. They all supported an extension of tenant rights in Ireland, see 'Ireland', *Spectator*, 13 November 1847.
171 Valentine Lawless, *Personal Recollections of the Life and Times, With Extracts From the Correspondence of Valentine Lord Cloncurry* (Dublin: J. McGlashan; London: W.S. Orr, 1849), pp. 503–504. A number of cases were reported to have taken place in County Galway, see 'The alleged case of cannibalism', *Belfast News-Letter*, 8 June 1849.

172 Ibid., p. 506.
173 'Prorogation of parliament', *Hansard*, 28 August 1846, vol. 88, c. 1066. Initially, parliament was to reconvene on 4 November 1846, but there is no evidence that this took place.
174 'Ireland', *Spectator*, 28 November 1846.
175 Ibid.
176 'Starvation-deaths-Whig rule', *Kerry Evening Post*, 16 December 1846.
177 'Ireland', *Hansard*, 19 January 1847, vol. 89, cc. 67–166.
178 'The Famine', *Irish Ecclesiastical Journal* (January 1847), p. 78 (Dublin: Grant and Bolton).
179 'Meeting of Parliament', cc. 1–3.
180 Russell, 'Corn and navigation laws', *Hansard*, 21 January 1847, vol. 89 cc. 210–268.
181 Ibid., col. 216.
182 'House of commons', *Times*, 22 January 1847.
183 Christine Kinealy, *Daniel O'Connell and the Anti-Slavery Movement* (London: Pickering and Chatto, 2008).
184 Destitute Persons (Ireland) Bill, *Hansard*, 8 February 1847, vol. 89, cc. 942–945.
185 Society of Friends, *Transactions of the Central Relief Committee During the Famine in Ireland in 1846 and 1847* (Dublin: Hodges and Figgis, 1852).
186 Rob Goodbody, *A Suitable Channel: Quaker Relief in the Great Famine* (Dublin: Pale Publishing, 1995), p. 78. To enable the Soup Kitchen Act to become operative, the Quakers provided the government with 284 large soup cauldrons.
187 For more on Quakers see Kinealy, *Kindness of Strangers*, pp. 63–84.
188 Trevelyan to Jonathan Pim, 24 August 1848, Treasury Papers, T.64 367 B/2, National Archives of England; Pim to Trevelyan, 5 June 1849, *Transactions*, pp. 452–454.
189 Kinealy, *Kindness*, p. 258.
190 *The Dublin University Magazine*, vol. 38 (William Curry, Jun., and Company, 1851); in 1851, Edgar published *Irish Industry – Women's Work and Women's Worth* (Belfast, 1851), p. 118.
191 See Christine Kinealy, 'A Polish count in county Mayo: Paul de Strzelecki and the Great Famine', in Gerard Moran and Nollaig O Muraile (eds), *Mayo: History and Society* (Dublin: Geography Publications, 2015), chapter 20.
192 'Skibbereen', *Freeman's Journal*, 29 December 1846.
193 One hundred years after he undertook the journey, Dufferin was praised for his graphic descriptions and objective writing, 'This happened today: From Oxford to Skibbereen', *Irish Press*, 21 February 1948.
194 Warren was an innovative farmer from Brighton, Mass. See *Magazine of Horticulture, Botany, and All Useful Discoveries and Improvements in Rural Affairs* (Hovey, 1843, vol. 9), p. 459.
195 Trevelyan, Treasury to Burritt and Warren, 3 February 1847, in 'Famine in Europe', *Niles National Register*, 1 May 1847, p. 138.
196 'Extracts from Irish papers', *Leinster Express*, 6 March 1847.
197 Charles Northend (ed.), *Elihu Burritt; a Memorial Volume Containing a Sketch of His Life and Labors With Selections From His Writings and Lectures, and Extracts From His Private Journals in Europe and America* (New York: D. Appleton, 1879), p. 52.
198 Ibid.
199 Society of Friends, *Transactions of the Central Relief Committee*, p. 40.
200 'State of the streets', *Cork Examiner*, 3 March 1847.
201 *Friends Quarterly Examiner*, fourth month, 1889, pp. 162–163; Sir Edward Fry, *James Hack Tuke: A Memoir* (London: Macmillan and Co., 1899), p. 50.
202 'Rome', *Westmeath Independent*, 13 March 1847, contained reports of heavy snow and freezing temperature in France and Britain.

203 From *Farmer's Gazette*, 'Effects of frost and snow on vegetation', *Newry Telegraph*, 25 March 1847.
204 'British ladies clothing association', *London Daily News*, 17 May 1847; ibid., 12 June 1847.
205 William Bennett, *Narrative of a Recent Journey of Six Weeks in Ireland: In Connexion With the Subject of Supplying Small Seed to Some of the Remoter Districts* (Dublin: Charles Gilpin, 1847).
206 *Spectator*, 28 November 1846.
207 Peter Gray, 'National humiliation and the Great Hunger: Fast and famine in 1847', *Irish Historical Studies*, 32.126 (November 2000), pp. 193–216.
208 The *Standard*, quoted in the *Spectator*, 6 March 1847.
209 'Miscellaneous', *Spectator*, 20 March 1847.
210 Philip Williamson, 'State prayers, fasts and thanksgivings: Public worship in Britain 1830–1897', *Past and Present*, 200.1 (2008), pp. 121–174, 153–154.
211 Gray, 'National humiliation', Abstract.
212 *Irish Ecclesiastical Journal* (May 1847), p. 141, Dublin.
213 Paul Cullen, Rome to Daniel Murray, 13 February 1847, Cullen Papers, CUL/144.
214 Ibid., Dr Cullen, Rome, to Daniel Murray, Dublin, 28 February 1847, Cullen Papers CUL/1450.
215 'A Bill for the temporary relief of destitute persons in Ireland' was introduced on 28 January 1847.
216 'Ireland', *Spectator*, 13 March 1847.
217 *Treasury Minute*, 20 March 1847; Lord George Grey to Lord Lieutenant, quoted in 'Ireland', *Spectator*, 27 March 1847.
218 *Report of British Relief Association for the Relief of Distress in Ireland and the Highlands of Scotland* (London: Richard Clay, 1849), p. 127.
219 *Times*, 24 March 1847; *Nation*, 27 March 1847.
220 Christine Kinealy, *Charity and the Great Hunger in Ireland: The Kindness of Strangers* (London: Bloomsbury, 2013), chapter nine.
221 Ibid. For the role of the Society of Friends during the Great Hunger see chapter three.
222 Alexis Soyer (1809–1858) was born in France but left during the July Revolution in 1830. In 1837, he was appointed chef of the Reform Club in London. While in Ireland, he wrote *Soyer's Charitable Cookery*, giving part of the proceeds to charity.
223 Alexis Soyer, *Délassements Culinaires: Culinary Relaxations* (London: W. Jeffs, 1845).
224 Helen Morris, *Portrait of a Chef: The Life of Alexis Soyer, Sometime Chef to the Reform Club* (Cambridge: Cambridge University Press, 1938), pp. 75–88.
225 *Dublin Evening Mail*, 7 April 1847.
226 The Royal Barracks are now Collins Barracks (*Dún Uí Choileáin*) located in the Arbour Hill area of Dublin.
227 *Dublin Evening Mail*, 7 April 1847.
228 Mrs A. Nicholson, *Annals of the Famine in Ireland, in 1847, 1848, and 1849* (New York: French, 1851), p. 143.
229 'Ireland', *Spectator*, 22 May 1847.
230 Ibid.
231 Clarendon to Henry Reeve, Clarendon Letter Books, Bodleian Library, 5 January 1847.
232 Ibid., Clarendon to Charles Wood, Chancellor of the Exchequer, 2 August 1847.
233 Ibid., Clarendon to Russell, 8 August 1847.
234 Ibid., Clarendon to Russell, 5 July 1847.
235 Ibid., Clarendon to Wood, 21 July 1847.
236 Anthony Howe, *Free Trade and Liberal England, 1846–1946* (Oxford: Clarendon Press, 1997), pp. 45–46.

237 George Poulett Scrope (1797–1876) was an English political scientist and politician. He was critical of the policies of the British government during the Famine, accusing them of treating the Irish poor as 'human encumbrances'. His alternative was to propose peasant ownership of the land in Ireland. In the short term, he believed that the Irish poor should have a right to relief.
238 Lord George Bentinck, 'Railways (Ireland)', *Hansard*, 4 February 1847, vol. 89, col. 801.
239 'Ireland', *Spectator*, 20 February 1847.
240 Bentinck, 'Railways', *Hansard*, col. 801.
241 *Times*, 8 March 1847, 9 March 1847.
242 Quoted in *Roscommon and Leitrim Gazette*, 3 April 1847.
243 'Deaths (Ireland)', *Hansard*, xciii, 9 March 1847, vol. 90, col. 1101.
244 Ibid., cc. 1148–1150.
245 'Mortality in Ireland', *Hansard*, 29 March 1847, vol. 91, col. 574.
246 'Poor relief (Ireland) bill', *Hansard*, 29 March 1847, vol. 91, cc. 597–598.
247 *Times*, 22 February 1847, 12 March 1847.
248 'Answer to the Famine', *Irish Press*, 22 September 1948.
249 The legislation consisted of three separate acts, the main one being, 'An act to make further provision for the relief of the destitute poor in Ireland', 8 June 1847, 10 Vic., c. 31.
250 'Ireland', *Spectator*, 4 September 1847.
251 Ibid.
252 *Nation*, 21 July 1847.
253 'Ireland', *Spectator*, 4 September 1847.
254 'An act to make further provision for the relief of the destitute poor in Ireland', 8 June 1847, 10 Vic., c. 31.
255 'Ireland', *Spectator*, 4 December 1847.
256 The Poor Relief (Ireland) Bill of 1843 made landowners responsible for paying poor rates on property valued at less than £4.
257 'Ireland', *Spectator*, 20 February 1847.
258 *Connaught Telegraph*, 22 July 1846.
259 Lord Sligo to Lord Monteagle, 8 October 1848, Monteagle Papers, NLI, MS. 13,395/5.
260 *Connaught Telegraph*, 5 July 1848.
261 'Papers relating to proceedings for relief of distress, and state of unions and workhouses in Ireland', *BPP*, 1848, fifth series, 4 January 1848, p. 368.
262 Ibid., 1848, sixth series, 25 March 1848, p. 63.
263 O'Rourke, *Irish Famine*, p. 204.
264 Quoted in G. P. Gooch, *The Later Correspondence of Lord John Russell 1840–1878* (London: Longmans, Green and Company, 1925, vol. 1), p. 225.
265 *Times*, 10 October 1847.
266 Report of Joseph Bewley and Jonathan Pim, 1 December 1847, *Transactions*, p. 146.
267 Nicholson, *Famine*, p. 166.
268 *Spectator*, 4 December 1847.
269 'Ireland', *Spectator*, 13 November 1847.
270 Quoted in *Spectator*, 4 December 1847.
271 See *Annual Report of the Commissioners for Administering the Laws for Relief of the Poor in Ireland With Appendices* (Dublin: Alexander Thom, 1849).
272 *Tuam Herald*, 2 September 1848.
273 *Nation*, 26 October 1849.
274 *Report of the British Relief Association*, p. 135.
275 Robin Haines, *Charles Trevelyan and the Great Irish Famine* (Dublin: Four Courts Press, 2004), pp. 549–542.

276 *Morning Chronicle*, 28 November 1848.
277 Major-General Francis Plunkett Dunne (1802?–1874) was an officer in the British Army, an Irish landowner in Queen's County and a Conservative MP in Westminster. In 1848, he made a demand for an enquiry into the operation of the extended Irish Poor Law. This was granted in 1849, see *Illustrated London News*, 10 February 1849.
278 'Scraps from *Punch*', *Cork Examiner*, 6 September 1848.
279 Haines, *Charles Trevelyan*, p. 551.
280 'Order of the bath', *Newry Examiner and Louth Advertiser*, 6 May 1848.
281 *Morning Chronicle*, 28 November 1848.
282 'To the editor of the *Freeman*', *Tuam Herald*, 18 August 1849.
283 *Times*, 19 October 1849.
284 Lord Clarendon to Lord John Russell, 28 April 1849, Clarendon Letter Books.
285 Order for Third Reading, 'Poor laws (Ireland) rate in aid bill', *Hansard*, 30 April 1849, vol. 104, c. 991.
286 Clarendon to Russell, 12 March 1849, Clarendon Letter Books.
287 Evidence of Edward Twisleton, 'Select committee on the Irish poor law', *BPP*, 1849, xvi, pp. 711–714.
288 Ibid., p. 717.
289 'Subscription list', *Times*, 16 June 1849.
290 *Nation*, 27 October 1849.
291 *Times*, 19 October 1849.
292 *Nation*, 27 October 1849.
293 Dorian, *Outer Edge of Ulster*, p. 215.
294 *Cork Examiner*, 13 August 1849.
295 Ibid.
296 Victoria to Leopold, 6 August 1849, in Arthur Christopher Benson and Viscount Esher (eds), *The Letters of Queen Victoria: A Selection From Her Majesty's Correspondence Between the Years 1837 and 1862*, 3 vols (London, 1907), pp. 224–225.
297 Thomas MacHale, *Correspondence Between the Most Rev. Dr MacHale, Archbishop of Tuam and the Most Rev. Dr Murray, Archbishop of Dublin, Relative to an Address to Be Presented to Her Majesty Queen Victoria, on the Occasion of Her Visit to Ireland in 1849* (Dublin: M.H. Gill, 1885), p. 9.
298 See Kinealy, *Death-Dealing Famine*, pp. 139–141.
299 Mitchel, *The Last Conquest*, pp. 215–216.
300 *Times*, 18 July 1849.
301 *Illustrated London News*, 15 December 1849.
302 'Copy of a letter addressed by the poor law commissioners for Ireland appointing doctors Hughes and Hill as inspectors . . . for inquiring into the causes of the mortality in certain unions in the county of Clare', *BPP*, 1851, p. 442.
303 Kinealy, *Calamity*, pp. 270–276.
304 Kerby Miller, *Emigrants and Exiles: Ireland and the Irish Exodus to North America* (Oxford: Oxford University Press, 1988), p. 29.
305 See Bennett, *Six Weeks*.
306 Walsh, 'Epigenetics'.
307 Deane, *Field Day*, p. 204.
308 Terrence MacDonough, *Was Ireland a Colony? Economy, Politics, Ideology and Culture in Nineteenth-Century Ireland* (Dublin: Irish Academic Press, 2005).
309 A further difference is that the mass exodus that accompanied and followed the Great Famine took the story overseas and created generations of emigrants who believed that this was the reason why they had left Ireland. The desire to memorialize the Famine, most evidently since 1995, is a testimony to the resilience, hard work and long memories of the Irish diaspora.

310 Kinealy, *Kindness of Strangers*.
311 Julian Campbell, 'The artist as witness: James Mahony', in Crowley, *Famine Atlas*, pp. 473–475.
312 Melissa Fegan, 'The traveller's experience of Famine Ireland', *Irish Studies Review*, 9.3 (2001), pp. 361–371.
313 Burritt, Birmingham, to 'My dear sir', 6 February 1847, https://www.swarthmore.edu/library/peace/DG051-099/dg096Burritt/Burritt%20transcriptions_pdfa_18470206.pdf, accessed 28 October 2016.
314 'Skibbereen', 24 February 1847, Elihu Burritt Papers, New Britain Library, Connecticut, pp. 50–51.
315 At a meeting of the Repeal Association on 3 January 1848, John O'Connell referred to Trevelyan's article in the *Edinburgh Review* as 'a programme of the intentions of government with regard to Ireland', 'Repeal Association', *Tuam Herald*, 2 September 1848.
316 For alternative views of Trevelyan see Robin Haines, *Charles Trevelyan and the Great Irish Famine* (Dublin: Four Courts Press, 2004); Tim Pat Coogan, *The Famine Plot, England's Role in Ireland's Greatest Tragedy* (London: Palgrave Macmillan, 2012).
317 Christine Kinealy, 'The Stranger's Scoffing'. *Speranza*, the *Hope of the* Irish *Nation*. In the *Oscholars* Library at: http://www.oscholars.com/TO/Appendix/library.htm.
318 Spurgeon Thompson, 'Famine travel: Irish tourism from the Great Famine to decolonization', in Benjamin Colbert (ed.), *Travel Writing and Tourism in Britain and Ireland* (London: Palgrave Macmillan, 2011), p. 164.
319 Schultz, *Haunted Histories*, Blurb.

# Part I

# POVERTY AND PERSPECTIVES
Ireland before 1845

# 1

# GEORGE NICHOLLS, ESQ., *POOR LAWS – IRELAND. THREE REPORTS BY GEORGE NICHOLLS, ESQ., TO HER MAJESTY'S PRINCIPAL SECRETARY OF STATE FOR THE HOME DEPARTMENT* (BRITISH PARLIAMENTARY PAPERS, 1836–1838)

The debates that led to the passing of Irish Poor Law legislation in 1838 provide a valuable insight into how the Irish poor were regarded by politicians and political economists. Until that year, Ireland, unlike England, Wales and Scotland, did not possess a national system of relief. However, the writings of political economists, including the influential Thomas Malthus,[1] had created a perception that too generous a system of poor relief not only perpetuated poverty, but encouraged the recipients to breed.[2] A consensus formed, therefore, that the existing poor relief systems needed to be reformed or, in the case of Ireland, created with due caution. An enquiry into poverty and poor relief in England in the early 1830s led to the introduction of the 'new' Poor Law of 1834, which sought to eliminate outdoor relief.[3] It also provided an impetus for a similar investigation to be held in Ireland. Consequently, a nine-man team, chaired by Richard Whately, Anglican Archbishop of Dublin, was created in 1833. Daniel Murray, the Catholic Archbishop of Dublin, was also a member.[4] The resulting enquiry took three years to complete during which time an intensive and comprehensive survey was carried out in all parts of the island. The final report, based on a series of interim reports, was completed in 1836.[5] The recommendations were comprehensive and went beyond suggesting ways in which poverty could be relieved, to proposing projects that would assist in the longer-term economic development of the country. The Commissioners estimated that almost two-and-a-half million people a year would require some sort of support and they believed that a Poor Law alone, based on the English model, could not cope with such extensive demands. Instead, they recommended that the system of relief should be supplemented with public works and assisted emigration.[6] Such a comprehensive, practical and sympathetic approach to Irish poverty was beyond the ideological and financial limits of what the British government had expected or wanted. They responded by asking George Nicholls, an English Poor Law Commissioner, to undertake a visit to Ireland and report on the suitability of the English system of relief to Ireland.

George Nicholls been born in Cornwall in the south of England.[7] His first career was as a naval officer, he commanding his own ship before he was 30. In 1815, he left the Navy and moved to Nottinghamshire where he became a Poor Law administrator. He immediately proved skillful at bringing down costs, but his principal ambition was to end outdoor relief, that is, the relief that the poor received while still living in their own homes, which he regarded as both expensive and demoralizing. Nicholls published his recommendations, initially in a local newspaper, but shortly afterwards as a pamphlet.[8] Nicholls' career then took a different path as he undertook a number of entrepreneurial projects, before settling on banking. However, his achievements when working as a Poor Law overseer meant that he was consulted during the enquiry into the working of the English Poor Law. Its findings led to the introduction of the 'new' Poor Law of 1834, which sought to eliminate outdoor relief.[9] Nicholls was invited to be one of three new Commissioners, a position that he accepted. The new, more stringent Poor Law, was disliked by the poor and by progressives. Its cruelty was captured in Charles Dickens' *Oliver Twist*, which was published in serial form between 1837 and 1839 in the magazine *Bentley's Miscellany*.[10] Nonetheless, when a Poor Law for Ireland was being considered, Nicholls was considered an obvious choice to report on its suitability.

In late summer 1836, Nicholls undertook a six-week tour of Ireland that did not include the north-east on the grounds that he believed it was similar to England. He was an unsympathetic observer of Irish poverty and, unsurprisingly, he concluded at the end of his whirlwind trip that the English Poor Law, based on the workhouse system, was suited to Ireland. Moreover, his estimate for the numbers requiring relief was only 80,000, he achieving this lower figure by making a distinction between poverty and destitution. While the Commissioners had sought to eliminate poverty in Ireland, Nicholls simply sought to relieve the most desperate.

The death of William IV in June 1837 meant that parliament was prorogued and so passing a Poor Law Act was delayed. In the interim, Nicholls visited Ireland again. This time he included the north of the country. Although he modified some of his initial views, partly to answer earlier criticisms, he remained committed to the belief that the English Poor Law was suited to Ireland. Unsurprisingly, his recommendations were welcomed by the government, although they divided opinion in Ireland.[11] Opponents of Nicholls included the Irish political economist, Isaac Butt.[12] The Irish Poor Law was passed in 1838. The country was divided into 130 Poor law unions, each with a workhouse. The unions were also the unit of a new system of local taxation, known as poor rates. Although this was modelled on the English legislation, from the outset it was clear that the Irish poor were to be treated more harshly than the poor in other parts of the United Kingdom. Consequently, in Ireland no outdoor relief was permitted and no right to relief existed. This meant that if a workhouse became full, there was no obligation to provide alternative relief. In a country with a small industrial base and intermittent subsistence crises, a rigid system of Poor Law relief was not suited to the needs of the Irish poor. This was apparent in 1839, 1842 and after 1845 when additional relief measures were introduced to alleviate the food shortages.[13] In 1847, moreover, an extended Poor Law was made responsible for all relief in Ireland. George Nicholls had warned that 'where the land has ceased to be reproductive, the necessary means of relief can no longer be obtained from it, and a Poor Law will no longer be operative'.[14] His words, in this instance, were ignored, with disastrous consequences.

In April 1848, Nicholls was knighted. Charles Trevelyan of the Treasury was also honoured at this time. Nicholls retired due to ill health in 1851. However, he went on to publish separate histories of the English (1854), Scottish (1856) and Irish Poor Laws (1856). In total three reports on Irish Poor Laws were submitted by Nicholls – the first on 22 August 1836, the second on 3 November 1837 and the third on 5 May 1838. The final account included a report on the relief of the poor in Holland and Belgium. Only the first report is reprinted below.

## POOR LAWS — IRELAND. FIRST REPORT BY GEORGE NICHOLLS, ESQ., TO HER MAJESTY'S PRINCIPAL SECRETARY OF STATE FOR THE HOME DEPARTMENT (LONDON: W. CLOWES AND SONS, STAMFORD STREET, FOR HER MAJESTY'S STATIONERY OFFICE, 1838)

FIRST REPORT OF GEORGE NICHOLLS, ESQ. DATED 22nd AUGUST, 1836.

Lord John Russell's Letter of Instructions.

POOR LAWS (IRELAND). TO GEORGE NICHOLLS, ESQ., &c. &c. &c.

Sir,

Whitehall, August 22nd, 1836.
In order to arrive at a practical conclusion with respect to any measures to be introduced into Parliament during the ensuing Session, for the benefit of the Poor in Ireland, it is most desirable that a person well acquainted with the operation of the past and present system of Poor Laws in England, should visit that part of the United Kingdom.

There is no one to whom I can intrust such a duty, more able to perform it with judgment and diligence, than yourself. You will, therefore, proceed to Ireland in the first week in September, taking with you the Report of the Commissioners of Poor Inquiry in Ireland.

The chief objects to which your attention will be directed are,—that part of the Report which relates to the Relief of the poor by Money payments, and the resource of Emigration.

You will examine how far it is judicious or practicable to offer relief to whole classes, whether of the Sick, the Infirm, or Orphan children.

You will consider whether such relief may not have the effect of promoting imposture, without destroying Mendicity; and whether the condition of the great bulk of the poorer classes will be improved by such a measure.

You will carefully weigh the important question—whether a rate, limited in its amount rather than its application to particular classes, might be usefully directed to the erection and maintenance of Workhouses for all those who sought relief as Paupers. With a view to this question, you will inquire whether any kind of Workhouse can be established which shall not, in point of food, clothing, and warmth, give its inmates a superior degree of comfort to the common lot of the independent labourer. You will ask the opinion of experienced men, whether the restraint of a Workhouse would be an effectual check to applications for admission; and whether, if the system were once established, the inmates would not resist, by force, the restraints which would be necessary.

Supposing the Workhouse system not to be advisable, you will consider in what other mode a national or local rate might be beneficially applied.

You will examine the policy of establishing depots where candidates for Emigration might resort; and you will ascertain by what method it is proposed to avoid the evil, said to be likely to flow from the establishment of Workhouses, and which might arise in like manner from the formation of depots for Emigration.

You will specially direct your attention to the machinery by which any rates for the relief of the Poor might be raised and expended; the formation and constitution of a Central Board, of Local Boards, of District Unions, and of Parochial Vestries.

Your attention need not be very specially given to the plans for the general improvement of Ireland, contained in the Report of the Commissioners of Inquiry: but you will generally remark upon those, or any other plans, which may lead to an increased demand for labour.

You will also inquire whether, under the direction either of companies or individuals, the capital applied to the improvement of land, and reclaiming bogs and wastes, is perceptibly or notoriously increasing or diminishing.

You will also carefully read the Bills which have been brought into the House of Commons on this subject during the present year.

Lastly, I call your attention to the draft of a Bill prepared by one of the Commissioners of Inquiry, in conformity with their Report.

The Lord Lieutenant and Lord Morpeth will render you every assistance in their power.

I have the honour to be, Sir,<br>
Your obedient servant,<br>
J. RUSSELL.

## FIRST REPORT.

## TO THE RIGHT HONOURABLE LORD JOHN RUSSELL, HIS MAJESTY'S PRINCIPAL SECRETARY OF STATE FOR THE HOME DEPARTMENT.
London, November 15th, 1836.

My Lord,

1. I proceeded to Ireland in conformity with your Lordship's instructions, bearing date the 22nd of August, and, after having had an interview with His Excellency the Lord Lieutenant and Lord Morpeth, and having carefully inspected the House of Industry and the Mendicity Institution in Dublin, and obtained such other information there as seemed necessary, I proceeded to visit Carlow, Kilkenny, Thurles, Cashel, Tipperary, Clonmel, Cork, Killarney, Limerick, Galway, Connemara, Westport, Castlebar, Ballina, Sligo, Enniskillen, Armagh, and Newry,—everywhere examining and inquiring, in the several towns and districts through which I passed, as to the condition and habits of the people, their character and wants; and endeavouring to ascertain whether, and how far, the system established in England for the relief of the destitute, is applicable to the present state of Ireland.

2. The above route appeared to be most eligible, with reference to this inquiry, because the inhabitants of the manufacturing and commercial districts of the north and the east approximate more nearly to the English than those of the south, west, and central parts of Ireland. To the latter, therefore, it seemed advisable to direct my attention in the first instance; for, if the English system of Poor Laws should be found applicable to them, there can be no doubt of its applicability to the northern and eastern parts of the country.

3. I have not failed to attend likewise to the other points adverted to in your Lordship's instructions; and I have carefully considered the several Reports of Committees of Parliament on the state of Ireland, as well as the Reports of the late Commissioners of Irish Poor Inquiry, and the evidence collected by them. This evidence establishes so conclusively the existence of a state of poverty throughout Ireland, amounting in numerous cases to actual destitution, that I feel it unnecessary to exhibit any additional proof of the fact. It is enough to state, as the result of my own investigations, that the misery now prevalent among the labouring classes in Ireland, appears to be of a nature and intensity calculated to produce great demoralization and danger.

4. I propose to divide the observations which I have to submit to your Lordship's consideration into three parts:

I.—The first will exhibit the general result of my inquiries into the condition of the country, and the habits and feelings of the people; together with such observations as have occurred to me with reference to the introduction of a system of Poor Laws into Ireland.

II.—The second division will have for its object, to ascertain whether the Workhouse system can be safely established in Ireland, and how far the Workhouse may be there relied upon as a test of destitution, and a measure of the relief to be afforded; and, also, whether the means of forming Unions, and creating an efficient machinery for their management, exist in Ireland.

III.—In the third place, supposing these questions to be answered affirmatively, I shall submit to your Lordship in detail what appear to me to be the essential points requiring attention, in framing enactments for establishing a system of Poor Laws for Ireland.

5. It will be convenient to consider the two portions comprised in this division of the subject separately, and

I.—*In the first place,—As to the present condition of the country, and the habits and, feelings of the Irish people.*
I soon became satisfied, that it is only by a personal inspection that the condition of the Irish people can be accurately known. A general, and a tolerably correct notion of the state of the country may be gained, by the examination of Reports and Evidence; and deductions, pretty accurate in the main, may be drawn from them; but to arrive at definite and practical views, a personal inspection of the country is, I think, necessary.

6. The investigations and inquiries in which I have now been engaged, have led me to the conviction that the Condition of Ireland has, on the whole, during the last thirty years, been progressively improving. It is impossible to pass through the country without being struck with the evidence of increasing wealth, which is everywhere apparent, although, of course, it is more easily traced in towns than in the open country. Great as has been the improvement in England within the same period, that in Ireland, I believe, has been equal. There are towns and districts there, as there are towns and districts in England, in which little, if any, improvement is visible, or which, owing to peculiar circumstances, may even have retrograded; but the general advance is certain, and the improvement in the condition, and increase in the capital of the country, are still, I think, steadily progressive.

7. If it be asked how this accords with the apparent increase of misery and destitution among a large portion of the people, the answer I think is obvious. The capital of the country has increased, but the increase of the population has been still greater; and it therefore does not follow that there is an increase of capital or comfort in the possession of each individual, or even of the majority. The reverse is unhappily the fact.—Towns, exhibiting every sign of increased wealth, are encircled by suburbs composed of miserable hovels, sheltering a wretched population of mendicants. In the country, evidence of the extreme subdivision of land everywhere appears, and, as a consequence, the soil, fertile as it naturally is, becomes exhausted by continual cropping; for the cottier tenant, too often reduced to a level little above that of the mendicant, is unable to provide manure for his

land, and has no other mode of restoring its vigour but by subjecting it to a long and profitless fallow.

8. Farmers of three hundred acres, or even of two or one hundred, except in the grazing districts, have become almost extinct in Ireland. A variety of circumstances seem to have contributed to bring about this change. In some instances the proprietor has himself subdivided his land into small holdings of five, ten, or fifteen acres, with a view of increasing his rent-roll, or adding to his political influence. In other cases the land has been let on lease to a single tenant on lives, or for a term of years, or both conjointly,—and he has sublet to others, who have again gone on dividing and subletting, until the original proprietor is almost lost sight of, and the original holding is parcelled out among a host of small occupiers.

9. The occupation of a plot of land has now gotten to be considered, by a great portion of the Irish people, as conferring an almost interminable right of possession. This seems in some measure to have arisen out of the circumstances in which they have been placed: for, there being no legal provision for the destitute, and the subdivision of the land into small holdings having destroyed the regular demand for labour, the only protection against actual want, the only means by which a man could procure food for his family, was by getting and retaining possession of a portion of land; for this he has struggled—for this the peasantry have combined, and burst through all the restraints of law and humanity. So long as this portion of land, so acquired and so retained, was kept together, it was possibly sufficient to supply his family with a tolerable degree of comfort; but after a time he would have sons to provide for, and daughters to portion off, and this must all be effected out of the land;—until the holding of ten or fifteen acres became divided into holdings of two, three, or five acres. After a time, too, the same process of subdivision is again resorted to, until the minimum of subsistence is reached; and this is now the only resource of a large portion of the Irish peasantry.—Land is to them the great necessary of life. There is no hiring of servants. A man cannot obtain his living as a day-labourer. He must get possession of a plot of land, on which to raise potatoes, or starve. It need scarcely be said that a man will not starve, so long as the means of sustaining life can be obtained by force or fraud; and hence the scenes of violence and bloodshed, which have so frequently occurred in Ireland.

10. One of the circumstances that first arrests attention in Ireland, is the almost universal prevalence of mendicancy. It is not perhaps the actual amount of misery existing amongst the mendicant class, great as that may be, which is most to be deprecated; but the falsehood, the trickery, and fraud, which become a part of their profession, and spread by their example. Mendicancy appeals to our sympathies on behalf of vice, as well as wretchedness; and encouragement is too often afforded to the one, by the relief intended to be administered to the other. To assume the semblance of misery, in all its most revolting varieties, is the business of the mendicant. His success depends upon the skill with which he exercises deception. A mass of filth, nakedness, and misery, is constantly moving about, entering every house, addressing itself to every eye, and soliciting from every hand: and much of the dirty and indolent habits observable in the cabins, clothing,

and general conduct of the peasantry, may probably be traced to this source; and I doubt even if those above the class of labourers altogether escape the taint. Mendicancy and wretchedness have become too common to be disgraceful. It is not disreputable to beg, or to appear wretchedly clothed, or to be without any of the decencies of life: and the semblance of such misery is not unfrequently assumed for some special object, by individuals not of the mendicant class.

11. Another characteristic of the Irish is their intemperance. Drunkenness appears to be much more common than in England. The use of whiskey and tobacco appears to be excessive, although the evident poverty of the people would seem to forbid such indulgences. The number of spirit-shops in every town and village (for almost every shop in fact sells spirits), and the extreme cheapness of whiskey, afford facilities for drunkenness which seem irresistible. A man may get beastly drunk for 2d.; and I understand their potatoe [sic] diet renders the Irish people more easily affected by the spirit than others—it may possibly help to increase their love for it. I have been everywhere assured that the vice of drunkenness is increasing, and that many of the acts of violence and disorder which occur in Ireland are planned in some obscure whiskey-shop, and executed under the influence of the poison there imbibed.

12. The Roman Catholic Bishop of Kilkenny has set an admirable example, by putting a stop to drunkenness on Sundays throughout his diocese. It was at first supposed to be impossible to accomplish this, but by steady perseverance he at length succeeded, and is now rewarded by witnessing the improvement of the people in comfort and respectability. The new Act, prohibiting drunkenness on penalty of certain fines, seems to be working well in Ireland, and in some degree lessening the evil.

The public exhibition of drunkenness is an offence against decency, for which the community is justified in defending itself; and the police are properly active in enforcing the provisions of the Act.

13. During my progress through the country, it was impossible not to notice the depression of feeling, morally and personally, of the Irish peasantry, and this to an extent which a stranger could not witness without very painful emotions. It shows itself in their mode of living, in their habitations, in their dress, in the dress of their children, and in their general economy and conduct. They seem to feel no pride, no emulation; to be heedless of the present, and reckless of the future. They do not (speaking of the peasantry as a whole) strive to improve their appearance, or add to their comforts. Their cabins still continue slovenly, smoky, filthy, almost without furniture, or any article of convenience or decency. On entering a cottage, the woman and children are often seen seated on the floor, surrounded by pigs and poultry, in the midst of filth—the man lounging at the door, to approach which it is necessary to wade through mud; yet he is too indolent to make a dry approach to his dwelling; although there are materials fit for the purpose close at hand; his wife is too slatternly to sweep the place in which they live, or remove the dirt and offal, however offensive, from the floor. If you point out these circumstances to the peasantry themselves, and endeavour to reason with and show them how

easily they might improve their condition and increase their comforts, you are invariably met by excuses as to their poverty. Why are a woman, and her children, and her cabin filthy—whilst a stream of water runs gurgling at the very door?—the answer invariably is, "Sure, how can we help it ? we are so poor!" With the man it is the same; you find him idly basking in the sun or seated by the fire, whilst his cabin is surrounded by mud, and scarcely approachable from the accumulation of every kind of filth; and he too will exclaim, "Sure, how can we help it ? we are so poor !"—whilst at the very time he is smoking tobacco, and has probably not denied himself the enjoyment of whiskey.

14. Now poverty is not the cause, or at least not the sole and immediate cause, of this mode of living of the Irish peasantry. If they felt a wish to better their condition, or to appear better, they might do so; but they seem to have no such ambition; and hence the depressed tone of feeling of which I have spoken. This may partly be attributed to the remains of old habits,—for, bad as the circumstances of the peasantry now are, they were yet, I am persuaded, worse fifty or thirty years ago. A part also must be owing to a want of education, and of self-respect; and a part likewise to their poverty;—to which last cause alone everything that is wrong in Ireland is invariably attributed. Coupled with this assertion of their own poverty, I everywhere found the most exaggerated notions of English wealth, and a vague belief of certain great things that are by-and-by to be done by the influx of Englishmen and English capital. This, perhaps, is in some respects fortunate, for, although it may in a certain degree indispose the Irish themselves to present exertion, it will yet induce them to hail with favour whatever efforts may be made for bettering their condition, and developing the resources of the country.

15. The desultory and idle habits of the Irish peasantry are very remarkable. However urgent the demands upon them for exertion,—if, as in the present season, their crops are rotting in the fields, from excessive wet, and every moment of sunshine should be taken eager advantage of,—still, if there be a market to attend, a fair, or a funeral, a horse-race, a fight, or a wedding, all else is neglected or forgotten; they hurry off in search of the excitements and the whiskey which abound on such occasions, and, with a recklessness hardly to be credited, at the moment that they are complaining most loudly of distress, they take the most certain steps for increasing it. Their fondness for ardent spirits is, I believe, one cause of this; another, and probably the principal cause, will be found in their general position as part occupiers and part labourers. The work required upon their small holdings is easily performed, and may, as they say, "be done any day." Their work for wages is uncertain; hence arises a total disregard of the value of time, a desultory and sauntering habit, without industry or steadiness of purpose. Under these circumstances, it will not be a matter of surprise that the heaviest share of the work falls upon the females, who appear to do all the drudgery, and are commonly seen without shoes or stockings, whilst the men are in general supplied with both.

16. Such is too generally the character, and such the habits, of the Irish peasantry at the present day; and it may not be uninstructive to mark the close resemblance which these bear to the character and habits of the English peasantry in

the pauperized districts, under the abuses of the old Poor Law. Mendicancy and indiscriminate alms-giving seem to have produced the same results in Ireland, that indiscriminate relief produced in England; the same reckless disregard of the future—the same idle and disorderly conduct—the same proneness to outrage, and resistance to lawful authority, having then characterized the English pauper labourer, which are now too generally the characteristics of the Irish peasant. An abuse of a good law caused the evil in the one case, and a removal of that abuse is now rapidly effecting a remedy. In the other case, the evil appears to have arisen rather from the want than the abuse of a law; but the corrective for both will, I believe, be found to be essentially the same.

II.—*Secondly—As to the introduction of a system of Poor Laws into Ireland.*
17. The objections usually urged against an Irish Poor Law may be divided into two heads—*first*, those founded on an anticipated demoralization of the Irish peasantry—and, *secondly*, those founded on the probable amount of the charge.
18. The first objection derives its force from the example of England under the old law: but the weight of this objection is destroyed by the improved administration under the new law, which is rapidly eradicating the effects of previous abuse; and which will, there is good reason for believing, effectually prevent their recurrence. This belief is founded on the experience of the effects of the new system, in every instance in which it has been brought fairly into operation; and particularly in two important parishes in Nottinghamshire, where the workhouse principle was first established, in its simplicity and efficiency, fifteen or sixteen years ago; and where it has continued to be equally effective, up to the present time.[15] Similar results have invariably attended its application in the new Unions formed under the Poor Law Amendment Act, which are conducted essentially upon the same principle, but with a superior combination of machinery, and administrative arrangement.
19. With respect to the second objection, founded on the probable amount of expenditure,—it may be remarked, that the Irish population, like every other, must be supported in some way out of the resources of the country; and it does not follow, therefore, that the establishment of such a system of relief will greatly increase the charge upon the community, if it increase the charge at all. During the progress of my inquiries, I was often told that the recognition of any legal claim for relief would lead to universal pauperism, and would amount to a total confiscation of property. Many Irish land-owners appeared to participate in this apprehension,—under the influence of which it seems to have been overlooked, that the only legal claim for relief in England is founded on the actual destitution of the claimant; and that, as the existence of destitution is the ground of the claim, so is its removal the measure of relief to be afforded. This circumstance alone, if the destitution be rightly tested, will afford sufficient, and perhaps the best, protection to property. At present there is no test of destitution in Ireland; mendicancy is only the outward sign of it. The mendicant, whether his distress be real or fictitious, claims and receives his share of the produce of the soil, in the shape of charity, before the landlord can receive his portion in the shape of rent, and before

the tenant has ascertained whether he is a gainer or a loser by his labours and his risks. The mendicant's claim has now precedence over every other. If the whole property of Ireland was rated to the relief of the poor, it would be no more: but in this case the charge would be fairly and equally borne; whereas, at present, it is partial and unequal in the collection, and has, moreover, a direct tendency to evil in its application.

20. The voluntary contributions of Scotland have been strongly recommended as an example, rather than the compulsory assessments of England;[16] and the Dublin Mendicity Association,[17] supported on the former principle, has been referred to, and its working described as at once effective for the suppression of mendicancy, and the relief of the indigent within the sphere of its operations, without in any way lessening the sensibilities of individual benevolence. It appears to me, however, that the feelings of charity and gratitude, which it is delightful to contemplate as the motive and the fruit of benevolent actions, can only exist between individuals, and are incompatible with the operation of such associations. It matters not whether the fund to be distributed has been raised by voluntary contribution or by legal assessment, or whether it has been devised for purposes of general charity: the application of the fund becomes, in each case, a trust; it is distributed as a trust, and it is received as a right, not as a gift. Each applicant considers that he has a claim upon the fund, and regards every refusal as an individual injustice.

21. As regards the mode of providing relief for the destitute, which prevails in Scotland,—interwoven as it is with the habits and religious feelings of the people, and made up of partly voluntary, partly compulsory, contributions, (for a contribution may be rendered almost as compulsory by custom, as if imposed by legislative enactment,)—it seems only necessary to remark, that its existence in Scotland does not prove that it is applicable to a country so essentially different in all respects as Ireland, where no modification of voluntary contributions can be relied upon for rendering relief, from that source, permanent or effectual. Of this I was satisfied, after a careful examination of the Dublin Mendicity Association, which has with difficulty been kept in existence by the great exertions of the gentlemen constituting the committee, and by the threat of parading the mendicants through the streets. If so much difficulty is found in supporting such an institution in Dublin, how impracticable must it be to provide permanent support for similar institutions in other parts of the country!—and if the relief, professed to be afforded on certain conditions, is not steadily supplied, what mischief and misery may not ensue?

22. The practice of the Dublin Mendicity Association is, to receive all applicants, to supply them with sufficient food during the day, and, on dismissing them at night, to give each individual a penny to procure a lodging. Of the 2047 persons who were inmates when I visited the establishment, the far larger portion were seated in idleness. Some of the women and girls were occupied in spinning and knitting, and some in stone-breaking: this last seemed a favourite occupation, and the women could easily earn 1s. 8d. each per week at it, but they were not

permitted to earn more. The men who were able and willing to work, were occupied in grinding horse-corn, and in breaking limestone into gravel, and were not permitted to earn more than 2s. 6d. per week; but none were compelled to work, and the men, as well as the women, earning as above, were provided with subsistence, for which they were charged 1d. per day by the Association. The Dublin Mendicity Association has certainly done great good, and it must be admitted that the sudden closing of its doors would be productive of much suffering. It is, however, I think, evident that its tendency must be to hold out an encouragement to vagrancy, by ensuring a certain amount of support, on which the vagrant can fall back, under unfavourable circumstances, or a "run of ill luck," as it would probably be called,—thus operating, in fact, with respect to vagrancy, as a kind of voluntary labour-rate. The Dublin Mendicity Association, therefore, affords no precedent for general adoption as a medium of relief in Ireland; and the chief reasons in favour of such an institution seem to be, the absence of any general system of relief for the destitute, and the amount of suffering which would attend its sudden dissolution.

23. Some persons have contended, that relief for the indigent classes in Ireland ought to be provided in "Houses of Industry," similar to those now existing in Dublin, Clonmel, Cork, Limerick, &c, to be established and maintained by Government.[18] These institutions are in general tolerably well managed in the large towns. Some degree of classification of the inmates is enforced, and the sexes are invariably separated. In this respect they are decidedly superior to the old Gilbert's Incorporation Houses in England, although in most other respects they are nearly on a par with them.[19] But they are certainly not entitled to the designation of "houses of industry;"—there being little work done in any of them, and in some none at all. They are, in fact, places for the reception and maintenance of a certain number of poor persons, generally aged or infirm, and idiots, and lunatics. In some instances vagrants are committed to these "houses of industry" for one day or more; but, as a means of supplying needful relief to the destitute, and of testing that destitution, so as to detect and repel willful idleness, and thereby afford a new stimulant to exertion, they are, I think, totally inefficient.

24. Notwithstanding these objections, I found everywhere throughout my progress, after quitting Dublin, a strong feeling in favour of a general assessment upon property for the relief of the indigent. At present, the burthen of such relief falls almost exclusively upon what may be called the lower classes; whilst the higher classes generally, and the absentee proprietors entirely, escape from any immediate participation in it. A system of Poor Laws, similar in principle to the English system, would go far to remedy this inequality,—the people are aware of this,—and, as the general result of my inquiries, I have been led to the conclusion, that Poor Laws may be now established in Ireland, guarded by the correctives derived from experience in England, with safety and efficiency. I think, also, that such a measure would at the same time serve to connect the interest of landlords and tenants, and so become a means of benefiting both, and promoting the general peace and prosperity of the country.

25. The desire now so generally expressed for a full participation in English laws and English institutions, will dispose the Irish people to receive, with alacrity, any measure having a tendency to put them upon the same footing as their fellow-subjects of England. This is a circumstance particularly favourable to the establishment of a safe and efficient system of Poor Laws for Ireland at this moment. At another season, or under other circumstances, it might be difficult to surround a legal provision for the relief of the Irish poor, with such checks and counterpoises as to guard it effectually against abuse; and to prevent that which was intended for the relief of the unavoidably indigent, from being perverted to the support of indolence, or to the encouragement of vice and improvidence. At present, I think, little, comparatively, of such difficulty exists; and the Legislature may now venture to entertain the subject, having the experience of England before them, with a reasonable confidence of being able so to deal with it as to guard against abuse, and to bring the measure to a successful issue. All circumstances appear to be now favourable for the introduction of Poor Laws into Ireland; and if the landed proprietors and gentry will there perform the same part, which the proprietors and gentry of England are so zealously and beneficially performing in the administration of the new law, the result will be neither distant nor doubtful. That the landlords of Ireland will do this, it seems unreasonable to doubt, since every motive of public duty and private interest impels them to it; and it is, I think, impossible to over estimate the importance, morally and socially, of their thus taking their full share of the labour, as well as the charge, of local administration, and identifying themselves with the other classes of the community.

26. A system of Poor Laws, however, if established in Ireland, must not be expected to work miracles. It would not immediately give employment or capital; but it would, I think, serve to help the country through what may be called its transition period; and in time, and with the aid of other circumstances, would effect a material improvement in the condition of the Irish people. The English Poor Laws, in their earlier operation, contributed to the accomplishment of this object in England; and there seems nothing to prevent similar results in Ireland. Facilities now exist in Ireland for helping forward the transition, and for shortening its duration as well as securing its benefits, which England did not possess in the time of Elizabeth, or for a century and a half afterwards. By the term "transition period," which I have used above, I mean to indicate that season of change from the system of small holdings, allotments, and subdivisions of land, which now prevails in Ireland, to the better practice of day-labour for wages, and to that dependence on daily labour for support, which is the present condition of the English peasantry. This transition period is, I believe, generally beset with difficulty and suffering. It was so in England; it is, and for a time will probably continue to be so, in Ireland; and every aid should be afforded to shorten its duration, and lessen its pressure.

27. It has been considered, that the existence of the con-acre system in Ireland is favourable to such a transition.[20] I am disposed to concur in this view; and think that the frequent change, and annual hiring of the con-acre, will help to wean the Irish peasantry from their now eager desire for becoming occupiers of land, and

will thus lead them to become free labourers for wages. This eager clinging to land, and its subdivision into small holdings, is, I think, at once, a cause and a consequence of the rapid increase of the Irish people, and of the extreme poverty and want which prevail among them. It is not because the potatoe alone constitutes their food, that a kind of famine, more or less intense, occurs annually in Ireland, between the going out of the old, and the coming in of the new crops; but it is because the peasantry are the sole providers for their own necessities, each out of his own small holding; and being all alike hard pressed by poverty, and prone, therefore, to endeavour "to pull through," as they call it, with the smallest amount of means, they are very apt to undercalculate the extent of their wants, and often squander their store so early, as to be left without food before the new crop is ripe. In this emergency there is no stock provided to which they can have recourse, even if they had the means of purchasing: and misery and disease are the consequences. All the evidence bears out this view of the subject, and it is confirmed by my own inquiries. A Poor Law, if established, would lighten the pressure under such a visitation, by providing for the relief of the aged and infirm, the widow and the orphan, who now depend entirely upon the labouring classes for subsistence. The Poor Law machinery, too, would probably afford the best organization for obtaining present relief for the able-bodied, in their extreme need, as well as for preventing the occurrence of such a calamity in future.

28. It is impossible to mix with the Irish people, and not become sensible of the influence which the clergy exercise over their flocks. It seemed important, therefore, to ascertain the views of the clergy, and I discussed the subject with many of them, as well Catholic as Protestant, in all parts of the country, and took all opportunities of obtaining a knowledge of their views and opinions; and I found them, with few exceptions, decidedly favourable to a Poor Law. In the cases where they were not so, the adverse opinion appeared to be founded on some vague notion, that their immediate influence might be lessened by taking from them the distribution of some of that relief, which now passes through their hands: but this narrow feeling was of such rare occurrence, that I feel warranted in saying, that the clergy of every denomination are almost unanimously in favour of a system of Poor Laws for Ireland. This was, perhaps, to be expected; for the duties of the clergy lead them to mix more with the people, and to see more of their actual misery, than any other class of persons in Ireland. The shopkeepers too, and manufacturers and dealers generally, I invariably found favourable to Poor Laws. They for the most part declared that, independently of other and higher considerations, they should be gainers at the end of the year, whatever might be the amount legally assessed upon them; for that they could neither close their doors, nor turn their backs upon the wretched objects who were constantly applying to them for aid; whilst the landed proprietors, if resident, were in a great measure protected from such applications, and the non-resident proprietors were, of course, altogether beyond their reach.

29. A legal provision for the destitute is, moreover, I think, an indispensable preliminary to the suppression of mendicancy. If the state offers an alternative, it

may prohibit begging: it would be in vain to do so otherwise, for the law would be opposed to our natural sympathies, and would remain inoperative. This was the course adopted in England, where it was long endeavoured to repress vagrancy by direct enactments, but apparently with little advantage.[21] At last the offer of relief was coupled with the prohibition of mendicancy,—and, until our Poor Law administration had become corrupt, with perfect success. To establish a Poor Law, then, is, I believe, a necessary preliminary to the suppression of mendicancy. That it will be, on the whole, economical to do this in Ireland, it is, I think, scarcely possible to doubt: but the moral effect of removing such a pestilent plague-spot from society is, beyond calculation, important.

30. It is, I think, a circumstance favourable to the establishment of Poor Laws, that there is so much land lying waste and uncultivated in Ireland. A large portion of this land appears to be susceptible of profitable cultivation; and the order and security which the introduction of Poor Laws would tend to establish, would encourage the application of capital to such objects. If capital were to be so applied, considerable tracts would be brought under culture, and thus afford immediate occupation to the now unemployed labourers. I have no experience in the reclamation of bog-land, but the finest crops which I saw in Ireland, were on land of this description; and this often very imperfectly drained. Most of the recently-reclaimed bog which I saw in the western counties, was reclaimed by the small occupiers, who partially drained and enclosed an acre or two at a time; but such operations were without system or combination, and for the most part indifferently performed. In this way, however, the reclamation of these wastes will, of necessity, proceed,—constantly adding to the number of small cottier tenants, and consequently swelling the amount of poverty and wretchedness in the country,—unless proprietors and capitalists shall be induced to take the matter in hand, and, by inclosing and effectually draining whole tracts, secure the means of applying improved and economical management on a large scale. It appeared, from what I saw, and from all that I could learn by careful inquiry, that, wherever sea-sand, or sea-weed, or lime is to be obtained, bog-land may be cultivated to advantage,—presuming always that it is first effectually drained. Now Ireland abounds in limestone beyond any country that I have ever seen, and along the western coast sand and sea-weed, are plentiful. The elements of fertility, therefore, are at hand,—all that is wanted is capital and enterprise to call them into action. The enclosing and draining, and the whole process of reclamation, would afford employment to a large number of labourers, who are now, for a great portion of the year, idling about without occupation; and when the land so reclaimed becomes subjected to a regular process of cultivation, it will continue to afford them regular employment at daily wages, instead of the often miserably insufficient produce of their own small holdings, to which they now are compelled to cling as their sole means of support.

31. With reference to the establishment of a Poor Law, then, and to the passage of the labouring portion of the community through what I have called the "transition period," the reclamation of the bog and waste lands in Ireland is a most important matter of consideration. Such reclamation, too, will be perhaps equally important,

as affording almost the only unoccupied land, on which farms of sufficient extent for securing the advantages of improved cultivation and economical management, can now be established. In farms of small extent, there is not room for the division of labour, alternation of crops, and scientific and economical management, which are necessary for the profitable employment of capital in agriculture; and hence the striking fact stated in the Report of the Irish Poor Inquiry Commissioners,— that the average produce of the soil in Ireland is not much above one-half the average produce in England, whilst the number of labourers employed in agriculture is, in proportion to the quantity of land under cultivation, more than double, namely as five to two: thus ten labourers in Ireland raise only the same quantity of produce that two labourers raise in England; and this produce, too, is generally of an inferior quality. If the social and agricultural system of the two countries be assimilated, the produce of Ireland will be augmented, and the cost of production lessened. Hands, and capital, and enterprise will then be found for carrying on the fisheries, for which the coasts of Ireland are so favourable, but which have hitherto been almost or altogether neglected. Planting, likewise, will then be attended to by the landed proprietors of Ireland, as it has been by those of Scotland and England, and they will no longer allow extensive tracts of hilly and broken country, all capable of carrying timber, to remain without a tree. Ireland was evidently at one time a thickly-wooded country,—at present it is almost entirely stripped of wood, and every sapling is purloined by the people; but let planting become general, and such purloining will cease. It is the scarcity of wood, which now leads to the petty plundering, so destructive to young plantations.

32. In speaking of the reclamation of waste land, as an important auxiliary to the establishment of Poor Laws, I have presumed the land to be first effectually drained, which is an indispensable preliminary. An efficient system of drainage would also go far to correct the excessive humidity of the climate in Ireland. As drainage is now conducted, the water is not carried off the surface,—it is merely collected into pools and morasses, thence to be absorbed by evaporation, or else to stagnate and soak through the soil. But if, instead of this, the water was carried by effectual drainage into the great watercourses and rivers communicating with the sea, and the soil laid dry and warm, the climate would also become drier and warmer. There can be no doubt, I think, that the climate of Ireland, and particularly that of the western parts, was at one time less cold and humid than it is now; and that the growth of the bogs, by first retaining the rain as it fell, and then giving it back to the atmosphere by evaporation, instead of its being carried to the sea by the usual channels, has tended to make the climate and the soil more cold and wet. The size and character of the timber everywhere found at the bottom of the bogs, and over which they have grown in the course of years, proves this. Trees will not grow where these have grown; and the deteriorating process appears to be still in operation. If the wet and bog lands of Ireland were effectually drained, and properly cultivated, and the general drainage of the country duly attended to, I am persuaded that the climate would be improved, as well as the produce of the soil. Such drainage, however, will generally require the

co-operation of all the landowners of a district: and, to facilitate this object, the two Bills introduced in the last session by Mr. Lynch, if passed into law, would, I think, be highly useful. In addition to these measures, however, it would probably be found necessary to give large powers for the purpose of enforcing drainage, and charging the adjoining property with a fair proportion of the expense in certain cases; and also to appoint commissioners of sewers or drainage, as in England, to superintend the drains and watercourses, and to compel the occupiers of adjoining lands to keep them clear, with power to fine for any neglect of this very important duty.

33. It appears, then, I think, that a system of Poor Laws is necessary for relieving the destitution to which a large portion of the population in Ireland is now exposed. It appears, too, that circumstances are at present peculiarly favourable for the introduction of such a measure into Ireland. Poor Laws seem also to be necessary, as a first step towards effecting an improvement in the character, habits, and social condition of the people. Without such improvement,—peace, good order, and security cannot exist in Ireland; and without these, it is in vain to look for that accumulation of wealth, and influx of capital, which are necessary for developing its resources, agricultural and commercial, and for providing profitable employment for the population. Ireland is now suffering under a circle of evils, producing and reproducing one another. Want of capital produces want of employment—want of employment, turbulence and misery—turbulence and misery, insecurity—insecurity prevents the introduction or accumulation of capital—and so on. Until this circle is broken, the evils must continue, and probably augment. The first thing to be done is to give security—that will produce or invite capital—and capital will give employment. But security of person and property cannot co-exist with general destitution. So that, in truth, the drainage, reclamation, and profitable cultivation of bogs and wastes—the establishment of fisheries and manufactures—improvements in agriculture, and in the general condition of the country—and lastly, the elevation of the great mass of the Irish people in the social scale, appear to be all more or less contingent upon establishing a law providing for the relief of the destitute.—How such a law may be best formed, so as to secure the largest amount of good, with the least risk of evil, I proceed now to consider.

PART THE SECOND.

34. The two points which I propose to consider under this division of the subject, are of primary importance,—the whole question of a Poor Law for Ireland turning, I think, upon the conclusions to which they will lead.
These points are—

I.—Whether the Workhouse system can be safely established in Ireland; and, if so, whether the Workhouse can be there relied upon as a test of destitution, and a measure of the relief to be afforded.

II.—Whether the means exist generally, or partially, of forming Unions, and creating such a local machinery for their government, as has been established in the English Unions under the provisions of the Poor Law Amendment Act.

In my inquiries with reference to these two points, in the several districts of Ireland through which I passed, I endeavoured to exercise a care and vigilance proportioned to the importance of the object. I do not give—indeed I did not collect, detailed evidence on these and the other questions referred to me,—a sufficiency of such evidence being already accessible, in the Appendices to the Report of the late Commission of Irish Poor Inquiry, and your Lordship having required from me only practical conclusions, with a view to early legislation.

I.—First, then, *As to the establishment of the Workhouse as a test of destitution, and a measure of relief, in Ireland.*
35. I entered upon this inquiry, under great apprehension that the workhouse would be found to be less efficient in Ireland as a test, than experience has proved it to be in England: and that it would, probably, be applicable to the able-bodied in a limited degree only, if applicable to them at all. This impression had been somewhat weakened before my departure from London, by inquiries among the several workhouse-masters and parish-officers of St. Giles, Whitechapel, Stepney, and Shadwell, in each of which parishes great numbers of the Irish reside. All these officers assured me, as the result of their experience, that the Irish had just as much dislike to the discipline and regularity of a workhouse as the English, and would be as little likely to remain in the house, if they could obtain the means of support out of it. Notwithstanding these assurances, however, I arrived in Ireland with considerable misgiving on this point.
36. I felt very doubtful also, I confess, whether it would be practicable to control any considerable number of the able-bodied in a workhouse,—whether, in fact, the proneness of the Irish peasantry to outrage and insubordination was not, as had often been represented, such as would lead them to break through all restraint, and probably demolish the building and commit other acts of violence. The probability of outrage thus occurring amongst a people so excitable as the Irish, is strongly insisted upon by the Commissioners of Inquiry in their Report, and the same argument was urged upon me by some of the individuals with whom I communicated in Dublin; so that my apprehensions as to the applicability of the workhouse system, as well as the security of the workhouse itself, were rendered extremely sensitive when I commenced my investigations in Ireland.
37. I shortly found, however, in the progress of my inquiries amongst men most competent from experience to form a judgment, that there was no real ground of apprehension, either as to the applicability and efficiency of the workhouse for the purposes of relief,—or as to any danger of resistance to the establishment of such a system of discipline within it, as should constitute an adequate test of destitution. Indeed, if relief be limited to the house,—if no out-door relief whatever

be allowed,—it evidently becomes the interest of parties relieved, or seeking or expecting relief therein, to protect the premises, not to destroy them: by such destruction they would, in fact, deprive themselves of the only means of relief provided for them by law. It is true that, when congregated in large numbers, and excited by whiskey, the Irish peasantry are prone to outrage and insubordination; but this is not their invariable, nor even their habitual, character. I speak on the testimony of experienced witnesses when I state, that the Irish are easily governed, and easily led; and as in the workhouse they would be free from the influence of ardent spirits and other excitements, I anticipate no difficulty in establishing an efficient system of discipline and classification; and I consider, moreover, that there will be little danger of injury to the premises, or of violence against the functionaries.

38. In the several "Houses of Industry" established in Ireland, a strict separation of the sexes is enforced, and a discipline more or less approximating to our workhouse discipline is established. No spirits are admitted; but tobacco is generally allowed. On the whole, however, there is enough in these institutions to render them in some measure distasteful, as places of partial restraint,—the inmates being subjected to privations calculated, perhaps, more than any other, to excite them to resistance: yet from no governor of a house of industry could I learn that resistance had ever been made to their regulations, and a degree of surprise was even expressed at my thinking it necessary to make such an inquiry. I received the same opinion from the governors of gaols. In short, every man whom I conversed with, who had any knowledge or experience of the habits of the people, declared that the peasantry are perfectly tractable, and never think of opposing authority, unless stimulated by drink, or urged on by that species of combination for securing the occupancy of land, which has become so common in certain districts, and which is most generally formed and acted upon under the influence of whiskey. Neither of these influences are opposed to the establishment of a workhouse, or the regulation of its inmates, all of whom will have sought refuge in it voluntarily, and may quit it at any moment. Let the condition on which the inmates are received into the workhouse be clearly understood, and I think that there will be no resistance to the regulations by which it is governed.

39. As regards the security of the workhouse, therefore, and the establishment of a system of discipline as strict as that maintained in our English workhouses, I believe that there will be neither danger nor difficulty. How far the workhouse, if established, may be relied upon as a test of destitution and a measure of the relief to be afforded,—how far it will be effectual for the prevention of pauperism, and for stimulating the people to exertion for their own support, instead of seeking that support within its walls;—how far, in short, the workhouse system, which has been safely and effectually applied to dispauperise England, may be applied with safety and efficiency to prevent pauperism in Ireland, is a question now remaining for inquiry.

40. The governing principle of the workhouse system is this:—that the support which is afforded at the public charge in the workhouse, shall be, on the whole,

less desirable than the support to be obtained by independent exertion. To carry out this principle to its full extent, it might seem at first sight to be necessary that the inmates of a workhouse should be in all respects worse situated,—worse clothed, worse lodged, and worse fed,—than the independent labourers of the district.[22] In fact, however, the inmates of our English workhouses are as well clothed, and generally better lodged and better fed than the agricultural labourer and his family: yet the irksomeness of the labour, discipline, and confinement, and the privation of certain enjoyments which the independent labourer possesses, produce such disinclination to enter the workhouse, that experience warrants the fullest assurance that nothing short of destitution and of absolute necessity,—of that necessity which the law contemplates as the ground for affording relief,— will induce the able-bodied labourers to seek refuge therein : and, that if driven thither by their necessities, they will quit it again as speedily as possible, and strive (generally with increased energy and consequent success) to obtain their subsistence by their own efforts.

41. This has been invariably the result in England, and hence the conviction as to the perfect sufficiency of the workhouse test. If the party is actually and unavoidably destitute, the workhouse affords relief to his necessities: if not absolutely destitute,—if sustenance is in any way attainable by his own efforts— workhouse relief does not lessen the stimulus to exertion in search of it ; and there are instances without number of individuals so circumstanced, being successful in their endeavours, and thus securing an independent support for themselves and their families : whereas, under the old system they would have become confirmed paupers, ever after dependent upon the parish for their daily subsistence.

42. Let these facts be now applied to Ireland. It would, perhaps, be in vain, even if it were desirable, to seek to make the lodging, the clothing, and the diet, of the inmates of an Irish workhouse, inferior to those of the Irish peasantry. The standard of their mode of living is unhappily so low, that the establishment of one still lower is difficult, and would, I think, under any circumstances, be inexpedient. In Ireland, then, there would not, I believe, be found this security for the efficiency of the workhouse test, which is in some, although in a very slight degree, operative in England. There are countervailing circumstances in favour of Ireland, however, which appear to more than balance this circumstance, even if it were weightier than it really is. The Irish are naturally, or by habit, a migratory people, fond of change, full of hope, eager for experiment. They have never been tied down to one confined spot, to one limited settlement, as has been the case with the English peasantry. They have never been enervated by a dependence upon a misapplied system of parish relief. Rather than bear the discipline and the restrictions of a workhouse, the Irishman, if in possession of health and strength, would wander the world over in search of employment. All the opinions which I have collected from persons most conversant with the Irish character, confirm this statement. Confinement of any kind is more irksome to an Irishman than it is even to an Englishman. Hence, although he might be lodged, fed, and clothed, in a workhouse,

better than he could lodge, feed, and clothe himself, by his own exertions,—he will yet, like the Englishman, never enter the workhouse, unless driven thither for refuge by actual necessity; and he will not then remain there one moment longer than that necessity exists.

43. The test of the workhouse is then, I think, likely to be to the full as efficient in Ireland, as experience proves it to have been in England; and, if relief be there restricted to the workhouse, it will be at once a test of destitution and a measure of the amount of the relief necessary to be afforded; and will serve to protect the administration of a legal provision for the destitute poor in Ireland, from those evils and abuses which followed the establishment, and led to the perversion, of the old Poor Laws in England. In giving this as my deliberate opinion, I assume that the country is to be formed into Unions as in England, and that each Union is to be provided with a workhouse, adequate to the circumstances and wants of its population, and having a competent establishment of paid officers.

44. I have spoken of the workhouse as a test of destitution generally, without limiting its operation to age, infirmity, or other circumstances; for, independently of the difficulty of discriminating between those who may fairly be considered as aged and infirm, and those who are not,—as well as certain other difficulties, practical and theoretical, in the way of making any such distinction,—I have found in the state of Ireland no sufficient reason for departing from the principle of the English Poor Law, which recognises destitution alone as the ground of relief,—or for establishing a distinction in the one country, which does not exist, in the other. I propose, therefore, to empower the presiding authority to admit the claims of all alike, able-bodied as well as infirm, young as well as old, male and female, to relief within the workhouse on the ground of actual destitution; and I found this proposition upon a careful consideration of the present state of Ireland, as well as upon the experience of Poor Law administration in England.

45. The discipline, mode of employment in, and general management of, the workhouses in Ireland, should, I think, be as nearly as possible assimilated to the practice in England. In one respect, however, it will probably be found expedient to depart somewhat from this. In England it has been found that land, beyond an acre or two for a garden, is not a desirable appendage to a workhouse. Out-door labour on the land, is not found to be so efficient for workhouse purposes, as the labour which may be provided in the house, by means of hand cornmills, stone-breaking, &c. Looking at the circumstances of Ireland, however, and the possible influx of inmates at certain seasons, especially at the commencement of the system, I am disposed to think that a plot of land, varying from six to twelve acres, should be attached to each workhouse. This would be prudent as a first provision, and, if it should afterwards be found that it can be dispensed with, the land might be readily let off, or sold.

46. The expense necessary to be incurred for providing workhouses, will not, I apprehend, be so considerable as might have been anticipated. If the surface of

Ireland be divided into squares of twenty miles each, so that a workhouse placed in the centre would be distant about ten miles from the extremities in all directions, this would give about eighty workhouses for the whole of Ireland. A diameter of twenty miles was the limit prescribed for the size of Unions by Gilbert's Act, but it was often exceeded in practice—it may, however, be assumed as a convenient size on the present occasion. In some cases, owing to the positions of the towns to be taken as the centres of Unions, or other local causes, the Unions will probably be smaller; in others, especially in the thinly-peopled districts of the west, they will in all likelihood be larger: but still, there is, I think, every probability that the number of workhouses required will not materially, if at all, exceed eighty. In aid of this number, the Houses of Industry, and Mendicity and other establishments, which will be unnecessary as soon as a legal provision is made for the relief of the destitute, will become available at probably a small expense, or at no expense whatever. In some instances, moreover, barracks, factories, or other buildings suitable for conversion into workhouses, will not improbably be obtained on easy terms:—but, excluding all these favourable considerations, which are calculated to lessen the estimated expense, and even admitting that, instead of eighty workhouses, 100 will be required, and that the cost of erecting each will be about the same as for the largest class of our English workhouses, namely, about 7000*l*.—this would give a gross outlay of 700,000*l*. for the whole of Ireland,—a sum surely not large, when the nature of the object is taken into consideration.

47. If Government were to advance this sum, or so much as might be necessary for providing the workhouses, by way of loan, as has been done to the Unions in England,—requiring an instalment of 5 per cent, of the principal to be paid off annually out of the rates,—it would make the whole charge so easy, that it would scarcely be felt. With such an object in view, it will scarcely be contended that a payment of 35,000*l*. per annum for twenty years, with the interest on the constantly decreasing principal, would be considered as a hardship on Ireland; and this is in fact the whole of the new or additional outlay proposed : for, as regards the relief of the destitute, that, as I have said before, would not be a new charge, the destitute classes being now supported out of the produce of property: although in a manner calculated to lessen the amount of production, and consequently in the long run to lessen the income of the proprietors, as well as to injure and depress the general character of the people. No objection can, therefore, I think, be raised in Ireland, on account of this proposed outlay for the provision of workhouses.

48. It appears, then, from the foregoing statements, that the workhouse system, which has been successfully applied to dispauperize England, may be safely and efficiently applied, as a medium of relief, to diminish the amount of misery in Ireland. It appears, moreover, that the expense of providing the necessary buildings will not be so large, having reference to the importance of the object, as to cause any serious impediment to the measure; and that this expense may, with the

consent of the Legislature, be so spread over a period of years, that its pressure will scarcely be felt.

II.—Secondly, *As to the means of obtaining the benefits of combined management, and of creating a local machinery for the government of Unions in Ireland.*
49. If it was desired to establish, in the several parishes of Ireland a parochial machinery, similar to that which exists in England I believe the attempt would fail; for the description of persons requisite for constituting such a machinery will not be found in the great majority of Irish parishes. In some parts of Ireland, however, and especially in the north and the east, competent individuals would be found in many, if not in most, parishes. If an Irish Poor Law be established, the uniting of parishes for the purpose of securing the benefits of combined management, is, therefore, more necessary, even than it was for England; and by making the Unions sufficiently large, there can be no doubt that, in almost every instance, a Board of Guardians may be obtained, by way of election, of such intelligence and efficiency, as to insure the orderly working of the Union, under the system of strict supervision and control, which it would be necessary, for a time, to exercise over their proceedings.
50. In the first instance, and until a rate for the relief of the destitute is established, the contributors to the county-cess might be empowered to elect the guardians;[23] but in some cases an efficient Board of Guardians may not be obtainable by election; and this is most likely to occur at the commencement of a new system, when individuals will be ill instructed as to their duties, and when the public will, perhaps, have formed exaggerated and erroneous notions of what is intended to be done. To meet this contingency, it seems essential that large general powers should be vested in some competent authority, to control and direct the proceedings of Boards of Guardians, and even to supersede their functions altogether, when such supersession shall appear to be necessary. Power should also, I think, be given, to declare Unions, and to appoint paid and other officers to conduct the business, under the direction of the central authority, without the intervention of a Board of Guardians; and in order to guard against the confusion and mistakes to be expected in some districts, on the first introduction of an entirely new order of things, and to prevent the mischief that might ensue from failure or misconduct on the part of the local authorities at the outset, the central authority should also be empowered to dispense with the election of the first Board of Guardians, and to appoint such persons as may appear most fit and competent to act as guardians of the Union, either until the Lady-day next ensuing after such appointment, or to the Lady-day twelve months, as the central authority may decide.[24] The number and selection of such specially-appointed guardians to be entirely at the discretion of the central authority.
51. These powers are greater than those that were given to the English Commissioners by the Poor Law Amendment Act: but they are, in my opinion, necessary in the present state of Ireland; and as they will be openly exercised upon the

responsibility of the central authority, whose governing motive must be the success of the measure, there is the best guarantee for their proper application. With these powers confided to the central authority, no difficulty will arise for which it will not be prepared; and it will, I think, be enabled to establish the Unions, and to constitute an adequate machinery for their government throughout the whole of Ireland, with certainty and efficiency.

52. In England, all the county magistrates residing and acting within the limits of the respective Unions, are ex-officio members of the several Boards of Guardians. The number and position of the magistracy in Ireland seem to require a modification of this rule in its application to that country. The principle of Poor Law Administration established in England by the Poor Law Amendment Act, is based essentially upon popular representation. The guardians are elected by the actual occupiers and owners of the property rated, and in the hands of the guardians the administrative power is vested. The county magistrates, it is true, are admitted, in virtue of their office, to sit and act as members of the Board, having equal powers with the elected guardians: but this does not destroy the strictly elective character of the administrative body; for in every Union, the number of elected guardians so far exceeds that of the ex-officio guardians, that the popular and elective character of the Board is maintained; whilst, at the same time, by the infusion of a portion of the magistracy, who become in virtue of their office permanent members, and therefore connecting links between the successive Boards of Guardians, the whole machinery is greatly improved; and a degree of stability and continuity of action is imparted to it, which, if based entirely upon election, and changeable annually, it would not possess.

53. This is the constitution of the Boards of Guardians in the English Unions, and nothing can work better: but in Ireland I have found, upon inquiry, that the number of magistrates who would be entitled, under a similar provision, to act as ex-officio guardians, would in general greatly exceed the number usually found qualified in England, and in some cases would, in fact, probably outnumber the elected guardians.[25] If this should occur, the elective character of the Board would of course be destroyed; but even if this should not be the case, yet any undue preponderance of the permanent ex-officio guardians would detract from the popular character of the governing body, and lower it in the confidence and estimation of the people. On these grounds, and with a view of keeping as nearly as possible to the practical constitution of the English Boards of Guardians, I propose, in the Irish Unions,—1st. That the number of ex-officio guardians shall never exceed one-third the number of elected guardians: 2dly. That immediately on the declaration of a Union, the county magistrates residing and acting within its limits, shall nominate from among themselves a number nearest to, but not exceeding, one-third of the elected guardians,—which magistrates so nominated by their compeers, shall be entitled to act as ex-officio guardians of the Union, until the Michaelmas twelvemonth after such nomination;[26] and a list of their names, duly certified by the clerk of the peace of the county or division in which the Union is situated, shall be inserted twice in the county newspapers: and 3dly. That at each

succeeding Michaelmas, the magistrates entitled as aforesaid, shall proceed to a new election. These regulations will, I think, not only preserve a due proportion in the constitution of the Boards of Guardians, but also ensure the co-operation of the most efficient portion of the magistracy in the government of the Unions; as the magistrates will, of course, nominate those members of their body who are resident, and most active and able.

54. A different practice from that established in England seems also to be necessary for Ireland with respect to the clergy. Under the provisions of the Poor Law Amendment Act, ministers of religion of every denomination are eligible to fill the office of guardians, elected or ex-officio. In the present condition of Ireland, I fear that this would be attended with serious inconvenience, and might perhaps altogether destroy the efficiency of the Boards of Guardians. I therefore propose that no clergyman, or minister of any religious denomination, shall be eligible to act either as elected or ex-officio guardian. This exclusion is not proposed from any notion of the general unfitness of the clergy to fill the office of guardian; but with reference solely to the present state of religious opinion in Ireland, and to the importance of keeping the functions of the Boards of Guardians totally free from even the suspicion of any kind of bias. If the ministers of one persuasion were to be admitted, the ministers of every persuasion must be admitted; and then the deliberations of the Boards of Guardians would too probably, in some cases, be affected by religious differences. Many of the clergy of the Established Church, moreover, being in the commission of the peace,[27] would be entitled to act as ex-officio members of the Boards of Guardians, if no such general ineligibility was to be established; and this would probably be considered by many as giving them an undue preponderance in districts where the bulk of the people are Catholics. Ireland in this respect differs greatly from England, and seems to require the application of a different rule.

55. In the course of my very anxious inquiries on this point, it was several times suggested to me, that the clergy, and ministers of religion generally, ought to be members of the Boards of Guardians in virtue of their office, on the ground that they knew more of the wants and necessities of the poor than any other description of persons; and this was stated to be more particularly the case with the Catholic Clergy. It might, perhaps, be sufficient to state, with reference to this suggestion, that any such admission of the clergy, as a body, would be directly at variance with the principle of popular election established in England, under which the Boards of Guardians are constituted, and to which they continue amenable, the several members having to be elected annually; whereas the clergy, if they were to be admitted as suggested, would be permanent and irresponsible members of the Board. In addition to this objection, however,—which, as it involves a principle, must be considered as final,—it may be remarked, that, if the above suggestion was to be adopted, and all the ministers of religion within a Union were, as such, to become members of the Board of Guardians, it would make the Board far too numerous for the orderly and efficient dispatch of business. There would probably be much debate and contention, with but little progress in the affairs of the Union.

The experience already obtained in the working of the Unions in England, is decisive upon this point. The most numerous Boards of Guardians are invariably the least efficient, and the most open to be acted upon by partial and party views. If this be the case in England, how much more likely is it to occur in Ireland, where the incentives to party bias, religious and political, are so much stronger! In Ireland, therefore, it seems most important to extend the size of the Unions, for the purpose of obtaining an impartial Board of Guardians; and to limit the number of its members, in order to secure its efficiency.

56. The duty of a guardian will be altogether of a civil character, to be fulfilled in conformity with strict legal enactments, and having nothing in common with religious functions. If a clergyman were to become a guardian, he would be bound to act in that capacity as if he were a lay member; and the clergy of all persuasions, it appears to me, would be enabled to exercise a more legitimate influence within their districts, if they were not members of the Boards of Guardians, than if they were. As guardians, their course of action would be strictly prescribed: but, if not guardians, they may be guided by what they consider to be their general or peculiar duties; and they will be enabled, as teachers to whom the people look up for advice and instruction, to render most important service to the Union.

57. The Board of Guardians, in the faithful performance of its duties, will often have to refuse applications for relief, and to act with strictness, perhaps at times even with apparent rigour. If any minister of religion was to be a member of the Board, a part of the odium which would attend such acts, however necessary and proper they might be, would attach to him, and possibly affect his ministry. If clergymen are restricted from acting as guardians, no such consequences can ensue. — They may then moderate as well as inform, and become mediators between the poor on the one side, and the Union authorities on the other. The funds, too, which as clergymen they have to administer for charitable and religious purposes, must generally be distributed by them on a different principle from that which governs the administration of relief by the Board of Guardians. This circumstance, if they were members of the Board, and party to its proceedings, would probably embarrass their conduct in one or the other capacity. On no point have I taken more pains to arrive at a sound conclusion than on this, being fully sensible of the objections, on principle, to the exclusion of any class of men from office; but the great majority of the clergy themselves with whom I have conversed, Catholic, Presbyterian, and Protestant, have agreed in thinking that it will be, on the whole, inexpedient to admit any of the ministers of religion to act as guardians. After the fullest consideration and most anxious inquiry, therefore, I recommend that they should be declared altogether ineligible.

58. The clergy, both Catholic and Protestant, may, however, by their influence and exhortations, greatly facilitate the introduction, and help the working of a system of relief for the destitute classes; and this they will be enabled to do far more effectually, if they are not guardians. I rely upon the clergy, and upon the intelligent portion of the community in Ireland, for explaining the real objects of

the new law to the people, and thus preventing exaggerated notions as to what is intended. The Irish peasantry may otherwise be led to consider it as framed for their entire support, and be apt to look to the rates, instead of their own exertions. The application of the Workhouse Test, will, it is true, correct this after a time; but in the interim, and especially at the outset, inconvenience may be created, if this very possible evil is not guarded against, by explaining to the people that the relief which the new law provides, is intended solely for the destitute, and not for those who have ability to support themselves. Such explanations have been necessary even in England, where certain evil-disposed persons have occasionally laboured to persuade the people that they were entitled to be supported in idleness out of the rates: and similar practices may not impossibly be attempted in Ireland.

59. With a central authority possessing such powers as have been indicated, I see nothing, present or prospective, to prevent the establishment of Unions in Ireland, similar to, and in all respects as effective as, the Unions established in England, under the Poor Law Amendment Act.[28] In the less populous parts of the country, it might be desirable to have the chief police station near the workhouse, and the school would be close, if not attached to it. The dispensary too, and medical and surgical aid, if required, would be found there. The Union establishment would thus become a kind of colony, a centre of civilization, and the Unions might be made important engines for effecting improvements in the condition and habits of the Irish people, in whose clothing, cottages, and domestic economy, as well as in their agricultural and other management, there now appears a lamentable deficiency of the faculty happily so common in England,—namely, the faculty of making the best of everything.

60. In passing through Ireland, no person can fail to notice the several police stations, nor can doubt that the order and neatness which they generally exhibit will operate in the way of example upon the neighbouring cottagers. It may require time to produce any very sensible effect; but some effect will assuredly be produced. Man imitates good as well as evil; and if examples of the former are placed before him, they will not be altogether lost, even under ordinary circumstances; but the example set to a district by a Union establishment such as is above described,—exhibiting neatness, order, and comfort, with probably a portion of land for farming and gardening attached—must be of far greater influence than any insulated example could be. Such an establishment would be the centre of resort of the whole district; and might become the source and nursery of almost every kind of improvement in the moral and social habits, the domestic economy, and general operations of the surrounding peasantry and occupiers of land.

61. When there shall be a provision for the destitute at the common charge, the community will have acquired a right so far to interfere with the proceedings of individuals, as to prevent the spread of destitution, and to guard itself from loss or damage by the negligence, obstinacy, or supineness of any of its members. Under the old civil institutions in England, this interference was largely exercised, to the benefit of the community at the time, although in the present advanced state of society it has become unnecessary, and would now scarcely be tolerated. In

Ireland, the state of the rural community is in many respects similar to that which prevailed in England when the local headman of the village or parish was looked up to as an authority, in advising and directing to what was right, as well as in restraining from what was wrong; but in the majority of Irish parishes the whole population is nearly on the same level; there is no gradation, no man or class of men sufficiently prominent to possess control, or even to exercise influence : there is not the least approach to self-government observable. To select, from among the inhabitants of a parish, one or more of the most intelligent individuals, and to array them on the side of the law, good order, and improvement, and to clothe them with a certain extent of authority and local importance,—as was the case with the headborough or local headman,[29] and as is now the case with the parish officers in England,—would therefore, I consider, be productive of benefit as well as convenience in Ireland; and I recommend that the central authority should be empowered to appoint, or to direct the Board of Guardians to appoint, one or more wardens or officers for every parish, or for such districts of the Union as may be deemed most convenient.

62. The central authority should have power to define the duties of these officers or wardens, which would be to superintend generally the affairs of the district, to assist and observe the instructions of the Board of Guardians, especially with reference to measures intended to operate upon the habits of the laboring population. Parochial or district officers of this description might be made extremely useful in connecting the Board of Guardians with the several portions of the Union, thus extending its influence, and rendering it effective for the purposes of general improvement, as well as for the administration of relief. These officers, should, I think, be armed with the authority of constables or headboroughs; and should be second in local importance to the guardian, to which office theirs would probably often become preliminary. I propose to vest their appointment (subject to the control of the central authority) in the Board of Guardians, for the purpose of giving importance to that body within the district of which it is the head, an object obviously desirable. The appointment should be for a year, but the same persons might be re-eligible. Such officers would probably be found useful for other local purposes, with reference to the functions of Magistrates and Grand Juries; to which end it might be necessary to have one or more for every civil parish, according to its size, population, or other circumstances. This would be the first step towards self-government in the Irish parishes.—It has been said that the Poor Law Amendment Act has destroyed local self-government in England; but this is not the fact. It has not destroyed, it has on the contrary improved it, by centralizing and combining the best elements existing in a large district, in lieu of the scattered, desultory, and imperfect old parochial administrations. Such will also, I believe, be the effect of Unions in Ireland.

63. There are some other points connected with the creation of a machinery for Union government, to which it appears necessary to advert. In England, under the provisions of the Poor Law Amendment Act, every parish or township rated

for the maintenance of its poor, and included in a Union, is entitled to return a guardian. In Ireland it will, I think, be essential that the central authority should be empowered to fix the boundaries of a Union, without being restricted to parish boundaries. It should be empowered to divide parishes, either for the purpose of electing guardians, or for joining a portion of a parish to one Union, and another portion of the same parish to another Union. It should also be empowered to consolidate parishes for the purpose of electing one or more guardians, and likewise to form election districts for this purpose, without reference to parochial boundaries. And lastly, the central authority should be empowered to add to, take from, and remodel Unions, with or without consent, at any time that such change might be deemed to be necessary. These powers have been much wanted by the English Poor Law Commissioners, and would have enabled them to make their Unions more compact and convenient than they are at present;—local prejudices and local interests having frequently compelled the Commissioners to abandon the arrangement which, with reference to the general interest, they deemed the best. In Ireland, full powers in this respect are, I think, indispensable, not only on account of the size and uncertain boundaries of some parishes, but also to enable the central authority to deal with the various circumstances under which the Unions will there have to be formed.

64. I consider then, that with adequate powers confided to a responsible authority, and with such modifications as are herein before described, the principle of Union for the purposes of systematic and combined management, which has been established in England by the Poor Law Amendment Act, may be advantageously extended to Ireland; and that, as it has been shown that no insurmountable difficulty exists to impede the introduction of the workhouse as a test of destitution, and a measure of relief,—so neither will there be any insurmountable difficulty in establishing an adequate machinery for the government of the Unions when formed.

PART THE THIRD.

65. I think it has been shown that a system of Poor Laws ought to be established in Ireland; that the workhouse system may there be relied upon, as a test of destitution, and a measure of relief; and that the means of forming and governing Unions exist there, as well as in England. It now remains to describe, in detail, the several points which appear to require especial attention in framing a measure comprising these objects; and also to offer such further observations, as did not seem to come immediately within the scope of either of the preceding divisions of this Report.

66. I assume, as the governing principle to be observed in dealing with this portion of the subject, that the Poor Law of Ireland should assimilate in all respects as nearly as possible to the Poor Law System now established in England,—varying only in those instances, in which the relative circumstances of the two countries require a different practice.

67. The point first in order for consideration would naturally be the constitution of the central or chief authority, and the powers to be confided to it for carrying the measure of an Irish Poor Law into operation; but I postpone this part of the subject for separate consideration—assuming only, that a central authority is to be established, with powers similar in kind to those conferred upon the English Poor Law Commissioners, but more ample in extent.

This point being disposed of for the present, the other objects for consideration may be taken in the following order.

I. Relief.—The objects for relief, and the mode and conditions of its administration.

II. Local Machinery.—The appointment and authority of the parties by and through whom relief is to be administered.

III. Rating.—The mode in which the funds required for the purposes of relief are to be raised, and from whom.

IV. Settlement.—This subject would have properly come under the first head, but it will be more convenient to consider it separately.

IV. Mendicancy.

V. Bastardy.

VI. Apprenticeship.

VII. Pauper Idiots and Lunatics.

IX. Emigration and Migration.

X. Houses of Industry, Foundling Hospitals, Mendicity Establishments, and other Charitable Institutions.

On each of these heads I will now proceed to remark, in the order in which they are above placed.

I.—Of Relief.

68. The only legal claim for relief, in England, is founded upon the destitution of the party claiming it. I propose to extend the same principle to Ireland; and, as a test of the actual existence of such destitution, and to guard against the abuse and train of evils which have invariably attended the unrestricted distribution of out-door relief, (that is, of relief administered either in money or in kind to parties out of the workhouse, or at their own homes,) I further propose that, in Ireland, no relief should be given except in the workhouse. This limitation should be specified in the Act, in order to protect the central authority from the pressure which is not unlikely to occur upon this point, and which would otherwise possibly be at times too great for it to stand up against, if not so supported.

69. I do not propose to impart a right to relief, even to the destitute, but to place the ordering and directing of all relief in the hands of the central authority. The claim to relief in England may be said to be founded on prescription, rather than on legislative enactment; for, although the 43rd of Elizabeth provides for the levying a rate for the purpose of relieving the destitute poor, it invests them with no right

to claim relief, the administration of which is left entirely to the discretion of the local authorities; who are, however, of course, responsible for the exercise of such discretion and for the due administration of relief.[30]

70. The promulgation of rules for the administration of relief would, therefore, be vested in the central authority, limited by this proviso,—that relief is only to be administered by receiving the applicants into the house, and subjecting them to the regulations established for its government. It would rest with the central authority to declare when the workhouse should be so applied in each Union; and also to take care that no time was lost in providing competent workhouse accommodation, as well as to establish such regulations as might be necessary for the guidance of the local authorities in the interim: but it will be most safe to prohibit all relief whatever, until the test of the workhouse can be applied, rather than invest the central authority with a discretionary power of permitting or directing its administration in any case, without the intervention of such a test.

71. The strict limitation of relief to the workhouse may possibly be objected to, on the ground that extreme want is found occasionally to assail large portions of the population in Ireland, who are then reduced to a state bordering upon starvation; and ought therefore, it may be asserted, to be relieved at the public charge, without being subjected to the discipline of the workhouse. This, however, is an extreme case, and it would not, I think, be wise to adapt the regulations of Poor Law administration in Ireland to the possible occurrence of such a contingency. In a period of famine, the whole population become in a great degree destitute; but it surely would not be expedient to hold out an expectation, that, if such an event should unhappily occur, support for all would be unconditionally provided at the public charge. This would lessen the inducements to a provident economising of their means of support on the part of the people, by a timely resort to which the occurrence of actual famine may often be averted, although dearth and much consequent distress may still arise. This must in fact be the case in all countries, whenever a season of scarcity occurs. During such a visitation, the workhouse would not, in all probability, contain the numbers who might be anxious to crowd into it for support; but to the extent of its means of accommodation it would help to relieve the general distress, and the Union machinery would probably be found useful in the application of general relief, as well as for preventing the recurrence of the calamity.

72. The occurrence of a famine, however, if general, seems to be a contingency altogether above the powers of a Poor Law to provide for. It must be remembered, that then there is an actual deficiency of supply. As there is less to consume, less must be consumed. To assess the rate-payers, in order to enable the rate-receivers to continue their ordinary consumption, would only shift the suffering. If the famine is not general, but merely local, the resources of the country, or the districts which have escaped its visitation, must be brought in aid of those suffering from its ravages; and this would be most effectually done by the public and private exertions of the opulent and the charitable. It is, however, I think, impossible to

contemplate the longer prevalence of such a state of things in Ireland, as that in which any considerable portion of its population shall be subjected to the periodical occurrence of famine. As the habits, intelligence, and forethought of the people improve, with the increase of wealth and the progress of education, these visitations will be guarded against and averted. I do not therefore propose to make any exception, permissive of out-door relief in any shape, not even in kind; although it is still allowed to be so administered in certain cases in the English Unions: but I recommend, that in Ireland relief should be limited strictly to the workhouse.

73. It is also, I think, necessary for carrying out the workhouse principle in Ireland, that no individual of a family should be admitted, unless all its members enter the house. Relief to the father or husband is equivalent to relief to the child or the wife, and vice versa; and, while they continue one family, a part cannot be considered as destitute, and the rest not so; a family must be taken as a whole, and so admitted or excluded. This principle is established very generally in the English Unions, although in certain cases its direct application to the full extent has for a time been suspended, in consequence of the habits and abuses which had grown up under the old system, having rendered it difficult to enforce the principle at first in all its strictness. In Ireland, however, no such difficulty exists, and the rule should there be strictly and at once applied. In fact it is now acted upon in some of the Houses of Industry which I have visited, and with very good effect.

74. Whenever the community shall have provided for the protection of its members against the effects of destitution, it will have acquired a right to compel individuals to fulfil their natural duties towards their relatives; and the provisions of the 43d of Elizabeth, requiring parents to support children, and children to support parents, should be extended to Ireland. I would also propose that the affording relief by way of loan, provided for in the 58th section of the Poor Law Amendment Act, be extended to Ireland. It may in certain cases be useful, and, if exercised with discretion and firmness by the Boards of Guardians, can scarcely be productive of mischief.

75. The regulation of all relief being placed in the hands of the central authority, it is unnecessary to particularize several other points of detail, for which its powers would enable it effectually to provide. With respect to medical relief, it would of course, like any other kind of relief, be administered in the workhouse: but it may be a question whether, and how far, the medical aid now afforded by Dispensaries, and to which the people have become accustomed, shall be continued to outdoor applicants, in the event of these institutions being connected with the workhouse. This is a point of some importance, both in respect of principle, and as a matter of detail; and, in order that the central authority may be enabled to deal with it, I propose to give them the power to regulate all the Dispensaries. Independent medical clubs ought also, I think, to be encouraged in Ireland, as they have been in England, for the purpose of correcting the too prevalent disposition to rely upon gratuitous medical aid.

II.—Of the Local Machinery.

76. I propose that the local machinery for the administration of relief to the destitute in Ireland, under the direction of a central authority, should be the same as that which is provided in England by the Poor Law Amendment Act; namely, the union of a district for common management, under a Board of Guardians to be elected annually by the rate-payers, with paid officers to be appointed or approved by the central authority.

77. In forming the country into Unions, it will, I think, be necessary to observe the civil, rather than the ecclesiastical, boundaries of parishes; but cases will arise, in which it may be requisite to disregard all such boundaries—it being obviously more important that the district to be united should be compact, convenient, and accessible, and be naturally connected with its centre, than that the old and often inconvenient boundaries should be observed. This applies no less to county or baronial boundaries than to those of parishes or other divisions; and it cannot, I think, be too strongly impressed upon the individuals to whom the duty of forming Unions may be confided, that the point to which they ought to direct their attention in grouping the country into Unions, as regards size, form, and means of communication, is the general interest and convenience of the inhabitants.

78. The principle which has governed the Commissioners in the formation of the English Unions, whenever they have not been driven from it by local circumstances, has been, to fix upon some market-town conveniently situated as a centre, and to attach to it the whole surrounding district, of which it may be considered as the capital—the mart, in which the general business of the district, both public and private, for the most part concentrates. The roads of a district always converge upon the market-town. The communications with it are constant, and the people settled within the range of its influence constitute almost a distinct community. To form such a district into a Union, under one common government, for general as well as for Poor Law purposes, seems therefore an obvious course of proceeding: and I strongly recommend its being adhered to, as closely as possible, in the formation of Unions in Ireland. There may be parts of the country in which such a convenient centre does not exist, but this will be of rare occurrence, and the general powers of the central authority will be competent to deal with it wherever it does occur. The larger the Unions are made, the less of course will be the difficulty in this respect.

79. I have stated, in the second part of this Report, much of what appeared to be necessary, with reference to the members of the Boards of Guardians, both elected and ex-officio. The qualification for an elected guardian will consist of being rated at a certain amount; and this amount, as in England, the central authority will prescribe, as well as the regulations for governing the proceedings of the guardians, when elected. The central authority will also either appoint, or direct the appointment, and prescribe the duties, of the paid officers of the Union, together with the audit of the accounts, and the form in which they are to be kept.

80. The important question—in whose hands the right of appointing Guardians shall be confided, and in what way that right shall be exercised,—remains still to

be considered. In this, as in all other cases, the principle which has been established for England by the Poor Law Amendment Act, should, I think, be applied to Ireland, and the election or appointment of guardians be vested in the rate-payers and owners of property within the Union: but the circumstances of Ireland appear to require a certain departure from the English practice, in carrying this principle into operation. The owners of property, in England, are entitled to vote according to the scale which was established by the Select Vestry Act,[31] and which ascends, by gradations of 25*l*. each, from a rated value of 50 *l*. per annum, up to 150*l*. per annum, giving one vote for the former, and six votes for the latter. This scale, is, perhaps, open to some objection on the grounds of complexity and over-minuteness. It is, moreover, different from the scale of voting fixed for the rate-payers by the Poor Law Amendment Act, and which provides that rate-payers, if rated under 200L. shall have one vote; if rated at 200*l*. and under 400 *l*., two votes; and if at 400 *l*. and upwards, three votes.

81. The above scale of voting for rate-payers seems, on the whole, well adapted to the condition of England; but the amounts specified are, I think, too high for Ireland; and the scale is not sufficiently minute in its graduation, with reference to the subdivision of property which prevails there. Instead of adopting these English scales, therefore, or either of them, I would propose to establish one scale in Ireland, by which simplicity of detail, and a right result, will, I think, be more effectually secured; and I recommend the following for regulating the votes of owners of property, as well as occupiers, namely,

above 5 *l*. and under 50 *l* .... one vote.
50 *l*. and under 100 *l*. .... two votes.
100 *l*. ,, 150 *l*. .... three votes.
150 *l*. ,, 200 *l* .... four votes.
200 *l*. and upwards .... five votes.

This scale would, I believe, be found to work well and satisfactorily in Ireland. The cumulative votes of the owners and larger occupiers would serve to counterbalance the number of small rate-payers, and secure the return of competent individuals.

82. I do not propose to extend the right of voting below a rating of 5 *l*., on account of the vast number of small occupiers, especially in the west and south of Ireland; but I recommend, that, for all property rated under 5 *l*. value, the occupiers of which would thus be deprived of the privilege of voting at the election of guardians, the landlord, or owner of the property, should be required to pay the rate, and not the tenant. The aggregate rated value of the property for which the owner would so pay must, of course, be included in the amount by which the number of his votes will be regulated, according to the above scale. If, as a matter of arrangement or otherwise, the occupying tenant of premises rated under 5 *l*. value should have paid the rate, he must in such case be authorized to deduct it from the rent payable to the landlord. A form of rate-book should be prescribed, as in England, in which the owners' and the occupiers' name, and the fair estimated value, or net

rental of the property, should in every case be inserted; and this rate-book, unless appealed against, should be conclusive evidence of the right of voting in every instance.

III.—Of Rating.

83. The power to assess the property and levy a rate within a Union, for the purpose of relieving the destitute, must, I think, be confided to the Board of Guardians, by whom such relief is to be administered. The mode of assessing and collecting the rate, as well as its application, will be prescribed by the central authority. The central authority, moreover, ought, I think, to be empowered to direct a rate to be at any time levied by the Board of Guardians, or by such other local executive as it might have found it necessary to appoint, under the provisions already suggested.*[32]

84. The Parochial Assessments Act,[33] introduced by Mr. Poulett Scrope,[34] and passed in the last Session of Parliament, establishes the principle that the rates are to be paid upon the net annual value of property. This was always, I believe, the law in England, although it had been widely departed from in practice. As regards the principle by which the assessment of property should be regulated, therefore, it will be only necessary to extend the provisions of Mr. Poulett Scrope's Act to Ireland, substituting the Union for the parish authorities, and introducing such other modifications as the circumstances under which it will have there to be applied render necessary. The valuation of property for the purpose of rating need not, I apprehend, be made in every instance by surveyors and professional valuators. The fairly estimated value of the property is all that is really necessary; and there will probably not be much difficulty in ascertaining this, either with or without professional assistance, taking the Union district parish by parish. In many instances a valuation has already been made for the purpose of tithe commutation in Ireland. Wherever this or any other fair valuation has been made, it will, of course, be available for the purpose of rating to the relief of the poor.

85. Hitherto there has been no rate for the relief of the poor in Ireland. The destitute classes have gone on increasing in numbers, but still there has been no recognized or legal provision for their relief. Property has been acquired, capital invested, and contracts made, under this state of things. It will be impossible, therefore, suddenly to impose a rate upon property without affecting existing interests, and partially disturbing existing arrangements. The subject cannot be considered without our becoming immediately sensible of this consequence: but I believe that the effect will be slight, even at first, and that in the course of a very few years it will cease altogether. If the inconvenience were far greater than I anticipate, however, it will be as nothing when compared with the object to be effected; and all objections to the imposition of a rate on this ground are overborne by considerations of the public welfare.

86. The question as to who shall be liable to pay the rate, and in what proportions, requires to be very carefully considered. The parties immediately interested

appear to be the owner or person possessing the beneficial interest of the property assessed, and the tenant or occupier. Between these two, it seems, therefore, at once equitable and expedient to apportion the rate. Where the two characters are combined, the same person would, of course, be answerable for the entire rate. As to the occupier, he would be resident, and no difficulty could occur with respect to him; and for the owner, I would not propose to look beyond the person having the immediate beneficial interest, under whom the occupier holds, and to whom he actually pays his rent. On these parties I propose to confer the right of voting for guardians; and to apportion between these two alone the payment of the rate.

87. It appeared to be the opinion of the Irish Poor Inquiry Commissioners, that the owner should pay two-thirds of the rate, and the occupier one-third; and it seemed to me, at first, that this would be an equitable division. On further consideration and inquiry, however, I was led to abandon this proportion, and thought that each should be called upon to pay half the rate. I was mainly influenced to adopt this change of view by the consideration that at present nearly the whole support of the destitute falls upon the tenantry. It is to the occupiers that the mendicant resorts, and from them he receives his daily rations. There is thus, in reality, a compulsory rate now levied in Ireland, although not sanctioned by legal enactment; and no occupier, however limited may be his means, turns away the mendicant empty-handed from his door. There is an almost superstitious dread of doing so; and this motive operates, perhaps, as compulsorily as the law would act, in the raising of a regular rate.

88. It is, I think, in some measure the pressure of these constant calls upon the occupiers which bears them down, and keeps them at their present low level of subsistence. If, therefore, the destitute classes be relieved by means of a general rate upon property, of which the occupiers are called upon to pay half the amount, they would be relieved from nearly one-half their present burthen; for a Poor Law, if rightly administered, although it ensures relief for the actual destitute, will not increase their number, or tend eventually to swell the fund appropriated to their support. On the contrary, I believe it will help to lessen both. But, admitting that the number and the amount remain the same as at present, still the occupiers will then have to pay only one-half, the landlord the other; whereas now, in reality, the occupier contributes nearly the whole. For these reasons, it appears to me that the most equitable adjustment of the payment would be to divide the rate equally between the owner and the occupier. Whether the rate be paid in equal proportions by the landlord and tenant, or one-third by the latter, and two-thirds by the former, as already proposed, is, however, purely a matter of detail; of great importance it is true, but still involving no question of principle; and, in whichever way it may be decided, I feel that I shall have fulfilled my duty in thus stating my opinion, and the reasons on which it is founded.*[35]

89. There is yet, however, another consideration connected with this question, deserving of some attention. In England, the whole of the rates are paid by the occupiers of property; and, assuming it to be desirable to assimilate the practice in both

countries in all respects as nearly as possible, and even where a perfect assimilation is not at present practicable, to admit any exception which may be necessary, only with a view to its earliest abandonment—assuming this, it may be asked whether the law, with respect to rating in the two countries, should not be assimilated within a certain period; whether in short, at the end of (say) twenty-one years, the occupiers might not be made solely responsible for the payment of the rates in Ireland, as they now are in England?—However this question, and the general subject of rating, may be settled, it is important that it should be clearly defined and provided for in the Bill.

IV.—Of Settlement.
90. Parochial Settlement, as established in England, is almost universally admitted to have been productive of great mischief.
It has led to much litigation and expense; and, by fixing the peasantry to the narrow limits of their parish, beyond which the world was to them a blank, it has probably done more to injure their character, by destroying its elasticity, and banishing all self-dependence and resource, than any other part of the old English Poor Law system. It will not, therefore, I presume, be considered right to establish parochial settlement in Ireland. In the Poor Law Amendment Act, provision is made for the several parishes comprised in a Union becoming one for rating and settlement; and, although this may not be immediately achievable, the Commissioners are fully sensible of the extreme desirableness of the object, and spare no effort to hasten its accomplishment. This is now, in fact, the only practicable mode of correcting the evils of parochial settlement. In Ireland, however, no such practice has prevailed. The habits of the Irish people are migratory, their movements depending upon their own volition. To establish a Law of Settlement, would be to fix them to one locality. No such law has yet been established there; and it is therefore perfectly open to the Legislature to prescribe the limits, if a settlement shall be deemed advisable; or else to dispense with settlement altogether, leaving the whole of the country open to the whole of its people, as at present.
91. If it should be decided to establish a Law of Settlement, it will of course be a Union Settlement, making the limits of the Union the boundary. This would be open to fewer objections than a parochial settlement; an extension of the area necessarily lessening the amount of evil which must always result from fixing any limit whatever. The Union limits would be also the boundary for rating to the relief of the poor; and thus the Union would be one for rating and settlement in the sense provided for in the Poor Law Amendment Act. The chief difficulty in carrying such a Law of Settlement into operation, would arise out of the necessity of prescribing distinctly the individuals to whom the right of settlement should be imparted; so as to prevent doubt, and the occurrence of the dishonest trickery and expensive litigation, in which the English Settlement Law has been so prolific.
92. If a census of the population actually within a Union on the day of its declaration was to be taken as the basis of settlement, it would necessarily contain

a number of individuals who in fact belonged, in their own sense of the term, to some other part of the country, to which after a time they would probably remove. If, on the contrary, the names of those persons only were to be inserted who had been permanently resident, or who had resided three, five, or more years, (which seems the only other alternative,) many individuals would be excluded who might afterwards become permanently resident, and who would thereby be deprived of a settlement altogether. To establish settlement in a Union by means of a census, seems therefore open to serious objection, although at first view it appears to holdout a prospect of preventing litigation.

93. The English practice with respect to settlement is, I think, rather to be avoided than imitated; and apprenticeship, a year's hiring and service, or renting a tenement of 10*l.* value, will not, I presume, be approved as conditions for conferring a right of settlement in Ireland. The simpler the conditions on which settlement is made to depend, the better; and, in the event of a settlement law being established, I would propose generally to limit these conditions to two,—namely, birth, and actual residence for a term of years. These conditions would be retrospective as well as prospective; and individuals not coming within either, would have to be treated as casual poor. In order that families should not be separated, the wife must always take the husband's settlement, and the children that of their parents, until (say) fourteen years of age, or until they shall have acquired a settlement in their own right.

94. The right of settlement by birth is susceptible of the easiest proof. A copy of the register, or certificate from the clergyman, or parish authorities, would be sufficient to establish the claim; and this, once recognised, would remain in force, unless superseded by the acquisition of a new right acquired by residence. To impart a right of settlement, the residence ought, I think, to be an independent residence. The individual should have supported himself without public relief, and have paid all assessments to which he was liable. This would in fact amount to what has been called "Industrial Residence." The duration of such a residence for conferring a right of settlement, admits of question. Three, five, and seven years have each been recommended, but the first period seems to have been most generally approved; and for my own part I think a period of three years is, on the whole, the best term. An individual who had maintained himself independently during that time, and paid his portion of contributions towards the common charge, appears thereby to have entitled himself to relief from destitution, at the charge of the community. Three years' residence, moreover, is the period fixed by the Municipal Corporation Act, for conferring a full participation in municipal rights;[36] and on this, as well as on other accounts, it seems to be the best term for conferring a right of settlement. It may be noticed here, however, that three years is precisely the period of residence on which the acquisition of a right of settlement was founded in Denmark; but this was afterwards discovered to be productive of so much inconvenience, and to lead to so many forced ejectments, with a view of preventing the completion of the requisite term, that the period has now been extended to fourteen instead of three years.[37]

95. The example which Denmark thus affords of the tendency to abuse, whenever such artificial distinctions and divisions are forced upon a community, is of considerable value; and, when added to the dearly-bought experience in England of the effects of a Settlement Law, may well call for consideration as to whether any such law is actually necessary in Ireland, or whether settlement may not be there altogether dispensed with. This point is of vast importance, and I have endeavoured to work through the details in all their practical bearings, so as to arrive at an accurate estimate of the comparative advantages and disadvantages of establishing Poor Laws in Ireland, with a Union settlement, and without any settlement whatever;—and I have arrived at an entire conviction, that it will be better to dispense with settlement altogether. Some inconvenience may possibly arise at the first declaration of a Union, from an undue pressure for relief by persons not fairly forming a part of the Union population; but the general powers proposed to be confided to the central authority, will I think enable it to deal effectually with such cases. As the Unions increase in number, moreover, the inconvenience from this cause will become less; and, when the whole country shall be formed into Unions, it will nearly, if not altogether, cease. Even then, however, with the present migratory habits of the Irish people, there may be occasionally an undue pressure upon particular Unions; but the workhouse will, I am persuaded, prove a sufficient corrective in the long run; and the evil arising from this cause, supposing it even to be far greater than I anticipate, will still be as nothing, compared to the evils which experience has shown to be the invariable attendants of a settlement law.

96. Without a law of settlement, it is true, vagrants and mendicants from other districts may congregate in particular Unions, from accident or inclination, and may claim relief, or may be sent into the workhouse by the police; but, if the workhouses are all regulated upon the same scale of diet and discipline, there would be no inducement for the mendicant and vagrant classes to prefer one Union to another, and they would probably remain scattered throughout the country, much in the same proportions as at present. If such a preference was in any instance shown by them, it might be taken as a proof of inefficient management or lax discipline on the part of the favoured Union, and would be a signal for the central authority to interfere. Thus, if there should be no law of settlement, the numbers of inmates in the several workhouses would serve as a kind of index of the efficient management of each; and the local authorities would be compelled in self-defence to keep their Unions in good order, to prevent their being overrun with paupers. Such a competition, if well regulated, would go far to ensure the permanent efficiency of all the Unions. In speaking of vagrants and mendicants, I of course mean the existing race, and those whom the present habits of the people will for a time give rise to: but I confidently reckon on the extinction of mendicancy at no distant day—or at least that it will be so reduced in amount by the joint operation of the Union system and the Workhouse test, as to be no longer the source of evil and moral degradation, which unhappily it now is and long has been in Ireland.

97. If the Legislature should see fit to dispense with settlement altogether, great care and attention will be necessary in establishing the Unions, especially the

early Unions, to avoid imparting to any class of persons a right to relief, real or imaginary. The arrangements in the several Unions must be brought into operation gradually, the local authorities advancing step by step, and the central authority superintending their proceedings, and being always ready to afford assistance in the event of any pressure or difficulty occurring. With such management, I see no ground for apprehension as to the consequences of establishing a system of relief and Union government in Ireland, without a law of settlement. If, however, a different view on this point should be taken, and, for the purpose of guarding against the possible in conveniences which might at first occur, a Union settlement should be established,—it will then be deserving of consideration, whether provision should not be made for putting an end to such settlement, at the expiration of three or five years, or some other definite period, to be fixed by the Act, or determined by the central authority, whenever the whole country shall be formed into Unions.

v.—Of Mendicancy.

98. Whenever relief is provided for the destitute, mendicancy may be suppressed. A law, which says, "You shall not beg or steal, but you shall starve," would be contrary to natural justice and humanity, and would be disobeyed; but if the law first makes provision for the destitute, and then says, "You shall not beg, but you shall be relieved at the public charge," the alternative thus offered will enable the community to suppress a practice which is held to be injurious to its best interests. On these grounds, I think the law which establishes a system of public relief for destitution, should at the same time prohibit mendicancy.

99. The present state of Ireland, however, as regards beggars and vagrants, and the habits and feelings of the Irish people, throws considerable difficulty in the way of an immediate suppression of mendicancy. The number of such individuals is very great, and they are therefore of some importance as a class, and support and keep each other in countenance whilst following, what they seem to consider, no disreputable vocation. They enter the cottages of the peasantry as supplicants, it is true, but still with a certain sense of right; and the cottager would be held to be a bold, if not a bad man, who resisted their appeal. In fact, the appeal of the mendicant never is resisted,—if there is only a handful of potatoes, they are divided with the beggar; and there is thus levied from the produce of the soil in Ireland, for the support of mendicancy, I believe to the full as large a contribution as it is now proposed to raise by an equitable assessment of property, for the relief of destitution. The "sturdy beggars," adverted to in the 43rd of Elizabeth, must have been of a class very similar to that which is now common in Ireland.[38] Indeed the state of society at the two periods seems to have been nearly the same in both countries, the prevalence of begging in each being accompanied by the same general disposition to give, and this disposition of course causing a constantly progressive increase in the number of beggars. Such was the state of England at and prior to the time of Elizabeth, and such is now the state of Ireland.

100. The evils of mendicancy in Ireland can hardly be overestimated, and its suppression should certainly be provided for at the earliest practicable period. The best mode of effecting this object would probably be, to enact a general prohibition, and to cast upon the central authority the responsibility of bringing the Act into operation in the several Unions, as the workhouses became fitted for the reception of inmates. In furtherance of this object, the police should act in close communication with the Boards of Guardians; and the central authority might, I think, so regulate the progress of the measure, as that the now itinerant mass of mendicants, who may be really unable to provide for themselves, should be placed in the several workhouses with the least degree of coercion and inconvenience; and that the able-bodied, but idle vagrants and disorderly persons, should be compelled to provide for their own subsistence, by the application of workhouse discipline.

101. Time and forbearance will, however, be necessary in carrying such a measure into operation in Ireland, and these the flexible powers of the central authority will enable it to afford. The present generation will probably pass away before the disposition to encourage begging by indiscriminate almsgiving, which now prevails so generally among all classes in Ireland, will be corrected by the adoption of sounder views, and a more enlightened benevolence. It will then, we may hope, be seen, that the real friends of the people are those who lead them, even where necessary by compulsory measures, to active independent exertion, to a reliance upon themselves and their own efforts for support—not those who, by the constant doling out of what is called charity, entice and mislead the people into a state of dependence. It may minister to human pride, to be surrounded by a crowd of such dependents; but it surely is inconsistent with genuine benevolence to encourage, or even to permit this, if it can possibly be prevented. For wise ends, man has been subjected to various wants, as stimulants to exertion; and those persons are not the real friends of their race, who attempt to divert him from the exercise of the active faculties with which he is endowed, and to lead him to a reliance upon the volition of others rather than upon his own efforts. Looking at the present state of Ireland, it is, I think, much to be desired that correct views in this respect should be impressed upon the public mind. The clergy, it is to be hoped, will exert themselves in furtherance of this object, and particularly the Roman Catholic clergy, whose influence will be most valuable in bringing about a right understanding on this very important subject.

vi.—Of Bastardy.

102. As far as I had opportunities of observing and inquiring, the Irish females are generally correct in their conduct. I am aware that opinions somewhat different have been expressed; but I feel bound to state that my own impressions of the moral conduct of the Irish females are highly favourable. Their duties appear to be much more laborious than those of the same class of females in England. Their dress, too, is very inferior, and so likewise seems their general position in society;

yet they universally appear modest, industrious, and sober. I state this as the result of my own observation merely; and I do so here, because, if the Irish females have preserved their moral character untainted under the very trying circumstances in which they are placed, (as I believe in the main to be the case,) it affords a powerful argument for "letting well alone." If it had been otherwise, however, and if the extent of bastardy, and its demoralizing influence on public manners, had been much greater, I should still have recommended that the Irish females should be left, as now, the guardians of their own honour, and be responsible in their own persons for all deviations from virtue.

103. The abuses under the old English Bastardy Law, and the brief experience of the improved practice established by the Poor Law Amendment Act, warrant me in recommending that no such law should be applied to Ireland; but that bastards, and the mothers of bastards, in all matters connected with the relief of the poor, should be dealt with in the same manner as other destitute persons, solely on the ground of destitution. If, however, bastardy and demoralization should be actually more prevalent in Ireland than I apprehend to be the case, they are evils not, I believe, remediable by legislative enactments,—they must be left to the slow but certain amelioration which the diffusion of education, religious culture, and the increase of intelligence, industry, and wealth, will effect. These will in time improve the moral feelings of the people, and correct their social habits.

vii.—Of Apprenticeship.

104. The experience which England affords, as regards apprenticeship, is of a somewhat conflicting character, although the preponderance of testimony is certainly opposed to it. It has been open to much abuse, and has operated very mischievously in several parts of the country, by increasing that dependence upon the parish in the various contingencies of life, which under the old system of Poor Law Administration had become so entirely the characteristic of the English peasantry. It must, however, I think, be also admitted, that the apprenticing of orphan and destitute children, as provided for by the 43rd of Elizabeth, has in many cases been productive of good; and, if judiciously limited, and sparingly acted upon, so as not to be regarded as the ordinary mode of providing for the children of the labouring classes, but merely as a resource for the destitute and the orphan, it might still, I think, be continued with advantage.

105. I am aware that this opinion is rather more favourable to the system of apprenticeship than that which was entertained by the members of the late English Poor Law Inquiry Commission: but the evidence of abuse submitted to the Commissioners was taken under the old Poor Law Administration, which, in fact, converted everything which it touched into an abuse; and it does not follow, that, because apprenticeship helped to add to the accumulation of evils under such circumstances, (as it unquestionably did,) it is incapable of producing substantial good if differently conducted. It is on the different application of apprenticeship

that I rely, and on the different circumstances in which it will be now applied, as compared with the old Poor Law Administration. In the case of Ireland, none of the abuses exist which prevailed under the old parochial management in England; and, by the aid of the Union machinery, apprenticeship may, I think, be there safely applied to the placing out of destitute and orphan children, the number of whom is very considerable. Without some such provision, these children would too probably grow up without the training to habits of manual industry necessary for enabling them to support themselves, and to become useful members of the community. I consider, also, that the apprenticing of such children will gradually pave the way for the hiring of male and female servants by the occupiers of land. This will, perhaps, be the first step in that transition of which I have spoken, from the state of a mere cottier tenant, with a view solely to subsistence, to that of the agriculturist, occupying land with a view to profit.

106. It is essential, however, that the governing principle of Poor Law Administration should be adhered to in the apprenticing of pauper children, and that they should on no account be placed in better circumstances than the children of the independent labourer. This principle had been, in great measure, overlooked in our English practice; and hence, apprenticing by the parish, instead of being looked to as a last resort in cases of actual need, has been regarded as a kind of established right for disposing of all the children of a district. Like mendicancy in Ireland, its general prevalence took from it all sense of disgrace: and parents, instead of exerting themselves to get their children out into service, regularly applied to the parish, which most unwisely took upon itself the duties of a common parent in one of the ordinary affairs of life. In the fulfilment of the duty thus voluntarily undertaken, the old parish authorities were very frequently guilty of much jobbing, partiality, and oppression. Large premiums have been given, and weekly payments made out of the rates, on account of such parish apprentices, which never ought to have been allowed. Individuals too have been exposed to much expense and inconvenience, by having apprentices fixed upon them improperly. These abuses are now, however, for the most part remedied, wherever Unions have been formed; and the improved administration by Boards of Guardians, and the strict supervision of the Commissioners, may be expected to remove them entirely.

107. The Poor Law Amendment Act (sec. 15) empowers the Commissioners to frame rules, orders, and regulations, for apprenticing the children of poor persons; and I propose to extend this provision to Ireland, by which it may be hoped that all the beneficial effects of the law may be secured, whilst the evils which certainly have resulted from it in England will in great measure be avoided.

VIII.—Pauper Idiots and Lunatics.

108. For individuals of this description, if not dangerous, the Union workhouses may be made available. Dangerous lunatics, and insane persons, must of course be sent to the county and district lunatic asylums, as at present, to be there subjected to such treatment as each particular case requires;[39] and it is important, I think,

that these institutions should be kept totally distinct from Poor Law Administration. The deprivation of reason is a misfortune so extreme, that special and extraordinary efforts on the part of the community seem to be called for, in behalf of the unhappy individuals subjected to such a visitation. The careful supervision of such unhappy persons is moreover necessary, as a measure of police, for the protection of the community. On all accounts, therefore, the lunatic asylums should, I think, remain under the control of the magistracy and local authorities, as at present.

109. With respect to pauper idiots and lunatics, not in a dangerous state, the case is different;—these, I think, might be advantageously provided for in the several workhouses, where a lunatic ward should be prepared for such of them as might be unfitted to mingle with the other paupers of their class. There can be no hopes of the recovery of a confirmed lunatic, and medical treatment would therefore be unnecessary. Idiots, laboring under a deficiency, rather than a deprivation of reason, are capable of being employed in a variety of ways, and appear in general to feel contentment in proportion as they are employed; presuming, of course, that the employment is suitable for them. In a workhouse, such employment might be provided, and they would probably partake as largely of comfort as their unhappy state is susceptible of. I propose, therefore, that the provision of the Poor Law Amendment Act, permissive of the retention in a workhouse of idiot and lunatic paupers, not dangerous, be extended to Ireland, and that their mode of treatment and employment be in all cases subject to the direction of the central authority.

IX.—Of Migration and Emigration.

110. This subject opens a wide field for inquiry and consideration. A country may be so circumstanced, as to require that a portion of its population should migrate from one part of it to another, either permanently or occasionally; and may still, on the whole, have no actual excess of population. A country may also, with reference to its means of employment, labour under an excess of population; or both these circumstances may exist at the same time; and this appears, in fact, to be the state of Ireland at present. The Irish population seems to be excessive, as compared with the means of employment which the country affords; and the effects of this excess would, I think, be much more felt were it not for the opening which England presents for migration. Still, however, notwithstanding this relief, Ireland now exhibits all the characteristics of a superabundant population; but to what extent can scarcely be determined, as a small excess will operate prejudicially upon the whole mass.

111. It is difficult, if not impossible, to effect any material improvement in the condition of a people, whilst they continue thus circumstanced; for, as long as the labourers exceed the number required, so long will their competition for employment tend to depress their condition, and to counteract any efforts that may be made to improve it. The only alternative, therefore, in such case, is either to increase the amount of employment, or to decrease the number of labourers depending upon

it. Now, to effect an artificial increase in the amount of employment, may, under certain circumstances, be practicable for a time, I believe only for a short time: but this would merely mitigate the symptoms: it would not destroy the seeds of the disease. To bring about, by forced and direct interposition, any material increase of permanent employment, is in every view difficult, and, under common circumstances, perhaps impossible; for mankind will, in the aggregate, spontaneously do that which their interest dictates. Something, however, may be done indirectly in this respect, in the way of legislation, by the removal of impediments and the establishing of increased facilities for the application of capital; and something also perhaps by the intervention of Government : but all such aids must of necessity be contracted in their application, as well as remote in their operations— it is from spontaneous or natural employment alone, that the labourers of a community can look for permanent occupation, and the means of support.

112. By natural employment, I mean all those objects on which capital is expended and labour applied by the voluntary action of individuals, uninfluenced by the application of any forced or artificial motives. The establishment of manufactures, the reclaiming of waste lands, the establishment of fisheries, the laying out grounds, and improving, planting, and ornamenting estates, the making roads, and opening communications, for the facility of intercourse and transit of commodities,—these are all natural sources of employment, tending to augment the capital of the community, and to increase permanently the demand for labour. So long as employment from these and other legitimate sources keeps pace with the increase of population, the labourers generally will be in a satisfactory position; but whenever the number of labourers exceeds the means of employment, (as is now the case in Ireland,) distress and disorder must ensue, more or less intense, according to the quantum of such excess, and the character of the people.

113. To aim directly at effecting an increase of employment in Ireland, however desirable such an increase may be, seems beyond the powers, if it is not foreign to the province, of a poor law, the immediate object of which is to provide for the relief of the destitute. Now destitution may be alike caused by an excess of labourers, and by a deficiency of employment, which are in truth convertible terms; and if an able-bodied labourer becomes destitute from want of employment, however arising, he must, if actually destitute, be relieved at the common charge, like any individual reduced to a state of destitution by age or infirmity. Relief to able-bodied labourers in such case may be afforded in one of these three modes:—

1st. In the workhouse of the Union in. which he is located.

2nd. Or he may be assisted to migrate to some other district, where employment is attainable.

3rd. Or lastly, he may be enabled to emigrate to some British colony, where he will find a field open for his exertions.

114. With respect to the first, the offer of the workhouse would be the test of destitution, and the only direct relief to be afforded. The second should, I think,

be expressly provided for in the Act; but, to guard against abuse, it ought to be a condition that the consent of the central authority should be necessary to all such migrations at the expense of the rates, and that they should be conducted in conformity to such regulations as the central authority might issue. It is important, however, that such migration should never be forced, but be permitted to arise naturally out of an excess in one quarter, and a demand in another. The law may properly give facilities for correcting such inequality, but ought, I think, do no more. The last mode of relief is emigration, which requires a more extended notice, involving, as it does, considerations of principle as well as matters of detail.

115. Emigration ought not, I think, under any circumstances, to be looked to as an ordinary resource. An excess of population is an evil,—to relieve that excess by emigration is so far a good; but it may be doubted whether the parent stock is not enfeebled by the remedy thus applied. In general, the most active and enterprising emigrate, leaving the more feeble and less robust and resolute at home. Thus a continual drain of its best elements lowers the tone and reduces the general vigour of the community, at the same time that it imparts an additional stimulus to the tendency towards an undue increase of population, which was the immediate cause of disease.

116. In saying this, I do not contend against the resort to emigration as a relief from an existing evil, but merely wish to point out the inexpediency of encouraging it as an approved practice in our social system. The necessity for its adoption should be regarded as an indication of disease, which it would be better to prevent than thus to relieve. The means of prevention will be found in the education and improved moral and prudential habits of the community. In proportion as these prevail, will its general character be elevated; and individuals will feel a wholesome dread of entailing upon themselves burthens, which will depress their position in the social scale. In Ireland, unhappily, these prudential considerations do not prevail at all, or prevail in a very imperfect degree; and the consequence is, that marriages are daily contracted with the most reckless improvidence. Boys and girls marry, literally without habitation or any means of support, trusting, as they say, to Providence, as others have done before them. It is quite lamentable to witness the effects of this ignorant recklessness, which, by occasioning an excessively rapid increase in their numbers, tends to depress the whole population and to extend the sphere of wretchedness and want.

117. Emigration not only may, but I believe must, be had recourse to, as a present means of relief, whenever the population becomes excessive in any district, and no opening for migration can be found. The actual excess of population will be indicated by the pressure of able-bodied labourers upon the workhouse. If any considerable number of these enter the workhouse, and remain there subject to its discipline, it may be taken as a proof of their actual inability to provide for themselves, and of the consequent excess of labourers beyond the means of employ. Under such circumstances, emigration must be looked to as the best, if not the

only present remedy; and express provision should, I think, be made in the Act, for defraying the expense which this would occasion, as well as for the regulations under which it should be carried into effect.

118. With reference to the expense, I propose that the charge of emigration should in every case be equally borne by the Government and the Union from which the emigrants proceed. This division of the charge appears to me to be equitable; for, although the Union only is immediately benefited, yet eventually the whole empire is relieved, excess in one portion of it tending to occasion an excess in the whole. The emigration should, I think, be limited to a British colony, where such arrangements might be made, through the intervention of the Colonial Office, as would serve to protect the emigrants on their first arrival, and also ensure their obtaining employment at the earliest period. This is important, alike for themselves and the community; at home they were a burthen,—in their new position they will increase the general productive powers of the empire, as well as enlarge the demand for British produce. In every case, however, the emigration should be conducted under the control of the central authority, and be subjected to such regulations as the Government may deem it right to establish.

119. I propose also, that, whenever it shall appear that any owners and occupiers of land, within a period of (say) three years antecedent to the passing of the Act, shall have actually incurred an expense in effecting the emigration of labourers and others, a moiety of the actual outlay so incurred may, at the discretion of the central authority, be repaid to such land-owners and occupiers—the charge to be borne jointly by the Government and the Union in which the property of such landowner may be included: provided, however, that the moiety of such outlay so to be repaid shall in no case exceed (say) 5*l*. for each of such emigrants. This provision will enable the central authority to deal equitably with respect to certain individuals, who have recently, at great personal charge, effected the emigration from their estates and neighbourhoods of a portion of the surplus population; and as the Unions when established, and the whole community, will be benefited by what has thus been done, it seems right that they should bear a moiety of the charge.

X.—Of Houses of Industry, Foundling Hospitals, Mendicity Establishments, and other Charitable Institutions.

120. There is now a kind of Poor Law established in Ireland, under which the "Houses of Industry" are managed, but it is altogether partial and ineffective; and the several statutes providing for these Houses of Industry, and the other institutions intended for the relief of the poor, should, I think, be repealed, and the property and management of all such establishments placed under the central authority. With respect to institutions strictly charitable, and supported by voluntary contribution or otherwise,—these would of course remain, as at present, the property of their respective supporters; but it would, I think, be extremely desirable to invest the central authority with such a power of revising their rules and superintending their practice, as would ensure their acting in unison with the provisions of the

Act,—or which would at least prevent their acting in contravention of the principles which it establishes for Poor Law administration in Ireland. The "Houses of Industry" would generally become available as Union workhouses, for which they are for the most part well adapted; and, where of insufficient size, they may readily be enlarged. The other charitable establishments, where they are the property of the public, or provided or supported by Government, or by local grants from the county-rates, should, I think, be appropriated in like manner, under direction of the central authority.

121. The foregoing appear to be the only points requiring especial attention, in framing a measure for establishing Poor Laws in Ireland, although there are several other matters of minor interest which must not be overlooked. I would propose that the "Poor Law Amendment Act" should be taken as a guide in drafting the intended Bill, and that the language, order, and general provisions of that Act should be adhered to, except where the contrary is herein indicated, or where a variation is obviously necessary. There will, I think, be much practical convenience in thus assimilating the two statutes, which provide for Poor Law administration in the two countries.

## CONCLUSION.

122. A measure framed on the principles, and comprising the details, which I have endeavoured to develop in this Report, is, I think, necessary for Ireland. Unless the great mass of the Irish people are protected from the effects of destitution, no great or lasting improvement in their social condition can be expected. The establishment of a Poor Law is, I conceive, the first step necessary towards this end; and, followed as it must be by other ameliorations, to the introduction of which it is a necessary preliminary, we may hope that it will ultimately prove the means of securing for Ireland the full amount of those benefits which ought to arise from her various local advantages, and the natural fertility of her soil.

123. The disposition, everywhere observable, to rely upon the support of Government in all contingencies, rather than upon their own individual exertions, affords a painful proof of the disordered and enfeebled condition to which the social and moral energies of the Irish people are reduced. To restore, or create, the feeling of self-confidence—to revive, or establish, the habit of reliance upon their own efforts, I do not know any measure more effectual than one that shall compel them to acts of local self-government. This will obviously be the effect of the introduction of the Union system; and it does not therefore appear unreasonable to expect, that the establishment of a Poor Law, as herein recommended, in addition to the advantages from its direct enactments, will be attended with collateral advantages of no trifling importance in the present state of Ireland.

124. Supposing the recommendations contained in this Report to be adopted by His Majesty's Government, and sanctioned by the Legislature, the following, I presume, would be the order in which the measure will be introduced in Ireland:—
After carefully inquiring into the circumstances of the several districts, the central

authority would proceed to establish Unions, according as localities were found to be prepared for the measure; which would thus not be applied to every district at once, but be brought into operation gradually and successively, advancing step by step, until the whole country was in Union. This was the mode of proceeding in England, and this course would, I presume, be pursued in Ireland. It may thus, probably, occupy two years, or even more, before every district is put into Union; and possibly another two years, before the workhouses are all completed and in operation: but this will not be lost time, as it will serve to prepare the people for the measure, and to instruct them as to its objects. It is essential, I think, to proceed thus cautiously—pressing forward, or pausing, according to circumstances: but it is important, however, that there should be no more delay than is actually necessary, in carrying out the measure: for, until the whole country is in Union, the Unions which are established will be to a certain extent ineffective, and subjected to unequal action: but for this, and the other irregularities which may be expected to occur at the outset, before the system becomes fully established, the general powers of the central authority will enable them to provide.

125. With respect to individual Unions, the proceeding, I presume, will be nearly as follows:—After a careful investigation, the central authority would issue the necessary order declaring the Union ; the Board of Guardians would be elected, and certain paid officers appointed; steps would then be taken for providing a competent workhouse, with the least possible delay. In these, and in all the earlier operations, an Assistant Commissioner would aid by his presence and advice. When the workhouse is so advanced as to admit of any part of it being used, indoor relief would be afforded according to the means of accommodation, beginning of course with the aged and infirm. As soon as the workhouse is completed, and the machinery effective, measures would be adopted, with the aid of the police, for the gradual suppression of mendicancy, by sending into the workhouse those who are dependent upon begging for support. This might be done more or less stringently, according to circumstances. By thus advancing tentatively, the Union authorities would be enabled to introduce the system, and to establish the workhouse test, without danger, and with little risk of failure in any case—always presuming the Assistant Commissioner to be watchful, and that a central authority, armed with sufficient powers, superintends and regulates the whole.

126. In this way, I think, the Union system, as now in operation in England, may be established in Ireland, successively advancing until the whole country is formed into Unions. The duty of conducting this operation must, I apprehend, be confided to some responsible body, such as I have above designated by the term "Central Authority;" and I have reserved for this part of the Report, such observations as have occurred to me on this subject, its importance seeming to require a separate and special consideration.

127. I believe the proposed measure may be carried into operation, either by means of a separate Commission in Ireland, or by the existing English Poor Law Commission: one of these modes, I presume, must be adopted; and, before deciding upon the alternative, it will be necessary to consider the advantages and

disadvantages of each. In doing this, it is important to bear in mind, that it is the English Poor Law system which is now proposed to be established; and that the knowledge and experience acquired in working that system, can be made available for Ireland, only by employing there individuals conversant with the English practice.

128. If a separate commission should be issued for Ireland, it would therefore be necessary that the individuals to be selected as Commissioners under it, should be acquainted with English Poor Law as now administered; and this, I apprehend, would exclude most of those Irishmen, who might otherwise he deemed qualified for the office, if it did not exclude Irishmen altogether. Such exclusion, however necessary, would probably have a somewhat ungracious appearance to the Irish people, and might excite angry comment. But, admitting that three Irishmen, conversant with English Poor Law administration, could be found for filling a separate Commission, there would be no guarantee that they would carry out the system in all its details. The law would be similar in both countries, it is true, but the practice might, and probably would, become widely different in each, as was the case in different parts of England under the old Poor Law administration. With two Commissions there might possibly be no unity of principle,—there would certainly be no unity of action,—and consequently no identity of result. Unless the existing English Poor Law Commission should be unequal to the additional duty of introducing the proposed law into Ireland, or unless it should appear that the Commissioners ought not to be intrusted with the performance of this duty, the above reasons would seem to be conclusive against a separate Commission.

129. Now, it must be admitted that the official duties of the English Poor Law Commissioners have been, and in fact still are, very heavy. As a member of the Commission, and one too not unaccustomed to work, I may be permitted to say, that the labour has been throughout unceasing and excessive, to an extent that nothing but the hope of accomplishing a great public good would have rendered bearable. The success of the measure, however, in lessening the pressure upon the rate-payers, and in its improvement of the habits and condition of the labouring classes,—coupled with the support which has been afforded by Government, and by nearly all the intelligent portions of the community, have given the Commissioners encouragement and confidence; and, when the process of forming Unions shall be completed, as it will be in all probability by Midsummer next, their labours will become lighter. Under these circumstances, there would seem to be no insuperable difficulty in the way of the present Poor Law Commissioners being made the instruments of establishing the new law in Ireland; and, whatever may be the amount of difficulty at first, it will lessen as the amount of English business decreases, and the organisation of the Irish machinery is perfected. If, then, no other grounds of objection exist, and if it shall be deemed desirable, I see no reason to doubt that the English Poor Law Commissioners are competent to the additional duty of introducing the proposed measure into Ireland.

130. In stating this opinion, I beg to be understood as in no way compromising my colleagues, whom I have not felt myself at liberty to consult in this matter, and who are in no respect answerable for anything contained in this Report. I may venture to add, however, that I do not anticipate any material difference of view on their parts; and your Lordship will probably deem it right to ascertain their sentiments before coming to a final decision upon this subject.

131. The reasons in favour of placing the Poor Law administration in the two countries under the same Commission appear to be weighty:—the equable action, if so combined—the total freedom from all local, partial, or party influences—the impossibility of jobbing—the certainty of the same application of the same law, and the consequent equality of England and Ireland in this respect—and lastly, the saving the expense of a new Commission,—which ought not perhaps to be altogether overlooked, although this last consideration should not have the slightest weight, as opposed to the establishment of a separate Commission for Ireland, if such was in any way necessary.

132. Assuming that the charge of introducing the new Poor Law into Ireland should be confided to the present Poor Law Commissioners, it will then be necessary to consider whether any, and what, modifications are required, for enabling them to fulfil the large additional duties thus cast upon them. Mr. Senior,[40] whose opinions are always entitled to especial attention, after expressly stating that whatever may be done in the way of a Poor Law for Ireland ought to be intrusted to the existing Commission, and not to a separate authority,—suggested the addition of one or two members to the English Board, which now consists of three.[41] In practice, however, I believe it does not always follow, that the efficiency of a Board is increased by an increase in the number of its members. Three men may act harmoniously and effectively together; but the addition of a fourth, by destroying the proportion, may injure the harmony, and lessen the efficiency of the Board. I do not say that this would necessarily be the case, but there is obviously some danger of it; and as, in my judgment, no necessity will exist for increasing the present number of Commissioners, the danger need not be incurred.

133. In the way of arrangement, however, although not by a direct addition to its numbers, I think the efficiency of the present Commission might be greatly increased. If the Commissioners were empowered to confer what may be called brevet rank upon such of their Assistant Commissioners as they might for a time find it necessary or convenient to associate with themselves, as acting members of the Board, it would afford the means of supplying every defect which could arise from want of number; and that, too, with men already tried and trained, and whose minds would be in unison with the governing principle of the measure, with the previous administration of which they would be familiar. In practice, this would be found a great advantage; and it would probably be some recommendation, that it would entail no permanent expense, as the Assistant Commissioners, when the emergency was over, would of course fall back into their former position. By the 12th section of the Poor Law Amendment Act, the Commissioners are enabled to

delegate the full powers of the Board to any Assistant Commissioner, excepting only as regards general rules, the making of which is reserved to the Board. I do not propose, in the above suggestion, to impart so extensive a power as this; but merely to enable the Commissioners to associate with themselves one or more of the Assistant Commissioners whenever they find it necessary.

134. Another arrangement for increasing the efficiency of the Commission would be to constitute the Secretary a member of the Board in virtue of his office, whenever there are not two Commissioners present. This would be attended with great practical convenience in working the Commission. The precedents for such an arrangement are, I believe, numerous in the commercial companies, if not in other departments of public business; and there are especial reasons for thus rendering the Secretary eligible to act as a member of the Board, under the present Poor Law Commission, arising out of the extremely varied character of the business, of which no other individual (not a Commissioner) can have so intimate a knowledge. In this respect the Secretary stands far before any Assistant Commissioner, whose knowledge is necessarily local and particular, rather than general and comprehensive: and I would accordingly propose, whenever one Commissioner only is present, that the Secretary, in virtue of his office, should be entitled to act as a member, for the purpose of constituting a Board.

135. With these arrangements, the provision of the Poor Law Amendment Act, requiring the presence of two Commissioners to constitute a Board, might be complied with, whilst one Board sat in Dublin and another in London, which might occasionally be necessary, especially at first. There will be no risk of two Boards, so constituted under one Commission, differing materially in views or in practice; but, to ensure a perfect unity of action throughout, it might be provided that every document of a general character should be approved by both. Thus a general order or regulation prepared in London, would be submitted to the Board in Dublin before being issued; and, if in Ireland, it would be submitted to the approval of the Commissioners sitting in London. If a difference of opinion should occur between the two Boards, the decision of that Board to which the reference is made should be final. Each Board should regularly report its proceedings to the other; but each should be empowered to affix the seal of the Commission, where necessary, in the ordinary and current business of the office, without waiting for the sanction of the other; but it should nevertheless be open to either to raise a question as to the proceedings in any instance. In case of any difference of opinion arising between the Commissioners constituting a Board, the point should be referred to the other Board (if two Boards were sitting), whose decision thereon should be final.

136. I lastly recommend, as another arrangement for increasing the efficiency of the Commission, that the Board should be authorised to empower one of its members to visit a district and to associate with himself the Assistant Commissioner in charge, or any other; and the two should then constitute a quorum, and be competent to exercise within the particular district the authority of the

Commission, excepting only as regards general orders. A provision of this kind might occasionally be useful in England; but in Ireland it would be still more so, as it may there probably be requisite to visit and inspect the district before declaring a Union, and also afterwards to witness and regulate its working.

137. The first and third of the above-suggested arrangements seem to come fully within the spirit, if not within the letter, of the Poor Law Amendment Act. The second stands upon its own merits: but it appears so desirable, with a view to the practical working of the Commission, that I strongly recommend its adoption. To prevent all doubt and misapprehension, I further recommend that the whole should be provided for in the Bill, and thus be made a substantial part of the system.

138. The staff of able and active officers now attached to the Commission would immediately become available for Ireland, although it would, I think, be necessary to make some addition to the number of Assistant Commissioners, and to the office establishment, which might be done with the approbation of the Treasury, as at present. The Secretary, Assistant Commissioners, Assistant Secretaries, Clerks, and all other persons now in the service of the Commission, or who may hereafter be so, should be authorised and required to serve either in Ireland or in England, according to the directions of the Commissioners. These enactments would, I think, provide for the enlarged working of the Commission, and at the same time ensure its unity of action.

I have the honour to be,
My Lord,
Your Lordship's obedient and faithful Servant,
GEO. NICHOLLS.

ESTIMATED EXPENSE OF THE PROPOSED SYSTEM. (Memorandum.)
An estimate of the annual charge of such a system of relief for the destitute poor in Ireland, as is recommended in the preceding Report, may be desired. The following will probably be found to be a pretty near approximation; but there are no data on which such an estimate can be framed with any pretension to minute accuracy.

The population of Ireland being about eight millions, I assume that workhouse accommodation may occasionally be required for one per cent., or 80,000 persons;*[42] this accommodation to be provided in, say 100 workhouses, each capable of holding 800 inmates.

The cost of maintenance per diem, in the several mendicity institutions which I visited in Ireland, varied from 1½d. to 2½d. per head. Taking credit for good economical management, I assume that the average cost of maintaining the pauper inmates of the workhouses will be 1s. per week for each person. I assume also, that the average weekly cost of the establishment, including salaries, clothing, bedding, wear and tear, furniture, fuel, and other incidental expenses, will be about half that amount, or 6d. per head, making together a charge of 1s. 6d. per head weekly.

From these assumptions, the following results may be deduced:—

If the hundred workhouses, each capable of holding 800 Paupers, should be fully occupied throughout the year, the total charge of maintenance, salaries, clothing, wear and tear, &c, would be, per annum £312,000

If the workhouses were, on an average, to be occupied by only three-fourths of the full number throughout the year, the establishment and other charges continuing the same, the total charge would be, per annum £260,000

If the workhouses were to be only one-half filled, on an average of the whole year, the charge would then be, per annum £208,000

Our experience of workhouse administration in England would warrant the adoption of the last of the above assumptions for Ireland; but it may be safer to take the second, which will probably be found to approximate pretty nearly to the truth.

G.N.

## Notes

1 Thomas Robert Malthus (1766–1834) was an English political economist who taught at the East India Company's college in Haileybury, Hertfordshire, from 1805 until his death. One of his pupils was Charles Trevelyan. His influential 'An Essay on the Principle of Population' was published in 1798, in which he argued that unless checked, population growth would outgrow food production.

2 T.R. Malthus, *An Essay on the Principle of Population as it affects the future improvement of society, with remarks on the speculations of Mr. Godwin, M. Condorcet and other writers* (London: J. Johnson, 1798), Chapter V, pp. 39–45.

3 An Act for the Amendment and Better Administration of the Laws relating to the Poor in England and Wales (4 & 5 Will. 4 c. 76).

4 The other members were, Charles Vignoles, Richard More O'Ferrall, James Carlile, Fenton Hort, John Corrie, James Naper, and William Battie-Wrightson.

5 'Royal Commission for inquiring into the Condition of the Poorer Classes in Ireland: third report' (BPP), 43, 1836, xxx.

6 Ibid.

7 George Nicholls (1781–1865).

8 George Nicholls, *Eight letters on the Management of our Poor, and the general administration of the Poor Laws: In which is shewn the System that has been adopted, and the saving in the poor rates, which has recently been affected in the two Parishes of Southwell and Bingham, in the County of Nottingham, respectfully offered to the consideration of Magistrates, and earnestly recommended to the attention of all Parish Officers* (Newark: S. and J. Ridge, 1822).

9 An Act for the Amendment and better administration of the Laws relating to the Poor in England and Wales (4 & 5 Will. 4 c. 76).

10 *Bentley's Miscellany* was an English literary magazine, which commenced publication in 1836. Dickens was the first editor but argued with the owner, Richard Bentley, and left in 1839.

11  An example of the opposition was made by a landowner in Bushmills, Co. Antrim - Francis Workman Macnaghten, *Poor Laws - Ireland: Observations Upon the Report Of George Nicholls* (London: Longman and Co., 1838).
12  Isaac Butt, *The poor-law bill for Ireland examined its provisions and the report of Mr. Nicholls contrasted 1837* (Dublin: W. Curry, 1837).
13  Christine Kinealy, *This Great Calamity. The Irish Famine 1845 to 1852* (Dublin: Gill and Macmillan, 2006), chapter one.
14  George Nicholls, *A History of the Irish Poor Law: In Connexion with the Condition of the People* (London: John Murray, 1856), p. 357.
15  In 1818, a Mr Lowe of Bingham, appalled by what he perceived to be 'the demoralized state of the poor', instituted a reform of poor relief whereby outdoor relief was stopped and only workhouse relief was offered. The success of these measures paved the way for the reforms associated with the new English Poor Law of 1834.
16  Similar to the English Poor Laws, the Scottish Poor Laws dated back to the sixteenth century. In 1595, a Scottish poor rate was introduced, know colloquially as the 'buttock mail'. Money for poor relief could be raised in other ways, including from voluntary subscriptions.
17  The Dublin Mendicity Institute, which was established in 1818, provided the poor with food, clothing and lodging. Its original aim was to stop public begging, which had increased during the depression that followed the ending of the Napoleonic War. The Institute was funded by donations, which were requested in house-to-house collections made in Dublin. Collection boxes were also located in shops and business premises.
18  The first House of Industry in Ireland was established in Dublin in 1703, by an act of parliament. It was located in James Street, on the south side of the city. Initially, it was financed by taxes on sedan chairs, hackney coaches and households, but in 1772 the Irish House of Commons passed legislation providing for similar Houses to be established in every county. Following this, a second House was established on the north side of Dublin, and Houses were founded elsewhere. This legislation marked an important step in accepting public responsibility for the poor in Ireland.
19  The 1782 Poor Law Amendment Act in England, also known as Gilbert's Act, after its sponsor, Thomas Gilbert. It provided for parishes to group together and establish a joint workhouse. The able-bodied poor were not allowed to enter these workhouses.
20  Con-acre, or conacre, was a widespread system of letting land in strips in Ireland. It was usually only let from season to season, and usually for eleven months only. Farmers and Landowners used conacre as a way of employing a labour force, in lieu of paying wages.
21  The Vagrancy Act of 1824 (5 Geo. 4. c. 83), which applied to England and Wales, made it illegal to sleep rough or to beg. Punishment was up to one month's hard labour.
22  In Poor Law terms, this was referred to as the principle of 'less eligibility'.
23  County cess had been introduced in Ireland in 1634. It was a tax (cess) levied for the upkeep of local roads, bridges, and other public utilities.
24  A Lady Day, in both Ireland and Britain, was one of the four quarter days on which rents were paid. Traditionally, they coincided with the solstices and equinoxes, but were co-opted by the Christian Church to fall on four religious festivals. Lady Day fell on 25 March, which was the Feast of the Annunciation.
25  The office of resident magistrates was created in 1822. They were appointed by the Lord Lieutenant and paid a salary, but they were required to reside in the district.
26  Michaelmas was one of the quarter days. It fell on the 29 September, or the Feast of St Michael. In Ireland, it traditionally marked the end of the harvest. Rents were paid on this day, cattle were slaughtered, and hiring fairs for the winter were held.
27  Justices of the Peace, or Commissioners of the Peace, first appeared in Ireland in the fifteenth century. They enforced the law and could convene courts for civil and criminal cases. By the early nineteenth century, approximately ten per cent were Church of

Ireland clergymen (Catholics could not hold this position), while the rest were resident gentry.
28  Unions were the main administrative unit of the Poor Law. Each Union had its own workhouse.
29  The head of an administrative unit or borough
30  The Poor Relief Act of 1601 (43 Eliz. 1 c 2) was passed towards the end of the reign of Elizabeth I. It was the basis of poor relief in England and Wales, until the passing of the 'new' Poor Law in 1834, hence it being referred to as the 'old' Poor Law.
31  In fact, there were two acts of parliament, passed in 1818 and 1819, which regulated the giving of poor relief in England and Wales. The 1831 Vestry Act provided for ratepayers in urban areas to elect vestrymen.
32  Author's note. * *See sec. 50, Part the Second.*
33  Parochial Assessments Act, 1836, 6 & 7 Will. IV c.96. provided for a new, uniform method of rating for the relief of the poor, based on the net annual value of the property rated.
34  George Poulett Scrope (1797–1876) was an English geologist, political scientist and politician. He had a particular interest in poverty and the Poor Law, believing that Ireland would benefit from a national Poor Law. His ideas were explained in *Poor Law for Ireland* (1831). Scrope was critical of the policies of the British government during the Famine, accusing them of treating the Irish poor as 'human encumbrances'.
35  Author's note. * *In Scotland the rate is divided equally between the owner and occupier.*
36  The Municipal Corporations Act 1835 (5 & 6 Wm. IV. c.76) applied to England and Wales and provided for the reform of local government. A similar act was passed in Ireland in 1840.
37  The Poor Law in Denmark had its origins in the 17th century. From the outset, the poor had a right to relief—a right that was implicit, but not codified, in the English Poor Law.
38  From the 16th century, English Poor Law legislation made a distinction between the 'deserving poor' and the 'undeserving poor'—able-bodied beggars fell into the latter category. As a deterrent, 'sturdy beggars' could be whipped.
39  The first institution for the mentally ill had been opened in the 18th century, that is, St Patrick's Hospital in Dublin, which was opened in 1757. A few others followed but, following the passage of the Lunacy (Ireland) Act of 1821, the Criminal Lunatics (Ireland) Act (1838) and the Private Lunatic Asylums (Amendment) Act 1842, more 'asylums' were built. Collectively, they provided for a national network of institutions, and dictated the way in which mental illness was perceived and treated in the country.
40  Nassau William Senior (1790–1864) was an English lawyer and political economist who was a member of the Poor Law Inquiry Commission of 1832.
41  The Poor Law Commission appointed as a result of the 1834 legislation consisted of Thomas Frankland Lewis (1834–39), John George Shaw Lefevre (1834–1841) and George Nicholls (1834–47). Edwin Chadwick, who had hoped to be a Commissioner, was appointed Secretary. Internal divisions and public scandals led to the Commission being abolished in 1847, at which point, Ireland was provided with a separate Commission.
42  Author's note.* *In Kent, Sussex, Oxford, and Berks, the amount of in-door pauperism, as returned on the 29th of September last, was just one per cent, of the population. These four counties were among the most highly pauperised, have been longest under the operation of the new law, and are provided with the most effective work house accommodation.*

# 2

# LYDIA JANE FISHER, *LETTERS FROM THE KINGDOM OF KERRY IN THE YEAR 1845*. LETTER VIII (1847)

Lydia Jane Leadbeater Fisher was part of a small number of privileged women who traversed Ireland in the mid-nineteenth century and left a written account.[1] The elite group included Maria Edgeworth in the 1830s,[2] Asenath Nicholson in 1844 and again from 1847 to 1849,[3] Harriet Martineau in 1852,[4] and Queen Victoria in 1849, 1853, 1861 and in 1900, shortly before her death.[5] Although they were writing from different perspectives and motives, a common question was 'how could a nation so environmentally blessed be so disadvantaged socially and economically?'[6] Fisher toured County Kerry in 1845, on the cusp of the onset of the Great Famine. Unlike many other women commentators, she was Irish, and then living in Limerick.[7]

Lydia Leadbeater had been born in the Quaker village of Ballitore in County Kildare in 1800. She was the youngest daughter of Mary Leadbeater (1758–1826), a noted author, poet and diarist whose publications included *Cottage Biography, being a Collection of Lives of the Irish Peasantry* (1822) and *The Annals of Ballitore from 1768 to 1824*.[8] The two volume *Annals* were not published until 1862, and it is generally assumed that Lydia was the editor.[9] In February 1823, Lydia had married James Joseph Fisher, a well-known Quaker from Limerick.[10] James was a merchant and co-owner of 'Fisher & Quinlivan,' one of the largest corn mills in the city.[11] The mill burned down in 1850 and the family moved to Dublin where James became the Secretary of the Patriotic Insurance Company.[12]

Lydia is remembered for being a close friend of the writer and poet, Gerald Griffin, they first meeting in 1829.[13] Griffin referred to Lydia in verse, his unrequited love for her barely disguised:

> Remember me, Lydia, when I am departed.
> Live over these moments when they, too, are gone;
> Be still to your minstrel the soft and kind-hearted.
> And droop o'er the marble where he lies alone.[14]

Lydia herself wrote poetry, although it was not published.[15]

Lydia, as part of a larger party, toured around County Kerry in the summer of 1845. Although her account is largely concerned with the picturesque, amidst the beauty she also noted the dirt and poverty. Additionally, she was not sympathetic to Catholics, referring to them in this context as 'primitive people'.[16] Her love of Ireland, however, is evident throughout, explaining its poverty through the prism of colonization. The tour took place over July, August and early September 1845. It is unlikely that Fisher or her companions were aware that a new form of potato disease was appearing in the Dublin area.

*Letters from Kerry* comprises of twelve letters that were written by Lydia to her sister. They were initially published anonymously by a fellow Quaker, Richard Webb, in Dublin.[17] Webb had been educated at the Ballitore school by Lydia's father. The Preface, which is copied below, was written in 1847 to accompany the publication. By this stage, the Famine was devastating the places that Lydia had visited.

Lydia Fisher died in 1884 in Stradbally, Queen's County.[18]

## LYDIA JANE FISHER, *LETTERS FROM THE KINGDOM OF KERRY IN THE YEAR 1845* (DUBLIN: WEBB AND CHAPMAN, 1847)

### Preface [1847]

The reader must not expect to find, in the following pages, and reference to the present distressed state of those parts of Ireland which they attempt to describe. When I concluded these letters, it was far from entering my mind that such aggravation of their poverty and misery impended over the primitive people I had so recently visited. When we turned from their mountain land, their wants were many and their privations great; we deemed them sunk in the lowest depth of poverty. Alas! Lower deeps still were to be fathomed by them. The potato-crop was blighted; their staff of life was destroyed, and we now behold the awful result. My heart sinks within me as I picture their present situation, encompassed by their desolate mountains, buried in their barren wilds. What have they now to barter? What can they offer for their bare means of subsistence? and even if they were able to purchase, where can they procure the food? Famine, Disease, and Death stalk through the country, and how can the means of life be carried in sufficient quantities into those rugged and dreary wastes? Meanwhile, thousands upon thousands are being swept off the face of the earth. May God in his infinite mercy relieve the sorrows of my stricken country!

### Letter VIII [1845]               Dingle

My Dear S ----

William took me a most charming walk yesterday, along the cliffs over the harbour, to a high point which affords from its summit a view of the whole of the Dingle Bay on the one side, with Valentia and Skelligs in the distance, shadowy in the evening mists and tinted by the declining sun; on the other, Mount Eagle and his brother mountains rising in the empurpled gloom against the western sky, while Dingle, nestling in her hills, lay at the head of the harbor, her pretty church-tower just peeping above the trees, with which imagination might play whatever tricks she pleased, giving it 'a local habitation and a name' of her own. It was a glowing evening, such as we have found very rare in this land of clouds, and the whole panorama of mountain and sea looked after their very best fashion; several fishing boats, gliding out to their nightly toil, added a living interest to the scene. As we did not know the name of this point, we called it 'Merlin Cliff', and the lovely little cove near, with its fairy well, and group of children dancing on its firm bright strand, we named 'Elfin Cove'. How vexed I was for my companion throwing pence amongst them,[19] thereby awakening sordid passions, and disturbing the harmony of their innocent amusement! On our return, we found we had been close to a place renowned for the traces of hoar antiquity, and in our ignorance had passed it by. In 'Nancy Browne's Parlour' are rocks upon which are engraven sacred words in the Ogham character.[20] The next day, the two gentlemen set out in quest of the fair lady's sitting room and of its mystical lore; they could make nothing definite out of some tracing on the rocks, save that it did not resemble the Ogham writing.[21] Perhaps the writer was no accomplished scribe, but a poor priest, old and ill-taught, who carved with feeble fingers some holy words in this lone and mighty temple.

I suppose I possess a large organ of inhabitiveness, for I regret leaving Dingle notwithstanding its drawbacks, and would willingly prolong our fortnight into a month, if we had a private lodge and sea-bathing; but to be thus in deep water, vainly trying to cast anchor is tiresome. We saw a bill up in one window, and applied—the house was engaged; we went to another—the same reply; at another which particularly caught our fancy, for it was ornamated with enormous hydrangea in profuse blossom, the answer was 'Yes, it would be set, if the master did not marry', but it was suspected he would be wedded in a few days. Of course, we could not interfere with matrimonial arrangements, lest the bride, even in her bridal days, should become a 'Mrs. Caudle'—and with some reason.[22] Our party are so tired of Dingle, that we must leave—indeed it is no marvel that they should be, for our parlour is small, and our attendants and attendance is not very cleanly; but the beds are comfortable. Upstairs, there is a drawing room and chambers on the same floor; at present they are occupied by English folk; when they leave, if we survive them here, we are to get possession. The lady above is a botanist and I wanted William to introduce himself as a brother of the craft, but in vain.[23] We are truly like the dove seeking rest for her weary wing, or like the Israelites in search of the land of promise.

My only comfort is, I have seen so much of our native island that is new and intensely interesting, that it is a positive gain to my patriotic feelings.

As this will be one of our last days in Dingle, I must wind up with a final account of it. On one side of the principle street is a large stone, 'the holy stone of Dingle'.[24] Tradition says that St Patrick placed it there to contain holy water, until the adjacent church, which was being built, should be completed. The chapel is entirely gone—no trace of it left except one part of the wall, while the sacred stone still remains, and still there is the hollow for the blessed water, not only filled from the fountains of the sky.

By dint of the most persevering and impertinent enquiries, I have become in some ways intimate with the peculiar habits of this primitive people, and remark with sadness the very slight value they place on any of their possessions—least of all upon their time. For example, it is usual for the tenants to do the season work on the farms of their landlords, when there is a hurry to put it out of hand; such as the planting and digging of potatoes, reaping, hay-making, drawing home the turf etc. This is all done without payment, or the expectation of payment; and the labour is not even allowed in the rent. Their pay, when they are paid, is from sixpence to eightpence per day. While the men are thus employed for 'the master,' the women do their own farming work, and save the turf. No wonder that they become prematurely old; they lead a dreary life of hard work and privations, yet cheered by the blessed consciousness of fulfilling their duty. The ground is rented in a manner, I believe, peculiar to this part of Ireland, not by the acre, but by 'the hundred,' as it is called, for potato ground. The hundred is one hundred spade-lengths long by eighty or sixty wide, and this is set for ten or twelve shillings, the tenant to provide manure; the bargain lasts only for the crop, like our con-acre.[25] Other land is set for a continuance, at so much for the grass of one or two cows, or as many as are agreed for, the tenant being free to cultivate it as he likes. If a lease be required, he pays a higher rent; so that the power of improvement is taxed on the industrious, and he has to pay a penalty for the desire of making a home for himself and family; it seems to be a hard state of things for the poor peasant. All their stock for market use is held in unreasonable contempt as to value. A donkey's whole load of turf, in paniers, which they make with great hardship, and perhaps bring a distance of ten or twelve miles, will sell for fourpence or sixpence at the utmost. Geese are bought for sixpence each, turkeys for ninepence, and a pair of ducks for sixpence. Chickens, provided they are cocks, for one penny each, and sometimes three for twopence. Hens' eggs are their most valuable commodity, as the hucksters and pedlars buy them for the Cork exportation; therefore, they rear the hen chickens, while, if far from a market, they wring the head off the cocks, and throw them on the dung heap, as being not worth rearing! Beef is but twopence or twopence halfpenny per pound; mutton is higher, threepence or threepence halfpenny, and is of better quality. Milk and butter are not so cheap in proportion, on account of the Cork butter-buyers.[26] They live very independent of money; they make their own frieze, flannel, linen and stuff, and dye them bright colours with native dyes extracted from the roots and leaves of plants and grasses. Sheep being here in abundance, wool is cheap, and they grow their own flax very successfully; while peeled rushes dipped in grease afford them light. Their great luxury, which is esteemed beyond any other, is tobacco. A bit of prime tobacco will purchase more gratitude than thrice the worth of it in money. As for good will, good nature, and ready obligingness, they are the growth of the soil, and abound everywhere. The men appear to be idle, or else in this season they have little to do; we have met them strolling into market, two attending one donkey, with sixpenny worth of turf—the whole day's work of two men and the use of the beast forfeited for the sake of sixpence and a gossip in town! A man will walk ten miles into town for one pennyworth of tobacco, or two pennyworth of fish, and deem his day well spent. It is indeed a sorrowful state of things when time is so little prized; yet they are well and comfortably clothed from head to heel, and are strong, active, open-countenanced, and able-bodied race. As it is uncertain when the labour of the men will be required for the master's behoof, their wives must see that the provision for their own families is secured; therefore, winter and summer, the whole year round they have to work hard both within and without doors; so that a daughter is as valuable as a son to a poor man's hearth in Kerry. Yet hard as are their privations and labour, they make out time to yield observance to the claims of friendship. We met more than twenty blooming lasses one evening, on the road leading out of town, with saddened countenances under their hooded cloaks, some embracing, others walking with clasped hands; they frankly replied to our questioning, that eight of them were going to America, and the remainder were escorting them part of the way. They were dressed in their holiday garments, and looked very interesting, although their agitated countenances did not suit with their upright figures and free mountain tread.

I should have told you that the peasantry do not live each family on their own spot of ground, as with us, even if the ground be held by lease; but congregate in those hamlets of which I have before spoken, which are always built in a sheltered situation. On the whole, as far as my observations extend, they appear to be a peculiar people hereabouts. I am told their learning is great both in the Irish and in the dead languages, so, as the old adage says that 'learning is better than houses and land,' perhaps they are possessed of more true wealth than we imagine.

Amongst the curiosities of nature, I omitted to introduce to your notice a poor idiot, who is named 'Denis of Dingle'. He is possessed of extraordinary strength of body, and is frequently employed to put out loads of manure on potato ground. He will carry as much as a horse, and with as much apparent ease. It is told, that a gentleman who had urgent business in Tralee, and was disappointed of both horse and car, accepted Denis's offer to carry him thither for two pence—a distance of fifteen miles! The gentleman mounted and away went Denis up hill and down vale—all alike to Denis. Frequently his rider wished to dismount and relieve him; this Denis never would permit, but held his hands with his mouth, biting them if he attempted to struggle. At length, on coming near the town, the gentleman begged, and prayed, and offered him a guinea,[27] if he would allow him to dismount, and walk into Tralee; but Denis was inexorable, held him fast, and severely bit his hands to intimate his determination of fulfilling his part of the agreement; and at length he bore him, will-he, nill-he,[28] into the town, up to his hotel in triumph, where he set him down, and claimed his twopence; more he did not want, and more he did not take.

This time twelvemonths we were in England, reveling in the soft and verdant wealth of her landscapes, and the rich glory of her waving wood—her fields divided by hedge rows, and her plains stretching away to the horizon—a sea of verdure—all speaking of peace, industry and security! Alas, judge if the contrast between those well-remembered scenes and the terrible and sorrowful poverty of these wastes and wilds does not strike me with a saddening force, akin to envy. How much more melancholy is the difference between the domestic habits and comforts of the two nations! Here, toil, dirt, and hopeless poverty! There, fair remunerative wages allow the peasantry to surround themselves with decent comforts, which a sense of security permits them to fully enjoy. Enter an English labourer's cottage—the small grate with a bright little fire, upon which is the kettle for tea, first strikes your eye; then it wanders on from one comfort to another—luxuries in Ireland—absolute necessaries in England; the polished earthenware, the shining tin, the burnished copper, the bed-warmer, the ancient family clock, and the floor sanded in fanciful patterns—all so delicately clean; and above all, the neat dress of the grave matron, as she welcomes you in with a grave air of self-respect, which is of more value than all the rest. Nothing charmed me more than the quiet dignity of the English peasant matron.

I will not picture the frightful contrast. I will only insist that it is not the fault of my country that she is so different—so sorrowfully different—so inferior! What has she been but a conquered nation for ages!—plundered by invaders—a perpetual battlefield from the time of the Danes to her complete subjugation under the English yoke, and even still torn asunder by factions and dissensions!

England may be envied for her wealth, her order, her industry, her peace, and her security—yet, dear, dirty Ireland! we must ever feel for you, pity you, and love you; and dearly do I love you, my beautiful country!

## Notes

1. The publication sometimes appears as being authored by Mary Jane Leadbeater Fisher. See, for example: http://www.pnsbook.com/author/Mary-Jane-Leadbeater-Fisher, accessed 14 December 2016.
2. Maria Edgeworth (1768–1849) had been born in England but moved to the family estate, Edgeworthstown in Co. Longford, as a young child. She was a successful author of many novels and of children's literature. In her writings, she resisted stereotyping the Irish, presenting them as different, but equal, to the English. Her *Tour in Connemara and The Martins of Ballinahinch* (London: Constable, 1950), covered the period from 1834 to 1847 but was not published until 1950, by Harold Edgeworth Butler, Maria's great-nephew.
3. Asenath Nicholson (1792–1855) was an American Protestant who first visited Ireland in 1844 to learn more about the poor and to distribute Bibles. She returned during the Famine to provide relief. She was an acute, and at times, acerbic, commentator. See, Maureen O. Murphy, *Compassionate Stranger: Asenath Nicholson and the Great Irish Famine* (Syracuse University Press, 2015).
4. Harriet Martineau (1802–1876) was a feminist, abolitionist and early sociologist. Her publication was *Letters from Ireland* (London: John Chapman, 1852). Her interest continued, and she wrote approximately 50 newspaper articles on Ireland following this

visit. In her writings, she argued that Ireland's problems were social and not political, and that Ireland would benefit by remaining within the Union.
5 Queen Victoria (1819–1901) ascended to the throne in 1837. During her long reign, she only visited Ireland four times, the first visit taking place during the Famine, when she travelled along the east coast in what was a carefully choreographed stay. See, Christine Kinealy, 'Queen Victoria and the Great Famine' in *Atlas of the Great Hunger*, pp. 96–98.
6 Joel Scherer, 'Troubling Journey: Elite Women Travellers of Ireland and the Irish Question', *Madison Historical Review*, vol.11, article 5 (2014, 1–17), 1–17, p. 2.
7 In some ways, Fisher's account and letter format bears resemblance with fellow Irish woman, Edgeworth's, *Tour in Connemara and The Martins of Ballinahinch*.
8 Rev. Matthew Russell, *The Irish Monthly: A Magazine of General Literature*, vol. 15 (Dublin: M. H. Gill and Son, 1887), p. 250.
9 Christopher Moriarty, 'Mary Leadbeater and the Annals of Ballitore', *The Friendly Word*, November-December 2009.
10 Selected Records Transcribed from the Society of Friends (Quakers) Monthly Meeting Minutes: http://www.igp-web.com/IGPArchives/ire/carlow/churches/quaker-mar-12.txt (accessed 17 November 2016).
11 'Flour milling and the Corn Trade', *Limerick Leader*, 24 January 1920.
12 *Thom's Directory of Ireland for 1851* (Dublin: Alexander Thom, 1852), p. 1.
13 John Cronin, *Gerald Griffin (1803–1840): A Critical Biography* (Cambridge University Press, 1978), p. 108.
14 Ibid.
15 David James O'Donoghue, *The Poets of Ireland: A Biographical Dictionary, with Bibliographical Details* (London: the author, 1892–93), p. 73.
16 Scherer, *Troubling Journey*, 1–17.
17 Richard Davis Webb (1805–1872) was a publisher and abolitionist, who was one of the founders of the Hibernian Antislavery Association in 1837. Webb published Frederick Douglass's *Narrative* in 1845 and again in 1846. He was an important figure in the transatlantic Abolition movement.
18 O'Donoghue, *Poets of Ireland*, p. 73.
19 Pennies (pence) were British currency. There were 240 pennies in a pound.
20 The Parlour, a ledge of rock, was near to the Dingle lighthouse. It is close to a circle of Ogham stones at Ballintaggart. The origin of the marks on the Parlour remain disputed.
21 Ogham is an early Irish alphabet comprised of various strokes and lines. It was primarily used between the 3rd and 6th centuries, when it was gradually replaced with the Roman alphabet. Ogham was inscribed on stone monuments throughout Ireland, but was most prevalent in counties Cork, Kerry and Waterford. Ogham was also used in parts of Wales, Scotland, England and the Isle of Man.
22 *Mrs. Caudle's Curtain Lectures* were written by Douglas William Jerrold (1803–1857), an English dramatist. The 37 comic lectures first appeared in *Punch* in 1845, but later were published in book form. Mrs. Caudle was a nagging wife who usually complained to her long-suffering husband when they were in bed, and he was attempting to sleep.
23 This was possibly Anna Atkins (1799–1871), an English botanist who published on algae and seaweed in the British Isles. She pioneered the use of early photography to illustrate her publications.
24 The origins of the Holy Stone in Dingle are uncertain but it probably relates to an early medieval monastic site. Unusually, it contains a number of depressions, suggesting that it might have been a font for holy water. An alternative interpretation is that the stone predates the Christian era and is a type of standing stone, and the indents were used for a ceremonial pagan ritual. Another, non-religious, theory is that the large stone is a glacial erratic that was deposited by retreating glaciers.

25 The renting of land, usually for the growth of a single crop, the potato.
26 From the eighteenth century, Cork city was a major exporter of butter, initially to North America and the Caribbean, but after 1769, exports to Britain were permitted (they had been excluded from this market during the previous 80 years). Most of this produce was brought by horse and cart, in firkins, to Cork, with the main route from east Kerry to the Cork Butter Exchange being referred to as 'the Butter Road'. Cork's monopoly of the British markets lasted until the 1870s, when it was challenged by new techniques being used in Europe, particularly Denmark.
27 A guinea was worth 21 shillings (a pound comprised of 20 shillings). The name derives from the fact that the coin contained gold that came from Guinea.
28 Now more usually contracted into willy-nilly, meaning unwillingly.

# 3

# REPORTS OF MESSRS. KANE, LINDLEY AND PLAYFAIR, COMMISSIONERS, *ON THE POTATOE [SIC][1] DISEASE* (1845)

The alarm felt at the news of the potato disease that was sweeping Europe in mid-1845, finally appearing in Ireland in early September, was summed up by an editorial, written by Dr Lyon Playfair,[2] in the well-respected *Gardeners' Chronicle*:[3]

> We stop the Press with very great regret to announce that the potato Murrain has unequivocally declared itself in Ireland. The crops about Dublin are suddenly perishing . . . where will Ireland be in the event of a universal Potato rot?[4]

The answer was more dreadful and lethal than anybody could have imagined. Prime Minister Sir Robert Peel responded to the unfolding crisis with a series of measures, many of which had been used before.[5] One of his innovative measures was to introduce a Scientific Commission to investigate the cause of the blight and, if possible, find an antidote to it. He also requested that the Commissioners should suggest ways in which the diseased potatoes could be used. In addition, the Commissioners were to ascertain the true extent of the loss, on the grounds that, 'there is such a tendency to exaggeration and inaccuracy in Irish reports that delay in acting upon them is always desirable'.[6] The Commission initially consisted of two men, Dr Lyon Playfair, a Scottish chemist, and Dr John Lindley, an English botanist.[7] The third Commissioner was an Irishman, Sir Robert Kane.[8] Lindley, a friend of Peel, had recommended the other two men. Furthermore, he had promised that, in addition to the official reports, he would write privately to Peel daily.[9] The appointment of the Commissioners did not impress everybody in Ireland. The nationalist newspaper, the *Nation*, for example, was skeptical about the work of the 'triumvirate':

> The awful calamity with which it has pleased Providence to afflict the poor in the disease, scarcity, and enhanced price of their staple food, has afforded the Government an opportunity, as usual, of "seeing about it." First — They commissioned two Englishmen, Mr. John Lindley, and Mr. Lyon Playfair, with whom was associated one Irishman, Dr. Kane. These

learned triumvirs spawned some scientific balderdash, which few read, and fewer understood; it is enough that the reports of these gentlemen, very long, very learned, and very dull, answer fully the apparent intentions with which Government Commissioners set about their business, that of consuming precious time, and leaving matters exactly where they found them . . . the two learned Cockneys retired in triumph to their own country, their heads full of potatoes, and their travelling expenses in their pockets.[10]

The *Tuam Herald* was similarly dismissive. They suggested that the body should be renamed 'The Commission for the Destruction of Potatoes' pointing out that, 'in every instance where the direction of the Commissioners was followed, the potatoes were utterly destroyed'.[11] For Daniel O'Connell, leader of the Repeal Association, a key concern was that the Commissioners had underestimated the extent of potato crop lost, they calculating it to be in the region of 50 per cent. He articulated his concerns in a debate in the House of Commons, speaking with:

. . . great caution and diffidence on a question upon which so much learning and science had been employed, and which involved not only the comforts, but, literally speaking, the vital interests of a large portion of the community. He had every respect for the high character and attainments of Dr. Playfair and Mr. Lindley; but he must remark, that when in November they reported that at a low estimate one-half of the potato crop was destroyed, there was no practical man in Ireland who did not believe that they had been imposed upon.[12]

Despite the mistakes and miscalculations, the reports of the Commissioners did influence relief policies. In one respect, their lack of knowledge proved beneficial to the Irish poor, as they failed to build into their calculations on potato losses that the 1845 crop had been a bumper one—possibly six to ten per cent larger than usual.

Inevitably perhaps, the potato as a subsistence diet was disparaged within the Commissioners' reports. In the second report, they refer to it as 'one of the most inferior articles of food.' In his *Memoirs*, furthermore, Lindley claimed that 'the famine was not an unmixed evil to Ireland', on the grounds that it 'destroyed' dependence on the potato and 'compelled the Irish to live on more nutritious types of diet'.[13] The much-praised *Atlas of the Great Irish Famine*, published in 2012, reaffirmed this view, stating, 'The hegemony of the potato was broken by the Great Famine'.[14]

The reports were all addressed to Lord Heytesbury. Four were made public, they dating from 29 October to 7 November 1845. After that, the Commissioners corresponded privately with the Lord Lieutenant.

Interestingly, throughout the Report, the Commissioners do not refer to the disease as 'blight'—a word that was subsequently to be associated with the tragedy. Nor do they make any mention of the Lumper,[15] generally held to be the most widely grown, the most nutritionally inferior, and the most susceptible potato to blight in 1845.[16]

## REPORTS OF MESSRS. KANE, LINDLEY & PLAYFAIR, COMMISSIONERS, *ON THE POTATOE [SIC]*[17] *DISEASE* OCTOBER AND NOVEMBER 1845)

Board Room, Royal Dublin Society,[18]

24th October 1845

"My Lord – We, the undersigned commissioners appointed by her Majesty's government to report to your Excellency on the state of the disease in the potato crop, and on the means of its prevention, have the honour to inform your Excellency that we are pursuing inquiries with unremitting attention.[19]

We are fully sensible of the important and difficult nature of the inquiry, and therefore are unwilling to offer, at the present moment, any final recommendations, as we are still receiving evidence, and awaiting the results of various experiments now in progress. But at the same time we ought to state to your Excellency that we have reason to hope the progress of the disease may be retarded by the application of simple means, which we trust may appear worthy of adoption, until we are enabled to offer further recommendations.

In the present communication we avoid entering into any account of the origin or nature of the disease; but we would particularly direct attention to the ascertained facts, that moisture hastens its progress, and that it is capable of being communicated to healthy potatoes when they are in contact with such as already tainted. A knowledge of these facts, determined as they have been by experiment, and agreeing with the scientific information obtained as the causes and nature of the disease, lead us to propose the adoption of the following plan for diminishing the evils arising from the destructive malady: -

In the event of a continuance of dry weather, and in soils tolerably dry, we recommend that the potatoes should be allowed, for the present, to remain in the land: but if wet weather intervene, or if the soil be unnaturally wet, we consider that they should be removed from the ground without delay.

When the potatoes are dug out of the ground, we are decidedly of the opinion that they should not be pitted in the usual way, as the circumstances under which potatoes are placed in ordinary pits, are precisely those which hasten their decay.[20]

We recommend, that potatoes when dug should be spread over the field, and not collected into heaps, and if the weather continue dry and free from frost, that they should be allowed to lie upon the field for a period of time not exceeding three days.

The potatoes, after being thus dried and improved in their power of resisting disease by the means proposed, should then be sorted by carefully separating those which show any tendency to decay. Those potatoes which appear to be sound, should then be placed about two inches apart in a layer, and over each layer of potatoes should be placed a layer of turf ashes, or dry turf-mould, or dry sand, or burned clay, to the depth of a few inches. Thus will be formed a bed of potatoes, each potato being completely separated from the other by a dry absorptive material; upon this bed, another layer of potatoes should be spread in this manner, and be also covered with the dry materials employed; as many as four layers may be thus placed one above the other, and when the heap is completed, it should be covered with dry clay, straw, heath, or any other material adapted to protect it from rain.

In the event of weather becoming wet, these recommendations are not applicable. In that case we would advise the potatoes be packed in small heaps, with either straw or heath interposed, and well covered; in such a situation they should become as well dried as seems practicable under the circumstances. Where out buildings exist, it would be advisable that this mode of temporary packing should be carried on in those places. If there be no out houses, the heaps may be left in the open field. We, however, particularly recommend that potatoes should not be removed into inhabited rooms.

With regard to the treatment of potatoes already attacked with the disease, we have to state that in this early stage of our investigation, we do not feel justified in proposing to your Excellency any more positive treatment – this subject we reserve for a future report; but we may remark that exposure to light and dryness, in all cases retards the progress of alterations, such as the disease in question, and we therefore suggest that all such potatoes should, as far as possible, be so treated.

We do not mean to represent that these recommendations if carried into effect, will prevent the occurrence of disease in potatoes, but we feel assured that the decay will extend less rapidly and less extensively under these circumstances than if the potatoes were taken from the ground to be at once pitted in the usual manner. Neither do we offer these suggestions to your Excellency as a final means of securing the crop, but merely as a method of retarding the progress of an enemy whose history and habits are as yet but imperfectly known, whilst we endeavour to ascertain the means of more completely counteracting its injurious effects, if any such can be discovered.

All of which we submit to your Excellency's consideration, and remain.
Your Excellency's obedient and faithful servants,
Robert Kane
John Lindley
Lyon Playfair

To His Excellency, Baron Heytesbury, &c. &c. &c."

The Potato Disease – Second Report of the Commissioners.

To his Excellency, Baron Heytesbury, Lord Lieutenant of Ireland, &c., &c.

Board Room, Royal Dublin Society,

29th October, 1845

"My Lord – Having submitted to your Excellency, in a former report, some preliminary instructions intended to prevent improper treatment of the potato crop still remaining unaffected, we now have the honour to lay before your Excellency, our views regarding some process of treatment for the potato, which appear to us to be of practical value and importance.

We are deeply sensible of the incompleteness of form which this mode of presenting our results to your Excellency, necessarily assumes; but the exigencies of the case are such, that we consider it our highest duty to bring at once under the notice of her Majesty's government such principles or modes of practice as, upon due consideration, we feel ourselves authorised to recommend.

We have been engaged in the investigation of various plans for preserving diseased potatoes, as proposed by other persons, or suggested by ourselves, and we have been collecting precise information as to the experience of others in their endeavours to arrest the progress of the disease. From all the results that we have obtained, we feel justified in submitting to your Excellency the following observations:-

Plans of treatment have been proposed by persons possessing more or less chemical knowledge, in which by some acids are to be employed; in others, alkaline liquors; and in a third class, gases such as chlorine. These processes we dismiss from further consideration, as even did they, in the laboratory, answer the intended purpose, they are totally inappropriate to the circumstances of the produce off an entire country, and to a population such as that for whose welfare your Excellency is so deeply anxious. Other methods, apparently more practical, consist in the treatment of potatoes with chloride of lime – (bleaching powder) and salt, either separate or in mixture. The result of our own experiments, and the evidence we have received concerning trials made by persons in whom we have full confidence, authorize us at once to recommend the rejection of those materials. We have found the decomposition of the potato to be decidedly accelerated by their application with respect to lime, the results of our own experiments are not yet decisive; nor is the experience of others as yet satisfactory. We, therefore, reserve the point for further examination.

Whilst the disease is not yet very far advanced in the potato, it is certain, that after being boiled or steamed, it may be employed as food for immediate use, both for man and other animals without prejudices to health.

When the disease is more advanced, so as to have invaded a large portion of the potato, and when the tubers have acquired a disagreeable smell, their influence on the system is more questionable. We have put in operation a series of experiments, in order to determine this point, and will, in due time, report the result to your Excellency. As, however, the potato, when once affected, quickly runs into total decomposition if left to itself, it is evident that its consumption merely for the purpose of food cannot be sufficiently rapid; and it therefore becomes necessary to consider to what other uses it may be applied.

The extraction of starch from potatoes, and its use as food, having strongly attracted public attention, and conflicting, and, in many cases, inaccurate opinions having been entertained on this subject, we consider it of paramount importance at once to direct your Excellency's attention to the actual state of knowledge regarding this material. It is recognised that the potato, in relation either to its weight or bulk, is one of the most inferior articles of food. In its ordinary state of sound constitution, every hundred pounds by weight of potatoes contain, on an average, seventy-four pounds of water; of skin and fibrous matter, eight pounds; and of starch, sixteen pounds, whilst of gluten, the most nutritious of vegetable matters, and which predominates in corn, there is not more than two pounds in the above quantity. It is quite certain that starch, or materials corresponding to it, exists to a certain amount in every variety of useful food; but it is equally certain that in food starch is not the material which serves for the support of the animal frame; and an animal fed merely on starch dies of starvation nearly, if not quite as soon, as if totally deprived of food. Hence, starch extracted from the potato cannot be viewed as a substitute for the potato itself; and we consider it of great importance that whilst the attention of the people is directed to the real value of starch and the uses to which it may be advantageously applied, they should not be allowed to rest their hopes of nourishment during the succeeding season upon any store of it alone.

With this preliminary caution, we have to state to your Excellency that probably the best use to which diseased potatoes may be applied is the extraction of starch. In a commercial point of view, the starch represents a considerable proportion of the value of the potato, although it is not present in as large a quantity in the unsound tubers as in those which are free from disease. The extraction is simple, and consists in processes which we need not here describe, as they are given in the current publications of the day, and indeed are already practiced in most parts of the country.

Your Excellency is aware that we are directing your attention to the manner in which starch can be advantageously employed. It can be worked off, and with utility, as food, when mixed with proportions of oatmeal, bean-meal, or peas-meal, and such intermixture forms an excellent and economical article of food. It is also to be remarked, that the pulp remaining after the extraction of the starch from the diseased potato, contains a considerable quantity of nutritive material; and as the decomposing substance is, to a very great extent, washed out during the preparation; the pulp may, when dried; be applied with confidence to the nourishment of animals. Further, if the dried starch, extracted from the potato, be mixed up with the dry residual pulp, a material will be produced really representing the potatoe, equivalent to it as food, and, if kept dry, capable of being preserved for a considerable length of time; it, of course; must, be prepared for use by cooking or baking in the ordinary way.

The manufacture of the pulp and starch, on an extensive scale, in accordance with these suggestions, we venture to consider worthy of your Excellency's attention. It is an operation not suited to the circumstances of isolated cottiers, and just now might not be a proper object for mere commercial speculation.— But arrangements might possibly be made for carrying out this recommendation, through the agency of the Poor Law Unions, and other government establishments, in which mechanical power and intelligent superintendence could be speedily and economically applied. We feel, however, that even these facilities for the conversion of the tubers may be not sufficient to keep pace with the progressive injury which it is to be feared, the potato crop is sustaining. We, therefore, recommend a mode by which we believe the process of decomposition may be retarded. In our preliminary report, we mentioned to your Excellency the important influence exercised upon the disease, by moisture and dryness. Our subsequent investigations have confirmed this opinion, and we believe where means exist for a more complete drying of the tubers, such a method will prove the most efficacious plan for preserving the potato from further decay.— This most perfect drying cannot, however, be effected in this climate by mere exposure to air, it requires artificial heat, applied in some form of kiln, and without entering into mechanical details, we may name some simple contrivances which seem well adapted to the purpose. The corn-kilns 'extensively' distributed through the country may at once be applied to the drying of the potatoes, which will, however, demand a temperature, rendered gradually higher than that required for corn. But as in many cases those kilns are at present fully occupied, we would represent that every lime-kiln may be adapted to the purpose, without interfering with its ordinary operations, by erecting over it, at a suitable height above its mouth, a frame-work of hurdles upon which the potatoes may be spread in a thin layer, fresh potatoes being added as the others become dry and are removed. In localities where the previous means do not exist, or may not be on a sufficiently extensive scale, potatoes might be spread on a frame-work of hurdles, supported on a few props of stone, two or three feet high; one or more turf fires burning slowly under the hurdles, would effect the object. There need be no fear of the potatoes becoming slightly browned, as they are not injured thereby for future use; and the turf smoke would act favourably on the potatoes rather than otherwise.

In all these modes of drying, the potato should be cut into two, or if very large, into three pieces, so as to allow the water to escape.

Potatoes dried in any of the modes above described are certainly capable of being preserved when kept in a dry place, and stored, with the precaution described in our first report, until suitable opportunities arise for using them directly as food, or for converting them into starch or meal, according to the degree in which they were affected by the disease.

It is gratifying to us to find that our own opinion as to the advantages of thoroughly drying the potato in the manner we have recommended, and by processes such as those above described, are confirmed by the experience of highly intelligent persons who have simultaneously directed their attention to the subject.

We shall not hesitate to bring under the notice of your Excellency our further conclusions, and we have the honour to be, your Excellency's obedient and faithful servants,
Robert Kane
John Kindly [sic]
Lyon Playfair
To his Excellency Baron Heytesbury, Lord Lieutenant of Ireland, &c., &c., &c."

## POTATO DISEASE.

The following is the third report of the commissioners appointed by the government to examine into the potato disease.

*To His Excellency Baron Heytesbury, Lord Lieutenant of Ireland, &c., &c., &c.,*

Board-room, Royal Dublin Society,

3d November, 1845.
"My Lord, We have had the honour to lay before your Excellency, reports on the diseases in the potato crop, which have been distributed extensively throughout the country. Representations, however, have been made to us, that the recommendations being in the form of reports, are not likely to be of that use which the more simple form of instructions might enable them to be. We have, therefore, thought it advisable to prepare the accompanying directions, in the hope that the methods recommended may be easily understood and promptly carried into execution.

We shall immediately lay before your Excellency our views upon the course which should have been pursued with regard to seed for a future year.

We have the honour to be, your faithful and obedient servants,
Robert Kane,
John Lindley,
Lyon Playfair.

*Advice concerning the Potato Crop to the Farmer and to the Peasantry of Ireland.*

The dreadful disease that has attacked your potatoes is one, the effects of which you can only stop by strict attentention [sic] to the advice of those interested in your welfare. Many plans have been proposed, and, after examining them all, we recommend the following as the best.

All competent persons are of opinion that the first things to bear in mind are the following directions:-

1. Dig your potatoes in dry weather, if you can, and if you cannot, get them dry somehow as fast you can.
2. Keep them dry and cool.
3. Keep the bad potatoes separate from the good.
4. Do not pit your potatoes as you have been accustomed to do in former years.
5. Recollect that if they get damp, nothing can make them keep; and do not consider them dry unless the mould which sticks to them is like dust.
6. Do not take them into your houses unless you want them for immediate use.

DIGGING AND DRYING.—As you dig the potatoes leave them in the sun all day; and if you can, throw them upon straw, turning them over two or three times. At night you may gather them together and cover them with straw so as to keep off frost. Next day take off the straw, spread them out, and give them the sun again. Do this for three days running, if the weather permits. If you put straw enough upon them at night they will not suffer.

If the weather be unfavourable, and you have a dry loft, or outhouse large enough to hold them, you may spread them thinly on the floor, allowing a free circulation of air so as to dry them there.

They MUST be got DRY.

SORTING THE POTATOES.—As soon as they are dry you must sort them. Pick them one by one, and put in one heap the very bad ones, in another, those which are not so bad, and in a third, those that are sound. Treat the bad potatoes as shall afterwards be directed, and store the sound ones according to the directions given in the next paragraph. You will know the very bad potatoes by their unpleasant smell, and the second set by their skin looking brown, or dull, and not bright, as it generally does; a very little practice will teach you how to distinguish them easily from each other.

STORING.—When the potatoes are quite dry, and well sorted, proceed to store them thus:—Mark out on the ground a space six feet wide, and as long as you please. Dig a shallow trench two feet wide all round, and threw the mould upon the space; then level it, and cover it with a floor of turf-sods, set on their edges. On this sift or spread, very thinly, the dry mixtures, or any of the dry materials described below, and which you may call *packing stuff*. Also, get some dry slacked lime, and dust all the potatoes with it as well as you can. Then put one row of turf-sods, laid flat, on the top of the floor, all round the sides, so as to form a broad edge, and within this spread the dry potatoes, mixed well with packing stuff, so as not to touch one another. When you have covered the floor in this manner up to the top of the sods, lay another row of sods all round the first, so that half of each sod may rest, on the bed of potatoes, and the other half on she [sic] first layer of sods; this will make another edge one sod deep, which must be filled up with dry potatoes, and dry packing stuff, as before. Then lay another edge of sods in the same way, fill it again, and so go on till the heap is made. When the building of this pit is finished, it may be covered with sods at the top, and will be ready for thatching. If rightly made it will laok [sic] like the roof of a cottage cut into steps.

If you do not understand this, ask your landlord or your clergyman to explain its meaning, and we are sure that they will give you every assistance; also recollect that the recommendation applies only to sound potatoes, after being well dried.

You will lose nothing by applying these materials in storing, for the turf can be burnt as you use up the potatoes, and the mixture of lime with dry clay or ashes, which you are afterwards directed to employ, will form a good manure after having saved the potatoes. The only difference is, that you must get what you want now instead of waiting till another time.

After you have completed the heap, thatch it so as to throw off the waters into the ditch, and keep out the frost.

In districts where there may not be spare turf sufficient to form the pits in the above way, make them as follows:–Mark out the spot, and make the trench as before. Lay on the ground a floor of stones; about as large as apples, and over them as much heath, brushwood, or twigs, as will just cover the stones. On this floor form the heaps of potatoes, and packing stuff, just as described, for the turf pit. Cover the sides of the potatoes with more of the packing stuff, and thatch in the usual way.

We must again impress upon you that to pit potatoes in your usual way is certain destruction to them.

PACKING STUFF.–This, which is of the greatest consequence, may be prepared in either of the following ways– some of you may prefer the one, some the other:-
FIRST WAY.–Mix a barrel of freshly burned unslacked lime, with two barrels of sand or earth, as dry as you possibly can get it. The lumps of lime should be broken into pieces as large as marbles, and the mixture should be left 24 hours; at the end of that time, turn the heap well over, mixing together the lime and sand (or other dry materials) till no lumps of lime can be found.

SECOND WAY.–Mix well equal quantities of earth and broken turf, or dry sawdust, put a few sods of lighted turf on the ground, place the mixture on them by degrees till a large heap is made, in a few hours the fire will have spread through the heap, which is then to be covered with earth so as to put out the fire. In fact, this is to be managed just as if you were burning land. This burned mixture forms a very good kind of packing stuff, perhaps as good as the mixture of lime with dry materials.

WHAT TO DO WITH BAD POTATOES,—When potatoes are only slightly diseased, that is, when the disease shows itself only under the skin in small dark spots, or at most, spreading into the substance of the potato for about a quarter of an inch deep, with a yellow, or light brown, or blackish colour, and without any smell, they may be eaten by the family without danger. They should be peeled and the diseased parts pared off before they are boiled: the parts cut off should be kept for making starch. Potatoes thus treated are wholesome and palatable, but should be used for food as quickly as possible, as it is not quite certain that they will keep long with the greatest care.

It is a pity to destroy potatoes for starch if they will otherwise keep. Cut out the diseased parts, if it can easily be done, and dust over the cut parts with lime and the potato also. Get them dry as soon as you possibly can, and if you have outhouses or sheds you should keep the potatoes in them also, using the packing materials. In such cases you should allow the air to circulate freely in the sheds, and should frequently examine your potatoes, which should not be laid in layers above two or three feet in height. If you turn them frequently during the first two or three weeks and keep them VERY DRY; in this way they will probably keep. Although sheds or outhouses are to be preferred, if you have them not, and cannot construct them out of cheap materials, you should store the diseased potatoes by themselves just as we have recommended you to store the sound ones.

If, with all your care, the diseased potatoes still get worse, dry them THOROUGHLY in kilns, or on hurdles placed over lime kilns, or on screens or hurdles placed over low turf fires, after having cut the potatoes into two or three slices. It is only very bad potatoes that you should break up into starch.

HOW TO SAVE THE VALUE OF VERY BAD POTATOES.—

Although nobody knows how to make bad potatoes into good ones, or to prevent many of them from becoming worse, yet it is possible to extract from bad potatoes, or from bad parts of them, a great deal which is good. For this purpose proceed as follows:—Provide yourselves with the following things, a rasp or grater, which may be made of a sheet of tin or even of sheet iron bent round, and punched full of holes, with a nail—a common coarse linen cloth, or hair sieve, hand sieve, or common cloth strainer—and a pail, or tub or two to hold water.

To make the bad potatoes useful, wash them clean and then rasp them into one of the tubs of water; the finer they are rasped the more food will you procure from them. Having rasped a good many, take the cloth and place it on another tub, then put the pulp on the cloth, and pour water on it, allowing the water to run through. You have now two things to attend to—the pulp and the starch.

First—Attend to the pulp, squeeze out as much water as you can from what remains on the cloth. You should wash it, however, till no smell remains. After you have squeezed it pretty dry, complete the drying on a griddle, over a slack fire, and when it is dry, put it aside for use.

Next look to the milky water; it will then become clear, and the milkiness, which is starch, will have settled to the bottom. Pour off the water gently till the starch is tolerably well drained; then add more water, stir the whole well up, and let it settle again. As soon as it is again clear pour off the water, and when you have got rid of as much as you can, put the wet lumps of starch on a shelf or other place to dry. In a few days it will be fit to pack up.

Good wholesome bread may be made by mixing starch with the dried pulp, peasmeal, beanmeal, oatmeal or flour. You must bear in mind that starch is not food by itself.

There will be of course a good deal of trouble in doing all that we have recommended, and perhaps you will not succeed very well at first; but we are confident that all true Irishmen will exert themselves, and never let it be said that in Ireland the inhabitants wanted courage to meet difficulties against which other nations are successfully struggling.

ROBERT KANE,
JOHN LINDLEY,
LYON PLAYFAIR.
Board Room, Royal Dublin Society,
3d November, 1845."

## THE POTATO DISEASE.

The following is the fourth report of the Government Commissioners:–

"TO HIS EXCELLENCY BARON HESTESBURY, LORD LIEUTENANT OF IRELAND, &c. &c.

Board Room, Royal Dublin Society,

7th November, 1845.

"MY LORD–Having laid before your Excellency our views as to the best means of storing the potato; and converting to useful purposes such as are too much diseased to offer a probability of being preserved, we now have the honour to bring under your consideration the question of seed for a future year. If, in our former reports, we have found it difficult to determine what course, under the peculiar circumstances of Ireland, it might be most advisable to pursue, we are still more embarrassed, on the present occasion, in consequence of the conflicting testimony that has been presented to us, and the absence of all decisive evidence as to the cause of the potato disease. The want of experience, derived from previous visitations of the same nature, also renders it impossible to affirm in what manner the potato may be affected in the course of the next few months.

We have, however, endeavoured to ascertain all that is positively known upon those subjects; by the examination of great variety of published documents; both foreign and domestic; by personal observation, and by inquiries addressed to persons of practical experience or scientific reputation.

It is a very general opinion, and one entertained by men whose extensive knowledge entitles it to respect, that parasitical fungi, similar in their nature to those which produce mildew and dry rot, are the real cause of the malady. It is stated that one of these plants belonging to the genus 'botrytis,'[21] and similar to that which some years since produced great mischief among the silk worms of France and Italy, has attacked the potato crop. It is described as entering the potato plant by the breathing pores of its leaves, and then passing down through the interior of the stem into the tubers, in which its mycelium or spawn fixes itself, traversing the cellular mass, separating the cell themselves, causing alteration in their chemical condition, and thus producing decay. In other cases where the spawn is not apparently distinguishable, the diseased portions of potatoes, even by the most practised observers, it is suggested that the juices of the plant may be vitiated by the parasite which destroyed the leaves, and that particles of it, too obscure to be distinguished by the eye, may be circulating with the juices and producing disease by irritation. The presence of the parasite is not to be detected by the naked eye, unless it makes its appearance on the outside of the potato in the form of mouldy tufts; but its spawn may be detected in the diseased portions by the microscope whether any external indications of its presence can be perceived or not; hence it is inferred that it is produced exclusively from within. It is, however, within our knowledge, that when apparently sound potatoes are pitted in places where the mouldiness of a diseased potato is able to appear, that mouldiness rapidly establishes itself on the sound potatoes at every point where their surface has been wounded or bruised; and that under such circumstances the disease is immediately extended through the entire mass.

That the spawn of fungi is at present in large quantity in diseased potatoes is undoubted; the evidence of the best microscopical observers would be with us conclusive on that point, even if we had not verified the fact by personal examination. We also regard it as well ascertained, that these parasites spread rapidly in warm and damp situations, producing infinite mischief under such circumstances, and that their advance is only to be successfully resisted by dryness. But it does not appear to us, that their being the original cause of the disease has been well established. If it were so, it is difficult to conceive why fields of potatoes placed very near each other should be differently affected; or why certain varieties of this plant should be much less injured than others–the Irish Apple potato for example,[22] which appears to have suffered more extensively than any other. We are also unable to reconcile with the theory of the potato disease being caused by parasitical fungi, the remarkable fact that in its present form it is certainly of modern origin. That it may have always existed is possible, though of this we have no proof; but at least there can be no doubt that it has only manifested itself to any considerable degree within the last few years. We cannot suppose the botrytis which observers find to be the kind of fungus that attacks the potato, to be a recent creation. We must assume it to have been co-existent with the potato itself; and therefore we must conclude that some recent causes have come into operation favourable to its increase to the present alarming degree.

Without pretending to decide what that cause really was, we may state, that it seems to be connected with the cold, cloudy, ungenial weather, which has characterized the present year over the north of Europe; conditions highly unsuited to the constitution of a plant which, like the potato, is a native of a warm, dry, sunny country, and insufficient for the ripening of the tubers. Without adverting to solitary cases, which require to be examined with more care than we have the means of giving to them, we may state, that amidst the mass of conflicting evidence which we have obtained, the following facts appear to be established:–

1st.–That potatoes planted early in the season are more healthy than those planted later.

2nd.–That the crop has suffered less in dry, elevated, sandy districts, when the influence of the season was mitigated by the slowness of growth, or compensated for by the natural warmth of the soil.

3d.–That the late varieties of potatotoes [sic] are more diseased than early ones.

4th.–That the present disease seems to be confined to the Northern parts of Europe and North America, and to be unknown in the countries to the southward. If we are right in the conclusion at which we have thus arrived, there will not be cause for serious alarm as to the crop of another year, unless an equally unfavourable season should be experienced, or the supply of healthy seed should be insufficient, or that the parasite should be found to have so entirely taken possession of this year's plants, as to overcome the natural power of living bodies to repel the attacks of such enemies to healthy vegetation.

To Providence we must turn in the hope that a second season like this may not be visited upon us. Should the Almighty, in his infinite mercy, avert such a misfortune, we entertain confident hopes that the two other sources of danger may be guarded against by human foresight and diligence.

In providing seed for a future year, we may look with confidence to such potatoes of home growth, as shall have resisted all tendency to decay during the winter; and we trust, that a considerable quantity of them will be found remaining, where the precautions for storing, which we have recommended, shall have been observed. We do not anticipate any danger in the use of them, if they are planted early, especially, if before being planted, they are exposed to light till they become green. Another source of supply, may, doubtless, be found in the southern parts of Europe, where, we have reason to believe, that disease has not shown itself; and we would strongly advise the public to lose no time in securing what may be procurable from that quarter.

It is stated by M. Séringe, secretary to the commission appointed in the department of the Rhone, in a report just published by him on the potatoe disease, that it is unknown at Genoa, and in the warmer countries; our own advices describe the crops about Marseilles as being perfectly healthy, and therefore, we may conclude, that mercantile enterprise will make up by importations, a large part of the deficiency to be apprehended.

It has also been ascertained by actual experiments that potatoes, although diseased will grow and produce apparently healthy plants. The Reverend Mr. Berkely [sic], a gentleman eminent above all other naturalists of the United Kingdom, in his knowledge of the habits of fungi, and whom we have consulted on this occasion, states, that although there would certainly be some risk of raising a diseased progeny from a diseased stock, yet the growth of fungi so evidently depends on atmospheric conditions, that it does not follow that because germs are present they should be developed.

We cannot, however, recommend the use of diseased tubers for seed, except by way of experiment, or in cases of absolute necessity, and it will always be prudent to dust them with powdered lime before they are used. It would indeed be proper to do so even when sets, however sound in appearance, are employed; for this process will destroy the minute seeds of parasitical fungi, which may be sticking to the sets, and assist in repelling those which are lying in the ground. Of course, those potatoes being selected which, on careful inspection, show no sign of disease, and hence afford the fairest prospect of a sound and healthy growth.

Where home-grown sets are to be employed for another crop, we would suggest with very great confidence the adoption of the system of autumn planting; a method of cultivation which has been proved advantageous in regard to the crop, which is attended with no unusual expenses and which seems particularly adapted to the circumstances of the present case. It has been shown by Mr. Grey of Dilston,[23] that in Northumberland, his potato crop has been considerably increased in quantity by this practice, and that he has no disease in it this year. In 1844, his autumn planted crop, produced 100 and 111 loads, when the same quantity of spring-planted land yielded but eighty loads under the same circumstances. And in the present season, this gentleman states, that his autumn planted is one third better than his spring planted crop. There can, therefore, be no doubt, that the autumn planting may be safely practiced. On this occasion it has these peculiar advantages that it offers an additional chance of security against renewed attacks from parasitical fungi. On this point, the evidence of Mr. Berkley is positive. 'Autumn planting,' he states, 'seems to me to offer the best chance of obtaining healthy sets. What are now planted will produce their tubers before the atmospheric conditions requisite for the growth of the parasite in the leaves can be realized and without much growth, the particles, if present, will be too few to cause much evil. I think, under existing circumstances, the commissioners cannot do a greater service than by encouraging and enforcing as much as possible autumn-planting.' Concurring as we entirely do in this recommendation, we trust that the planters of potatoes who have it in their power to adopt it, will do so at once.

All that we conceive it necessary to state, with reference to this practice, is, that it should be performed at any time before the end of January; that the sets should be thoroughly dried by exposure to light and air, that they should also be well dusted with lime; and that they should be planted in drills six inches deep, with farm yard manure below the sets. We also recommend that where the potatoes are not large, they should be planted whole; and even large potatoes should be cut into not more than two pieces.

We have ascertained that autumn planting has already been practised throughout Fingal, for the early supply of the Dublin market; and that although the practice has been nearly discontinued, that has not happened for any reason that affects the present question. Neither do we learn that the early period at which the leaves appear above the ground in spring, is attended with any greater risk than what attends precarious crops like the potato in any season. The effect to be anticipated from autumn planting consists not merely in a probable increase of quantity in next year's supply, but in the saving of potatoes which may perish before spring, if the slow growth which goes on during winter is arrested, and in the early ripening of next year's crop in the event of a second unfavourable season supervening. We may add, that experience has shown the small refuse potatoes of the year to be suited to autumn planting, if sound, and prepared in the manner we have recommended.

It has been supposed by many persons that the potato has arrived at a state of general debility, and that the crop will continue liable to disease like the present, until new varieties shall have been raised from seed. We do not find any satisfactory evidence to support this opinion. It is doubtless true, that great constitutional differences exist among the varieties of the potato, and that some are much more delicate than others; but we do not find that the oldest varieties are the most tender, or the newest the most hardy. On the contrary, it is within our own knowledge that in the present season very healthy varieties, recently raised, have suffered much more than kinds that have been long in cultivation.

While, however, we withhold our assent to the proposition that newly-raised varieties of the potato are exempt in any peculiar degree from the attacks of disease, we fully admit the fact that some varieties are much more subject to it than others, and we therefore recommend the cultivation of the tender kinds to be discontinued, and that those alone be used for future cropping which the experience of the present year shows to be best suited to unfavorable seasons; and on this point we may further remark, that all concurrent testimony points out the Irish "cup" variety[24] as that which has suffered least from the attacks of the disease.

We are also of opinion that it will be imprudent to plant potatoes for the next crop, in land which has been just cleared of them. The latter is in all probability filled with the seeds of fungi, countless myriads of which must have been scattered over the tainted field; and, although they probably have been borne by the winds to every portion of the country, yet it may be conceived that soil will be more impregnated where diseased potatoes have just been growing, than in fields in which decaying matter was not actually present.

Under these circumstances, we are decidedly of opinion, that prior to putting any kind of crop, for the coming year, into land that has been this season under potatoes, it will be prudent, if not absolutely necessary, that the ground should be turned up and exposed to the action of the atmosphere with care, and that it should be thoroughly manured with lime. We have already recommended that the potatoes, whether whole or cuttings, used for seed should be dusted over with lime previous to planting; and we further urge that in the case of corn or seed crops of every kind, the seeds should be steeped in lime water, or in the solution of blue stone and salt, well known to farmers. Evidence has already been laid before us of injurious effects where such precautions as we have described have been neglected.

We forbear from adverting to the possibility of replenishing the dimished [sic] supply of potatoes by sowing the seeds formed by the flower. This is an operation which can only be carried on successfully in a garden—is unsuited to the means of the small cultivator—cannot in any way effect the question of immediate supply, and may be safely left to the intelligence of the gardeners scattered throughout the country.

Hitherto we have laid before your Excellency, for the purposes of publication, several reports in a merely popular form, suited to the present emergency. We are confident that the recommendations contained in them, if carried into effect, will tend to mitigate the evils arising from the attacks of the disease in the potato crop. We now propose to proceed forthwith to apply ourselves to the investigation of the important scientific questions involved in the subject and to report in due time the results of our inquiries, in order that from past experience, we may derive knowledge for future guidance. These investigations will occupy us for a considerable time, and while we do not contemplate the necessity of publishing further popular directions, we shall hold ourselves in readiness to give our immediate attention to any question which your Excellency may submit for our consideration, or to report from time to time for your Excellency's private information.

We have the honour to be, your faithful and obedient servants,
ROBERT KANE,
JOHN LINDLEY,
LYON PLAYFAIR."

## TO HIS EXCELLENCY THE LORD LIEUTENANT,

Royal Dublin Society,

Nov. 8, 1845.

"MY LORD–We take occasion to mention to your Excellency some facts regarding the action of peat or turf upon diseased potatoes, which we are anxious to make known without delay, although at the present moment we do not wish to put forward a formal report, or official recommendation.

We had early fixed our attention on the preservative action of turf, and in our first report gave some directions for its use, since which time we have received accounts of its decisive utility in many cases. We had also obtained very distinct evidence that in wet bog land the disease was in reality milder and less extensive than in dryer and more fertile soils. Upon these grounds we proceeded to institute experiments on the action of bog-water on diseased potatoes; and we find that certainly, when immersed therein the disease appears to be arrested, and the substance of the potato does not appear in any way to suffer.

Our trials having been made in Dublin, and but on a small scale, and also the pressure of circumstances forcing us to make known every plan likely to prove useful without loss of time, we do not wish to have this notice considered as decisively stating that steeping in bog-water will stop the progress of the disease; but we consider it highly important that the plan should be tried by persons residing in bog districts where circumstances render a possible failure in a certain quantity an object of no importance. We have accordingly applied be [sic] several gentlemen to institute trials on a large scale, and shall, when we learn the results, at once proceed to lay them before your Excellency.

We remain your Excellency's obedient and faithful servants,
ROBERT KANE,
JOHN LINDLEY,
LYON PLAYFAIR."

## Notes

1 A common spelling of potato in the nineteenth century and earlier.
2 Lyon Playfair (1818–1898) had been born in Bengal in India, but educated in Scotland. In 1843, he was appointed Professor of Chemistry at the Royal Manchester Institution. He was a founder and first editor of the prestigious *The Gardeners' Chronicle*.
3 *The Gardeners' Chronicle* was a British horticulture periodical that had been founded in 1841.
4 *The Gardeners' Chronicle*, 13 September 1845.
5 Robert Peel (1788–1850) was a Conservative politician who served twice as Prime Minister (1834 to 1835 and 1841 to 1846). Unlike many English politicians, he had personal knowledge of Ireland having served there as Chief Secretary for Ireland from 1812 to 1818.
6 Kinealy, *This Great Calamity*, p. 14.
7 John Lindley (1795–1866) had been born in Norwich in England. From 1829 to 1860, he was professor of botany at University College, London.
8 Robert Kane (1809–90) was born in Dublin. In 1831, he was appointed Professor of Chemistry at the Apothecaries' Hall in Dublin, which earned him the nick-name, the 'boy professor'. In 1845, he became the first President of Queen's College, Cork. He was knighted in 1846.
9 Lindley, *Memoirs*, p. 98.
10 *Dublin Weekly Nation*, 6 December 1845. The term was also used by the English press, eg 'Potato Triumvirate', *Times*, 20 October 1845.
11 'Dr Kane on the Potato Commission', *Tuam Herald*, 7 November 1846.
12 'FAMINE AND DISEASE IN IRELAND', House of Commons Debates, *Hansard*, 17 February 1846, vol. 83, col. 1076.
13 Thomas Wemyss Reid, *Memoirs and Correspondence of Lyon Playfair: First Lord Playfair of St Andrews* (London and New York: Cassell and Co., 1900), p. 100.
14 John Feehan, 'The potato: root of the Famine' in John Crowley, William J. Smyth and Mike Murphy, *Atlas of the Great Irish Famine* (Cork University Press, 2012), p. 28.
15 The Lumper was introduced to Ireland from Scotland in the early nineteenth century. Because of its high yields, it quickly became the mainstay of the poorer and cottier classes in Ireland, although there were marked regional variations. It had little

resistance to the blight. For more on Irish potato varieties, see: https://www.agriculture.gov.ie/media/migration/farmingsectors/crops/seedcertification/topspotatocentre/PotatoBook010610.pdf, accessed 3 January 2017.
16 Cormac Ó Gráda, 'The Lumper Potato and the Famine', *History Ireland*, issue 1 (Spring 1993), pp. 22–23.
17 A common spelling of potato in the nineteenth century and earlier.
18 The Dublin Society was founded in June 1731 'to promote and develop agriculture, arts, industry, and science in Ireland'. In 1820, it was renamed the Royal Dublin Society when King George IV became a patron. The Society was located in Ballsbridge.
19 The letters are address to Baron Heytesbury, the Lord Lieutenant of Ireland, who headed the Administration at Dublin Castle. Born William à Court (1779–1860), he was first elected to the House of Commons in 1812. Peel appointed him as Lord Lieutenant, a position he held from 17 July 1844 to 8 July 1846.
20 Traditionally in Ireland, after harvesting potato tubers were carefully stored in pits. The pits were usually in the ground and the potatoes could be dug up as needed. If the ground became wet, they were more likely to rot.
21 More usually *botrytis cinereal*, is a necrotrophic fungus. It is particularly associated with a rotting of grapes, and manifests itself as a grey mould.
22 The 'Apple' was generally regarded as superior in quality—but lower in yield—than the more widely grown Lumper potato.
23 John Grey (1785–1868), of Dilston, was an English land agent and agriculturist. His politics were liberal, he supporting the abolition of slavery and Catholic Emancipation. In 1833, the government put him in charge of managing estates owned by Greenwich Hospital in the north of England. While there, he focused on agricultural improvement. Grey was father of the feminist activist, Josephine Butler.
24 The 'Cup' was one of the varieties of potatoes grown in Ireland prior to 1845. It was introduced into the country around 1800. It was regarded as coarser, but hardier, than the Apple.

# Part II

# THE POTATO BLIGHT EXAMINED

# 4

# REPORTS OF THE MANSION HOUSE COMMITTEE ON THE POTATO DISEASE IN 1845 (1846)

The failure of the potato crop in 1845 and, more extensively, in 1846, resulted in the reconvening of a number of private relief committees that had come into existence during earlier periods of shortages. This was the case with the Mansion House Relief Committee in Dublin, which had first been convoked during the crisis of 1822 and reconstituted in 1831.

The origins of the new Mansion House Committee lay in a public meeting convened in Dublin on 31 October 1845. The name of the committee derived from the meeting place, the Mansion House on Dawson Street, the official home of John Arabin, the Lord Mayor.[1] The committee included some of the most powerful men in Ireland, drawn from across religious and political divides. Unlike many other committees, however, they were all Irish men. Two of its most prominent members were the veteran politicians Daniel O'Connell and Lord Cloncurry.[2] It was the latter who tried to persuade the Prime Minister, Sir Robert Peel, through his representative in Ireland, Lord Heytesbury, to intervene early in the approaching food shortages.[3]

The purpose of the committee was threefold: to collect information from the localities about the potato loss; to recommend appropriate responses, and to raise and distribute donations. Included in the series of practical measures proposed, was that the ports in Ireland should be 'opened' to allow the importation of foodstuffs, without the imposition of prohibitive taxes and freight charges. This measure had been used with some success previously and so there was a precedent. Moreover, other countries in Europe were enacting similar legislation.[4] But to the Tory and Liberal governments of Britain, it was too interventionist. Starvation, as it turned out, was preferable to intrusion in the market place.

The day following the public meeting, an Address was delivered personally to the Lord Lieutenant, the answer to which was deemed 'unsatisfactory' by the committee. The nationalist *Freeman's Journal* was more blunt, reporting that the delegation had been received 'very coldly' and that Heytesbury's attitude to the Irish poor could be summed up by the phrase, 'They may starve'.[5] Following this, the committee sat daily, with each member contributing £5 to cover his expenses. On 8 November, the committee sent over 3,500 questionnaires to all parts of the country. Armed with the responses, they made a further appeal to the government, this time directly to the Prime Minister, Sir Robert Peel. Their letter was emphatic in stating that they had not exaggerated the state of the country, fear of exaggeration being one of Peel's motives for establishing a 'Scientific Commission'.[6] They also warned that if he hesitated, people would 'die in countless numbers'. Peel's response was evasive, saying he would forward the information, while he assured the committee that Ireland was receiving the 'unremitting attention' of his confidential advisors. Disappointed, the committee tried the direct approach of sharing their information with the Scientific Commissioners in Dublin. Although the Secretary of the committee, Thomas Synnott,[7] claimed to have been met with the 'utmost courtesy and kindness', the Commissioners had made it clear that co-operation was not an option.[8]

Despite the various rejections, the Mansion House Committee continued with their work, sending out a further questionnaire on 10 December. They made a synopsis of their findings, in the hope that the government would make use of it.[9] Regardless of the vast amount of detailed information collected by the committee, there is no evidence that the Scientific Commissioners or any other government department ever did consult it.[10] Throughout their reports, Lord Cloncurry, the chairperson of the committee, repeatedly appealed to an invisible social contract between the government and the Irish people, the latter being in need of the 'protection of government'. Time and time again, however, the government and its representatives proved elusive in responding to this call. More successfully, the committee made direct appeals to the public through the Irish press. This information was picked up by some newspapers in North America.[11]

Regardless of the overt rejections by the official relief commissioners, the Mansion House Committee believed that their work had had a positive impact. At a public meeting of the Repeal Association on 28 January 1846, O'Connell informed the audience:

> I ought to be somewhat proud of the exertions of the gentlemen who acted with me on the Mansion House Committee, for I find that every allegation we made with respect to the potato disease has been verified by the prime minister (hear, hear). Those allegations have got even into the Queen's speech, and the prime minister has, by that document acknowledged that we as truthfully described the extent of the calamity, as we were incapable of concealing anything of importance (cheers).[12]

O'Connell repeated these sentiments at a meeting of the Mansion House Committee that he chaired at the beginning of September 1846. At the meeting, it was also decided that, regardless of the reappearance of the potato blight, there was no need for the Committee to resume its fact-finding activities, trusting in the newly installed Whig government to provide adequate relief.[13] This trust was sadly misplaced.

In the decades that followed the Great Famine, Ireland repeatedly suffered from a number of harvest failures that resulted in varying degrees of hunger and starvation. In 1862, 1879–81 and 1898, the Mansion House Committee again convened to come to the aid of the poor of Ireland.

## *REPORT OF THE MANSION HOUSE COMMITTEE ON THE POTATO DISEASE*
(DUBLIN: J. BROWNE, 1846)

REPORT OF MANSION HOUSE COMMITTEE.

YOUR Committee report that a public meeting of the citizens and others interested, was called by The Right Honourable JOHN LADAVEZE ARABIN, the LORD MAYOR of the City of Dublin,[14] on the 31st day of October, 1845, at the Music Hall, Abbey-street,[15] to take into consideration the alarming accounts of the failure of the Potatoe crop, at which meeting it was resolved, that a Deputation be formed, consisting of the Right Honourable the LORD MAYOR, His Grace the DUKE of LEINSTER,[16] The Right Honourable The Lord CLONCURRY,[17] ALDERMAN DANIEL O'CONNELL, M. P., The VERY REVEREND DR. YORE,[18] V. G.[19] & P. P., REV. CHARLES SHERIDAN YOUNG,[20] &c. &c., to prepare and present an Address to His EXCELLENCY BARON HEYTESBURY, the Lord Lieutenant of Ireland, laying before His Excellency the awful state the kingdom was likely to become reduced to, if Government did not at once step in to prevent as far as possible, by all human means, the dreadful scourge of anticipated famine and pestilence.

An adjournment of the meeting above mentioned was held on the fourth day of November, 1845, at the same place, to receive the answer of His Excellency to the Address presented by said Deputation on the 1st day of November, 1845.

His Excellency's answer to the Deputation not being considered sufficiently satisfactory, it was resolved that a Committee be appointed to sit daily at the Mansion House, Dawson-street, and be called "The MANSION HOUSE COMMITTEE," each member of said committee to pay Five Pounds to cover the necessary expenses.

In pursuance of that resolution, your Committee met at the Mansion House on the 5th day of November, 1845, when the following plan of proceeding was determined on-

*First*, to inquire into the extent of the calamity.

*Second*, inquiry as to modes of arresting or curing the disease, and especially as to the practical efficacy of each plan.

*Third*, modes of alleviation, by the introduction of food, and prevention of loss of food already in the country, and above all, the procuring of employment for the people.

Nos. 1 and 2, to be carried out by the following circular, addressed to the Clergy of all religious denominations, the Lieutenants, Deputy Lieutenants, Sheriffs, and Poor Law Guardians, throughout Ireland, amounting to Three Thousand Five Hundred and upwards:

*Mansion House, Dawson-st. Dublin,*
*8th November,* 1845.
SIR,
I am requested by the Committee appointed at the late Meeting held in this City, on the 4th instant, the Right Hon. the Lord Mayor in the chair, to submit the following queries for your consideration, and respectfully to solicit a reply at your earliest convenience.
I have the honour to be, Sir,
Your obedient servant,
CLONCURRY,
*Chairman.*

1st—Whether the crop of potatoes was in point of quantity an average crop.

2nd—What proportion of the crop has been already lost by decomposition, or otherwise?

3rd—What is your opinion as to the probability of the remaining portion continuing sound during the year?

4th—What modes of preventing the disease, or of curing it, if any, have been found practically efficacious in your district?

5th—Have any, and what modes been used for the above purpose, which have proved inefficacious or injurious?

No. 3, to be carried out by

1st—That every effort should be made to increase the quantity of provisions.

2nd—That it is the unanimous opinion of this Committee that the ports should be opened for the free importation of all description of human food.

And resolved–That we forthwith write to Sir R. PEEL,[21] pointing out to him the exact state of this country, and the pressing and imminent danger of famine, and calling on Government to take immediate and efficacious precautions to avert the otherwise certain and impending calamity.

*Mansion-House, Dawson-street,*
*7th November,* 1845.
As Chairman of a Committee consisting of highly respectable gentlemen of all classes of religious and political opinions, appointed at a recent public Meeting of the citizens of Dublin, the Right Honourable the Lord Mayor in the chair,
It devolves upon me as a public duty, to address you, as responsible adviser of our Most Gracious Sovereign, and which I do with unfeigned respect, and in the most anxious manner to call for your fullest and most immediate consideration to the present afflicting and most dangerous state of the people of Ireland.

We can assure you that our information is both accurate and extensive, that it reaches over all parts of Ireland, and is derived from sources altogether unaffected by any political party motive whatsoever.

Be assured, Sir, we tell you but the simple truth, when we inform you that the danger of famine is immediate and pressing, and if not averted by the activity of man, and the blessing of a merciful Providence, must result in a pestilence of a most frightful nature.

We do solemnly assure you of our perfect knowledge that the destruction of the potatoe crop is extremely extensive, with some slight mitigation in particular localities; but, as a general calamity, is extending to all the provinces and counties in Ireland. Nor does the evil rest here, for day after day the disease is extending; quantities of potatoes apparently in the most healthy state one day, are found on the ensuing partially, if not entirely, unfit for human or even animal food. The disease is in its nature expansive, and is to our knowledge daily and hourly expanding; nor is there any rational evidence to show that this wide spreading rottenness will find any other limit than in the destruction of the entire potatoe crop.

We do not intend you any disrespect—quite the contrary; but we do wish to impress upon your mind the awful responsibility which, as Her Majesty's principal advisor you incur, if your government hesitates to adopt the most speedy and extensive possible modes of alleviating the impending calamity. Whilst you hesitate, if hesitate you shall, the people of Ireland are about to perish in countless numbers.

May we respectfully refer you to Lord Devon's Report of last session,[22] where you will find, or indeed whence we take it for granted you are already informed, that the Irish agricultural labourers and their families are calculated to amount to more than four millions of human beings, "whose only food is the potatoe, whose only drink is water, whose houses are pervious to the rain, to whom a bed or blanket is a luxury almost unknown, and who are more wretched than any other people in Europe."

We respectfully call your attention to the fact, that the foregoing description of the state of the Irish peasantry, was published long before there was or could be the least suspicion of the most afflicting visitation of Providence in the destruction of the present crop.

If then such was the condition of a large portion of the Irish people even in favourable harvests, you will, in your humanity, easily judge what must be the horrors of their situation, if the approaching famine be allowed to envelop the entire population.

We implore of you, Sir, not to allow yourself to be persuaded that we exaggerate the horrors or certainty of the approaching famine; we have no motive under heaven of misleading or misinforming you; and even if we had, you may believe we are utterly incapable of acting on such a motive; our only object is to impress on your mind what we know to be the fact—that famine and pestilence are at our door, and can be averted only by the most extensive and active precautions.

The season for receiving supplies of foreign food is rapidly terminating, the northern ports of Europe, as also the ports of the British American colonies, as well as other Northern American States, will soon be closed, until it will be too late to receive supplies from these countries.[23]

Other foreign countries afflicted by a similar calamity, have already been before us in the market, and are daily enhancing the price of those supplies which our Government might otherwise calculate on.

The lives of the people of Ireland are in the hands of your Government: if you determine not to take immediate precautions, we are unable to contemplate the extent of the horrible consequences resulting from the destruction of the people's food, and from the neglect of the protection of Government.

We are incapable of using any language that could be construed into dictation, but we respectfully declare it to be our conviction that it is the imperative duty of the Government to adopt some or all of the following measures, together with such others as that Government may deem advisable, to meet the impending evils:

1st. The opening of the ports of Ireland for all kinds of human food, free of duty.

2nd. The closing the ports of Ireland against the exportation of oats, either ground or whole.

3rd. That the consumption of oats by cavalry regiments in Ireland be diminished as much as it possibly can with safety to the public service.

4th. That the distillation from grain be suspended in Ireland, due precaution being taken to prevent illicit distillation.

5th. That there be immediately raised money by way of loan, to the extent of One Million and a-Half at the least, and chargeable upon Irish resources, such as the department of Woods and Forests, &c., and that the amount of such loan be applied in the first instance to the increasing the quantity, and decreasing the price of food in Ireland.

6th. That we earnestly recommend the forming of grannaries [sic] in each of the Poor Law Unions, and other localities throughout Ireland, so as to bring food within the reach of all its inhabitants.

7th. That we also earnestly recommend the setting the people to work without any delay, by urging on and assisting the construction of Railways, and also in works of Drainage, as recommended by Government Commissioners, and other works of general or local utility.

I have the honour to remain, Sir,
Your obedient servant,
CLONCURRY.
The Right Hon. Sir ROBERT PEEL, Bart.

On the 12th of November, your Committee received the following reply from Sir ROBERT PEEL:
*White-hall, November 10th,* 1845.
MY LORD,
I have the honour to acknowledge the receipt of the communication of the 7th of November, which bears your Lordship's signature, earnestly calling the attention of Her Majesty's Government to the calamity with which Ireland is threatened by

the failure, through disease, of the Potato crop, and suggesting for the consideration of the Government the following measures, [as already appear in the letter addressed to Sir Robert Peel].

I give full credit to the assurance that in making this communication your Lordship, and all those who are parties to it, are influenced by no other motive than the desire to aid the Government in the efforts which they are making to avert or mitigate the impending evil.

I shall without delay submit this, as I have submitted all other representations which have reached me on this painful subject, to my Colleagues in the service of Her Majesty.

Although considerations of public policy and of public duty prevent me from entering, in this acknowledgment of your Lordship's communication, into a discussion in respect to the advantage of the particular measures recommended for immediate adoption, yet I beg to assure your Lordship that the whole subject is occupying the unremitting attention of Her Majesty's confidential advisers.

I have the honor to be, my Lord,
Your most obedient servant,
ROBERT PEEL.
The LORD CLONCURRY.

It having been ascertained that the Government had appointed a Commission to sit in Dublin to inquire into the extent of the potato disease, the Right Honourable the Lord Mayor was requested to solicit an interview with Sir THOMAS FREEMANTLE [sic],[24] Chief Secretary for Ireland, and to inform him that your Committee were ready and willing to place in the hands of the Government all the information they had obtained on this painful subject, and to submit to their inspection all the letters they had received from all parts of the country. The Lord Mayor having obtained the interview sought for, received the following answer: "That the Government would feel obliged to the Committee for such information as they may deem of importance, and that the Committee might rest assured that the Government are fully prepared to take such steps as may be found necessary, for the protection of the people, when the emergency shall arise." Your Committee deeming all the information received by them important, directed their Secretary to make abstracts of all letters received, and hand over the originals to the authorities at the Castle.

Your Committee having received four very important returns from the County of Clare, adopted the following resolution :—

"That the Secretary be directed to take the documents received this day, and marked A, B, C, D, to the Commissioners now sitting at the Castle, and to call their attention to the facts contained therein, and in particular to point out statements in reference to the townland of Killard, in the parish of Killard, County Clare, shewing that such townland contains sixty-six families, composing three hundred and seventy-four individuals having out of their crop of ten hundred and ninety barrels of potatoes, but one hundred and six barrels fit for human food. That in the townland of Doonbeg, same parish, there are forty-five families, comprising two hundred and seventy individuals, with but eighty-five barrels of good potatoes, out of a crop containing six hundred and sixty-six barrels. That in the townland of Kilfeira, same parish, there are eighty-eight families, whose total produce of potatoes was four-teen hundred and fifty barrels, of which one hundred and eighty-seven barrels only were fit for human food. That in the additional returns from the townlands of Dunmore and Doonbeg, same parish, there are twenty-nine families, or one hundred and twenty-seven individuals, whose total produce was three hundred and seventy-two barrels, of which there were but fifty-eight barrels fit for human use. That in the townlands of Frureere and Donoughboy, at least three fourths of the crop are lost. And that the Secretary be further directed to call the attention of the Commissioners in the most respectful manner, to the length of time those enquiries have lasted, and to the extensive and melancholy information afforded them by this Committee; and to request, with all due deference, explicit information from the Commissioners, what steps it is the intention of Government to take, to meet the impending and inevitable calamity; at all events to request the Commissioners to inform the Committee, what they purpose to recommend Government to do, under the present afflicting circumstances."

The Secretary reported, that he had, in compliance with the foregoing resolution, waited on the Commissioners at the Castle, and they declared that they did not feel at liberty to state what they were about to recommend to the Government; and that with regard to the intention of Government, an application on that head ought to be made to other quarters.

Your Committee having had a "Synopsis" made of the answers to their circular dated 8th November, (*see Synopsis No. 1.*) from which it was evident that famine was approaching with rapid strides, resolved upon issuing the following circular to the parties from whom they had received answers to their former communication; in order, if possible, to elicit still more decidedly the then actual state of the potato crop, and to awaken the public mind to a sense of the impending evil:-

*Mansion House, Dawson-street,*
*Dublin,* 10*th December*, 1845.

SIR,

I am requested by the Mansion House Committee to return you their grateful thanks for the honour you have done them by your communication in reply to theirs of 8th November.

They take the liberty of submitting the following Queries for your kind consideration:

1st. Is there any change, and especially is there any favourable change, in the Potato Crop in your vicinity, since the date of your last letter?

2nd. Do you see any reason to alter or add to the opinions given by you in that letter? If so, be so good as to state the same.

3. What, according to your judgment, is the present prospect of their [sic] being a sufficiency of Potato Food for the people in your locality, for the coming season?

4. What quantity of the Potato Crop in your neighbourhood do you consider to have become unfit for human food?
You are respectfully requested to answer the above Queries at your earliest convenience.
I have the honor to be, Sir,
Your obedient servant,
CLONCURRY.

Your Committee being most anxious to lay before the public all the information in their possession, ordered a "Synopsis" of the answers to their circular dated 10th December to be made out. (*see Synopsis No. 2.*)
In addition to the account contained in the above Synopsis, of the appalling effects of the failure of the potato crop in the agricultural districts, your Committee are enabled to state on unquestionable authority, that the miserable condition to which the poor inhabitants of the Cities and Towns in Ireland are reduced in consequence of the same failure, call equally for prompt and effectual measures of relief.
Having thus laid before the public the appalling evidence of approaching famine and pestilence, and being totally uninfluenced by any party motives, we deem it most prudent to allow the facts to operate upon the mind of the Government and the Public, under the awful responsibility of that Government to procure for the Irish people the means of preventing, or at least alleviating, the fearful calamities that appear to us with perfect certainty to be fast approaching.
CLONCURRY,
*Chairman of Committee.*
THOMAS L. SYNNOTT,
*Secretary.*

## Notes

1 Since 1715, the Mansion House had been the official residence of the Lord Mayor of Dublin. It was originally built by the entrepreneur, Joshua Dawson, after whom Dawson Street was named.
2 Valentine Brown Lawless (1773–1853) was the 2nd Baron Cloncurry. He was politically radical, sympathizing with both the 1798 and 1803 risings. He later supported Catholic Emancipation, but not O'Connell's Repeal movement. He was highly critical of the government's policies during the Great Famine.
3 Valentine Lawless, *Personal recollections of the life and times, with extracts from the correspondence of Valentine Lord Cloncurry* (Dublin: J. McGlashan; London: W.S. Orr, 1849), pp. 502–504.
4 Christine Kinealy, *A Death-Dealing Famine. The Great Hunger in Ireland* (London; Pluto Press, 1997), pp. 83–91.
5 *Freeman's Journal,* 4 November 1845.
6 Charles Stuart Parker (ed.) *Sir Robert Peel from his Private Papers*, vol 3, (London, 1899, 2nd ed.), p. 225.

7 Thomas Lambert Synnott (1810–1897) was a Catholic merchant who was a supporter of O'Connell's campaign for Repeal. In addition to his work with the Mansion House Committee, he was also Secretary of the Indian Relief Fund and worked with Archbishop Murray to help distribute relief to local Catholic priests. From 1849 to 1865, he served as a Governor of Grangegorman Female Prison.
8 *Freeman's Journal*, 4 December 1845.
9 Dublin Mansion House Committee for the Relief of Distress in Ireland, *Report of Mansion House Committee (MHC) on the Potato Disease* (Dublin: J. Browne, 1846), pp. 7–11.
10 W.P. O'Brien, *The Great Famine in Ireland and a Retrospect of the fifty years 1845–1895* (London: Downey and Co., 1896), p. 58.
11 For example, 'The Mansion House Committee. The Potato Disease', appeared in the *Boston Pilot,* 31 January 1846.
12 'Irish Parliament' in *Boston Pilot*, 28 February 1846.
13 *Freeman's Journal*, 7 September 1846.
14 John Arabin, the Lord Mayor in 1845, was a political Liberal. His official residence was the Mansion House in Dawson Street, Dublin.
15 The Music Hall was situated on Lower Abbey Street. It hosted both theatrical and political events. John Classon, a wealthy Dublin merchant, was the proprietor (see *Slater's Commercial Directory of Ireland* for 1846), p. 242.
16 The title of the Duke of Leinster was the premier Dukedom in Ireland. The title had been bestowed on the family in 1776, although the Fitzgerald family had been in Ireland since the arrival of the first Anglo-Normans in the 12th century. Augustus Fitzgerald (1791–1874), the 3rd Duke of Leinster, owned extensive properties in Dublin and in Kildare (67,000 acres). A staunch Whig, he had supported Catholic Emancipation and other liberal measures. He resided in Ireland and looked after his estates. During the Famine, he served on a number of relief committees. In 1849, during Queen Victoria's first visit to Ireland, she made a brief visit to his estate in Carton, Co. Kildare.
17 Valentine Brown Lawless, Baron Cloncurry, had been born in Merrion-square, Dublin (1773–1853). Despite his privileged background, he had been sympathetic to the United Irishmen and opposed the Act of Union.
18 Rev. William Gore was parish priest (P.P.) of St Paul's on Arran Quay, from 1828 to 1864, was later made Vicar-General of the Dublin Diocese. He was a noted advocate of temperance, and had assisted Daniel O'Connell in the establishment of Glasnevin Cemetery (initially referred to as Prospect Cemetery).
19 V.G. - Vice-Guardian – of a workhouse. 130 Poor Law Unions (each with its own workhouse) had been established in Ireland in 1838. They were administered by a Board of Guardians, both elected and ex-officio. Dublin had two Unions—on the North and South side respectively.
20 Charles Young was Church of Ireland Curate at St Paul's Church on North King Street. This church had been completed in 1824 and built on the site of an older church dating from the 18th century.
21 Robert Peel (1788–1850) was an English Tory politician who, unusually, had first-hand knowledge of Ireland, having served as Chief Secretary from 1812 to 1818. He held the office of Prime Minister twice (1834–1835 and 1841–1846), the second period coinciding with the first failure of the potato crop. Although not generally regarded as being sympathetic to Ireland (Daniel O'Connell had nick-named him 'Orange Peel', on the grounds of his alleged ultra-Protestant views), during his administration he introduced a series of relief measures that proved effective in saving lives. His decision to repeal the Corn Laws split the Tory Party, allowing the Whig Party to come into office.

22 The Devon Commission was appointed in 1843 by Peel's government to investigate land holding in Ireland and suggest improvements. It reported in 1845.
23 Due to freezing conditions, a number of ports in North America did not operate over the winter months.
24 Sir Thomas Fremantle (1798–1890) was an English Tory politician who served as Chief Secretary in the Dublin Castle administration from 1845 to 1846.

# 5

# ALFRED SMEE, *ON THE CAUSE OF THE POTATO DISEASE: APHIS VASTATOR* (1846, 1847 AND 1878)

In 1843, a previously unknown disease destroyed the potato crop in parts of North America.[1] From there, it made its way to Europe, facilitated by the new, fast steam ship crossings. The destructive blight appeared in Belgium, Germany, France and Switzerland. The arrival of the potato disease was formally reported in Britain in mid-August 1845 by Dr. Thomas Bell Salter, who referred to it as a 'blight'.[2] Within a few weeks of his commentary, the same disease had occurred in diverse locations in Britain. The arrival of blight in England, and the likelihood of it spreading to Ireland—where approximately forty per cent of the population depended on this tuber—led to a lively discussion by horticulturalists and others as to its cause and cure.

One of the most prolific of these commentators was Alfred Smee.[3] Smee was the second son of William Smee, accountant-general to the Bank of England. In 1834, he had become a medical scholar at King's College, London, where he proved to be a brilliant, prize-winning scholar. As a surgeon, he specialized in diseases of the eye.[4] Smee's interests, however, were wide ranging. In 1840, when only in his early twenties, his interest in electro magnetics led him to invent a chemical battery, a silver zinc sulphuric combination, popularly known as the 'Smee Battery'.[5] The following year, he was elected a Fellow of the Royal Society. In later life, Smee devoted himself to horticulture, establishing an experimental garden in Surrey in the south of England.[6] One outcome of this period was the much-praised publication, 'My Garden; its Plan and Culture' (1872).

In 1840, Smee married Elizabeth Hutchinson and together they had three children, one son and two daughters. His son, Alfred Hutchison Smee (1842–1901), was also a surgeon with an interest in epidemic diseases.[7] Like his father, he was a prolific writer, his publications including 'Sewage, sewage produce and disease'.[8] Also, like his father, he had an interest in horticulture, and cultivated orchids and produced experimental hybrids. *Saccolabium smeeanum* (or Smee's Schoenorchis) was named in his honour.[9]

Smee's theories on the potato disease appeared in many newspapers in 1846 and 1847. In June of the latter year, his text was accompanied by his own detailed illustrations in *The Illustrated London News*.[10] Thirty years later, Smee's daughter,

Elizabeth,[11] created a memoir of her father, bringing together his writings on the potato disease.[12] In it, she variously referred to Smee as 'my father' or 'Mr. Smee'. Elizabeth, in turn, had married the noted chemist, William Odling,[13] in 1872.[14] Interestingly, Alfred Smee regarded the Roman Catholic religion as being based on 'mummery'.[15]

## ALFRED SMEE ON THE CAUSE OF THE POTATO DISEASE IN, ELIZABETH MARY ODLING, *MEMOIR OF THE LATE ALFRED SMEE, F.R.S.* (LONDON: BELL, 1878)

... In the summer of the same year a disease appeared in Europe among potato plants, which caused the tubers to decay. The first communication of the fact was in the 'Gardeners' Chronicle,' on the 16th of August, 1845, by Dr. Bell Salter.[16] No sooner had this letter appeared than other communications were sent to that journal, stating that the disease had existed to a large extent the previous season, although such an important statement had not previously been chronicled. The disease was at first considered a totally new malady, but Mr. Smee found, on inquiry, that in Germany, in 1830, Martius wrote on the subject, and that he attributed its effect to a fungus. Berkeley, the great fungologist[17]—who, though differing in opinion from Mr. Smee, always carried on the controversy in the most courteous manner, and whom my father held in great respect and esteem—considered the fungus called the Botrytis to be the cause. My father became interested in the subject, and began making his own researches. He concluded that the first cause of the disease was occasioned by an aphis[18] which punctured the leaf, sucked the sap, and destroyed the relation between the leaf and the root, thus causing the leaf or some other part of the plant to become gangrenous, and die. After the attack of the aphis, fungi grew, which 'growth,' he writes, 'is probably in many cases materially assisted by the prior attack of the aphis.' The results of Mr. Smee's inquiries and researches on aphides, and their relation to the potato and other plants, became so numerous, that he was led, in 1846, into embodying his views on the subject in a treatise containing 170 pages, which is well known by the title of the 'Potato Plant, its Uses and Properties, together with the Cause of the Present Malady.'*[19] In this book, which is dedicated to the late Prince Consort,[20] the properties and growth of the potato plant are set forth, as is also its individuality, and the chemistry and use of that plant, &c.; its gangrene, or present disease, and the chemistry of the disease; the relation of the disease to internal and external causes; the effect of temperature, light, electricity, upon the disease; the relation of the disease to soils and manures, to fungi; the relations of gangrene to animal parasites. The various aphides are then described. The insect that attacked the potato plant he considered to be an aphis, which, when fully grown, is about a tenth of an inch long, and its colour, either white, olive-green, brown, or inclined to red. This aphis, the destroyer of the potato, he found was identically the same which had been previously known to infest the turnip, and

# THE POTATO BLIGHT EXAMINED

which is called by Curtis on that account the *Aphis rapse*.[21] On the great confusion attending such a nomenclature, Mr. Smee determined, for the sake of perspicuity, to call it the *Aphis vastator*, or destroyer of our best provisions: for the *Aphis vastator* destroys, in a similar manner as it does the potato, the turnip, the swede, the beetroot, the cabbage, the broccoli, the radish, the horse-radish, the various wild Solani, some kinds of henbane, the Stramonium, the Belladonna, the clover, the groundsel, the Euphorbia, some sorts of Murex, the mallow, the shepherd's purse, the holy thistle, some kinds of grass, and even wheat, the Jerusalem artichoke and the sweet potato, and perhaps other plants.

There are many other kinds of aphides, besides the *Aphis vastator*, which destroy other plants, and even trees, and we had, about five years ago, some large willow-trees totally destroyed by their ravages at 'my garden' at 'Wellington.'*[22] Many of these different sorts of aphides and injuries caused by them are also delineated in this work on the potato disease. He also shows the relation of the Vastator and other aphides to fungi; and he then gives the natural and artificial remedies for the present diseases among plants. The work is illustrated by ten lithographs of potato plants in health and in disease, of diseased carrots and turnips, parsnips, and mangold-wurzel, of the *Aphis vastator* and of other aphides, and of various fungi. Mr. Curtis, the distinguished entomologist, blamed Mr. Smee for having violated the established custom, in not having used the prior name of the aphis. 'But it appears,' says my father, 'that Mr. Curtis named this self-same creature *rapte*, when it had the former name, *dianthi*, assigned to it, as Mr. Walker has informed me.' Thus we have *Aphis vastator* (the destroyer) alias *rapes*, alias *dianthi*. How many more aliases will this dire scourge to mankind receive?

The moment this book on the potato plant was published, it was assailed in the most extraordinary way. The writers did not attempt to attack his facts or his reasoning, but they misrepresented his views, and indeed but too frequently made my father say the very reverse of what he did say, and then they wrote their own fabulous versions of his writings.

The controversy which ensued during this potato pestilence, and the violence of various parties, were truly a reproach to science. At last, as my father has said:

Foolish people used to amuse me by sending threatening letters by nearly every post (many of these have been collected together), cautioning me that I should be amply punished if I dared to continue to write upon the subject (his life was even threatened). Notwithstanding all this, it was very curious to notice how kindly the public used to supply me with facts for my guidance; and I received valuable communications, some of them of great length, though, when the controversy was at its height, they were sent anonymously. By the middle of summer nearly every agriculturist was made acquainted with my investigations despite this rancorous animosity.

I can just remember the time of the potato disease. Our drawing-rooms were ornamented with innumerable specimens of diseased potatoes. Potatoes were on the mantelpieces; potatoes were on the tables; potatoes innumerable were on the floor. I am by no means sure that the chairs were not occupied by potatoes! Wherever the eye glanced, diseased potatoes met the view.

In the Appendix, No. XV.B., will be found a selection from the voluminous correspondence which Alfred Smee carried on in various newspapers on the potato disease during the years 1845, 1846, and 1847.[23]

Besides the rancorous animosity of the ignorant and of the bigoted, Mr. Smee was subjected to be taken off in humorous skits. Mr. Punch,[24] of course, was not behindhand.

In the pantomime at Drury Lane appeared :—
>    *Scene, a Village Fair with Shows, &c. &c.*
>    *Little Boy looking at a peep-show.*
>
> *Showman.* This is the *Aphis vastator*, as you may see,
> Very much magnified by Mr. Smee.
>
> *Boy.* Please, sir, which is the aphis and which is the tater?
> *Show-man.* Whichever you like, my young investigator.
> *The Knight and the Wood Demon; or, One o'clock.*

In one of the newspapers appeared the following humorous lines:—

*Lines on reading Mr. Smee's Account of the Aphis vastator, supposed by him to cause the Potato Blight.*

Well! this confounded *tater* blight

> Is now clear'd up by Smee;
> And for a cure all people must
> To fumigation flee.

> Let all peruse his handsome book
> About the wondrous fly,
> Which is the cause of all the ill—
> So says his theory.

> On reading first the title-page
> (I say it in no joke),
> From seeing F.R.S., I thought
> The thing must end in smoke.

> That some large bugs have been the cause
> We've had some keen debaters;
> But none till now thought little flies
> Could turn out such vast (e)aters.

> That this vast-eating insect thrives
> On its new kind of food,
> There is no doubt, for milliards are
> Born daily to the brood:

Which shows potatoes 'mongst all plants
Still hold the foremost place,
In making insects breed in swarms,
As well's the human race.

Alas! how many other crops
This aphis now will finish!
And though we may have *gammon* left,
We'll have no more of spinach.

On turnips, carrots, and on beets,
They jump about in flocks;
Even dandelions are not free,
Nor nettles, grass, nor docks.

Let some strong dose be now devised
By chemic speculators,
To massacre, this very year,
These terrible vastators.

Other lines appeared elsewhere, such as –

'The butcher, the baker, the candlestick-maker,
All jump'd out of Alfred Smee's rotten potato' –

and others I might enumerate had I space so to do.

But in the midst of the investigations, in the midst of the bitter controversies and the humorous skits on the subject, the disease still went rapidly on, till the scourge became so great that a famine ensued in the land, and in Ireland the people were dying of starvation. Then, in the midst of their distress, the people bethought them of turning to Heaven for assistance; and accordingly, we find that, on the 11th of October, 1846, prayers to the Almighty were offered up in all the churches and chapels in England and Wales, for relief from the dearth and scarcity then existing in parts of the United Kingdom. A few months later, on Wednesday, the 24th of March, 1847, a form of prayer was used in all churches and chapels throughout England and Ireland, that being the day appointed by proclamation for a general fast and humiliation.[25]

Meanwhile, my father was trying various experiments to ascertain how far other kinds of food might be employed for the relief of the poor starved population of these realms. On Saturday, the 6th of February, 1847, he held a large soiree at his residence in Finsbury Circus, expressly to exhibit his famine food, at which between 200 and 300 of the most distinguished professional and literary men of the metropolis were present. The account of the various kinds of bread constituting the famine food is given in the Appendix, No. XV.A.

The company tasted all the samples prepared, and pronounced Mr. Smee to have succeeded beyond expectation in his attempt. Though a mere child at the time, I have a distinct recollection of the nauseous taste of the Iceland moss bread; but the hay bread and the hay biscuit I remember having found very sweet and palatable. It should here be added that my father did not himself believe that any of these breads, excepting the cereal breads, could compete with wheat in nutritive power or price, so that, besides being inferior in quality, they could never be brought into use from their additional cost.*[26]

On the 10th of March of the same year Mr. Smee delivered a lecture at the London Institution[27] on aphides being the cause of the potato disease. Whenever he delivered a lecture or wrote a book, he always drew up on a card, or on one sheet of paper, the plan of the lecture or of the book. This he called the 'skeleton.' And in lecturing he only employed such brief notes as were contained in his 'skeleton.' I will here subjoin the skeleton of the lecture he delivered on the cause of the potato disease, as it is a very good example of all of them. The lecture clothed in its proper form will be found in the Appendix, No. XV.B.

    Insect Plagues. 800,000, St. Augustine. Barnes, 2000 miles covered by them.
    Aphides.
    Demonstration:
      1. Live plants.
      2. Healthy.
      3. Sucks juices.
      4. Impairs qualities.
      5. Alters properties.
      6. Bad sap not nourish.
      7. Imperfect tissue dies.
      8. Death local, remote.
      9. Remote death entirely kill the plant.
      10. Wild plants resist better than cultivated.
      11. Cultivated plants ill resist.
      12. Deposition of fibre.
      13. Propagation of diseased fibre.
      14. Injury to plants hastens transformation.
      15. Growth of fungi.

Destroyers of aphides—ladybirds, gauze-wings, synphidae, ichneumons, Chalcidida, birds.

Great fleas and little fleas have smaller fleas to bite 'em;
These smaller fleas have lesser fleas, so on *ad infinitum*.

    Aphides live on all plants.
    Vastator potato no novelty.
    Gangrene.

Vastator, name, leaf, root, history, anatomy, chemistry. Subsistence.

Tendrils. Oxyhydrogen. Microscope.
Future prospects, transitions.

'I will rebuke the devourer for your sake, and it shall not destroy the fruits of the ground.'
Whenever my father found a plant infested by an aphis, he used to secure some specimens, put them in a pill-box, and in the evening place them in Canada balsam[28] so as to carefully examine them. In this way he preserved all his evidences upon this point for future reference, and the name of the plant on which the insect fed was immediately scratched on the glass with a diamond, so that no source of error could possibly arise. The mode of fixing the insect in Canada balsam was very simple: a slip of glass was warmed over a candle, and a drop of the balsam was then placed upon it; the insect, whilst yet alive, was then placed on the balsam, and the glass was again very gently warmed in order to kill the insect; another piece of the glass was then heated over a candle and placed on the insect, when the creature was hermetically sealed up for ever.
It is necessary (he says) that the insect should be dry when it is mounted, and we must take especial care not to apply too much heat, which will corrugate the antenna and destroy the form of the insect. I strongly recommend to all entomologists this mode of preserving small insects; and having once properly secured them, they will last for an indefinite period, and can be handled without the slightest risk of injury.*[29]
Mr. Smee mounted many hundreds of these microscopic preparations of the *Aphis vastator*, and of slices of diseased potatoes; and these slides have, after the lapse of nearly thirty years, been the means by which this great controversy on the potato disease has probably at last been settled. For in the winter of 1876, when Mr. Worthington Smith[30] was investigating the subject of diseased potatoes, my father placed in his hands for examination 360 slides of diseased potatoes and of aphides, all of which the latter had himself mounted during the great potato murrain of 1846–1847. On placing these slides under a powerful microscope, Mr. Smith discovered that some of the aphides were completely filled with the fungus internally and covered with it externally, and that gentleman has further demonstrated that this insect punctures the potato, and inserts in it the fungus. A full account of these recent observations of Mr. Smith, together with two drawings which that gentleman has kindly made for me from my father's mounted specimens of the *Aphis vastator*, and of a diseased potato showing the resting spore of the fungus within the aphis, will be found in the Appendix, No. XV.c. By this it would appear that the primary cause of the potato murrain of 1846–1847 was the aphis, and the secondary cause the fungus. The following question, which my father addressed to a well-known actuary, is transcribed for the amusement of those who may be fond of figures:—
An aphis arrived on my cucumber, January 1, 1861. It had ten young ones at the end of ten days, ten more in ten days' time, and every succeeding ten days. Every

young one had ten young ten days after birth, and again every other ten days, till December 31st, 1861. How many aphides in all, if the mother aphis and her whole progeny were alive on the 31st of December?

Every aphis weighed one-tenth grain. What was the total weight of the aphides so produced?—ALFRED SMEE.

*Answer.*

Let $a$ = total number of generations from the mother aphis = 36.
Let $b$ = the number at each birth = 10.
The formula will be $1 + ab + (a - 1) b1 + (a - 2) b* +$ etc. $(a - 35) b^{36}$.
The answer to the first question, *i.e.* what number of aphides in all, is—
1,234,567,901,234,567,901,234,567,901,234,567,861 aphides, or nearly one and a quarter sextillions of aphides.
The answer to the second question is— 78,728,820,231,496,422,293,148,463 tons weight, or nearly 783 quadrillions[31] of tons weight.

Besides interesting himself with aphides, we find him occupied on other subjects; for in 1816, in conjunction with one of the managers, he was engaged on the ventilation of the theatre of the London Institution...

## Notes

1 Frederick Bravender, *The Potato Disease & how to Prevent it* (London: Farm Journal Office, 1880), p. 25.
2 Thomas Bell Salter (1814–1858), a physician and botanist who also practised medicine.
3 Alfred Smee (1818–1877) was a brilliant surgeon with an interest in chemical and electrical studies. He also loved horticulture, achieving notoriety for growing ferns at his home in Finsbury Circus in London. He was subsequently appointed Chairman of the Fruit Committee of the Royal Horticultural Society.
4 'Obituary', *Gardeners' Chronicle,* 20 January 1777.
5 Kevin Desmond, *Innovators in Battery Technology: Profiles of 95 Influential Electrochemists* (North Carolina: McFarland, 2016), p. 207.
6 Plarr's Lives of the Fellows Online, Royal College of Surgeons: http://livesonline.rcseng.ac.uk/biogs/E003537b.htm, accessed 10 January 2017.
7 Alfred Hutchinson Smee (1842–1901) was an English doctor and plant collector. His obituary read: 'Mr. A. H. Smee, M.R.C.S. Eng., a director and chief medical officer of the Gresham Life Assurance Society, died on Friday at the Grange, Hackbridge, Surrey. Mr. Smee contributed many articles to the medical and daily Press on the purity of water supplies and the prevention of epidemic diseases. A few days ago he published a book dealing with comparative rates of mortality', *Times,* 11 November 1901.
8 London: W.H. & L. Collingridge, 1873.
9 Global plants http://plants.jstor.org/stable/10.5555/al.ap.person.bm000392495 (accessed 10 Jan. 2017).
10 'Re-Appearance of the Aphis Vastator on the Potato Plant' plus Illustration, for *The Illustrated London News,* 12 June 1847.
11 Elizabeth Smee (1843–1920) was born in London.
12 Elizabeth May (Smee) Odling, *Memoir of the Late Alfred Smee, F.R.S. by his Daughter, with a selection from his miscellaneous writings* (London: George Bell and Sons, 1878).

13 William Odling (1829–1921) was a professor of chemistry who assisted with work on the Periodic Table. Like his father-in-law, he was appointed a fellow of the Royal Society of London.
14 'Obituary Notices of Fellows Decease', *Proceedings of the Royal Society of London*, Series A, Containing Papers of a Mathematical and Physical Character, Vol. 100, No. 707 (Mar. 1, 1922), pp. i-ix.
15 'Remarkable Trials. Knox v. Smee', *The Annual Register for 1864*, vol. 106 (London: Rivingtons, 1865), p. 232.
16 Bell Salter, who resided in the Isle of Wight, wrote a letter to the *Gardeners 'Chronicle*, in which he referred to the disease as, 'A blight of an unusual character'.
17 Probably Miles Joseph Berkeley (1803–1889) an English cryptogamist, Anglican clergyman, and expert on fungi and plant pathology. He was mentioned in the report by the Scientific Commission.
18 A genus of insects, notorious as agricultural pests.
19 Alfred Smee, *The Potatoe Plant, Its Uses and Properties: Together with the Cause of the Present Malady* (London: Longman, Brown, Green and Longmans, 1846). *Author's Note: This book is still in print, and is published by Messrs. Longman and Co., Paternoster Row.
20 Prince Albert of Saxe-Coburg and Gotha, husband of Queen Victoria, died in 1861, when aged 42.
21 J. Curtis was a prolific author on insects that attacked plants and vegetables. He was particularly known for his work on the turnip beetle.
22 Alfred Smee, *My garden, its plan and culture together with a general description of its geology, botany, and natural history. Illustrated with one thousand two hundred and fifty engravings* (London: Bell and Daldy, 1872). *Author's Note: See 'My Garden,' second edition, p. 477.
23 * Author's Note: In the 'Annual Register' for 1805 it is stated in an article upon the aphis, 'In some years the aphides are so numerous as to cause almost a total failure of the hop and *potato plantations;* in other years, the peas are equally injured, while exotics, raised in stoves and greenhouses, are frequently destroyed by their depredations.' In the Linnaean Transactions Mr. W. Curtis states, 'To *potatoes,* and even to corn, we have known the aphides to prove highly detrimental, and no less so to melons.' Mr. Curtis further states that 'the aphis is the grand cause of blights in plants, and that erroneous notions are entertained, not only by the vulgar and illiterate, but even by persons of education, that aphides attack none but sickly plants, with other notions as altogether false in fact as unphilosophical in principle.' * Author's Note: 'Instinct and Reason,' p. 263.
24 Mr. Punch (and his wife, Judy) were puppets. The show had its origins in the 17th century, but travelling puppet booths were popular in the 19th century. Punch came to symbolize a subversive character who could say and do outrageous things.
25 These days were officially instigated by the monarch, Queen Victoria. Also see, Peter Grey 'National humiliation and the great hunger: fast and famine in 1847' in *Irish Historical Studies*, vol. 32 (2000), pp. 193–216.
26 * Author's Note: * See 'Instinct and Reason,' p. 106.
27 Founded in 1806, the London Institution was educational organization that had a particular focus on promoting scientific knowledge. Initially, it was intended for Dissenters, who were barred from attending Oxford and Cambridge Universities.
28 A pale yellow resin obtained from the balsam fir, which was used for mounting preparations on microscope slides because it dried to a clear transparent film.
29 * Author's Note: See 'Potato Plant,' p. 14.
30 Worthington George Smith (1835–1917), an English artist and plant pathologist. In 1875, he published a paper about *Phytophthora infestans*, earning him the Royal Horticultural Society's Knightian gold medal.
31 A large amount—usually one thousand to the power of five.

# Part III

# APPEALS, PRAYS AND PHILANTHROPY

# 6

# DR JOHN EDGAR, *AN APPEAL IN BELFAST FOR THE PEOPLE OF CONNAUGHT* (OCTOBER 1846)

The part played by proselytizers during the Famine has cast a long shadow over the role of private charity during those tragic years. Moreover, the work of proselytizers in encouraging the poor to convert was primarily directed at the most vulnerable group in society, children. Consequently, 'souperism', as it was referred to in Ireland, remains a derogatory epithet in Famine memory. However, relative to other philanthropic activity, proselytism existed on a small scale and was confined to certain districts. It was also condemned by many within the Protestant churches. Nonetheless, the mixing of hunger with religious conversion only served to deepen the divisions between the main churches at the time and it continues to be a reviled part of Famine relief.

The repeated failure of the potato after 1845 was regarded by a number of Protestant evangelicals as an opportunity to renew their attempts proselytize the Catholic peasantry.
Dr John Edgar,[1] Moderator of the Presbyterian Church in Ireland, was one of those who regarded the Famine as an opportunity to intensify his involvement. Edgar was closely associated with two organizations that were formed in Belfast in the wake of the second potato failure, the Ladies' Relief Association for Connaught and the Belfast General Relief Fund. The Belfast General Relief Fund was formed largely at Edgar's recommendation. It had first convened on 2 January 1847 and comprised of leading Presbyterians as well as Anglicans from the town.[2] Dr Thomas Drew, the Anglican Minister of Christ Church in College Square, was Secretary of the Fund. Drew, also an evangelical, was known for his anti-Catholic, sectarian views.[3] The members of this body were all male.

The Ladies' Relief Association for Connaught was the first ladies' association to be formed in Belfast. The association had been the idea of Edgar who, when travelling in Connaught in the autumn of 1846, had witnessed the distress of the people first-hand. He realized that, 'if relief do not come speedily, [hundreds] will in a few weeks die of hunger'.[4] Edgar penned his concerns to the editor of the *Banner of Ulster*, a newspaper founded on Presbyterian principles.[5] In one letter he warned, 'Private benevolence must awake at once, and give and work for those that are ready to perish'.[6] The appeal was successful and resulted in a number of donations being sent. The money raised was distributed to Catholics, Episcopalians and Presbyterians.[7]

Upon his return to Belfast, Edgar convened a public meeting in the May Street Presbyterian Church, his lecture entitled, 'An Appeal for the People of Connaught'. A number of Presbyterian women were the first to respond, they forming the kernel of the Ladies' Relief Association. Edgar published his lecture as, *A Cry from Connaught: An appeal from a land which fainteth by reason of a famine of bread and of hearing the words of the Lord.* It sold 26,000 copies and raised £16,000.[8] Part of the funds were given to Dr. Feeny, the Roman Catholic Bishop of Killala, who was duly grateful.[9] This ecumenical goodwill proved to be short lived. In his many public appeals, Edgar's deeply-held evangelical views and his longer-term desire to make converts were apparent. However, these were tempered by his sympathy for the poor and aspects of their culture. Consequently, he argued that relief should be given without regard to religion, and that saving lives, rather than souls, should be their immediate concern. Edgar was more forthright about his ultimate ambitions when he appealed to evangelicals in America, through their Synod, to support his proselytizing missions in Ireland. At the same time, he alerted them to the dangers of the influx of so many Roman Catholics to their country, Edgar making a distinction between 'the *Northern Scotch-Irish* emigrant, and the *Southern Roman-Irish* emigrant'.[10] The American Synod appointed a committee that reported favourably, explaining that:

> The zeal and energy with which this Mission has been prosecuted by our brethren of the Presbyterian Church of Ireland call forth our admiration; and the success with which their operations have been attended in the evangelization of the Roman Catholic districts of Ireland cannot but be most gratifying to all the friends of evangelical truth, and encouraging to those who are immediately engaged in this good work.[11]

By the end of 1847, the 72-strong Ladies' Relief Association had raised £4,615–6–1.[12] At this stage their mission changed with all future income to be used to establish 'industrial schools' in which the children would be taught needlework and knitting. While the children worked, they were also taught to read 'and made familiar with the Scriptures'.[13] By the beginning of 1851, Dr Edgar had fifty-six female teachers working with 2,000 pupils and their families. In keeping with Edgar's admiration for Irish culture, many of his missionaries were fluent in Irish and used vernacular versions of the Bible.[14] Nicholas Murray, an immigrant to America who had converted from Catholicism to Presbyterianism,[15] and then engaged in public wrangles with fellow Irish immigrant, Archbishop John Hughes, visited the industrial schools in 1853. He was fulsome in his praise, opining that 'the only cure for Ireland is that which these schools are applying, to instruct and to evangelize the people. When the knowledge of the Bible and of Jesus Christ supplants the wretched idolatry of Popery, the days of Ireland's mourning are ended'.[16] Not all within the Protestant churches were as complimentary. For example, Rev. Richard St. George, the Rector of Crossmolina, published a number of letters accusing Edgar and his followers of gross exaggeration, while claiming that the Church of Ireland had been more successful in its proselytizing work, which pre-dated that undertaken by Edgar.[17] In general, however, Edgar was critical of the work of the Anglican Church during the Famine, in particular of their attempts to proselytize through the medium of the English language, he averring: 'Is it at all surprising that the Reformation made small progress in Ireland when those in authority persisted in attempting to spread it by means of a language which the people did not understand?'[18]

In 1866, Edgar died of throat cancer, while seeking treatment in Dublin. His remains were returned to Belfast by train, for burial in Balmoral Cemetery.[19] Twenty years after the publication of his appeals on behalf of Connaught, Edgar's interventions were generally regarded negatively in that part of Ireland, he even being likened to Baron Munchausen (a master of exaggeration) for inflating the success of his proselytizing missions.[20]

## DR JOHN EDGAR, *AN APPEAL FOR THE PEOPLE OF CONNAUGHT* (1847), REPRINTED IN WILLIAM DOOL KILLEN, *MEMOIR OF DR JOHN EDGAR* (BELFAST: C. AITCHISON, 1867)

### APPEAL FOR THE PEOPLE OF CONNAUGHT.

It is religious and wise to say that the present great calamity on our native land will be overruled for good, for the hand of God is in it; and however dark the dispensation may be to us, all is for good, and all will in the end be well.

But there is a species of heartless philosophy current which says this calamity will, in the end, be good for Ireland, because it will cure the Irish of their laziness, and force them to seek a better food than potatoes. As to the latter part of this philosophy, all I have to say is, that, if the potato be an evil, it is one which millions would gladly bear; and may the poor of our country never have a worse evil than good potatoes and plenty of good milk and butter to them.

As to the laziness of the Irish, I don't believe it; I don't know of any country where people work hard for the mere love of work, neither do I know any country where people work well who are not well paid. In Connaught, where I have lately been, men are paid eightpence, and sometimes sixpence a-day, board wages; and I put it to yourselves, is a man called on to work himself to death for eightpence a-day.

But this talk about laziness, and about potatoes being bad food, does not touch the real merits of the case. It distresses me to hear men talking very learnedly and very coldly about the necessity of teaching the Irish, in present circumstances, a taste for luxuries, for the comforts of life, and so forth; because such talk evidences melancholy apathy, and ignorance too, of the real state of the case.

The real state of the case in regard to the districts of Connaught, for which I wish to engage your sympathies, is this: the land, in general, is unproductive, and the population is so overflowing, that a father of a family, of perhaps six or eight, thinks himself fortunate in having got hold, at a high rent, of three or four acres. These acres would not grow wheat; and suppose that they were all sown in oats, they would not afford food to his family, even had he not a farthing of rent to pay.[21] What, therefore, is he forced to do? He is forced to have recourse to potatoes, simply because an acre of potatoes furnishes as much food as four acres of corn.

The real fact of the case, I repeat, is this: the poor Connaught man eats none of his own corn, none of his own butter, none of his pig; corn, butter, pig—all go to pay his rent; and whatever potatoes remain after the pig is fed, are the only food, the only support of his family.

It is a libel, therefore, on the poor Irishman to say that he is too lazy or too savage to seek for better food than potatoes; his only nourishment is potatoes, because the other products of his farm go to his landlord, and because potatoes are the only crop sufficiently productive to save himself and his family from starvation.

It is mighty fine for Englishmen, or even Irishmen here in Ulster, to talk of luxuries, where there are so many manufactories, and where, not only a man himself, but his wife and children, can earn good wages; but the Connaught man has no manufacture, no employment for his family; and for himself, only partial employment as a day-labourer, at eightpence a-day.

When distress comes on a man in humble life here, he has some little store on which to draw—if not money, at least furniture, or extra clothing, which he can place in 'pawn'; but the Connaught man has no clothing but what he wears; and as for furniture, you might enter house after house in Connaught, as I have, and find no table, no chair, no cupboard, no bedstead deserving the name, no spoon, no knife, no anything, except a square box, and a potato pot, which a pawnbroker would take in pawn.

In fact, a large proportion of the houses are not fit for anything that we would dignify with the name of furniture. They have no chimney, no window, their floors are fearfully damp, their roofs are often not watertight, and the general custom is to have cow, pig, ass, and geese, all in the same apartment with the family—all sleeping together, and all going out and in by the same door.

Such, then, being a true picture of the people of the Mayo district of Connaught, whose claims I advocate—such being their condition, even in the best seasons—their houses cheerless, and dark, and damp, and smoky, and filthy too, as asses, cows, pigs, and poultry can make them—their corn the property of the landlord—their only food potatoes—what, I ask you, must be their state, when, in an awfully mysterious Providence, their only food has been entirely destroyed?—what, I ask you, is the remedy which, in such circumstances, you propose.

Let the landlords, do you say, not demand their rent for the present year? Some landlords there are willing, I am sure, to do everything that justice and mercy demand. No people can have a better landlord than the Earl of Arran.[22] I heard high praises of an excellent family resident at Easky. Mr. Jones, who has established a mail communication to Ballina, deserves all praise for his public spirit and enterprise; and in the heart of Connaught there lives a John Knox, worthy of his great name, because he is all that a resident landlord and a Christian gentleman ought to be.[23]

There are, however, other landlords of a very different spirit—some non-resident, some resident—who have no heart to feel for the poor. I have heard of eight guineas an acre having been charged for land because it lies along a bay, where there was a good fishing-station; and though it has long ceased to be good, the land sets for four pounds ten shillings an acre yet. To seize the poor man's barley on that land for rent, in such a year as this, is surely cruel. Deeply as I detest whisky-drinking, I never detested it more thoroughly than when I looked into a room, one evening, and saw a man sitting drinking punch, after having that day seized the grain of his poor tenants for rent.[24]

But even though all the landlords were willing to forego their rents, many of them have it not in their power, being themselves deeply in debt, and their property heavily mortgaged to their creditors, who are the real receivers of their rents.

It is not for me to speculate what amount of assistance Government will afford. Where there are a few poor among many rich, something effective can be done for them; but where nearly all are poor—where young and old, healthy and sick, male and female, able-bodied and infirm, are in one mass of destitution and starvation—what can be done for them? Government must give cautiously—must give for work done—must give in small proportions—must give chiefly in the frontier towns; and how can such charity meet the whole case? Here is a family with a widowed mother at its head; there is another with a bed-ridden father; and here again are two or three maiden sisters living unprotected in the same wretched hovel. Who is to earn money at the public works for them? and, supposing meal to be given out, a stone at a time, to each family, when a poor, hunger-bitten, debilitated creature travels eight or ten miles to and from the Government store, and hangs in the street for half a winter's day, waiting his turn, won't he have earned his stone of Indian meal very hard and sore, when, wet and weary, he has brought it to his comfortless home?

Whatever Government may do or may not do, there is a plain duty and a blessed privilege before us. God calls us to contribute generously and at once, to prevent our own countrymen, our own brothers and sisters, from dying of hunger. Famine is not an evil threatened, or at a distance; it has actually begun, and there is not a moment to lose. The potato crop is not a twentieth part of what it used to be; and it is all bad, wholly unfit for human food. The only potatoes fit to eat were at scattered stalks from last year's seed, growing here and there among the corn, and they have been all grubbed up and consumed. What, then, is to be done? Do you expect a family to live on the handful of cabbage in the garden? or if they have a few stooks of barley, are they to defy the landlord and the law, and eat them, and leave for next year no seed and no hope of life at all? Even were they to attempt this, I don't see how it is to be done; for over large districts of many square miles, there is no such thing as a mill; nobody, even in the best of times, making meal; nobody, except perhaps a mother with a child at her breast, tasting such a luxury as stirabout; and the old querns only used for grinding malt for private stills, being too slow and rough a machine to make, in any reasonable time, or indeed to make at all, a sufficient quantity of good meal.

Happy, therefore, are they who, in such circumstances, live within three or four miles of a town, and one or two of a turf bog; for, if they have an ass, and have paid for a bit of bog, they can send a couple of creels full to town,[25] and sell them for two pence! Amid poverty and starvation, it is refreshing to look on the pleasant faces, and hear the cheerful conversation of the little girls along the roads, mounted behind their creels, driving without bridle or halter the obedient ass. Let any man who wants to learn genuine politeness go and learn it from these little girls. One day, when I gave a penny to a boy, his sister, riding on an ass before me, immediately thanked me most courteously. The shabby suspicion arose in my mind that this was a civil hint for a penny to herself—but no, it was genuine gratitude—genuine honest politeness; and when, after some conversation with her, I was passing away from her along a different road, perhaps never to meet her again, her affectionate 'God speed you on your journey,' so cheerful and so kind, forced me to feel how much I was her inferior in real good manners, and perhaps in real religion too.

But, suppose that this genuine lady of God's own making behind the creels, were not mistress of an ass or of turf, what then must be her fate? During harvest, for a very few weeks, she might struggle to keep body and soul together, by following the example of another very interesting girl whom I overtook, with a rough, heavy creel on her back, climbing up a steep rock in the channel of the torrent, where her native village is built, lest it should occupy any arable land that might bring the landlord four guineas an acre. 'Ah,' said I, 'my good girl, it is too hard to make you carry turf upon your back in such a creel as that; have you no ass to relieve you of your burden?' 'Sir,' said she, modestly, 'it is not turf, but heads of barley, I carry.' 'And where do you get them?' 'I gather them after the reapers.' 'And what will you do with them when you go home?' 'I will beat them, Sir, with a stick.' What an interesting illustration of Scripture, thought I—what a genuine Irish Ruth is here![26] I wish that some accomplished artist, like him who painted the picture of Ruth, which I see hanging on so many drawing-room walls, would paint a likeness of our modern Irish Ruth, and hang it up before the eyes of all Irishmen, to wake up in their hearts some gallant and generous spirit on behalf of their poor starving countrywomen, forced to serve as beasts of burden, and eke out, in hunger and nakedness, a wretched existence; while pampered lap-dogs and tabby cats are smothering in their own fat.

It is to me a source of sincerest gratification that I should be honoured with even the humblest place, as an advocate of a people so highly deserving as those who claim an interest in your sympathies now. They are genuine native Irish, far away behind their own bogs and mountains from the contaminating influence of a mercantile, polished, refined, hypocritical world.

You call them ignorant, and I don't deny it; but remember that the vast majority of them are able to speak fluently two languages, and that is what a very small part of the present audience could do.[27] They are ignorant, you repeat; well, it may be so, but they are willing to learn, and I have examined hundreds of them, and, had time permitted, I might have examined thousands of them, who can read English well, and who, from love to their own mother tongue, the Irish, have, at great sacrifices, learned to read in it, and understand the blessed Book of God.[28]

They are bigoted Romanists, you say, steeped in superstition, and the slaves of priestcraft. The more shame for us, I reply, who have not exerted ourselves as we should, to enlighten them and convert them to God; and the greater shame and the deeper disgrace will it be to us still, if we do not embrace the opportunities which Connaught is offering now, for its people are accessible—they are inquiring, they are reading, and arguing; there are noble spheres of usefulness open, and spiritual fields are white to harvest. This, however, is not my subject now; I hope soon to have an opportunity of directing public attention to spiritual famine in Connaught, but our effort now is to save the perishing body; and, whether our countryman and brother be a Protestant or Romanist, we acknowledge the claim which, in the day of his deep distress, he has on our purses and our hearts. Our brother is starving, and, till we have satisfied his hunger, we have no time to inquire whether he is Protestant or Romanist. If we would act the part of the good Samaritan, it is enough for us to know that the cry of distress comes from a poor mortal like ourselves, and our first enquiry, our first anxiety, will be how best to do him good.

In acting thus kindly towards the people of Connaught, you will only be imitating the great kindness which the poorest among them would show you, if you were living or travelling among them. In the midst of abject poverty and absolute destitution, their generosity and hospitality are most affecting. They make no inquiry whether you are Protestant or Roman Catholic; it is enough that you are a man and a stranger, for with them stranger is a holy name, and whatever their house contains is at your service. 'How sorry I am,' said a woman to me, 'that I was not at home when you called, that I might have had the happiness of welcoming you to my house.' This house of hers was a hole in a bank, with something at the fire-side like a hen roost, or what flax is dried on in Connaught, as the only bed for a large family;[29] and so many holes in the roof, unto the top of which I stepped off a ditch, that the smoke was a chief thing to prevent the sun from shining inside the house as clearly as out-side, though there was nothing anywhere except in the roof, pretending to be a window. One day, after hungry and weary travelling for nine hours, I found my companions squatted round a little four penny loaf in rather a respectable sort of establishment, for there were two jugs, and one or two tea cups, out of which we drank huge quantities of water, yet, though our hospitable host's poor loaf did not leave a wreck behind, and his hen's nest was left without even a nest egg, not a farthing of recompense would he receive; no, no, he was too happy to have the honour of receiving under his poor roof such honourable gentlemen, and it was only by contriving to slip something into the hand of his child, that we got off with a safe conscience from a family on whom we had pounced with such an omniverous appetite.

Another day, when passing, hungry and faint, by a house at which we had called in the morning, the mistress cried after us—'Sure, you're not going to pass without tasting a bit of what I have prepared for you.' Right glad to hear the news, we rushed in, and could scarcely believe our eyes, to find that our visit had been the death of two unfortunate hens, which, while we devoured, the good woman insisted on attending us, and, in the true patriarchal style of Abraham's politeness, when he entertained the angels, both she and her husband refused to sit down with guests, whom they wished most highly to honour.[30] Such, in this case, was the style of superior politeness, and disinterested high-minded hospitality, that every one of our party felt that it would be esteemed a distressing affront to offer anything in the shape of remuneration; and we could, therefore, only tender our warmest expressions of gratitude.

Hospitality, it is said, is the virtue of savage life; but life in Connaught is not savage; it is peaceful, remarkably peaceful; it is polite—eminently polite; it is social in the best sense of the term, it is delightfully grateful; and I trust that your liberality will make Connaught gratitude flow as a river of oil; both to strangers, and to friends, and neighbours, the Connaught peasant is pre-eminently kind. It is a melancholy fact that Romanism, to a fearful extent, profanes the Sabbath day; yet, while on the evening of Sabbath eight days, I passed over some dozen miles of country to preach, almost the only violations of the Sabbath which I witnessed were by poor fellows, here and there trying to find, in their desolate field, a few blighted potatoes, for a comfortless supper.

There was one exception, however, and I expressed surprise and grief at seeing a large boon of reapers spread over a whole field, in full work on the Sabbath evening. The explanation was this—and I give it as I got it, without comment— 'The field belongs to a poor widow, whose husband lately died. These people have hard scraping, every week-day, to collect as much as will keep themselves from starving, and they are embracing the opportunity of the Sabbath's rest, for doing an act of kindness and mercy for one, who, like Duncan's widow, is forced to cry to her orphan children—

> The oak is fallen, the sapling bow
> Is all Duncraggon's shelter now.'[31]

Had you been present at the funeral of that husband, you would be able to testify, as I can from personal observation, to the strength of the ties of good neighbourhood and good fellowship which bind Connaught hearts together. The abominable service of whisky at funerals is not there, which draws together many thirsty throats in districts of our own province; men and women come in large numbers, solemn and serious, to testify friendship for the living, and honour to the dead; each relation and intimate acquaintance enters the house of mourning with suitable expressions of sorrow, and, as Campbell says—

> Woman's softer soul in woe dissolves aloud.[32]

No hired mourning women are there, such as those to be found in some parts of Ulster, and such as the prophet Jeremiah refers to,[33] when he says, 'Call for the mourning women that they may come, and send for cunning women, that they may come, and let them take up a wailing for us, that our eyes may run down with tears, and our eyelids gush out with waters.' The first time I heard the Irish cry in a part of county Down, it impressed me with the deepest solemnity and melancholy;[34] but my feelings were turned to disgust and indignation, when I happened to look to the mourning women, and saw their levity. The funeral I lately attended in Connaught was orderly, solemn, deeply impressive—every countenance was pensive, every expression was sad, passengers stood silent and grave at the side of the road, till the cart containing the honoured remains was far away, and horsemen, whatever their speed, reined in, and leaned pensive over the saddle, till the mournful procession passed by. There was no keening along the road, as is customary in the north, no women appointed to make melancholy melody in the dismal coronach; I feared, while I stood pensive and alone in the venerable graveyard of Easky, that in expectation of hearing the Irish cry, I had followed the funeral in vain. All at once, at my side, a woman, kneeling with her face down upon a grave, commenced the mournful wail; it was a wail of real woe for a departed friend, and forthwith the old ruined church and the whole field of graves resounded with loud and bitter lamentations, from wives, and sisters, and mothers, pouring forth the unrestrained sorrow of their hearts, over their beloved and honoured dead.

Would I have deserved the name of man, if, amid such scenes as these, I had not deeply sympathised—had not given away so as to be obliged to borrow money for carrying me home—had I not resolved, in God's name, to appeal to the Christian public, as I have done, and as I now do again, lest many an Irish cry should rise, loud and wild, over whole families starved; lest, over whole districts, there should be none to kneel and wail upon the full grave, as the devouring pestilence crowded into the narrow house, what the murderous famine had spared.

Brethren, I detain you no longer. I afflict your hearts and my own no more. I have come from the barren bog and the wild mountain glen, to present the petition of the starving to the liberal and rich of prosperous Ulster, and more especially to those whose hearts the liberality of the gospel has enlarged. I come from the valley of the shadow of death to the world of light, and competence, and comfort, to cry on behalf of God's poor, to every one whom my voice can reach, 'If thou draw out thy soul to the hungry, and satisfy the afflicted soul, then shall thy light rise in obscurity, and thy darkness be as the noonday.'[35]

It is to me a subject of sincerest joy, that the first effort in Ulster on behalf of the Roman Catholics of Connaught, has been made by those who have also taken the lead in seeking their spiritual good—in supplying them with the bread from heaven, of which if a man eat he shall hunger no more. In answer to my former appeal, I have already received fifty pounds, and the collection this night will show our Connaught brethren, still more fully, that all our efforts on their behalf are prompted by love; that, therefore, they may trust us, that the religion which we teach them is a religion of love; and that the Bible which we put into their hands is the book in which God's own Spirit teaches many such a lesson as this—'Is not this the fast that I have chosen? Is it not to deal thy bread to the hungry, and that thou bring the poor that are cast out to thy house; when thou sees the naked that thou cover him, and that thou hide not thyself from thine own flesh.'[36]

## Notes

1 John Edgar (1798–1866) was born in Ballynahinch in Co. Down, the eldest son of Rev. Samuel Edgar, who also taught at the Belfast Academical Institution.
2 'Destitution', *The Belfast News-Letter*, 5 January 1849.
3 In 1857, Drew's virulently anti-Catholic sermon to local Orangemen is thought to have led to two months of sectarian rioting. See, Hugh McLeod, *European Religion in the Age of Great Cities: 1830–1930* (London: Routledge, 2005), p. 151.
4 'Famine in Connaught' reprinted in William Dool Killen, *Memoir of Dr John Edgar* (Belfast: C. Aitchison, 1867), p. 203. Killen (1806–1902) was an Irish Presbyterian minister and church historian, who had been born in Ballymena in Co. Antrim.
5 The *Banner of Ulster* had been founded in June 1842, by the Rev. William Gibson, minister of Rosemary Street Presbyterian Church in Belfast.
6 Killen, 'Famine in Connaught', p. 207.
7 'Famine in Connaught. Dr Edgar's Appeal', *Belfast News-Letter*, 13 October 1846.

8 'Rev. John Edgar (1798 - 1866) Clergyman and philanthropist' in *Dictionary of Ulster Biography:* http://www.newulsterbiography.co.uk/index.php/home/viewPerson/2007, accessed 15 December 2016.
9 Killen, *Memoir*.
10 Dr John Edgar, *An appeal on behalf of the Home Mission of the General Assembly of the Presbyterian Church in Ireland, respectfully addressed to their Christian brethren of all evangelical denominations in America* (Belfast, 1847), p. 2.
11 'Report of the Committee on the Appeal from Ireland', *The Evangelical Repository . . . by the Associate Synod of North America* (Philadelphia: W. S. Young, 1847), p. 36.
12 *Transactions of the Central Relief Committee of the Society of Friends during the Famine in Ireland, in 1846 and 1847* (Dublin: Hodges and Smith, 1852), p. 46.
13 William Dool Killen, *The ecclesiastical history of Ireland from the earliest period to the present time* (London: Macmillan and Co., 1875), p. 496.
14 Shaftesbury Society and Ragged School Union, *The Ragged School Union Magazine*, vol. v (London: Partridge and Oakey, 1853), p. 190.
15 Nicholas Murray (1802–1861) was born in Ballinasloe, Co. Galway but emigrated to New Jersey in America. Despite being a convert from Catholicism, he rose to be Moderator of the General Assembly of the Presbyterian Church in the United States of America. He wrote his polemical articles under the pen-name, 'Kirwan'.
16 Kirwan, *Men and things as I saw them in Europe* (New York: Harper and Brothers, 1853), pp. 253–54. Kirwan was the pen-name of Nicholas Murray, see above.
17 Letter by Rev. St George, 'The Church in Connaught', *The Irish Ecclesiastical Journal,* no. 101 (December 1848), pp. 186–188.
18 Quoted in *Dictionary of Ulster Biography*.
19 'Funeral of Dr Edgar', *Freeman's Journal*, 31 August 1866.
20 'Ballina is the Belfast of the North-West', *Telegraph or Connaught Ranger*, 20 June 1866.
21 A farthing (originally, a fourthling), was equal to one-quarter of an old penny. The first farthing was minted in 1806. Prior to that, people would cut a penny into two or four pieces to create a smaller valued coin.
22 Philip York Gore (1801–1884), the fourth Earl of Arran, held land in Tirawley Barony, Co. Mayo. It had been granted to the family under the Act of Settlement of 1662. The Earl was a career diplomat. The *Mayo Constitution* wrote favourably of his relief efforts, following the second failure of the potato crop, he directing his agent, John Symes, to purchase a large quantity of oatmeal for distribution amongst his tenants.
23 There were a number of landlords of this name. Possibly John Knox of Castlereagh (1783–1861), one of the group of landlords who, in November 1846, privately purchased a cargo of Indian Meal in Liverpool for distribution and sale amongst their tenants (*Tyrawly Herald,* 26 November 1846). Alternatively, Captain John Knox of Greenwood Park, who was a Guardian of the Ballina Poor Law Union.
24 Edgar was a keen supporter of temperance. In 1829, he inspired the founding of a temperance movement in Ulster by symbolically pouring his own whiskey out of a window.
25 A creel (Irish – *cliabh*) is a wicker basket that can be used for a number of purposes. Traditionally in the west of Ireland, they were used for carrying turf. Smaller ones could be carried on the back, and larger ones, on a donkey or ass.
26 Ruth was a young widow in the Old Testament, known for her goodness and loyalty. Many images depict her gleaning in a field of wheat or barley, or carrying a sheaf of corn.
27 In 1841, an estimated four million people could speak Irish as their first language. By 1891, it had fallen to 680,000. For practical purposes, many of these people also spoke English.

28  An Irish language version of the Bible had first been completed in the mid-seventeenth century. Edgar, who was a champion of Irish culture, encouraged his missionaries to learn Irish and to use an Irish language version of the Bible.
29  Linen production, based on the growth of flax, had been traditionally carried out in Co. Mayo but, by the mid-nineteenth century, the industry had become highly concentrated in Ulster, this province effectively having a monopoly after 1850.
30  An Old Testament story in which Abraham and his wife, Sarah, entertain three visitors, who turned out to be angels.
31  From the narrative poem, 'The Lady of the Lake' (1810) by Sir Walter Scott (1771–1832), an Edinburgh-born writer who helped to revive an interest in Scottish culture. He was a Lowland Presbyterian. The poem is based on an Arthurian legend. The actual lines are:

> The oak has fall'n, the sapling bough Is all
> Duncraggan's shelter now . . .

32  Thomas Campbell (1777–1844) was a Scottish poet who authored *Gertrude of Wyoming; A Pennsylvanian Tale* (1809). It was set in 1778, during the American Revolution, when 300 Revolutionaries had been killed by Loyalists. Its historical accuracy was later called into question.
33  Jeremiah is sometimes called the weeping prophet as he was distressed by impiety. He was one of the four major prophets in Hebrew Scripture.
34  Keening (from the Irish *caoineadh*, meaning to cry or to weep) is a vocal lament for the dead. The keening woman (*bean chaointe*) would sometimes rock or clap her hands. Because if its association with Ireland, it was sometimes referred to as 'the Irish cry', although it was also used in Gaelic Scotland. Edgar had a personal interest in this funeral practice. Keening was one of the mourning rituals that was little observed during the Famine as the levels of mortality proved to be overwhelming.
35  From the Book of Isaiah, who was a prophet in the Old Testament.
36  Also from the Book of Isaiah.

# 7

# THE QUEEN'S LETTER FOR IRELAND (JANUARY 1847) AND CONSEQUENT PARLIAMENTARY QUESTIONS

Similarly to Charles Trevelyan, Queen Victoria remains a controversial figure both in folk memory and the historiography of the Great Famine. A widespread belief, that was popularized by Charles Stewart Parnell, was that she made no private contribution to Famine relief.[1] In fact, in January 1847, she made a donation of £2,000 to the British Relief Association, thus making her the largest individual donor to Famine charities. Moreover, her involvement extended beyond this intervention. As early as October 1846, Victoria, in her capacity as head of the Established Church, had called on Anglicans to observe three consecutive Sundays of prayer for 'relief from the dearth and scarcity now existing in parts of the United Kingdom'. In Ireland, the prayer days were to extend to late November. Additionally, the 20 November 1846 was to be observed by Anglicans in Ireland as a day of humiliation.[2] The impetus for these requests actually came from Prime Minister, Lord John Russell, but a call for national religious observances had to be issued by the monarch.[3]

On 13 January 1847, Victoria issued a Queen's Letter.[4] Again, she was acting at the behest of the Prime Minister.[5] In it, she made an appeal to Anglicans in Britain to raise subscriptions for Ireland and, to a lesser extent, for Scotland.[6] The Letter, which was published in a number of newspapers, was addressed to the Archbishop of Canterbury, with a copy made to the Archbishop of York.[7] At the same time that this appeal was made, a 'Day of Fast and Humiliation' was called for. Privately, the Queen was skeptical of the value of such an activity, as were a number of leading Anglican clerics including Archbishop Whately in Dublin.[8] Moreover, public opposition was led by the London *Times*, who warned that, 'A general fast in the British metropolis in the middle of the nineteenth century on account of a remote provincial famine will supply abundant materials to the witty and the dull'.[9] The Society of Friends and the Catholic Church did not observe the Day of Fast, although the latter held special prayers on that day.[10] The Reverend Dr. Adler, Chief Rabbi of the Jews in the United Kingdom,[11] issued a form of prayer to be used in the synagogues within his control on the day of the general fast.[12]

The date set for the fast was 24 March. On that day, a Wednesday, the Queen, Prince Albert and the royal household attended a divine service in the private chapel of the Palace.[13] The Stock Exchange and other major businesses in London and elsewhere closed for the day, while prayers were read in the House of Commons before the Members proceeded to hear a service in St Margaret's Church.[14] Whatever else the impact of the day proved to be, it served to reinforce a providentialist interpretation of the Famine, thus lessening the role of human agency and responsibility.

The Queen's Letter raised £170,571 0s. 10d. for Irish relief. A second appeal was issued in October, but it had less support within the government and clearly within the country; it only raising £30,167 14s. 4d. Public opposition to a second Queen's Letter was again led by the *Times* who claimed, with some accuracy:

> Where a sovereign was given last year, it will be half a crown this; where half a crown then, a shilling now; where a shilling, nothing at all. The result will be that public benevolence, which at all times is rather hard to keep alive, will go out altogether...[15]

The question of how the money donated as a result of the Queen's Letter should be used was debated in parliament. It was decided that the proceeds of the two Letters should be entrusted to the British Relief Association, an organization that had been formed by wealthy merchants and bankers in London in January 1847. From the outset, they had worked closely with the government, in effect, with Trevelyan, which gave them valuable access to information and resources, but also allowed the meddlesome civil servant to have some say in how the money should be expended.

In addition to the Letters, the Queen showed her support for charity in other ways. In March 1847, she attended a benefit performance at Her Majesty's Theatre, in London, 'in aid of the fund for the distressed Irish and Scotch'.[16] The event produced over £1,300.[17] Most private donations dried up at the end of 1847, leaving the poor at the mercy of a newly amended Poor Law.[18] Despite evidence of extreme suffering, the government remained reluctant to intervene. In June 1849, in an effort to rekindle charitable interventions, a number of politicians made donations to Ireland. Victoria contributed £500. The proceeds were again entrusted to Count Strzelecki of the British Relief Association.[19]

Shortly afterwards, in August 1849, the Queen and her family visited Ireland. It was her first visit to the country and her stay was brief and confined to the east of the country, she travelling between locations on the royal yacht. Ostensibly, her public reception was warm, but it also proved divisive, with the fiery Archbishop of Tuam, John MacHale, refusing to put his name to a welcome address from the Catholic Church hierarchy.[20] Victoria returned to Ireland again in 1853 and 1861. Her fourth and final visit took place in April 1900, when she was aged and infirm. In protest, advanced nationalist Maud Gonne penned an article entitled, 'The Famine Queen'.[21] The sobriquet persisted and contributed to the myth of a Queen who had done nothing to assist her starving Irish subjects.

## THE QUEEN'S LETTER OF 13 JANUARY 1847 (REPRINTED IN THE *TIMES*, 22 JANUARY 1847)

The Right Hon. the Home Secretary on Wednesday transmitted to the Lord Primate, and also to the Archbishop of York, the Queen's Letter in aid of the subscription for the distressed population in Ireland and the Highlands of Scotland.

The following is a copy of the document:

QUEEN'S LETTER TO HIS GRACE THE ARCHBISHOP OF CANTERBURY FOR A COLLECTION IN AID OF THE SUBSCRIPTIONS ENTERED INTO FOR THE RELIEF OF A LARGE PORTION OF THE POPULATION IN IRELAND AND IN SOME DISTRICTS OF SCOTLAND.

Victoria Regina.

Most Reverend Father in God, our right trusty and right entirely beloved councillor, we greet you well. Whereas a large portion of the population in Ireland, and in some districts of Scotland, is suffering severe distress owing to the failure of the ordinary supplies of food; and whereas many of our subjects have entered into voluntary subscriptions for their relief, and have at the same time humbly prayed for us to issue our Royal letters, directed to the Lord Archbishop of Canterbury and the Lord Archbishop of York, authorizing them to promote contributions within their respective provinces for the same benevolent purpose:

We, taking the premises into our Royal consideration, and being always ready to give the best encouragement and countenance to such humane and charitable undertakings, are graciously pleased to condescend to their request; and we do hereby direct that these our letters be by you communicated to the several Suffragan Bishops within your province,[22] expressingly requiring them to take care than publication be made hereof on such Sunday in the present or the ensuing month, and in such places with the respective dioceses, as the said Bishops shall appoint; and that upon this occasion the ministers in each parish do effectively excite their parishioners to a liberal contribution, which shall be collected the week following at their respective dwellings by the churchwardens or overseers of the poor in each parish; and the ministers of the several parishes are to cause the sums so collected to be paid immediately into the hands of the Bank of England, to be accounted for by them, and applied to the carrying on and promoting the above mentioned good designs.

As so we bid you very heartily farewell.

Given at our Court of St James, the 13th day of January, in the 10th year of our reign.

By Her Majesty's Command,

G. Grey.[23]

To the Most Reverend Father in God, our right trusty and right entirely beloved councilor, William Lord Archbishop of Canterbury, Primate of all England, and Metropolitan.

## COST OF RELIEF (IRELAND). House of Commons Debates, *Hansard,* 28 January 1847, vol. 89, c. 506.

### MR. G. A. HAMILTON[24]

said, he had a question to ask of the right hon. Baronet the Secretary for the Home Department,[25] of which he had given him intimation. It appeared there was a collection about to be made under the authority of a Queen's Letter, for the relief of the distressed poor in Ireland; the question he had to ask—and he believed the amount of the collection would be influenced considerably upon the answer—was this: whether the sum to be collected was to be distributed by paid commissioners—paid out of the fund, as was the case with the Newfoundland collection,[26] and which caused some dissatisfaction—or whether, the fund, being collected from the Church in this country, it was intended to administer it by an agency with which either the heads of the Church, or the clergy of the Established Church in Ireland, with whom their brethren in this country deeply sympathized, were to be in any way connected?

### SIR GEORGE GREY

stated, in answer to the question of the hon. Member, that it was not intended that there should be any paid commissioners, as was the case with the collection made under the Queen's Letter for the distressed people of Newfoundland. It was the intention of Government to place the fund to be collected at the disposal of the London committee, which comprised some gentlemen of the highest character in the country, and many of the dignitaries of the Church;[27] and, in answer to the latter part of the question, the fund would be distributed through the local relief committees in Ireland, comprising, as was well known, the clergymen of the Established Church in each parish within the district.

## THE QUEEN'S LETTER (IRELAND). HOUSE OF COMMONS DEBATES, *HANSARD*, 8 FEBRUARY 1847, VOL. 89, C. 942

### SIR R. H. INGLIS[28]

was anxious distinctly to understand the Secretary for the Home Department on the subject of the distribution of the money which had been, and he hoped would be, collected for Ireland under the Queen's Letter. Through what channel would the money thus obtained be distributed? Much might depend upon the answer of the right hon. Baronet.

### SIR GEORGE GREY

The same question was put to me a few evenings ago, and I then stated that Government thought that the best mode of distributing the subscriptions would be to place them at the disposal of the committee of the British Association for the Relief of Distress in Ireland, and in certain districts of Scotland. That committee possesses a high character and standing in the country, and they have published the details of the plans upon which they proceed in their distributions. A very large sum has already been disposed of by them, and they are acting in connexion with the Government. I think that the mode they adopt is most effectual in rendering the money available to the utmost extent.

## Notes

1 This claim was made by Charles Stewart Parnell during a tour of North America in early 1880. It was immediately refuted by Lord Randolph Churchill, *Inangahua Times*, vol. 11, 22 March 1880, p. 2.
2 Lord John Russell to the Archbishop of Canterbury, 8 September 1846, Russell Papers, National Archives of England (NAE), 30/22/5C.
3 Philip Williamson, 'State Prayers, Fast and Thanksgivings: Public Worshipping in Britain 1830–1897', *Past and Present,* 200, 1(2008), pp. 121–174.
4 'The Queen's Letter', *Times*, 22 January 1847.
5 Lord John Russell to Queen Victoria to Archbishop of Canterbury, 6 January 1847, Royal Archives, Windsor, folio 16/6.
6 The potato had also failed in the Highlands of Scotland. One-sixth of the money raised by the British Association for the Relief of Distress in Ireland and the Highlands of Scotland was given to Scottish relief.
7 William Howley (1766–1848) served as the Archbishop of Canterbury from 1828 until his death. The Archbishop of Canterbury was the most senior bishop and principal leader of the Church of England. He was the symbolic head of the international Anglican Communion. The Archbishop of York was second to him, and also served as an ex-officio member of the House of Lords. At this time, the Archbishop was Edward Venables-Vernon-Harcourt (1757–1847), who died in November of that year.
8 Peter Gray, 'National Humiliation and the Great Hunger: Fast and Famine in 1847' in *Irish Historical Studies,* 126 (November 2000), p. 195.
9 *Times*, 24 March 1847.
10 The Quakers preferred that the two fast days would be spent working on behalf of the starving Irish, rather than in idleness, *Launceston Examiner,* 8 September 1847.
11 Rabbi Nathan Marcus Hakohen Adler (1803–1890) was the Orthodox Chief Rabbi of the United Kingdom and the rest of the British Empire from 1845 until his death. He had been born in Hanover in Germany, then an appanage of the English crown under George III, which made him a British subject.
12 'Miscellaneous', *Spectator*, 20 March 1847.
13 Ibid., 'At Court', 27 March 1847.
14 *Courier* (Hobart), 3 July 1847.
15 *Times*, 9 October 1847.
16 'Ireland', *Spectator*, 20 February 1847.
17 Ibid., 6 March 1847.
18 See, Christine Kinealy, *Charity and the Great Hunger. The Kindness of Strangers* (London: Bloomsbury, 2013).
19 Subscription List, *Times,* 16 June 1849.
20 See, Thomas MacHale, *Correspondence between the Most Rev. Dr MacHale, Archbishop of Tuam and the Most Rev. Dr Murray, Archbishop of Dublin, relative to an*

*Address to be presented to her Majesty Queen Victoria, on the Occasion of Her Visit to Ireland in 1849* (Dublin: M.H. Gill, 1885), p. 9.

21 'The Famine Queen', *United Irishmen*, 7 April 1900.
22 In the Anglican Church, Suffragan Bishops were subordinate to Diocesan Bishops.
23 George Grey (1799–1882), the third Earl Grey from 1845, was a British Whig politician. In 1846, Lord John Russell appointed him Home Secretary (a position that he was to hold on two subsequent occasions). Grey took a hard line on the issue of assistance during the Famine, regarding a strict adherence to the Poor Law as a vehicle for bringing about the moral reform of Ireland.
24 George Alexander Hamilton (1802–1871) had been born in Downpatrick, Co. Down, the son of an Anglican minister. He served as Conservative MP for Dublin University from 1843 to 1859. He was a vociferous defender of Protestantism and Orangeism.
25 Sir George Grey.
26 A Queen's Letter had been issued in 1846 to raise money for a devastating fire that had taken place in June of that year in Newfoundland, then a British colony. The fire had left almost 60 per cent of the population without accommodation. The local legislature imported food and banned the exportation of goods from St. John's, while the Fire Relief Committee had paid the fares of those who wished to emigrate.
27 Grey's statement was misleading, suggesting that the British Association for the Relief of Destitution in Ireland and the Highlands of Scotland was closely allied with the Anglican Church. In fact, it had been the initiative of Jewish banker, Lionel de Rothschild (1808–1879). Rothschild's brother was also an active member. In 1858, Lionel de Rothschild became the first practicing Jew to sit in the House of Commons.
28 Sir Robert Harry Inglis (1786–1855) was an English Conservative politician who served as MP for Dundalk 1824 to 1826 and between 1829 and 1854, for Oxford University. He was a fierce defender of High Church Anglicanism, leading him to oppose Catholic Emancipation, Jewish Emancipation, the 1845 grant to Maynooth. Despite these views, he sympathized with the suffering in Ireland. During a debate in the Commons on 1 February, he quoted from reports by the Society of Friends, but admitted that he was so moved by them that he 'could hardly trust himself to read [them] aloud', See, *Hansard,* 1 February 1847, vol. 89, c. 618.

# 8

# BISHOP HUGHES, *A LECTURE ON THE ANTECEDENT CAUSES OF THE IRISH FAMINE IN 1847* (NEW YORK, MARCH 1847)

Irish-born John Hughes was a formidable figure within American religious and political circles, combining a love of his native country with loyalty to America and its Constitution.[1] Hughes was ordained a priest in America in 1826. Within a decade, he had risen to prominence within the Church, being consecrated a Bishop in 1838. A champion of the rights of Irish Catholics on both sides of the Atlantic, his fearlessness earned him the sobriquet, 'Dagger John'.

Hughes visited Ireland in 1839 and again in 1843. During the latter visit, he attended a repeal meeting in Dublin, addressed by Daniel O'Connell. Describing Ireland as 'England's weakness and shame', he averred, 'nothing short of Repeal will be of much use to Ireland'.[2] Reflecting on his visit to his native land, he said, 'my feelings got so much excited by the poverty and the oppression, the patriotism, the indifference, and the perfidy which I witness in that lovely land, that it is a relief to escape from the spectacle'.[3] Although a supporter of O'Connell and Repeal, in 1848 he became caught up in the revolutionary fervour that was sweeping America, even donating $500 to a fund to support a rising, although with a proviso that his money should be used to purchase shields, not weapons.[4]

Like many within the Catholic hierarchy in Ireland, Hughes did not adopt a providentialist interpretation of the Famine. Similarly to Archbishop MacHale in Tuam,[5] and Bishop Maginn in Derry,[6] he took a critical view of the British government's policies. In his lecture, Hughes was disparaging of the current government's adherence to laissez faire, but argued that it had to be viewed within the context of centuries of colonization and dispossession.

Hughes was greatly saddened by events in Ireland after 1845. In February of that year, he had issued a Diocesan Letter appealing for a collection on behalf of a theological seminary. On reflection, he decided to divert the money thus raised to Ireland to avert 'death by starvation'. This raised approximately $14,000 which he forwarded to the Irish bishops.[7] Tickets for Hughes' 1847 lecture in the Tabernacle cost $1 each. One newspaper report, described Hughes as being, ' . . . about 50 years of age, of dark complexion, Milesian features, stoops slightly, and has very much of that air which somehow always characterizes the Romish ecclesiastic'. Proceeds from the lecture raised $529–11, from which $4–50 was deducted for advertising.[8] In August 1848, Hughes also spoke in New Orleans where he raised $6,000 on behalf of famine relief.[9]

Hughes' contact with the Famine was not to remain an abstract one, as the hunger brought hundreds of thousands of poor Irish to North America. As a consequence of this influx, by the mid-nineteenth century, eighty-seven per cent of foreign-born unskilled labourers living in New York were Irish. Writing in 1849, he described them as, 'the poorest and most wretched population that can be found—the scattered debris of the Irish nation.'[10]

In 1850, Hughes became the first Archbishop of New York. In 1861 and 1862, he travelled in Europe winning support for the Union cause during the Civil War. During this time, Hughes visited Ireland for what would be the last time. He died in January 1864. President Lincoln paid tribute to the Irish man for his 'loyalty, fidelity and practical wisdom'.[11]

Bishop John Hughes, *A Lecture on the Antecedent Causes of the Irish Famine in 1847. Delivered under the auspices of the General Committee for the Relief of the Suffering Poor of Ireland By the Right Rev. John Hughes, D.D., Bishop of New York, at the Broadway Tabernacle, March 20th, 1847* (New York: Edward Dunigan, 1847).[12]

THE year 1847 will be rendered memorable in the future annals of civilization, by two events; the one immediately preceding and giving occasion to the other, namely, Irish famine, and American sympathy and succour. Sympathy has, in its own right, a singular power of soothing the moral sufferings of the forlorn and unfortunate. Where is no heart so flinty, but that, if you approach it with kindness, touch it gently with the magic wand of true sympathy, it will be melted, like the rock of the wilderness, and tears of gratitude on the cheeks of the sufferer, will be the prompt response, to those of interest, of pity, of affect in imagination, he will have discovered on yours. Who will say that Ireland is not an unfortunate sufferer? But since her sufferings have become known to other, and happier nations, who will say that she is forlorn? America offers her, not a sympathy of mere sentiment and feeling, but that substantial sympathy which her condition requires. When the first news of your benevolence, and of your efforts, shall have been wafted across the ocean, it will sound as sweetly in her agonized ear, as the voice of angels whispering hopes. It will cause her famine-shrunken heart to expand again to its native fullness, whilst from day to day the western breezes will convey to her echoes of the rising wing, the swelling chorus, the universal outburst, in short, of American Sympathy. The bread with which your ships are freighted, will arrive too late for many a suffering child of hers; but the news that it is coming, will perchance reach the peasant's cabin, in the final hour of his mortal agony. Unable to speak, gratitude will wreath, in feeble smile, for the last time, his pinched and pallid countenance. It is the smile of hope, as well as of gratitude; hope, not for himself, it comes too late for that, but for his pale wife and famished little ones. He will recline his head more calmly, he will die with yet more subdued resignation, having discovered at the close of his life, that truth which the whole training and experience of his hard lot in this world had almost taught him to deny? namely, that there is humanity in mankind, and that its blessings are about to reach even his cabin, from a quarter on which he had no other claim, than that of his misfortune.

But I have not come here to enlarge upon the feelings of sympathy that have been aroused in our own bosoms, nor yet on those of gratitude that will soon be awakened in the breasts of the Irish people. I come, not to describe the inconceivable horrors of a calamity which, in the midst of the nineteenth century, eighteen hundred and forty-seven years after the coming of Christ, either by want or pestilence, or both combined, threatens almost the annihilation of a whole Christian people. The newspapers tell us, that this calamity has been produced by the failure of the potato crop; but this ought not to be a sufficient cause of so frightful a consequence: the potato is but one species of the endless varieties of food which the Almighty has provided for the sustenance of his creatures; and why is it, that the life or death of the great body of any nation should be so little regarded as to be left dependent on the capricious growth of a single root? Many essays will be published; many eloquent speeches pronounced; much precious time unprofitably employed, by the State economists of Great Britain, assigning the cause or causes of the scourge which now threatens to depopulate Ireland. I shall not enter into the immediately antecedent circumstances or influences, that have produced this result. Some will say that it is the cruelty of unfeeling and rapacious landlords; others will have it, that it is the improvident and indolent character of the people themselves; others, still, will say that it is owing to the poverty of the country, the want of capital, the general ignorance of the people, and especially, their ignorance in reference to the improved science of agriculture. I shall not question the truth or the fallacy of any of these theories; admitting them all, if you will, to contain each more or less of truth, they yet do not explain the famine which they are cited to account for. They are themselves to be accounted for, rather as the effects of other causes, than as the real causes of effects, such as we now witness and deplore: for in the moral, social, political, and commercial, as well as in the mere outward physical world, there is a certain and necessary connexion between cause and effect, reaching from end to end, through the whole mysterious web of human occurrences. So that, in the history of man, from the origin of the world, especially in his social condition, no active thought, that is, no thought which has ever been brought out into action or external manifestation, is, or can be isolated, or severed from its connection with that intricate universal, albeit mysterious, chain of causes and of consequences, to which it is, as it ever has been, the occupation of mankind to add new links every year, and every day.

If the attempt, then, be not considered too bold, I shall endeavour to lay before you a brief outline of the primary, original causes, which, by the action and reaction of secondary and intermediate agencies, have produced: the rapacity of landlords, the poverty of the country, the imputed want of industry among its people, and the other causes to which the present calamity will be ascribed by British statesmen. I shall designate these causes by three titles; first, incompleteness of conquest; second, bad government; third, a defective or vicious system of social economy. Allow me first, to say a word of the country itself.

Ireland, as you know, is not larger in its geographical extent than two-thirds of the State of New York. An island on the western borders of Europe, its bold coast is indented with capacious bays and safest harbours. For its size, it has many large and navigable rivers; and it is said that no part of the island is more than fifty miles from tide-water. Its climate is salubrious, although humid with the healthy vapours of the Atlantic; its hills, (like its history,) are canopied, for the most part, with clouds; its sunshine is more rare, but for that very reason, if for no other, far more smiling and beautiful than ever beamed from Italian skies. Its mountains are numerous and lofty; its green valleys fertile as the plains of Egypt, enriched by the overflowings of the Nile. There is no country on the globe that yields a larger average of the substantial things which God has provided for the support and sustenance of human life. And yet, there it is that man has found himself for generations in squalid misery, in tattered garments, often, as at present, haggard and emaciated with hunger; his social state a contrast and an eye-sore, in the midst of the beauty and riches of nature that smile upon him, as if in cruel mockery of his unfortunate and exceptional condition.

The invasion of Ireland took place toward the close of the twelfth century, under the Anglo-Norman King, Henry II. An Irish chieftain had been expelled from his country by the virtuous indignation which a flagrant act of immorality had aroused against him, in the minds of his countrymen and of his own subjects. He had recourse to the British monarch:[13] the king merely gave him letters patent, authorizing such adventurers as were so disposed, to aid him in recovering his estates. Such adventurers were not wanting. They embarked and landed under the banner of invasion, upheld by the criminal hand of an Irish traitor.[14] They succeeded in effecting a partial conquest. The native population were driven out of that portion of the country which stretches along the east and southeastern coast, which afterwards became known in history as the English Pale.[15] This portion of the kingdom—less than one-third—may be considered as having been really conquered by the adventurers; but the rest of the island continued as before, under its ancient princes and proprietors; some of them having simply recognized the monarch of England as their superior lord, by agreeing to pay a mere nominal tribute. Here is the real point in history, at which the fountain of Ireland's perennial calamities is to be placed. Many a tributary streamlet of bitterness came afterwards, to swell the volume of its poisoned waters; but this is the fountain which supplied and gave its direction to the current. The king displayed, when he visited Ireland, an authentic or a forged document from the Pope, authorizing the invasion. There is no evidence, however, except what rested on the royal testimony, that such a document had been granted; but whether or not, it had no more effect in the success of the invasion, than if it had been so much blank Parchment.

The success of the invasion was due, on the one side, to the superior skill of the adventurers, guided, if not led on by an Irish chief; and on the other side, was owing to immemorial, and apparently interminable, divisions among the Irish leaders themselves. They prosecuted their own private piques against each other, as I fear they would do again, no matter how formidable the common enemy of the common weal that might be thundering at their gates. If the invaders had prosecuted the contest to a final issue, that issue might possibly have united them for once; but the English, whether from weakness or from policy, were satisfied with what had been already achieved.

The conquest was thus cut short, almost at the opening of the book; and the calamities that have resulted to Ireland, from that time until our own days, are but so many supplements, many of them bloody ones, to complete the volume. The invaders were pleased to consider themselves as having conquered the Irish nation; and as having acquired right of supreme dominion over the Irish soil. The king divided the lands of the whole kingdom into ten sections, or regions, and bestowed them upon as many of his principal followers. Having flung this apple of discord between the old and new race of the Irish people, he sailed back to England—had the emerald gem of Erin's sovereignty set among the jewels of his crown—and called himself Lord of Ireland. The consequence of his distribution was, from this time, that every portion of the Irish soil, every estate, had two sets of owners; the one, owner by justice, hereditary title, and immemorial possession; the other, owner by assumed right of conquest, and the sign manual of Henry II. If Henry had conquered the country, he might have made these grants a reality; but as it was, they were simply as royal letters-patent, authorizing the iniquities and disorders of all kinds which make up the history of the relations between the Irish people and what was called the English Pale.

The invaders regarded the natives as illegal occupiers of the soil—as barbarians, who stood between them and the peaceable possession of their property. To attempt to dispossess the native population, however, by force, would have been a dangerous experiment; and it makes one shudder to see the persevering ingenuity with which the aid of inhuman legislation was invoked, with which laws for the protection of cruelty and treachery of every description were enacted, to accomplish *by piecemeal* and *by fraud*, the complete conquest which they were too feeble or too politic to refer, once for all, to the more humane decision of the battle-field.

If we look at the legislation of the Pale for the entire period of four hundred years, we will find the tone of its enactments to be always in harmony with this purpose—laws against intermarriages with the natives—laws against their language—laws against their manners and customs—and even laws making it criminal for a liegeman of England to allow a native horse to graze on his pasture. In the minds of the invaders,—in the acts of Parliament,—in royal proclamations, during all those centuries down to the reign of Queen Elizabeth, the natives are designated as aliens and Irish enemies. No part of the soil of their country was recognized as theirs. They were denied all share in the benefits of English laws; the iniquities of the royal grant, supported by the iniquities of legislation, made it lawful for the invaders to kill or rob "the mere Irish," as the accidents of opportunity, or the caprice of expediency, might direct. If any of the natives appealed to the law for redress, it was enough for the defendant to prove, that the would-be plaintiff was a mere Irishman, and did not belong to any of the five families to whom the protection of the British laws had been, by special favour, extended. This plea arrested all farther proceedings in the court. Frequently, during this long interval, had the natives petitioned and implored to be admitted into the Pale, and under the protectorship of the laws; but as often was their petition rejected. On the other hand, their own sovereignty was paralyzed and rendered impotent by the invasion, and the disorders which resulted from its incompleteness. They were broken up and divided, so that they were deprived of all opportunity for social or physical improvement, by any legislative organization of their own. This sketch conveys a faint idea of the condition of Ireland, during nearly four hundred years after the invasion.

The English Pale, meantime, instead of enlarging its boundaries, had often been obliged to curtail them; and as late as the reign of Henry VIII, it was restricted to only four counties out of the whole kingdom. Enough has been said, I think, to illustrate the principle with which I set out, that to assume the fiction of a conquest; to accomplish it by halves; to leave it incomplete; to repair its deficiency, which must be repaired, by other means, which must be fraudulent, is the most cruel policy, as well as the most injurious to both, that a strong nation can employ in the subjugation of a weak one. If it must be done at all, it will be mercy to do it thoroughly—so that the sword shall have determined, to the conviction of all parties, the reality of the new relations that have sprung up, by its decision, between the conquerors and the conquered. The bad policy of the incomplete conquest of Ireland had to be repaired, or rather completed, in the sixteenth century, by commencing the work anew: for, it was only under Queen Elizabeth, who was no half-way ruler, but who, whatever else she may have been, was, I had almost said, a king every inch of her, that Ireland was finally crushed, if not conquered.

It would have been, however, too humiliating to British sovereignty to supply the original defect, under the original name, of conquest. It was, therefore, now to be accomplished under the title and form of "reducing insubordinate and rebellious subjects:"- although it required the help of a strong legal fiction to regard as rebels, those who had hitherto been repulsed from the protection of the law. But even this reduction could not be accomplished, it seems, without cruelties, for which the annals of mankind, in the most barbarous ages of the world, furnish no parallel. It is a singular coincidence and full of admonition, that in this second conquest, British statesmen recommended—and military officers employed—and lord deputies approved of – FAMINE, as their most effectual instrument and ally in the work of subjugation.

The occupation of the troops, from year to year, was to prevent the cultivation of the land, to destroy the growing crops already planted, for "*famine*," says the English historian who records the fact, "was judged the speediest and most effectual way of *reducing* the Irish." The consequences were, that whole provinces were left desolate, without an inhabitant, except in the towns and villages; that those whose misfortune permitted them to escape the sword, sometimes offered themselves, their wives and children, to be slain by the army, rather than for that slow, horrid, death of famine and starvation, which had been reserved for them; for we can all conceive that, compared with the deliberate use of this instrument of war, against a rural and scattered agricultural population, the Indian's tomahawk becomes a symbol of humanity. Meantime, the old chieftains of clans, the owners of the soil, the leaders of the people, the "great rebels," as they were called, were becoming fewer and fewer. Some perished on the battle-field—they were the most fortunate; others gave themselves up on the word of honour and protection, and were then impeached and executed. Some were slain at the festive board of the invading commander, whose invitation to the banquet they had accepted, thinking foolishly, that the laws of truce and hospitality made all their rights not only secure, but even sacred, under the tent of a true soldier; and thus, in few years, the Irish aliens, the Irish enemies, or the Irish rebels if you will, were indeed reduced; and now there was a prospect of the invaders being permitted to enter into peaceable possession of those estates which, by right of conquest, as they understood it, had been theirs from the first invasion.

Elizabeth proposed to colonize the whole province of Ulster with English settlers, but she did not live to accomplish her project.

The plantation of Ulster remained to be carried into effect by her successor, James I. He secured to himself a new and better title; he confiscated to the crown six entire counties of Ulster, in one day; and parcelled them out, chiefly among his *Scotch* rather than his *English* friends—the native, the hereditary population having been, of course, sent adrift. The king and his ministers congratulated themselves, and compared this act of his Majesty to the conduct of a wise and thrifty husbandman, who transplants his trees according to the soil in which they will grow best. After James came Charles I, and the civil wars in England. When other resources failed the monarch, the fragments of property, real and personal, that still remained to the Irish people, were strained into the supply of his empty coffers. He obtained from them, by royal promise, £120,000 sterling, for what was called "Graces;" the principal of which was, what every American inherits by birthright—liberty of conscience.

He pocketed the money, but I am sorry to say he refused the "Graces." His deputy in Ireland projected and carried out a system for the confiscation, in detail, of private estates, under a "Commission" for inquiry into defective titles. The jury that refused to find a verdict for the crown, under this system, was punished and ruined; and as to the judges, the lord deputy writes to his royal master, that he had got them to attend to this business, as if it were their own personal affair, by promising four shillings in the pound to the judge who presided at the trial, out of the first year's income from all confiscated estates. Under the Commonwealth, Ireland is the scene of new exterminations—new confiscations,—new foreign settlers, amidst the wrecks and ruins of the native population. On the Restoration, the loyalists of England and Scotland were reinstated in their rights; but in Ireland, the loyalists were abandoned by the crown; and the followers of Cromwell confirmed in their possessions. Nay, James II came in on the title of a Cromwellian, and appropriated to himself, in one instance, no less than from 70,000 to 100,000 acres, that had been confiscated by Cromwell to punish the fidelity of its rightful owners for adhering to the cause of that miserable James' unfortunate father. Finally, that country which had been conquered so often, submitted at last to William III, successor to James on the English throne—submitted, but still not to the *sword* of a conqueror, but to the faith of a *king*, stamped on a written instrument, mutually agreed upon by him and the last representative of unconquered Ireland, called the "Treaty of Limerick." But every article of it, autograph, royal seal, and all, was repudiated the moment it was safe to do so.

The enactment of the entire penal code, soon afterwards, is evidence of the entire and deliberate violation of all the articles of the treaty of Limerick. By that code, the inhabitants of Ireland were again divided into two classes; the one consisting of those whose conscience would allow them to take the State oath, on the subject of religion: to them high privileges were secured. But penalties were enacted against those who could not, or would not, swear that oath. The great overwhelming majority of the Irish people refused the test; and the penal law came quickly to punish them, even in their family relations and domestic circle. It invested any child, who might conform to the *test* prescribed, with the rights of property enjoyed by his father. It invested the wife with rights of property over the husband. If any of those who had refused to swear, purchased an estate for any amount of money, any of the others, who *had* taken the oath, could dispossess him without paying one shilling for such estate. If any of the former class owned a horse worth fifty or one hundred pounds, any of the latter class had a right, by law, to tender five pounds and tell him to dismount. If any of the former class, by his skill and industry in agriculture, raised the value of his land, so as to yield a profit equal to one-third of the rent, any of the latter could enter on the profits of his labour, and take possession of his land. These laws continued for between eighty and ninety years, down to the period of American Independence. And in this enactment, we see what a penalty was inflicted on the agricultural industry of the Irish—what a premium was held out to encourage that indolence which British statesmen now impudently complain of.

The same system has been continued to the present day: as if some cruel law of destiny had determined that the Irish people should be kept at the starving point through all times; since the landlord, even now claims the right, and often uses it, of punishing the industry of his tenant, by increasing the rent, in proportion to the improvement the tenant makes on his holding. If then it be true, that the Irish are indolent, which I deny, the cause could be sufficiently explained by the penalties which a bad government has inflicted upon them, in their own country, for the crime of being industrious. Then, if it be said, as a reproach, that the Irish are ignorant, let it be remembered that this same code of penal laws closed up the schools of popular education; that the schoolmaster was banished for the crime of teaching, and if he returned he was liable to be treated as a felon. If ignorance of the people, then, be the cause of the famine, enough has been said to point out the cause of the ignorance itself.

The melancholy training of so long a period of oppression served to bring out, in the shades of adversity, virtues which perhaps would not have bloomed or borne fruit in the sunnier atmosphere of national prosperity. Filial reverence, domestic affections, always congenial to the Irish heart, had here ample opportunity of proving themselves, and were never found wanting. The law put it in the power of any son, by declaring himself a Protestant, to enter immediately upon the rights of property enjoyed by his father and his family; but no son of Irish parents was ever known to have availed himself of the law. As a matter of expediency, it was customary for the Catholic proprietor, for the protection of his property, to vest the legal title in some Protestant neighbour, and again it is consoling to know that, notwithstanding the temptations presented by these iniquitous laws, there is no instance of that private confidence having been violated. These laws originated at the close of the seventeenth century, and continued in force until two years after a British general, Burgoyne,[16] turned the point of his sword to his own breast, and presented the hilt to the hand of his conqueror, after the battle of Saratoga.[17] Then came the only brief, bright period of Ireland's history: the period of her volunteers, of her statesmen and orator—her illustrious Grattan[18] rousing the patriotism of his country, and emancipating her long enslaved Parliament. The period of her Bushe,[19] her Flood,[20] her Curran,[21] add the other great names that have made Irish eloquence as immortal as the Anglo-Saxon tongue. But the sun of her brief day soon declined and set, shrouded in clouds of blood, for it closed by the banishment or martyrdom of her patriots—her noble-hearted Emmets[22] and Fitzgeralds.[23] It was brought to an end by a new policy, conducted in the old spirit. A rebellion had been deliberately fomented by the agents of a foreign government, until it reached the desired point of precociousness ripeness, and then it was crushed with promptness and with cruelty. Martial law for the people, gold for the senate—a bayonet for the patriot who loved Ireland, and a bribe for the traitor who did not, led to the Act called the Union, in which the charter of Irish nationality was destroyed, but I trust not forever.

The rest you are all acquainted with; it has occurred in our day, and within our memory. It will be manifest from what has been said that the causes which have prevented the prosperity of Ireland, the development of her material resources, the cultivation of her mind, have existed from an early date; and, under one form or another, have been in perpetual activity. She has hardly been permitted to enjoy repose sufficient even for a fair experiment of improvement. During the first four hundred years after the invasion, her people were outlawed because they were mere Irish. Afterwards, when the English laws were extended to her, in 1610, her people were again outlawed or worse, not now because they were Irish, but because they were Catholics. By adhering to their old religion, their rulers supposed them to have shipwrecked their hopes of happiness in another world, which would have been misfortune enough, without inflicting punishments for their mistake so well calculated to destroy their prosperity here. At the commencement of these changes the law required them to attend the church and service of the State religion; if they attended, they did not understand a syllable of that service, which was conducted in the English language: if they did not attend, their property was seized by fines for their nonattendance, £20 a Sunday. Then, either by grants or confiscations, under Charles the First, to whose cause they were loyal, their property was still diminished. Under Cromwell, they were punished and plundered both as idolaters, and because they had been faithful to their king. Under the Restoration, all preceding iniquities as regarded the ownership of property were confirmed. Under William III and his successors, the penal laws were applied in the same way, not to the body politic at large, but with an ingenuity of detail, to every joint, and sinew and muscle, as if the object were to paralyze all effort at national amelioration. Just in proportion as the struggle of these colonies for independence was successful, in that proportion did the policy of the British government relax the pressure of this weighty bondage of the Irish people.

We sometimes hear comparisons instituted between the prosperity, industry, and moral, or at least, intellectual condition, of the Scotch, and the poverty of all kinds of the Irish; and the conclusion is generally averse to the latter, either on the score of national character or of religion. Some even assert that the Catholic religion is in reality the cause of the poverty and degradation of Ireland. I have said enough to show that it has been at least an occasion; but I am willing to go farther, and admit that in one sense it has been a cause too; for I have no hesitation in saying that if the Irish, by any chance, had been Presbyterians, they would have, from an early day, obtained protection for their natural rights, or they would have driven their oppressors into the sea. The Scotch escaped nearly all the calamities I have described; they were never conquered; their soil was never taken from beneath their feet; they merged themselves spontaneously at their own time, and on their own terms, into the State of England. They kept also, the property of their old religion for their own social and religious use. Already, before the change, parish schools were established in Scotland; after the change these were multiplied, improved, and endowed out of the old church property.

But in Ireland, everything was the reverse: church buildings, monasteries, glebes, tithes, from year to year, all went by the board: all were subtracted from the aggregate of the national wealth. And even in modern times, we read of incumbents appointed to ecclesiastical livings, entering on their cure or rather sinecure, penniless, and after a few years, by the probate of their own wills, leaving to their foreign heirs, in some instances, as much as three, and four, hundred thousand pounds sterling.

I have ventured to suggest a defective or vicious system of social and political economy as the other great cause of Ireland's peculiarly depressed condition. By social economy I mean that effort of society, organized into a sovereign state, to accomplish the welfare of all its members. The welfare of its members is the end of its existence- "Salus populi, suprema lex."[24] It would be a reproach to say that Christianity conceived a meaner or a lower idea of its obligation. This idea, it may not, perhaps, be possible to realize fully in practice under any system; but it should never be lost sight of the system which now prevails has lost sight of it, to a great extent. It is called the free system,—the system of competition,—the system of making the *wants* of mankind a regulator for their supplies.

It had its origin in the transition of society from that state of mitigated slavery which was called feudalism and serfage, as they prevailed in England. As regards the mere physical position, food, clothing, lodging, of the entire people of England, there is no doubt that the old system provided better for it than the present one. The old Barons never allowed their serfs to die of a hunger which they were not willing to share. As the latter emerged from serfdom, and before they were able to take their ranks with advantage, in a more honourable sphere of free labour, the church property, with its great means constituted a Providence of protecting for this class. When the church property was distributed among the nobles of England this resource failed, and then it was that Poor Laws were enacted, and taxes began to be levied by the State, from the poor, for the support of the pauper. Until then, the aggregate physical comfort, if not the aggregate wealth, of the English people, taking them altogether as members of one State, was greater than it ever has been since, or so far as we can see, is likely ever to be again. There were not, indeed, those colossal individual fortunes which now exist, but neither were there on the other hand those abysses of physical and moral destitution, which are now yawning on every side for the new victims, whom the pressure of the present system is pushing, every day, nearer and nearer to their fatal brink. By this system England has, I admit, become the richest country on the globe; but riches are by no means synonymous with prosperity, when we speak of the social condition of a whole people. And this system, though it may work well, even for national prosperity, in certain given times and circumstances, yet carries within it, in the palmiest days of its success, a principle of disease, which acts first on the lower extremities of the social body; and with the lapse of time will make itself felt, at the very heart and seat of life. It is an appalling reflection that out of the active and productive industry of Great Britain and Ireland, provision must be made for the support of between four and five millions of paupers. This number will be increased by every depressing crisis in commerce and in trade; by every blight of sterility which

Providence permits to fall on the fields of the husbandman; and the experiment of Sir Robert Peel, in imposing on the *wealthy* an income tax, may be regarded as a premonitory warning that, although the time may not yet have arrived, it is approaching, and, perhaps, at no very remote distance, when the mountains of individual wealth in England shall be made comparatively low, and the valleys of pauperism will be partially filled up. I am aware that in speaking on this subject, I will go as it were in opposition to the almost universal sentiment of this age, but for the expression of my opinion I will offer you this apology, that provided you do me the honour to hear, I will not ask you to coincide in so much as one of the conclusions at which my mind has arrived in regard to it.

I know that no living man is accountable for the system of which I am about to complain; it is older than we are, it is the invisible but all-pervading divinity of the Fiscal, the unseen ruler of the temporal affairs of this world. Kings and Emperors are but its prime ministers, premiers and parliaments but its servants in livery; money is the symbol of its worship, we are all its slaves, without any power to emancipate ourselves; the dead and the dying in Ireland are its victims.

It will not be disputed, I presume, that the present system of social and political economy resolves itself, when analyzed, into a primary element of pure selfishness. The principle that acts, the mainspring that sets all its vast and intricate machinery in motion is self interest; whether that interest assume a national form in the commercial rivalship of States, or an individual form in the pursuits, the industry, and enterprise of private persons. The conqueror, indeed, carries off great spoils from the contest; but his enjoyment of them would be disturbed if he could only hear the cries of the wounded and the dying who have fallen in the battle.

The true system, in my opinion, would regard the general interest first, as wholly paramount, and have faith enough to believe that individual interest would, in the long run, be best promoted by allowing it all possible scope for enterprise and activity within the general limits. Then individual welfare would be the result and not the antecedent, as it is when the order is reversed. The assumption of our system is, that the healthy antagonisms of this self-interest, which, as applied to the working classes, its advocates sometimes designate pompously "the sturdy self-reliance of an operative," will result finally in the general good. I am willing to admit, that in the fallen condition of human nature, self-interest is the most powerful principle of our being, giving impulse and activity to all our individual undertakings, and in that way, to the general operations of life. But unfortunately, this system leaves us at liberty to forget the interest of others. The fault which I impute to it, however, is that it values wealth too much, and man too little; that it does not take a large and comprehensive view of self-interest; that it does not embrace within its protecting sphere, the whole entire people, weak and strong, rich and poor, and see as its first and primary care, that no member of the social body, no man shall be allowed to suffer or perish from want, except by the agency of his own crime. The fault that I find with it, is, that in countries of limited territorial surface and dense population, by a necessary process it works down a part of the community, struggling with all their might to keep up, into a condition not merely of poverty, but also of destitution; and then treats that poverty, which itself had created, as a guilt and an infamy.

The fault that I find with it, is that whilst it allows, and properly so, competition to be the life of trade, it allows it also to be, oftentimes, the death of the trader. The premier of England is reported to have said not long since, "that nothing prevented him from employing government vessels to carry bread to a starving people, except his unwillingness to disturb the current of trade." Never was oracle of a hidden and a heartless deity uttered more faithfully, or more in accordance with the worship of its votaries, than in the language here imputed to the British minister, who may be fairly regarded as the living high priest of political economy. To put public vessels in competition with merchantmen, in the low business of mere trade, would indeed have been wrong and unworthy of a great ruler; but if the profits of trade had been curtailed in the proportion of three or four per cent per annum, during this crisis of the famine, it would have saved many lives, and yet not have inflicted a wound or a scar on the health of commerce.

The fault that I find with the system, then, is, that it not only allows but sanctions and approves of a principle which operates so differently in two provinces of the same State, divided only by a channel of the sea. It multiplies deposits of idle money in the banks on one side of that channel, and multiplies dead and coffinless bodies in the cabins, and along the highways, on the other.

The fault that I find with it, is, that it guarantees the right of the rich man, to enter on the fields cultivated by the poor man whom he calls his tenant, and carry away the harvest of his labour, and this, whilst it imposes on him no duty to leave behind at least food enough to keep that poor man alive, until the earth shall again yield its fruits. The fault that I find with it, is, that it provides wholesome food, comfortable raiment and lodgings for the rogues, and thieves, and murderers, of its dominions, whilst it leaves the honest, industrious, virtuous peasant, to stagger at his labour through inanition, and fall to rise no more! O! if this system be all in all, why did he not, in his forlorn state, entitle himself to its advantages? Why did he not steal or commit murder? for then the protection of our modern Christian governments, would be extended to him, and he would not be allowed to die of want.

I may be told that I avail myself unfairly of an extraordinary calamity to prove the defects of our present system; I may be told that the famine in Ireland is a mysterious visitation of God's providence, but I do not admit any such plea. I fear there is blasphemy in charging on the Almighty, what is the result of his own doings. Famine in Ireland is, and has been for many years, as the cholera in India, indigenous. As long as it is confined to a comparatively few cases in the obscure and sequestered parts of the country, it may be said that the public administrators of social and political economy are excusable, inasmuch as it had not come under their notice; but in the present instance, it has attracted the attention of the whole world. And yet they call it God's famine! No! no! God's famine is known by the general scarcity of food, of which it is the consequence; there is no general scarcity, there has been no general scarcity of food in Ireland, either the present, or the past year, except in one species of vegetable. The soil has produced its usual tribute for the support of those by whom it has been cultivated; but political economy found the Irish people too poor to pay for the harvest of their own labour, and has exported it to a better market, leaving them to die of famine, or to live on alms; and this same political economy authorizes the provision merchant, even amidst the desolation, to keep his doors locked, and his sacks of corn tied up within, waiting for a better price, whilst he himself is perhaps at his desk, describing the wretchedness of the people and the extent of the misery; setting forth for the eye of the first lord of the treasury,[25] with what exemplary patience the peasantry bear their sufferings, with what admirable resignation they fall down through weakness at the threshold of his warehouse, without having even attempted to burst a door, or break a window.

Such conduct is praised everywhere; even Her Majesty, in a royal speech, did not disdain to approve of it; and it is, in truth, deserving of admiration: for the sacredness of the rights of property must be maintained at all sacrifices, unless we would have society to dissolve itself into its original elements; still the rights of life are dearer and higher than those of property; and in a general famine like the present, there is no law of Heaven, nor of nature, that forbids a starving man to seize on bread wherever he can find it, even though it should be the loaves of proposition on the altar of God's temple. But, I would say to those who maintain the sacred and inviolable rights of property, if they would have the claim respected, to be careful also and scrupulous in recognizing the rights of humanity. In a crisis like that which is now passing, the Irish may submit to die rather than violate the rights of property; but on such a calamity, should it ever happen, which God forbid, the Scotch will not submit; the English will not submit; the French will not submit; and depend upon it, the Americans will not submit. Let us be careful, then, not to blaspheme Providence by calling this God's famine. Society, that great civil corporation which we call the State, is bound so long as it has the power to do so, to guard the lives of its members against being sacrificed by famine from within, as much against their being slaughtered by the enemy from without. But the vice which is inherent in our system of social and political economy is so subtle that it eludes all pursuit, that you cannot find or trace it to any responsible source. The man, indeed, over whose dead body the coroner holds the inquest, has been murdered, but no one has killed him. There is no external wound, there is no symptom of internal disease. Society guarded him against all outward violence; it merely encircled him around in order to keep up what is termed the regular current of trade, and then political economy, with an invisible hand, applied the air-pump to the narrow limits within which he was confined, and exhausted the atmosphere of his physical life. Who did it? No one did it, and yet it has been done.

It is manifest that the causes of Ireland's present suffering have been multitudinous, remote, and I might almost say, perpetual. Nearly the whole land of the country is in the ownership of persons having no sympathy with its population except that of self-interest—her people are broken down in their physical condition by the previous calamities to which I have directed your attention. Since her union with England, commerce followed capital, or found it in that country, and forsook the sister island. Nothing remained but the produce of the soil. That produce was sent to England to find a better market, for the rent must be paid; but neither the produce nor the rent ever returned. It has been estimated that the average export of capital from this source has been equal to some 25 or perhaps 30 millions of dollars annually, for the last seven and forty years; and it is at the close of this last period, by the failure of the potato, that Ireland, without trade, without manufactures, without any returns for her agricultural exports, sinks beneath the last feather, not that the feather was so weighty, but that the burthen previously imposed was far above her strength to bear. If it be true that the darkest hour of the night is that which immediately precepts the dawn, may we not indulge the hope that there are better days yet in store for this unfortunate people. They have been crushed and ruined in all the primary elements of their material happiness, but yet they have never forfeited any of the higher attributes of a noble, generous nature. They might, perhaps, have shared with the other portions of the empire in the physical comforts and improvements of modern civilization, if they had renounced their religion, at the period when the others saw fit to change theirs; but after the present famine shall have been forgotten, the high testimony which the Irish people bore to the holiness of conviction within their soul, at all risks, and through all sacrifices, will be considered an honour to humanity itself. They believed, whether rightly or not is not now the question, but right or wrong, they believed that to profess religion which had no hold on their conviction, would offend God, and involve them in the double guilt of falsehood and hypocrisy—that it would degrade them in their own minds, that it would entitle them to the contempt of the world—and sooner than do this, they submitted to everything besides. There was this one sovereignty which they never relinquished—the sovereignty of conscience, and the privilege of self-respect. Their soul has never been conquered; and if it was said in Pagan times that the noblest spectacle which this earth could present to the eye of the immortal gods, was that of a virtuous man bravely struggling with adversity; what might not be said of a nation of such men who have so struggled through entire centuries? Neither can it be said that their spirit is yet broken. Intellect, sentiment, fancy, wit, eloquence, music and poetry, are, I might say, natural and hereditary attributes of the Irish mind and the Irish heart; and no adversity of ages was sufficient to crush these capacities and powers; who will say that such a people have not, under happier circumstances, within themselves a principle of self-regeneration and improvement, which will secure to them at least an ordinary portion of the happiness of which they have been so long deprived? The charity of other countries, and among them preeminently of England herself; the sympathy of distant and free states, on this occasion, in themselves have an effect. They will show Ireland that she is cared for; they will inspire her with the pleasing hope that she is not to be always the down-trodden and neglected province, the outcast nation among the nations of the earth.

## Notes

1. John Hughes (1797–1864) was born in Annaloghan in Co. Tyrone. His emigrated to America in 1817 to join his family. Initially a gardener, he achieved his ambition of becoming a priest in 1826. In 1838, he was consecrated Bishop of New York, and in 1850 was raised to Archbishop.
2. John Hughes, written from London, July 1843, *Life of Archbishop Hughes: With a Full Account of His Funeral . . .*, vol. 1 (New York: American News Company, 1864), pp. 129–130.
3. Ibid.
4. Christine Kinealy, *Repeal and Revolution. 1848 in Ireland* (Manchester: Manchester University Press, 2009), p. 218.
5. John MacHale (1791–1881) was born in Co. Mayo. In 1814, he was ordained a priest at Maynooth Seminary, and 20 years later was appointed Archbishop of Tuam, despite the opposition of the British government. He was a friend and supporter of Daniel O'Connell, and was an outspoken champion of Catholic Emancipation and later, Repeal. He was disturbed by the poverty of Ireland, believing that it resulted from British misrule. Initially, he took a providentialist view of the potato blight, but by 1846 was criticizing the relief policies of the government.
6. Edward Maginn (1802–1849) was born in Fintona in Co. Tyrone. He was ordained in 1825 and, like many Catholic priests, supported Daniel O'Connell's quest for Catholic Emancipation and later for Repeal. He blamed the British government— 'a professedly Liberal, Whig government, of which Lord John Russell was Premier'—for mortality during the Famine.
7. John Rose Greene Hassard, *Life of the Most Reverend John Hughes, D.D.: First Archbishop of New York*. Part 4 (New York: D. Appleton & Co., 1866), p. 303.
8. Quoted in Christine Kinealy, *Charity and the Great Hunger. Kindness of Strangers* (London: Bloomsbury, 2013), p. 98.
9. Kinealy, *Repeal and Revolution*, p. 128.
10. Ronald H. Bayor, Timothy Meagher (eds), *The New York Irish* (Baltimore, MD: John Hopkins University, 1997), p. 20.
11. Letter from President Lincoln to the Very Rev. William Starr, Administrator of the Diocese of New York, 13 January 1864, Mazyck Andrews, *John Hughes and the Civil War* (Chicago, IL: University of Chicago, 1935), p. 15.
12. The Dunigan brothers were leading Catholic publishers in the America. They were Edward (1812–1853) who was born in New York to Irish immigrant parents, and his half-brother, James Kirker (d. 1868).
13. At this stage, there was no united British monarch. Henry II (1133–1189) ruled over the 'Angevin Empire' (or *espace Plantagenet*) which consisted of parts of England and France, and, intermittently, Scotland, Wales and Brittany. To this, he added the Lordship of Ireland in 1171.

14 Diarmaid (Dermot) Mac Murchadha (c. 1110–1171) was the King of Leinster who solicited help from Henry II in order to regain his kingdom.
15 The Pale, also known as the English Pale, was the area of Ireland directly ruled by England, which fluctuated in size. They never controlled more than two thirds of the island and, by the end of the fifteenth century, this area had shrunk to the counties of Dublin, Kildare, Louth and Meath.
16 John Burgoyne (1722–1792) was a British soldier and politician. He is associated with the American Revolutionary War, his surrender at Saratoga being a turning point in the conflict. He was Commander-in-Chief between 1782 and 1784.
17 The Battle of Saratoga was more correctly two battles fought in autumn 1777. General Burgoyne was victorious in the first battle, but surrendered during the second. This battle persuaded the French to enter the war on the side of the colonists.
18 Henry Grattan (1746–1820) was a Dublin-born politician who led the Patriot Party within the Irish Parliament. He is associated with a period of legislative independence for Ireland that commenced in 1782. After 1800, he led the opposition to the Acts of Union.
19 Charles Kendal Bushe (1767–1843) was an Irish judge, known for his eloquence. He served in the Irish parliament after 1796. He was opposed to the Acts of Union in 1800.
20 Henry Flood (1732–1791) a politician who first entered the Irish House of Commons in 1759 and became a founder of the Patriot Movement, whose aim was to achieve legislative independence.
21 John Philpot Curran (1750–1817) was an Irish orator, lawyer and politician. After 1783, he served in the Irish Parliament. He opposed the Acts of Union.
22 Robert Emmet (1778–1803) was an Irish republican leader. He was found guilty of high treason for his leadership of the 1803 Rebellion and was executed in Dublin. Before being sentenced, he made his famous speech from the dock.
23 Lord Edward Fitzgerald (1763–1798) was the son of the Duke of Leinster. He joined the British Army and fought against the colonists in the American Revolutionary War. He was elected to the Irish parliament in 1783. Fitzgerald's support for the French Revolution led to his dismissal from the Army. In 1796, he joined the Society of United Irishmen. He was wounded in the lead-up to the 1798 rebellion and died in prison some weeks later.
24 Latin: 'The health of the people should be the supreme law'.
25 The First Lord of the Treasury was the British Prime Minister. In 1847, this was Lord John Russell (1792–1878).

# Part IV

# VISITORS TO IRELAND

# 9

# ELIHU BURRITT, *A JOURNAL OF A VISIT OF THREE DAYS TO SKIBBEREEN, AND ITS NEIGHBOURHOOD* (FEBRUARY 1847)

Elihu Burritt was born in 1810 in New Britain, Connecticut. Following his father's death, when Burritt was aged about 17, he apprenticed himself to a blacksmith. Regardless of this humble beginning, his ability as a linguist (his range of languages including Sanskrit and Arabic) and his overall erudition, earned him the title, 'the learned blacksmith'.

By the 1840s, Burritt, already a supporter of abolition and temperance, was becoming increasingly interested in peace. In June 1846, he sailed to England, to promote this issue. He also wanted to develop an 'Ocean Penny Post', to make transatlantic communications cheaper. On arrival in Liverpool, Burritt sought a meeting with Richard Rathbone,[1] from a family of nonconformist merchants, who were known for their philanthropy.[2] Shortly afterwards, he founded the League of Universal Brotherhood, which was dedicated to using peaceful means to end war.[3] Burritt's plan was to lecture in England for a few months and then to travel to France. Events in Ireland, however, led to a change in his plans, and an unscheduled visit to Skibbereen in the south west of Ireland.

Before travelling to Ireland, Burritt made various entreaties on behalf of the Irish poor, both to the British government and to his fellow Americans. One of his appeals was read out at a meeting in Worcester in Connecticut in mid-February 1847, which proved to be:

> ... much the largest meeting ever held for such a purpose in this town. The large Town Hall was well filled and the proceedings showed that a deep sympathy pervades the breasts of the people. We trust that it is universal throughout the country, and that it will be manifested in such a manner that will carry hope and joy to thousands of hearths now desolate. The Catholic Society in this town has already raised and awarded $300 and they intend making it up to $1000. Besides that, many individuals have remitted considerable amounts to their own friends in Ireland. The case was stated at the meeting of an Irish servant girl who took all

the savings of her wages and then anticipated her earnings sufficiently to make up the amount to $50 and sent it on.[4]

Burritt also worked with William Rathbone,[5] Richard's brother, who was assisting the New England Relief Committee to bring aid to Ireland.[6]

Burritt was to claim subsequently that his appeals to the people of Massachusetts were the impetus for the American government's decision to send the relief-laden *Jamestown* to Cork from Boston.[7] This claim, however, was misleading. The resolution to allow two decommissioned men-of-war ships to undertake errands of mercy to Ireland had been taken in Washington in the wake of a meeting on behalf of Ireland convened by the Vice President.[8]

Burritt travelled to Skibbereen via Dublin and Cork. On 13 February, when visiting a private soup kitchen in Dublin, he first came into contact with 'famine-stricken people', whom he described as 'haggard, unwashed and ragged'. Regardless of the desperation of the scene, Burritt noted the sadness was mitigated by 'the broad Irish humour that prevailed, and that queer genius for repartee and sallies of wit, done in the richest Hibernian, diffused a sunshine over the scene'.[9] After Dublin, Burritt travelled to Kilkenny, Cork and Bandon, finally arriving in Skibbereen at 10.00 pm on 19 February.

Burritt's account opens on the day after he arrived in Skibbereen. The final entry was made on Monday, 22 February. What the pamphlet does not show (but Burritt's private journals do), is that he curtailed his visit to the town, and his stay in Ireland, because after two days in Skibbereen he awoke feeling feverish, while his clothes were 'saturated with nauseating effluvia of the cabins'.[10] A local doctor gave him medicine, also advising him not to expose himself again to such scenes and to stay in his room. The following day, Burritt felt better but he decided to return to Cork, and from there go immediately to England.[11] In total, he had spent two weeks in Ireland.

Burritt's *Three Days in Skibbereen and its Vicinity* was published only weeks after he had left Ireland. Although it was printed in England, Burritt's comments were directed to a primarily American audience. The preamble to the pamphlet was written by Burritt's friend, Joseph Sturge, an English Quaker, who was also an abolitionist and a pacifist.[12] Even before Burritt's arrival in England, the two men had been in correspondence, with Sturge donating money to Burritt's Olive Leaf missions.[13] Sturge's solution to the Famine in Ireland was to make the owners of soil responsible by giving the poor a right to relief, similar to the system in England.

In return for his services to the Irish poor, Burritt had been offered a free passage home on board the *Jamestown*, the ship that had brought relief to Cork from New England. He turned this down on financial grounds (see letter below). His illness while in Skibbereen, however, may also have made him reluctant to return to Ireland. Moreover, Burritt, assisted by Sturge, was engaged in organizing the second international Peace Conference, which was held in Brussels in September 1848.[14] Overall, Burritt's direct involvement in the Famine may have been short-lived, but he helped to raise awareness and enlist aid for Ireland, while his eyewitness account provided additional evidence of the inadequacy of the British government's policies.

## ELIHU BURRITT, *A JOURNAL OF A VISIT OF THREE DAYS TO SKIBBEREEN, AND ITS NEIGHBOURHOOD*[15] (LONDON: CHARLES GILPIN; BIRMINGHAM: JOHN WHITEHOUSE, 1847)

EXTRACT FROM THE SPEECH OF LORD JOHN RUSSELL,
On the Irish Poor Relief Bill, March 12th, 1847.[16]

"A gentleman who lately called upon me, and whom I have every reason to trust, gave me a letter from a person resident in that union (Skibbereen) stating, that though the property within the union is rated to the poor as being of the value of £8,000 a-year only, its actual value is no less than £130,000 a-year, and that, until September last, no rate had been made exceeding sixpence in the pound, but that, in November, a rate was made of ninepence in the pound ; but that rate has never been levied. (Loud cries of 'Hear, hear.')" – See "The Times" of Saturday, March 13.

ELIHU BURRITT, well known on both sides of the Atlantic by his devoted labours for the good of mankind, especially in the promotion of peace and universal brotherhood, has recently paid a visit to some of the distressed parts of Ireland, principally with a view of sending a statement of facts, from his own observation, to his native country, together with an appeal on behalf of the sufferers under the awful pressure of famine and disease.

In this appeal, which was sent to the United States by the last steam packet, Elihu Burritt, speaking of the locality he had visited, says: – "I have come to this indescribable scene of destitution, desolation, and death, that I might get the nearer to your sympathies; that I might bring these terrible realities of human misery more vividly within your comprehension. I have witnessed scenes that no language of mine can portray. I have seen how much beings, made in the image of God, can suffer on this side the grave, and that too in a civilized land."

The reader will judge for himself, when he has perused the following record of only three days of this journey, whether the foregoing language is too strong. Although the fearful facts Elihu Burritt relates may have found a parallel in the statements of others, it is thought desirable to publish them in this country, as he recently witnessed them in the very district to which the sympathies of the English have been, for several months past, particularly directed, and for which locality large subscriptions have been specially contributed. A single individual is reported to have given £1000 for Skibbereen.[17] Yet, notwithstanding all that has been subscribed, up to the period when this journal was written, no effectual means had been adopted for the decent interment of the dead, or even for their timely removal from the hovels of the living, and the great expenditure of the British Government, appears to have effected, at least in this district, but little mitigation of the fearful calamity.

There are many noble instances of individual sacrifices by personal attention to the sufferers, and other efforts for their relief, but nothing short of a law to give the poor of Ireland the right to claim support from the owners of the soil, before they are reduced to starvation, will effectually meet the evil, or be any security against its recurrence.

The Poor Law of England admits the claim of the people for support from the land and other fixed property; and, until this is given, neither landlord or mortgagee is entitled to rent or interest.

This should be fully applied to Irish legislation, and partial and unjust laws removed, including those of primogeniture and entail. To the neglect of these measures and that of giving the cultivators of the soil a proper security for the labour and expense which they bestow upon it, is mainly to be attributed the fact that a country possessing some of the finest natural advantages in the world, and which could be rendered capable of supporting in comfort at least three times its present population, is now overspread with such extreme human misery that the awful scenes portrayed in the following pages cease to excite a thrill of horror.
JOSEPH STURGE.[18]
Birmingham,
3rd Month, 15th, 1847.

## THREE DAYS AT SKIBBEREEN, AND ITS VICINITY.

Skibbereen, Saturday, February 20. – Rev. Mr. F---,[19] called with several gentlemen of the town, and in their company I took my first walk through this Potter's Field of destitution and death. As soon as we opened the door, a crowd of haggard creatures pressed upon us, and, with agonizing prayers for bread, followed us to the soup-house. One poor woman, whose entreaties became irresistibly importunate, had watched all night in the grave-yard, lest the body of her husband should be stolen from his resting place, to which he had been consigned yesterday. She had left five children sick with the famine fever in her hovel, and she raised an exceedingly bitter cry for help. A man with swollen feet pressed closely upon us, and begged for bread most piteously. He had pawned his shoes for food, which he had already consumed. The soup house was surrounded by a cloud of these famine spectres, half naked, and standing or sitting in the mud, beneath a cold, drizzling rain. The narrow defile to the dispensary bar was choked with young and old of both sexes, struggling forward with their rusty tin and iron vessels for soup, some of them upon all fours, like famished beasts. There was a cheap bread dispensary opened in one end of the building, and the principal pressure was at the door of this. Among the attenuated apparitions of humanity that thronged this gate of stinted charity, one poor man presented himself under circumstances that even distinguished his case from the rest. He lived several miles from the centre of the town, in one of the rural districts, where he found himself on the eve of perishing with his family of seven small children. Life was worth the last struggle of nature, and the miserable skeleton of a father had fastened his youngest child to his back, and with four more by his side, had staggered up to the door, just as we entered the bread department of the establishment. The hair upon his face was nearly as long as that upon his head. His cheeks were fallen in, and his jaws so distended that he could scarcely articulate a word. His four little children were sitting upon the ground by his feet, nestling together, and trying to hide their naked limbs under their dripping rages. How these poor things could stand upon their feet and walk, and walk five miles, as they had done, I could not conceive. Their appearance, though common to thousands of the same age in this region of the shadow of death, was indescribable. Their paleness was not that of common sickness. There was no sallow tinge in it. They did not look as if newly raised from the grave and to life before the blood had begun to fill their veins anew; but as if they had just been thawed out of the ice, in which they had been imbedded until their blood had turned to water.

Leaving this battle field of life, I accompanied the Rev. Mr. F---, the Catholic minister, into one of the hovel lanes of the town. We found in every tenement we entered enough to sicken the stoutest heart. In one, we found a shoe-maker who was at work before a hole in the mud wall of his hut about as large as a small pane of glass. There were five in his family, and he said, when he could get any work, he could earn about three shillings a week. In another cabin we discovered a nailer by the dull light of his fire, working in a space not three feet square. He, too, had a large family, half of whom were down with the fever, and he could earn but two shillings a week. About the middle of this filthy lane, we came to the ruins of a hovel, which had fallen down during the night, and killed a man, who had taken shelter in it with his wife and child. He had come in from the country, and ready to perish with cold and hunger, had entered this falling house of clay. He was warned of his danger, but answered that die he must, unless he found a shelter before morning. He had kindled a small fire with some straw and bits of turf, and he was crouching over it, when the whole roof or gable end of earth and stones came down upon him and his child, and crushed him to death over the slow fire. The child had been pulled out alive, and carried to the workhouse, but the father was still lying upon the dung heap of the fallen roof, slightly covered with a piece of canvass. On lifting this, a humiliating spectacle presented itself. What rags the poor man had upon him when buried beneath the falling roof, were mostly torn from his body in the last faint struggle for life. His neck, and shoulder, and right arm were burnt to a cinder. There he lay in the rain, like the carcass of a brute beast thrown upon a dung heap. As we continued our walk along this filthy lane, half-naked women and children would come out of their cabins, apparently in the last stage of the fever, to beg for food, "for the honour of God." As they stood upon the wet ground, one could almost see it smoke beneath their bare feet, burning with the fever.

We entered the grave-yard, in the midst of which was a small watch-house. This miserable shed had served as a grave where the dying could bury themselves. It was seven feet long, and six in breadth. It was already walled round on the outside with an embankment of graves, half way to the eaves. The aperture of this horrible den of death would scarcely admit of the entrance of a common sized person. And into this noisome sepulcher living men, women, and children, went down to die; to pillow upon the rotten straw, the grave clothes vacated by preceding victims and festering with their fever. Here they lay as closely to each other as if crowded side by side on the bottom of one grave. Six persons had been found in this fetid sepulcher at one time, and with one only able to crawl to the door to ask for water. Removing a board from the entrance of this black hole of pestilence, we found it crammed with wan victims of famine, ready and willing to perish. A quiet listless despair broods over the population, and cradles men for the grave.

Sunday, February 21.—Dr. D----[20] called at two o'clock, and we proceeded together to visit a lane of hovels on the opposite side of the village. The wretchedness of this little mud city of the dead and dying was of a deeper stamp than the one I saw yesterday. Here human beings and their clay habitations seemed to be melting down together into the earth. I can find no language nor illustration sufficiently impressive to portray the spectacle to an American reader. A cold drizzling rain was deepening the pools of black filth, into which it fell like ink drops from the clouds. Few of the young or old have not read of the scene exhibited on the field of battle after the action, when visited by the surgeon. The cries of the wounded and dying for help, have been described by many graphic pens. The agonizing entreaty for "Water! water! help, help!" has been conveyed to our minds with painful distinctness. I can liken the scene we witnessed in the low lane of famine and pestilence, to nothing of greater family resemblance, than that of the battle field, when the hostile armies have retired, leaving one-third of their number bleeding upon the ground. As soon as Dr. D---appeared at the head of the lane, it was filled with miserable beings, haggard, famine-stricken men, women, and children, some far gone in the consumption of the famine fever, and all imploring him "for the honour of God" to go in and see "my mother," "my father," "my boy," "who is very bad, your honour." And then, interspersed with these earnest entreaties, others louder still would be raised for bread. In every hovel we entered, we found the dying or the dead. In one of these straw-roofed burrows, eight persons had died in the last fortnight, and five more were lying upon the fetid, pestiferous straw, upon which their predecessors to the grave had been consumed by the wasting fever of famine. In scarcely a single one of these most inhuman habitations was there the slightest indication of food of any kind to be found, nor fuel to cook food, nor anything resembling a bed, unless it were a thin layer of filthy straw in one corner, upon which the sick person lay, partly covered with some ragged garment. There being no window, nor aperture to admit the light, in these wretched cabins, except the door, we found ourselves often in almost total darkness for the first moment of our entrance. But a faint glimmering of a handful of burning straw in one end would soon reveal to us the indistinct images of wan-faced children grouped together, with their large, plaintive, still eyes looking out at us, like the sick young of wild beasts in their dens. Then the groans, and the choked, incoherent entreaties for help of some man or woman wasting away with the sickness in some corner of the cabin, would apprise us of the number and condition of the family. The wife, mother, or child would frequently light a wisp of straw, and hold it over the face of the sick person, discovering to us the sooty features of some emaciated creature in the last stage of the fever. In one of these places we found an old woman stretched upon a pallet of straw, with her head within a foot of a handful of fire, upon which something was steaming in a small iron vessel. The Doctor removed the cover, and we found it was filled with a kind of slimy seaweed, which, I believe, is used for manure in the seaboard. This was all the nourishment that the daughter could serve to her sick mother. But the last cabin we visited in this painful walk, presented to our eyes a lower deep of misery. It was the residence of two families, both of which had been thinned down to half their original number by the sickness. The first sight that met my eyes, on entering, was the body of a dead woman, extended on one side of the fire-place. On the other, an old man was lying on some straw, so far gone as to be unable to articulate distinctly. He might have been ninety or fifty years of age. It was difficult to determine, for this wasting consumption of want brings out the extremest indices of old age in the features of even the young.

But there was another apparition which sickened all the flesh and blood in my nature. It has haunted me during the past night, like Banquo's ghost.[21] I have lain awake for hours, struggling for some graphic and truthful similes or new elements of description, by which I might convey to the distant reader some tangible image of this object. A dropsical affection[22] among the young and old is very common to all the sufferers by famine. I had seen men at work on the public roads with their limbs swollen almost to twice their usual size. But when the woman of this cabin lifted from the straw, from behind the dying man, a boy about twelve years of age, and held him up before us upon his feet, the most horrifying spectacle met our eyes. The cold, watery-faced child was entirely naked in front, from his neck down to his feet. His body was swollen to nearly three times its usual size, and had burst the ragged garment that covered him, and now dangled in shreds behind him. The woman of the other family, who was sitting at her end of the hovel, brought forward her little infant, a thin-faced baby of two years, with clear, sharp eyes that did not wink, but stared stock still at vacancy, as if a glimpse of another existence had eclipsed its vision. Its cold, naked arms were not much larger than pipe stems, while its body was swollen to the size of a full-grown person. Let the reader group these apparitions of death and disease into the spectacle of ten feet square, and then multiply it into three-fourths of the hovels in this region of Ireland, and he will arrive at a fair estimate of the extent or degree of its misery. Were it not for giving them pain, I should have been glad if the well-dressed children in America could have entered these hovels with us, and looked upon the young creatures wasting away unmurmuringly by slow consuming destitution. I am sure they would have been touched to the liveliest compassion at the spectacle, and have been ready to divide their wardrobe with the sufferers.

Monday, February 22.—Dr. H.---[23] called to take me into the Castle-haven parish, which comes within his circuit. This district borders upon the sea, whose rocky indented shores are covered with cabins of a worse description than those in Skibbereen. On our way, we passed several companies of men, women, and children at work,[24] all enfeebled and emaciated by destitution. Women with their red, swollen feet partially swathed in old rags, some in men's coats, with their arms or skirts torn off, were sitting by the road side, breaking stone. It was painful to see human labour and life struggling among the lowest interests of society. Men, once athletic labourers, were trying to eke out a few miserable days to their existence, by toiling upon these works. Poor creatures! Many of them are already famine stricken. They have reached a point from which they cannot be recovered. Dr. D--, informs me that he can tell at a glance whether a person has reached this point. And I am assured by several experienced observers, that there are thousands of men who rise in the morning and go forth to labour with their picks and shovels in their hands, who are irrecoverably doomed to death. No human aid can save them. The plague spot of famine is on their foreheads; the worm of want has eaten in two their heart strings. Still they go forth uncomplaining to their labour and toil, cold, and half naked upon the roads, and divide their eight or ten pence worth of food at night among a sick family of five or eight persons. Someone is often kept at home, and prevented from earning this pittance, by the fear that some one of their family will die before their return. The first habitation we entered in the Castle-haven district was literally a hole in the wall, occupied by what might be called in America, a squatter, or a man who had burrowed a place for himself and family in the acute angle of two dilapidated walls by the road-side, where he lived rent free. We entered this stinted den by an aperture about three feet high, and found one or two children lying asleep with their eyes open in the straw. Such, at least, was their appearance, for they scarcely winked while we were before them. The father came in and told his pitiful story of want, saying that not a morsel of food had they tasted for twenty-four hours. He lighted a wisp of straw and showed us one or two more children lying in another nook of the cave. Their mother had died, and he was obliged to leave them alone during most of the day, in order to glean something for their subsistence. We were soon among the most wretched habitations that I had yet seen; far worse than those in Skibbereen. Many of them were flat-roofed hovels, half buried in the earth, or built up against the rocks, and covered with rotten straw, sea-weed, or turf. In one which was scarcely seven feet square, we found five persons prostrate with the fever, and apparently near their end. A girl about sixteen, the very picture of despair, was the only one left who could administer any relief; and all she could do was to bring water in a broken pitcher to slaken their parched lips. As we proceeded up a rocky hill overlooking the sea, we encountered new sights of wretchedness. Seeing a cabin standing somewhat by itself in a hollow, and surrounded by a moat of green filth, we entered it with some difficulty, and found a single child about three years old lying on a kind of shelf, with its little face resting upon the edge of the board and looking steadfastly out at the door, as if for its mother. It never moved its eyes as we entered, but kept them fixed toward the entrance. It is doubtful whether the poor thing had a mother or father left to her; but it is more doubtful still, whether those eyes would have relaxed their vacant gaze if both of them had entered at once with anything that could tempt the palate in their hands. No words can describe this peculiar appearance of the famished children. Never have I seen such bright, blue, clear eyes looking so steadfastly at nothing. I could almost fancy that the angels of God had been sent to unseal the vision of these little patient, perishing creatures, to the beatitudes of another world; and that they were listening to the whispers of unseen spirits bidding them to "wait a little longer."

Leaving this, we entered another cabin in which we found seven or eight attenuated young creatures, with a mother who had pawned her cloak and could not venture out to beg for bread because she was not fit to be seen in the streets. Hearing the voice of wailing from a cluster of huts further up the hill, we proceeded to them, and entered one, and found several persons weeping over the dead body of a woman lying by the wall near the door. Stretched upon the ground here and there lay several sick persons, and the place seemed a den of pestilence. The filthy straw was rank with the festering fever. Leaving this habitation of death, we were met by a young woman in an agony of despair because no one would give her a coffin to bury her father in. She pointed to a cart at some distance, upon which his body lay, and she was about to follow it to the grave, and he was such a good father, she could not bear to lay him like a beast in the ground, and she begged a coffin "for the honour of God." While she was wailing and weeping for this boon, I cast my eye towards the cabin we had just left, and a sight met my view which made me shudder with horror. The husband of the dead woman came staggering out with her body upon his shoulder, slightly covered with a piece of rotten canvass. I will not dwell upon the details of this spectacle. Painfully and slowly he bore the remains of the late companion of his misery to the cart. We followed him a little way off and saw him deposit his burden alongside of the father of the young woman, and by her assistance. As the two started for the grave yard to bury their own dead, we pursued our walk still further on, and entered another cabin where we encountered the climax of human misery. Surely thought I, while regarding this new phenomenon of suffering, there can be no lower deep than this between us and the bottom of the grave.

On asking after the conditions of the inmates, the woman to whom we addressed the question answered by taking out the straw three breathing skeletons, ranging from two to three feet in height and *entirely naked*. And these human beings were alive! If they had been dead, they could not have been such frightful spectacles, they were alive, and, *mirabile dictum*,[25] they could stand upon their feet and even walk; but it was awful to see them do it. Had their bones been divested of the skin that held them together, and been covered with a veil of thin muslin, they would not have been more visible, especially when one of them clung to the door, while a sister was urging it forward, it assumed an appearance, which can have been seldom paralleled this side of the grave. The effort which it made to cling to the door disclosed every joint in its frame, while the deepest lines of old age furrowed its face. The enduring of ninety years of sorrow seemed to chronicle its record of woe upon the poor child's countenance. I could bear no more; and we returned to Skibbereen, after having been all the afternoon among these abodes of misery. On our way we overtook the cart with the two uncoffined bodies. The man and young woman were all that attended them to the grave. Last year the funeral of either would have called out hundreds of mourners from those hills. But now the husband drove his uncoffined wife to the grave without a tear in his eye, without a word of sorrow. About half way to Skibbereen, Dr H---proposed that we should diverge to another road to visit a cabin in which we should find two little girls living alone, with their dead mother, who had lain unburied seven days. He gave an affecting history of this poor woman; and we turned from the road to visit this new scene of desolation; but as it was growing quite dark, and the distance was considerable, we concluded to resume our way back to the village. In fact I had witnessed as much as my heart could bear. In the evening I met several gentlemen at the house of Mr. S--, among whom was Dr. D---. He had just returned from a neighbouring parish, where he visited a cabin which had been deserted by the poor people around, although it was known that some of its inmates were still alive, though dying in the midst of the dead. He knocked at the door; and hearing no voice within, burst it open, with his foot; and was, in a moment almost overpowered by the horrid stench. Seeing a man's legs protruding from the straw, he moved them slightly with his foot; when a husky voice asked for water. In another part of the cabin, on removing a piece of canvas, he discovered three dead bodies, which had lain there *unburied for a fortnight;* and hard against one of these, and almost embraced in the arms of death, lay a young person far gone with fever. He related other cases too horrible to be published.

ELIHU BURRITT.

PRINTED BY J.W. SHOWELL, TEMPLE-STREET, BIRMINGHAM.

LEAGUE OF Universal Brotherhood.
        London, April 23/47
My Dear Sir,
It almost makes my heart heavy to think that I could not participate in the joy and honor of witnessing the dispensation of the <u>ammunition</u> of the <u>late</u> sloop of war *Jamestown* among the poor Irish. O it would have been a scene fraught with happy associations, and an ample reward for all the spectacles of misery I witnessed in my recent tour in Ireland. I should have been rejoiced to witness this novel demonstration of brotherly sympathy in Jonathan, but, to tell the truth, I have not enough left in my locker to pay my fare to Cork & back. Besides, I am

pressed to the ground with arduous and increasing labour. I congratulate you on being present to witness this auspicious token of the better day coming. I have already written to Captain Forbes, that I would try to tread the deck of this gallant ship before it returned to America, but I must now relinquish that hope. May God bless him forever for his act of heroic beneficence. I wrote to Sumner some time since. Thank you for your kind letter.

Adieu !<br>Elihu Burrritt

5 Bishopsgate Without[26]
London.

## Notes

1. Richard Rathbone (1788–1860) was part of the Rathbone family of Liverpool who were successful merchants and ship-owners. They were also prominent abolitionists and philanthropists.
2. From Burritt, Browns Hotel, Clayton Square, Liverpool, to Richard Rathbone, 6 July 1846, Elihu Burritt Library, Central Connecticut University (CCU) Archive: http://library.ccsu.edu/help/spcoll/burritt/burrletters2.php, accessed 5 October 2016.
3. 'LEAGUE OF UNIVERSAL BROTHERHOOD', *The Advocate of Peace and Universal Brotherhood*, vol. 1, no. 10 (October, 1846), pp. 243–247.
4. 17 February 1847, the *Daily Spy* (Worcester's leading paper).
5. William Rathbone V (1787–1868) was Richard's brother and business partner. He was active in supporting social reforms, especially in his home town of Liverpool. He was a supporter of Catholic Emancipation and of the work of Father Mathew (1790–1856) the Irish temperance reformer. During the Famine, he oversaw the distribution of relief from New England to Cork.
6. The papers of the New England Relief Committee are held in Liverpool University, Special Archives and Collections.
7. Chas. Northend (ed.), *Elihu Burritt: A Memorial Volume Containing a Sketch of His Life and Labors, with Selections from His Writings and Lectures, and Extracts from His Private Journals in Europe and America* (New York: D. Appleton, 1879).
8. Christine Kinealy, *Charity and the Great Hunger. The Kindness of Strangers* (London: Bloomsbury, 2013), pp. 24–44; 'Debates in Congress', *National Era,* 25 February 1847, 4 March 1847.
9. Journal, Dublin, 13 February 1847, in Northend, *Elihu Burritt*, pp. 35–36.
10. Ibid., pp. 50–51.
11. Ibid., writing from Skibbereen, 24 February 1847, p. 51.
12. Joseph Sturge (1793–1859) was a Birmingham-based businessman. A supporter of abolition, in 1839, he was a founder of the British and Foreign Anti-Slavery Society. Sturge supported other progressive issues, including Chartism and the Peace Society.
13. Sturge, Birmingham, to Burritt, 3 March 1847, CCU Archive.
14. Both men were in touch with Richard Dowden (1794–1861) a prominent Unitarian and businessman from Cork City, who supported Catholic Emancipation, Repeal, abolition and temperance, and the work of the Peace Convention. See Cork Archives: www.corkarchives.ie/media/U140web.pdf, accessed 10 January 2017.
15. The original pamphlet contains many typographical errors, which have been corrected in the preceding text.

16 In spring 1847, Russell's government decided that the Poor Law would be extended and, after August, be made responsible for both ordinary and famine relief. This change effectively threw the whole financial burden for supporting relief on Irish landowners. See, Christine Kinealy, 'The role of the Poor Law during the Famine', in Cathal Póirtéir (ed.) *The Great Irish Famine* (Cork: Mercier Press, 1995), pp. 104–122.

17 It is generally believed that this donation came from the young Lord Frederick Dufferin, who undertook his own journey to Skibbereen in the spring of 1847, during Spring Break at Oxford University. See, Lord Dufferin and G. F. Boyle, *Narrative Of A Journey From Oxford To Skibbereen During The Year Of The Irish Famine* (Oxford: John Henry Parker, 1847). The proceeds of this booklet were also sent to Skibbereen.

18 Sturge established the Birmingham branch of the Society for the Promotion of Permanent and Universal Peace, a pacifist organization that had been founded in London in 1816.

19 Father John Fitzpatrick (1803–1892), the Roman Catholic priest in Skibbereen. He worked tirelessly to raise funds and distribute relief. He wrote many letters to the British and Irish press, describing conditions in the area. In 1851, Fitzpatrick was moved to Midleton parish.

20 Dr. Daniel Donovan (1807–77), a native of Rosscarbery, commenced his medical career in Skibbereen in the late 1820s. When the local workhouse opened, he was appointed its first Medical Officer. Throughout 1846 and 1847 he wrote his 'Diary of a Dispensary Doctor', which was published in the Cork-based, *The Southern Reporter,* but reprinted elsewhere. Donovan also wrote on the origins and consequences of the fever in the *Dublin Medical Press*, 1 March 1848.

21 Banquo is a ghostly spectre in William Shakespeare's play, *Macbeth* (1606).

22 Dropsy, now more usually referred to as edema, causes a swelling of the legs, which can spread to the entire body. One of its causes is malnutrition and a prolonged lack of protein.

23 Dr David Hadden, a Methodist doctor in Skibbereen. He was a regular contributor to the medical journal, the *Lancet*.

24 The Public Works Scheme was initially intended for men, but the deliberately low rate of wages meant that women and children also applied to it. Their lack of utility is summed up in the phrase, 'Roads that lead nowhere; walls that surround nothing'. See, 'An Act to extend and consolidate the powers hitherto exercised by the Commissioners of Public Works in Ireland, and to appoint additional Commissioners' (26 August 1846).

25 Literally, 'wonderful to relate'.

26 Burritt used the address of his publisher, Charles Gilpin, as his posting address. Gilpin (1815 -1874) was an English-born Quaker publisher and politician, who was related to Joseph Sturge. He was liberal, supporting abolition, prison reform, the ending of the death penalty and the Peace Society. He managed the London publishing company from 1842 to 1853, many of the works that he printed being written by progressive writers. His papers are now held by Duke University: http://library.duke.edu/rubenstein/findingaids/gilpin/, accessed 3 January 2017.

# 10

# WILLIAM BENNETT, *SIX WEEKS IN IRELAND* (MARCH AND APRIL 1847)

William Bennett had been born in London in 1804 to a Quaker family involved in the tea trade. In 1828, he married Elizabeth Trusted, a teacher of the poor, who later authored of a number of religious books for the Society of Friends.[1] In the wake of the second failure of the potato crop, Quakers in both Dublin and London had formed committees, not simply to raise funds, but also to distribute the relief personally. Although small in numbers, and mostly concentrated in urban areas, British and Irish Quakers were well respected for their stance on many social issues, including Abolition.[2] They were part of an international network that was noted for its philanthropy and humanity. Consequently, their involvement was both practical and personal, with members of the Society undertaking arduous and dangerous journeys to the poorest parts of Ireland in order to provide relief. In keeping with their belief that God was present in everyone, Friends treated the poor with sympathy and respect. Bennett too, proved to be kind and respectful when dealing with the Irish poor. The involvement of the Quakers in providing aid during the Famine was widely praised, both at the time and subsequently.[3]

In the spring of 1847, Bennett arrived in Ireland, accompanied by his eldest son, with the intention of 'touring the worst-hit areas'. Unlike a number of other visitors who came merely to observe, Bennett came to distribute relief, in this case, 'small seed'. Bennett's visit took place in March and April 1847, thus coinciding with the closing of the public works, which had left many people with no means of support. During this hiatus in relief provision, it was often private charity that provided a vital lifeline to the poor.[4] Unfortunately, it coincided with an unusually hard and prolonged winter, with frost and snow adding to the suffering of the poor.[5] Initially, Bennett had intended to visit only counties Mayo and Donegal but, following his return to Dublin, he decided to extend his stay and visit counties Tipperary and Kerry.

Rather than focus on providing immediate relief, Bennett chose to use his resources to help the poor become more self-sufficient. He believed that as the potato had proved to be an unreliable source of food, there was a need to encourage a greater diversity of crops. To this end, he purchased seed from W. Drummond and Sons in Dawson Street in Dublin. Drummond's Company also provided Bennett with both verbal and printed advice. Bennett's preferred choice of nourishment was turnip seed together with carrots and mangelwurzel. He later included cabbage, parsnip and flax. In addition to distributing seed, Bennett took £50 in cash, three large bales of clothing, and a plentiful supply of arrowroot and ginger, in whose medicinal properties he was a firm believer. The clothes were provided by the London Ladies' Committee (of which Bennett's sister was a member), Quaker women providing an essential service in providing clothes to the poor.[6]

The impact of Bennett's charitable endeavours was acknowledged by one recipient. Reverend Samuel Stock, the Church of Ireland rector in the Kilcommon parish in north Mayo—one of the poorest and remotest districts in Ireland—was unequivocal in his praise. At the end of 1846 and again in October 1847, Stock wrote to the British Prime Minister, pointing out that because of the delay in providing government relief, thousands of people had perished in the area. He also accused the government of having no plan for the coming months.[7] In a separate letter, Stock claimed that the distribution of turnip and carrot seed, 'had prevented the perishing of thousands'.[8]

*Six Weeks in Ireland* belongs to a genre of writers who observed the Great Famine first hand.[9] When he is not directly commenting on the poverty, his writings have the feel of a travelogue. Bennett's backdrop to the human suffering is the rugged, natural beauty of Ireland, which he comments on at length, and which provides a stark juxtaposition with the ugly reality of starvation. Bennett's narrative was comprised of letters, which were written to his sister, who herself was involved in relief activities in London.

Bennett's book was published only four months after his return to England. The income from the publication was to be used for 'Irish relief'. A further purpose was to encourage more donations for Ireland.[10]

Bennett died at his home in Westminster in England in February 1873.[11]

## WILLIAM BENNETT, *NARRATIVE OF A RECENT JOURNEY OF SIX WEEKS IN IRELAND, IN CONNEXION WITH THE SUBJECT OF SUPPLYING SMALL SEED TO SOME OF THE REMOTER DISTRICTS: CURRENT OBSERVATIONS ON THE DEPRESSED CIRCUMSTANCES OF THE PEOPLE, AND THE MEANS PRESENTED FOR THE PERMANENT IMPROVEMENT OF THEIR SOCIAL CONDITION* (DUBLIN: CHARLES GILPIN, 1847).

"Nor will I give the slightest countenance to any consideration of Ireland as a thing separate and apart from ourselves."—OLD MS.

LONDON: CHARLES GILPIN, BISHOPSGATE WITHOUT. JOHN HATCHARD & SON, PICCADILLY. DUBLIN: J. CURRY, Jun. & CO. M.DCCC.XLVII.

"In the morning sow thy seed, and in the evening withhold not thine hand; for thou knowest not whether shall prosper, either this or that."—Ecclesiastes xi. 6.

ADVERTISEMENT.

THE following record of a simple individual effort is from memoranda and letters written principally to my sister, one of the working members of the Ladies' Irish Clothing Committee of London.[12] It is not that an additional testimony is needed to the depth and extent of the visitation which has been permitted to desolate our sister-isle; nor to their patient endurance of sufferings, which it is believed are unparalleled among any other people, at least in Europe and in modern times. It is simply, that in a protracted period of such severe and wide-spread calamity, the field is open to every variety and extent of labour, while the humblest contribution is kindly received. In the prosecution of the object, likewise, some spots have been visited which had not before obtained the same degree of personal investigation. Some account is also felt to be due to those who have lent their aid and sympathy, and to the general interest and inquiry which have now been awakened in the way of information on whatever may concern the present state or more permanent welfare of Ireland; and which is disposed to look with indulgence on every practical effort to mitigate one pang of her accumulated and varied sufferings, to counteract in any degree those causes which have left her peasantry without resource on the constant verge of famine, or to grapple with the evils resulting from her social condition.

Should these notes and observations, which the writer feels have been crudely put together under much difficulty, create any additional interest in the state of some of the remote and neglected corners of the sister-land—in the wide field there offered for humanity and usefulness—in the means of her permanent improvement—in the features of her attractive and magnificent scenery,—should they have any effect in abating one prejudice—in awakening any fresh sympathy, or in keeping up any warmth of feeling and affection, he will be amply repaid and his object answered. They have been written out rather as a debt; and, the journey having extended from north to south, and twice from east to the extreme west of the island, over a distance of not less than 1,500 miles, much beyond what was at first anticipated, they have unconsciously swollen under his hands. Having often enjoyed her simple and social hospitality, it is felt as a tribute not less due in this her hour of deep tribulation and anguish, of humility and woe. The whole journey has been a gainful, but now upon the retrospect, a most deeply interesting one. He has endeavoured to confine these Letters to such details only as are characteristic of something in the state and circumstances of the people, or otherwise closely connected with his subject: and it was never his intention to have written a BOOK.

The proceeds will be devoted to Irish relief.

*London, 1st of 7th mo.* 1847.

## SIX WEEKS IN IRELAND.

LETTER I. BALLINA. *6th*—13th *of 3rd mo.* 1847.

APPREHENDING there could not be a much greater service, or more beneficial appropriation of some small funds, than in the purchase of seeds for green crops, and the distribution of them in some of the most remote districts of Ireland, where they could not otherwise have been obtained by the poor people, I started on this mission, accompanied by my eldest son, on the 6th day of the 3rd month. I had previously conferred with the Relief Committee of the Society of Friends in London, in the hopes they would give the subject a wider range, by taking it on their own hands. They kindly gave me every personal encouragement, but were too full-handed, and, as a Committee, did not feel at liberty to take it up any further. A Friend, too well known for his unbounded liberality and large contributions through almost every channel opened for Irish subscriptions, to need being mentioned by name, on hearing of my object, immediately sent an authority which *doubled* the sum I had been able to appropriate to this purpose. Several other Friends kindly sent me smaller amounts. The Ladies' Irish Clothing Committee placed at my disposal £50, and three of their largest bales of clothing, besides a box of arrow-root and ginger,[13] for distribution wherever I saw need. These unsolicited and substantial proofs of sympathy in the object were a great encouragement, but they added much to my feeling of responsibility in entering upon the undertaking.

Thus strengthened, we proceeded direct to Belfast; spent two or three days in obtaining information, seeing parties, and attending the Quarterly Meeting for Ulster, held at Lisburn; and left for Dublin on the 10th. It was a heavy snow storm on the way to the train, but did not continue long. We heard the most distressing accounts of the state of the Lurgan poor-house, and of the mortality within its walls.[14] Along the road there was a fair quantity of agricultural labour going forward; and from all our inquiries, we have reason to believe there is a considerably greater breadth of land under corn, and likewise of the better qualities, in this part of the country, than usual; and far more potatoes were likely to be set than had been anticipated. The Mourne mountains came out grand, and almost alpine, under their canopies of snow, which remained on all the higher ground. One could fancy the towns looked dull, and many shutters were observed up in passing through, but there was no marked appearance of distress along the public road.

I attended the sitting of the Central Relief Committee in Dublin on the 11th.[15] Their organization and mode of transacting business appeared complete; and it was said they had as extensive a correspondence to conduct as any mercantile counting-house in Dublin. Some Friends devote almost their whole time, giving up day and night to its concerns and management, and to the work of the sub-committees. The supply of seed, however, they thought a very questionable mode of rendering relief, and requiring great caution. An opinion was even expressed, that all which had been done for Ireland in the way of relief has only acted injuriously. The unwearied labours and devotedness of the Committee themselves bespeak another hope and sentiment. Some statements on the great saving in human food, amounting to a large percentage—a most important consideration in times like these—that would be effected by the use of "whole meal" instead of fine flour, were made by a Friend, whose opinion likewise, on its greater wholesomeness for all classes, is entitled to no small weight, as a member of the medical profession.

My arrangements for the supplies of seed were made with the house of W. Drummond and Sons, Dawson-street, whose agricultural museum at Stirling I had the opportunity of visiting last summer with great interest.[16] I have to acknowledge the readiness and liberality with which the resident partner entered into my views, and afforded every information and assistance, in the way of recommending the best and most suitable sorts, which their great local knowledge and extensive experience enabled them to do. They had facilities likewise for subsequent transmission to the different remote localities; and they sent a copious supply of their simple printed directions for sowing and cultivating each particular sort. My selection consisted of the several varieties of turnip, principally Swedes, the white Belgium carrot, and mangel-wurzel. A small quantity of cabbage, in sorts, some flax, and some parsnip seed, were afterwards added. Two hundred weight, in proportions of each, were packed up to take with us, being as much as could very conveniently be carried by coach; and a few agricultural pamphlets of their recommendation for distribution.

Thus equipped, we left Dublin on the 12th, by day-coach, for Boyle. The provision-boats on the canal near Mullingar were guarded by policemen on board, needlessly as it seemed to me. The first evidence of the extreme distress of the times we witnessed was in the spectacle of a corpse exposed in the public road, death having apparently been the work of starvation. Not far from this, in an angle of the way side, under a low temporary erection of straw, was a poor family down in fever. We met along the road multitudes of emigrants, mostly on foot, with their bundles on their backs, proceeding to Dublin. A few had more than they could thus carry; and it was an affecting sight to observe numerous whole families, with their worldly ALL packed up on a donkey-cart, attempting to look gay and cheerful, as they cast a wistful glance at the rapidly passing by coach passengers; and thus abandoning a country which should have nourished them and their children. We met several hundreds in the course of this morning only, and the guard assured me it was the same every day, and thicker at the week's commencement. Except in the increased beggary in the towns,—always great in Ireland,—wherever the coach stopped, and which was particularly importunate in Longford, there was no other unusual appearance of poverty along this line of road. The land, however, was evidently much neglected, or lying wholly waste. The absence of pigs was also a remarkable feature to an eye accustomed to Ireland. The difference in the face of the country, and in the appearance of the peasantry and their habitations, from the influence of a resident benevolent and kind-hearted family, was particularly evident about Edgeworth's-town,[17] and again in the neighbourhood of Lord Lorton's,[18] before entering Boyle.

Our guard was one of those shrewd, intelligent, well-informed, clear-thinking men, not unfrequently met with in that and similar capacities in Ireland. A gentleman who got up on the coach, full of the one-sided views and oblique mode of reasoning so common among a certain class, had no chance with him in argument, on the subject of Ireland's grievances. He quoted Latin and Shakspere [sic] with great fluency and appropriateness. Land is let in this part at £5, £7, £12, and £14 per acre, on the *conacre* plan. I afterwards heard of £20 per acre, but was not able to substantiate so high a rental. The word "Gombien," [sic][19] and prevalence of the "Gombien system," was new to me; though I find it exposed and commented on in the able letters of the "Times Commissioner,"[20] No. 20. I cannot but think that it only requires to be fully brought out to the light, and generally known, to cease to exist altogether. The poor cottier having taken his plot of ground on conacre,— that is, for the present crop, and no further interest in it,—requires seed, and having no money to purchase it, he goes to a Gombien man. This man sells him potatoes, or oats, or whatever else it may be, on the *credit of the harvest*, taking his I. O. U. at 50, 70, and even 100 p cent, profit, according to circumstances, on the current market value of the article. Under any accident or failure, or even in fair seasons, he is often unable to pay this exorbitant price when the time comes round. The Gombien man enters his process for the recovery on the I. O. U., and generally gets the full amount awarded, and often forces the sale of the crop, or anything else the poor fellow possesses, to *himself*, at his own price. Not only is seed-corn, but meal for his present subsistence, – often purchased in this way. The poor fellow is hopelessly ground down by this system, which is sufficiently calculated to feed and encourage his natural recklessness and improvidence, and is the fruitful source of innumerable disputes and heart-burnings. I was happy to hear that one of the assistant barristers in the county of Roscommon had set himself resolutely against the system, refusing to award more than fair market price at the time of contract, with customary interest. The practice is prevalent all over the west, and particularly in Mayo.

The want of any direct and permanent interest in the improvement of the soil, and the non-requital of the actual cultivator, arising from the land being usually the only source from which several grades of holders have to extract all the profit they can,—falling therefore with accumulated weight on the last or actual occupier,— is one of the sorest evils of Ireland. While large tracts of land have been let on low terms, and underlet, or leases sold for lives renewable *for ever*,—so that the great proprietor has little interest in, or power over them,—they get divided and subdivided, each at an increased rental, until the small holder pays those enormous rates we hear of under the conacre system. The average rent in Ireland at which arable land is let, is probably more than double the same in England; so that what with conacre rent for his land, and Gombien price for his seed, and ditto for his food, while he tills the land, it is not surprising that the Irish peasant has been kept at the lowest verge of pauperism; for all inducement to industry, beyond the barest living, is in fact withdrawn. A poor man got up on the coach who held 1½ rood taken from the bare bog,[21] for which he paid 30s. at first; built himself a cabin, and was now raised to 35s.; and did not doubt he would have his rent again raised, or be turned out, if he *improved it any more*. His immediate landlord paid 7s. 6d. *p. acre, under lease.*

From Boyle we took a car across the country to Ballina. The shores of Lough Garra are wild and dreary, and the whole district increasingly so on approaching the small town of Tobercurry. We here first encountered the public works so called. These consisted in making new roads and altering old ones, in many cases worse than useless, and obviously undertaken without judgment, for the mere sake of employment. Independently of the moral effects of useless labour,—which it is impossible should be otherwise than listlessly pursued,—it was melancholy and degrading in the extreme to see the women and girls withdrawn from all that was decent and proper, and labouring in mixed gangs on the public roads.[22] Not only in digging with the spade, and with the pick, but in carrying loads of earth and turves on their backs, and wheeling barrows like men, and breaking stones, are they employed. My heart often sunk within me at the obviously deteriorating effects of such occupation, while the poor neglected children were crouched in groups around the bits of lighted turves in the various sheltered corners along the line. I need scarcely say that the soil was totally neglected here. I conversed with several of the men, and the overseers in many of the gangs,—the car with great difficulty getting along, and having to go walking pace over miles of alterations. The pay was *6d.* and *7d.* p. day to the girls and women, and *8d.* to the men; which being the lowest we met with anywhere, though never exceeding *10d.*, I shall not have occasion to mention again.

Thrashing out corn in the *middle of the public road*, where every wheel must necessarily pass, was a novelty to me, and clearly indicated the wasteful, as well as backward state of agricultural ideas, and the want of farm buildings.

The country became very dreary, and but thinly inhabited, soon after leaving Tobercurry. It is a cross road but little frequented, winding up among wild hills until it reaches the solitary elevation of Lough Talt,—bounded by the bleak repulsive heights of Slievh Gamph [sic][23]—the northern shore of which it skirts, and then descends into the plain, extending to the shores of Lough Conn, beyond which the eye rested on the broad shoulders of the Nephin range.

At Ballina our first enquiry was for our dear friend Wm. Forster, and his companions, Joseph C. Harvey and Abraham Taw,[24] whom, to our great pleasure, we found had not left the town. W. F. had been engaged a day or two at Killala and Ballycastle, and had only just returned. We lost no time in communicating with them.

LETTER II. BALLINA — BELMULLET. *14th—16th of 3rd mo.* 1847.

THIS was First-day morning.[25] At 11 o'clock we went to sit down with Wm. Forster and his companions, at their hotel. It was probably the first time a Friends' Meeting had been held in this place; and the circumstances were such as to awaken many deep reflections. I think I was never more sensible of the value and privilege of our simple views, in the belief that acceptable worship may be performed, where 'two or three' are gathered together in silence and retirement, without dependence upon place, or building, or appointed ministration.

We returned to spend part of the afternoon and evening with them. It did not require to be long in their company to become conscious of the great personal labour our dear friend had undertaken; which indeed he could hardly have got through but for very able assistance. Wm. Forster's mind seems wholly occupied with his mission; which only those who are able to enter into a little of its working and details can have any idea of the weight and burden of. Besides the journeyings and various labours of the day, the filling up needful arrangements, and the necessary writing and correspondence usually occupied them far into the night. W. F. introduced me to a gentleman residing in one of the extreme corners of Erris, of whom I shall have occasion to say more hereafter.

Next morning, under the guidance of Abraham Taw, we proceeded to visit a widow lady about four miles off, on the old Killala road, who had called upon them, and whose case had much interested them, though not coming exactly within their province. We found a small, but neatly-furnished cottage, with signs of having been used to comfort and even elegance. She held about forty acres, on three lives and thirty-one years, and had come to the property, I think, since the decease of her husband. Her tenants had all deserted her in arrear; and the land was consequently lying waste and neglected, being all thrown upon her own hands, without the means of cropping it, and no rental whatever. She had little doubt of being able to obtain labour if she had seed. Here then commenced our first distribution: we left with her sufficient to cover about one-fourth of her land, if carefully and economically laboured, with the printed directions for the culture of green crops, as everywhere else where they were not much known. In Ballina we found a Protestant clergyman who was doing all he could to influence the poor people not to neglect their land, and had commenced employing eight whom he knew in preparing their respective plots, in the hope of procuring them seed. We had much pleasure in giving him a supply of such as we had; in this, as well as in every future case, taking an acknowledgment of the purpose for which they were given, and requesting a return of results, under the several heads.

Ballina has more the appearance of one of the new-born American cities than perhaps any other place in Ireland. There is a fine river, broad quays, large newly-built piles of warehouses, and a country around it still in the rough. It had a rising trade, and was rapidly increasing, until checked by the present calamity. In the afternoon we took the mail-car to Belmullet in Erris.[26]

It is an old saying concerning this remote district of Ireland, that "he who goes into Erris once will certainly go there again." I think the saying may have originated in the exceeding rarity of any one going there *at all;* for until within comparatively these very few years there was no road whatever into any part of this "ultima thule"[27] of the British isles. I know not how this may be, but certain it is that very few have ever visited any portion of the far west of Ireland without having had their admiration drawn forth by its wild and noble scenery, and their best affections awakened for its simple and kind-hearted peasantry, not unmingled with the deepest sympathy. I have sat round the basket of potatoes, in the wilds of Connemara, or among the mountains of Donegal, on some old log or broken stool, in friendly equality with the whole family,—pig and cow inclusive, while they had them,—without guide or protection of any kind; and partaken of their simple but hearty hospitality, with the greatest unwillingness on their part to accept of the smallest return and on leaving, often attended, to be shown the way further "for the love of your honour's company." I have watched the progress of the present calamity, too well knowing what the loss of the potato must be to them. The truly pristine state of the country may be best illustrated by the following anecdote, which we heard as a fact, with names, and not a witty invention.

The carriage of the engineer who constructed the present post road was the first wheeled vehicle that had ever been seen in the Mullet. How it got there was a mystery to the good people; but it was not accomplished without taking sufficient planks with them, which were placed down before the carriage, step by step, for it to be dragged over the bogs. At the further extremity of the Mullet, he was not a little surprised and delighted to find a most respectable lady and her daughters living in the best style circumstances around them enabled. The young ladies were charmed beyond measure with the novelty of the carriage, amusing themselves greatly by running up and down, in and out, shutting each other in, and such like gambols. They were acquainted with six different languages, could paint, sing, and play on the piano, but had never seen *a tree, a bridge, a flight of stairs, or a wheeled carriage of any kind.* Their accomplishments were accounted for by the circumstance of a foreign vessel having been driven in distress some years before, and landed a young artist, who acted as tutor, with a piano, and other auxiliaries.

The afternoon proved stormy and wet. The driving mist and rain, really painful with the violence of the blast, from which there is no protection in these open cars, hid the view of Lough Conn and the bases of the great Nephin mountains; but their summits were occasionally seen looming above the clouds. We found in Father ------------, Roman Catholic priest in Belmullet, our only fellow-passenger, a gentleman who gave us much local information concerning this capital, that is, the *only town* in the wide barony of Erris.[28]

The poor little town of Crossmolina exhibited great wretchedness. Beyond this there is not a tree to be seen. The country becomes one dreary waste of bog and moorland, here called "mountain," while the more elevated ground is designated "hill." The barony of Erris is entered at Corragh bridge, just where the Owenmore, coming down from the northern hills, crosses the road, and makes a sharp turn to the left, to avoid Nephin Beg, and the still nearer and loftier Slievh Cor.[29] The deep winding ravine through which the Owenmore now forces its way, and accompanies the road to Bangore, is wild and romantic in many parts. This river was said to be one of the most attractive in Ireland for the angler. Lough Carrowmore, which drains into it further on, but two miles from the sea, is also "full of the finest fish," including abundance of salmon, uncaught for want of skill and the requisite appliances. We lost the beautiful views of Broadhaven on the one hand, and Blacksod Bay on the other, with the mountains of Achill, and the many islands and promontories indenting the ocean, for want of daylight.

The whole of this wild country is full of traditions of old heroes and giants, and of the doings of the fairies, and of the "good people" or "gentry," so called; and certainly no tract or region could seem to be better adapted to a belief in their freaks and vagaries. A sensible man who rode some way by the side of the car, one of the small independent farmers, who was wishing to sell what he had, and be off to America while he had anything left, told us of a skeleton he had himself found, fourteen Irish feet in length,[30] while occupying a part of the island of Inniskea, off the coast.

The car was hailed by a voice, somewhat startling at that time of night and place, calling me by name, which proved to be that of a man-servant, kindly sent on the look out by our friend residing within about a mile of the town, and whose thoughtful hospitality, with even this little shortening of the journey, we were truly glad to make certain of, in exchange for the chance and unknown accommodation that might be met with in the town.

Our friend was the rector of Kilcommon,[31] with whom we had had much correspondence on the state of this district, from the first of the calamity assuming its more dreadful forms. The parish under his charge is 22 miles from north to south, 16½ from east to west, containing 146,000 Irish acres, and is therefore about the size of the county of Middlesex. It contains *(contained)* 20,000 inhabitants, of whom about 450 are Protestants. He had estimated the deaths in his vicinity from absolute starvation, up to this period, at *upwards of one thousand.*

The morning burst upon us in great beauty. Immediately beneath my window lay the sparkling estuary of Broadhaven, stretching right and left, like a great American river. On a sand-bank left by the tide, near the centre, three or four seals were disporting themselves. The contemplation of the beauty of Nature was, however, soon broken into, by evidences that we were indeed in the land of woe. From early daylight the poor people began to crowd the door. During breakfast they thronged the windows, which presented framed pictures of living groups of want and wretchedness, almost beyond endurance to behold; yet to keep them off the family had long found impossible. One of the valuable bales of clothing from the Ladies' Committee of London had just been received; and the first thing after breakfast we had the pleasure of seeing it partly distributed by the minister's wife and sister. The difficulty of selection was very great, where the supply, though so good and serviceable, was but a drop in the rolling ocean of destitution and nakedness; and of course there was a reserve made for known cases at home. We next visited the soup-kitchen, which they had set up themselves, on a small scale at first, in one of their own outhouses, and now extended by assistance received from Wm. Forster and Friends. The lady had also recently instituted employment for thirty poor women in spinning, and the manufacture of a coarse flannel, for which she pays them 2s. per week, and proposes to sell the flannel at as cheap a rate as she can to keep the employment going, or according to the support she may obtain. We saw them at work; and she spoke of the improved appearances of the poor women already, their cheerfulness and gratitude for the help and shelter thus afforded, and the circumstance of being employed.

We now proceeded to Belmullet, kindly accompanied by the minister. The miserably clad female forms we met along the public road were disgraceful,— disgusting. This is probably the newest town in Ireland, having just attained its majority of twenty-one years, within which time it has sprung up entirely.[32] Its site is most advantageous, precisely on the narrowest part of the isthmus connecting the Mullet with the main land, here not above three quarters of a mile over. Through this isthmus it is intended to cut a canal, thus giving the town the advantage of the transit, as well as the two sea-boards. Broadhaven on the north is navigable for small craft only. Blacksod Bay, on which the town more properly stands, is capable of sheltering any navy in the world. The town is regularly built, with a centre, and streets radiating in each direction towards the sea; and possesses a neat quay, an hotel, a school-house, stores and shops supplying most useful articles, and several places of worship.

Our first visit was to the station for curing fish, lately established by Government, for the encouragement of the fisheries, and as a model for private enterprise,[33]—having a parcel of fishing-tackle, from a Friend of Dublin, for the superintendent. We found this gentleman—sent for from Scotland for the purpose—intelligent and obliging, and ready with any information required.[34] The object is to open a market for the poor fishermen, by purchasing their fish, which the officer is prepared to do, in any quantities brought in, at a fair price, but not to interfere with any other channel, if they can find sale elsewhere. The fish is cured and sent to distant markets for sale. He spoke of the establishment having been quite successful, even thus far, in point of profit; and that Government were most desirous of exciting private enterprise in this branch of industry, for which they would lend every practical assistance. In the curing-vats we saw magnificent specimens of ling and haddock. Cod and turbot abound on the banks a little further out; an improvement in the craft, and the application of skill and a little capital, being all that is requisite to open an abundant field of industry, and insure an ample return.

The school was attended by about ninety children,—two-thirds Catholics. The priest does not object to the simple Scriptures being used. It is supported principally by the aid of the rector. A description of the scenes within the Mullet I must defer to the next letter.

LETTER III. BELMULLET. *16th of 3rd mo.* 1847.

WE now proceeded to visit the district beyond the town within the Mullet. The cabins cluster the road-sides, and are scattered over the face of the bog, in the usual Irish manner, where the country is thickly inhabited. Several were pointed, out as "freeholders;" that is, such as had come wandering over the land, and "squatted" down on any unoccupied spot, owning no fealty, and paying no rent. Their neighbours had probably built them the cabin in four and twenty hours; expecting the same service in turn for themselves should occasion require it,—which a common necessity renders these poor people always willing to do for each other. Whatever little bit of ground they may reclaim around the cabin is necessarily done as much by stealth as possible; and the appearance of neglect and wretchedness is naturally carried out to the utmost; for should there be any visible improvement, down comes the landlord or his agent, with a demand for rent. The moral effect of such a state of things is obvious to the least reflecting mind. How far does its existence lie at the very basis of the low social condition of the people? I mention it here not as peculiar to this district. It is an element pervading large portions of Ireland; entering into the very growth of a population ever—by habit and education—on the verge of pauperism, and of whom the landlord, rarely coming near the property, knows little, and unfortunately in many instances cares less. The superior landlord,—the nominal owner of a wide domain,—has often very little interest, and no direct influence; or from incumbrances and limitations,—perhaps ever since it came into his possession,—he finds it a disagreeable and vexatious property, and dislikes it; or is really poor, and yet cannot relieve himself by reason of these difficulties. Here is society dislocated at *both ends*. Is Irish disorganization anything surprising? The natural influences and expenditure of property in creating artificial wants and means of livelihood, withdrawn from their own sources, and the people thrown back entirely upon the soil, with a bounty upon the veriest thriftlessness and least remove above the lowest animal conditions of life! Under such a state of things,—not the accident of to-day, but the steady and regular growth of years and a system,—a population is nurtured, treading constantly on the borders of starvation; checked only by a crisis like the present, to which it inevitably leads, and almost verifying the worst Malthusian doctrines.[35]

Many of the cabins were holes in the bog, covered with a layer of turves, and not distinguishable as human habitations from the surrounding moor, until close down upon them. The bare sod was about the best material of which any of them were constructed. Doorways, not doors, were usually provided at both sides of the bettermost—back and front—to take advantage of the way of the wind. Windows and chimneys, I think, had no existence. A second apartment or division of any kind within was exceedingly rare. Furniture, properly so called, I believe may be stated at *nil*. I would not speak with certainty, and wish not to with exaggeration,—we were too much overcome to note specifically; but as far as memory serves, we saw neither bed, chair, nor table, at all. A chest, a few iron or earthen vessels, a stool or two, the dirty rags and night-coverings, formed about the sum total of the best furnished. Outside many were all but unapproachable, from the mud and filth surrounding them; the same inside, or worse if possible, from the added closeness, darkness, and smoke. We spent the whole morning in visiting these hovels indiscriminately, or swayed by the representations and entreaties of the dense retinue of wretched creatures, continually augmenting, which gathered round, and followed us from place to place,—avoiding only such as were known to be badly infected with fever, which was sometimes sufficiently perceptible from without, by the almost intolerable stench. And now language utterly fails me in attempting to depict the state of the wretched inmates. I would not willingly add another to the harrowing details that have been told; but still they are the FACTS of actual experience, for the knowledge of which we stand accountable. I have certainly sought out one of the most remote and destitute corners; but still it is within the bounds of our Christian land, under our Christian Government, and entailing upon us—both as individuals and as members of a human community—a Christian responsibility from which no one of us can escape. My hand trembles while I write. The scenes of human misery and degradation we witnessed still haunt my imagination, with the vividness and power of some horrid and tyrannous delusion, rather than the features of a sober reality. We entered a cabin. Stretched in one dark corner, scarcely visible, from the smoke and rags that covered them, were three children huddled together, lying there *because they were too weak to rise*, pale and ghastly, their little limbs—on removing a portion of the filthy covering—perfectly emaciated, eyes sunk, voice gone, and evidently in the last stage of actual starvation. Crouched over the turf embers was another form, wild and all but naked, scarcely human in appearance. It stirred not, nor noticed us. On some straw, soddened upon the ground, moaning piteously, was a shrivelled old woman, imploring us to give her something,—baring her limbs partly, to show how the skin hung loose from the bones, as soon as she attracted our attention. Above her, on something like a ledge, was a young woman, with sunken cheeks,—a mother I have no doubt,—who scarcely raised her eyes in answer to our enquiries, but pressed her hand upon her forehead, with a look of unutterable anguish and despair. Many cases were widows, whose husbands had recently been taken off by the fever, and thus their only pittance, obtained from the public works, entirely cut off. In many the husbands or sons were prostrate, under that horrid disease,—the results of long-continued famine and low living,—in which first the limbs, and then the body, swell most frightfully, and finally burst. We entered upwards of fifty of these tenements. The scene was one and invariable, differing in little but the number of the sufferers or of the groups, occupying the several corners within. The whole number was often not to be distinguished, until—the eye having adapted itself to the darkness—they were pointed out, or were *heard*, or some filthy bundle of rags and straw *was perceived to move*. Perhaps the poor children presented the most piteous and heartrending spectacle. Many were too weak to stand, their little limbs attenuated,—except where the frightful swellings had taken the place of previous emaciation,—beyond the *power of volition when moved*. Every infantile expression entirely departed; and in some, reason and intelligence had evidently flown. Many were *remnants of families*, crowded together in one cabin; orphaned little relatives taken in by the equally destitute, and even strangers, for these poor people are kind to one another to the end. In one cabin was a sister, just dying, lying by the side of her little brother, just dead. I have worse than this to relate, but it is useless to multiply details, and they are, in fact, unfit. They did but rarely complain. When inquired of, what was the matter, the answer was alike in all,— "*Tha shein ukrosh*"—*indeed the hunger*.[36] We truly learned the terrible meaning of that sad word "*ukrosh*." There were many touching incidents. We should have gone on, but the pitiless storm had now arisen, beating us back with a force and violence against which it was difficult to stand; and a cutting rain, that drove us for shelter beneath a bank, fell on the crowd of poor creatures who continued to follow us unmitigatedly. My friend the clergyman had distributed the tickets for meal to the extent he thought prudent; and he assured me wherever we went it would be a repetition of the same all over the country, *and even worse* in the far off mountain districts, as this was near the town, where some relief could reach. It was my full impression that *one-fourth* of those we saw were in a *dying state*, beyond the reach of any relief that could-now be afforded; and many more would follow. The lines of this day can never be effaced from my memory. These were our fellow-creatures,—children of the same Parent,—born with our common feelings and affections,—with an equal right to live as any one of us,—with the same purposes of existence,—the same spiritual and immortal natures,—the same work to be done,—the same judgment-seat to be summoned to,—and the same eternal goal.

In returning through the town we called on Alfred Bishop, the Government commissariat,[37] whose affecting letter, describing similar scenes to those we had witnessed, is published in the Report of the Belfast Ladies' Relief Association for Connaught.[38] I had much conversation with him, and he afterwards came to spend the evening with us at the minister's. This gentleman had been in all parts of the world. He had been among the native tribes of the most uncivilized countries. In answer to my enquiries, as to whether he had ever seen a people living in so low and degraded a condition as the poor Irish had evidently long been suffered to remain, he replied, "No, not even the Ashantees or wild Indians." He was much grieved that the stores recently landed by the Society of Friends, the only food— among considerable supplies that had now been poured into the town—for gratuitous relief, should for one moment be lying unavailable, as was stated to be the case at that time, for want of powers, or any one in authority to distribute, while this frightful distress was raging around them.

Several of the gentlemen I much wished to see were absent just then. A disgraceful action, in which he was cast in heavy damages, was going on at the Castlebar Assizes, against one of the great landed proprietors, which had required the presence of most in the neighbourhood. This rather shortened my stay in the Mullet. It is hardly necessary to say that the soil—some, perhaps, as fine as any in the country for the growth of green crops—was lying wholly neglected; and nothing could more affectingly illustrate the deep-sunk poverty of the peasantry than the total absence of live stock, aforetime, so teeming in the cottages. One solitary pig, a single ass, no cow, one pony, and a few fowls, were all we saw in the whole morning's round. The few dogs were poor and piteous, and had ceased to bark. We left with the minister, and the neighbouring agent of the principal proprietor, a considerable quantity of carrot, turnip, and mangel-wurzel seed, for the benefit of such of the poor as they could influence and control; and £10 with the minister's wife, from the Ladies' Committee of London, for the promotion of her adult school of female industry, whose number, we soon afterwards heard, was increased to forty.

Before closing this letter, I should like to mention one other cause of the increase of a pauper population, in those districts where they are mostly Roman Catholics, as is the case to an overwhelming majority in the west. It is the encouragement of early marriages by the Catholic priests. Being the principal source from which they derive their income, this is almost inevitable under the present constitution of things. It is well known there is scarcely a greater sin than depriving the priest of his dues. We are aware this is not peculiar to the Catholic Church, but it is more a personal thing, where there is no State maintenance. While these early connexions are a source of great evil, as promotive of reckless and improvident habits, the fee attached to the solemnization of the rite, which the most indigent always manage to scrape together for the purchase of the blessing on these occasions, operates greatly on the vigilance of the priests on the side of morality. The Protestant clergy discourage early marriages.

## LETTER IV. BELMULLET—ROSSPORT. *17th- 18th of 3rd mo.* 1847.

HAVING given Samuel Bourns[39]—the name of the party I have before mentioned as residing in one of the extreme corners of Erris—an expectation of visiting him, we found him this morning at the breakfast table, having walked over a distance of twelve miles, to meet us. The scene about the minister's house was the same as yesterday, only, I think, a larger number, but orderly and well-behaved. I cannot describe this gentleman's house in any better terms than as the "metropolis" of the poor of the neighbourhood. There were more than two hundred waiting when we came away.

Some idea may be formed of the interest excited by the visit of a stranger to this remote district, when I say that we had scarcely started above a mile for the house of S. Bourns, on foot, when we were overtaken by his neighbour, the only other respectable resident for many miles round, who, with his son, had brought his car, and been to Belmullet in search of us, to give us a lift on the way. We took the north coast road for some miles, through a region dreary and brown, at this season, but affording ample pasturage for sheep and cattle in the summer time,— now, alas! reported to be nearly swept from the face of the country. Behind, the bold cliffs and promontories of Achill formed a noble outline; and distant views of the great Nephin were obtained on the right. We met many poor persons coming eight, ten, twelve, and we were assured sixteen Irish miles,[40] for a quart or two of meal. This is a great hardship, and arises from the deficiency of stores in a country where the people have been accustomed to grow all they wanted beneath their feet. We met with cases of labourers who, after they had earned their pittance on the roads, had to be out two days and a night, before they could return, with the purchased necessaries, to their families.

A mountain road struck off to the left, which was the right direction for all of us, and brought us to the house of our new acquaintance. He has about 3000 acres under long lease, and is one of those, who, after residing here all his life-time, and bringing up a family, is now cast down by the impoverished state of his small tenantry, and of everything around him, and would be glad to sell out his property, and emigrate elsewhere. It is a wild mountain district; but some fine land, handsomely sloping down to a navigable tide estuary. Just by was the old burying-ground of Kilcommon, where more than one funeral was going on at the time. Here we took boat for the opposite shore, the residence of our friend who had so kindly come to conduct us. There was no road, at present, of any kind to his house.

Rossport, the name of this truly isolated abode, is prettily situated in a nook of the eastern shore of the noble estuary of the Greyhound river, commanding from the house—between the bold promontories of Erris-head and the point of Runroe—a fine peep of the rolling white-crested Atlantic. The tide rises rapidly, and sweeps in with the strong current of a broad swift river. The property is bounded on the other side by an arm of the sea, so that it forms a peninsular, containing about 1300 acres, held from the lord of the soil, on a lease for lives renewable for ever, at a rent little more than nominal; and is therefore nearly of the value of freehold, as a purchase or security. The soil is various and sufficiently good, with the most admirable facilities for manuring with sand and sea-wrack,[41] all round. Samuel Bourns occupies a portion himself, and has besides a small tenantry of about seventy families upon the estate. His best tenants, however, as in other places, are gone away, some in arrear, and the remainder so reduced, from the common failure, as to be in the greatest distress; and involving himself and his family in the universal calamity. Having been a shopkeeper before he purchased this property and removed here, he continued the shop for the general convenience, being the only one where any of the useful articles of daily life could be obtained for twelve miles in one direction, and upwards of twenty in any other. His is the only Protestant family residing anywhere near, and is almost a patriarchal one, consisting of himself and wife, a grown-up son, two daughters, and three younger children, his own mother, his wife's mother, his wife's sister, and an English lady visitor, who had been much over the world, but was so charmed with this locality that she had taken up her residence with them, and now gave her kind assistance to the soup-kitchen, &c., as occasion required.

We lost no time in visiting the cottier tenantry. We found them poor and destitute enough, and without any means of being able to maintain themselves, or raising any return from their little allotments of land,—the potato-plot and oat-field of last year lying equally unprepared for the future. This was St. Patrick's day;[42] the day on which it is considered agricultural labours—always late in the west—should commence in earnest, and the peasantry are usually busy on their holdings. The present contrast was truly melancholy. There were also, among the cottagers we visited, decent tailors, carpenters, and shoemakers, all entirely out of work, and unable to purchase food, much less to pay any rent or arrears. They had hitherto been supported on the small stocks of last year, now nearly exhausted. We saw some cases of great distress; but not so utterly beyond hope and remedy as the extreme and appalling scenes we had witnessed in the Inner Mullet,—yet what must soon come to it without timely help. Our friend, unable to stem the daily gathering flood of destitution, and his own resources being utterly extinguished, had written the previous day an emphatic appeal to a leading gentleman in the Methodist connexion in London,[43]—to which he was himself attached,—for assistance in the purchase of seed oats, by way of loan, with security on his unencumbered property,—understanding that body had large funds at their disposal for this very purpose. He had previously applied to take £500 of the Government loan, to employ his own people, on his own land; but found the Committee sitting at Belmullet would have the right of selecting the labourers, and of sending their own paupers to be so employed, with a great loss of time in getting it, and other limitations and encumbrances.

Among other persons who had left his vocation and emigrated was the schoolmaster, so that the school was now abandoned. From the assistance granted by Wm. Forster, on behalf of the Society of Friends, the school-house was fitted up into a soup-kitchen. We attended the giving out of the soup; and it appeared under the excellent management of the lady before mentioned, and S. Bourns's son. Without this timely assistance, he declared, a large portion of his tenantry must have perished. The poor people came a very long way, from other districts, in hopes of partaking of the bounty, and were not sent empty away. While at the soup-kitchen, we received a visit from Lieutenant Carey, the coast-guard officer of these parts,[44] whose station was at the point on the other side of the creek, and who, with our host and his opposite neighbour,—the only three residents of respectability within a radius of ten to fifteen miles,—formed the Relief Committee. With him an engagement was made for the morrow.

The sun set gloriously across the great Atlantic, and brought out the magnificent features of the coast in bold relief. The scenery wants foliage, but nothing else, to render it most attractive.

The forthcoming morning we had again the pleasure of witnessing a barrel of clothes, from the London Ladies' Committee, distributed to the numerous applicants. We had overtaken it the day before in a country cart, with the singular address of "S. Bourns, North Coast, Mayo," which somewhat indefinite direction had nevertheless found its destination quite correctly. The delight and admiration infused into the countenances of the poor people, at sight of some of the articles, was worth the journey to behold. I trust the Society will not be charged with underhand proselytism, from the droll figures occasionally cut by some of the poor natives, under the new set-out of a well-proportioned left off "Friend's" coat.[45]

After breakfast, according to appointment, we started for Lieutenant Carey's, to visit, under his guidance, the magnificent scenery of the north coast of Erris. A little rising of the weather prevents much of it being accessible, and the day looked squally and doubtful. Samuel Bourns's boat carried us safely down the rapid estuary of the Greyhound river, to a point on the opposite shore, from which it was a walk of about a mile along the strand to Lieutenant Carey's. He had already decided that it was too uncertain and stormy to venture round the point of Runroe, and so by Kid Island, and the cliffs of Benwee. The great cave there, is only to be entered in very calm weather. We therefore walked across, about four miles, to Portacloy, a small fishing and coast-guard station on the north coast. There are new roads making throughout this district, under the Board of Works,[46] which will be very useful if ever the resources of the country are fairly developed. As a specimen of the great distress of the poor country people, and the want of a market, he told me he had just bought a very pretty cow and calf for £2. 5s taking them as a favour. This gentleman gave it as his opinion that ten years of successive good harvest would not place the people where they were two years ago. We saw one poor fellow who had had a horse and four sheep "driven" for 25s. rent. They had been sold that morning for 20s.

The coast-guard galley was soon ordered out, under the lieutenant's directions, manned by four of those sturdy and intrepid characters peculiar to this arduous service. Portacloy is a deep rift in these hostile cliffs, otherwise wholly inaccessible for many miles. There is scarcely any proper landing, the beach being high and rough with rocks; and so great is the swell and turbulence of the ocean that accidents not unfrequently happen. A man had recently been swept off the rocks while catching crabs; and two poor women, we afterwards heard, met with the same fate that very morning, while gathering sea-weed for food. With all their skill, our boat, while hastily getting us on board, was struck by a sea, thoroughly drenching two or three of those on that side, and obliging us to put out instantly, with one short of our complement of men, for fear of being beaten on the rocks; seizing another opportunity, between the waves, for taking him on board. The rocks rise on each side of this opening as if riven asunder by some recent catastrophe, the fragments being strewed below. On approaching the mouth of the harbour the Stags of Broadhaven are distinguished on the left, apparently a promontory of the main land when first seen, but gradually break off from the coast, and then separate from each other, exhibiting their singular structure, and the deep fissures between them, as the boat makes way. On rounding a point eastward, the most fearful scenery bursts at once upon the astonished beholder.

An amphitheatre of cliffs rises stupendous, rugged, black, perpendicular,—their summits sharply pinnacled against the sky, and with some remarkable twists in their structure, that give them a most impending appearance. These inaccessible strongholds are still the resort of eagles, several of which we saw, both soaring aloft and perched fearlessly on projections of the rock. The wild fowl are innumerable. Innismuck, or Pig Island, formed the extremity of this wonderful range, through which there is a natural archway, impassable at all times. The eddies are so uncertain, and the gusts so violent, on this terrific coast, that a sail is not allowed to the revenue boats. The spot was pointed out where, some time since, a coastguard boat was lost, and all, including an inspecting officer, perished, save one man who escaped off the rocks most wonderfully. After making what appeared to us some dangerous passages between the surging boiling rocks, we appeared to be directly approaching the perpendicular cliff, in one of the highest parts. The seaman in command at the bow-oar inquired if we thought there was a passage *through*. Startled,—as we were now approaching the solid facade of impending cliffs, with a rapidity that seemed to bring them all about us, and were within a few boats' length,—I replied, "Impossible." "Steady boys,—keep your seats,—pull!" and instantly an archway appeared, at the base of those adamantine barriers, of width just sufficient for the oars to play, and within which we caught sight of the sea, wreathing and roaring like some prostrate monster enchained. "Back in an instant!" shouted our commander. There were some stationary moments before the boat could be recovered, and the motion reversed, during which it seemed as if the suckage of the sea would gain the mastery, and draw us down irrevocably into its jaws; and those who can enter into the rushing-by of the trees and hedges, from within a vehicle in motion,—or the shore, from a vessel rapidly propelled,—can easily imagine, that with the rising of the boat on the swell of the surge, the archway and overhanging cliffs—close under them as we were—seemed at the moment instinct with motion, and in the act of falling, as if in concert with the ocean to close in upon us, and seize their prey. It was altogether the most sublime and exciting combination of reality and imagination I have ever experienced. The superincumbent mass of nature's masonry was at least 600 feet above the archway, and it was marked with a deep furrow or channel from the summit to the entrance of the orifice. There was no real danger, and the experienced boatman would not have hesitated with his crew alone; but from the state of the tide, the sea—chafed within that narrow gorge—was running higher than he expected, and one or two of the company had exhibited symptoms of timidity, from which there might have arisen danger, which he thought it safest not to risk.

We afterwards rowed round to the other opening of this natural tunnel. The sea seemed moderately placid, but there were some ugly rocks in case of a boat becoming unmanageable. The whole coast is truly wonderful. The loftiest cliffs are however westward, rising 900 feet at Benwee. There is a continuation of magnificent scenery, with the extraordinary passage of Moista Sound, eastward to Bealderrig.[47] Our landing was curiously effected, through a wilderness of rocks, at Porturlin—another coast-guard station—from whence we walked back over the mountains to Rossport, crossing a creek in a manner by no means unusual in this part of the country, by hailing a stout fellow at a distance, who voluntarily offers his back, and is more than satisfied by a few pence from the stranger.

LETTER V. ROSSPORT—SLIGO. *18th—20th of 3rd mo.* 1847.

I HAD become so much interested about S. Bourns and his property, and so well acquainted, in this day's excursion, that we seemed to form quite part of the family in the evening. He believed a very large field to be open, in agriculture, in fisheries, and in some other channels, if only skill and capital could be attracted to the spot. He offered me forty acres,—not of mountain or moor, but of land that had been reclaimed,—for ten years, for nothing; simply for the sake of getting it under improved cultivation, or any cultivation at all. This I could not undertake. But I did agree, before the evening was out, to supply the seed, and pay the labour *for five acres of flax*, he finding the land, and his son the superintendence,— the produce to be divided; and an agreement to this effect was regularly signed. A Friend at Belfast, a member of one of the first mercantile and manufacturing houses there, had particularly desired I would seize any opportunity that presented for the introduction or encouragement of flax, especially in new districts; and though I did not feel it so much within my province as the endeavour to fill up, in some degree, the immense vacancy in human food, occasioned by the loss of the potato,—yet I was quite willing to undertake this little speculation, from the belief that flax is the crop which, on any given quantity of land, employs the greatest amount and variety of manual and mechanical labour, from first to last, of any crop whatever. My friend—of whose House I came to order the flax seed, when subsequently in Belfast—was so pleased with the experiment, and the circumstances of its being undertaken in a new locality, that he generously doubled the quantity, as a free gift, to the party in question,—to whom, also, I arranged to send a supply of turnip and carrot seeds, for the service of himself and his poor tenantry, and also some for his opposite neighbour; to which was afterwards added some of the best varieties of the cabbage, and a small assortment of handy agricultural implements, from means supplied by a Friend. Five pounds from the Ladies' Committee of London was likewise left with Maria Bourns,[48] for the institution of some employment she had in view for the poor women, in the way of providing coarse clothing material.

The excursion and walks above-mentioned gave ample opportunity for becoming acquainted with S. Bourns and his property, and for conversation with Lieut. Carey, an experienced officer, who had been stationed in various parts of the world. His opinion coincided with everything we had heard and met with, as to the orderly and peaceable disposition and patient endurance of the people, under unheard-of privations and sufferings, and also of the rich, but neglected capabilities of the country. He had ocular demonstration, daily, of what might be done in the way of fisheries, from what was brought in by the poor fishermen with their miserable craft and tackle at the several stations under his command. He mentioned the sperm whale was occasionally seen off the north coast in numbers. We noticed all the estuaries abounding with seals.

I had previously remarked to a gentleman, that the peasantry we had met, especially the men, did not look so very miserably clad along the public road before reaching Belmullet. "You don't know how that is, I dare say," he replied; "they have often only one decent suit among a whole family, or among half a dozen, which he who wants to go out makes use of, the others remaining in bed, or at least at home. I won't vouch for the literal truth of it," said he, "but I was told, that there was but one hat in the whole island of Achill, some time ago, which was considered common property, and he who wished to visit the main land regularly borrowed!"

Having a long day's walk before us—for we were wholly out of the reach of conveyances—without any stopping place short of twenty miles, we were up betimes in the morning,—the tide also serving early to take us the whole navigable distance up the Greyhound river. It is a fine broad estuary for some miles, narrowing rapidly into a mountain torrent, beyond the tide reach. Our friend would not do otherwise than accompany us as far as his boat could go, which was within about a mile of Glenamoy bridge,—a great saving of distance, but not so much in point of time, for it was a strong head-wind to work against, and a heavy boat. From the quantity of wild fowl on the bosom and banks of this river, it could be but rarely disturbed by the sound of sportsman's gun. Duly provisioned by the kind forethought of the ladies, it was not without emotion that we took leave of our host at this solitary spot, and after having clambered the rough bank, watched the last mutual wave of the hand, till the lessening boat disappeared behind a bend of the stream.

At Glenamoy bridge we gained the north coast road from Belmullet to Ballycastle. The wind was very violent to contend against, and our distance great. The country was dreary on both sides, rising in monotonous masses, with nothing but intervening bog and moor-land, yet thickly peopled in parts. As the road approached the coast it became much more interesting, revealing the magnificent promontories behind us, with the Stags far out at sea. It was a noble walk along the edge of the cliff, a considerable height above the whitening ocean. A deep glen drove us inland, until the road, by a great bend, could descend sufficiently to cross it; and after rising again, we looked straight down into one of the loveliest of bright emerald basins, shut in and sheltered by black mural precipices,—and forward to the long, singularly inclined, causeway-like headland of Downpatrick, with its end broken off. On this fragment are the remains of buildings of some extent, plainly visible from the verge of the main-land cliff, and evidently the handy-work of man, but now perfectly inaccessible, and have been so for ages. Of course the tutelar saint has many traditions here.

Ballycastle occupies a bleak, but fine position. Up a valley, opening southward, the eye is saluted by the appearance of a few trees; but we were now out of Erris. It was two miles to Mount Glen, an address we had the favour of; and the increased planting, the appearance of hedgerows and agriculture, the busy evidences around a mill on the property, bespoke the resident gentleman. While partaking of the lady's hospitality, and conversing about the distress of the neighbourhood, which she described as almost overwhelming in the rural districts around them, the gentleman and his son came in. They spoke in the highest terms of Wm. Forster's visit, and of the service it had been to them in the hour of need. The lady having mentioned that W. F. had signified to her his intention of endeavouring to obtain a package of clothing for her destitute poor, than which she said there could be no greater boon, I had no hesitation in ratifying the same, by engaging to send her one of the bales placed at my disposal by the London Ladies' Committee. This gentleman being a justice of the peace, I conversed with him about the objection raised against doing anything for the poor peasantry in the way of providing them with seed, on the ground of its being likely to serve the landlord only, who would come down upon the crop. Whatever liability might apply to grain in this respect, he replied, there was none whatever to be apprehended in regard to green crops. They were not worth the landlord's while, and he had never known an instance of their being taken. He offered his guarantee, as a magistrate, against such being the case, where he had any influence or authority. His son was most earnest for a supply of small seeds, however limited, being difficult to obtain in their remote quarter; and undertook the charge of distribution, and to answer for the right use.

It was still ten miles to Killala, and dark some time before we reached it. The Presbyterian minister and his wife,[49] residing near this town, are among those who are devoting their time and utmost energies to the help of the poor, and the mitigation of their severe sufferings, but are almost overwhelmed by the extent and magnitude of the calamity on every side. I believe we have no idea of the daily exertion, self-sacrifice and agony of spirit they have to go through, whose lot is cast, almost single-handed, in the midst of these fearful scenes of want and suffering, without the power to relieve. Some have been ready to fly their homes in terror and despair, but for the paramount sense of higher duty and kindred compassion. They do indeed require the warmest sympathy, and their hands to be effectively upheld. Unless such devoted instruments had been here and there raised up, the country must have become depopulated. We were much disappointed in not being able to call upon the pastor of Mullaferry, but the lateness of the hour in an unknown locality, and being strangers, forbad. This did not prevent opening a correspondence, which resulted in the supply of a bale of clothing from the London Ladies. "Truly"—the wife of the minister, had previously written in a letter to Dr. Edgar, of Belfast,[50]—"they need clothes almost as much as food. Their rags are reduced to such a state, that nothing but a sense of duty could induce me to come in contact with them."

Finding nothing very attractive in the narrow streets and accommodation of Killala,—though an old place full of recollections, an ancient bishopric, and with a very interesting round tower,[51]—and being but a short stage, we ordered out a car, and pushed forward to Ballina, receiving, though late, a most hearty welcome from one or two familiar faces at our former comfortable hotel, on our safe and happy return.

We took the mail, next morning, from Ballina to Sligo. The country appeared tolerably well cultivated after what we had left; the cottages decent, and more live stock about them. There were several respectable homesteads, and even the novel and refreshing sight of a drove of pigs along the public road. The beggary about the coach, wherever it stopped, was very violent; and we heard sad tales of the distress in the villages, particularly along the shore. It is a fine ride the whole distance. The Ox mountains are on the right; the varied indentations of the sea, Knocknarea, and distant views of the Ben Bulben range, on the left. A beautiful river with vast water power comes rushing down at Ballisadare, where the Sligo and Dublin mail meets the western mail from Castlebar.

Again, the tide of emigration—increasing on all the roads in proportion to the proximity and size of the port—is truly affecting. The obvious strength of the country is departing with those who go. They are in no case—except where assisted by the landlord, or other funds—the very paupers [*sic*]. These have not the means. But they are just those who have still a little left, able and calculated to do well with a fair chance and encouragement, and are going to enrich other and better constituted lands, with the same materials beneath their feet. The expressions of despair at the state and prospects of the country, emanating from persons of respectability and reflection,—not the mere outbursts of excited or party feeling, but arising from their strong sense of the sad reality,—such as, "poor Ireland's done,"—"the country's gone for ever,"—"it can never again recover,"—"if Government won't send us seed corn, they'd better send soldiers at once to destroy the people; it would be far more humane,"—were of constant occurrence. Of course, one meets with many short-sighted and bitter reflections from those who suffer.

We reached Sligo early in the afternoon, and our first enquiry was for Wm. Forster and his companions, who were to come here from Ballina. Learning they had not left, I went down immediately to their hotel, and just caught our dear friend W. F., and Joseph Harvey, already seated in a car, in the act of departing for Manor Hamilton. I took a seat for a short distance out of the town, for the privilege of company and conversation. It was the next day that Joseph Harvey was laid up with fever at Manor Hamilton, which seemed to come very close home to us.
Not feeling we had much to do with the large towns, the only call I made in Sligo—except needful arrangements with the shipping agent, for the transit of goods—was on a lady, well known for her energetic and devoted benevolence on behalf of the poor, with whom we spent the evening. She is a widow

lady, and her health was then suffering, from being much overdone. She has long had a school for the most indigent, under her care and influence; and now gives a dinner of bread and soup to upwards of 120 poor children every day. The unrivalled attendance at her school, in consequence of this attractive meal, has set the heads of other schools at work to distribute also,—the beneficial example having met with general approbation. She follows up many of these "forlorn little ones" to their cheerless homes, and extends the helping hand to endeavour to keep dying fathers, or sick and lonely widows, from an untimely grave. She is also much interested in the promotion of female industry, in the way of manufacturing cheap clothing; and I left with her £5, on behalf of the Ladies' Committee of London, for the encouragement of a work in which she is engaged,—which, she has since written, has gained more than other five pounds, for the same cause.

LETTER VI. SLIGO—DUNGLOE. *21st—23rd of* 3rd *mo.* 1847.

FROM Sligo to Ballyshannon is a truly glorious ride. We took it leisurely by hired car. The pleasing aspect of Sir Robert Gore Booth's property exhibits the presence and effects of an excellent resident landlord.[52] At Drumcliff there is an ancient pillar, and something more than the stump of a round tower, on passing which, the driver had the satisfaction of informing me, that I was "not the wisest man in the world;"—for, lucky escape! "whenever *he* goes by, it will fall down upon him."

We were now rounding the foot of Ben Bulben. The acute angles and flat tops of the different members of this group are very striking. From the north side they have every appearance of an ancient range of sea-cliffs; and with their precipitous and shelving sides, and their different headlands stretching far away to the east, I know of nothing for their height, which does not exceed 2000 feet, more magnificent than this noble mountain range. The cottages are mostly neat, stone built, and white-washed. Lord Palmerston possesses considerable property here.[53] Beyond Ahamlish the road approaches the sea. The coast is low, but rocky; and the fine swell of the Atlantic is seen to great advantage, booming over the reefs, with the Donegal mountains on the other side of the bay. County Donegal is entered at the thriving little bathing place of Bundoran; and soon after the town of Ballyshannon, through a long dirty narrow street of irregular cabins, and crossing the bridge, up a steep ascent to the better part of the town.

This is one of those towns of great natural capabilities almost wholly neglected. A glance at the map will exhibit its position in the sheltered corner of a fine bay, within three or four miles of the noble navigation of Lough Erne, one of the most varied and beautiful in the whole kingdom, extending into the very heart of the country, and thence connected by the Ulster canal with the town of Belfast. The river, the only outlet of the waters of Lough Erne, has falls within the town, presenting an unfailing and inexhaustible water power; and a canal this short distance would render Ballyshannon the natural emporium of all the central counties. We found Cockburn's hotel, in Main-street, very comfortable.

Through Ballyshannon the country continues of increasing interest. The characteristic rocky undulating scenery of county Donegal is set off by the pleasing aspect of the cottages; and considerably more tillage appeared to be going on. On the estate of St. Ernan's, near Donegal,[54] it was quite animating to see a large number of men employed upon the land, evidently under the superior influence of a gentleman who took an interest in his property, with ornamental trees, and handsome plantations around.

It was not my first visit to the town of Donegal; but I think I was even more struck with the natural beauty and advantages of its situation, than on the former occasion. The bay of Donegal is of the very first character, sheltered by bold promontories, and backed by lofty mountains. There is abundant sea-bathing, and an excellent spa in the immediate neighbourhood. In the town is a fine old ruin. We arrived here by the mail,[55] being on the great high road between Londonderry and Sligo. To illustrate the sort of communication that exists with other parts, I inquired, immediately on alighting, for the mail car, that we had understood ran to Glenties after the arrival of the mail. We were informed by the coach master that "*sometimes* it went, and *sometimes it did not*." "Well, but would it go today?" "He would send for the man and let us know." This occupied an hour, and we then learnt it had been discontinued! We could take the mail-car to Killibegs, five miles on the same road; but the remainder would be out of the way. We, therefore, ordered a post-car,[56] perhaps the object of the landlord. However, the difference in expense is not so alarming as with hired vehicles in England. The rate for a one-horse post-car varies in different parts, from as low as 6d. per Irish mile—more than one and a quarter English—which is all we were charged in several places, to 8d. for two passengers, the usual rate where no bargain is made, and 9d. to 10d. per mile if there are three or more. On the low rates an extra 6d. was sometimes charged, on account of the high price of oats, which was but reasonable. The drivers expect much the same as in England, but there are no turnpikes in the west.[57]

The road keeps the north side of the bay. The small town of Mountcharles crowns a long steep ascent, repaying by ample views of the bay, and of the mountains on both sides. On leaving the main road to Killibegs, we turned direct to the north, and the picturesque character of the scenery was soon exchanged for dreary brown moor, black bog, and barren mountain. We seemed to be entering the very heart of the wildest mountain region. On every side the distant peaks rose one above the other, revealing range after range still loftier, as we wound amongst them, and left the nearer hills behind. The afternoon was one of those rare and lovely ones, that especially in elevated regions, shed an indescribable flood of solemnity and beauty on everything around. There is a repose amid mountains the populous plain knows not of. Their vast piles cut the clear sky with a peculiar grandeur, all their own. The sun was now setting, and lit up the distant peaks—at first blue from the clearness of the atmosphere—with the fires caught from his horizontal beams, each varying in hue according to their features and character, —their sternness all subdued. The seaward range to the west grew black and massive. Where a wild glen opened there were a few cultivated patches; but otherwise the wretchedness of the miserable hovels, and the deplorable neglect and poverty everywhere visible, contrasted most painfully with the grandeur and magnificence of nature. The hand of improvement was, however, most agreeably apparent on approaching this "city of the wilderness," as, from its lone mountain-girt situation, Glenties may truly be called. Since my former visit some years ago, a neat court-house, a magistrate's residence, a new poor-house, and many tidy looking buildings had sprung up, and a small, but decent hotel in the town, in fact, more than one,—where in passing through before, I remember the feeling of thankfulness at not being put to the test of attempting to pass a night there. Though not visiting poor-houses generally,[58] as this was the one which William Forster found in such a deplorable and affecting state,[59] I made a point of inspecting its present condition. The master was laid on a sick-bed at the time W. F. was here; and they were overtaken by the calamity as a flood, with means altogether unprepared and inadequate to meet its sudden pressure and extent, at the worst season too of the year. The building is well constructed and airy. It was satisfactory to find it in a fairly comfortable state as to food, cleanliness, and order: the greatest deficiency appeared to be the want of adequate instruction to the number of poor children there collected. But the distress without and disease within were fearful and increasing. The number of inmates was 500, of whom 102 were in the infirmary. But what was told us by the master of the poor-house, depicts most powerfully the wretched condition of the poor peasantry. He said, the crowds who were every day refused admittance for want of room, watched eagerly the daily deaths, for the chance of being received into the house. I conversed with him a good deal, on the means of bettering the condition of the peasantry, and the supply of a little seed, which they had no means whatever of procuring for themselves. He said there was scarcely any one here to take any interest in them. He spoke of the Roman Catholic priest as an excellent and devoted man, doing all that lay in his power for the benefit of his flock. With him, therefore, I had an interview, in company with the clerk of the poor-house, and arranged for a supply of seed under his charge, for distribution. The parish contains 31,000 inhabitants, nearly all Catholics.

Finding the car-road to Dungloe was some miles further round, we arranged to start in the morning, with the advantage of "Her Majesty's" foot-mail, as guide over the mountains. His time was six o'clock, but not being very punctual, we were out on the road first; and learning the mail was at breakfast, and would soon overtake us, we proceeded forward, having been put into the right road. It was not long before we saw a ragged-looking urchin, scarcely decent as to outer garments, with an ancient post-bag slung across his shoulders, rapidly gaining upon us, who proved to be that important functionary. He was a shrewd, intelligent lad, however, and gave us much information. The ascent was long and toilsome over the mountain, with nothing but vast barren wastes, and very few habitations, and those of the most inferior character. The clouds were low, and tending downwards with a wetting mist, which added to the dreary and sombre hue of the face of the country. The descent was down to the estuary of the Gweebarra river and ferry, where we had to wait some time for the boat to be hailed from the opposite shore: it was about half a mile over, and by no means so much unlike the Killery of Connemara, but not so grand. Our fellow-passengers were five poor women, going to gather sea-weed on the other side, for breakfast, as they assured us. A mile further on, at a point just half way, sheltering himself under a peat-stack, until his companion came up, we met the corresponding mail, a similar lad, but rather more respectably clad, who after exchanging bags in due form, took us under convoy the remainder of the way. We passed through some wild rocky scenery, and round the head of a most romantic little lake, with its solitary island. But the rain coming on heavily, the long reaches of the road became tiresome, as it climbed one after another, ridge after ridge, with no variety in the wide waste of bog—"a killing *every* day's march,"—as our guide called it,—until after one more tough ascent, we dropped down upon the little town of Dungloe, seated at the head of its rocky bay, among rocks as rude, and backed by the wildest mountains. Its wreathing smoke was a welcome sight; and, being thoroughly wet, we were too glad of a comfortable fire, and anything in the shape of a breakfast, to be very critical about the accommodation; and in the way of civility and attention, it could not be surpassed.

After drying without and invigorating within, we set off, though it still rained, for Maghery, the residence of Valentine P. Griffith, the officiating minister of the parish,[60] four miles along the southern shore of the bay. I mention this gentleman by name, because it is appended to two public documents, making known the state and condition of this large and destitute parish.[61] You distinguish, a long way off,— by the number of poor people surrounding them,—the residences of those who are devoting themselves to endeavouring to mitigate the severity of this awful crisis. I believe this gentleman and his family to be among the excellent of the earth. This is the large and neglected parish of Templecrone, or "the Rosses." It is hemmed in by the sea on one side, and bleak mountains on the other, over which the roads are often impassable, and no market-town within the distance of thirty miles. It has not the natural advantages of sea-board, the whole line of coast being foul, rugged, and inaccessible, except in the calmest weather. The rude and backward state of agriculture in this isolated district, cannot be more strongly shown, than in one of the documents above alluded to, wherein it is stated, "that in a parish, the area of which is 52,921 acres with a population of 10,000 souls, dispersed through wild mountains, and thickly inhabited islands, there is neither the recollection, nor the tradition, of a *plough* ever having been used throughout it." Of course, there can be no resident gentry here. The mass of ignorance, poverty, and destitution, remains therefore unalleviated, beyond the personal exertions of the few who signed the above document. I have rarely received the impression of more heart-felt zeal and devotedness in the cause of the poor, than was manifested by this gentleman and his family; but they seemed indeed almost cast down and overborne by the rising tide of famine and desolation at their very doors, and by the hopelessness of the future. Everything, they said, was getting worse and worse; and where it would end, except under the over-ruling hand of Divine Providence, save in famine and pestilence consummating the work of depopulation, they were unable to conceive. The stubbornest heart would break beneath the sight of the harmless multitude— men, women, and little children—pining away in want and misery,—our own fellow-creatures and countrymen,—in this boasted land of wealth, civilization and humanity. The streams of individual and public charity have been noble; but what are they to the enormous gulph? AND OUR TRANSATLANTIC BRETHREN HAVE SHAMED US. And do, or do not, the *causes and the responsibility* lie with us? It was Dispensary day at the house of the minister, which gave us the opportunity of an introduction to Dr. Brady, the medical superintendent of the district,[62] with whose kind accord we made an appointment to visit the island of Arranmore the following day.

In company with V. P. Griffith, we visited a number of the mud cabins constituting the miserable village of Maghery, immediately adjoining his residence. In filth and wretchedness they were equal to anything we had seen, and the victims of disease were becoming daily more numerous under the continued privation of food and clothing. It was publicly stated that the agent of the landlord, early in the season, had promised seed to the poor tenantry, from which they had been induced to consume what few oats they had in reserve. The defence of the noble owner is one of the most touching and pathetic records in the whole of Irish history. We thought this a most suitable place for some supply of our seeds; and gave also £5 on behalf of the Ladies' Association of London, to Elizabeth L. Griffith,[63] for the special purpose of providing shoes, of which the want was very great, interfering with the ability to work of the few men who could get employment.

Having intended our next call to be upon Francis Forster, the able and intelligent agent of Lord George Hill,[64] residing four miles on the other side of Dungloe, our friend the clergyman had kindly arranged to put us across the bay in a boat. We accordingly found a six-oared galley ready, at a small pier on the glebe property, to which he conducted us down, and is constructing for the sake of giving some useful employment. The row was about six miles over, and certainly a most curious and interesting passage. The afternoon had cleared up beautifully, revealing a splendid admixture of land and water scenery. Snow lay upon the higher mountains, among which the great cupola of Errigal, the loftiest in the north of Ireland, rose above all; while Slievh Snaght and some others were still cloud-capped, black, and threatening. The sea, or rather the sheltered lagoons, through which our passage lay, was smooth as glass. The rocks were low, and of a reef-like character; and we steered through narrow winding channels, opening the connexion between one basin and another, just where there seemed an impossibility to further progress, in the most extraordinary and interesting manner. The lighting up of the great waters westward, as we occasionally caught sight of them outside these barriers, through some opening, rolling and glittering in the setting sun, was truly glorious. It was dusk when we landed at Burton port, from which it was but a short distance to Roshine Lodge, the residence we were in quest of. Francis Forster had just started to Gweedore with a gentleman who has recently purchased (or was about purchasing) a portion of the property adjoining Lord George Hill's; but the hospitality of the house was pressed upon us in a way so kindly, that could not be refused, in competition with the additional walk of four miles back to Dungloe after such a day, in the dark, and with untried accommodation.

LETTER VII. ARRANMORE. *24th of 3rd mo.* 1847.

NOTHING could be more favourable than the next morning for the proposed visit to the island of Arranmore. Dr. Brady was true to his appointment at the breakfast table; and from his local knowledge and acquaintance with the islanders, as medical visitor, we could not have enjoyed a more fortunate opportunity than under the auspices of that gentleman.

Not deeming it right to go empty-handed among the hungry multitude, we provided ourselves in all with fifty-six tickets, for a stone of meal each, for distribution. The distance from Burton port is about four miles, not open sea, but interspersed with rocks and islands. The waters were dancing in the greatest brilliancy. We met one or two crews of the Arran people crossing the bay, and the light coracle was gliding to and fro. We called at the coast-guard station, on a small island near Rutland, to see the officer, but he was not there just then. On Rutland Island, opposite, are the remains of a custom-house, quay, and other buildings, formerly erected by Government, at great expense, but now in ruins, and almost buried by the encroachments of the sand. Clearing these, the whole island of Arranmore lies stretched before the eye. It rises gradually towards the centre, presenting varied slopes to the south and east, and terminated northward and westward by cliffs and caves of considerable interest. As our visit was wholly unexpected, we landed about mid-way on the eastern shore without much observation. The presence of a stranger, however, soon attracts attention, and especially one so well known as the medical superintendent; and no sooner did the work of visiting the cabins commence, than the crowds collected became shortly so dense, that ingress and egress were difficult, and sometimes force had to be used. It was a warm sunny day, and we walked leisurely over the whole of the more thickly inhabited portion of the island, which lies principally towards the main land. The agent of the Irish Island Society was absent; and they had not yet their soup-kitchen in operation. In another part of the island, was a soup-kitchen established by the "Appeal Committee," (a committee formed of the gentlemen who signed the address before alluded to), but under the worst management; which, as Dr. Brady, who was himself one of the committee, witnessed with the greatest pain, would unquestionably be remedied by this visit. The great difficulty of control and management at such a distance, where there is not a single resident to be depended upon, and the few on the main land have their hands and hearts so full and overburdened, are serious obstacles. We spent the principal part of the day upon the island, in a walk of about six miles, through most of the villages, and, in spite of their repulsive features, entering the cabins, as long as our tickets lasted, endeavouring to search out such as lay more in the interior, had not claimed much notice before, or were the most destitute. There was indeed but little to choose, where misery and want were all so palpable. Throughout the island, there was a remarkable equality,—one mass of deep-sunk poverty, disease, and degradation. The details I need not attempt; it has been done before most vividly. The dwellings, upon the whole, were perhaps, externally, a shade better than the mere turf-hovels of Erris; but all within exhibiting the truth of the words (still I believe in MS.) of a vigorous and acute observer from another land, who went herself "to see the poor peasant by way-side and in bog, in the field, and by his peat-fire, and read to him the story of Calvary."[65]

Of a similar neglected district, she says, "I had learned to a *demonstration*, that man, left to instinct alone, will not make himself as comfortable as the beasts of the field, or birds of the air; *they* will construct their nests and habitations when wanted, with perfect system, and even mechanical taste; while *man*, with no stimulus to activity, but barely the food that sustains him, will lie down in stupid content, in the most filthy, disorderly habitation, and even make a *merit* of doing so." I fear to state the number of families in which seaweed and limpets appeared to be the only substitutes for food; although the ravages of famine and pestilence were still short of the harrowing scenes we had witnessed in the Mullet. There were the same gaunt looks in the men, and the peculiar worn-out expression of premature old age, in the countenances of the women and children; but the latter still clutched, with an eagerness I shall never forget, at the sight of some biscuit I had brought with me, when offered them to eat with their seaweed,—very different to the apathy and vacant stare, yet more heart-piercing, with which the unaccustomed sight was regarded, by those with whom the very desire and volition were past. We thought there were exhibited marks of a longer period of neglect and degradation; as if these poor islanders had never known any other state, and expected nothing better. Their importunity was also not without rudeness and abuse, when the tickets were exhausted, and there was nothing more to be had. The bits of paper, in the way of petitions ready prepared, constantly thrusting into our hands, evinced an older trade in beggary. We detected, too, instances of exaggeration; and, under any other circumstances, some amusing ones of pretence. My son, who was more at liberty to observe, discovered girls and children were up and running about as soon as we were fairly cleared off, who had on our approach thrown themselves on their miserable sleeping places, and beneath what they had of covering, as if sick. The feature that struck me most forcibly was, that among this whole population, estimated at 1,500, there was not a single particle of work of any description that we could see going forward, either inside the cottages, or outside upon the soil, except one old woman knitting.

Sometimes we thought proper to exercise the right of lecturing; and made the levelling of the mud floor, the filling in some filthy puddle, or the removal of some abominable heap from *in* to *outside*, the condition of our gift. Even in the midst of such wretchedness and misery, we were not without proof of the native wit and readiness of the lower order of Irish. One poor fellow, so immured in thick darkness, that it was some time after entering his cabin, before we could find him out; on asking him "why he did not knock a hole in the wall to let in the light and air?" replied, "It's I, your honour, that am not fit to be seen in't!"

There were no public works going on, and no school at present in the island. We took boat again at a rocky knoll, by an unenclosed burial-ground, not far from the Catholic chapel,—the only place of worship. Near this spot was a charming little cove, with delightful sands for the bather. The sea-views, the islets, the deep bays, and rocky indentations of the main land, with the grand mountains beyond,—the cone of Errigal rising in the midst and over all,—formed an assemblage of the most attractive land and water scenery. We gazed upon the island, as we left its shores, crowded with those wretched beings, with very mingled feelings, thinking what it might be under other circumstances, and of what it might still become,— of great capability and beauty, the abode and nursery of a vigorous race.

In returning, on a low, but inaccessible point of rock, sat a splendid golden eagle. As if conscious of his security he allowed the boat to approach within easy gun-shot. Two knowing gulls, by their marked evolutions, were evidently teasing his majesty, or they might have a nest near, but taking excellent care to keep *above* him, until he spread his noble wings and slowly moved away, when they were off in an instant.

On calling again at the former island, we found R. K. Thompson,—inspecting officer of the coastguard, who interests himself warmly in the state of the poor, and is one of the Appeal Committee,—at home. He received us very courteously. The provisions landed by the "Albert," and six boilers were still without instructions.

After again partaking of the hospitality of Roshine Lodge, and leaving £5, on account of the Ladies' Association of London, to be laid out in clothing materials, with Charlotte Forster, who is occupied from morning to night in the service of the poor; and to whom we had subsequently the pleasure of consigning the last of the bales so kindly entrusted to my care by the same Committee; and just visiting with her a soup-boiler they had set up, and would put in operation as soon as they could get materials,—we set forward on foot, still favoured with the company of Dr. Brady, for the Gweedore hotel. It was well we had so good a guide, for other-wise we should never have been able to have tracked this very intricate road after twilight came on. At first it was a continuation of the same characteristic scenery on land, as we had the day before at sea, in crossing the bay,—a perfect wilderness of rocks, through which it was curious to thread the way. A long, solitary, winding, craggy freshwater lake, was crossed by a bridge in the narrowest part, and then an arm of the sea on the sands, as the tide was out. A series of sandhills, very intricate and tiresome succeeded, and another strand, and then between a large freshwater lake and the sea, until we came to the estuary of the Gweedore river, opposite Lord George Hill's store at Bunbeg. The ferryman had to be roused. It might be three quarters of a mile over. The shores looked picturesque, but both distances and objects are deceptive in the grey light. A car was in waiting by previous arrangement from the hotel, of which we were glad enough to avail ourselves, the remaining four miles.

## LETTER VIII. GWEEDORE-DUNFANAGHY *24–25th of 3rd mo.* 1847.

WHEN last in this part of the country, on a pedestrian tour through the wilds of Donegal, my companion and I came wandering one morning, over bog and mountain, from the shores of Lough Swilly; and having ascended Errigal, came down to the village at the foot of that mountain, tolerably jaded out, by night-fall. It was the only place then marked in the map,—the Society's and Betts's[66] were not then published,—and in fact in existence anywhere near; and in consequence, being distinguished with LARGE LETTERS, gave us reasonable expectation of affording fair accommodation. We found the inn to be a little way-side public-house or drinking-shop, with a mud floor, the guest-chamber, kitchen, and family sleeping-room being *all one;* and a slight partition, behind which there was a second *shake-down,*[67] made the only other apartment. We certainly looked at each other, but there was no remedy. To proceed further was impossible, for there was nowhere to proceed to. So the landlady made us fresh oaten cakes on the hearth. We fortunately had some tea with us;[68] and mustering all the odd pieces of crockery they possessed, we managed to make the uninebriating beverage in a basin,— for the first time in the house,—and gave some to the host and hostess, and to two country lasses who came in, to their no small admiration and delight; and thus amused an hour or two, till first the children, and then the landlord and landlady, wished us "good night," and very comfortably got into bed. My friend retired to the shake-down. I had seen enough of its *outward* condition; and any toilet accommodations were out of the question. So I entertained myself as well as I could in eagerly watching for day-break. What a contrast—thanks to Lord George Hill— did the excellent accommodation of the Gweedore hotel present to this![69]

The situation of the hotel, except for its wild mountain grandeur, would appear to the eye of a stranger, visiting it for the first time, bare and uninviting enough.[70] All around what has been won from the desert is still the brown moor. But this is a great conquest, and the marks of improvement are everywhere going forward. The building itself is substantial, and well arranged for comfort and convenience.

The river Clady flows at the bottom of the garden. There is a pretty bridge thrown over it, and a boat is kept for excursions to the lake. There is a capital horse and car, and ponies for the mountains in the summer time. The summit of Errigal is about five miles from the hotel, and the lovers of wild and solitary scenery may here take their full. There are good roads made, and more making. It is four miles to the sea at Bunbeg, where there is a store supplying all useful articles, a mill, and a dispensary. There is also a new school-house. The former miserable hovels have been converted into neat white-washed glazed cottages, throughout the property; and the system of "rundale," or holding land in common, has been abolished.[71] Inclosures and draining have been introduced, with green crops and a better tillage. The growth of flax has been added this year. An interest is given to the tenantry in the improvement of their farms, and there is an experienced resident agriculturist. All this has been accomplished, and is carrying out, by the public spirit, and determination of the noble proprietor, against every disadvantage, and, at first, against the violent opposition and prejudices of the tenantry,—under the active co-operation, and unremitting zeal, perseverance and ability of his agent, Francis Forster.[72] A more untoward and discouraging set of circumstances, and greater practical difficulties, could hardly have been collected together than upon this property. They have been met and conquered. What has been done in one locality, of a most unpromising character, and under every disadvantage, is comparatively of easy execution, and more rapid recompense, in other localities far more favourably situate. If any one doubt the practicability of improving either the soil or the people of Ireland, let them read the 'FACTS FROM GWEEDORE,' a little book which ought to be in the hands of every Englishman, and every Irishman really interested in the welfare of his country.[73] Independent of the practical results exhibited, it possesses all the graphic interest of a simple and truthful tale. But to obtain the same results, the same means must be adopted, and among these are the personal exertions of Lord George Hill himself. He was not at the hotel when we were there, but had been the previous two severest months, and was now gone to London, I believe, on the seed question. In this deficiency, let me take the character of this truly benevolent nobleman in a letter from a friend. "Lord George Hill is doing all that man can. I do not know what would become of this part of the country were it not for him. From morning to night he is occupied with the poor. He spares no exertion, and never thinks of himself. I have seen a great deal of him latterly, as I stay entirely with him when here."

On arrival at the hotel last evening, we had the pleasure of finding Francis Forster, at whose house we had previously been so kindly entertained; the gentleman who was becoming the new proprietor of the lands adjoining; and another gentleman, whom I well knew by name, and much wished to meet with. They most kindly invited us to join their party.

The numerous interesting subjects of discussion at that time and place I need not mention. This one evening was all too short. It must not be supposed that Lord

George Hill and his tenantry have not suffered severely under the present calamity. It has been a serious drawback on that nobleman's personal sacrifice and unwearied exertions, that just as the fruits were beginning to appear they should be overtaken and retarded by a blight like the present—destroyed they cannot be. But the pecuniary loss alone, by the destruction of the potato, is a most serious consideration in the absorption of the means of what may truly be designated a rising family; and it is one of the strongest and most affecting proofs of the depth and extent of this awful calamity, that distress has reached even the estate of Lord George Hill.

I had fully intended re-visiting the scenery and establishments at Bunbeg in the morning, as Dr. Brady had kindly proposed going over to some of the smaller islands which lie scattered along this coast, and had scarcely been visited before with a view to their condition and relief. But in the morning I found the Doctor had been summoned out in the night, almost back again to where we had come from. The duties of Francis Forster, who is also a magistrate, took him likewise out for the day. We therefore accepted seats in the car with the other gentleman, who was going to Dunfanaghy, and whose intimate local knowledge and experience, as Inspector of Public Works for the district, made his company particularly valuable. But we did not leave without arranging with Francis Forster to place some seeds under his care, for the benefit of the poor in his own immediate neighbourhood. To this gentleman, along with Dr. Brady, and the officiating minister of Templecrone, was afterwards consigned the greater part of the box of arrow-root and ginger, belonging to the Ladies' Committee, for the aid of the sick in those extensive districts.

The road continues along the course of the river Clady, and the lake which supplies it, and then, rounding the base of Errigal, strikes due north. This mountain, which is the great feature in the landscape for many miles round, and is a striking object from the hotel, assumes a hard and repulsive aspect on nearer approach. Its vast shoulders of bare granite appear inaccessible on this side, and the region around its base consists of dreary and desolate moors, bounded only by other masses of sterile uninhabited mountains. A tolerably well-cultivated valley succeeds, with some pleasing cottages, and more live stock and comfort about them, and the country people better clad, than we had been accustomed to of late. It is true there was a fair going on at the little town of Cross-roads,—or the far more euphonious [sic] Irish name of Falcarrow,—on which occasion the women and girls always come out in their best. But it was pleasant to see they *had a best* to put on, and shoes and stockings once more, and a gay-coloured shawl or cloak—the true delight of an Irish peasant girl of the west; and to catch an arch smiling face or two underneath, or the actual merry sound of a laugh. It may appear but a light or a wrong thing, but my spirits rose perceptibly at these simple, though of late unaccustomed signs, which perhaps only proves the point of previous depression. It seemed like walking out of the valley of death into the verdant plains of life once more. On the left, the high promontory called the Bloody Foreland,—the most north-westerly point of land,—looked more dismal perhaps from its name. Tory Island, far out at sea, presents a most remarkable and abrupt outline; and the peninsular of Horn Head stretches far eastward, in something of the contour which gives it its name.

On passing a village, with a long Irish name I could never have recalled, but for the pleasure of having just received a note dated "Raymunterdoney Glebe," my friend and companion pointed it out as the residence of a clergyman, who was most actively engaged in endeavouring to influence and encourage his poor parishioners to prepare their land, and especially in some degree for flax seed, in the hopes of obtaining it for them, but did not as yet know from what quarter.[74] I thought I could not appropriate a sum of five guineas—which had been intrusted to me by a friend, for the general object, without specific instructions—better than to the aid of this effort. I extract the following from the note above mentioned. "You will see, from the inclosed receipts, that the money has been expended in the purchase of flax seed, as you desired, for the benefit of the poor tenants on the immense glebe lands of this parish. . . . I am personally and altogether responsible for the welfare of 500 human beings, occupiers of this wild, boggy, and mountainous territory. I gave about three gallons of flax seed to each head of a family, so far as the quantity extended, and the people were delighted with your gift."

Dunfanaghy is situated at the bottom of one of the deep inlets of Sheep Haven. It has a good market-house, lately built by a neighbouring proprietor, one broad street of tolerably respectable houses, and some trade, with great facilities for its extension, although I think I understood the mouth of the harbour was encumbered with an unfortunate bar. The country around is very poor and destitute, and the agriculture low. The Commissioner under the New Temporary Poor Law Bill[75] was sitting in the parlour of the hotel, which gave us an immediate introduction to several highly respectable gentlemen of the town and neighbourhood, who were assembled there to meet him. One gentleman of considerable property, and rector of the parish, to whom we had the further verbal introduction of Wm. Forster, most kindly gave up his time to us afterwards.[76] He and his family take a deep interest in the condition of the poor, and in all measures calculated for their benefit and improvement. With him we visited the soup-kitchen, partly set up and sustained by the assistance of Friends, which we found in excellent working order. He next took us to the school-house, where we found his lady, and several others, in a room crowded with poor folk, weighing out wool with her own hands, to give out to the women to spin. It was the most busy and animating sight of the kind I had met with. She stated her stock of wool for this truly kind and charitable purpose was nearly exhausted; and as I saw it in practical operation to some extent, I felt justified in appropriating £10 from the funds of the Ladies' Association of London to this object. We afterwards accepted of their kind hospitality. The house was in a fine situation on the Head, about a mile out of the town. The lady there showed me substantial specimens of the work produced, of several kinds, mostly blanketing of great durability and strength; and I brought away one of the vests of their make, as a specimen for Wm. Forster. As the poor cottiers were represented as suffering much for want of seed, and the soil as well adapted to the growth of green crops, I ordered a supply to this gentleman's kind care, for distribution in the neighbourhood.

At the hotel, in the evening, I found the Commissioner most courteous and obliging in affording every information on the subject of his new appointment.

## LETTER IX. DUNFANAGHY—DUBLIN. 26th–31st *of 3rd mo.* 1847.

WE left Dunfanaghy this morning early, accompanied a short distance by the Commissioner, per mail-car, to Letterkenny. The pass by Glen Lough to Kilmacrenan, is almost equal to anything in Scotland for wild and savage grandeur. The day was gloomy; and the huge bare mountain masses, wrapped in clouds, had their true elevation veiled on both sides,—a state which I think always adds to the impressive character of this description of scenery,—for the towering rocks seemed piled upon each other as far as the imagination gave play. It was a new road lately cut with admirable skill through this singularly wild and rocky gap. The post was previously carried to Dunfanaghy by horse or footman, as the case might be, over the mountains sometimes taking two days, and not unfrequently exposed to accidents, with loss of life. On emerging from this dark glen, the country rapidly improves; and about the prettily situated town of Letterkenny, assumes a cultivated and prosperous aspect. Trees, plantations, and genteel residences adorn the landscape. Proceeding by car, interesting views of the long and varied expanse of Lough Swilly are obtained from the risings of the road. The fine stream of the Mourne is crossed by a bridge of several arches directly out of Lifford; the county of Tyrone is entered, and almost immediately the thriving town of Strabane. The mail, upon which we had here calculated, came up full. We had therefore to continue by post-car, which, though throwing us late in the evening, gave much more opportunity of observing and enjoying the country. The noble valley of the Mourne, with here and there a factory, and one or two handsome bridges spanning the river, appeared rich and flourishing, and the several towns through which we passed, respectable and thriving, perhaps only in contrast with the bogs and mountains, the neglected capabilities, and squalid population of Mayo and Donegal, to which we had been so long accustomed. After Newtown Stewart the road is accompanied by the Strule, a branch of the Mourne, to Omagh. Soon after Ballygawley, darkness and rain came on, so that we missed what appeared to be very interesting features about the neat little town of Caledon, and on entering the handsome city of Armagh.

Our object being to reach the annual examination of the children at Brookfield Agricultural School,[77] we took the first conveyance in the morning to Portadown, and thence to Moira by rail.[78] The aspect of the country around Armagh is highly beautiful. Efficient measures of relief had been in early operation, and although distress was so much less apparent, generally speaking, in this province than in the west, we afterwards heard most fearful accounts of the ravages of fever, extending upwards in the scale of society, and spreading dismay and consternation among all ranks in this highly respectable city and neighbourhood. We heard of so many deaths occurring the very day of our being there that I am afraid to mention, lest it might not be credited. We heard of the number dying in the infirmary being so great, that separate graves had been abandoned, and the poor were buried together in one large square hole, service being performed over several at the same time, by both Protestant and Catholic clergymen. The Presbyterian minister and two physicians attending the infirmary had been carried off; and the third, it was reported, had fled, so that for a day or two they were without medical attendance. The poor house at Lurgan was closed, from either egress or ingress.

The examination at Brookfield School we had much satisfaction in attending. I have long looked upon this school as one of the most successful educational experiments in the kingdom. Not, perhaps, in dazzling results, but in adaptation to wants and circumstances; in bringing a sound practical education to the nearest within self-support; and the establishment of the principle, that a proportion of manual labour assists the development of mind. The organization of such schools all over Ireland, would, under the Divine aid and blessing, be one great means towards her regeneration.

All the remaining seeds we had with us, were left under the kind care of William Shannon, the superintendent of that establishment.[79] On coming down to the school shortly after, we found his family busily occupied in making them up into small parcels for distribution to the neighbouring poor. He afterwards sent me a list of fifty-eight names to whom he had given each a little, besides some handed to another Friend, "who would divide it with *his* poor neighbours, who he was sure, would be glad to get it," and "many," he adds, "are going away disappointed since the seeds have been exhausted." I had much pleasure in ordering a further quantity to William Shannon's charge, on arriving again at Dublin.

The next day or two were spent in Belfast, in arrangements for the transmission of the flax seed and bales of clothing, and in other needful matters; and an interview with the secretary to the "Society for the Promotion and Improvement of the Growth of Flax in Ireland," to whom I was introduced by one of their liberal subscribers. I was unacquainted with the operations of this Society before; but I found their Reports, and the information therein contained most interesting; and I believe this Society has the strongest claims to support, and is among the institutions calculated to do the greatest amount of good in the country. The secretary immediately offered to open a correspondence with both the parties I was interested about in respect of flax seed, and to send one of their trained agents to *superintend the sowing* and for *subsequent instruction* to each of those remote localities in Mayo and Donegal. The secretary further writes, "I have succeeded also in getting a number of flax-spinners here to join and send fifty barrels of flax-seed to Mr. Hewetson,"[80] (the gentleman we had the pleasure of travelling with from Gweedore to Dunfanaghy) "to be distributed among the farmers about Rossgarrow, who have no means of procuring seed."

I must not omit to mention here the great kindness we received from the members of both the Ladies' Associations of Belfast. The older one, specially for "Connaught," originated in the exertions of Dr. Edgar,[81] one of the first to awaken public attention and sympathy to the threatening calamity, and the real condition of the Western peasantry. His little pamphlet entitled "Famine in Connaught" was widely circulated,[82] both in this country and America, and produced a great effect; his personal visit to that province, having at the same time opened a very extensive and interesting correspondence. At that period, the extent and depth of the calamity was neither known nor apprehended. It was presumed the extremities of neglect and destitution were nearly confined to Connaught; and no conception was then entertained, that it would extend equally into other districts, and, as it were, over-spread the land. This called up the second Ladies' Association, with a wider sphere. Both have been most active and zealous; and both have had their successful bazaars. Both also have looked beyond the present emergency; and propose rendering themselves permanent for educational and industrial objects, and are worthy of the best support. Among other things, Dr. Edgar gave some hopes of being able to supply the deficiency of a school master at Rossport, through the means of his Society. Distress was rapidly spreading in Belfast, and most parties seemed full of despair at the prospects of the country; though a little revived by the great fall which had just then taken place in the price of Indian meal,—alas! how soon to be annihilated. Yet their active and enterprising spirit will not be readily laid.

The following is the acknowledgment addressed to one of the active ladies of the Connaught Committee, with whom the sum mentioned was left on behalf of the ladies of London, to be remitted to a clergyman of whose exertions in endeavouring to promote industry, chiefly in woollen-spinning and weaving, in a very poor district, we had witnessed practical proofs. "Castlebar, Mayo, April 2nd, 1847. I received your letter of the 30th of March, enclosing £5, for re-productive works of industry, for which I am very thankful. I am happy to say the object in view is going on very favourably, as far as the money at our disposal enables us to work. My daughters have sixty poor females employed, and I have as many spinning and weaving. They are preparing articles for the public sale in Dublin. We have labour cheap; all we want is skill, energy, and a little capital to set us going. I hope, if the Lord will, to live to see the day, when Mayo will be like the North of Ireland. Prices of food are coming down, but alas! the land lies waste,—little or no tillage, no seeds." Again, under date April 7th. "We got a woman to instruct our girls in knitting and spinning. Enclosed is a specimen stocking, which appears very soft and good. Such would be made to order at one shilling a pair, we finding all materials. I also send two specimens from the looms I am setting to work. They are good; the next pieces will be better

I hope, these are the first." Enclosed were the specimens, with size and price, and labelled as "made by poor starving persons in Mayo, in a loom set up in the clergyman's stable," &c.

We had much pleasure in ordering a supply of seed, on an application from one of the members of the London Ladies' Committee, to a party residing at Castlerea, Roscommon, after a satisfactory correspondence. Following, as we did, in several places the footsteps of William Forster, I think it right to bear testimony to the high terms in which his mission was everywhere spoken of; the stimulus given by him to the exertions of others; and the effect the part taken by the Society of Friends, irrespective of creed and opinion, and entirely above the suspicion of partiality, was leaving upon the minds of the people. We met with several inquiries after our principles, in places where Friends were hardly known or had been heard of before; and in one or two cases promised books. We were favoured to reach Dublin again in safety, on the last day of the third month.

LETTER X. DUBLIN—CAHIRCIVEEN. *1st—7th of 4th mo.* 1847.

AT the house of my earliest friend in Ireland—to whose kindness and assistance we were almost wholly indebted for the success of our first enterprise many years ago in the west, and which have been continued to the present time—we met an American lady, of singular and strong character, whose first acquaintance with the Irish peasantry, in the garrets and cellars of New York, had ripened into a feeling of sympathy and commiseration, which had induced—I believe I may say compelled—her to come over on a mission of philanthropy, in order to visit the people she had so much pitied and admired, in their own homes; and to learn what soil had nurtured such a hardy and impetuous,—such an intelligent yet down-trod,—such a poor but generous race.[83] She came almost without scrip[84] or purse, and has now spent upwards of two years in walking over nearly every part of Ireland, going from cabin to cabin wherever she found access, that is, almost everywhere among the poor, administering according to her measure and ability, both to their physical and spiritual destitution. I found her with limited and precarious means, still persevering from morning to night in visiting the most desolate abodes of the poor, and making food—especially of Indian meal—for those who did not know how to do it properly, with her own hands. She was under much painful discouragement, but a better hope still held her up. Having a considerable quantity of arrow-root with me, at my own disposal, I left some of it with her, and £5 for general purposes.

At the sitting of the Central Committee, in William Street,[85] this morning, in addition to the usual business, an arrangement—offered through the liberality of the Government—was detailed, by which it was proposed that the latter should become, as it were, the Bankers of the Committee for the stores now arriving, and in transit from the American continent. On the lodgment of the bills of lading with the proper officers, at any of the ports where cargoes of provisions for Friends arrived, the Committee were to have credit for them at the market-price of the day, and to be allowed to draw upon them at once, either in kind or value, at any other port where the Government had depots. The facilities thus afforded, and the saving of time and carriage, expense and risk, as well as the convenience, were great and obvious. The arrangement was subsequently carried into effect, by which means the (representative) food was, in some cases, in the mouths of the recipients even before it was actually landed.

The clearness and consistency of the Committee, in becoming the almoners of any of the Slave States, after having declined acceptance of a sum forwarded by Lord John Russell from a theatrical source, was also discussed. A protest, against any accrediting of the principle of Slavery being thereby involved, was subsequently issued.[86] Two members of the Committee, one of whom was one of the secretaries, had gone down on a mission to the far west.

In the evening we made a very interesting call on H. Pendleton,[87] Secretary to the Irish Island Society.[88] The house was identified immediately on entering it, by the sacks and bales of food and clothing obstructing the passages, and by the active work going on within. There is no doubt this Society is endeavouring to promote the good work. One hundred weight of seeds, for such district as they might think most in need, was consigned to their charge.

It is necessary to attend a sitting of the Clothing Sub-committee, in Cole Alley,[89] to be able to appreciate their labours and incessant pains-taking, in order to insure, as much as possible, the articles passing through their hands being suitably applied in the first place, and to diminish the chances of their being in any way improperly appropriated afterwards. As the Ladies' Clothing Committee in London had applied to the General Committee, for a grant to enable them to purchase some arrow-root, for the inclosure of a few pounds in each of their made-up bales, I thought one of the packages which the Sub-committee in Dublin had kindly warehoused for me would prove acceptable to them for the same purpose, and would by this means get well distributed. They also took charge of the little assortment of two dozen and a half of simple agricultural implements, with an additional small bale of clothing, for forwarding to Samuel Bourns, of Rossport. Let me here acknowledge the kind, attentive, unwearied, and essential services of Joseph Crosfield, of Liverpool,[90] in the receipt and forwarding of goods for Irish relief; as well as the liberality of the railroad and steamboat companies, in the transmission of the same.

It was not part of my original intention to have visited more than those remote districts of Mayo and Donegal, lying beyond the reach and influence of most of the Committees that had been formed; but having still some seeds left, and being favoured with good accounts from home, I felt desirous of completing the journey, by proceeding to some of the more distressed parts of counties Tipperary and Kerry. With the remainder of our seeds and arrow-root, we again left Dublin on the 3rd instant, by first train to Carlow. It was a delightful morning, exhibiting the beautiful scenery of the Wicklow mountains from along the line, in great variety and perfection, their loftier snow-clad peaks thrown up, and glistening in the brilliant sunshine. The whole range of country appeared to us smiling and prosperous after the west, and the various towns we glanced by, strikingly excellent. At Carlow we took the coach to Clonmel. There are many genteel residences in coming out of the town. The road is accompanied by the river Barrow, until crossed at Leighlin Bridge. Beyond this the country becomes more flat and dreary, with apparently an inferior soil.

The approach to the ancient city of Kilkenny is imposing. The fine serpentine sweep of the river Nore is overhung by the noble residence of the Ormond family,[91] as seen from the bridge, on entering the town. This is a locality fixed upon for one of the new colleges; and a remarkably chaste and handsome building has arisen, in an admirable situation, just out of the town. One cannot but be struck with the neatness and beauty of much of the architecture seen in various places along this road, in which the handsome grey limestone of the country is freely used.

Soon after Callan, the county of Tipperary is entered at a bleak wild spot, where the road ascends considerably, in order to surmount the shoulder of Slievh Naman.[92] It continues over a dreary elevated plain, until the white jagged peaks of the Commeragh range are caught on the other side, just before the descent, by a narrow winding defile, into the great central valley lying between the Knockmeiledown and the Galtee mountains. Stories of recent murders were here told us; but they are almost always connected with, or to be traced to, what is conceived to be some injustice or oppression with regard to the possession of land.

There is no small increased appearance of wealth in approaching the town of Clonmel—"retreat" or "valley of honey." The numerous large establishments, the genteel residences with avenues and plantations, and the improved agriculture, spread an air of substantiality to which we had been quite unused. The wheat grown in this district is among the finest in the country, and, with the great waterpower derived from the Suir and its tributaries, has given rise to the extensive milling trade for which this town and its neighbours are so well known.

Our intended destination being the house of a Friend, about one mile on this side Clogheen, we pushed forward by hired car. The first part of the ride, along the banks of the Suir on one side, and through rising plantations—bordered by laurestinus in full blossom, and other ornamental evergreens—on the other, is extremely beautiful. At Ardfinnan there is an ancient castle and ruined tower, picturesquely overlooking the river, just where it is crossed by a bridge. Beyond this the daylight failed.

Ballyboy House, the residence of Susanna Fennell, proved half a mile out of the public road, and quite solitary. A letter of introduction, which we expected would have preceded us, had been delayed. The family had not very long occupied this house, and had not been without disturbances from persons of suspicious character intruding themselves, and endeavouring to obtain an entrance upon one pretence or another. We were strangers, and wholly unexpected. The sound of unknown wheels, the excited state of the times, and the hour considerably after dark, were all questionable circumstances. It was therefore some time before the door was opened,—amid the clatter of a variety of dogs,—and admittance obtained from the servant girl with evident reluctance. A further period elapsed before any of the family were visible; and I must say we began to feel a little awkward, at the fear of not being able to give a good and satisfactory account of ourselves, and the pain of having been, most innocently, the cause of creating a moment's alarm. At last Wm. Fennell, the only son then in the house, made his appearance; and after some explanations and recognitions, and the gradual restoration of confidence, I need not say with what a grateful sense we have now to recur to the hospitality with which we were entertained and received into the bosom of this truly kind family. They had recently drank deeply of the cup of affliction; and there is that which is felt by those whose pathway has been beneath the great waters, although unknown before.

The Meeting at Cahir, being eight miles distant, gave us a cursory glance over so much of the country there and back. There are many beautiful spots about this neighbourhood, among which is Cahir Abbey, close to the town; and the town itself is rapidly improving, under the patronage of Lord Glengall, its owner. In the evening, accompanied by Wm. and Joshua Fennell,[93] we walked a few miles into the poor district over the river, behind their house, along the foot of the Knockmeiledown mountains. The land is stony, and for the most part sterile, yet thickly scattered over with cabins of the usual character. Selecting one of the worst looking as a specimen, those who entered first were wholly baffled in detecting the internal contents, either animate or inanimate, on account of the smoke and darkness. After some time, however, a "lump of darkness" moved from between the eye and a few turf embers, which proved to be one of the inmates. The man soon after entered, and we found it belonged to a "squatter," who had never paid any rent, nor his father before him, and had no means of livelihood whatever. The family obtained soup daily from the soup-kitchen at Castle-grace, which was under the especial care of Susanna Fennell and family. The situation of Ballyboy House is immediately at the foot of the Knockmeiledown mountains, commanding likewise most noble views of the Galtee chain in front. A dense mass of rolling clouds had obscured the summit of Galtee-more—the loftiest in this part of Ireland—the whole of the day; but partly clearing off towards evening, there was a gain of those grand successions of light and shade, and noble outline on either hand, which take place in endless variety wherever the majestic mountain is the character of the scenery.

At breakfast next morning we had the company of a gentleman, closely allied to a noble family of the county, who is one of those actively engaged in endeavouring to mitigate the condition of the poor in his neighbourhood, and had himself given up some expenses and luxuries habitual in his rank of life. He was then occupied upon the new Government relief measures, which he considered impracticable, from the non-existence—if from nothing more—of the presumed machinery of persons willing and qualified according to the Act; and the impossibility of working it, from what may be called its mere friction. For instance, he stated, that in one district alone it would require 13,000 signatures of the noble chairman, in duplicate!

Wm. Fennell had kindly arranged to give up the day to a circuit among the poorer villages lying at the foot of the Galtee mountains, much as is described in page 26–27 of the Dublin Reports, No. 2. While waiting for the car at the hotel in Clogheen, I was much gratified with the simple and unaffected affability of Lord Lismore, who had occasion to enter the room at the inn, in his magisterial capacity.[94] He is one of the resident landlords attentive to the welfare of his tenantry; and being the landlord of our friends, and learning our mission, he courteously invited us to call at Shanbally Castle,[95] if in our way. Proceeding along the high road, the little town of Ballyporeen, where we struck off to the mountains, is very poor indeed. There was reported to be much distress further along, upon the Kilworth mountain, on the borders of the county.

We first stopped at the village of Burnt-court, [sic][96]—retaining its name and ruin from the deed of Cromwell,[97]—proceeding next to Tencurry, where the soup-kitchen is established in buildings belonging to a Friend; and then to Tubrid, where the arrangements appeared extensive and excellent. All these were established in very poor and destitute localities, at a distance of four to five miles asunder, principally by the personal exertions of Wm. Fennell, actively co-operated with, and assisted by, the eldest son of Lord Lismore. At the two latter places, 3,200 quarts of soup, or rather porridge, were distributed daily, to upwards of 800 families,—at one of them the boilers being filled four or five times. The amount of distress thus mitigated is beyond calculation, and was stated to be apparent even in the looks of the poor people since the soup-kitchens had been in action. It was delightful, in passing along the roads, to mark their becoming and orderly conduct, as we met the women and girls radiating from the different centres of attraction; many a really graceful figure bearing her vessel on her head, and groups collected, not wholly unworthy the Greek or Italian artist.

Before leaving, Susanna Fennell kindly accepted of some arrow-root we had brought with us, for the use of the poor in this large district; and Wm. Fennell of a small supply of our different seeds, specially for the old labourers about their former paternal residence of Rehill, which was situated in the very centre of this day's excursion.

Not liking to be so close in the neighbourhood without seeing the celebrated caves,[98] we had ordered a car to be in readiness directly after breakfast. They lay scarcely out of the line between here and Mitchellstown; but wishing to vary the route, we struck off from Clogheen to Shanbally Castle,[99] the seat of Lord Lismore, whom we met just at the corner of a country lane unattended, and who reined his horse with great affability to speak to us and renew his invitation to call. At the entrance lodge a soup-kitchen is established, under the personal superintendence of the noble owner's sister, a lady who devotes her time to the purpose. The castle is approached by a handsome drive through the domain, and is a remarkably chaste and elegant modern castellated building. The plantations and walks are laid out in the highest degree of taste, and contain every variety of wood and water, open glade and shady vista, wild copse and trim flower-garden, all shut in and secluded by dark magnificent mountain boundaries. The ornamental evergreens are remarkably fine and thriving, and here and there is a noble oak. This beautiful demesne evinces what can be done by design and culture, being taken out of a hard and dreary region,—a perfect oasis in the surrounding desert.

The entrance to the caves is not far from the further gate of the park. Their position is truly disappointing. I had anticipated a clamber half up the side of the mountain, and then some vast rift or chasm, not attainable without difficulty and danger. Their entrance is close to a small village, in a plain field, by something like an abandoned quarry, and in no way remarkable. They were discovered fourteen years ago, quite accidentally, by the man who acts as guide. Not expecting visitors, being rather before their season, he was absent; but a man and a boy to carry the candles, and a couple of lasses who knew the caverns, were soon mustered. The mouth of the cave is kept under lock and key, and is very narrow and steep down at first. Being the first visit this season, a ladder had to be adjusted to a fault in the rock, of about ten to twelve feet perpendicular, and then all difficulty is over, except occasionally stooping in some parts of an irregular passage, of about 100 yards in length, and in some subsequent galleries. In general terms, the caves may be described as a series of great chinks in the limestone rocks, at different depths, opening out into chambers of various forms and dimensions, and all connected together by their several ramifications. These are variously incrusted with stalactitic formations, and mimic architecture more or less perfect; some depending [sic] from the roof like enormous icicles or chandeliers, depositing the like matter underneath, and thus constantly approximating, until, having met, they assume the form of pillars supporting the roof. These are in every stage of formation, sometimes assuming singular and grotesque shapes, according as the process may have been interrupted from some cause, or taken an irregular direction; and all sorts of names have been bestowed, according to their fancied resemblances. There is the House of Commons, and the much grander House of Lords. There is Adam's organ; Queen Elizabeth's ruff; the chandler's shop; the tower of Babel; the beehive; the wheel and spindle; the Turk's cap; the waterfall; the £50 pillar, from that sum having been refused for it; &c., &c. The regular guide, having heard of his visitors, had hastened back from Clogheen, and met us in the caves as we were just returning, without having visited the lowest one, which is about 200 feet beneath the surface, and our junior guides had been fearful of the water it might contain. He soon took a light, and ordering one of the girls to remain behind with her candle, conducted us down a long, steep, irregularly arched gallery, and then requested us to look back and upward through the long vista. The effect was most extraordinary. The girl had placed her taper behind a semi-transparent screen of stalactite, in order to bring out its fine hues, and the ruddy light, mellowed by the gloom into a soft glow, fell upon the rich sun-burnt features of her full bust— miniatured in by the fretwork and distance—with a tone and colouring I have never seen approached by any work of art, and perfectly inimitable. In another part we came to the Cross-roads, where two passages intersect at right angles,— more than one, the guide said,—extending a mile. Last year, a curtain closing one of the passages was broken through, and a further long gallery discovered, leading past a deep chasm, terminating in a spacious and splendid chamber, called, after the noble owner, "Lord Kingston's Hall." There are twenty-four large chambers, besides many smaller ones, and three miles of gallery in all, at present discovered; several of which have never been traced to the end, and additions are being made every year. Some of the spar is very beautiful, and it is altogether one of the most wonderful specimens of Nature's handy-work under ground.

We had spent so long time in the caves, as to find ourselves too late for the public car on reaching Mitchellstown. This gained us, however, more time to look round, and the drive through the park, permitted to private vehicles. Mitchellstown is a much larger and better place than I had anticipated. The lodge offices form a long range on one side of a large square in the centre of the town, and the Kingston Arms Hotel occupies nearly another.[100] Lord Kingston is likewise a resident landlord, and excellently spoken of. The castle is of the same style and date,[101] but much larger and more massive than Lord Lismore's; and the domain is fine, but not such a complete gem. The country, for some miles through Kildorrery, wears an improved aspect; it is watered by several fine streams, the land well cultivated, with slated houses, trees, and hedgerows, several substantial farms, and flocks and herds in the fields. A large breadth we understood to be under wheat, and the roads were excellent where not interfered with by the public works.

The cabins by the road-side became deteriorated on the approach to Mallow, as is usually the case in the vicinity of all the larger towns. The main street looked substantial. We found the inn full, in consequence of the Assizes.[102] An excellent horse had brought us here; and being promised another equally good, we had no hesitation in pushing forward, though a stage further than we had intended.

The river Blackwater adorns the landscape for several miles, and the country appeared pleasing as long as the twilight held out, but with increased signs of poverty and neglect in the neighbourhood of Kanturk. In this out of the way thoroughly Irish town, we had rejoiced ourselves at the appearance of a white-fronted genteel-looking hotel, nearly detached, in the centre of the town, approached by a handsome flight of steps, to which the car drove up. Our congratulations were soon cooled by its proving inside everything that was bad and abominable, in attendance, food, and filthiness; and glad enough we were to get away the next morning, though in an uncomfortably wetting Scotch mist, that seemed likely to last the whole day.

The road to Killarney passes through a coal district, which formerly gave employment to a considerable number of men, but is now much reduced in consequence of the price of the coal and preference of the poor to turf. The country is not interesting until the great mountains begin to loom on the left, and first the Paps, then Mangerton and the Turk mountains, and finally Macgillicuddy's Reeks, heave into sight. The clouds, however, were on the summits of them all day. Killarney was as dirty and poor as ever; and there we dare not stop. I had seen the lakes before, and onward to the far west was now the motto. We just caught sight of the Lower Lake, with Ross Castle, and the lovely Innisfallen, and drove round by the new Victoria Hotel,[103] but everything was shrouded in the increasing mist. The river Laune—the outlet of the lakes—falls into Castlemaine Haven at Killorglin. Lough Garra is on the left, with a fine salmon stream running out of it. The country here becomes very wild and dreary. We changed horses at a neat little place, kept by an Englishman, called Glenbay or Brookes's, just halfway, where a very comfortable night's lodging may be had, and we should have been glad to have taken, had we known of it before. Just beyond, an uncommonly fine mountain, crowned with plantations, and a wild stream sweeping round its base, seems to oppose the thoroughfare. This passed, the road takes to the coast, and is conducted, at a great height, along a most noble range of headlands, one after the other, with nothing for the eye to rest upon but the vast rock and soaring mountain on the one hand, and on the other sheer down into the ocean, lashing for ever those majestic and inaccessible barriers. There were some fearful glens, and the view both before and behind appeared at times completely sea and mountain-locked. The road leaves the coast to avoid a mountain on the right, and appears to enter a truly savage region; but darkness overtook us an hour before entering the town of Cahirciveen.

LETTER XI. CAHIRCIVEEN—KENMARE. *8th—9th of 4th mo.* 1847.

WE arrived at Cahirciveen late last evening, in the dark and very wet. I am therefore not able to do justice to the approach to this new city of the west. Behind it rises a lofty mountain, and before it flows the estuary of the Valentia river. In it there is nothing particularly interesting: the country around is wild and dreary. Magnificent cliffs continue all along the coast; but this is several miles from the town itself. About one mile before reaching the town, the house is pointed out where Daniel O'Connell was born.[104] It is nothing remarkable at the present time.

The accommodation at the "Royal Mail Hotel and Post-Office" is not of the first-rate character. We preferred a very small room to ourselves, rather than a three-bedded one shared with another gentleman. I should strongly recommend any one coming this way, and not bound by business, to be two hours earlier, and cross over to Valentia Island, where there is a very comfortable new hotel immediately on landing.

At the hotel in Cahirciveen we met several gentlemen, members of the Relief Committee, and others. Maurice O'Connell,[105] though residing at his father's, fifteen miles (Irish) off, usually attends the Relief Committee weekly, and was fully expected that day. He was spoken of as very attentive to the wants and sufferings of the neighbourhood, and as maintaining a most hospitable house.

It was still a most unpromising driving rain, and blowing heavily when the landlord called us in the morning. He declared it was too stormy to be able to get over to Valentia Island. The ferry at Rynard Point is about three miles from the inn. Having made our arrangements for the car over-night, we were determined to go down, at all events, to the water-side, to see for ourselves. It looked rough and unpleasant, and the boat was on the other side. But the island of Valentia was stretched out before us; and if the boat could come over for us, we did not think there would be much risk in its taking us back again. The weather, too, had now begun to clear up, and the wind was obviously abating. It took some time for the ferry-boat to make its way across, to get on board, and push off again. It was still blowing fresh, but no kind of danger; and we much enjoyed the "long pull and the pull altogether," and the splash and dance over the strait, of about three quarters of a mile, which took half an hour. When safely landed, we had occasion to congratulate ourselves, in the exchange from the other side, over a very comfortable breakfast, with everything clean and good, and agreeable attendance. During breakfast the Protestant clergyman came in,[106] and wished me to call on an English resident gentleman, who works the celebrated slate quarries at the back of the island.[107] After much interesting conversation, I arranged to send a small supply of seeds, under his care and that of the minister, for the benefit of the poor inhabitants, who would not otherwise have obtained any.

Finding the master of the ferry, who had crossed over with us, a respectable and intelligent man, and that we should save time thereby, we accepted the offer of his services to conduct us over the island. The weather, in the mean time, had cleared up wonderfully; and the sun came out with that extra joyousness and brilliancy, as if to make up for lost time, when he seems to get the better of falling weather, and triumphantly drives the mist and clouds away. We took the middle road through the island, as commanding the most to be seen, which leads past the chapel, with a moderate ascent sufficient to overlook the bay. The island is the property of the Knight of Kerry, whose residence we look down upon on the right. The slate quarries are some distance further, on the same side. At a considerable elevation our guide requested us to pause: and oh! what a glorious picture! Beneath our feet lay the noble harbour of Valentia, where all the navies of the world might ride in safety. At the narrow opening between the island and Innisbeg, the Atlantic appeared to be pouring in. It has depth sufficient for vessels of any size, in any state of the tide; is accessible in all weathers, and perfectly sheltered within. It is further protected by the noble projecting foreland of Doulas Head [sic],[108] against which the great Atlantic was beating with a force and fury that sent the spray spouting up as if discharged by some powerful artillery beneath; while the subdued waves within were curling and cresting among the rocks, and in the sweet little bays, as if in the most beautiful pastime. It only required looking across to the Dingle side to be convinced of the excellency of the advice taken the previous day. I had much wished to have visited the opposite peninsula, by taking the route from Tralee to Dingle, and crossing the bay to Valentia, but was strongly advised against it at Killarney, on account of the navigation being foul and uncertain, and by no means always to be accomplished with the boats of the country; in which case there would be no alternative but waiting for fair weather, or coming all round by land, which would have incurred the loss of a day or two, I did not feel to be at command. Surveying the ocean across the bay, it was obviously impracticable, or the attempt was what we should not have ventured upon. The mist had not entirely cleared off in the distance, but on the other side we could plainly see the Blasquets,[109]—the most westerly of all our islands; the Eagle mountain,—the property and patronymic of Lord Monteagle;[110] and, just distinguishable in the further distance, Brandon, 3,126 feet in altitude. Leaving these charming land and water prospects, we passed some rocks that looked most inviting habitats for some of the rarer ferns; and then, turning the crest of the high ground, obtained a view of the whole island south-westward. The cottages in the interior are very poor, and the people undergoing much hardship, but there did not appear to be that intense degree of misery and suffering we had witnessed in some other parts. We spoke to one poor man at work on his plot, inquiring what he was going to set. "Faith, God knows," was his answer, "I have nothing at all, at all." He had the first patch of potatoes we had seen anywhere up; and, seeing his industry, we had much pleasure in telling him to prepare all the land he was able to, and apply to the clergyman, or the other gentleman, in a week's time.

The Protestant and Catholic inhabitants are about as one to twenty. Our walk over the island impressed us greatly with its beauty and capability. The climate is remarkably mild.[111] Snow is rarely seen, and ice the thickness of a shilling is an uncommon occurrence. We left the island at the point opposite to Portmagee,—where we had ordered the car to meet us,—ferried over by the man and three stout girls.

The ferryman occupied a small farm, on which he gave employment to as many as his means allowed; and, though things pressed very hard upon him, seemed anxious to mitigate the still greater want and poverty of his neighbours. Believing him to be an honest man, I proposed to send him a small supply of seed, which he has since received, and acknowledges in the following terms, under date 4th of May.

"I have distributed your parcels of turnip and Belgian white carrot seeds to the different persons in my neighbourhood. They send you their blessing, and offer up their prayers for you, and all persons who would be willing to serve them."

Along the southern shore of this strait the country is poor and ill cultivated. The cabins, spread over the moor, are merely turf-built, and very wretched. But many of the occupiers were "squatters." This is part of the O'Connell property. I must, however, in justice, say, that the state of it is attributable to the system rather than to the man. Holding, as I do, that the domestic character of any one is that only upon which he is to be trusted,—that he only who ruleth his own household well is fit to rule others,—and that he who feels the Christian duties which property imposes upon him, and who as a landlord performs those duties, is alone qualified to make laws for the property of others, or to have any voice or influence in the government of a Christian country,—I was one of those who was much influenced in my opinion of the "Liberator" by the statements of the "Times Commissioner."[112] An immense mass of valuable information, all bearing upon one point, was brought together by the industry and courage of that gentleman. But there was no reason why Daniel O'Connell should have been selected as an example *per se*. That there is a large amount of poverty upon the remote, wild, and in many respects very unfortunately situated estates, which he either owns or holds, is undoubtedly true,—too sadly true. But many of his lot-holders are those who have been driven away—"mercilessly evicted," as he himself says, from other estates, and have found refuge here; and "by this means have been saved from a worse fate, and rescued from starvation." Most of these poor tenantry had their cow, their pig, or their goats, last year, by which they supported themselves on the potato patch, paying little or no rent. The live stock are almost as clean swept from the face of the country as is the potato itself, and the poor cotters are consequently reduced to the greatest misery. Daniel O'Connell, by the universal report of the neighbourhood, has the character of being a kind, indulgent, and improving landlord; and bad as is the condition of many of the tenantry on his estates, they would be much worse off without him; and they are, by appearances, better and more comfortably off than those on the adjoining estates of some standing very high in the government of the country.

There is a considerable mixture of the old Spanish blood—transmitted likewise in the names of many of the places—all along the western coast of Ireland. Amid their extreme neglect and indigence, the fine figures, the elevated features, and the native grace and beauty of many a Kerry peasant girl, is often striking. The whole race of peasantry are perhaps among the most simple and affectionate, harmless and peaceable, hardy and intelligent, of any within our islands.

Proceeding towards Waterville by Eeny bridge,[113] the country is bare and solitary in the extreme. Vast mountains, with many a wild stream and lonely lake, rear their desolate forms as far as the eye can reach, almost without inhabitant.

The few there were, in sheltered spots or near the coast, appeared with more marks of industry about them than in many other parts. For such an out of the way place, there is a comfortable little inn, cheap, and a very civil landlord, at Waterville, on the fine bay of Ballinskelligs. Close by, on a small river coming out of Lough Curraun,[114] is one of the most productive salmon weirs in the country, the property of a resident gentleman of the name of Butler. Beyond this the road ascends rapidly, and scaling the mountain side in sight of the sea, presents, I think, for the distance of four or five miles, the grandest succession of sublime scenery I know of anywhere. The height attained cannot be much less than 1000 feet; and the road is hewn among enormous blocks of impending rock, piled up to the summits of the mountains on one side, and shelving right down into the sea on the other. Out at sea, between Boulas Head and the singular long projection of Hog Head, are seen the pinnacled forms of the Great and Little Skellig. On turning the crown of the ridge, through a gap, a still more varied and magnificent panorama bursts upon the sight. The long stretching peninsula terminated by Dursey Island, with the Bull, the Cow, and the Calf further out,—the noble opening of the river and bay of Kenmare, seen almost their whole length, with the Slievh Miskisk and Caha mountains for boundaries,—the islands of Scariff and Dinish (the property of O'Connell) nearer at hand, with many others,—and the innumerable indentations, bays, creeks, rocks and promontories of both shores, with the sea curling and wantoning around and amongst them,—formed a wonderful assemblage as seen from this height. The descent was rapid, among wild rocks, down to Derrynane.

Not knowing the position of the family, and being without letters of introduction, I felt great hesitation in calling at Derrynane Abbey,[115] though with repeated assurances of the hospitality of the house. To this I must add my warmest testimony. After the first difficulties of introduction were over, I may say, we were not *allowed* to proceed that day, by Maurice O'Connell. He personally took us round to the various interesting objects,—to the walk by the beach,—to the arsenal, where there was a moderate-sized boat re-building,—to the garden, showing us his father's favourite seat, in full view of the notorious Derrynane Beg,—and to the store, where a considerable number of persons were being supplied with meal, and where he exercised his magisterial functions by taking a deposition or two. He seemed to take great pleasure in pointing out his father's and his own alterations and improvements. The house is an unpretending one, built at different periods, with more attention to comfort and convenience within, than to appearance and symmetry outside. The situation comprises every variety of wild and romantic land and water scenery. The party at the dinner table was small and plain, and perfectly without ceremony. The state of the country, the inefficient measures of Government, the relief works, the poor-laws, and of course Repeal, were topics of conversation, in which any idea of dismemberment of the empire was emphatically denied.[116] No one could speak in stronger terms of invective against the filthy habits of the Irish poor when left to themselves, and their apathy to the introduction of new crops. He said the potato had not so completely failed in this part as in some others; and that most had still enough left for seed, which would be sown. Before leaving in the morning he called his steward, and to his trust I committed the last of our seeds.

We had now a long day's work of 26 Irish miles before us, without any conveyance, or anything of any kind to be had on the road. It is a winding ascent from Derrynane, wild, but highly interesting. The district is very poor, and we heard of some bad cases of starvation along the coast. A long dreary ascent, somewhat inland, conducts on the other side to Sneem,—a poor, dirty village, without accommodation. Notwithstanding the previous caution, I had hoped to have got something here in the way of refreshment; but the only place bearing any appearance of supplying the wants of the traveller was so dismally dirty, and so full of other people, squatted before the peat fire on the ground, that we were glad to make our escape into the outer air without sitting down,—if there had been anything in the house to sit down upon. The road again became extremely fine as it gained the coast once more. The gorse, in full bloom, was a great ornament. There is a charming bit of scenery at Blackwater bridge, looking down into a deep chasm,—ornamented with hanging foliage above,—on to a wild black river below. Dromore Castle, the newly-built residence of a clergyman of property,[117] who was highly spoken of as providing seed for his tenantry and as caring for the poor, occupies a fine position on the north bank of the estuary. We found it a long day's march before reaching the town of Kenmare.

LETTER XII. KENMARE WATERFORD. *10th—17th of 4th mo.* 1847.

KILLARNEY, Kenmare, Glengariff, are names which have long been associated with all that is lovely and beautiful in the Sister Isle. The first-named I had visited on a former occasion; the two latter were new ground to me, but an investigation of the scenery was not now the object.

It was late in the evening when we arrived at Kenmare,—tired, and a good deal exhausted. I had looked upon our painful mission as now completed, not having any idea of the awfully wretched condition of this town and neighbourhood, until accounts had begun to reach us, the last day or two, on approaching its vicinity. We were beset immediately with the most terrific details of the want and sufferings of the people: indeed it could not be concealed. The sounds of woe and wailing resounded in the streets throughout the night. I felt extremely ill, and was almost overcome.

In the morning I was credibly informed that NINE DEATHS had taken place during the night, *in the open streets*, from sheer want and exhaustion. The poor people came in from the rural districts in such numbers, in the hopes of getting some relief, that it was utterly impossible to meet their most urgent exigencies, and therefore they came in literally *to die;* and I might see several families lying about in the open streets, actually dying of starvation and fever, within a stone's throw of the inn. I went out accordingly. In the corner of an old inclosure, to which my steps were directed, on the bare ground, under the open heaven, was a *remnant of three*. One had just been carted away who had died in the night; the father had died before; the rest could not long survive. A little further, in a cask, placed like a dog-kennel, was a poor boy, who had lain there some time, in high fever, without friends or relatives. I proceeded down the main street. In the middle of it, on a little straw, under an open erection, made by placing two uprights and a board across them, were two women, horrible to behold, in the last stages of consumptive fever, brought on by evident starvation. The town itself is overwhelmed with poverty; and the swollen limbs, emaciated countenances, and other hideous forms of disease to be seen about, were innumerable. In no other part of Ireland had I seen people falling on their knees to beg. It was difficult to sit over breakfast after this. Two clergymen, hearing of our being there, came in, along with Captain Herbert, the Government Inspector,[118] who had just come down under the new relief measures. With one of the former, I immediately went to visit a family he had just come from. The house itself was not so completely wretched; but the scene within was the counterpart of what we had witnessed in Erris. He could have shown me many such. At his earnest request and representations, I engaged to visit his additional parish of Tuosist, lying along the southern shore of the Kenmare estuary, which I had previously heard described as in the most awfully destitute condition. The other clergyman, who officiated in Tuosist and Kilcatterin, still further down, was returning home. We all started together, the first-mentioned clergyman accompanying us about two miles.

A handsome suspension-bridge leads out of the town, and is a work of great public utility. The passage was often difficult, and liable to much detention, especially to the poor, before its erection,—to which the Marquis of Lansdowne,[119] the principal owner of the town, and of the property in the neighbourhood, contributed liberally. But his influence does not extend to the welfare of the peasantry on his estates in the parish of Tuosist. We took the car as far as Kilmichalog, about ten miles along the coast. It is a wild alpine region; the inhabitants being mostly self-dependent, and in ordinary times holding very little communication with the rest of the world. The clergyman depicted their present state and condition in the most affecting terms. He could think but of two persons at all in the condition of gentlemen residing in the whole district. He declared it to be his belief, that out of a population of upwards of 30,000, there were 10,000 who had no other means of subsistence, at the present moment, than seaweed and shell-fish from the rocks. There existed considerable remains of clanship among these mountaineers. He described them as a highly moral, a careless, but a peaceable and contented race, with great kindness and simple hospitality, and strong family attachments; but now the bonds of natural affection were fearfully broken and destroyed, under the pressure and sufferings of their present calamity. Their cattle, as in other places, had almost wholly disappeared. Cows had been parted with for 20s. to 25s.; sheep 3s. 6d. to

5s., being brought in by the poor people to sell for anything they would fetch. At parting I handed him £5 for immediate urgency; and ordered to Kenmare two small bales of clothing I had remaining in Dublin. The Central Committee have since responded to an application on behalf of this district.

From the spot where we parted with the car we struck directly up the mountains. There was a new road making under the public works, and a truly magnificent one it will be; requiring not a little first-rate engineering to carry it in the best way over the mountains. We pursued its yet only rough-hewn course with considerable difficulty—carried a great height above the lovely and secluded, but little known Lough Glenmore, until the works and work-people disappeared in the ascent, and we could no longer track it. We then made a short cut over the crest of the mountain, somewhat arduous, and down a tremendous defile to the junction with the new line on the other side; which—after some noble vistas into deep, abrupt-looking valleys, alive with the voice of waters, and the motion of many graceful white-threaded streamlets coming down from the heights—brought us out at Adragool, one of the sweet secluded harbours on the north side of Bantry Bay. The boundary line between the counties Kerry and Cork is passed on the summit.

We were deceived in the distances, and found the walk along the coast long and toilsome, though very fine. It is needless to caution the experienced traveller against the length of the Irish miles. They are in proportion to the English, as 11 to 14, but in the rural unmeasured districts they know nothing of real distances. The people along this line are poor and distressed. The want of clothing is as great as the want of food. The wan, aged, and sunken countenances, and the silent beseeching look, *without a word spoken,* of some of the women and girls, is what enters into the heart deepest, and is the most difficult to bear. To describe properly the state of things in some of these wretched districts, is a vain attempt. It is impossible,—it is inconceivable. STARVATION,—a word that has now become so familiar, as scarcely to awaken a painful idea,—is NOT being two or three days deficient of food. *It is something quite different;* and the effects of dwindling and insufficient nourishment upon a whole population,—upon the mass of men, women, and the little children; the disease,—the emaciation,—the despair,—the extinction of everything human beyond it,—are utterly past the powers of description, or even of imagination, without witnessing. I am in possession of details beyond anything that has appeared in print, or, I believe, in private circulation; in fact, for the sake of poor humanity, unfit to communicate. My mind was at times so struck down, that for days together the pen has refused its office; the appalling spectacles have seemed to float between, whenever I attempted it, and to paralyze every effort. The loss of a parent, of a child, we know what it is in any one of our families. If the causes are, or appear to have been, in any way within the reach of neglected assistance, or of human control, we know how manifold the agony is increased. Multiply this into all the cabins, the populous way-sides, the far-off solitary mountain hamlets,—vivify the details of famine and pestilence, by thousands and tens of thousands, throughout the length and breadth of Ireland,—and we may have some idea of the voice of anguish and lamentation that now ascends from her whole land.

We had to regret the darkness overtaking us in the latter part of this walk. After losing sight of the bay and the opposite mountains, it was a very long ascent, and then it seemed an almost endless descent; in the course of which we first looked down upon, and then rounded the foot of a most romantic mountain-locked lake. Ravines were crossed, that looked fearful in the twilight, with the rushing sound of wild waters below; and the last forms of the mountains that were visible were truly grand.

We had no time left to investigate the beauties of Glengariff. To all appearances it was a most delightful spot, combining perhaps the lovely and the grand, the mighty rock and the secluded bower, the sweet cove and the majestic mountain, in the highest degree possible. The remainder of the journey was a rapid return through Bantry, where we heard the distress was very great; Skibbereen, where distress and fever had much abated—we were informed, that in the barony of West Carberry, comprising the south-west corner of the island, out of a population of 97,000 probably one-fourth had been carried off; Roscarberry, Clonakilty, and Bandon, to Cork. In this great city fever was much on the increase, and ascending in the scale of society. There were stated to be 22,000 extra paupers in the city at that time. From Cork we proceeded by Watergrasshill and Rathcormuck, through the handsome town of Fermoy by Clogheen to Clonmel. Here we had the satisfaction of attending the Quarterly Meeting for Munster,[120] and of visiting, in company with a very kind friend, the soup-kitchen, jail, auxiliary poor-house, additional fever-hospital, and the lunatic asylum, all which appeared to be under the most efficient management. I must here acknowledge the kindness of C. Bianconi,[121] in forwarding the various parcels of seeds to the far west, free of expense, on application. I think it right to mention the terms of esteem and gratitude in which, throughout this whole journey, I heard the efforts of England and Englishmen towards Ireland everywhere spoken of, under the desolation which has been permitted thus mysteriously to sweep over the land.

From Clonmel we took the public car to Waterford; visited the admirable soup-kitchen established under the care of Friends in that city; and came off by mail-boat to Milford, on the morning of the 16th, and were favoured to reach home in safety the following day,—thus exactly completing an absence of Six Weeks in Ireland.

CONCLUSION.

It may now be naturally inquired,—what is the result? Has any good been accomplished?—*can* any good be accomplished for Ireland? Is there any improvement? Have we a more cheering prospect for the future? or is there any *possibility* of a change for the better? Are there any remedies that can be applied to prevent the recurrence of the same evils?

The simple travelling of an Englishman in Ireland, at the present juncture, with his mind open, and his heart in his hand,—the interchange of information and experience,—the mere expenditure of the money,—I believe to be a great good. The result of our individual seed-sowing has yet to be shown. We have reason to believe upwards of 2,000 poor cottiers have been more or less set to work on their own plots, with the stimulus of obtaining, by their own labour, some future supply of food for their families, where they would not otherwise have had any; and introducing new ideas, as well as the necessity of better habits of agriculture, than dependence on the one unfortunate root. Female industry has been upheld and promoted in several places, by the funds placed at our disposal by the Ladies' Committee of London; and flax-sowing to some extent has been encouraged in two fresh quarters. The sight of a stranger in some of these remote localities is like that of a friend; and I do trust we have been made instrumental in holding up the hands of individuals here and there, who were devoting their *all* in some of the distressed districts, in endeavouring to alleviate the misery around them, but were ready to faint, and all but borne down by the weight and extent of the calamity. We have felt it a great privilege to be thus employed, at whatever sacrifice. I expect a full report will be received from every locality in which the seeds have been scattered. In these Letters I have endeavoured to give a bird's-eye view, as it were, of the distressed portions of Ireland, drawn upon the spot, with the vivid delineations of truth, but without exaggeration or colouring, and as concisely as possible; accompanied by such details as might serve to illustrate the actual condition of things, to indicate the causes that have operated, and the elements that are still at work, or exist to be worked upon, in her domestic and social constitution. Any of these might have been expanded into a volume. What is the picture? Take the line of the main course of the Shannon, continued north to Lough Swilly, and south to Cork. It divides the island into two great portions, east and west. In the eastern there is distress and poverty enough, as part of the same body, suffering from the same causes; but there is much to redeem. In the west it exhibits a people, not in the centre of Africa, the steppes of Asia, the backwoods of America,—not some newly-discovered tribes of South Australia, or among the Polynesian Islands,—not Hottentots, Bushmen, or Esquimeaux,—neither Mahomedans nor Pagans,—but some millions of our own Christian nation at home, living in a state and condition low and degraded to a degree unheard of before in any civilized community; driven periodically to the borders of starvation; and now reduced, by a national calamity, to an exigency which all the efforts of benevolence can only mitigate, not control; and under which *absolute thousands* are not merely pining away in misery and wretchedness, but are dying like cattle off the face of the earth, from want and its kindred horrors! Is this to be regarded in the light of a Divine dispensation and punishment? Before we can safely arrive at such a conclusion, we must be satisfied that human agency and legislation, individual oppressions, and social relationships, have had no hand in it.

I am aware of the immense amount of prejudice that has to be met in approaching this subject. I am aware that in conversing with a large class of well-intentioned persons in Ireland, one is met with the notions in which they have been educated, and with all sorts of doubts and discouragements; such as, that the question is surrounded with difficulties; dangerous to meddle with; and what is worse than all, with their very imperfect acquaintance with Ireland, gleaned only from the particular prejudices and the partial influences in their locality, being mistaken for a knowledge of the whole land and people. I do not believe in the reality of the difficulties. They are the creations of fear, of interest, or the want of faith in principle,—the lion in the way of the slothful man. If one prejudice is opposed by another, the stronger will gain the mastery. But I never yet knew any prejudice able to withstand the undermining influence of the power of reason and evidence, when silently applied; nor falsehood and usurpation to resist the light of truth, where each had equally fair play.

Some of the social evils under which Ireland peculiarly labours have been hinted at, as occasion occurred, in the course of these Letters. There is, I believe, scarcely another country where the proprietary is so small, and have so little direct interest in the soil: that is, where the number of acres, divided by the number of lords of the soil, gives so large a result. Add to this the almost universality of absenteeism in the west, and let the two facts be treasured up.

Emigration is proposed as a remedy. So long as there is land that would repay the expense of labour lying unreclaimed, and much more land only half cultivated, it is opposed to every mercantile principle to send that labour away. We have in Ireland the two great elements that lie at the foundation of all national and individual wealth,—land and labour. We have them both in superabundance. With an immense amount of labour lying idle, which might be applied to the equally idle soil, the waste of national wealth is beyond calculation. The want of national policy is as great as the national sin in this neglect. Place these three or four million Irish in a fair position, enable them to earn the necessities and decencies of life, and we have a finer market opened at home than any of our hard-earned and expensively maintained possessions abroad: and Ireland is capable of maintaining several times its present amount of population. At the best, emigration can only be like the medical man's remedy of bleeding, which can but be done at the expense of the constitution.

Poor-laws are offered as a remedy. While it is freely admitted that the labourer has the first claim to maintenance upon the soil which produces abundance, the principle of unearned compulsory support is the worst form in which this right can be enforced, and is known to be most deteriorating both to character and morality. Every reflecting mind, while it acknowledges the necessity and the Christian duty, under the present affecting circumstances of Ireland, deplores the consequences of the gratuitous relief that has been pouring in on all sides, knowing that it must inevitably breed a mass of corruption; and, with their natural inclinations, was almost the worst thing that could be done for her people, unless powerfully counteracted by other means, and the influence of active principles.

Loans upon a large scale have been suggested, and eagerly sought for as a panacea. While real capital is essential in healthy action, artificial capital but inflames the evils in a diseased and unhealthy state. No mercantile or banking establishment would lend its money for the sake of supporting a concern, however rich in itself, that did not make proper use of its own resources, or where those resources were so ill employed as to be converted in expense and extravagance. A sound discretion, wishing to benefit its best friend, would say,—Justify your accounts; give us some guarantee or security on your present resources, as the basis of profitable investment or occupation of more; or if you are so embarrassed and involved as to be unable to do the best, get rid of your incumbrances, wind up the old order of things, and begin anew, and then we will help you: otherwise additional means will be wasted or worse,—the catastrophe may be deferred, but the ultimate dividend will be diminished.

Is there anything inherent in the national character fatal to improvement? The Irish are accused of being lazy, improvident, reckless of human life. I doubt their being much more so than the English, the Americans, or any other nation would be under the like circumstances. The distances to which an Irish labourer will go for work, and the hardships he will submit to, are notorious; and the private correspondence of all who have entered into the subject teems with evidence of the alacrity of the poor women and peasant girls for employment of any kind, and of the teachableness and skill they exhibit. The appeal to a wider range of facts is irresistible. Who come over in such numbers to reap our harvests, dig our canals, construct our railroads, in fact wherever hard work is to be obtained? Who save up what money they can, during harvest-time, and suchlike seasons of extra employment, to take back to their families at home? Who, in a country where labour is better remunerated, send over sums exceeding all that the wealthy have raised in charity, to comfort those they have left behind, or help over their poor friends and relatives to what they think that happier land? The generosity of the Irish was never questioned. Their peaceableness has been put to the severest test. In no other country, probably, could such a state of things have endured so long, and to such an extremity, without ten-fold more outrages than have been committed. They are naturally a contented and a happy race. The charge of recklessness of human life—apart from those deplorably aggravated deeds arising invariably out of natural jealousies—is answered by the perfect safety of a stranger amongst them; and it has further been placed on the right shoulders in another quarter, more fearlessly than I durst have penned it here.

Is their religion the cause of the low and degraded state of the Irish people? The influence of an Established Church, not in harmony with the sympathies of the people, and compulsorily maintained, I am bound to believe injurious. The paramount injustice, and the deteriorating and disorganizing effects among all classes, are, I believe, among the sorest burdens and greatest detriments in every way that afflict Ireland. The Protestant form of doctrine I most sincerely believe to be nearer the original sources, and far more favourable to the development of industry, and of individual and national independence, intelligence, and enterprise. I regard the claim to allegiance spiritual, of which the Roman Catholic Church is the exponent, as the key-stone of priest craft; and, under whatever form or denomination, as the great barrier to human progress. But if I hear the Irish disinclination to cleanliness attributed to their religion, I cannot help remarking—the Scotch are Protestant; or if their idle and improvident habits placed to the same account, I must answer—the Belgians are Catholic. Isolate the poor Irishman from the circumstances that depress him,—place him in any other part of the world,—give him the same reward for his labour,—the same hopes and prospects of success as another, and look at him then, with or without the form of his religion unchanged. I need hardly refer to the services which have been rendered to this country in every department of literature and the arts, at the Bar, and in the State, and in some fields with which I cannot sympathize, by distinguished Irishmen.

What, then, is the grand cause of the constant depression of a country and a people formed by Nature to be one of the richest in the world? What is it that makes our Sister a continual beggar and a drain upon us, our weakness and deformity, a spot upon our escutcheon, instead of, as she might be, our pride, our beauty, and our strength? Let us look narrowly at unjust and partial legislation. Has she been treated as a Sister? a Bride? or as a captive slave won by the force of arms, kept by coertion, [sic] and therefore unattached and restless, miserable, and easily to be won by others? Has she not ever been treated as a conquered province? We know how even the Act of Union was brought about.[122] Have not the alterations and ameliorations up to the present time been wrung by fear, or granted as eleemosynary favours, and not as due and equable rights? Has it not been coertion here and indulgence there,—a manacle and a sop? and is this the way to educate a rational and intelligent people? There is nothing in the state or position of Ireland that has required her being on any but the same or an equal footing with the ancient kingdoms of Wessex or Mercia,[123]—with Cornwall or Northumberland,—if we wished her to constitute an integral part of the same empire. Still though the Legislature can do much, in removing or mitigating the elements of evil, we must not look to legislative means for doing everything towards the regeneration of Ireland. I wish to put this on the right basis. I have little faith in the power of human Governments for active good. The true mission of Government is to repress evil, to withstand the encroachments of individuals, and to counteract the oppressions and the constant tendency to arbitrariness, which the various combinations of selfishness exercise towards individuals, or towards one another, in an artificial and competing state of society. Whenever Government attempts to do positive good, it mistakes its functions, and rarely does more than exchange one form of oppression for another. It is by individual exertion, regeneration and development, that active and permanent good can alone be effected. By setting free their latent and long-smothered energies,—by awakening their industry, their self-reliance, their feeling of duty and responsibility,—virtue is born and nurtured among the masses. You cannot force freedom on the slave, economy on the spendthrift, duty on the unconscientious, religion on the wrong or the orphaned in heart, by any legal enactments or outside observances. The internal principles must be brought into activity, the self-supporting powers developed, or you are building without foundations upon the sand,—you are placing leaves and branches on a life-less stump, in expectation of having fruit therefrom.

The difficulties of Ireland lie more in the remnants of the hereditary and inveterate selfishness of the old feudal times,—the laws of entail and primogeniture,—the principle of serfdom in the tenure of land, being there left in greater vigour,—and in the partial and class legislation by which they are maintained, than in any other cause. The powers of the soil and the talents of the people, now lying waste and idle, require simply to be liberated, and to be brought into mutual and healthy action and co-operation one with another. The duty of Government, when it has no crooked policy, no party interests to serve, is plain and straightforward,—to grant freedom to the utmost point of safety, whether in reference to land, to labour, to manufactures, or to the multitudinous products and blessings of the soil,—and to turn to the best account for all. The great principles of right and justice are therein involved. The time is gone by when the old doctrine, "that a man had a right to do what he liked with his own," is held to be true, either as regards individuals or Governments. A man or a Government has only a right to do its duty with its own, improperly so called. There is no right without a duty, and the right ceases if the duty is not performed. This principle lies at the bottom of all social compacts, and of all legitimacy. If a man has 100,000 acres, and either does not or cannot occupy them,—if he does not turn them to profitable account, or improve the talent entrusted to him, he forfeits his title, because it is a violation of the compact by which he holds it, and an injury to others, and to the State under whose authority alone he obtains that title. Not that the same should be taken away by force; but the State is justified—nay called upon—to interfere, and require him to part with to others what he cannot use or properly maintain himself, at what it is worth under *his* management. Our Government has made a move in the right direction, by setting free the trade in corn. Where would Ireland or England have been now, and what fertilizing streams of benevolence from America would have been stopped in their sources, but for this righteous amelioration of a mistaken code? The next natural step forward is to set free the land. Facilitate its transfer, in every legitimate way, from the hands of nominal to those of real proprietors,—from those who will not or cannot perform the duties incumbent upon property, to those who can. The one would be as glad to get rid of the burden as the other to purchase the boon. Free it from all those unnatural and impolitic incumbrances and embarrassments which oppress the soil, and see the effects in Ireland, where things can scarcely be worse, and where the opposite system has for so long worked so badly. Everything I have seen, heard, or read, points to one simple and natural measure for Ireland—FREE TRADE IN LAND. I believe the liberation of the land from its incumbrances and mismanagement,—the bringing it to a free, fair, and open market,—would be felt immediately to vibrate throughout Ireland, in its invigorating influence, like pouring new life-blood into her veins. Capital, which in a commercial country is like the lubricating oil between the labourer and his raw material, would instantly commence flowing in legitimate and healthful channels; as it can never fail to do, where the cheapest markets are opened, be it in land or labour, or any other element of productive industry;

increasing the value in proportion to its free access, and giving value to what was worthless before. The millions of uncultured, and at present worthless acres, would put on a value, and be brought under the productive labour of the millions of unemployed poor, whose social position would be raised, as they would be taught of necessity the wants and the comforts of life. Every class would be benefited; and no one would be injured unless those who prey upon the mystifications and incumbrances at present involving the tenure of land, inflicting a fearful amount of inequality and injustice, the accumulation and behest of the feudal bye-gone ages, which must be swept away to make room for a simple and effective measure. Without it I believe all our temporary measures, our subscriptions, our societies, our new poor-laws, our emigrations, our industrial schools, our religious missions, will prove vain and fruitless,—mere palliations, that can no longer be maintained when the excitement is past, or serve only to inflame the evil eventually. All will be smothered beneath the incubus that oppresses the country, or sink back and be swallowed up in the same order of things, with the same results, one dire calamity treading in the footsteps of another, each with a still more fearful train of horrors.

It is but a faint picture that has ever yet been drawn of the miseries and sufferings of Ireland. It has been difficult to confine the narrative within limits. Volumes might be written without detailing a tithe of the shocking truths. Some of the scenes have retained their grasp upon the imagination day and night. Such a state of things as has long existed in Ireland would not have been suffered by England in any foreign country, without pouring forth its missionaries. Such abandonment of duty and responsibility would not have been endured in England. I have elsewhere written, that if the *animals* had been anywhere allowed to live and die off in the manner of these poor people, the nation would have been up in arms against the owner of that estate.

To conclude, in the words of a late visitor to some of these districts, "Let us not consider our duty to Ireland fulfilled, by the effort to meet its present necessity. Its general and permanent condition is a subject in itself almost too dreadful to contemplate. Famine is there no new cry. It is a periodic disease. Every year there are districts where prevails somewhat of that misery that now rules the land. For a large portion of its population, all the great purposes of existence are forgotten in the struggle with death. I would not now discuss the causes of this condition, nor attempt to apportion blame to its authors; but of this one fact there can be no question, that the result of our social system is, that vast numbers of our fellow-countrymen,—of the peasantry of one of the richest nations the world ever knew,—have not leave to live. Surely such a social result is not only a national misfortune, but a national sin, crying loudly to every Christian citizen to do his duty to remove it. No one of us can have any right to enjoy either riches or repose, until, to the extent of his ability, he strive to wash himself of all share in the guilt of this fearful inequality, which will be a blot in the history of our country, and make her a bye-word among the nations."

# APPENDIX

APPENDIX A.

Dr. Harvey states,[124] in a letter addressed to the "Central Relief Committee of the Society of Friends," with a copy of which he has favoured me, that the saving by the adoption of "genuine brown bread, made from the best whole wheaten meal, which meal is the wheat well ground, but retaining the whole of the bran, in place of the more usual white bread used in families," and, especially if made by a process without fermentation, is under-estimated at 25 per cent. He supports his statement by the following extracts.

"It has been calculated that the people might produce for themselves five million quarters of wheat before the next harvest, simply by eating brown bread. It is well known that out of 112 lbs. of wheat 28 lbs. are taken in the shape of brans and coarse flour, leaving only 84 lbs. of fine flour. Now, if the brans only were taken out, which would in no case exceed 8 lbs., there would be left 104 lbs. of nutritious flour, more wholesome and more digestible, as every man can testify, than the flour now used; so that, as 104 exceeds 84 by one-fourth, twenty million quarters, which is believed to be about our consumption annually, would, if dressed in this way, produce as much flour as twenty-five millions."

"Fermentation destroys part of the flour or meal. We find in consequence, that a sack, or 280 lbs., which makes 360 lbs. of bread, or 90 quartern loaves, by fermentation, gives 408 lbs., or 102 quartern loaves, by effervescence. The loss by refining is still greater. A quarter of wheat, weighing 520 lbs., or 65 lbs. per bushel, produces 512 lbs. of meal; but these, after a course of screening, yield only 416 lbs. of flour,—a diminution of 96 lbs. or 18 per cent. Thus it appears, that a quarter of the best wheat, ground for meal, and manufactured by the simple but efficacious process now brought into notice, will give 746 lbs. of the most nutritious bread; but if converted into flour 'by officiously separating what Nature has beneficially combined,' and further reduced and deteriorated by fermentation, the product will not exceed 534 lbs., exhibiting a loss in quantity of bread, to say nothing of its inferior quality or inability to sustain life, of 212 lbs., or 106 such loaves as are usually seen in the shops and at our tables."

"The total loss by fermentation and by refining, taken together, independent of the cost of labour and machinery, is under-estimated at 25 per cent. Now, by the common computation, 18 millions of quarters of wheat are made into bread annually, in England and Wales. The annual waste of human food in these divisions of the United Kingdom, is, therefore, at the rates given, 4,500,000 quarters of wheat, equivalent to 3,357,000,000 lbs. of bread, or 8 ounces per day for every member of the community, old and young, and nearly twice the quantity usually supplied by importation, amounting in money value, at only 50s. per quarter, to £11,250,000—an absolute loss to the nation, lessened only by the produce of the bran, or rather by the difference between that and the cost of labour and machinery expended in separating it. The question of economy is therefore one of much interest to the public as well as to individuals; and the illustration of it might be extended with advantage, particularly at the present time."

"The bread of unrefined flour will sustain life, while that made with refined will not. Keep a man on genuine brown bread and water, and he will live and enjoy good health; give him white bread and water only, and he will gradually sicken and die. The meal of which the brown is made contains all the ingredients essential to the composition or nourishment of the various structures composing our bodies. Some of these ingredients are removed by the miller, in his efforts to please the public; so that fine flour, instead of being better than the meal, is the least nourishing; and, to make the case worse, it is also the most difficult of digestion. The loss is therefore in all respects a waste."

Dr. Harvey goes on to say,—

"I could multiply opinions and facts, but have confined myself to a few, which I deemed absolutely necessary to assure you, and the public, of the many advantages that would result from the adoption of genuine brown bread, in place of the white bread now generally used. As to its advantages over our common brown bread, scarcely more need be said. If the authorities and facts adduced should have satisfied you of the principle advocated, I doubt not you will be willing not only to act upon it as respects yourselves, but will, without loss of time, so precious in the urgency of the circumstances, call the attention of the Government and public to the subject. And, I would further suggest, the support and encouragement, by you and by all, of such baking establishments as may be willing to adopt the receipts and manner of preparation of the bread, as have been and may further be laid down by practical and scientific men."

The same principle "that not only as a matter of feeling, but as a matter of imperative duty, as well as economy, the upper and middle classes ought to impose the strictest regulations with regard to the consumption of the staff of life in their families," has been publicly advocated on both sides the House of Lords. An advertisement, signed by many peers of the realm, binding themselves to the same course, has appeared in the public papers. The Queen has likewise been pleased to issue her commands, "that from the date of this order, no description of flour except seconds shall be used for any purpose in her household."

## APPENDIX B.

Having in every case supplied model dibbles,[125] made by W. Drummond and Sons, with a view to the greater economy of seed, and more employment, where labour was so superabundant, I transcribe (with permission) the following letter, exhibiting the striking results of dibbling tillage, as applied to the great grain crops, originally addressed to the editor of the Leinster Express.

"Though unused to obtrude my views upon the attention of the public, the very appalling circumstances in which this country is now placed by the general, and all but total failure of the potato crop, has induced me to request the insertion of some observations, accompanied by a statement, showing the very considerable advantages, present and prospective, that would have resulted from, and may yet in a great measure be obtained by the adoption of an improved system of tillage, peculiarly adapted to the present emergency.

"The people of Ireland are now suffering from an infliction that has created an extent and severity of misery and destitution hitherto unprecedented in the history of any civilised country; and by the accounts received each day, and from every district, it is quite evident that the amount and extent of the misery and destitution are increasing and extending each succeeding hour, and what at first was confined to the rural population has now spread to the tradesmen and artizans, and will shortly be severely felt by the shopkeepers and merchants.

"Famine and its associates, fever and dysentery, are carrying off the population by thousands, and though the higher classes have been hitherto blessed in their freedom from the first, the latter scourges, more rapid in their spreading from the lower to the higher classes, have already caused dismay and sorrow in many families, whose inmates were far removed from want. The horrors arising from these inflictions are rendered still more awful to contemplate, by the consideration and dread that the ensuing harvest may bring no alleviation of suffering, by reason of this fact, that a great proportion, more especially in the western and poorer counties, of the hitherto occupied land, still remains uncropped and untilled; nor has any stock of compost been as usual collected.

"I would therefore most earnestly call upon all landowners and farmers, as well as upon all of every class interested in and for the safety and welfare of Ireland, to take the present circumstances of the country into instant consideration, that some measures may he adopted and carried out, by means of which the arable land now lying idle may be tilled and cropped, and the fullest possible provision made for the wants of the ensuing year; and I would solicit attention for the following statement, believing that the calculations are so framed as to exhibit results very much within the really attainable advantages. Where no two authorities were found to correspond, it was impossible to obtain such exact data as would insure freedom from error in these calculations; actual correctness is therefore neither insisted on nor pretended to; but numerous cases, showing results from the system of dibbling tillage, much higher than merely bearing out these calculations, can be brought forward and certified.

## STATEMENT.

"The quantity of WHEAT grown in Ireland annually, on an average of 10 years, is about 2,500,000 quarters, or 4,285,714 barrels, of 20 stones to the barrel. This, at 7 barrels to the statute acre, would make 612,245 acres under wheat.

"To sow this number of acres would take, at 12 stones to the acre . . . 367,347 brls.

"If the like breadth of land was sown by a system of dibbling, the quantity of seed required would not be over 28 lbs. per acre, viz., 612,245 acres, at 28 lbs. per acre

. . . 61,224 brls.

"By a still more careful system of dibbling, the quantity of seed required might be lowered to 18 lbs. per acre

... 39,358 brls

"By a system of good drilling, the quantity of seed required per acre would be about 4 stones

... 122,449 brls.

"Thus by the most careful method of dibbling, a saving of seed to the amount shown as underneath would be attained, viz.—

| | |
|---|---:|
| "612,245 acres, at 12 stones per acre | 367,347 brls. |
| "612,245 acres, at 18 lbs. per acre | 39,358 brls. |
| "Attaining a saving of | 327,989 brls. |

applicable to the consumption, being one half of the amount annually exported from Ireland.

"To sow the like number of acres at 28 lbs., would require 61,224 barrels, attaining a saving of 306,123 barrels.

"And to sow the same ground, by drill tillage, at 4 stones, 122,448 barrels, attaining a saving of 244,899 barrels.

"The quantity of OATS annually grown in Ireland is about 16,000,000 quarters, which, at 40 lbs. per bushel, or 320 lbs. per quarter, would be 26,122,449 barrels, at 14 stones per barrel, which, at 10 barrels per statute acre, would make 2,612,244 acres under oats.

"2,612,244 acres would require for seed, at the rate of 17 stones per acre

... 3,067,010 brls.

"If the like breadth of land was sown by careful dibbling, the quantity of seed required would not be over 28 lbs. per acre ... 373,177 brls.

"Attaining a saving, applicable to the consumption of this country, of ... 2,693,833 brls. being an amount greater than the average annual export of oats from this country. This saving would of course require an increased expenditure, consequent upon the improved tillage, but which increased expenditure would be repaid by a very great increase in the acreable produce.

"By ordinary, well-conducted drill tillage, the quantity of seed required might be lowered to 4 stones per acre ... 746,354 brls.

"Attaining a saving of ... 2,320,656 brls.

being still over the average annual export.

"The foregoing statement shows, if correct, that, were a system of dibble tillage generally adopted throughout Ireland, the saving on the number of acres hitherto for many years cultivated under wheat and oats, would amount to 133,897,960 lbs. of wheat and 527,991,268 lbs. of oats, together making 661,889,228 lbs., or nearly 295,482 tons of food, applicable to the consumption of this country; and it is to be borne in mind, that this saving is irrespective of barley and other crops somewhat similarly circumstanced.

"Now, most important as such a saving of seed would be, and paramount in such a time as the present, the whole amount is trifling indeed, in comparison to the extent to which such a system of tillage would add by the increased acreable produce of the ensuing harvest.

"Supposing that potatoes should not again become the staple food of this country, and that the people become henceforward a breadstuff-fed people, it would require fully three times the present breadth of land to be brought under tillage to support the population, admitting the tillage to remain as defective as it has been.

"In many parts of the western counties, hitherto producing excellent crops of potatoes, say averaging 12 tons to the acre, or 26,880 lbs., giving 73⅔ lbs., or 5¼ stones per day, the produce of oats per acre—with a sowing of 14 stones of seed—averages little more than 7 barrels, of 14 stones to the barrel. Now, as oats require to be of good quality to produce 112 lbs. of meal per barrel, the produce of an acre of oats would be but 784 lbs., or 2 1/7 lbs. per day; this very great difference of acreable produce of food must be, by some means, made up, or the population cannot be supported.

"Had the labour expended on the public roads this season, uselessly or injuriously, as regards *present* purposes of locomotion, been usefully expended on the land, under a system of dibble tillage, with its scanty proportional requiring of seed, how very different would have been the prospects of the coming season. It is, therefore, that I would so earnestly call the attention of the Government, the landowners, and of all parties interested in the safety and welfare of the country, to this most important subject.

"It is quite apparent, unless unhappily famine shall fearfully thin our population, that we shall next season require a much greater amount of produce than we ordinarily do; and yet, notwithstanding this fact is admitted by all, a great proportion of the ground hitherto under tillage is now lying idle, without any apparent appearance of its being cropped, and this to an extent not much short of the one half of our usual extent of land under tillage.

"I am, very respectfully,

"WILLIAM TODHUNTER."[126]

"Dublin, 9th of 3rd mo. 1847."

The same party, under a later date, writes,—

"Though a very warm advocate for dibbling under certain circumstances, yet I do not so strongly recommend it where the ground is rich and well cultivated. But under the peculiar circumstances of our country last year, it was most unfortunate, and deeply to be regretted, that the system was not generally adopted. Had it been, no one solitary acre of the counties of Donegal, Londonderry, Leitrim, Mayo, Galway, Clare, Cork or Kerry, need have been uncropped, while as it is, part of some, and a great portion of the others, still remain unsown; and of the portions actually cropped, the tilling, as well as the sowing, are equally insufficient.

"The difference of the result, had the plan proposed by me been adopted, would have amounted to a quantity of food four times, at least, greater than all the imports we can possibly obtain from all quarters, for the past, present, and coming year.

APPENDIX C.

To show that these fearful anticipations have been but too fatally realized, I transcribe the following from the rector of the parish.

"Belmullet, 4th May, 1847.

"The people themselves, heaps upon heaps, are dying; it is said the third of them will not survive; and upon sober calculation, I should say fully one half must sink under a calamity unparalleled in the memory of man. What you witnessed was but trifling to the awful state we are now reduced to; and notwithstanding the aid afforded us by the British Association,—and it is great,—the mortality and pestilential disease seem only to be on the increase.

"Yours very faithfully,

"SAML. STOCK."

George S. Bourns says, Rossport, 19th May,—

"They are dying,—absolutely dying,—over their spades. They try to work, yet from exhaustion are not able. . . . The number of deaths each day, within four or five miles of this, is fearful in the extreme . . . The people were in an awful state when you visited Mayo,—they are *much worse now*."

The distress did not appear so raging in the neighbourhood of Ballycastle as in some other districts, when we were there. The following exhibits the downward progress since.

"Mount Glen, Ballycastle, Killala,

"19th May, 1847.

"As you expressed a wish to know how the poor may be getting on in this locality, I beg to inform you, that poverty and real distress is considerably on the increase, since I last had the pleasure of writing to you. It is truly awful to contemplate the condition of the starving poor at this moment; they are dying fast, through actual want. It is impossible to supply the one half of the applicants for relief, with the scanty funds at my disposal. They are coming to my place in crowds every day, with imploring cries for one morsel of food. It is truly heart-rending to witness the scenes of awful destitution which present themselves every moment in the day. I earnestly entreat, if you have any influence with any of the benevolent societies in England, that you will try and induce them to send more relief to these poor creatures . . . My son will furnish you, in a short time, with a list of the distributions of the seeds. The number of applicants were so many, that he had to give it out in small quantities. The poor farmers seem most anxious to obtain the seed; he could not supply half the applicants, notwithstanding that he gave it sparingly. He would consider it troublesome to ask for more seed . . . I applied in another quarter for some, but have had no reply.

"Yours very sincerely,

"JOHN FAUSSETT, J.P."[127]

The safe receipt of the bale of clothing, "to the inexpressible delight of the poor people," has since been acknowledged. A copy of the above letter I thought it best immediately to forward to the Central Committee in Dublin, who I have reason to believe will be able to support the application, from the grant of seeds now placed at their disposal by the liberality of the Government.

The following touching picture, from another quarter, of the *effect* of daily witnessing these scenes, upon the feeling mind, is from a letter to a friend.
"Achill Sound, 26th May, 1847.
"Since I wrote you last I find myself almost a changed being. The *scenes of death and misery* which I daily witness are now to me a mere matter of course, and although I go beyond my means to relieve the sufferers, yet there is a cold iron stiffness in my heart which I cannot account for. I pay an immense district of labourers weekly, and as I drive along near Westport, Newport, and other places, the assembled hundreds that are watching here and there to meet their paymaster present an appearance truly wretched. Other paymasters go *armed, and with an escort of police*. I travel without fire-arms or police,—often at night from Westport home,—*and am perfectly safe*. I make this remark merely to show that in whatever situation of life we are placed, to read the character of the persons we have to deal with, and act a straightforward independent part, will in the end be better than arms.
"This country is now in its last struggle. Fever and starvation go hand in hand. Many respectable persons have fallen victims. Many are sick. To draw a picture would fail me . . . I have not time to write any more; crowds are around my house at this moment."

APPENDIX D.

The following is the description of the state of the island of Arranmore, by eye-witnesses, published so long ago as the middle of last winter.

"In consequence of the expressed anxiety of many friends, as well as in accordance with what we conceived to be a duty, we visited Arranmore—the largest and most populous (it contains about 1,500 inhabitants) of the group of islands off the north-west coast of Donegal—on Wednesday, the 13th of January, to ascertain, by personal investigation, how far the report of disease and great destitution, said to be existing there, was founded on fact.

"Apprehending that there might be ample foundation for such a report, we went into the island provided with the means of administering some relief, both to the sick and hungry.

"That our apprehensions were well grounded, the following cases, met with in our walk, may prove. We shall merely premise, that most of the cabins we visited were small, smoky, dark and loathsome; destitute of the meanest articles of furniture—the solitary chest being frequently applied to the varied uses of table, chair, and dresser; the whole arrangements of the hovels, in many instances, resembling more the wretched resources of savage life than those which might be expected to be found within the precincts of a civilized nation.

"Jack Connaghan, of Libranagh, has a family consisting of ten persons, his wife having a child on the breast, three weeks old. The entire group, crouched around an indifferent fire, presented a picture of unqualified misery. The father does not possess a single four-footed animal, cannot obtain any employment whatever, and the whole family (excepting the infant) had not partaken of anything, save seaweed, during the forty-eight hours previous.

"Condy Molloy, of Libranagh, aged seventy, his wife, of the same age, and both infirm, with one daughter, have existed on 'BARNAGHS' (or Limpets) for the last fortnight, and are now scarcely able to move from consequent exhaustion.

"Widow Connaghan, of Libranagh, does not possess any money, has a family of five, the eldest child about eleven years old. The widow was preparing a large potful of seaweed *(called Doolamin)*[128] as we entered her cabin, and assured us, that upon such she and her children had existed three days. When we inquired if she had not some meal in the house, she exhibited about half-a-pound, tied carefully up in a *nightcap*, which she said she had got from a neighbour 'for God's sake.'

"John Gallagher, of Ballintra, has eight of a family, none of whom had tasted food that day; one of the children was apparently *dying of starvation;* the wasted mother had a child on the breast, six months old, not so large as the infant of a month.

"Widow Mooney, of Ballintra, with a family of seven daughters and one son, has not any meal, or other provisions in the house, nor the means of procuring them. The son observed, that he must leave the island, and, 'like the dogs, provide for himself.'

"Denis Connaghan, of Ballintra, with his family of six, has existed during the previous two days on one naggin [sic][129] of meal, which he borrowed; and three days prior to that, they had eaten nothing but Doolamin, which produced violent diarrhoea, from which they are now suffering.

"Connell Gallagher, with a family of six, has existed for the last fortnight on five pounds of meal, helped out, of course, by sea-weed and limpets. The wasted form of the father, and the still more reduced appearance of the children, testified to the truth of his terrible statement.

"Widow Mooney, with five orphans—her husband and one child had been buried the day before our visit. That they died of starvation we readily believed, as the widow asserted there had not been *any food whatever* in the house for several days. The children, even under their fresh affliction, presented a gaunt, unmeaning, vacant stare, characteristic of inanition; their very lips having become blanched and shrivelled from prolonged destitution.

"Hugh Boyle, of Gort-Car, has a family of nine. He and his daughter were *lying in the same bed* ill of dysentery. Previously to one of us entering this house, it was intimated that the man's son *had fever*, and shared the *identical apartment*. On its being asked where he was—for the room was too dark, for a person coming in from the light of day, to observe him—the sick father pointed to a corner. The blankets being removed from about his son's head, the fetid stench that issued forth was overpowering; and there is little reason to expect that this young man can survive under the multiplied evils he is exposed to. This is a specimen of the many cases of fever and dysentery that prevail on the island.

"Daniel Boyle, of Fallagowan, having a family of twelve, all living in a very confined cabin, is not able, from want of food, to go out fishing. He tried it one day, and was obliged to return, owing to hunger and weakness.

"James Gallagher has a family of eight. When we were on the island we believed him to be in the agonies of death. His son told us that the family had not eaten anything for the forty-eight hours previous, but a few spoonsful of barleymeal, given to them by a neighbour woman.

"Denis Gallagher has eight of a family—his wife dropsical.[130] In their chest about half-a-stone of meal was found by us. On inquiry, we ascertained that it had been purchased the evening before; the sum with which it was bought being the produce of *four days' labour, at four-pence a-day*.

"Edward Gallagher, of Leabgarrow, whose family consisted of six, had his arm broken. The appearance of the children was wonderfully similar; their prominent jawbones and sunken cheeks fearfully indicating the progress of starvation. A very sickly infant sat up in its cot, whilst we remained in the house; the face was deadly pale; it was endeavouring, with a beseeching look and melancholy whine, to attract the attention of its anxious mother, who was heedless to it for a moment, in her anxiety to secure our sympathy for her famishing offspring. Long will it be ere the anguish of that infant's languid eye, expressive only of mortal agony, will fade from our memory.

"The bounty of some charitable persons enabled us to issue tickets for about half-a-ton of Indian meal: the number of applicants was vast, but it was only the most awfully destitute amongst them we could help. In order, therefore to dole out our supply the more extensively, we determined to give but one stone of meal to any individual, except in very dreadful cases; yet, so irresistible was the eagerness to gain even such a trifling quantity, that, though the people were under the conviction (and they are generally very timorous) that a man and child had died of an infectious disease, a couple of days before, in a house we stood in, they, notwithstanding, crowded about us for tickets; and, to give additional weight to the force of this statement, we may add, that they crossed the sea, a distance of four miles, the next day, *though it was rough and stormy*, for the sake of the *one single* stone of meal.

"We were particularly struck by the number of *widows*, many of them having lost their husbands by drowning, which rendered the bereavement the more ruinous, on account of the sudden destruction thus brought upon them.

"It was no wonder that the biscuits we took in were eagerly seized and ravenously devoured, for, in the minute scrutiny we made through the cabins, the only articles of food we discovered were—half-a-stone of meal, the half-pound tied up in a nightcap, and about a stook[131] of unthrashed barley.

"The island itself exhibits one uniform scene of unmitigated desolation, not a single stack of corn having been observed by us far or near, throughout those parts of it which we visited; in some places, the land had been dug over *three times*, in the hope of procuring an occasional potato.

"While *all* the inhabitants are manifestly drooping from the effects of famine, *many* are lying in fever; and it is grievous to think, that the poorhouse—the last refuge of the destitute—appears to be the nursery from which disease is disseminated throughout the district, so that it is dreaded and fled from as a literal pesthouse. Employment is not to be had, nor are public works going on in the island; and it is altogether impossible that the islanders could daily attend work on the main land, owing to the intervening sea passage.

"In since calmly reviewing and reflecting upon the harrowing and revolting incidents that were crowded into our hurried walk through *but a part* of the island, and on a short winter's day, we feel astonished and dismayed at the accumulation of misery that presented itself to us; and we mourn as we persuade ourselves, that such afflictions are but the shadows of things to come, and the beginning of unutterable sorrows.

"VAL. POLE GRIFFITH,
"*Officiating Minister.*

"G. FRAZER BRADY,
"*Medical Superintendent of the District.*

"Templecrone Glebe, Dungloe, County Donegal,
"Jan. 19, 1847."

See also George Hancock's account of his visit, in the 'Dublin Reports,'[132] No. 2, page 10–11, and in the 'Friend,'[133] No. 52, page 76.

## APPENDIX E.

Since the text was written, the man whose name has occupied more space in the country than any other, both within the walls of Parliament, and without among the people,—the man of unquestionably the greatest moral influence upon the minds of his countrymen since the days of Napoleon,—Daniel O'Connell, has been gathered to his fathers.[134] How differently was this influence employed! The party interests that cramp and sway their minds, and the personalities of our great men, interfere too much with each other to allow them to do one another justice while living. But it is the English nature to sink the errors and failings of those who are gone. Daniel O'Connell has raised himself from one of the furthest corners of the land; and in estimating his personal character, the only question worth asking is,—whether he was habitually found on the side of the injured and oppressed? Did he, throughout a long and laborious life, advocate the great principles of freedom, right, and justice, or did he not? And accordingly let his memory live, or his monument be engraved.

## APPENDIX F.

In reference to the destitution of Kenmare, the following has since been received from the clergyman of the united parishes. After acknowledging, in very grateful terms, the aid in food afforded by the Central Relief Committee, on a direct application, he goes on to say,—

"I fear I am justified in stating, that the amount of destitution and sickness has been on the increase instead of the decrease since you were here. This fact that I am now about to relate bears me out, I think, in forming this opinion; and I state the circumstance on the authority of Captain Herbert, the Government Inspector of our Relief Committee, viz.—that out of a population of 7,580, in the parish of Tuosist, there are 6,000 receiving out-door relief. This is that parish through a part of which I accompanied you in your car the day you left Kenmare; and out of a population of 5,000, in the parish of Kenmare, over 2,000 are receiving out-door relief. This is an alarming amount of pauperism to exist in a parish,—nearly two-thirds of the inhabitants of the Union reduced to absolute want, and obliged to be fed gratuitously by the Government. Fever prevails in almost every cabin; the interior of each as wretched and more so than the house you visited with me in Kenmare. The deaths from starvation are perhaps not so numerous, but numbers are being daily swept off from the fatal complaints. Another sad feature in the picture is, that a considerable part of the land lies waste. On this point I am disposed to hope that you may be enabled to confer a great benefit upon the country; for if I recollect right, I think you said, that one object of your visit to Ireland was to assist distressed localities with a supply of turnip and parsnip seeds. When you were here, there was then plenty of time to have cropped the land with barley, and we were in daily expectation of a considerable grant of barley seed being sent into the country.

I regret to say that we have been disappointed in that expectation, and now it is vain to hope for barley, as it is almost too late to sow that grain. Turnips I believe are now the only crop that can be sown. It is rather late for the best description of turnip, the Swedish, though I have had them very good that I sowed in the first week in June. If you can still hold out any hope of assisting us with a supply, however small, of turnip seed,—the yellow or purple-top Aberdeen I should like to get,—you will confer a vast benefit upon us, for which we shall be ever grateful.

"Yours faithfully,

"CHAS. P. THOMAS."[135]

"Kenmare, 15th May, 1847."

Being an extension of the journey, our seeds were exhausted when we reached Kenmare. But I had much pleasure in immediately ordering two hundred weight of turnip seed, in reply to the above, from additional means most seasonably furnished by a friend.

APPENDIX G.

On the deteriorating effects of gratuitous and compulsory relief, the following portion of a letter from a gentleman referred to in these pages, and holding the position of Deputy Lord Lieutenant of the County, addressed to the Sub-committee of the Society of Friends in Dublin, is emphatic.

"St. Ernan's, Donegal, 22nd May, 1847.

"The gratuitous relief given under the new plan has certainly saved many lives, which would have fallen victims to famine had no aid been given; but it is a fearful thing to see hundreds of able-bodied men, willing to work, lounging in discontented idleness round the soup-kitchens, while thousands of acres are lying in a comparative state of unproductiveness, for want of the labour of those men being applied to them. The demoralization increases, and every day that the compulsory idleness continues the demoralization takes a deeper root, and throws up a more luxuriant growth of sin and shame.

"You will be glad to hear that my agricultural improvement-works promise well; and in a visit I made, a few days ago, to a wild and remote district, where my son labours (Fintown), I saw luxuriant corn crops on land eight months ago not worth 2*d.* an acre, and this to a very considerable extent. The tone and expression, and whole bearing of the few hundred men employed by us, is quite different from the miserable, dejected, yet impudent look of the crowds degraded at the soup-kitchens. You will understand me as not speaking against *any* gratuitous relief, but as deprecating the system which makes *no attempt* to cause or encourage useful employment, but, on the contrary, *taxes* it for the benefit of non-employing owners and farmers of land, and of nonworking paupers. I look upon the madness that leads to legislation of this nature as *the* curse we are suffering under, and not the failure of the poor potato. The kind of aid you send is, however, both needful and a blessing. May it prove a blessing indeed, a gift twice blessed, to the giver and to the receivers!

"I am, yours faithfully,

"JOHN HAMILTON."

APPENDIX H.

See the Speech of Samuel Tuke,[136] at the Meeting on the condition of Ireland, reported in the 'Friend' and 'British Friend' of the present month.

EDWARD NEWMAN, Printer, 9, Devonshire Street, Bishopsgate.

## Notes

1. Elizabeth (née Trusted) Bennett's (1798–1891) publications included *My Mother's Meeting* (London, 1863) and, with William, *Pages from the Life of the Apostle Paul* (London, 1873).
2. John Greenleaf Whittier, *The Letters of John Greenleaf Whittier* (Harvard University Press, 1975, vol. 1), pp. 313–314.
3. Rob Goodbody, *A Suitable Channel - Quaker Relief in the Great Famine* (Dublin: Pale Publishing, 1995).
4. Christine Kinealy, *Charity and the Great Hunger. The Kindness of Strangers* (London: Bloomsbury, 2013), pp. 277–292.
5. From *Farmer's Gazette*, 'Effects of frost and snow on vegetation', in *Newry Telegraph*, 25 March 1847.
6. For more on clothing and nakedness, see Daphne Wolf in Christine Kinealy et al. *Women and the Great Hunger* (Quinnipiac Press and Cork University Press, 2016).
7. Re. Samuel Stock, Belmullet, Co. Mayo, to Lord John Russell, 28 October 1847, reprinted in *Howitt's Journal*, vol. 2 (London: W. Lovett, 1847), p. 341.
8. Ibid., W.H., 'Frightful Condition and Prospects of Ireland'.
9. For more on visitors to Ireland see Glenn Hooper, *The Tourist's Gaze. Travellers to Ireland 1800–2000* (Cork University Press, 2001), p. 79.
10. *Six Weeks*, p. vii.
11. *Annual Monitor for 1874 or Obituary of members of the Society of Friends in Great Britain and Ireland for the year 1873* (London: Samuel Harris and Co. 1873), p. 5.
12. In 1846 and 1847, this committee raised £9,533-4-0. See *Transactions of . . . the Society of Friends* (1852), p. 46.
13. Arrow-root was viewed as beneficial to people with digestive problems; ginger was believed to have a wide range of health benefits, especially in alleviating stomach discomfort.
14. At the beginning of 1847, mortality in the Lurgan Workhouse equaled that of the poorest workhouses in counties Cork and Mayo. See Gerard MacAtasney, *'This Dreadful Visitation'. The Famine in Lurgan/Portadown* (Belfast: Beyond the Pale, 1997).
15. This committee had been established by leading Quakers in November 1846.
16. W. Drummond and Sons, Seed Merchants. The business had been founded in Stirling by Scottish nurseryman, William Drummond (1760–1824). The Drummond family

were pioneers in swede development, some of the varieties carrying their name. In 1833, they had opened Drummonds' Agricultural Museum in Stirling. The Dublin premises were opened in 1843 by David Drummond, grandson of William.
17  The writer, Maria Edgeworth (1768–1849), although in her eightieth year, was indefatigable in appealing for funds, a portion of which she used to set up shoe (brogue)-making workshops. See, Kinealy, *Kindness of Strangers*, pp. 156–58.
18  Robert Edward King, Lord Lorton (1773- 1854) who owned Rockingham Estate, was a resident landlord. Between 1831 and 1854, he served as Lord Lieutenant of Roscommon.
19  More usually 'gombeen' (from the Irish, *gaimbín*—meaning a bit or small amount), a pejorative term for a local businessman or money-lender who made loans on very unfavourable terms to the borrower.
20  Also referred to as the 'Times Special Commissioner'. Partly to counteract the sympathetic conclusions of the Devon Commission, at the beginning of 1846, John Delane, editor of the *Times*, appointed Thomas Campbell Foster (the 'Commissioner') to provide an authentic view of Ireland. It can be regarded as part of a campaign by the British press to demonize O'Connell and reinforce the Irish people as 'the other'. The reports, however, were influential in shaping perceptions.
21  An English unit of measure equal to one quarter of an acre or 10,890 square feet.
22  Public works had first been introduced by Peel's government. They were re-introduced by the Whig government in August 1846, but with more stringent conditions attached. Wages were deliberately kept below local wages rates, despite rising food prices. One of the consequences was that women and children sought employment on the works, despite the fact that they received lower wages than men.
23  More usually, *Slieve Gamph* (Irish: *Sliabh Gamh*)—a mountain range in Co. Sligo.
24  Quakers, who were distributing relief and fact-finding in the west of Ireland. William Forster (1784–1854) was a veteran campaigner, known for his work in anti-slavery and prison reform. He was praised in the *Freeman's Journal* (2 January 1847) for his honest and sympathetic reporting of the condition of the poor. Joseph Harvey and William Harvey travelled together distributing relief. They were both members of the Quaker Cork Auxiliary Committee. See, *Transactions of The Society of Friends During the Famine in Ireland* (1852). Abraham Taw was a Quaker London tea merchant. He was involved in the distribution of clothing in Ireland.
25  The First Day meeting was held on Sundays, in silence, unless a participant was moved to say a message.
26  Belmullet was almost 50 (English) miles from Ballina. Despite its isolation and the unusually cold weather, a number of Quakers, including William Forster and Richard Webb visited the area in early 1847. Count Strzelecki of the British Relief Association (BRA) had visited the district in February, the journey from Ballina taking him three days. He had established 7 sub-relieving stations. See Report of the British Relief Association (BRA), pp. 92–93.
27  Latin – in ancient geography, a place that lay beyond the known world.
28  Forster had reported acrimony between the Catholic and the Anglican priests. Strzelecki of the BRA, however, had entrusted them with looking after relief.
29  Probably Slieve Carr, which is described as the most remote mountain in Ireland.
30  Irish measures tended to be longer and larger than the equivalent ones in Britain. The Weights and Measures Act of 1824 was intended to standardize them throughout the United Kingdom, but with little success outside of Dublin.
31  Probably Samuel Stock, rector and vicar of Kilcommon. He worked tirelessly on behalf of the local poor, including writing to the Prime Minister asking for relief (see *Howitt's Journal*, quoted earlier).
32  The town was established by William Henry Carter, a local landlord, in 1825.
33  Fish curing stations had also been established at Roundstone in Galway and Killibegs in Donegal.

34  William Joshua Ffennell (1799–1867) had been born in Co. Tipperary. He had visited Scotland to learn about fish curing there. He was responsible for the passage of a number of acts giving police protection to salmon fishing. See, *Dictionary National Biography*, vol. 18.
35  Rev. Thomas Robert Malthus (1766–1834) was a prominent writer on political economy and demography, largely due to his influential *An Essay on the Principle of Population,* published anonymously in 1798. His argument that population growth would outstrip food production was frequently applied to the Famine.
36  Possibly *Tá ocras orainn*, meaning 'We are hungry'.
37  The Commissariat was a uniformed civilian service. In 1842, Bishop had been promoted from Commissary-Clerk to Deputy Assistant Commissary General (*Edinburgh Gazette*, No. 5175, Nov. 29 1842), p. 501. For these 'Extraordinary Duties on the Relief Service', Bishop was paid 5 shillings a day (House of Commons Papers, vol. 54, H.M.S.O., 1848, p.11).
38  The Belfast Ladies' Relief Association for Connaught was founded in 1846 by Dr. John Edgar. D.D., of Belfast, who was also its President. It was a Protestant body that, in addition to providing relief, also provided 'Industrial Scriptural Education'.
39  Probably Samuel Bourns (also rendered as Bournes), the owner of Rossport House, who was married to Maria Watts, daughter of Andrew Watts of Ballinglen, Co. Mayo. See Landed Estates Database: http://landedestates.nuigalway.ie:8080/LandedEstates/jsp/estate-show.jsp?id=341, accessed 3 December 2016.
40  The Irish mile was longer than the English mile, being 2240 yards and 1760 yards respectively.
41  A species of sea-weed.
42  17 March – generally believed to be the day on which Patrick died.
43  The Methodist Connexion, also referred to as the Wesleyan Methodist Society, generally saw the Famine as a punishment from God. During the shortages of 1822 and the Great Famine some of their members undertook proselytizing activities. See Kinealy, *Kindness of Strangers,* pp. 268–270.
44  Frederick Carey was an Inspector of the Coast Guard in Dunkeehan, near Belmullet; 14 men were stationed there.
45  Many Quakers wore 'plain dress'. Coats generally had no collar or tucked-in waist, and dyes produced by slave labor would not have been used.
46  In the early stages of the Famine, the Board of Works was responsible for providing public works throughout Ireland. Colonel Harry Jones (1791–1866) was the chairman of the three-person board.
47  More usually, *Belderrig*.
48  Samuel's wife.
49  Probably David Rodgers, who was minister in Killala until 1849, when he became infirm. Thomas Armstrong, who was appointed to Ballina Presbytery in November 1845, in his memoir, wrote about the visitors to Ireland in 1847, and singled William Forster out for particular praise. See, Thomas Armstrong, *My Life in Connaught: With Sketches of Mission Work in the West* (London: Elliot Stock, 1906), p. 10.
50  Dr. John Edgar was appointed Moderator of the Presbyterian Church in 1842. In 1847, he was appointed Honorary Secretary to the Presbyterian Home Mission. His work with the Ladies' Committee was tainted by some accusations of proselytization.
51  The Round Tower in Killala is believed to be about 1,000 years old. It is approximately 84 feet high.
52  Lissadell House in Co. Sligo was built by Sir Robert Gore-Booth, 4th Baronet (1805–1876), between 1830 and 1835. It was later immortalized in a poem by W.B. Yeats. Although Gore-Booth did evict tenants (most controversially during the 1830s), in the famines of 1845–52 and 1879–81, the family provided relief to their tenants.

53 Henry John Temple (1784–1865), the third Viscount Palmerston, owned estates in Sligo. He had a long career in British politics which included serving as Foreign Secretary and as Prime Minister. He was one of the first landlords to finance his starving tenants to emigrate during the Famine. The condition of a number of the vessels that he chartered were severely criticized by emigration agents in Canada. Nonetheless, in 1847 approximately 2,000 of Palmerston's tenants were part of the emigration scheme.

54 Probably John Hamilton (1899–84), who inherited the Brownhall Estate in 1821. Shortly afterwards he started building a home on St Ernan's Island. His generosity to his tenants meant that only one is recorded to have died during the Famine, his actions earning the praise of the local parish priest, Father John Doherty. Hamilton's journals form the basis of the book on the life of John Hamilton by Dermot James, *This Recklessly Generous Landlord*.

55 The development of a network of cars (carriages) was pioneered by Charles Bianconi (1786–1875) in 1815. By 1845, Bianconi had over 100 cars and mail carriages traversing the country, which could each carry from four to 24 passengers. They travelled at eight or nine miles an hour, and the cost averaged a farthing (a quarter of a penny) per mile. The passenger service did not run on Sundays.

56 The post-car, or post-chaise, was a fast carriage. It usually had a closed body on four wheels, sat two to four persons, and was drawn by one, two or four horses. It was meant for passengers, while the mail-car was primarily intended for mail, but could carry passengers.

57 Turnpike roads, which charged tolls, operated in Ireland between 1729 and 1858. The highest concentration was around Dublin.

58 Another name for a workhouse. The Glenties workhouse was one of the 130 institutions provided for by the 1838 Poor Law. Although completed in September 1845, no inmates were admitted until July 1846, making it one of the last workhouses to be operative. It was built to accommodate 500 - a capacity that was reached in the wake of the second potato failure.

59 William Forster travelled to Donegal in December 1846, through heavy snow falls. He visited a number of the local workhouses.

60 Rev. Valentine Pole Griffith (1806–1886) was minister of Templecrone (also referred to as the Rosses). In October 1846, he was one of the signatories of an appeal for aid for the parish. It described the local poor as 'peaceable, orderly and patient', but warned that they were on the verge of starvation. The letter was also signed by the local Catholic priest, James McDavitt, and by Dr. Brady. See, *The British Magazine and Monthly Register of Religious and Ecclesiastical Information* (Vol. 31, J. Turrill, 1847, p. 95).

61 At the beginning of 1847, Rev. Griffith and Dr. Brady visited Arranmore Island and published their report on 19 January 1847. They concluded by warning, 'such afflictions are but a shadow of things to come, and the beginning of unutterable sorrows'. See *Transactions*, pp. 188–189.

62 Dr. George Frazer Brady. He was a member of an 'Appeal Committee' on behalf of Arranmore Island.

63 Elizabeth Lucy Griffith (née Murphy, d. 1869). She and her husband, Valentine, married in 1830 and are buried with their children in St Ann's Church of Ireland, Tullaghobegley, Co. Donegal.

64 Lord George Hill (1801–79) features in many accounts of the Famine, including Asenath Nicholson's. He was a resident, 'improving' landlord, whose cold, rational approach to evictions made him unpopular with his tenants. During the Famine, he served on a number of relief committees, both locally in Donegal and in Dublin.

65 The 'observer' was Asenath Nicholson (1792–1855) an American Protestant Evangelical and Abolitionist, who visited Ireland in 1844, in order to understand the Irish poor and to distribute the Bible. She provided an account of her visit in *Ireland's Welcome*

*to the Stranger*. Nicholson returned to Ireland during the Famine, but in order to distribute relief, not Bibles. She met Bennett, and a number of the other Quakers during her tour of Ireland, which provided the basis of her *Annals of the Famine in Ireland in 1847, 1848 and 1849* (first pub. in 1851).

66 John Betts, a London publisher, was known for his maps and atlases.
67 An improvised bed.
68 Tea was first introduced to Ireland in the mid-eighteenth century, but its usage became more popular following the removal of tariffs in 1784, its popularity eventually spreading to the poorer classes.
69 Lord George Hill (1801–1879) was the fifth son of the second Marquis of Downshire. Following an army career, he came to Gweedore in 1838, purchasing about 23,000 acres there. Regarding himself as an 'improving landlord' he sought to modernize the traditional agricultural practices on his estate.
70 The building of Gweedore Hotel by Hill was part of his plan to modernize the town and to attract more visitors to it.
71 Upon purchasing Gweedore, Hill had ended the old Rundale system of land tenure which he viewed as a barrier to any attempt at improvement. Tenants who did not comply were evicted.
72 Forster worked closely with Hill in the modernizing project. Forster, of Roshine Lodge, died in Brighton in England in 1858. He was aged 59. See, *The Gentlemen's Magazine*, July-December 1858, p. 537.
73 Written by George Hill, the book quickly went into three editions – in 1845, 1846 and 1854.
74 Rev. Richard Gibbings had been appointed to the parish in 1842. See, *The Churchman's monthly review*, 1842, p. 736.
75 The Temporary Relief Act, also known as the Soup Kitchen Act, was passed in February 1847. It allowed for the establishment of soup kitchens which, for the most part, provided gratuitous relief. As its title suggested, it was regarded as a short-term measure, free relief being disliked for creating a permanent culture of dependency.
76 Possibly Rev. William Archer Butler (c. 1814–1848), the local vicar who was also a well-respected philosopher. As a teenager, he had converted from the Roman Catholic to the Established Church. Shortly after ordination, he was appointed the prebend of Clondehorka in Co. Donegal. During the Famine, he postponed his writing on literature, philosophy, and divinity so that he could devote himself to the poor. He died in July 1848 of fever. See *Dictionary of National Biography, 1885–1900*, vol. 8.
77 Brookfield Agricultural School, near Moira, was opened in 1836 by the Quakers as a boarding school for abandoned children. It consisted of a house and 24 acres of farmland. The male pupils were taught agricultural skills, girls mostly learned household duties, while both were trained in moral and religious principles. The school closed in 1922.
78 The Moira train station was opened in November 1841.
79 William Shannon, assisted by his wife Sarah, was Principal of the school from its opening in 1836 until 1852. They were from Wexford.
80 Nicholson (see above) also spent some time with the Hewetson family.
81 The Belfast Ladies' Industrial Association for Connaught, which was the brainchild of Dr. Edgar, sought to instill industrial habits in women in the west of Ireland. Its approach to relief was to combine both temporal needs with spiritual ones.
82 John Edgar, *The Women of the West. Ireland helped to help herself* (Belfast: Banner of Ulster Office, 1849).
83 Asenath Nicholson (see above).
84 A form of credit.
85 57 South William Street was the headquarters of Central Relief Committee.
86 The Society of Friends were ardent supporters of Abolition. For more on these debates see Kinealy, *Kindness of Strangers*.

87 Henrietta Pendleton, the Honorary Secretary. See, Alfred Clayton Thiselton, *A memorial sketch of the life and labours of Mrs. Henrietta Pendleton, forty years Honorary Secretary of the Irish Island and Coast Society* (Dublin: Hodges, Foster and Co., 1875).
88 The Irish Island and Coast Society was originally formed for the propagation of the English language and the Protestant religion. Prior to the Famine they had 19 teachers in various locations in the west, who were supported by funds raised in Britain. They published annual reports of their missionary progress. See, Thomas Walter Freeman, *Pre-Famine Ireland: A Study in Historical Geography* (Manchester University Press, 1957), pp. 136–7.
89 Cole's Alley was an early Quaker settlement in Dublin, containing a Meeting House. See, George Newenham Wright, *An historical guide to the city of Dublin, illustrated by engravings, and a plan of the city* (Dublin: Baldwin, Cradock, and Joy, 1825), p. 103.
90 Joseph Crosfield from Merseyside accompanied Forster to Ireland, during his first visit at the end of 1846. He was in his early 20s, and one of the many young Friends to travel with the older man. His family owned a soap-making business near to Liverpool.
91 The Earldom of Ormond was associated with the Butler family. Since 1391, the family seat had been Kilkenny Castle.
92 More usually *Slievenamon*, which is a mountain situated northwest of Carrick on Suir.
93 A Tipperary Quaker family: Joshua Fennell died 1905, aged 83 years; Susanna Fennell died 1889, aged 71 years; William Fennell died 1868, aged 52 years.
94 The title had been created in 1806 for Cornelius O'Callaghan, 1st Viscount Lismore (1775–1857). He owned land in the Galty-Vee Valley and served as an ex-officio Poor Law Guardian for the Clogheen Union, and played a major role in bringing relief to the areas. See, Edmund O'Riordan, *Famine in the Valley*: http://www.galteemore.com/Fam%20in%20Val.pdf, accessed 4 December 2016.
95 Shanbally Castle, designed by architect, John Nash, was built for Cornelius O'Callaghan, the first Viscount Lismore, around 1812. Controversially, it was demolished by the Irish government in 1960.
96 Burncourt Castle by Sir Richard Everard in 1641. Sir Richard was sympathetic to the Catholic Confederates. The Castle was burned in 1650, during the Cromwellian War. Sir Richard was hanged the following year for taking up arms against Cromwell's army.
97 Oliver Cromwell (1599–1658) was an English military and political leader who, during the inter-regnum, served as Lord Protector of England, Scotland and Ireland. The years 1649–53, marked the Cromwellian War in Ireland, which was characterized by brutality. Cromwell personally led the first year of the campaign.
98 The Mitchelstown Cave is situated on the border of Cork and Tipperary. The calcite columns include the huge Tower of Babel. It was discovered accidentally by a farm worker, Michael Condon, in 1833. He subsequently acted as a guide.
99 Shanbally Castle was built for the first Viscount Lismore, around 1810, by the noted English architect, John Nash.
100 In 1846, the hotel was described as 'an excellent inn', See, The *Parliamentary Gazetteer of Ireland: Adapted to the New Poor-law, Franchise, Municipal and Ecclesiastical Arrangements, and Compiled with a Special Reference to the Lines of Railroad and Canal Communication, as Existing in 1814–45*, Vol. 2, A. Fullarton and Company, 1846.
101 Galtee Castle was built c.1780 by the second Earl of Kingstown. In the 1850s, due to accumulated debts, the family had to sell the estate. See, 'The Encumbered Estates of Ireland' [Reprinted from the London *Daily News* of Aug. and Sept. 1850.] (London: Saunders and Sons, 1850), p. 44.

102 Assizes were criminal courts that operated outside of Dublin. The modern Irish legal system had derived from the English common law tradition
103 The Victoria Lake Hotel opened c.1835. It was regarded as one of the grandest hotels in the area. It later re-designated itself, The Royal Victoria Hotel, the Queen having visited Killarney in 1861, and alleged having spent some time in the hotel. In the late 20th century, it was renamed Castlerosse Hotel.
104 Daniel O'Connell (1775–1847) was a Kerry-born Catholic nationalist and promoter of human rights, including Abolition. His parents were poor, but his education was sponsored by a wealthy uncle, enabling him to become a lawyer. His role in winning Catholic emancipation in 1829 made him simultaneously despised and admired. The British media often singled him out for criticism, including the influential, but frequently anti-Irish, London *Times*.
105 Maurice O'Connell (1803–53) was Daniel's eldest son. Like his three brothers, he was brought up on 'principles of Catholic faith and national feeling'. Regardless of his abilities, his restless temperament meant that his brother, John, was the preferred political heir of their father's political movement. See, *History of Parliament*: http://www.historyofparliamentonline.org/volume/1820–1832/member/oconnell-maurice-1803–1853, accessed 10 February 2017.
106 The Protestant minister is possibly Rev. John Godfrey Day of Laharan, Valentia.
107 The slate quarries had only recently been developed by the Knight of Kerry, who brought an English industrialist to the island to oversee this process. Some of the slate was used in the newly built Houses of Parliament in London. See, F.C. Westley, *Spectator*, vol. 18 (1845), p. 225.
108 Possibly Douglas Head.
109 The Blasket Islands (*Na Blascaodaí* in Irish).
110 Lord Monteagle, Thomas Spring Rice, (1790–1866) was a Whig politician who served as Chancellor of the Exchequer between 1835 and 1839. Although opposed to O'Connell's nationalism, he supported Catholic Emancipation. As early as September 1846, he had written to Charles Trevelyan warning him of the extent of relief needed, and he later chastised the PM for the inadequate policies of the government. His brother, Stephen, was an active member of the British Relief Association. See Kinealy, 'The British Relief Association and the Great Famine in Ireland', *L'association britannique de secours et la grande famine irlandaise*, XIX-2014: La grande famine en irlande, 1845–1851, pp. 49–66.
111 Valentia Island lies in the Gulf Stream current, which provides a mild climate and allows for sub-tropical plants to grow.
112 The *Times* Special Commissioner, in reality, Thomas Campbell Foster, wrote a series of articles that cast opprobrium on O'Connell as a landowner and described the poverty of his tenants.
113 Possibly the old stone bridge that spans the Staigue River. Many of these bridges date from the Cromwellian period.
114 More usually, Lough Currane, noted for its salmon and sea trout.
115 Probably a confusion with Derrynane House, the ancestral home of the O'Connells. The oldest parts date back to 1702. Daniel made a number of additions, including adding a chapel in 1844. The ruined Abbey and the House are close to each other.
116 The fear of dismemberment of the empire if Repeal of the Union was permitted had been used with great effect by Peel in 1843. See Kinealy, *Repeal and Revolution. 1848 in Ireland* (Manchester University Press, 2009).
117 Dromore Castle, located at Templenoe, overlooking the Kenmare River, was completed in the late 1830s. It was the property of Denis Mahony, the Church of Ireland minister. Mahony was alleged to be a renowned proselytizer, viewing the famine as an opportunity to make converts. Although he opened a soup kitchen at Dromore, he

was very unpopular, and his property was vandalized. See, 'The Mahonys of Kerry (continued)', *Kerry Archaeological Magazine*, 4.20 (1918), pp. 223–55.

118 Captain Herbert was one of the many Royal Navy personnel who assisted with relief. In October 1847, he was moved to Donegal where he was made a Temporary Inspector to assist with dispensing relief under the extended Poor Law. See, *Annual report of the commissioners for administering the laws for relief of the poor in Ireland with appendices* . . . (Dublin: A. Thom, 1848), p. 7.

119 The fourth Marquess of Lansdowne (1816 -1866) was a Liberal politician. He served as a Lord of the Treasury from 1847 to 1848. His estate included the Kenmare Poor Law Union, one of the poorest in the country. He sent as many as 5,000 paupers to North America, believing it was a cheaper and better option than life in the workhouse.

120 More usually, Quarter Sessions, which were local courts held four times a year - at Epiphany, Easter, Midsummer, and Michaelmas. They were held in Carrickfergus, Cork, Derry, Dublin, Galway, Kilkenny, Kinsale, Limerick, Waterford, and Youghal.

121 Charles (Carlo) Bianconi (1786–1875) was born in Italy, but moved to Ireland in 1802, during the Napoleonic Wars. In 1815, he established regular horse-drawn carriage services on various routes in Ireland, contributing to a transport revolution. Travelling on board a 'Bian' cost one penny farthing a mile. Bianconi served twice as Mayor of Clonmel.

122 The Acts of Union of 1800 created the United Kingdom of Great Britain and Ireland, governed by a single parliament in London. The Dublin parliament was bribed, bullied and coerced to vote itself out of existence.

123 Anglo-Saxon kingdoms in Britain.

124 Possibly Joshua Harvey, MD.

125 A gardening implement with a pointed end that is used to make holes in soil, especially used for planting bulbs or seedlings.

126 William Todhunter.

127 John Faussett was minor Church of Ireland gentry. He died in 1856. J.P. denotes that he was a Justice of the Peace.

128 More usually, *Dúlamán*, an edible seaweed, which is associated with periods of hunger.

129 Noggin – a small mug or cup.

130 Dropsy (from the Middle English dropesie) was a term used for the swelling of soft tissues due to the accumulation of excess water.

131 A small number of sheaves.

132 George Hancock was a Quaker from Liverpool who was involved in the distribution of relief.

133 'A Religious and Literary Journal', which was devoted to Quaker affairs.

134 Daniel O'Connell died in Genoa on 15 May 1847 while on his way to Rome. His final speech in the House of Commons, in February, had been on behalf of his starving country people.

135 Charles Thomas was the Anglican curate of Kenmare from 1840 to 1847. The parish registers of St Patrick's Church, Kenmare are held at the Representative Church Body Library, Dublin.

136 Samuel Tuke (1784–1857) was a Quaker from York in the north of England. He was a proponent of more humane treatment for the insane. Samuel's son, James Hack Tuke (1819 – 1896), assisted in famine relief both during the Great Famine and in the forgotten famine of 1879 to 1882. See, Charles Tylor, *Samuel Tuke, His Life work and Thoughts* (London: Headley Brothers, 1900).

# Part V

# OFFICIAL RESPONSE AND REACTION

# 11

# ISAAC BUTT, *A VOICE FOR IRELAND, THE FAMINE IN THE LAND. WHAT HAS BEEN DONE AND WHAT IS TO BE DONE* (1847)

Isaac Butt had the dubious distinction of featuring in a 1989 history book, *Worsted in the Game*.[1] The sub-title, *Losers in Irish History*, gives an indication of where Butt has been viewed on the historical spectrum in Ireland. However, this brilliant and, at times, tortured figure was a champion of the Irish poor during the Famine, using his knowledge of political economy to carefully critique the policies of the British government.[2] In some ways, the Famine was a part of his ideological journey from being a conservative unionist to a home rule nationalist.

Isaac Butt was born in Glenfin in County Donegal in 1813, the son of a Church of Ireland rector. He grew up in a Protestant, pro-Union environment and his own politics as a young man reflected this upbringing, he being both a supporter of the Tory Party and a member of the Orange Order.[3] Between 1836 and 1841 he was professor of political economy at Trinity College in Dublin, after which he pursued his career as a barrister. The experience of the Famine and the Young Ireland rising in 1848 contributed to Butt increasingly sympathizing with the nationalist perspective. After 1852, he served in the Westminster parliament, where he proved to be a vocal champion of his countrymen.[4] In 1870, he founded the Irish Home Government Association, which developed into the powerful Home Rule movement. However, he was superseded as President in 1878 by the younger and more radical Charles Stewart Parnell.[5] At the time of his death, Butt had little political influence and he was in debt, his chaotic demise overshadowing his very real contribution to nationalist politics in Ireland.

In 'The Famine in the Land', Butt appealed for cross-party unity for the benefit of 'the common country of all'. He believed that there should be a legal right for the Irish poor to receive relief – a right that had not been part of the legislation introduced in 1838. This suggestion was in keeping with the fact that Butt was a unionist, who argued for a genuine union—in which Ireland would be an equal partner and all component parts of the United Kingdom would be treated alike. Butt also supported the idea of a 'United Empire', and so believed that the 'calamity' should be relieved out of imperial resources—an idea that also resonated with nationalists. Butt, at this stage a Tory, believed that the policies introduced by Sir Robert Peel's government had 'recognized the duty of government to feed the people to the utmost extent to which all the resources of the empire could accomplish that end.'[6] Furthermore, Butt believed that if Sir Robert Peel had remained in power, he would have expanded relief to meet the needs of the poor, a claim that had no substance.

Butt's criticisms were reserved for the Whig Party, which had come into power in June 1846. For him, the largest mistake made by the Whig government was leaving the supply of food to private enterprise. In this viewpoint, he mirrored the perspective of nationalists. Butt also chastised the new government for a number of failures, including the prorogation of parliament at the end of 1846, when it met to implement emergency policies. In fact, parliament did not meet again until it reconvened on 19 January 1847 when they discussed the condition of workhouses in Ireland.[7] At this stage, the measures introduced included the closing of the public works and a direct intervention in trade by suspending the Navigations Laws and the duties on the importation of foreign corn.[8] For Butt, it was too little and too late.

'The Famine in the Land' was first published in the *Dublin University Magazine* in April 1847. The *Dublin University Magazine* was a literary and political journal, which Butt had helped to found in 1833, when a student at Trinity College. The article was reprinted, unaltered, as a pamphlet later in the year.

ISAAC BUTT, ESQ., Q.C.,[9] *A VOICE FOR IRELAND, THE FAMINE IN THE LAND. WHAT HAS BEEN DONE AND WHAT IS TO BE DONE* (DUBLIN: JAMES MCGLASHAN, 21 D'OLIER-STREET; WILLIAM S. ORE AND CO., 147 STRAND, LONDON; FRASER AND CO., EDINBURGH, MDCCCXLVII). REPRINTED FROM 'THE DUBLIN UNIVERSITY MAGAZINE'

INTRODUCTION,

THE following pages contain a reprint of an article which appeared in the DUBLIN UNIVERSITY MAGAZINE of last April.[10] It is reprinted because it has been suggested that its publication in a separate shape, with whatever additional sanction the sentiments might derive from being printed with the name of the writer, might possibly be of use to the cause of the country.

I could have wished, in republishing this article, to have had time to have altered and revised it, so as to have made it more suitable for its present form of publication; it is, however, reprinted without the alteration of a line, as it was originally written for the pages of a periodical. Those who read it now, in its separate shape, will make allowance for many things which, though well suited to the form in which it originally appeared, are not, perhaps, equally well adapted to the present shape of its publication.

The months which have passed since this article first appeared, have not in the slightest degree altered the conclusions, or invalidated the reasonings it contains. The imminent peril to all Irish interest still continues the same. The necessity for active, vigorous, and immediate exertion in increasing the productions of the country, to prevent the total confiscation of its property, continues as urgent as before. Perhaps the temporary respite that is now felt from the severer pressure of the famine—a respite not altogether anticipated in these pages—has but increased the danger, by leading the indolence of too many to believe that with the promised plenty of the approaching harvest the difficulties of the country will pass away. A delusion more fatal to the interests of the country could not be entertained.

The harvest, however abundant, cannot enable the country to support upon a corn diet the population formerly fed upon the potato, without trenching, and trenching largely, upon the portions of that harvest which in other years went to the other classes of the community. It is quite true, that by the exportation of wheat we will be able to purchase cheaper kinds of grain, and thus make our land, by means of commerce, more productive for our peoples' wants—a consideration, I may observe, which appears to be overlooked by those who urge an embargo upon exportation as a remedy for our deficient supply of food. By exporting the dearer, and importing the cheaper bread stuffs, we will make, it is true, our acres of wheat equivalent in effect to a much larger surface of rye or Indian corn;[11] but, making every allowance for this, it is still manifest that, to support our labouring population in the altered circumstances of the country, we must either increase the amount of produce of all kinds raised in the country, or apply to the wants of that population the income that has hitherto belonged to other classes of the community—that is, in other words, EITHER THE GENERAL RESOURCES OF THE COUNTRY MUST BE CALLED INTO IMMEDIATE AND VIGOROUS ACTIVITY, OR IRISH POVERTY SUPPORTED FOR A TIME (AND IT CAN BE BUT FOR A TIME) BY THE CONFISCATION OF IRISH PROPERTY.

This great and startling truth is the one fact that ought now to be presented to the mind of every Irishman. It ought, may I be permitted to say it, to supersede all party and all political considerations. No party interest can survive our country; and, while we are struggling for party or class interests, the common country of all is itself crumbling away beneath our feet.

If parliamentary inquiries are to be relied on, the impossibility of supporting our population out of our present resources, without reducing all to a common level of pauperism, is matter of arithmetical demonstration. The Commission of Poor Inquiry, in 1835, contrasted the agricultural population of Ireland with that of Great Britain, and also the quantity of cultivated land, and the produce in each. The result is stated in their report to be this, that there are—

|  | *IN GREAT BRITAIN* | *IN IRELAND* |
| --- | --- | --- |
| Acres of cultivated land.. | 34,254,000 | 14,603,000 |
| Value of produce .... | £150,000,000 | £36,000,000 |
| Labourers, including occupiers who do not employ labourers | 1,055,082 | 1,131,715 |

The problem, therefore, that is now presented to the Irish nation is this—to support the 1,131,000 labourers of Ireland, out of a produce worth £36,000,000, in the same manner as Great Britain supports 1,000,000 of labourers out of a produce worth £150,000,000.

The solution is obvious. Let the labourers still continue the same in number—let the produce be the same in amount—and utter beggary to all grades and classes in Ireland is the inevitable result.

These figures I brought forward I believe upon more than one occasion, at a meeting of the Irish Council—subsequently I perceived that they were quoted in Parliament. They make it matter of demonstration, that unless we can increase the quantity of what is raised in Ireland, every interest in the country must share a common ruin.

To reiterate this truth—to keep it constantly present to the minds of our people—ought now to be the object of every well-wisher of his country, until every man in Ireland shall learn the lesson, that to increase the productiveness of Ireland's resources is no longer a matter of patriotism, but of self-preservation.

Some of the means by which this might be effected, the following pages imperfectly and inadequately endeavoured to point out. Suggesting, however, immediate remedies, they were not conversant with one great and necessary object, which must be comparatively the growth of time, but to forward which much perhaps may be speedily done—I mean the REVIVAL AND ESTABLISHMENT OF IRISH MANUFACTURES. The figures I have quoted demonstrate that we cannot support our population as agricultural labourers—no conceivable increase in our agricultural produce will enable us to do so. The choice is, whether we will support a portion of them as manufacturers or as paupers.

The question, however, of Irish manufactures is one too large to be discussed in a few cursory remarks. Ireland once was, to a large extent, a manufacturing country, and there is nothing to prevent its being so again. The history of nations abundantly teaches the means by which manufactures may be introduced or fostered among a people.

Holding and expressing these strong opinions as to the possible confiscations of all Irish property that may be involved in the attempt to support, out of our present resources, our pauper population—these pages have been charged with inconsistency, in approving of the new poor-law, which gives, for the first time, to the pauper population, the right to that support. However unpopular with many persons in Ireland the support of an extended poor-law will be, I for one will never shrink from declaring my conviction, that until every man in Ireland is given, by law, the right to earn his bread, we cannot hope for the real improvement of the country.

The question of a poor-law for Ireland is one in regard to which I have long been anxious to place before the public views which I am deeply convinced are founded alike in justice, expediency, and truth. I am convinced that it ought to be a first principle of every social system, that every man who is willing to work should have guaranteed to him by law a right to obtain wages adequate to his decent support. A law of this nature for the able-bodied—and a law, furnishing at the same time, under proper restrictions, medical relief and necessary sustenance for the sick, and relief for those unable to work, would alone, in my mind, satisfy the requirements either of Christian legislation, or comply with the dictates of social expediency and prudence.

To the fact that England had, from the days of Queen Elizabeth, such a law[12]—while the poverty of Ireland was left without legal provision for its support—may be traced much of the difference in the condition of the two countries, and in the character of the people. In the case of nations, as of families and individuals, the neglect of moral obligations brings with it its inevitable consequences of physical misery and distress. The moral crime which has been committed in Ireland, of leaving our poor without a legal right to support, has entailed upon us the consequences of a pauperised population, and of the deterioration of their character. I say deliberately, the deterioration of their character—for so far from believing that a poor-law properly administered either degrades or demoralizes a people, I am sure that the absence of a legal right to support, is that feature in the social system which tends, of all others, to create in the labouring population habits of idleness, imprudence, and dependence; and that in no country where that right is not recognised, can we hope to have an independent, a thrifty, or an industrious peasantry.[13]

These views of the effects of a poor-law on the character of a people are, I know, directly opposed to those which have been advanced in quarters that are deemed of high authority. It is impossible, in these few pages, to discuss a question of this nature. I hope ere long to be able to make an attempt to vindicate from this and other objections that have been urged against it, the great principle of the right of the poor to earn their bread. I can now only ask of those who imagine that a poor-law demoralises a people, to reconcile with their theory the fact which Mr. Godley[14] has brought forward in the admirable pamphlet referred to in the following pages—that in every country in which, the poor have a legal right to support, the habits of the labouring population are thrifty and industrious, and their bearing bold and independent—in every country in which they have not, the character which they exhibit is directly the reverse.

I feel, however, all the difficulty of introducing anything like the principle of such a law into a country where long neglect of the rights of the poor has permitted pauperism to make such fearful progress; I feel, too, how immeasurably that difficulty is aggravated, by selecting as the time of its introduction the period when a fearful calamity has at once embarrassed the property and prostrated the energies of a country. The ministerial measure comes short, indeed very far short, of the requirements of a law that will give to our poor their just rights. It has however, established the principle that the property of Ireland shall support its poverty. It unjustly applies that principle to the distress which the recent calamity has created—a distress which I shall ever think ought entirely to be relieved from imperial resources. Whether this principle shall mean that the poverty of Ireland shall eat up its property, depends upon this—whether the great resources of the country shall be stimulated into immediate and active productiveness. If Irishmen will combine to forget party, and obtain for their country measures of practical advantage, there are elements enough of wealth in the country to supply all the demands that even this unprecedented crisis makes upon our resources.

A belief entertained by some persons that the republication of these pages might conduce, however humbly, to this result, has induced me to reprint them. I have delayed their publication, in the hope of being able to throw the substance into a form better suited for separate publication. The article is now reprinted exactly as it appeared in the pages of the Magazine for which it was written.

I.B.

LEESON-STREET, July 27th, 1847.

A MELANCHOLY duty we have proposed to ourselves to discharge in treating of the subject indicated in the title we have prefixed. The history of Ireland, since the commencement of the fearful blight with which it has pleased an all-wise God to visit the food of her people, is one in which there is but little to please, although possibly there may be much to instruct. Little is there in her present condition on which the mind can dwell with any feeling but that of the most intense pain. And gloomy as is the retrospect, and appalling as is the spectacle around us, we grieve to add that in the prospect there seems nothing to vary the monotony of horror. Nevertheless, it is a duty to look all this boldly, we cannot say fearlessly, in the face. With a deep, and we had almost said, an awful, sense of the solemnity, and, at the same time, the magnitude of our task, we proceed to do what poor service we can to our afflicted country, in recording the history of the calamity by which her people have been stricken down—in commenting upon the nature of the means by which that calamity has been attempted to be met—in tracing the effects of that calamity and those measures upon the condition of her people—and in suggesting what yet may be done to mitigate the evils that are still future, or improve this opportunity for good.

Ireland is now, in one sense, in the midst, in another sense, we fear in the beginning of a calamity, the like of which the world has never seen. Four millions of people, the majority of whom were always upon the verge of utter destitution, have been suddenly deprived of the sole article of their ordinary food. Without any of the ordinary channels of commercial intercourse, by which such a loss could be supplied, the country has had no means of replacing the withdrawal of this perished subsistence, and the consequence has been, that in a country that is called civilized, under the protection of the mightiest monarchy upon earth, and almost within a day's communication of the capital of the greatest and richest empire in the world, thousands of our fellow creatures are each day dying of starvation, and the wasted corpses of many left unburied in their miserable hovels, to be devoured by the hungry swine;[15] or to escape this profanation, only to diffuse among the living the malaria of pestilence and death.

As we proceed, we trust it will be seen that we have no inclination either to exaggerate or unnecessarily to alarm; but it were criminal to disguise the extent of the calamity, or to shrink from telling all the hideous truth. We must presume there are none of our readers to whom the evidences upon which this statement rests are not familiar, in the appalling narratives that have filled the journals of the empire for the last few months. It is long since the coroners gave over in despair the task of holding inquests upon the bodies of those whom starvation had stricken down. Our journals have become unable to record, our people to communicate, the deaths which in some districts result from insufficient food. 'Death by starvation' has ceased to be an article of news; and day by day multitudes of our population are swept down into the pit—literally into the pit—in which the victims of the famine are interred.

We will not take up our space by repeating the testimonies, which prove incontestably that this is no exaggeration. It is not, perhaps, the least appalling feature of this calamity, that it is difficult, if not impossible, to obtain accurate information upon the extent of devastation that has already taken place. Nearly a month ago, the deaths that had resulted in one shape or other from starvation were estimated at 240,000. Long before the same period, the deaths that were occurring each day in Ireland, beyond those of the same period in the preceding year, were estimated at 1,000–1,000 each day—a number, we apprehend, below the truth. In many of the workhouses deaths occurred in numbers that would lead to a much greater estimate of the loss of life in the entire country. In one electoral poor-law division of the county Cork—one not within the fatal district of Schull or Skibbereen—out of a population of 16,000, the deaths in the early part of March were averaging seventy a-day, a rate of mortality that would sweep away the entire population in about eight months. There are parts of Mayo, Galway, and Sligo, in which the deaths were nearly in the same proportion. It is impossible, however, to form more than an approximation to the real extent of the calamity. It is an incident of the neglect with which the people, when living, have been treated, that we have no note of them when dead. The occupation of Death has not been interfered with, even by registering the number he has carried off.[16]

It is, however, enough, to say that multitudes in Ireland are starving—that each day is striking down new victims of want of food, and that there is not in Ireland sufficient food to supply her whole population with subsistence for many weeks to come.

So many topics press upon us in relation to the fearful subject we have undertaken, that we scarcely know how to commence its treatment. Let us recall the attention of our readers to the commencement of the potato blight.

In the autumn of 1845, it was discovered that a disease had attacked the potato in Ireland, and in several other parts of the world.[17] Of the actual existence of such a disease there was no doubt. Its extent was, like most questions in Ireland, made a party one—and, we grieve to say, the Tory party were in the wrong. Some of the journals in Ireland, supposed most to represent the aristocracy, persisted in vigorously denying the existence of any failure to more than a very partial extent. The question of the corn laws, then pending, gave this question an imperial interest. The potato famine in Ireland was represented as the invention of the agitators on either side of the water. So far was party feeling carried, that the Conservative mayor of Liverpool, honestly we are sure, refused to convene a meeting for the relief of Irish distress[18]—a committee which sat at the Mansion House, in Dublin,[19] and first declared their belief in the approach of an overwhelming calamity, were stigmatized as deluding the public with a false alarm. Men's politics determined their belief. To profess belief in the fact of the existence of a formidable potato blight, was as sure a method of being branded as a radical, as to propose to destroy the Church.

Thus in the very outset of this sore trial did Ireland encounter that which has ever been her bitterest curse—that questions of fact are made party questions, and the belief or disbelief of matters of fact is regulated in each man's mind, not by the real state of the case, but by his own political prejudices or opinions.

Sir Robert Peel was then at the head of affairs, and the ministry certainly foresaw the coming calamity. Inquiries were made as to the substance that would be the best and cheapest substitute for the potato. Indian corn was adopted, and without any public excitement on the subject, orders were given by the government for the importation of Indian corn to the amount of £100,000. This timely precaution, and the subsequent judicious distribution of this store, had the effect of bringing the people through the winter that closed the year 1845, without exposing them to any very severe privations. Arrangements were made by the government for the supply of provisions in biscuit and rice, to a much greater extent, if needed. However men may differ as to the merits of Sir Robert Peel as a politician, whatever estimate may be formed of his measures, it is impossible to deny that for the limited distress that existed consequent upon the partial failure of the potato crop of 1845, provision was made with the most consummate skill—at least with the most complete success. Uninfluenced by party representations, the minister had evidently accurately informed himself of the nature of the calamity, and clearly foresaw its extent. That he erred in fixing too early a period for its full realization, subsequent events have proved; but this was an error on the right side: and all that Sir Robert Peel predicted of the fearful extent of calamity which he anticipated in the summer of 1846, has been more than realized in the spring of 1847. There is no man of any party in Ireland who does not now feel the debt which Ireland owes to the minister for the precautions that enabled us to meet the difficulties of 1846, or who is not thoroughly convinced that an imitation, and, with the extended occasion, an extension of that policy last autumn, would have obviated most, if not all, of the suffering in which Ireland is now paying the penalty of the adherence of the present ministry, not to the doctrines of political economy, but to an utterly mistaken application of them.

It was, however, the misfortune of famine-stricken Ireland, and a deep misfortune almost all men in Ireland now feel it to be, that party combinations (we say not now, how justifiable or honorable) removed from office the man who had shown himself alone, perhaps, of living statesmen, alive to the exigencies of the crisis, and capable of boldly and efficiently meeting them.[20] It was an occasion upon which no statesman could efficiently serve the country out of office—a lamentable proof of this we have later in this sad history, in the rejection of Lord George Bentinck's bill;[21] and with the removal of Peel from office he lost the power of even assisting to obviate the danger, which, we do believe, had he remained in office, he would successfully have met.

Our sketch of this part of our history would be incomplete without alluding to the repeal of the corn laws, by which the session of 1846 was ushered in. On that question, this periodical has already strongly and distinctly expressed its opinion, and that opinion it forms no part of the object of this article to qualify or retract. Sir Robert Peel stated, however, in parliament, that the determination of ministers to settle the question was forced on by their anticipation of an Irish famine—that he and his colleagues felt it would be impossible to maintain the protection during that famine—and that the ports once opened to avert starvation, never could be closed—that the agitation of the question of corn laws in a famine, when arguments in favour of cheap bread could carry with them such a deep appeal to the passions and sympathies of the human heart, would go far to break up society altogether. The coming of the Irish famine was that which he stated forced the ministry to perhaps a premature decision upon this question—and we well remember the deep and solemn warning in which, with all the authority of premier, he predicted the coming of a calamity in Ireland, of which no one could know or measure the extent.

It has, however, been the misfortune of Ireland, that everyone, from the highest to the humblest, who has attempted to make the public mind sensible of the full extent of her danger has been disbelieved. From this fate Sir Robert Peel was not exempt. That prediction, however cheered it might be for party purposes, was in reality disbelieved; and we fear the manly and fearless declaration of his belief damaged the premier in public estimation, especially when the time which he had fixed on for the fulfilment of his predictions had passed by, and left them still unrealized.

Far is it from our intention to discuss the policy of the corn law repeal—equally remote from our wish to determine whether the famine in Ireland formed a sufficient reason for undertaking, at that crisis, the settlement of the corn law question—whether the very pressure of this calamity did not disqualify both ministers and legislature from calmly considering a great question. It may be that the councils, prompted by the clear view of this terrible calamity, were those of

"Metus et malesuada fames,"[22]

and that these counsels were too hastily adopted by a 'frightened parliament'—to borrow the language of Lord Brougham in the upper, and Lord John Manners in the lower house.[23] But time has already done justice to the speech to which we have referred. Predictions that even from Sir Robert Peel were looked upon as the exaggerations of the politician, events have proved to have been but the language of caution. Every man now can feel the pressure under which he acted in the nearer view which he took of the calamity that is now upon us; we can appreciate the sagacity that foresaw the full extent of the calamity that was coming, and we can understand the feeling under which the premier sacrificed party associations, and power, and cherished friends, to what he believed to be his duty; thus far, at least, time has vindicated his conduct, and who is there that does not feel with what immeasurable power for evil over the passions of the multitude, the agitator for a free trade in corn could now direct the fury of the mob against the corn law lords, by denouncing their monopoly as the cause of the horrors of Skibbereen. All this, it is true, leaves untouched the question, whether the corn laws ought to be maintained or not; but a calm and impartial estimate of events must decide, that of all the motives which, in that memorable speech, Sir Robert Peel declared to have influenced his mind, time has proved and tested the power and the strength.

We will not pause long to review the measures by which Sir Robert Peel met the difficulties of the partial failure of 1845. The early purchase, at a very low rate, of large quantities of Indian corn by the government—the direction of the attention of merchants to its importation, while the government supply prevented them from realizing exorbitant prices—the distribution of assistance through relief committees, under the superintendence of a commission appointed on the 27th of November, 1845[24]—the keeping in reserve a store of biscuits, ready, if necessary, to be applied to the feeding of the people—and some additional preparations to obtain, at a short notice, an additional supply of Indian corn. These simple arrangements enabled Sir Robert Peel effectually to meet all the distress that then existed in Ireland, and but for these arrangements we would have had, last year, deaths by starvation, not, indeed, as numerous, but still numerous enough to have afflicted the country, disturbed its trade, and probably interfered with its cultivation.

These arrangements recognized the duty of government to feed the people to the utmost extent to which all the resources of the empire could accomplish that end. That duty, under the more trying circumstances of this year, we are satisfied, Sir Robert Peel would have discharged, and by a larger expenditure of money, but still an expenditure utterly insignificant in comparison with the revenue of England, he would have fulfilled it with equal ease as he had done the year before. Sir Robert Peel, however, paid the penalty which, perhaps, it is well public men who change their conduct on any great question should pay. He lost the confidence of his party, and in an evil day we shall never cease to believe for the suffering poor of Ireland, in an evil day for the greatness of the British empire, he resigned the seals of office, and with them the power and the opportunity of doing good. The question of Irish destitution was one for the minister, not the legislator; it could only be met even in legislation by those who have the power, the responsibilities, and the information of the official servants of the crown.

The summer of 1846 saw the place of Sir Robert Peel filled by Lord John Russell, and upon the present premier and his colleagues devolved the responsibility of meeting the heaviest calamities of the famine. Scarcely had the present cabinet been formed, when men began to be convinced that all hope of the preservation of the potato crop of that year must be given up. As in the former year, the question was made, indeed, a party one. Those who wished to see Peel disparaged, persisted in representing his alarm as groundless. Confident reports were still published of the probability of an average supply. The journals, who had from the very beginning appeared to make it a point of political conscience to disbelieve in the existence of the scarcity, persevered in their delusive hopes of abundance. It was elaborately calculated that the abundance of the produce of the potato and the great excess of the wheat and hay crops, for which last harvest was remarkable, would at least make up for the potatoes that were lost, and thus Ireland still have her ordinary supply of food, while in the increased prices obtained for their oats, the farmers would find the year one of profit. Alas! the representations of party cannot stay the progress of nature's blight.

While these calculations were amusing and deluding the public mind, the potatoes were rotting in the ground, and before the end of September the conviction had been fixed upon the mind of the most sceptical that the potato crop, as a means of support for the people, was destroyed, and that of the ordinary food of the people there was not a supply to support them for many weeks to come.

Parliament was not then sitting. The measures which ministers considered necessary to meet the exigencies of the crisis had been passed. We cannot believe that previous to the prorogation of parliament ministers foresaw the full extent of the destitution which they had to meet. Ignorance of that extent is the only possible excuse for their measures. Their Labour Rate Act was,[25] in truth, applying to meet the exigencies of a famine, the very principle of the Poor-Law of Queen Elizabeth, and applying it in the very worst possible way, compelling enormous waste of the resources of the country upon useless works; and we cannot help regarding as a great and a fatal mistake the determination to leave the supply of food entirely to the chances of private enterprise.

Were it altogether too late to retrace these disastrous errors, comment upon them might now, perhaps, be thrown away. But vast as is the mischief inflicted upon Ireland, which no repentance can now mend, and no change of legislation repair, there is something yet to be gained by an abandonment of the pernicious system which has desolated so many districts of our land. In this belief we deem the time not thrown away that will be spent in reviewing the sad catalogue of mistakes, and neglects, more fatal than mistakes, which the history of ministerial dealing with Ireland presents.

The destruction of the potato crop entailed a double misery upon the poor. It destroyed their food, and at the same time it took from them their income. Let the corn of England fail, and you have indeed the distress among her population that a scarcity of the means of subsistence will occasion, but the capacity of the great mass of the people to purchase that subsistence, were it offered at the accustomed price, is left unimpaired. Far different, however, was the effect of the withering of the potato gardens and the con-acres of Ireland. The poor man's store was altogether gone: a purchaser of his provisions he never had been—the means of purchasing them he never had. Send the potatoes into the market at the usual price, and the cottier who never had wherewithal to purchase, if unrelieved by the charity of others, must still starve. His whole wealth has perished in his potato ridge: not only was the usual quantity of provisions removed from the country, but his power of commanding a share of those that were, or might be in it, was gone.

These two evils were to be met. A supply of provisions must be brought into the country to take the place of the perished potatoes; and the poor man who had lost his all, in losing his patch of potatoes, must be supplied with the means of purchasing the imported food.

Before the prorogation of parliament, ministers announced the mode in which they proposed to deal with Irish distress. The means of purchasing provisions were to be secured to the poor by an enactment which enabled, or, perhaps, we ought to say, obliged the cess-payers,[26] in districts which the Lord Lieutenant proclaimed as distressed, to tax themselves for what were termed public works—the money for the expenditure to be advanced by the Treasury, but to be repaid by a rate upon the taxed districts in a period not exceeding twenty years. A sum of £50,000 was voted by way of grant, and in this measure was summed up the whole of the ministerial plan for meeting the exigencies of Irish distress !!

The introduction of the Labour Rate Act was coupled by a declaration on the part of the premier, which appeared almost to amount to a pledge that with the supply of food to the country government did not intend to interfere; that this should be left entirely to the ordinary resources of commercial enterprise; and that government was resolved in no manner to interfere with the ordinary operations of the speculators or traffickers in human food.

This fatal declaration of the minister was the grand mistake of his policy—it was the doom of myriads of the Irish people to death. Combined with measures of a character very different from any that ministers have ventured to propose, this determination would still have perilled, upon an experiment of social economy, the lives of thousands of Irishmen. Coupled only with such a remedial measure as the Labour Rate Act, it was consigning this ill-fated country to the horrors of starvation.

The expectation that the enterprise of merchants would bring to Ireland, under the circumstances in which the country was then placed, the additional supply of food that was needed for her people, appears to us, we confess, to have been one of the most unnatural expectations which an ignorance of the principles of social economy could permit any man to entertain, supposing the extent of the calamity to have been fully understood.

There can be no doubt that if any change in the circumstances of Ireland were to cause Ireland permanently to need an importation of Indian corn, and if the same change of circumstances were to endow her people with the means of paying for it, in a few years trade would accommodate itself to this new market, so as to afford the required supply. Shipping, probably, would be built to carry on the new transit—capital would be gradually withdrawn from other occupations, to be embarked in the trade—merchants would build stores, and carriers establish conveyances, to distribute the imported produce through the country; retail dealers in the towns and villages would gradually spring up, and in the course of a few years the new social machinery which the altered habits of the people demanded would be called into existence.

But all this must be, in any event, the work of time, and it could only be the work of time where there was a market existing, and people with the means of purchase known to exist in their hands; but to expect all this to be done as if by magic, to meet a sudden emergency, and this to supply the wants of a people known not to have the means of purchase in their hands, whose ability to pay must depend upon the successful application of the provisions of a questionable statute—to expect this economic miracle to be wrought, would indicate the most miserable misapprehension of every principle and law that regulates the system by which the wants of mankind are supplied.

The process by which extraordinary demand produces within certain limits additional supply, is one not very difficult to understand. The retail dealer of an article finds the calls of his customers for that article increasing; he correspondingly increases his orders to the merchant, who again, if the article be one of importation, gives larger orders to his correspondents abroad. By what delusion could any man persuade himself, that by the natural operation of this process, Indian corn could find its way to the wilds of of [sic] Mayo, or the village of Carberry? There were neither retail dealers nor merchants in the article required. The people whose food was gone were, in fact, beyond the pale of all mercantile system—they had lived upon the produce of their potato gardens, and had been customers of no shop. To trust to mercantile enterprise to supply a country so circumstanced, was to expect men suddenly to embark in the trade of supplying Ireland with food, not by any of the ordinary processes by which merchants are led into the affording of additional supplies, by orders coming in the usual way of trade, but upon some vague and uncertain speculation that a country of which they knew nothing would have a demand for corn, and the still more uncertain speculation that the pauper inhabitants of that country would have the means of paying for that demand.

We say nothing of the difficulty, upon such a sudden emergency, of finding in the ordinary way of trade the shipping necessary for the additional transit; from what other branch of commercial marine were they to be withdrawn? what trade was to have all its contracts disturbed—its promised freights retarded—its orders for importation disregarded? and all this to meet an emergency for which no calculation had prepared men. While this difficulty was aggravated by the obstinate refusal of ministers, up to the very meeting of parliament, to suspend the navigation laws, and permit foreign vessels to assist in the task of transit, to which the British marine was inadequate.

The refusal or neglect to suspend the navigation laws, was the climax of infatuation.[27] While food was deficient in the country, and the freight of corn from America had risen to three times its ordinary rate, not a vessel of any foreign nation would have been permitted to unload a cargo of grain in any one of our ports.

If ministers resolved to trust the lives of the Irish people to private enterprize, was it not common sense and common justice to them that private enterprize should be unencumbered by any restrictions in the execution of the task of supplying, at the notice of a few months, provisions to five millions of people; yet, during the months in which food might have been imported into the country, the ministry left the importation of corn impeded by the restrictions of the navigation laws, and subject to a duty on importation which an order in council might have removed.

It is difficult to trace this history without indignation. We can understand the verdict of the coroner's jury, who, in days when inquests were held in Ireland upon the bodies of men found dead upon the highway, returned upon the body of a man who died of starvation while toiling at the public works, and fell dead of exhaustion with the implements of labour in his hand, a verdict of murder against the ministers who had neglected the first responsibility of government. Can we wonder if the Irish people believe—and believe it they do—that the lives of those who have perished, and who will perish, have been sacrificed by a deliberate compact to the gains of English merchants, and if this belief has created among all classes a feeling of deep dissatisfaction, not only with the ministry but with English rule.

Let us not be misunderstood. Of any such compact we acquit the ministers. In the resolution they originally formed, they were actuated by a sincere, but most mistaken belief, that they could best secure a supply of food to Ireland by declaring their determination to leave all to be done by the ordinary operations of trade. But these must be excused, who, while they witness the scenes of horror that too many in Ireland are daily seeing, believe that the subsequent deliberations of the cabinet were too much influenced by the fear of offending powerful British interests—that the omission to remove the duty from the importation on corn—to suspend the navigation laws—and to import provisions into Ireland at government expense, when it became manifest that by no other means could the emergency be met, indicated a tender regard for the interests that might have been affected by a change in their policy, which gave too much weight to those interests, and too little to the safety of the Irish people, and which, in all probability, would not long have delayed remedial measures, had the interests to be sacrificed been Irish ones.

The folly of relying on private enterprize to supply the deficiency, is proved incontestably by the result. Private enterprize has not saved us from the horrors of the famine. With Indian corn at the price of 15s. 4d. a quarter on the other side of the Atlantic, and 60s. in London! with wheat 32s. and 73s.! private enterprize has failed to import it. The applications of the best established principles of political economy would have enabled any man of ordinary sagacity to have foreseen this result. All the ordinary demands of civilized life are, doubtless, best met by those spontaneous processes in which the self-interest of man directs his activity and energy in the channels best adapted to supply these demands; but sudden and extraordinary emergencies must be met by other means. These are the occasions upon which it is of value to all that great resources should be wielded by the governing power to effect rapidly great ends.

If ever there was an occasion upon which practical proof could be given of the value to every member of the state of that association of men into states, that permits the government to wield mighty powers for the common good—if ever there were a time when men in the remotest corners of Ireland might have been taught the lesson that they have a deep interest in the strength and greatness of the United Empire, this famine presented that occasion. Tell us not that it was beyond the power of the combinations which the strength of the British empire could have wielded, to have brought to the ports of Ireland subsistence for all her people. Who is there that will say, that in such an empire all that strength should not have been put forth? What nobler triumph of British greatness could be imagined, than to have collected in the ports of famine-stricken Ireland, vessels of all nations laden with food? This would have been an exhibition of British power and British greatness, compared with which the most glorious of her fleets, or the vastest of her arsenals, would bring to the mind but a poor idea of majesty and strength. Six months ago it was possible to have done all this. The opportunity was lost; and Britain is now branded as the only civilized nation which would permit her subjects to perish of famine, without making a national effort to supply them with food.

In what parallel case do we find statesmen willing to trust to the ordinary operations of commerce, to supply in any country a sudden and unexpected demand for human subsistence? If England had occasion to send an army into some country destitute of food, would her statesmen content themselves with seeing that the soldiers were provided regularly with their pay, and trust to the speculations of private enterprize to follow them with the necessary articles of food? Multiply that army to four millions, and you have exactly the case of the starving Irish in this year.

Four millions, it is calculated, annually subsisted each year upon the potato. This sustenance interfered in no way with the commercial operations, either of export or import, in which the country was engaged. It was supplied independently of all of which the laws of the market could take cognizance. With the withdrawal of the supply, which in other years had been found in the potato garden beside their hovels, these people for the first time started into existence as elements of calculation in the economic problem of the supply of Ireland's food—they became for the first time claimants upon a share of the general resources of the country. The effect was exactly the same as if Ireland had been, in previous years, a country raising only her grain and her pasture produce with a population of about half her present; and, suddenly, four millions of additional human beings had been placed upon her shores. Suppose this case actually to have occurred—suppose four millions of people to become located in any state of things upon a country altogether unprepared for them, would any man in his senses venture to locate that mass of human beings upon the shores, let us say of Spain, fruitful as is her soil, and content himself with giving them each a very small amount of money, and trust to the speculations of merchants to follow them with food? If any man were mad enough to do so, would we be surprised if starvation were the lot of multitudes of his victims?

The case, however, of Ireland was exactly analogous to that of a country into which such an addition to the population, to be supported out of its resources, had suddenly been poured.

We do not under-value the activity, the omnipresence of commercial enterprize, compared with the partial and cumbrous effects that the best directed commissariat can make. Government might, however, have fulfilled this duty without throwing over the aid of this enterprize; its contracts with merchants for two or three million of quarters of wheat and Indian corn, might have still left all of commercial activity and enterprize in the service of this supply. We confess, compared with the magnitude of the occasion, we see no reason why government might not have contracted for a supply of Indian corn sufficient to prevent any man in Ireland from starving. The offer of such a contract would have stimulated, not retarded, commercial enterprize. It would have bid the corn of the world to our shores; it would have made the poor Irish peasant a sharer in the supremacy of the British empire, and saved this country from the horrors with which it is now inflicted.

Early in last autumn, it was the clear and bounden duty of the government to have suspended the navigation laws; to have opened the ports to the free importation of foreign corn; and we believe it to have been their equally bounden, although, perhaps, not their equally clear duty to have, by some means or other, secured, by the expenditure or the pledge of the national resources, an adequate supply of bread-stuff to the Irish ports.

To fix the details of such a plan is far beyond the object or the capabilities of any writer of an article like this. We can, however, point to the general principles upon which it ought to have been carried into effect.

Let us, however, be just. If we condemn the ministry for want of exertion, and want of foresight, let us remember the unprecedented circumstances in which they were placed, with a calamity literally, as well as metaphorically, working underground, upon the progress or extent of which it was alike impossible to calculate with certainty. Unequal as they proved themselves to meet the emergency, let it not be forgotten that the emergency has been one which men seldom have been called on to meet. Their mistakes in the measures which preceded the prorogation of parliament, were at least excusable, but, we confess, it is difficult, with every disposition to make allowance for the circumstances in which they were placed, to find excuse for the obstinacy which last autumn persevered in their fatal policy of inaction, which refused to convene parliament, when the full extent of the calamity, and the inefficiency of their measures became plain, and which postponed the suspension of the navigation laws, and the removal of the duty on corn to a period when it was too late for either measures to be of much use.[28] The only palliation that can be found for their conduct is in the too general acquiescence of Irishmen themselves. Some men were silent, because they sincerely believed it wrong to embarrass, or even to question the measures of those upon whom the responsibility of providing for the exigencies of the crisis had devolved—others, like the ministers themselves, were bewildered by the pressure of the calamity upon the country. Political motives contributed a less creditable share to the silence of the nation. There were patriots who would not for all the world censure the minister, because places were given to their friends. Others, again, who were sore at the conduct of Sir Robert Peel, determined to see nothing wrong in those who had taken his place, and in the shortsightedness which is too often the attendant of resentment, and degrades it into spite, would hazard no attack upon the policy of the ministry that might bring back the ex-premier. In truth, men of all parties were dissatisfied with the measures of the ministry, but the motives at which we hinted, combined with a want of appreciation of the full extent of the danger, kept all men silent, while a large proportion of the nation felt, and in private acknowledged, that they wished, for this crisis at least, Sir Robert Peel once more at the helm of affairs.

While ministers thus declined all exertion of government to increase the supply of food, the Labour Rate Act, as the autumn deepened into winter, came into operation in the country. Of the merits and demerits of this measure, the country has had abundance of discussion. It is not our intention now to repeat all that has been said and written upon its subject. The question, after all, lies in a narrow compass.

The provisions of the Labour Rate Act were simple enough. In every barony which the Lord Lieutenant proclaimed in a state of distress, extraordinary presentment sessions were to be held, at which the magistrates and cess-payers were to have the power of presenting for public works to an indefinite extent, subject only to the control of the Board of Works. The sums so presented were to be at once advanced by the Treasury, to be replaced by instalments that would spread the repayment of the entire, with interest, over a period varying, at the discretion of the Treasury, from four to twenty years. Questions were raised at first, whether the duty of making these presentments could be enforced or not. A very short experience of its working proved how unimportant were such questions. In every district that was proclaimed, the gentry and the farmers vied with each other in voting away money with a reckless prodigality, to be accounted for only by the circumstances in which they were placed. Roads, bridges, and quays, it was found, were the only things that could be considered as public works; and roads were made through every district of the country where no intercourse ever had existed, or ever could exist. Hills were cut down, on which a horse had scarcely ever felt a draught. The highways of the country became impassable, from the improvements of the public works. In the month of February 700,000 men were thus employed, making, with their families, upwards of two millions of people, supported in laborious idleness by a taxation upon the country.

Before we proceed to observe upon the operations of this act, let us make the observation which the self-imposition of this enormous taxation naturally suggests. It is the best, the most triumphant refutation of those who have charged the resident gentry of Ireland with indifference to the necessities of the poor. Want of sympathy with the class below them, in the proper sense of the word sympathy—that is, an absence of identity with their feelings—respect for their habits—or cordiality and confidence of intercourse, unquestionably does exist. This the unfortunate circumstances of Ireland's past and present position have produced. But to understand by the charge of want of sympathy, an accusation of hard-heartedness, of disregard to the sufferings, of indifference to the privations of the poor, this were grossly to libel the gentry of this country. It may be, that in the unfortunate estrangement to which we have adverted—an estrangement to inquire into the causes of which would give this article a controversial character, which, of all things, we are most desirous to avoid—it may be that this estrangement is, in its practical effects, the same as indifference to their welfare; but nobly have the gentry of Ireland proved themselves ready to disregard every selfish, nay, every prudential consideration, when the hand of calamity pressed upon the people, and in the very recklessness of the prodigality with which they consented to pledge their estates to the repayment of the enormous sums which the presentment sessions voted, they proved how false was the charge that slandered them as the oppressors of the poor.

In addition to the enormous expenditure under the Labour Rate Act, it must be remembered that, in many districts, the landed proprietors undertook to employ all the poor, independently of any such provision; that, in others, the provisions of the summary Drainage Act were made available for the same purposes,[29] and that sums that never were, or can be, calculated, were distributed as gratuitous relief—sums unostentatiously given, which appeared in no list of charity subscriptions, which yet form by far the largest proportion of what has been so given; and, remembering all this, some estimate may be formed of what has been done by the holders of property in Ireland for the suffering poor.

If this enormous expenditure has been, except, so far as giving immediate relief to the people, altogether misplaced—if roads that lead to nothing,[30] and public works, that never can be of any public or private advantage, have been constructed, this has not been the fault of the gentry, but of the legislature, who called upon men assembled in sessions, with every motive influencing them that could disturb their judgments, with the great object pressing on them, not to select works of utility, but to employ the people, to forward applications of labour, which, within the limits of public works, it would have puzzled a staff of engineers profitably to discover.

The enormous expenditure of the national resources, upon works that could not profit, was, perhaps, not the greatest of the evils of the Labour Rate Act. Pitiable, indeed, it was to see labour that, judiciously applied, might have multiplied the means of the future productiveness of the country, squandered upon cutting up the fields into useless roads, or in making the old highways impassable; doubly pitiable at a time when there was need for husbanding every available resource that could make the country better able to meet that portion of the calamity that must extend over future years. Men seemed, in the pressure of the present, wholly to have forgotten the future, and the importance of providing for the present wants of the people was so exaggerated to the mind, that they never bestowed a thought upon the question, whether it was not possible to combine with this something that could supply at the same time means for the future. But the effect of all this upon the labourer was bad. The Irish are an acute people, and they understood as well as their Employers that the works upon which they were set were valueless; the inference was not an unnatural one, that the less labour they could bestow upon them the better. They knew that the labour was but a pretence for giving them wages, and they made as little of the pretence as possible suffice. Hence the public works became schools of idleness, in which men met to teach other how little it was possible to do in a day's work. The indolence which the long absence of the proper rewards of industry has fostered into a national habit, supplied but too ready pupils to these normal schools of busy idleness, until men have absolutely been known to refuse higher wages from the farmers with whom they must have laboured to earn the money, and prefer the lower wages and dignified ease of labourers upon the public works.

We believe and trust that the demoralizing effect of this upon the habits of the Irish labourer have been overrated; partly, perhaps, because the Irish labourer had few lessons or habits of patient industry to unlearn. What we regret is, the lost opportunity of inculcating better habits. Had these labourers been taught to feel that they were employed upon that which it was of real importance should be done—had they been employed, under active discipline and careful superintendence, in the formation of the earthwork of a railway, or engaged in the reclamation of some waste land, how well might they have been taught the lesson, that the remuneration of labour must, in the long run, depend, in a great degree, upon its productiveness. The employment given under the Labour Rate Act had a double fault; the wages were too low, and the work too light; it taught the people neither side of the lesson which employers and labourers in Ireland equally need to learn—"a good day's wages for a good day's work."

The real nature of the Labour Rate Act soon began to be understood. Men began to be alarmed at the prospect which this unproductive expenditure of the national resources opened. They asked themselves, how is this money to be repaid? They began to ask, how is next year to be provided for? It was felt, that if the people must be fed at the expense of the holders of land, something might be made of their labour, either for those holders, or for the country, or for both. It was asked why railroads, the great iron highways to modern civilization, were to be the only highways to which the labour of the people could not be applied. With the field unreclaimed and undrained on one side of the ditch, and the roads cut up upon the other, men did begin to think that the gang of labourers might at least as well be employed in improving the fields, as in destroying the roads. With the ministry, however, no remonstrance seemed to have effect. Like the Irish navigator in a fog, they knew no rule but too keep steady to their "nor'-east course"—they heaved no lead—they kept no reckoning. The labour rate was passed, and that was the panacea for all the evils. It will be a melancholy and a startling instance of the folly of the present generation, that in a year, when the national resources have been prodigally squandered upon setting labourers to work, we will not be able, at the end of it, to point to one single useful work. While we have employed and paid able-bodied labourers enough to have made a viaduct on a level from the Giant's Causeway to Cape Clear, we have not opened a single road, the construction of which will not be felt as a positive nuisance to the locality upon which it has been inflicted. Of all the money that has been expended within the last six months, not a shilling[31] has been advanced to forward those works, which, above all others, emphatically deserve the name of public works—those railroads, the general construction of which through the country would do more than any other conceivable project to develop the resources, increase the productiveness, and civilize the people of Ireland.

In the policy of refusing all assistance to railways, the government steadily persevered with an obstinacy that almost deserves the name of infatuation; they declined to enable the railway companies, whose operations had been suspended in the unprecedented depression of the times, by a comparatively small, and abundantly secured, advance of public money, to give employment to the people. Every effort to induce them to take this course was disregarded.[32] This, at least, was not the fault of the Irish people. In favour of such a measure, the opinion of all classes in Ireland was clearly, if not very energetically, expressed. One county (Meath) went so far as to present for the earthwork of a railway, under the provisions of the Labour Rate Act. No measure appeared more simple or more in accordance with the declared object of the Act, but it did not suit the predetermined policy of the ministry, and no railroad has been made.*[33]

Perhaps we ought in sorrow rather than in anger to say, that even here some portion of the blame must be cast upon the want of public spirit and public opinion, which is, from whatever cause, the unfortunate characteristic of this country. The landed interests did not support as they ought to have done the demand that *railways* should be constructed with the labour that Ireland was forced to employ. It is the misfortune of every movement in Ireland, that each class looks to what immediately affects itself, and forgets the interest that all have in the common prosperity of the whole. While merchants and traders and the inhabitants of towns held their meetings for assistance to the railways, most of the gentry, and those immediately connected with them, urged a claim of what is termed profitable expenditure on the soil, with an exclusive zeal, and each demand, inconsequence of this unfortunate separation of interests, came to ministers only with the authority of a class. The landlords were, on the whole, more successful than the railway companies. For once, the obstinacy of the English cabinet was forced to give way; Lord Besborough [sic], himself an Irish landed proprietor,[34] and one who we believe is not responsible as a statesman for any of the fatal supineness that has marked the policy of our rulers, took upon himself the responsibility of dispensing with the provisions of the Labour Rate Act, so far as to allow presentments to be made for works of profitable cultivation of the land; and a letter from the Chief Secretary stated the terms and conditions upon which this departure from the enactments of the statute would be allowed.

Great praise is, beyond all question, due to the wisdom and the boldness of this measure—one, for the benefit of which Ireland is, we believe, altogether indebted to the strong representations of Lord Besborough. But we cannot help thinking its effect has been ridiculously exaggerated by the apologists of government. It was, perhaps, making the best of the Labour Rate Act that could be made of it, without a total contravention of its principle; but this could neither supply its deficiencies nor obviate its mischiefs. The employment of the labour was still to be impeded by the cumbrous machinery of presentment sessions, and its remuneration loaded with the enormous expense of pay-clerks and officials. It could not neutralize the evil effects of the indolent habits fostered by employment which the people felt to be eleemosynary. To say that this latter would have enabled the gentry, by cordial co-operation with the government, to mitigate entirely the evils of the former act, as has been said by advocates of the government, whose opinions we respect, strikes us as utterly wild. To remedy these evils required measures very different from those which any Lord Lieutenant could venture to carry, on his own authority, into effect. Far be it from us, however, to detract from the praise and gratitude that Lord Besborough has received for even this slight approximation to a better order of things. We cannot but believe that if the suggestions of the men who dictated this policy, had received more attention in Downing-street,[35] Ireland would not now complain of the utter neglect of her interests manifested in the imperial councils for so many months.

Condemning, as we do, the Labour Rate Act, it would be unjust to deny the good that it has effected. Whatever evils have been attendant on its train, it has been the means of preserving the lives of thousands of Irishmen. God forbid that any man should have raised, should even now raise, his hand to stop its operations, until some substitute is put in its place. By its operation, masses of the people have been fed, who, but for its existence, would, in all probability, have perished. We must never forget that this has been effected by its means. We may complain,— indeed, we do complain, that this has been done with a mixture of danger and evil from which more comprehensive measures would have saved us, while they did this more efficiently; but to the positive good it has accomplished we cannot shut our eyes.

Nor can we help observing, that those who look upon the state of Ireland as only to be remedied by a poor law that will fully recognize the right of every man to earn his bread by his labour, saw with satisfaction, not unmingled with surprise, that this principle, from which modern legislation appeared to be departing, was now, in the pressure of this calamity, embodied for the first time in an enactment relating to Ireland. What was the principle of the Labour Rate Act? That it was the duty of each locality to give to every man within it, who was willing to work, the means of livelihood. This is just the principle of the much misunderstood and maligned poor law of Queen Elizabeth.[36] If it be just and expedient in time of famine, it cannot be wrong or inexpedient in a country in which a great portion of the population are always bordering upon famine. We confess we were among the number of those who saw with satisfaction this great principle for the first time even partially acknowledged in Irish legislation. We are perfectly convinced that until it be fully and honestly carried out, Ireland can never become prosperous. We cannot hope to lay the foundation of any solid Irish prosperity upon the hopeless slough of misery and despair that forms the substratum of our social state. Even the imperfect recognition of this principle were worth to the country a great price. But the man badly reads the signs, and ill understands the policy of legislation, who can be surprised that the ministry, who proposed to feed the people in time of famine by a Labour Rate Act, were prepared to follow it at no distant day by extending to Ireland's habitual destitution the remedy of outdoor relief.

The new year opened gloomily on Ireland. By this time the appalling extent of the calamity, and the inefficiency of the measures adopted to meet it, were, at least, partially understood. A vague sense of alarm possessed men's minds. The terror was, perhaps, exaggerated, because the evils apprehended were indefinite. The public eye was shocked by whole columns of the daily newspapers occupied exclusively with deaths by starvation. Men's hearts failed them with fear, for looking for the things which should come. The landlords saw ruin in the enormous imposts which the Labour Rate Act placed upon their estates—the merchant and the trader feared it in the general stagnation which they anticipated as the consequence of general distress. Rents were, in many parts of the country, withheld, and alarmists stated they were so universally. It is impossible to conceive a more gloomy picture than that presented by Irish society at the close of the disastrous year '46, yet all men looked forward to the meeting of Parliament with something like hope. The Irish people looked with confidence to Sir Robert Peel, in office or out of office; they calculated that his practised sagacity and comprehensive mind would have pointed out the inadequacy of what had been done, and suggest what ought to be done; and one fortnight before the meeting of Parliament, had the choice of premier depended on the suffrages of the Irish nation, Sir Robert Peel would have commanded their almost unanimous votes.

These expectations, perhaps unreasonable, have been disappointed. The Queen's speech, and the debate on the address, spread through Ireland the conviction that Parliament was as supine as the ministry.[37] Nor ought it to be disguised that the part of the session which is past has shaken the attachment of many to the Imperial and British constitution. Men have asked themselves, to what is to be attributed the apparent acquiescence in a policy which, right or wrong, has resulted in the sacrifice of such multitudes of our fellow Christians by the most horrible of all deaths? They have asked if the house in which this sacrifice has called forth so little inquiry, represent indeed the commons of the empire. How is it that the GRAND INQUEST of the nation has made no inquiry as to the death of thousands of the people? Men who have hated democracy all their lives, began seriously to reflect whether the people had influence enough upon a Parliament in which their sufferings were so little heeded. Irishmen, too, began to feel that they were legislated for by men ignorant of the condition and circumstances of their country. From this feeling arose the meeting of the landed proprietors in January last, which for one day assumed the form of an Irish convention;[38] from this emanated the resolutions of many of the grand juries of Ireland, in which were propounded sentiments bordering very closely upon those of Federalism, if not of Repeal.

This unfortunate state of feeling has been aggravated by the rejection of the measure known as Lord George Bentinck's bill[39]—it has been exasperated, as well as aggravated, by the manner in which senators, not, perhaps, of much character or influence in either house, have spoken of the Irish nation—language, of which we scarcely know whether we should most wonder that Englishmen were found base enough to speak it, or that, when it was spoken, Irishmen were not found adequately to resent.

We know that in the feelings of these spiteful malignants, the English nation do not participate; it is among the few blessings of the crisis that Irishmen have been taught how deeply the better heart of England sympathizes with their affliction. The aid which Englishmen have generously sent to Ireland has produced this counteracting effect: but Irishmen do still believe that in these feelings of good will, the parliament does not represent the people of England, and contrasts are drawn in the mind of many of the warmest advocates of British connexion, between the manner in which a British parliament have met, and an Irish parliament would have met, the calamity that has befallen us.

What can be more absurd—what can be more wicked, than for men professing attachment to an imperial Constitution to answer claims now put forward for state assistance to the unprecedented necessities of Ireland, by talking of Ireland being a drain upon the *English* treasury? By such declamation as this some English senators opposed the proposition of Lord George Bentinck, not to advance the money, but to pledge the credit of the empire to facilitate undertakings in this country, which, in enriching Ireland would have increased the strength of the empire at large. If the Union be not a mockery, there exists no such thing as an English treasury. The exchequer is the exchequer of the United Kingdom. Its separation into provincial departments is never thought of when imperial resources are to be spent, or imperial credit pledged, for objects principally or exclusively of interest to the English people. Ireland has been deprived, by the Union with England, of all separate power of action. She cannot do now, as in the days of her parliament she might have done—draw upon her own resources, or pledge her own credit, for objects of national importance. Irishmen were told, indeed, that in consenting to a Union which would make them partners with a great and opulent nation, like England, they would have all the advantages that might be expected to flow from such a Union. How are these expectations to be realized, how are these pledges to be fulfilled, if the partnership is only to be one of loss, and never of profit to us? if, bearing our share of all imperial burdens—when calamity falls upon us we are to be told than we then recover our separate existence as a nation, just so far as to disentitle us to the state assistance which any portion of a nation, visited with such a calamity, had a right to expect from the governing power? If Cornwall had been visited with the scenes that have desolated Cork, would similar arguments have been used? Would men have stood up and denied that Cornwall was entitled to have the whole country share the extraordinary loss?*[40]

Language like that to which we have alluded must force on inquiries, by the full prosecution of which, we believe, the claims of Ireland will not lose. Men will ask how much of food Ireland has sent to England as a subsidy, without return, whether to pay the rent of her absentees, or to contribute her share to the general revenue of the country; they will inquire how much of that revenue is spent in Ireland, and how much in England; what amount of revenue the Commissioners of Woods and Forests derive from the crown lands and rents of Ireland,[41] and when and how that income has been spent. These, perhaps, are questions of which the accomplished financiers, who talk so flippantly of drains upon the English treasury, have never dreamed. It is enough, perhaps, to tell them that to talk of an English treasury is, in effect, to declare the Union repealed. Some of them have made it a boast that England could now amply punish Ireland by repealing the Union, and leaving her to struggle, unaided, with the crisis. But if the partnership were to-morrow to be dissolved, and a fair account to be taken of all dealings between the partners, the items of charge upon the side of Ireland would exhibit at this moment no inconsiderable balance in her favour, were it struck between the sums she has contributed to the imperial treasury, and those which that treasury has expended in this country for Irish objects.

We trust it is not necessary for us to give proof of our adherence to the cause of British connexion in Ireland; it is in no spirit of unfriendliness that we tell British statesmen, that the last few months have silently set thoughts at work, and called passions into existence, which bode more peril to the Union than all the insurrectionary movements and monster meetings of 1843.[42] A little more of insult and contumely heaped upon the Irish people; a little more disregard of Irish interests and feelings in legislation; a little more treatment of Ireland as a conquered country, to be parcelled out in legislation as pleases her masters, and he would be a bold man who would promise many years' continuance of the Union.

We know that there are men in England—we trust not among her statesmen—who believe that those possessing the property of the country, of both creeds, and the bulk of her Protestant population, are so impressed with the opinion, that the ascendancy of an intolerant and bigoted democracy would be the inevitable result of a repeal of the Union, that no amount of ill-treatment will make these parties unite in the demand for a separate legislature. The reliance, at best, is an ungenerous one—it is as unsafe as it is ungenerous. These feelings are, from whatever cause it proceeds, losing their activity. The removal from the stage of Irish politics of some of those most prominently connected with the feuds of former times; the pressure of the calamity of the country, making men feel that no state of society can be worse than what they see; only one of a thousand accidents of the almost innumerable fluctuations that change the direction of public opinion, may prove the falsity of such security as this. The policy that makes the maintenance of the Union depend upon our divisions, must calculate on its ceasing with the termination, or even the first suspension of our mutual distrusts.

We have brought down our history to the meeting of parliament; we have now to deal with the measures that, in the present session, ministers have proposed.

The suspension of the navigation laws,[43] in favor of the importation of food, and the abolition of the duty on importation, were measures so obvious that the only observation that can be made upon them is, that their adoption, the moment parliament met, is the strongest self-condemnation of the policy that deferred them so long—that put off the permission to import grain in foreign bottoms until the ice upon the greater rivers of Europe was a barrier against their employment almost as effectual as the navigation laws. At the time when parliament suspended the navigation laws, many of the ships that would, at an earlier period, have been employed in bringing us food, were lying icebound in the Elbe.

Ministers felt themselves compelled to remit the re-payment of one-half of the sums advanced to Ireland under the Labour Rate Act. Common justice required such an arrangement. It is now proved that almost the entire of these sums had been spent, without the slightest permanent benefit to any one—that they had been so spent in opposition to the earnest remonstrances of the Irish landed proprietors who offered to make themselves responsible for the repayment of the very same sums—giving to the people at least the same wages, if they would be allowed to direct the labour to increasing the productive power of the soil—in opposition to the remonstrances of a large number of the Irish people, who had earnestly pressed upon the government to spend the same sums in aiding the construction of railroads, and thus at once benefit the country, and relieve the landed interests from the pressure of taxation.

This remission of half this sum—misspent as it was through the mistake of ministers, with the very trifling addition of the sums advanced by way of gift, is the entire amount of contribution from the imperial treasury, to meet the loss which Ireland has suffered by the unprecedented visitation that afflicts her—a loss which cannot be estimated, in its direct effects, at less than fifteen millions, and which, in its indirect effects, must be calculated at much more. If the principle be true—a corollary from the Union it appears to be—that this loss, as the best of English statesmen have admitted, ought to be considered not as an Irish but an imperial one, this contribution is inadequate. Poor, however, as it is, it was forced by circumstances—it was to repair the mistakes of the ministers. The principle of the Labour Rate Act was to throw upon the landed interests of Ireland the entire reparation of the loss that had accrued—a principle we believe to be unjust; but the application of this principle was accompanied by regulations which deprived the Irish rate-payers of all control over the expenditure. Had parliament declared that Ireland must bear the burden—and enacted, that the property of Ireland must find employment and wages for all the destitute, but left it at the same time to local and domestic arrangement to determine how that employment was to be directed, the grievance would have been less than that which is felt in the provisions of an enactment, which at once threw upon one class in Ireland the entire burden of the distress, and, at the same time, provided that by the plans, the caprices, or the obstinacy of the Imperial or the English cabinet, the money raised from that class should be spent, in opposition to their remonstrances, in an utterly unprofitable expenditure.

It must be remembered, too, that to a very large class in Ireland, upon whom the loss of the potato crop has fallen heavily, no assistance whatever has been given from the Imperial treasury; we mean THE LANDED PROPRIETORS AND THE TENANT FARMERS of Ireland. The former, in many instances, found their incomes suddenly stopped. The latter have not only lost severely by the loss of the potatoes which they had planted on their farms; but many of them who had paid their farm-labourers by giving them a portion of ground to plant the potatoes, as their wages by anticipation for the year, were obliged in the autumn either to give up their labour, or to pay them over again in money; and we believe we do not exaggerate when we say, that the majority of the small farmers in Ireland have not at this moment the means of paying in cash for the labour that is necessary for the cultivation of their farms, while, in too many instances, the landlords have been left entirely without the means of assisting them.

To these two classes, both of whom have suffered severely from this visitation, no assistance whatever has been given. Nay, it appeared sufficient to condemn any proposition if it could be shown that its effect would be to benefit these proscribed classes. If there be any truth or justice in the principle that the losses occasioned by a calamity like this—a calamity against which no prudence could guard, and which no fault on the part of the sufferers produced—should be borne, not by the immediate objects of the visitation, but, in some part at least, by the resources of the empire at large, it is difficult to see why nothing should be done to assist these two classes. On the contrary, they who themselves were heavy sufferers by the visitation, were selected out of all classes in the British empire, out of all the classes in Ireland possessing property or income, as the persons to bear the entire burden of meeting this extraordinary destitution of the classes below them.

The one expedient of ministers appears to be to tax the land. Amid these measures, indeed, of unprecedented impost upon the landed interest, one ominous measure of relief to the proprietors is promised. The boon that is offered to the owners of the soil is, "A bill to facilitate the sale of encumbered estates in Ireland."[44]

The principle of the measures of this year is the same as that of last. The entire burden of the loss of the potato crop is to be thrown upon the proprietors and tenant-farmers of the land. No expedient certainly can be more simple, and admirably is its simplicity preserved. It is unenumbered [sic] by any measure to improve the condition of the country at large, and thus assist the proprietors or occupiers of the soil to hear the burthen that is cast upon them. A general railway bill would have marred the simplicity of the ministerial policy. Can it be wondered at if there are men who regard these measures as nothing but measures of confiscation. Lord Clare[45] stated in the Irish House of Lords that the entire soil of Ireland had been confiscated three times. The next Chancellor who speaks in an Irish parliament will have probably to add to the catalogue of general confiscations a fourth.

The entire measures which ministers contemplate for the relief of Irish famine, are to be found in an act which, on the 26th of February, received the royal assent, entitled an act for "The Temporary Relief of Destitute Persons in Ireland."[46] The Poor Law Act admitting for the first time of out-door relief, although forced on, no doubt, by the exigencies of the present crisis, is one of a permanent, not a temporary nature. Its provisions require, therefore, a consideration distinct in some respect from the present circumstances of the country.

The provisions of the new act have unquestionably an immense advantage over those of the Labour Rate Act. They give at least the opportunity of boldly and efficiently meeting the destitution in Ireland, as far as the time that has been lost will permit it now to be met. But never was there an act passed, the result of which so much depends upon the administration, because everything is left to the arbitrary power of those who are to carry its provisions into practice.

Relief Commissioners or Finance Committees, appointed by the Lord Lieutenant, are given by this act an unlimited power of taxing the landed interests of Ireland—a power that may indeed be exercised so as to amount to a confiscation of all landed property in Ireland. In every electoral division, under the poor-law, in which the Lord Lieutenant considers it expedient that the act should be put in force, a Relief Committee is to be formed, consisting of all justices of the peace resident within the district, the guardians of the poor, the clergy of the different churches, and the three highest rate-payers not included in any of these descriptions. This committee are to make out lists of all persons within their districts entitled to be relieved, and the estimate of the expense; but both lists and estimates are subject to the revisions and alterations of finance committees, appointed by the Lord Lieutenant, and removable at his pleasure, upon which the Lord Lieutenant issues his warrant to the poor-law guardians to assess upon tenements liable to the poor-rate that sum, and all the expenses of the staff necessary for the execution of the act, either upon the union at large or the electoral division, as he shall judge expedient; the entire amount of such expenditure, unlike that of the Labour Rate Act, must be levied by an immediate rate. The treasury is indeed authorized to advance a sum of £300,000, in anticipation of these rates, but this is plainly a mere temporary accommodation, pending the collection of the rate. So far as this act provides, the entire cost of maintaining the destitute poor in Ireland, until the 1st of October next, is cast upon the landed proprietors and tenant farmers of Ireland—a measure which may be carried out so as to involve both classes in utter ruin, and amount to a total confiscation of landed property in Ireland.

The act, however, does contain a provision that these relief committees shall receive and distribute voluntary contributions, and the Commissioners may apply such grants as may be granted hereafter from the treasury, either by way of gift or loan, in aid of these local rates.

The mode of relief, the manner in which it is to be granted, and the terms of its distribution, are left entirely to the discretion of the local committees, acting under the complete control of the Relief Commissioners, whose orders and directions they are bound to obey. The act, however, contemplates a complete departure from the policy of leaving the supply of food to the people to the ordinary operations of commerce, since it authorizes the distribution, the sale, and even the culinary preparation of food under the direction of these committees.

Such are the provisions of an act, to the administration of which we look with fearful and trembling anxiety. If it be administered in a wise and generous spirit—if it be accompanied with large and liberal measures for this country—if it be assisted with the aid which Ireland, we say boldly all classes in Ireland, have a right to DEMAND from the imperial legislature, its machinery is capable of immense application for good. If, on the other hand, it be administered in a grudging or penurious, and an un-Irish, we do not wish to say anti-Irish spirit; if no measures of general utility accompany it—if no aid be given from the imperial treasury to mitigate the pressure upon all classes in Ireland; if, in a word, this act be put in force in that spirit of confiscation, of the existence of which, in some influential quarters, the owners of the land in Ireland have had abundant indication, then, we say, this act will result in temporary, and only temporary, relief to the destitute, in the ruin of all who derive their income from land in Ireland, in confusion and distress to all classes of her people, and in a state of things which will amply realize the expression—national bankruptcy.

It is, in the first place, manifestly impossible to expect that the destitution which must, for months to come, exist in many districts in Ireland, can be met, as this act proposes, by the assessment of a rate upon these districts, to be levied within the year. We do not now speak of the justice or expediency of such a course, but we speak of its physical impossibility. What rate could be levied in Scariff or Skibbereen that could supply the destitution that in these districts is to be provided for? It may be very easy to assess a rate, but its collection would be utterly impossible. Gratuitous subscriptions must supply the wants of such localities as these, or parliament must make liberal advances from the imperial treasury. This, again, may be done in two ways—either as a grant, or as a loan, to be repaid by instalments out of future rates. When we remember the pressure that must be upon these future rates by the operation of out-door relief, we do not hesitate to say that to relief committees in districts like these, and they are many in Ireland, large sums must be given, and given not as a loan but as a grant.

For our own parts, we confess we regret that another source was not provided to bear a portion of the burden—of the burden, we mean, that must fall upon exclusively Irish resources. We do not understand why property in land alone should be taxed for this purpose. Did machinery exist for the collection of such a tax, or if it be possible to create it, we see no reason why every man in Ireland, no matter whether his income be derived from the funds, from mortgages, or from official or professional sources, ought not to be compelled to contribute, in proportion to his income, to that portion of the expenditure which must be raised in Ireland within the year. That portion of the expenditure of this year, which is to become a continuing tax upon the industry of the country, in fairness ought to be charged upon the property which is of a permanent character; but to the expenditure that is cast upon this year's income, all income ought to contribute. For a measure of this nature it is now, perhaps, too late to hope. The landed interests of Ireland have, however, a right to expect that of the extraordinary supplies required to meet the extraordinary emergency of this year, a large proportion, if not the entire, shall be borne by the consolidated fund. The taxation of the Labour Rate Act has placed on the landed interest a burden for many years to come, which, with the increased taxation of the out-door relief, will be as much as it will be able to bear. There is neither wisdom nor justice in throwing upon that interest the entire loss occasioned by the calamity of last year.

Our first demand for Ireland is—we brave the scorn of the legislators at whom we have glanced in making it—that the taxation of this temporary relief act should, in every district where such aid is needed, be accompanied by large and liberal grants from the consolidated fund.[47]

The mode in which relief is to be dispensed under this act is, we have said, to be left to the discretion of those who are to administer it, and we see nothing in the act to prevent that relief being given in part in the shape of wages to persons to be employed in the useful work of cultivating the land. This is a subject of the very first importance to the country. Exaggerated, no doubt, the accounts have been which have alarmed us by representing whole districts as left waste; but still it is a melancholy fact, that in many districts numbers of the tenant-farmers have not, from causes we have already explained, the means of either purchasing seed, or paying the labour that is necessary to the cultivation of the land. Of the money that must be paid away in relief, we suggest that so much as may, in each district, be considered by proper authority advisable, be expended in paying the wages of workmen for either landlords or farmers, who want them for works of profitable cultivation, and will give for the repayment of those wages the security of the produce of the labour they employ. The farmer might thus obtain seed and labour to stock his farm, perhaps, on the security of his next harvest crops—the landlord labour for profitable undertakings, upon his personal security and a charge upon his estate.

No doubt there would be difficulties in the way of administering such a plan—but a crisis like the present is not to be met without difficulties; there are none which a little firmness and a little prudence cannot avoid; and unless plans like this are grafted on the measures for temporary relief, we confess we see nothing to result from that measure but a repetition of the wasteful expenditure of the Labour Rate Act, with more certain ruin to all connected with the landed interests of the country.

And, above all, to make this act effectual even for the sustentation, during the summer, of the poor, government must take immediate steps to insure, by every possible means, an importation of food into Ireland. Commercial enterprise will, we fear, prove as inadequate to supply the wants of the summer as it has of the winter. The last few days, indeed, have brought to us increased importations, and lowered the prices of grain in our market. But let us beware of placing too much reliance upon this. Fearful is the responsibility ministers will incur, unless they have information, which the public have not, of the operations of trade, if, with the experience of the winter, they leave the supplies of our food to resources proved to be precarious. Five long months must pass away before the next harvest can be available for the people's food. It is a solemn duty which the Queen's ministers owe to the Irish people and to our sovereign, to increase, by every means that the resources of the empire can command, the supply of food to Ireland. If that supply be unhappily deficient in July or August, the scenes of the summer will cause the horrors of the winter to be forgotten. The pestilence that in the history of Ireland has invariably marked the famine will be upon us—want will increase as endurance of suffering makes men less able to resist it. The famine is creeping up in society—men who had some little money stored have been living on their stores, and one by one they will drop into the class of paupers, and become victims of the famine. No Relief Act can give bread to the people, unless the quantity of bread in the country be sufficient to be distributed among all, and this, we fear, it will not be, unless the resources of the state are applied to increase, in the end of summer, the importation of food.

The new harvest of Indian corn that is now wasting on the prairies of the Missisippi, because it is of no value, will be floated down to New Orleans, in large quantities, if once it is known that the British government will buy. There is no vessel that the government can bribe, ay, or press into such a service, that they ought not to employ. The vessels of war that now lie idle in ordinary, may, at very little expense, be freighted for this service.

Shippers, if sufficiently tempted by high freights, will employ their vessels in bringing food; we can employ the quantity of steam ships belonging to our own country in this trade; we can hire the vessels of the merchants of other nations.

And when we speak of other nations, need we fear the jealousy of other nations, above all, of that great nation by whose cordial co-operation an enterprise of this nature might be made easy. Is there in the history of the world a nobler trait of national character than that which is exhibited in the recent proceedings in America, in relation to Irish distress? If the American people offer us corn, is it too much to ask of our own government to find the freight that is to convey it to us? We say *our own* government, for, despite of the malice of the malignants, the British government is our own. If, in very truth, it be not, what Irishman will advocate the continuance for one hour of the Union?

While Britain, last autumn, refused either to suspend the navigation laws, or to purchase bread stuffs for her people, France had done both. Ministers ask where were they to find food, food for the Irish people; they ask this question triumphantly of men who have no means of information such as ministers possess. We believe they could have found it. Let us ask them to account for the difference in the price for corn in America and in London. Do they know that last autumn a Dublin merchant was compelled to abandon a cargo actually purchased abroad, because foreign bottoms would not be allowed to import it. The enormous difference of price to which we have referred, abundantly proves we have not derived the supply that other countries could yield us.

But have endeavours been made to ascertain the extent to which government interference could be carried? Have ministers, with all the information they possess, which no private individual can possess, exhausted the efforts of ingenuity in discovering by what new means food can be supplied—what new fisheries might yield to us unknown supplies—what countries might send us new supplies of coarser animal or vegetable food? With a summer of unprecedented scarcity before us, has any effort, even now, been made to prepare to bring into the stock of that summer's food the supply that might be obtained from the deep sea fisheries round the Irish coast.

Three steps we believe indispensably necessary to make the Temporary Relief Act safe or efficient for the purposes of relieving the distress. The funds to meet the demands it will entail must be provided, in a very considerable degree, by grants or loans from the state. Full power must be left to the local committees to employ the labour as they see best, even though that employment be in the service of individuals upon profitable works; and lastly, and above all, the ministers who have indeed in this act undertaken the commissariat of the Irish people, must be prepared to apply all the available resources of the state to procure a sufficient importation of food.

When all this is done, Ireland must still undergo destitution and misery during the next summer, which we fear it is beyond the reach of human power to avert. No power but that of the Great God can now avert the pestilence which, if all former experience can be relied on, will most assuredly follow with the hot days of the summer the want of sufficient food. Fever is already in its ravages anticipating our prediction. In many of the workhouses the deaths have arisen to a fearful per centage of the inmates.In one work-house we read of deaths to the amount of two hundred a-week. But this is but the beginning of the plague. We tremble to think of what is before us. We know not whether, in their preparations for the summer, the government have calculated on this fearful element in the misery that is before us; but sure we are that every day that leaves our population with insufficient food, will fearfully aggravate this worst and last evil of the famine.

When we ask for grants from the imperial Treasury to meet the purposes of the Temporary Relief Act, let it not be supposed for an instant that we wish to shield the property of Ireland from contributing its fair share to the support of our poor. To meet the ordinary destitution of the country, we believe that property ought to be taxed; but to impose upon a class of the holders of Irish property, and that class the most embarrassed, the entire burden of this, which is justly admitted to be an imperial loss, appears to us, we confess, to be a measure of confiscation, as complete in principle as if the landed property of Ireland had been declared forfeited to pay the expenses of the Chinese war.[48] We advocate, be it remembered, the imposition of a tax in which personally we would be much more concerned than in any tax upon land. If government wish boldly and honestly to make Irish property contribute to Irish distress, let them put a tax for this year upon all who have property in Ireland—let them tax the holders of mortgages, and the owners of bank shares and stock—let there be now put an income tax[49] on Ireland, to meet the exigencies of the present year, but let its amount be fixed, according to what it may be deemed the holders of moneys in Ireland ought reasonably to pay; in addition to this, let the Treasury be empowered to advance to any district, a sum that will bear a fixed proportion to the value at which its property is rated to the poor—let this be repaid by instalments, on the principle of the Labour Rate Act; and let these advances be expended as far as possible in the wages of labour, to be employed on works that will ultimately increase the productiveness of the soil. The amount of taxation thus to be levied, either directly within the year, or in future years, to repay these advances, should be limited to the amount which a fair and impartial estimate may deem the property of Ireland fairly liable to contribute. Beyond the amount that can by these means be placed at the disposal of the Relief Commissioners, Ireland has a just and reasonable claim to have this extraordinary exigency met from the funds of the state.

Let it not be supposed that the emergency will pass away with the next harvest. We leave out of our considerations apprehensions too horrible to dwell upon, that are entertained, groundlessly we trust, that the wheat crop is showing symptoms of failure. We admit all calculations of the loss that will accrue from ground that must, even in spite of all exertions, remain untilled. To expect the potato crop to be resuscitated next year, is visionary and wild. All calculations agree that the quantity of ground which, planted in potatoes, will feed three persons, sown with wheat will do little more than supply sustenance to one—a calculation that leaves out the not unimportant item, that by the very waste of a potato diet, the swine and the poultry were fed. Perhaps the calculation would be more accurate which set against the one person maintained by the wheat, three persons and a pig to be fed upon the potato. If, then, the potato ground next year be all grown with corn—a supposition far too favourable for the country—where are we to find the food of four millions*[50] who have hitherto been supported by the potato produce of that ground? If in corn, it can do little more than sustain a million and a-half; it is taking, indeed, a short-sighted view of the effects of the potato failure, to believe that even its extraordinary effects will pass away with next harvest, or even the harvests of 1849, or 1850.

The country must prepare itself for a permanent change in the diet of the great mass of the population. We earnestly hope that never again will the potato be the staple food of her people. In dependency of those frequent failures which have brought periodical distress upon our poor—the difficulty of its transport—the impossibility of storing it up in a year of abundance to meet the wants of a year of scarcity—apart from all these objections which economists have so frequently pointed out as existing to its adoption as the staple food of a country, we believe the potato diet of the population, in the manner in which they subsisted on it, to have had the most injurious effects upon the character and habits of our people. It might appear almost fanciful to say, that the necessity of its culture fostered those habits of filth which have given so squalid an aspect to the wretchedness of an Irish hovel. The dunghill before the cottage was almost the necessary adjunct of the potato garden in the rear.[51] The pig, the most unclean of all animals, the inmate of the hut, was the product of the same prolific source of degeneration.[52] We will not inquire how far those philosophers are right who attribute to the physical qualities of "the dirty weed," the overabundance of our population. But it does not require the aid of any questionable philosophy to trace to the mode in which our labouring classes subsisted on the potato, the evil habits of these classes. The dunghill, the pig, and the potato garden were the poor Irishman's world. Receiving no money-wages, he neither knew the value of money, nor what it was to save. Men who toiled for their daily wages, and purchased their loaf with their shilling, would soon learn the value of husbanding a penny out of each shilling;[53] but the man who received his wages by the process of digging a basket of potatoes from his ridge, would never have suggested to his mind the idea of saving one potato out of twelve. The worst of this mode of subsistence was, that it shut out the man who so existed from any contact with the mercantile and social world. In the simple process by which he heaped up his dunghill, manured his potato garden, and dug out the root as he wanted it, requiring nothing but the process of boiling to make it fit for food, he was never driven to rely on the help of his fellow-man. What room, in such a miserable and wretched process, for that mutual dependence, that division of labour, even in its rudest form, to which we owe all the progress of the most refined civilization! What lessons of prudence were to be learned! what habits of frugality to be acquired in the solitary monotony of this unsocial existence! The very fact that throughout the whole process, the man might subsist without ever handling a coin, was enough to account for his knowing but little of the value of either industry or money. Living without exchange or barter, scarcely ever exchanging the products of his own industry for that of others, except when the price of the pig left him surplus enough after paying the rent, the means of purchasing something like clothing for himself or his family. It is impossible to conceive a mode of life less calculated to offer incentives to exertion or motives to frugality, or one better calculated to form the habits of the labourer to idleness, imprudence, and, worse almost than either, contentedness with the wretchedness of his condition. Earnestly do we hope, then, that once we have passed the ordeal of their loss, potatoes may never again be the staple of our food, or conacre the form in which the wages of our labourers will be paid.

In the transition from such a mode of livelihood to one more approaching to civilization, Ireland must unquestionably pass through great difficulties; and measures which contemplate only the present year, are, in reality, inadequate to the demands of the condition of the country—measures that will supply what is wanted, must, like the calamity that has called them forth, extend their operations far beyond the present year.

Of measures professing to go beyond the 1st of October next, ministers have only proposed the bill for extending the poor law system to one of out-door relief.[54] Although introduced in company with measures to relieve the destitution, and forced by the fearful disclosures which that famine has made of the wretchedness of our people, this measure is not properly one of those by which they propose to meet the emergency of the present time. To the permanent prosperity of Ireland, we believe an extension of the poor law, even more liberal than that now proposed, to be an indispensable requisite. No matter at what expense to the upper classes, we hold that no state can prosper in which the right of every man who is willing to work to be fed is not fully and liberally recognized. The rights of property do not arise until this obligation is discharged. Unquestionably, the habits and character of the people make the administration of a poor law in Ireland difficult, and, perhaps, dangerous. But still the obligation to provide for all the destitution of the country in ordinary years, is one from the fulfilment of which we are sure it is not the real interest of the owners of property in Ireland to be exempt.*[55] All our sympathies have been with those who have long laboured to establish in Ireland a legal provision for her destitute; and the attempt to narrow that provision to the miserable mockery of our workhouse relief, was, in effect, to leave Ireland without a poor law at all. To the principle of the poor law bill of the ministry, we give our cheerful and cordial assent. It is not, indeed, the measure by which famine can be, or ought to be met. Introduced two years ago, it would have commanded our cordial and unqualified assent. Intended as a measure for the permanent government of this country, we believe it to be one absolutely required; but if upon its provisions be thrown the burden of providing for the temporary destitution, it is not difficult to see that, in words which we remember to have seen applied on a similar occasion, "It will desperately deserve the name of a poor law, because it will be a bill for making all Ireland poor."

This bill proposes to introduce into the poor law system of Ireland two changes, the magnitude and importance of which it is impossible to overrate. IT RECOGNIZES, FOR THE FIRST TIME IN ANY CLASS OF PERSONS, A RIGHT TO SUPPORT, AND IT AUTHORIZES, IN CERTAIN CIRCUMSTANCES, OUT-DOOR RELIEF.

The persons whose right to relief is fully recognized by this bill, are those who are "permanently disabled from labour by means of old age, infirmity, or bodily or mental defect;" and it directs relief to be given to them in or out of the workhouse as the guardians may deem expedient.[56] Practically, there can be no doubt that this will be, and ought to be, a full and unqualified recognition of the right of such persons to be supported by outdoor relief, leaving the possibility of enforcing the workhouse test as merely the means of detecting and obviating attempts at imposture.

Such a provision as this is one which the first dictates of Christianity, of humanity, obviously demand.

In addition to this, the able-bodied poor, "when destitute and unable to support themselves by their own industry, or by other lawful means," acquire by this bill a partial recognition of their right to be maintained—that is, the guardians are bound by this proposed act to take order for relieving and setting to work in the workhouse, all such persons, whenever there is sufficient room in the workhouse for them to do so.

If, however, the workhouse should be full, or unfit for the reception of inmates, from the pressure of infectious disease, then comes the much-dreaded provision of out-door relief. In this case the Poor Law Commissioners are empowered to make an order for the extension of out-door relief to the able-bodied poor: this order cannot extend beyond a period of two months, and the relief shall only be given in food.

In addition to this, a relieving and a medical officer are to be appointed in each union, and the relieving officer is empowered, in cases of urgent necessity, to give immediate relief in lodging, food, or medical attendance.[57]

The difficulties attending on the recognition of the right to relief without a law of settlement,[58] are for the present at least escaped, by the expedient of simply recognizing the right to relief, and leaving it to the Poor Law Commissioners to frame regulations under which the applications must be made and the relief administered. But these regulations must, it is evident, be framed so as to secure the relief, the right to which the bill recognizes—that is, in all those permanently disabled, an unqualified right to relief; in the able-bodied destitute poor, a right to be relieved to the full capacity of the workhouse to which they may be directed to apply; when that workhouse is full or unfit for their reception, a right, subject to the control of the Poor Law Commissioners, to be supplied with food outside its walls.[59]

To these provisions, we confess, we cannot understand how anyone can object, who is not prepared to leave the destitute population of Ireland to a state of misery and wretchedness unparalleled in the civilized world. Twelve years ago that destitution was laid bare to the legislature and the empire, in the report of the Commissioners of Irish Poor Law Inquiry.[60] What effort was made to relieve it then? With the statement in that report, that two millions of people were for a considerable portion of each year in want of sufficient food, a measure was introduced which could not do more than feed 80,000 people in workhouses.[61] What effort has been made to relieve that destitution since? We left our poor to the helpless misery in which they were proved then to drag out a wretched existence, supported often upon the seaweeds of the rocks. Statesmen contented themselves with having given to Ireland a poor-law, and the national conscience, which had been startled by the fearful revelations which the poor law inquiry had brought to light, was too easily satisfied with the excuse, and legislators turned away from the embarrassing subject of Irish destitution with the feeling that they had passed a poor law. It was something certainly to have established, even in its most niggard form, the great principle, that there should be relief for the destitute; this we owe to the poor law of 1837.[62] Ten years have been sufficient to see that principle extended to a modified one of out-door relief. So true is it that the great principles of social charity, like those of the Christianity that teaches them, are expansive and progressive in their innate power. A few years more, and Ireland will have a poor law that will satisfy all the requirements of Christian legislation for the poor.

We are speaking, be it remembered, of the poor law as a measure to be enforced in the ordinary condition of the country, not as a measure to meet the emergency of a famine. It is the measure by which the ministry have, for the first time in Irish history, given to the poor man equality with his English neighbour; entirely do we agree with the memorable words of a writer in the *Standard*, of the 24th of May, 1836, when propounding the truth, that a poor law for Ireland was "that real and substantial equalization of the Irish with the British people, which must supply the basis of all sound schemes of uniformity." We may be told, indeed, that a poor law tax will press heavily upon the landlords. Be it so—every man must suffer a share of the poverty of his country. The man who has, must and ought to suffer whatever of inconvenience belongs to being the owner of property in a poor country. The social system that places the landlord of a poor and wretched tenantry in as good a situation as the landlord of those who are comfortable and happy, is based upon injustice, and most probably upon oppression. Let any man read over the evidence collected by the Poor Law Inquiry Commissioners in 1836, let him read the pitiable pictures of destitution that evidence discloses, and, having done this, let him vote against the out-door relief, proposed by the ministry, IF HE CAN!

The subject, however, of this extension of the poor law is one that must demand from us a separate discussion upon a future occasion. While, however, for any ordinary destitution existing in the country, we believe such a poor law to be the proper remedy, we cannot too strongly reiterate our conviction of the monstrous injustice of applying its provisions to meet the necessities of an extraordinary visitation. So long as the temporary relief act is in force, the out-door relief provisions of the poor law will obviously not be in force. They will, in fact, be carried into effect by a different arrangement, and, we earnestly hope, by funds provided from a different source;[63] but, by present arrangements, the provisions of the temporary relief act expire on the 1st October next. If we be right—as we have shown to demonstration that we are—that the pressure of extraordinary distress will not pass away with the next harvest—that in all probability three millions of people less by those whom famine and the pestilence and emigration has removed, will still be in want of their ordinary food—it is plain that to throw the support of them upon the poor rates of next year, will be to plunge all classes in Ireland into confusion, embarrassment, and distress. To the very success of the great measure of justice and humanity which ministers have introduced, it is essential that the powers of the temporary relief act should be continued until after the next meeting of parliament—it is equally essential that the funds necessary for carrying out that act should not be raised from the poor rates of the year.

Earnestly do we entreat of the owners of land in Ireland to look after these things. Measures that may involve the confiscation of their entire estates—measures that will involve it, unless properly guarded and accompanied, are in progress; measures which may, indeed, if well administered, be the means of raising Ireland from her abject state of poverty and degradation, but which, ill-administered, will ruin the landlords without benefiting the people. It is for them now to press the just claims of their country and themselves upon the ministry and the nation; making common cause with the people in their demand, that by vigorous and imperial efforts the calamity that now afflicts Ireland may be met; but we warn them, they must not shrink from admitting their readiness and their liability to bear all obligations which belong to property in England, and then they may with justice and reason demand, that in this extraordinary emergency, their country shall receive the same assistance which, under a similar calamity, any portion of England would, most undoubtedly, receive.

Intermediately in character between the Temporary Relief Act and such measures as the new Poor Law—between the measures by which the present necessity is to be met, and those by which the future state of Ireland is to be regulated—there are measures which deserve consideration—measures which we believe ought to be adopted—which will at once relieve, in some degree, the pressure of the present distress—facilitate the progress of the country through the transition through which it must pass—and assist in laying the foundation of her prosperity in a future, and what wise measures will make a better and a happier state of things.

The measures of this character which have been suggested may, perhaps, be classed under three heads. Measures to improve the country, by facilitating the construction of railways; measures to facilitate emigration of the destitute; and, lastly, measures to increase the productiveness of the soil by the reclamation of waste lands, or the improvement of those already under cultivation.

Our readers who have followed us so far, and who feel, perhaps, that we have trespassed unreasonably upon their time, will not expect from us a full discussion of the large subjects that questions upon such measures involve. It is the difficulty of considering Ireland's present condition, that to deal with it aright subjects must be taken into account of the most varied and the most comprehensive character. No partial or narrow view of her circumstances will suffice. This is the penalty of years of neglect. Had the whole social state of Ireland been reviewed in 1836, when the Report of the Poor Law Inquiry disclosed the destitution of great masses of her people, we would not need now to crowd the page of remedial suggestions with subjects involving all interests in the country. But the malady under which Ireland labours, produced, though it may be now by an accident, is not the result of that accident alone, but an aggravation of long settled constitutional disease. True it is, the immediate evil of the accident must be met; but no man can venture to prescribe the remedy, who will not estimate the effects of the constitutional derangement, and frame the remedy with regard to its effects upon the system of the patient. Recovered health assuredly will only follow the application of the remedies that will improve the constitution, as well as cure the temporary malady of the patient. Indeed in the social, as in physical science, it is vain to attempt to recover the temporary malady without checking the constitutional disease.

As to measures for promoting the construction of railways. Scarcely had parliament assembled, when Lord George Bentinck, to whom appears to have been awarded by unanimous consent, the place of leader to the party now termed the Protectionist party in the House of Commons, in conjunction with Mr. Hudson,[64] a name celebrated in the annals of railway enterprise, introduced "a bill to stimulate the prompt and profitable employment of the people, by the encouragement of railways in Ireland." This measure proposed an advance of sixteen millions, to be distributed among such Irish railways as could give the security of the expenditure of capital to half the amount required from the state. With the debate and the votes that followed, Ireland is unhappily too familiar.

Prominent among the measures which—IF RUIN IS TO BE AVERTED FROM IRELAND—must be passed in conjunction with any such enactments as the Temporary Relief Act, we place some measure similar in its provisions to that of Lord George Bentinck. It is impossible to add anything to the facts and reasoning by which the noble lord supported the measures he introduced. It is impossible, let us add, for any to appreciate that noble lord in the character of a statesman, who has not read and studied his masterly speech—the title of which we have prefixed to this article. We cannot say the speech failed to bring conviction to the mind of the House of Commons; unfortunately, however, it failed in commanding votes. With surprise, we confess, and grief, we number among the opponents of the measure it advocated, Sir Robert Peel.

The measure of Lord George Bentinck would have given relief to all grades and classes of the Irish nation, without costing the British Treasury one penny. It would have employed our destitute labourers; it would have stimulated our stagnant trade; developed the resources of our soil, about to be subjected to novel and unprecedented burdens; and poured into Ireland, rapidly and yet naturally, an amount of capital, productively employed, that would have arrested the evil effects of the present calamity upon her commerce and her trade.

It is impossible to bestow too much or too high praise on the speech of Lord George Bentinck in introducing this bill.[65] It was spoken in a spirit worthy of the best days of British statesmanship, with a reliance upon the energies of the country, to which, in better days, a British House of Commons would proudly have responded, and in a generous spirit to Ireland, that proved the difference between genuine and mock liberality to this country—between the liberality which contents itself with taking privilege from one class of the people to give it to another, and the liberality that sympathizes with the distress, vindicates the character, and would employ the resources of the empire for the benefit of all.

These qualities we value almost more than the unanswerable demonstration, the clear argument, and the accurate knowledge by which he proved the case he had undertaken to make out. It is impossible to read that speech without being convinced of the shortsightedness of the policy, and the wastefulness of the economy which refused to Ireland this aid. One of the railways now stopped for want of funds traverses near the doomed district of Skibbereen; another runs to the shores of Bantry Bay: two more traverse the most destitute districts of the west—districts in which hundreds of thousands have been lavished from the imperial treasury, upon useless roads, and in which yet famine numbers its victims by thousands.

That speech incontestably proved, that for the return of the sixteen millions to be advanced under the proposed regulations, the Irish railways would afford ample security—it established the fact, that wherever railways have been constructed, civilization and wealth have sprung up; and it showed, that in the increased consumption of excisable articles, the revenue would permanently gain to an extent almost impossible to calculate, while in the very sums that were to be expended in the purchase of land, and paid over to the landlords and the occupiers of estates, new means of employment would be given—let us add, new means of impetus to the general trade and industry of Ireland.

Upon the employment of the people we must permit the speech to speak for itself: –

> Suffice it for me that this great fact stares us in the face, that at this moment there are 500,000 able-bodied persons in Ireland living upon the funds of the state; that there are 500,000 able-bodied persons

commanded by a staff of 11,537 persons, employed upon works which have been variously described as 'works worse than idleness;' by the yeomanry of Ulster, as 'public follies;' and by the Inspector of the Government himself, Colonel Douglas, as 'works which will answer no other purpose than that of obstructing the public conveyances.'[66] Sir, I say that I feel with others that a great calamity is overhanging Ireland; but at the same time I cannot say that I look with any despondency at the present state of affairs. Sir, I do hope that we, who in former times have arisen from difficulties far greater than these, shall not be appalled at a calamity which consists in the loss of property to the value of £10,000,000 sterling; that we who at one period of the war were expending, upon an average for three years, £103,000,000 sterling a year, will not be down-hearted at having to provide for a deficiency and for a disaster that may be estimated at £10,000,000. On the contrary, sir, I look with confident hope that good will rise out of evil, and that so far from lying down and weeping over our misfortune, like children lost in a wood, we shall have the spirit to look our difficulties fairly in the face, and to be resolved to exercise a firm determination to overcome them.

The great question now arises, and it is this: How many men can you, by your scheme, find employment for? We know by experience—at least I know by information received from Mr. Stephenson,[67] the engineer of the line—that the London and Birmingham Railway employed 100 men per mile in its construction, for four consecutive years. The London and Birmingham line, however, was one far more expensive in its works than the Irish lines, of which the outside average cost is estimated at £16,000 per mile. The estimate of Mr. Stephenson is, that, taking one line with another throughout Ireland, to execute the whole of them would require the services of sixty men per mile for four consecutive years. Sixty men per mile, for 1500 miles, would give constant employment, for four consecutive years, to 90,000 men on the earthworks and line alone (hear, hear); but it is estimated that the employment given to quarrymen, artificers, and others, not actually engaged on the line of road, would occupy six men per mile for the whole number of miles under construction. This would give 9000 men more, to which is to be added—that which experience teaches is the fact—that when a new railway passes through a country, the new fences to be made, the fields to be squared, the new drains and courses to be cut, and the new roads to be constructed, also occupy at least six men per mile, making altogether a total number of 108,000 men. But there are other miscellaneous employments to which the expenditure of so large a sum of money gives rise, and it is thought to be putting the number very low when we estimate the able-bodied men required to be employed at high wages, in order to accomplish 1500 miles of railway in Ireland at 110,000, representing, with their families, 550,000 persons (hear, hear). Then, Sir, if, as I have shown, without cost to this country, and in the end adding greatly to the wealth of this country, we could by such a measure as this, for four consecutive years, feed, by means of good wages to the heads of families, 550,000 of the population of Ireland, it must be admitted that we should go a great way in assisting my noble friend to carry out his new Poor Law Amendment scheme for Ireland.

If there be truth in the views we have urged, as to the continuance of the necessity for exertion; if next year, and the year after, must feel the effects of the famine of last year; if we have truly pointed out the dangers of the Temporary Relief Act, and the extension of the poor law, with what almost immeasurable force do all these arguments apply! How overwhelming is the demonstration that if we could avert ruin from all classes in Ireland; some measure resembling in all its main features, if not identical with, Lord George Bentinck's rejected measure, must be passed!

It is impossible to do justice to the argument of this speech, without quoting the entire. The immense increase which railways have always secured to the productive powers of the country—the stimulus which the very example of their formation gives to enterprise—these arguments were all urged, and urged in vain.

No other measure has been suggested that will give a stimulus to trade. To one feature of Ireland's coming misery, even at the risk of being deemed prophets of alarm, and perhaps meeting the fate which the selfishness of those that aim at ease too often awards to the unprofitable predictions of Cassandra,[68] it is our solemn duty to call attention—we mean the certain ruin that awaits a large number of the shopkeepers and small traders of the country. It was singular that a long interval elapsed, before the distress that had visited the poorer classes in Ireland, so far reached the high as to interrupt the ordinary operations of trade. This was because the people, whose food was withheld, were, as we have said, beyond the pale of the ordinary mercantile system. Those within that pale proceeded in their ordinary routine, scarcely being conscious that these wretched beings were left without their ordinary sustenance. This could not last. As the gentry became gradually aware of the full extent of the misery that surrounded them, their expenditure on all but works of charity was stayed, or in a great degree curtailed. By the beginning of the new year trade began sensibly to feel the effects of the alarm. By the middle of the month of March, so far had the stagnation proceeded, that houses of the first respectability, in the leading streets in Dublin, have closed their establishments on a Saturday night, *without having effected one pound's sale during the week*. Tradesmen in every department are dismissing the workmen from their employment. These workmen who last year were happy and independent, supporting themselves by their labour, will, in a few weeks from the time in which we write, be an additional burden to the rates of the Temporary Relief Act. While such of their masters as had some little capital stored, are at this moment living upon it; such of these as have not, have no resource before them but the *Insolvent Calendar* and the poor-house.

All this portion of the calamity could have been avoided, had the measure proposed by Lord George Bentinck been passed. It may yet be avoided, if some measure like that be yet enacted. Such a promise of good to our country *would have given heart to all classes*; and who is there can overrate the value and importance of this, in a calamity like the present. Hands that now hang listless, would have moved to active employment—hearts that now despair, would have beat to the pulses of energetic and stirring exertion. Who can estimate in millions of pounds, the value of inspiring courage and confidence, at this fearful crisis, in the Irish people?

But again we are driven to ask, where is the public opinion, where is the public spirit of Ireland?
Not many years ago we remember when Ireland's nobility and leading merchants summoned the citizens of Dublin to a meeting, to call on government to construct railways in Ireland, when no such pressing necessity existed as there does now? Why have we not now a requisition to call forth the voice of the nation in favour of such a measure as Lord George Bentinck's bill; in the name of our starving people we ask the question. There have been occasions upon which the peers and the gentry of Ireland, in their respective parties, have stood forward in imposing requisitions to convene meetings for party purposes, to express the opinions which they honestly held; for once, let party feuds be merged; let class interests be forgotten; let a great requisition summon Irishmen to demand that assistance to her railways which even yet may save Ireland from ruin, and no ministry will take on themselves the responsibility of refusing their sanction to a measure like Lord George Bentinck's bill.

It is in no spirit of invidious signalizing of individual defaulters, in the midst of national neglect, that we ask, where is the Duke of Leinster,[69] with the honours and the responsibilities of the descendant of the Geraldines upon his head? Where is the Marquis of Ormond,[70] with a descent at least equally illustrious in the history of Ireland? Why does Lord Glengall[71] content himself with a letter as Chairman of the Waterford and Limerick railway company, pointing out to the English Treasury the number of men that company could profitably employ!! or Lord Rosse[72] with publishing those admirable letters to which, though sent with the name of the noble lord, an English journalist refuses to give a place in his columns. Let these four men head a requisition convening a meeting in this very month, in the city of Dublin, to petition parliament for aid—large and liberal aid—to Ireland in her present distress, and we are bold to say that, responded to as that requisition will be, no English minister will dare to take on himself the responsibility of refusing it.

Demanding for Ireland that the government should now give large and liberal assistance to the speedy construction of railways in the country, we pass to the next class of measures which have been suggested as necessary for the transition state through which Ireland must pass; that class of measures includes those which propose

## II. A LARGE ENCOURAGEMENT TO EMIGRATION.

Emigration is not, perhaps, a popular word—we do not wonder that in Ireland it should not be so, because it has hitherto been associated with the loss of the best and bravest of her people. So long as emigration is left to the unaided efforts of the emigrants themselves, it must be the natural result that the most industrious and most enterprising of our peasantry should be those who would hazard the adventure of a new world. Emigration, besides, requires some little expenditure to make it productive; and in former years it has been our duty, in the pages of this very periodical, to point the attention of our rulers to the tide of emigration which was rapidly draining Ireland of her Protestant population—the yeomanry of Ulster. To recommend emigration, too, appears to favour the harsh doctrine of political economists, which represents the increase of population as the origin of all the evils of the human race. The recommendation may be answered by many specious arguments, and met by many plausible appeals to facts.

Nevertheless, emigration was from the beginning the destiny assigned to the human race—"Be fruitful and multiply, AND REPLENISH THE EARTH," was the Creator's primeval command to the family of man. It is in truth the necessary condition of his existence upon earth. How much of all the misery we deplore in the state of civilized society may, perhaps, be traced to the neglect of the primeval injunction of our race. Men are crowded in the manufactories of Lancaster or the alleys of London, while wide plains of South America—the fairest portion of the globe—are untrodden by the foot of man; human beings have been for years famishing in Ireland for lack of food, while one valley on the Mississippi lies uncultivated, that would raise corn enough to supply the whole human race with food. Men have been fruitful, and they have multiplied, but they have not replenished the earth.

Attention has been latterly turned to emigration, as a means not only of relieving the present distress of Ireland—to that task it is inadequate—but as a means of enabling the country to pass through the ordeal that is yet before it. Lord Ashburton and Lord Ripon, in the House of Lords, have expressed themselves favourable to such a plan. Mr. Murray, Mr. Shafto Adair, and Colonel Torrens, have urged strongly in the pamphlets the titles of which we have prefixed, the necessity of encouraging emigration. Among the English journals, the *Morning Herald* has recommended the adoption of a system of emigration,[73] with equal perseverance and ability; and to the advocates of an extended emigration—although his valuable letters on the state of Ireland were not written directly with reference to this subject—we can add, on the testimony of these letters, the honoured name of the Earl of Rosse.

The policy, the actual necessity of emigration from Ireland, is, indeed, so obvious, that it needs only to look fairly at the actual condition of the country to be aware of its indispensable importance. The difference to which we have already adverted between the quantity of ground necessary to give sustenance to a human being on a corn and on a potato diet, is in itself demonstration, that it is impossible for the country to pass from the one mode of subsistence to the other—and pass, we believe it must—without the most fearful suffering and confusion, if its present population continue to crowd its soil. Apart, however, from the present circumstances of Ireland, the population of the country has been too dense, not for its capabilities of supporting them, if properly called forth, but too dense for the circumstances in which the country has been placed. Ireland, to support eight millions of people, would have required, at least, all her present agricultural produce, and many other things besides. We should have had the accumulated products of the industry of many former years—works upon which former generations had spent their savings—factories in which the savings of the present would enable the owners to advance food and sustenance to thousands of workmen, who now are wretched squatters on her bogs or her fields; a soil highly improved, the result of a long and careful tillage, farmsteads provided with all the appliances of high and successful cultivation, and all the means of large expenditure within the reach of the farmer; we should, in a word, have in the hands of all the different classes of society what political economists have called capital; we should have the whole country filled with the accumulated products of by-gone industry, and more than this, we should have a population trained to skill, and taught in industrious occupations. Were Ireland such a country as this, it could support, from its natural resources, far more than its present population. But how different from such an Ireland is the Ireland with which we have to deal—bare, naked, and unimproved!—no capital in the hands of its people—its population unskilled—its natural advantages unemployed—such an Ireland is incapable of supporting its present population.

Could we accomplish all these requisites in a day—could we give to the farmers all the appliances they would need for successful cultivation of the soil—could we endue them with knowledge so to apply them—could we stud our country with these evidences of capital, which must be the growth of the expenditure of years; and could we, after all these miracles of transforming the habits of our people—of enduing the wretched cottier with the skill of the artisan—of fitting our rural population for pursuits that are utterly opposed to the long-formed habits of their lives—then, indeed, the millions who now inhabit Ireland might be supported in comfort and independence within her shores; but if all this be but the dream of a fairy tale, to be used in sober argument only as an illustration of impracticability—and if the country, as it is now, cannot support its present population, what expedient is there but to remove a portion to scenes where energy and enterprise will raise for them a comfortable subsistence and a happy home.

What instance does the history of civilization afford of a country in which the population have multiplied, as they have done in Ireland, without the progress of these improvements which would have fitted the country to sustain them, emerging from such a state? The beginnings of improvement belong, in the natural order of a nation's progress, to a time when population is thin, and its advance should at least keep pace with the increase of numbers; but a dense population of paupers presents a problem in the economic condition of man, in which it is not easy to discover the means by which they are to rise from such a state. In every effort at improvement, they must be in each other's way. How forcibly is this felt in Ireland. What plans for social improvement does not the density of the population obstruct? Here is the evidence of Mr. Murray,*[74] to whose practical wisdom, and intimate acquaintance with the circumstances of the country, every one in Ireland will pay deference:—

> There is abundance of means, as regards money, intelligence, and energy, amongst the tenantry in Ireland, to improve the country and make it productive in proportion to its natural capabilities, but that tenantry so often stand in the way of each other as to render it impossible for a movement to be made. In every townland there is to be found, as in every other condition in life, one, two, three, or more men as tenants who, by reason of their greater intelligence, industry, and carefulness, are capable of holding positions greatly above those they now occupy; but they could not, and dare not, venture to extend their usefulness for their own benefit and that of their country, because they could only do so by the ejectment of their neighbours from their homes and places of refuge. Upon these men, and such as them, however, would devolve the regeneration of Ireland, if the way were prepared for them. Their savings, in place of being deposited in the National Savings' Banks of the country, the present place of safety, would soon be invested in the improvement of a grateful soil, as far more remunerative. The course of that improvement would be gradual,— but pave a course for it, and set it in motion, and like the stone in the proverb, its progress would be vastly accelerated as it proceeded. The labour to be afforded in this way would be natural—the wages of labour would be increased, and as these were permanently increased, and steady and continual employment obtained, emigration would naturally cease. The increased wages of labour would be amply compensated by the annually increasing produce of the soil, and each succeeding year would add to its productiveness.

We ask again, from what analogy are we to expect an overcrowded population of paupers to civilize themselves? In their very struggles for existence, they must, as has been finely said, trample each other down into indigence.

Mr. Shafto Adair, in his "Winter in Antrim,"[75] one of the ablest pamphlets which for many years has issued from the press, urges strongly the necessity for emigration, not only as a means of meeting the change that Ireland must pass through in losing the potato, but still more as a safe and necessary adjunct to the great social revolution which must be created by the new poor law act:—

> "And here I would distinguish between emigration—by which I understand the thrusting forth of unwelcome inmates from the parent home, as young ravens are driven into the wilderness—and colonization, by which systematic facility is afforded to industrious men to found, under other skies, British homes within the circumference of the British empire.
>
> I view, as among the worthiest objects of a statesman's ambition, the extension of the British race, and its institutions, through all lands. Broad regions lie ready for our occupancy: the crowded multitudes, who might find happy competences, and lead honoured lives in those yet unbroken solitudes, trample down each other in their fierce fight for existence on the over-burdened native soil. Many a brave heart has sighed forth its last during this dreadful winter, which might have animated, had it been cared for, another hardy settler to a British colony.
>
> Therefore systematic colonization must, for years to come, be adopted as a principle in the social management of Ireland; and the circumstances of the times, while they increase the facility, furnish additional proof of the necessity of such a step. . . . . . .
>
> The tendency of the new state of things will be to enlarge holdings, and to convert the cottiers into labourers. It is probable, therefore, that a much larger class, willing to emigrate, will crowd upon you, and that the newly-opened channels of employment may not be choked, it will be well to assist them. The Union has already power to assist in emigration; but the co-operation of government is necessary, in order to conciliate the public mind to the extensive assessment that would be necessary, even to the half of the actual outlay. The labouring poor should be taught to feel that colonization was not an engine for banishment, but to promote the positive well-being of the colonist; the ratepayer should be enabled to appreciate at once the prospective relief to be obtained by a partial expenditure of his contributions, for the purpose of relieving the labour market; and the government, as trustee for the empire, should take care that those whom the mother country could not employ, should find the means of honest subsistence in her scarcely-peopled colonies.
>
> But government alone, and unassisted public bodies, are not equal to the task of colonization, from which all possible benefits might be derived. The necessary funds should be furnished by the two parties to the operation—by the Union, in consideration of the actual relief, and as acting for the benefit of the pauper emigrant; and by the government, on

behalf of the empire, whose solid power is augmented by every emigrant transplanted to her colonial possessions."

Colonel Torrens,[76] long known and valued for his labours in the cause of emigration, has shown the possibility of locating a population much larger than could be taken away from Ireland, in British colonies. There may, indeed, be difficulties in providing for the support of a large number of emigrants when landed upon one of these colonial shores. But as we have already said, men cannot meet a famine, the like of which the world never saw, without difficulty. Those who wish for demonstration that it is possible, by a well-arranged system of colonization, to provide amply for the comfort and welfare of the emigrant, will find it in the admirable Essay of Colonel Torrens.

The *Morning Herald*, a journal which has advocated Irish interests always with generosity and ability, generally with accurate knowledge of the circumstances of this country, has recently referred to a very striking statement in the report of the commission to inquire into the state of the Irish poor. The statement and the comment embody, in clear and truthful language, facts of the utmost importance in estimating the value of emigration, either in relation to the general state of Ireland, or the measures that are in progress:—

The statement to which we refer is contained in the following passage, to be found in the first passage of the commissioners' report:—

> "It appears that in Great Britain the agricultural families constitute a little more than a fourth, while in Ireland they constitute about two-thirds of the whole population; that there were in Great Britain, in 1831, 1,055,982 agricultural labourers; in Ireland, 1,131,715. Although the cultivated land in Great Britain amounts to about 34,250,000 acres, and that of Ireland only to about 14,600,000, THERE ARE IN IRELAND ABOUT FIVE AGRICULTURAL LABOURERS FOR EVERY TWO THAT THERE ARE FOR THE SAME QUANTITY OF LAND IN GREAT BRITAIN."

> Thus we have in the outset the quantity of land that in this country would support two agricultural labourers, in Ireland supporting five. Suppose, then, the produce of that quantity in each country to be the same; suppose the share of the produce allotted to the reward of labour to be the same, and still you find the Irish labourer in a condition not half as comfortable as that of the English or Scotch. Some small, very small, allowance we know must be made in this calculation for the fact that the Irish agricultural labourer is himself, in many instances, the lessee and occupier of the soil, and so adds to his share what in England would be the profits of the farmer on this small holding; but the accuracy of the stubborn figures that supply the data of the calculation is indisputable.

But this supposition is far too favourable to the condition of the Irish labourer. The very same report supplies us with the means of calculating that *the quantity of land upon which, in Ireland, five labourers are located, produces very little more than half the value produced by the same quantity in England, upon which there are but two.* Here is the short statement of the miserable and depressed condition of the population of Ireland. Give to this state of facts what name you will—call it superabundant population—designate it as a want of efficiency in agricultural labour—describe it as want of capital—express it by the nomenclature of any favourite theory or science that you please, in the end you must come round to the plain stubborn statement of fact, that five agricultural labourers squat themselves upon a piece of ground in Ireland which, in England, would be tilled by two; and that, after all, there is raised from that piece of ground about half as much as is yielded by the corresponding piece in England.

Is it too much to say that here is demonstration that no measure of relief can permanently improve the condition of Ireland that does not contemplate, either by direct means, or indirectly as a consequence, the removal of no inconsiderable proportion of this agricultural population from the soil? Distribute as you will the produce of the land—nay, increase that produce as you will, and leave the five labourers still to receive the same share that two receive in England, and the destitution of Ireland is not removed. Increase the taxation of the poor law until you give each of the five as much as each of the two has in England, and you pauperize all classes. Will you leave 100,000 persons in Ireland depending upon agricultural labour more than there are in England so depending, no legislative enactment can raise the condition of the Irish labourers to a level with ours. The importance of the statement we have quoted from the commissioners' report it is impossible to over-rate. It is the key to Ireland's destitution; it is the warning of the dangers that must attend the attempt to relieve Irish distress by the mere enactment of a poor law; in our minds, it points to the safe and practicable remedy. What is that remedy? We say with Mr. Murray, in the able and well-timed pamphlet with which we have already made our readers familiar, 'in one word—emigration.' If the plainest calculations of arithmetic can be relied on—if the rules of addition and subtraction be not cheats— you cannot permit the present population still to prey upon the soil, and hope to see the country elevated to a level with England. What is to be done with those whom you must remove, in a country where there are no manufacturers to receive them, even were they fit for such employment—where they are too numerous to be located on the waste lands, even were all the waste lands capable of being reclaimed? No dictate of common sense appears more axiomatic than that which would prompt us to remove this population to those fruitful and vast plains of other regions in which man has yet new conquests to make, and new stores of subsistence to command. Shall one grand effort be made to do this now, when the people will co-operate with us; or shall we permit this wretched population to continue to trample each other down into indigence, until insulted nature vindicates her own laws, and periodical visitations of famine, and its sure attendant, pestilence, depopulate an over-burdened and neglected land?

We stated, on Tuesday, our conviction, that were the circumstances of the Irish landlords prosperous, they would, at their own cost, avail themselves of the eagerness now manifested for emigration by their cottier tenants. We have heard, and we believe with truth, of one Irish nobleman (better known, however, as an English statesman) whose agents have actually contracted for the removal to Canada, at his expense, of 2,000 persons, cottier tenants, and their families, who have thankfully accepted the boon that removes them from destitution to a region where their industry will find them bread.

There is not an estate in Ireland upon which, to a greater or less extent, the same offer, made in a kindly spirit, and with proper additions, would not now be received as a boon. Once more we ask of our rulers, shall the opportunity be lost?"

We have quoted this statement at length, because, while we do not entirely assent to all its reasonings, we feel that it forcibly calls attention to one great fact in the economic condition of Ireland, which must never be forgotten or overlooked, we mean the superabundance of the agricultural population on the soil of Ireland, compared either with its produce or the necessities of its cultivation. In every consideration of Ireland's condition, in every proposition for the improvement of the country, this fact meets us as one of the landmarks of her social state.

Foremost among the advocates for emigration we must place Mr. Murray. He it was who first called attention to the fact, that this year the small holders of land in Ireland *were, for the first time as a body, willing to emigrate*. By how many evidences this is now confirmed, no one who has watched the progress of events in Ireland needs be told. Every seaport is crowded with emigrants, leaving behind them this land of horrors. The neglect of tillage, which Mr. Labouchere was led to charge as a crime upon the people of some districts,[77] proceeded from their determination to depart from the country. Such few of the landlords as have the means, are now doing that which in former years no price could have commanded ridding their estates of the pauper tenants for whose location upon them they never were responsible. Miserable in Ireland, these very people will, in another state of social existence, exhibit qualities of industry, of enterprise, and of prudence, which no one could have dreamed of discovering in the listless or turbulent idler here, while their departure will leave room for others of their countrymen to exhibit the same qualities at home. One extract from Mr. Murray's pamphlet we cannot refrain from the satisfaction of quoting. Let us see what we may expect from our people when fair open is given to the fine qualities, moral and physical, with which nature has endowed them. It is a passage in which the writer feelingly details the remittances which Irish emigrants are in the habit of sending across the Atlantic to their relatives at home :—

> "You have been accustomed," he says, addressing the statesman to whom he writes, "to grapple with and master figures, whether as representing the produce of former tariffs, or in constructing new ones, or in showing the income and expenditure of the greatest nation on the earth. Those now about to be presented to you, as an appendix to this communication, are small, very small, in their separate amounts, and not by any means in the aggregate of the magnitude of the sums you have been accustomed to deal with; but they are large separately, and heaving large in the aggregate, in all that is connected with the higher and nobler parts of our nature—in all that relates to and evinces the feeling of the heart towards those who are of our kindred, no matter by what waters placed asunder, or by what distance separated. They are large, powerfully large, in reading lessons of instruction to the statesman and philanthropist, in dealing with a warm-hearted people for their good, and in placing them in a position of comparative comfort to that in which they now are. These figures represent the particulars of 7,917 separate Bills of Exchange, varying in amount from £1 to £10 each—few exceeding the latter sum; so many separate offerings from the natives of Ireland who have heretofore emigrated from its shores, sent to their relations and friends in Ireland, drawn and paid between the 1st of January and the 15th of December, 1846—not quite one year; and amount in all to £41,261 9s. 11d. But this list, long though it be, does not measure the number and amount of such interesting offerings. It contains only about one-third part of the whole number and value of such remittances that have crossed the Atlantic to Ireland during the 349 days of 1846. The data from which this list is compiled enable the writer to estimate with confidence the number and amount drawn otherwise; and he calculates that the entire number, for not quite one year, of such bills, is 24,000, and the amount £125,000, or, on an average, £5 4s. 2d. each. They are sent from husband to wife, from father to child, from child to father, mother, and grand-parents, from sister to brother, and the reverse; and from and to those united by all the ties of blood and friendship that binds us together on earth."

Who will not assent to the justice of his comment ?—

> "These remittances show by evidence incontrovertible that it is the want of opportunity alone that prevents the population of Ireland from raising itself, and becoming prosperous. That opportunity cannot, as Ireland is

circumstanced, be given at home; let it be afforded elsewhere. If Ireland were not 'sea-girded,' would the population have become what it is? Certainly not: it would long ago have relieved itself.

If we turn from the physical capacity of the population, as strongly manifested by these remittances, to raise itself, so as to enable it to support relations and friends, to the evidence which is afforded by them of the moral qualities of the population, there is proof equally incontestable of the heart of that population being in the right place. The first savings of labour are sent to aid those who were nursed in the same arms, and reared under the same roofs, with the emigrants, or to those who nursed and reared them."

Imperfect, of necessity, as has been our review of the facts and arguments that incontrovertibly establish the absolute necessity for extended emigration from this country, we have sufficiently examined the subject to demonstrate, that among the remedial measures for Ireland, emigration or colonization must hold a prominent place. The enormous voluntary emigration that is this year taking place, evidences how favourable is the opportunity. Unhappily, however, this emigration is just of the class that it is desirable to keep at home. Those who are able to leave the country without assistance are persons who must take with them means and enterprise that the country can but ill spare. The landlords share too deeply in the calamity of the visitation, to be able in general to give to their other tenants the means of removing themselves and their families.

After all, might not the best charity be, when we have failed in bringing the food to the people, to spend our money in enabling the people to go to the food. The ships that are bringing us provisions from beyond the Atlantic, might thus, in their transit each way, feed the hungry—on one passage bringing the corn to the land of famine—on the other, taking the people from the land of famine to the corn.

Emigration cannot, however, be carried on so as effectually to relieve the condition of Ireland, without assistance from the state. Unfortunately in this, as in other matters relating to the present state of Ireland, time, precious time, has been lost, that can never be recalled. We know that it is impossible for the government, as a government, to interfere in emigration to any but colonies of their own; we know also that government cannot be expected to undertake to superintend the shipment of emigrants to those colonies, without having made proper provision for them on their arrival—all this we know and feel, and, therefore, we fear that, in this year, it is vain to look for any very extended system of colonization from Ireland. To some extent, even this year, it may be carried. In some, at least, of the colonies, the colonists are even now ready to receive emigrants, as farm labourers, upon terms upon which our poor people would be happy to go; and it is not easy to calculate the number who, even this year, government might thus locate. But why should not government at once assist with the means any landlords who will be willing to give to their cottier tenants the means of emigration, leaving to the parties themselves the entire responsibility of selecting the place of destination. This, we believe might safely be done this year, supplementary to any direct amount of colonization which government might take upon themselves.

Valuable opportunities will unquestionably have been lost in the present year; but next year they will recur. The effects of the famine will not pass away for years. And next year will witness a readiness for emigration similar to the present. The administration of the new poor law ought to be so managed that no person who continues to be the holder of land should be entitled to relief. The opportunities for promoting voluntary emigration will not soon pass away. It will rest with the British ministry to be prepared to avail themselves of them. In every colony of Great Britain, preparations should be made to receive as many as possible of those who, next year as well as this, will be prepared to accept thankfully the means of transit from Ireland. Canada, Australia, New Zealand, the Cape of Good Hope, and even Ceylon, may all be ready to afford a home to some. But why should new colonies be formed? Is the splendid territory at last peaceably secured to us in the Oregon to remain a waste?[78] Why should not a British and an Irish colony people that splendid country, which the early habits of those who would emigrate from Ireland would fit them to till. We expose, perhaps, our plan to the hazard of objections, by entering into these details. It is not possible for any man, without the information of a colonial minister, to fix the locality or localities to which the surplus population should be removed. Enough for us to prove that the well-being of Ireland demands that her agricultural population should be made less dense—that unless it be so, the measures intended for her improvement can only perpetuate and deepen her poverty—and that in the present circumstances of the country an opportunity is offered of removing, with their own full consent, such a portion of the overcrowded population of Ireland as will leave room at home for the enterprise and energies of those who are left, to make Ireland a prosperous nation; while those who are thus removed will provide the colonies of Great Britain with a bold, an ingenious, and as they have ever proved themselves, under happier circumstances, an energetic and industrious race.

It remains with us to say a few words upon the third class of measures to which we have adverted :—

III. Measures for improving the productiveness or extending the surface of the cultivated land in Ireland.

Upon the first of these objects we have, in a great degree, anticipated our comment. The Drainage Act of last year supplies,[79] unquestionably, most valuable facilities for the permanent improvement of estates; and were the suggestion followed, of permitting proprietors and farmers to relieve the burden of the

Temporary Relief Act, by taking the labourers to works of profitable occupation, giving some similar security for the repayment to that which we have suggested, we believe much might be done this year in making the soil of Ireland more productive. Let government, however, by offering facilities for emigration, give the opportunity of removing the cottier paupers, who have hitherto kept the land less than half tilled—let them increase the demand for the produce of the soil by a general measure of railways to facilitate intercourse through the country, and the permanently improved cultivation of the soil of Ireland may safely be left to the energies of the people themselves.

The question of the reclamation of the waste lands is one of difficulty and magnitude. The exact nature of the measure which ministers intend to propose upon the subject we do not know. It will involve, probably, the power of taking these lands from the owners who have not the means or the capacity to improve them, and the improvement of them at the expense of the state. In the waste lands of the country will be found, to a very great extent, the means at present of usefully employing the labour we must purchase, and the means permanently of locating in comfortable circumstances a portion of that population, which Ireland, in the existing state of her agriculture, is no longer able even to feed. In the same waste lands may, perhaps, be found the means of establishing in the country a class of yeomen proprietors, if it be desirable to establish them—a proposition, we confess, of which we have serious doubts.

In whatever way, or by whatever tenure, the reclaimed lands are to be disposed of, their reclamation does appear the plainest and the most obvious of all remedial measures for Ireland. It must not be forgotten that almost all the measures which are now called for Ireland are, as Mr. P. Scrope observes,[80] the procrastinated measures of former years. Emigration and the reclamation of the waste lands were urged upon the ministry of 1837, as remedies for the state of Ireland, without which the poor law of that year would be a mockery—they were urged in the insulted and discarded report of the Commissioners of Poor Law Inquiry, the suggestions of which Lord John Russell contemptuously flung aside, to legislate for Ireland upon the report of a six weeks' inspection.[81] If out-door relief is now alarming the more timid of the Irish proprietors—if Irish distress is now embarassing the British ministry, let us remind both of the legislation of 1837. An opportunity then presented itself of improving permanently the condition of the Irish nation. A royal commission had then deliberately suggested the calm and careful consideration of the very measures of emigration and reclamation of the waste lands, which will now be carried into effect by an agitated parliament and a terrified proprietary. From comprehensive measures, the responsibility of which they feared, the ministry of that day escaped by Mr. Nicholls and the workhouses;[82] but look back to the debates, and see what evidence is there of the Irish representatives urging upon the nation the measures that then ought to have been taken to raise the condition of the Irish people—what do we find? miserable debates about details, and, on the part of some, a mere vain attempt—as there is now—to resist the obligation of a poor-law—an attempt which failed then as it has failed now, and only damaged the character of those who made it, and with them, unfortunately, the character of the Irish gentry.

It is impossible to read the letter of Mr. Poulett Scrope and the evidence selected by him from that taken by Lord Devon's commission,[83] without being convinced that in the waste lands of Ireland, of which there are about a million and a-half of acres reclaimable for tillage purposes, and nearly two millions and a-half for that of pasture—there is a resource to which we may confidently look for the support of a considerable portion of the population for whom, in the social revolution through which Ireland is passing, we must provide a subsistence and a home. To believe, however, that upon those waste lands can be located the whole, or even anything like a large proportion of her rural surplus population, is an exaggeration of the wildest and most mischievous character. No! we must have—unpleasant, perhaps, as the conclusion is—we must have colonization abroad. All men who have turned their attention to the state of Ireland, have felt the evil of her overburdened agricultural population. Schemes, apparently the most opposite, all have reference to this one giant mischief of our state. Home colonization, and foreign colonization, or emigration, however apparently different, are just the same in principle—an attempt to locate that population elsewhere than upon the soil they now overcrowd. To the sense of the same ever present evil may be traced the attempts that have been made to turn a portion of that population to manufacturing pursuits, by reviving or establishing native manufactures. The mind is slow in receiving the conviction which we have endeavoured in a previous part of this article to express, that a dense population, steeped in pauperism, can never extricate themselves from the degradation of their condition, until a portion of them are removed.

We have, however, land at home, upon which some, at least, of that population may be located; obvious indeed is the policy which prompts the selection of this home soil for their location, and collateral with the extensive colonization of our people abroad, we earnestly hope that measures will be introduced to reclaim and appropriate to the use of man, the extensive tracts which now lie waste and unproductive, within the circle of our shores.

We have concluded the task which we assigned to ourselves in reviewing the sad history of the famine, and suggesting the measures by which the evils of Ireland may be met. Unreasonable as is, perhaps, the space which this article has occupied of the pages of this periodical—unreasonable, certainly, were the question we have discussed, one less vital than the very existence of our country—we feel how wholly inadequate and imperfect has been our consideration of the matters we have included in our review. We feel, too, that in suggesting so much of detail as we have done in these pages, we have exposed the plans we recommend to cavils which a more prudent adherence to a general outline might have escaped. If, however, the general outline of the measures we have suggested be just, and expedient, and right—let those who quarrel with any particular items of our plan—remember that until the general principles we have put forward can be displaced, our argument is not affected, by showing that the writer of those pages has not the information, or perhaps the capacity, to shape these measures into unexceptionable detail.

No doubt the measures we have pressed will involve an advance, to no inconsiderable amount, of the money or the credit of the state—a little more, perhaps, as a loan, than Ireland and England jointly gave as a gift to carry out the project of negro emancipation.[84] All our measures are based upon the principle that this calamity ought to be regarded as an imperial one, and borne by the empire at large. If this be not conceded—if the state be not, as we have said, our government—if we are not to receive the assistance which government can render upon such an occasion—what alternative is there for any Irishman but to feel that the united parliament has abdicated the functions of government for Ireland, and to demand for his country that separate legislative existence, the necessity of which will then be fully proved.

It is true, no doubt, that the united empire can bring to the task resources far greater than any which a separate Irish government or parliament could command. But for a partnership in such extended resources—individuals first, and small communities afterwards—consent to lose their particular existence, or merge it in the combination of mighty states. These are the occasions upon which may be realized the memorable words of Pitt,[85] in advocating that very Union, the first principle of which those who would throw this burden exclusively upon Ireland assail—that "we have all a greater stake in the strength and prosperity of the empire at large, than we can have in any petty and separate interest of its component parts."

There is not one of the measures we have proposed which would not abundantly repay the imperial exchequer twice over—we say not in the increased strength of the empire—in the changed condition of Ireland—but estimated in pounds, shillings, and pence, in the increased revenue which, with our improved condition, our people would pay. No more profitable investment for state expenditure than Ireland now presents, was ever offered to the exchequer of a great nation.

To a liberal and generous policy to Ireland, the next few years will bring returns in the peace, the content, and the prosperity of this country, which no calculations of finance can measure, and for which no expenditure can be too great—but even in the legers of the financier a very short period will, in the increased contributions to the revenue which rising opulence will bring, blot out the largest entries of expenditure for which the measures we have demanded could call, and leave on the other side of the account a perpetual source of income and strength.

Estimated even by the low considerations of finance, no draught which the permanent improvement of Ireland demands upon the imperial exchequer ought now to be refused. Considerations of a higher character than these leave no doubt of the course that the nation is bound to pursue. The first duties of government imperatively require the effort of which present circumstances present the opportunity to raise Ireland in the scale of civilization. To avert, as far as human efforts can, the terrible calamity of famine, were a task to which one might think we would not summon the government of England in vain, were the sufferers the inhabitants of the remotest island upon which the flag of England was ever planted. To raise the condition of Ireland, so that the fearful occurrences of last year may never again disgrace the civilized world, is surely an object upon which all the energies of the empire might be well employed. Contemplate the stupendous exertions of England in the continental war, and we cannot help asking, in amazement, whether the nation that made these exertions is now permitting—when her means, with her opulence and her population, are doubled—is permitting her own subjects and kindred to perish at her very door?

When gigantic subsidies were then voted to the allies of Britain abroad—or mighty fleets and armaments fitted out—the arguments were not heard that the raising of the necessary sums would derange the money market upon 'Change.[86] This was yet the argument, the only argument by which Lord George Bentinck's bill was met. Were Ireland in rebellion instead of famine, and the money asked for an armament to conquer her, would this argument have prevailed? Miserable and short-sighted policy, even of finance! It never entered into the calculations of those who adopted it, to consider whether the ruin of all classes in Ireland would bring no derangement to the money market upon 'Change.

The assistance we ask for is a matter of humanity, of prudence, of duty; but it is more—it is, by the treaty of Union, a matter of national faith. To the claims of prudence, humanity, and duty, are superadded those of good faith—with Englishmen, perhaps, the strongest of all. All measures that have yet been proposed by ministers are framed upon the principle that Ireland herself must bear the burden of this unprecedented visitation; while the aid that imperial credit might afford her for the development of her own resources is either altogether refused, or given in so niggardly and procrastinating a dole that it becomes useless. A perseverance in this principle, short-sighted, narrow-minded, and unjust as it is, is the sentence of confiscation to the property of Ireland, and of beggary and ruin to all classes of her people. If Ireland be left to struggle through the crisis which now agonizes her, with such measures and such assistance as have been offered, it is not difficult to foresee the embarrassment and confusion that must come upon all. We have traced already the process by which the loss of the people's food has spread upwards through society, until the calamity is now beginning to be felt by all. From the gentry to the tradesman, from the tradesman to the merchant, embarrassment and distress are, at this moment, silently perhaps, but surely, spreading. We do not now reiterate the arguments by which we have shewn the inevitable result of leaving Ireland to grapple, unaided, with the giant malady that afflicts her. The process of national ruin is one not difficult to trace. In the ruin of the landed interest, the downfall of all classes is involved; and at no distant day a universal bankruptcy will complete the horrors of Ireland's social revolution.

Is England prepared for this? Have English statesmen calculated its effect upon their own people? Let them not believe that Ireland can become one wide field of confusion and distress, and England not share in the calamity. Little, perhaps, as Englishmen may be disposed to think of the confiscation of the estates of the Irish gentry, and the confusion that such a process must bring upon all property in Ireland, they must not delude themselves with the idea that the process will not react fearfully on England herself. The monetary and commercial systems of this great empire have too many complications to admit of such a result. If Ireland be now left to her fate, the British empire itself may not stand the shock by which its stability will be tried.

In a thousand ways that no man can predict, the contiguity of such distress as we anticipate in Ireland will produce upon the sister country its disturbing and dangerous effects. Were we to look no further than the emigration into England of the destitute Irish to whom you are refusing to give the means of transportation to more distant lands, but who have not the means of living at home—take this one instance of the danger of the continuity of pauperism. The English people complain of it already. Let us wait, however, until the legitimate occasion for such immigration arises with the harvest, when annually the English farmer has to invoke their aid. What multitudes of reapers will next autumn see pouring upon your fields? What power on earth can prevent this? The Irish, indeed, are threatened with being sent back—nay those who send them menaced with persecution.[87] But statesmen will scarcely be prepared to treat Ireland like the ill-fated ship, the Eclaire,[88] and prevent her ill-fated inhabitants from escaping from the plague.

But these are physical and material instances, or emblems rather, of the manner in which Irish distress must act upon English prosperity. But the credit—the commerce of the two countries, are too deeply involved in mutual complications, to permit Irish society to be convulsed by an economic revolution, without shaking the credit of the commercial and monetary system of England to its foundation. Who can calculate the ultimate financial embarrassment that all classes in England may now escape, by liberality in the expenditure of imperial resources upon this ill-fated land? If we be right in the views we have taken, that a liberal application of the imperial resources is necessary to avert ruin from Ireland, then is it matter of demonstration, that the effect of a niggard policy towards Ireland will be, in permitting the evils of famine to eat away the fabric of Irish society, to cause it to undermine the fabric of British prosperity itself.

Were, then, the advances our plans involve ten times larger than those which they can possibly require, still all the considerations of prudence, of duty, of revenue, of good faith—every sense of the duties of states—every feeling of respect for treaties—nay, every motive of self-interest, should prompt the British nation cheerfully to acquiesce in the measures we propose. Speaking of a far distant province, to a people comparatively uncommercial in their character, and in an age when the relations of commerce were not so complicated as they are now, the Roman orator addressed the Roman people in language which, surely, is not less applicable to the claims we have urged on the British nation:

> "Erit igitur humanitatis vestrae magnum civium numerum calamitate prohibere, sapientiae videre multorum civium calamitatem a republica sejunctam esse non posse. Non enim possunt una, in civitate multi rematque fortunas amittere ut non plures secum in eandem calamitatem traherent, a quo periculo prohibete rempublicam; et mihi credite, id quod ipsi videtis, haec fides atque hajc ratio pecuniarum quas Romas quae in foro versatur implicata est cum illis pecuniis Asiaticis et cohaeret. Ruenre illae non possunt et hasc non eodem motu labefactata concidant. Quare viclete num dubitandum vobis sit omni studio ad id opus incumbere in quo gloria nominis vestri, salus sociorum, vectigalia maxuma, fortunae plurimorum civium, una cum republica defendatur."[89]

What expression of this is inapplicable to the present circumstances of this country - not even the last, "una cum republica?"[90] In the fortunes of Ireland now, we believe the destinies of the British empire itself to be involved. It is, alas, too possible that, by the policy of ministers, Ireland may be ruined or lost—it is NOT possible that it can be either without shaking British power to its base. If weakness, and unwise and wasteful parsimony, and an ungenerous spirit to Ireland, now govern the councils of the nation—the theories which have been mistaken for the doctrines of science may be adhered to—immediate outlay may be saved—the favourite plan of those whose liberality knows nothing more liberal than a scheme to ruin the Irish landlords, may be triumphantly carried out; but in the misery and starvation of the poor that is present, and the confusion and beggary of all classes that must follow in no distant day, will be the sure forerunners of the dissolution of the British empire.

Time, indeed, has been lost, that can never be recalled—lives have been sacrificed that might have been saved—pangs and agonies endured, the remembrance of which humanity might have been spared. But the worse calamities that are yet to come, it is, even now, in the power of a bold, a liberal, and a generous policy to avert. No nobler object was ever yet proposed to statesmen than that which the state of Ireland now presents. Like all tremendous crises in the history of nations, it has brought with it deep calamities and peril; but with them, like all such crises, to those who know how to use them, also great openings for good. Singular, indeed, is the law in the history of nations which ordains that social or physical calamities should seldom visit communities without removing, in their fearful progress, obstacles to improvement, and opening up, with new vigour, scenes and new feelings, opportunities for amelioration of whatever was defective in their state. These opportunities are the compensation by which national calamities, that threaten utter destruction to a people, have been often more than atoned for, in the results for which they made way. Let Ireland now be dealt with by no ignorant, no procrastinating, and no niggard hand; let all the energies of the empire be directed to do all that her necessities require, and an opportunity is presented for altering her social condition, for which centuries might have waited in vain. From the results of the very calamity that oppresses her, it is possible for British statesmen to make her an ally and support of England's honour and strength, no longer the cause of her shame and weakness, and in elevating her people from their prostrate condition, to a state of comfort they never knew before, to conciliate the affections of an entire population, and thus increase the strength, and extend the resources of what will then be, in heart and affection, this united empire.

It is for the British Ministry, and the British House of Commons, to decide whether objects like these should be sacrificed to the dictates of an unwise and ungenerous parsimony, of which even the experience of the present troubles has already taught us, that it is always the most expensive in the end.

QUAKE VIDETE NUM DUBITANDUM SIT VOBIS OMNI STUDIO AD ID OPUS INCUMBERE IN QUO GLORIA NOMINI NOSTRI SALUS SOCIORUM VECTIGALIA MAXIMA, FORTUNAE PLURIMORUM CIVIUM UNA CUM REPUBLICA DEFENDANTUR.[91]

We cannot close this article without pausing, earnestly to thank the ministry for an act which has drawn on them rebuke from some of whom we had hoped better things—we mean the appointment by the Sovereign's proclamation of a day of solemn humiliation and prayer.[92]

Never, perhaps, was the lesson so fearfully taught, as in the recent visitation, how vain is all the wisdom and the strength of man, to secure happiness to a people. Never was there an occasion upon which it was more fitting that our Sovereign and her people should bow in submission to the mysterious will of the great Being who rules us all—and earnestly implore his mercy for a suffering land; and that blessing, without which the wisest of human legislation is in vain. And believe it sincerely and reverently we do, that the supplications, in which millions of our fellow-countrymen have fervently and earnestly joined, have not ascended up to heaven in vain. Just now, perhaps, the subject is too sacred and solemn for controversy—alas, that it should call forth any. But we could not close this article without expressing our deep gratitude to the advisers of our Sovereign, for this step, conceived and carried out in a manner worthy of a Christian nation, without recording our deep and earnest conviction, that the solemn offering up of a nation's confession and prayer to God, is not the mere homage of a ceremony and a form, but a reality, from which, with the deepest reverence, and without daring in presumption to point out how the prayers of the people and the Sovereign may be answered, we yet may humbly and confidently look for an answer, and a blessing on the nation from on high.

THE END.

Dublin: Printed by EDWARD BULL, 6, Bachelor's-walk.

## Notes

1 W. J. McCormack, 'Isaac Butt and the Inner Failure of Protestant Home Rule' in Ciaran Brady (ed.) *Worsted in the Game. Losers in Irish History* (Dublin: Lilliput Press, 1989), pp. 121–131.
2 Isaac Butt (1813–1879) was multi-talented and multi-facetted. In 1836, when only in his 20s, he was appointed Whately Professor of Political Economy at Trinity College in Dublin. In 1838, he was called to the bar, proving to be a brilliant barrister. At this stage, his politics were conservative and unionist, he opposing the Repeal campaign of Daniel O'Connell (1775–1847).
3 The Orange Order was an exclusively Protestant organization that had been founded in Co. Armagh in 1795. Initially its membership consisted of members of the Anglican or Established Church, but by the 1830s, Presbyterians were increasingly admitted. As its name suggests, the society honoured William of Orange, in particular his victory at the Battle of the Boyne in 1690.
4 Butt represented Youghal from 1852 to 1865, and Limerick from 1871 to 1879.
5 Charles Stewart Parnell (1846–1891) was born in Co. Wicklow to a family of Anglo-Irish landowners. He ousted Butt as President of the Home Rule Confederation of Great Britain, which Butt had founded. His achievements as leader of the Home Rule movement led to him being regarded as 'the uncrowned king of Ireland', until his spectacular fall from grace in 1890.
6 Sir Robert Peel (1788–1850) was a British Conservative politician who served as Prime Minister twice. His second incumbency coincided with the appearance of potato blight in Ireland. He used the food shortages as an opportunity to repeal the protectionist Corn Laws, losing him the support of many in his party. In June 1846, he resigned as PM.
7 'Workhouses in Ireland' and 'Answer to the Speech', House of Common Debates, *Hansard,* 19 January 1847, vol. 89, cc. 67–166. It was the radical MP, George Poulett Scrope, who questioned the Home Secretary.
8 Ibid., Lord John Russell, Corn and Navigation Laws, 21 January 1847, vol. 89, cc. 210–268.
9 Q.C. denotes 'Queen's Counsel', an honorific title given to the most distinguished lawyers. Because of their distinctive silk gown, Q.C.s are also known as 'silks'.
10 *Dublin University Magazine* was published from 1833 to 1882. It had been founded by a number of students from Trinity College (including Isaac Butt), who wanted to defend Tory political principles.
11 Indian corn was a form of maize, which was a major food source for the native people in both North and South America. It was also known as 'flint corn' because of

the hardness of its shells. In November 1845, Robert Peel had secretly ordered the importation of £100,000 of Indian Corn to Ireland, giving rise to the nickname, 'Peel's brimstone'. It was to be resold to the poor, who initially had no knowledge of how to prepare it for consumption.

12  The Elizabethan Poor Laws, which were codified between 1597 and 1601, were administered in England by parish 'overseers'. They provided relief for the aged, sick, and infant poor, in addition to work for the able-bodied in special institutions known as workhouses. A major revision of the Poor Laws took place in 1834.

13  The 'new' English and Welsh Poor Law of 1834 recognized the right to relief; the Irish Poor Law, introduced in 1838, did not.

14  John Robert Godley (1841–1861) was born in Dublin, the son of an Anglo-Irish landowner. During the Famine, he proposed emigration to Canada as a way of alleviating the suffering—an idea opposed by many Catholic priests. He was author of *Observations on the Irish Poor-Law* (1847).

15  There were numerous contemporary reports of debilitated people being eaten while still alive by animals—pigs, dogs and rats.

16  Official mortality statistics were not kept. This issue was debated in the House of Commons, with Benjamin Disraeli leading the criticism of the Whig government. See Kinealy, *Great Irish Famine*, Chapter Two.

17  The disease was *phytophthora infestans,* which infected the plant through its leaves, leaving behind shriveled, decomposing and inedible tubers. It was not until 2013 that, by using a DNA sequencing of plant specimens dating from the mid-19th century, the pathogen was identified.

18  Thomas Berry Horsfall (1805–1878) was a Conservative politician who became mayor of Liverpool in 1847, succeeding his father, Charles Horsfall (1776–1846). The younger Horsfall, who was associated with the support of ultra-Protestantism, opposed the grant to Maynooth in 1845.

19  The Mansion House Committee was formed in October 1845 by the Lord Mayor of Dublin, John Arabin. It included some of the most powerful men in Ireland, including Daniel O'Connell. They sent questionnaires to all parts of Ireland in order to understand the true extent of the crop lost.

20  A reference to the defeat of Sir Robert Peel and his resignation.

21  Lord George Bentinck (1802–1848) was a Conservative politician who, as leader of the 'Protectionists', led the opposition to Peel. He proposed a bill to loan £16 million to Ireland for the building of a railway network, which would provide employment, and thus relief, to the poor. It was defeated. See, the *Spectator,* 20 February 1847.

22  Latin for 'fear and famine'.

23  Henry Peter Brougham (1778–1868), who was born in Scotland, had helped found the *Edinburgh Review* in 1802. In the 1830s, he served as a Whig politician who was known for his opposition to slavery. He responded to the onset of famine in Ireland by declaring free trade to be a 'sacred right'. Lord John Manners (1818–1906) was an English Conservative politician. In 1841, he had written, 'Let wealth and commerce, laws and learning die, but leave us still our old Nobility!'

24  In keeping with the government's desire to keep famine relief separate from the permanent Poor Law, a Temporary Relief Commission was formed in November 1845 to oversee the distribution of food, collate information, and coordinate relief efforts. The members of the first Commission represented the various government departments in Ireland including the Dublin Castle administration, the Constabulary, the Coast Guard, the Poor Law and the Commissariat.

25  The Labour Rate Act (9th and 10th Vict. cap. 107) was introduced by the British government in August 1846. It gave the Treasury greater control over relief provision and introduced the principle of 'piece work'. However, wages did not keep pace with food prices.

26 The cess was originally a tax imposed to maintain the Tudor garrison in Ireland. In 1634, a new cess was introduced by local grand juries to maintain local roads, bridges and other public utilities.
27 The Navigation Acts had their origins in the seventeenth century. They restricted the use of foreign ships for trade with the British colonies except with ships registered in England. They were temporarily suspended at the beginning of 1847 by the Whig government to facilitate food imports into Ireland. They were repealed in 1849.
28 These temporary measures were announced by the Prime Minister to the House of Commons on 21 January 1847. For the text of the debate see, Corn and Navigation Laws, House of Commons Debates, *Hansard*, 21 January 1847, vol. 89, cc. 210–68.
29 The Labour Rate Act (9th and 10th Vict. cap. 107).
30 The public works introduced by the Whig government not only were more draconian than those used in the previous year, but they were to intended to serve no useful purpose, leading to the expression, 'walls that surround nothing and roads that lead nowhere'.
31 A shilling was a unit of currency. There were twelve pennies in a shilling and twenty shillings in a pound (£ or *l*).
32 The proposal to invest in railways during the Famine is generally associated with Lord George Bentinck (1802–1848), a Conservative politician who led the opposition to Peel over the repeal of the Corn Laws.
33 * Author's note. It appears that since parliament has met, government have consented to some such presentment on the Limerick and Waterford line!
34 John William Ponsonby (1781–1847), the 4th Earl of Bessborough, was an English Whig politician, who owned property in Ireland. He served as Lord Lieutenant of Ireland from 1846 until his death in May 1847. He was generally sympathetic to the victims of the blight, arguing for more government spending.
35 Downing Street was the official residence of the British Prime Minister.
36 The Elizabethan Poor Law (43 Eliz. 1 c. 2) provided a national system of relief for the poor of England and Wales, both in their homes and in workhouses. By the 19th century, it had become discredited as being too liberal. Following the introduction of the 'new' Poor Law in 1834 (based on more stringent principles) the Elizabethan legislation was referred to as the 'old' Poor Law.
37 The Queen's Speech was delivered at the opening of the new parliamentary session. On 19 January 1847, the speech opened with reference to Ireland and the relief measures about to be introduced by the government. Unfortunately, the Speech also drew a connection between Irish poverty and crime (outrages) in the country.
38 In January 1847, a large meeting of Irish peers, members of Parliament, and landed proprietors was held in the Rotunda in Dublin, during which they proposed measures both to alleviate the Famine and for the future prosperity of Ireland.
39 Lord George Bentinck, the leader of the Protectionist Party, had unsuccessfully introduced a bill for the extension of railways in Ireland as a means of providing employment while developing the infrastructure. His proposal was much praised in Ireland. He died, possibly of heart failure, when aged only 46.
40 * Author's Note. This article, was unfortunately actually in print before we had the opportunity of seeing the very able and temperate pamphlet, which, under the title we have prefixed to a note at its commencement, discusses the right we here assert for Ireland, in language strikingly corroborative of these views. This pamphlet bears internal evidence of being the production of a profound thinker, an accomplished scholar, and a lawyer deeply read in the history and constitution of the country. If surmise as to its authorship be correct, it furnishes a striking proof how entirely the sentiments we have expressed are shared by classes that English statesmen, perhaps, believe inaccessible to their influence.
41 The Commissioners of Woods, Forests, Land Revenues, Works and Buildings for the United Kingdom was established in 1810 to look after Crown Lands.

## OFFICIAL RESPONSE AND REACTION

42  Nationalist leader, Daniel O'Connell, had declared 1843 to be the year in which a repeal of the Act of Union would be achieved. A mass meeting to be held in Clontarf in October was banned by the authorities. O'Connell's compliance, which was in keeping with his pacifist methods, lost him support from a number of his followers, including the more radical Young Ireland.
43  The suspension was a temporary measure, introduced by parliament in January 1847.
44  The Encumbered Estates Acts of 1848 and 1849 were introduced to facilitate the sale of estates that were mortgaged and in debt.
45  John Fitzgibbon, Earl of Clare (1749–1802), was born near Donnybrook in Dublin. He was Attorney-General for Ireland from 1783 to 1789 and Lord Chancellor of Ireland from 1789 to 1802. He was controversial—in 1780 declaring that British rule of Ireland was 'a daring usurpation of the rights of a free people', yet supporting the Union and opposing emancipation for Catholics. His son, the 2nd Earl of Clare (1792–1851), was Deputy Lieutenant of Co. Limerick from 1846 to 1849.
46  The Temporary Relief Act, also referred to as the Soup Kitchen Act, for the first time allowed gratuitous, outdoor relief to the Irish poor. As its name suggested, it was a temporary measure only, to act as an interim between the closing of the Public Works and the introduction of an amended and extended Poor Law. Three separate acts heralded a change in Poor Law relief in 1847, which allowed the granting of outdoor relief in Ireland. They included 'An Act to make further Provision for the Relief of the destitute Poor in Ireland', passed on 8 June 1847 (10 Vic., c.31).
47  A 'consolidated fund' is usually the main bank account of the government. The Consolidated Fund Act of 1816 merged the services of Great Britain and Ireland into the single Consolidated Fund of the United Kingdom.
48  The Opium War (1839–1842), between Britain and China, concerned the former's right to interfere with the latter's trade. The war arose from China's attempts to suppress the opium trade, which was largely facilitated by British traders. A second Opium War was fought from 1856 to 1860.
49  The modern form of income tax was introduced in Britain by Prime Minister, William Pitt, in 1798 to pay for weapons and equipment for use in the wars against France. Regardless of the Act of Union, an income tax system was not introduced into Ireland until 1853.
50  Author's Note. * In estimating the number of persons supported by the potato at four million, we do not calculate that so great a number of persons were exclusively fed upon that food; calculating those partially supported by it, the result would be found, in the whole, equivalent to four million, entirely depending upon it. This estimate is rather below the truth.
51  Many visitors to Ireland noted the proximity of the dung heaps to the homes of the Irish poor. The dung was used as fertilizer for the potato crop.
52  The common perception was that pigs were dirty and unclean. In fact, pigs are clean and by eating potato left-overs and providing dung, they were an essential part of the potato economy.
53  British currency comprised of pounds, shillings and pence (with smaller units known as the half-penny and the farthing). It was shorted to £. s. d.
54  The Poor Law Extension Act consisted of three separate acts, the main one being 'An Act to make further Provision for the Relief of the destitute Poor in Ireland' (10 Vic., c.31.). It was passed on 8 June 1847, and came into effect in August. It provided for relief outside of the workhouse, and gave a right to relief to certain categories of paupers.
55  Author's Note. * We think we are justified in saying that it is unjust to represent the landed gentry of Ireland as universally, or even generally, opposed to the legal enforcement of this obligation. Two of them—Mr. Godley, and Mr. Adair—have written upon the subject; and both of them advocate the ministerial measure of outdoor relief. Mr.

Adair's pamphlet, with singular eloquence and ability, advocates a poor law that would be still more efficient. The information, and ability, and honesty of Mr. Godley's letter, must command the respect—we would almost hope convince the understandings—of the most determined opponents of out-door relief.

56  Poor Law Guardians (two-thirds of whom were elected, one third was ex-officio) were in charge of administering relief.
57  Relieving Officers were Poor Law officials who assessed claims for relief and determined how much should be given. The 1847 Extension Act permitted them to provide emergency relief.
58  A law of settlement had been part of the English Poor Law (since 1662), but not the Irish one. It provided for relief to be provided in the parish in which a 'settlement' had been established, through birth, residence, marriage etc.
59  The 1847 Extension Act provided for a Chief Commissioner to be appointed in Ireland who, together with the Chief Secretary and Under Secretary, constituted 'The Commissioners for administering the Laws for the Relief of the Poor in Ireland'.
60  The Irish Poor Law Inquiry (official title, Royal Commission on the Poorer Classes in Ireland). Its thorough investigation, which took three years to complete, was rejected by the British government, who instead commissioned a report from George Nicholls, an English Poor Law Commissioner.
61  In the wake of the completion of the Poor Inquiry, George Nicholls (1781–1865), an English Poor Law Commissioner, was sent to Ireland to inquire into the extent of destitution in the country. His estimate of 80,000 people requiring relief was far lower than the two million suggested by the Inquiry.
62  The Irish Poor Law was enacted in 1838, and provided for the first national network of relief.
63  The Temporary Relief Act, which provided for the establishment of soup kitchens, which were financed by local poor rates, although some of the poorest unions received small loans or grants from the government, subject to the approval of the Treasury.
64  George Hudson (1800–1871) was an English railway financier who, by the 1840s, controlled one-third of the railway network in England, earning him the nick-name, 'The Railway King'. He also served as a Conservative politician in the House of Commons. He supported Bentinck's Railway Bill, which was defeated.
65  Bentinck introduced the Railway Bill to the House of Common's on 4 February 1847, see 'Railways (Ireland)', House of Commons Debates, *Hansard,* 4 February 1847, vol. 89, cc. 773–846.
66  Lieutenant Colonel Douglas was initially appointed as an Inspector of Relief Committees etc. in Ireland in December 1846 by the Treasury. He was one of four military men appointed following complaints of mismanagement of funds by the local relief committees.
67  George Stephenson (1781–1848) was an English civil engineer who, in 1830, opened the first railway line in the world that used steam locomotives.
68  A mythological Greek princess who had the power of prophecy, which nobody believed, even when it was true.
69  Augustus Frederick FitzGerald, the 3rd Duke of Leinster (1791–1874) was born in Ireland, the family owning properties in both Dublin and Co. Kildare, including the prestigious Carton House. He was one of the only two dukes resident in Ireland. During the Famine, he was President of the Mansion House Committee, while his son, the Marquess of Kildare, worked with the Dublin Central Relief Committee. Queen Victoria visited briefly the Carton Estate in August 1849.
70  John Butler, 2nd Marquess of Ormonde (1808–1854) was an Irish politician and peer, who represented Kilkenny from 1830 to 1832. Between 1841 and 1852, he held the office of Lord-in-Waiting, a peer who served in the Royal Household of the Sovereign, Queen Victoria.

71 Richard Butler, the 2nd Earl of Glengall (1794–1858) of Cahir in Co. Tipperary was a Tory politician. He died without male heirs.
72 William Parsons, the 3rd Earl of Rosse (1800–67), was born in England but inherited a large estate in King's County (now Co. Offaly). He was renowned for building telescopes, including the much-praised, *Leviathan,* which was first used in 1845, although regular use was deferred for two years due to the Famine.
73 The *Morning Herald* was a daily newspaper, printed in London. When the paper had been founded in 1780 its focus was liberal but, by the 1840s, it identified with the Conservatives.
74 Robert Murray (d.1865) was manager of Joplin's Provincial Bank of Ireland, where he gained a first-hand insight into how emigration was being financed. In his pamphlet, he suggested that government intervention was necessary to assist in emigration. The Provincial Bank had been established by Thomas Joplin in 1825.

Author's Note. *Mr. Murray has been for many years, indeed we believe since its establishment, the chief manager in Ireland of all the concerns of the Provincial Bank; an establishment which is said to owe much, if not all of its present high position to its indefatigable industry, and great ability, and tact. The letter to Sir Robert Peel, in which he has urged the necessity of emigration, is one of the best timed and most valuable contributions to the cause of Ireland which her present calamity has called forth.

75 Robert Shafto Adair (1811–1886) was born in Ballymena, Co. Antrim. He was elected to parliament as a Whig member in 1847. His publication, *The winter of 1846–7 in Antrim: With remarks on out-door relief and colonization* (London: James Ridgeway, 1847), provided a rare contemporary insight into the impact of the Famine on the north east of the country.
76 Robert Torrens (1780–1864), a marine officer, political economist and colonization commissioner, was born in Ireland in Co. Derry. He was active in promoting emigration to Australia. He also wrote extensively on what he perceived to be threats to Britain's imperial greatness.
77 Henry Labouchere, the 1st Baron Taunton (1798–1869) was a British Whig politician. In 1846, he was appointed Chief Secretary for Ireland, a position that he held for one year. He is associated with the 'Labouchere Letter' of 5 October 1846, which provided for drainage works in Ireland, to augment the public works.
78 The 1846, the Oregon Treaty had settled the long-running 'Oregon Border Question' by establishing a border between British North America and the United States along the 49th parallel.
79 A Drainage Act had been introduced by Peel's government in March 1846. In August 1846, the Whig government renewed the Public Works, although generally under more stringent terms.
80 George Poulett Scrope (1797–1876) was an English political economist, who was an MP from 1833 to 1867. He disagreed with the population theories of Thomas Malthus and with David Ricardo's Theory of Rent. He disliked workhouses, preferring emigration as a way of alleviating poverty. Scrope was an avid writer, especially of pamphlets. He referred to the Irish poor as 'human encumbrances'.
81 The recommendations made by the three-year Poor Inquiry were disliked by the government for being too expensive and too interventionist. Instead, George Nicholls, an English Poor Law Commissioner, undertook a six-week visit to Ireland to report of the suitability of a Poor Law for that country.
82 George Nicholls (1781–1865) was an English Poor Law Commissioner under the 'new' Poor Law of 1834. In 1836, and again in 1837, he undertook two brief trips to Ireland to report on the suitability of a Poor Law. His reports provided the basis for Irish Poor Law Act of 1838 (1 and 2 Vict. c. 56), which made workhouses responsible

for relief. Although a champion of the Poor Law for Ireland, Nicholls stated that it would be beyond its capacity to deal with a famine.
83 The Devon Commission had been appointed by Sir Robert Peel to look into the occupation of land in Ireland. It sat between 1843 and 1845.
84 When slavery was ended in most of the British Empire in 1833, the slave owners in the Caribbean were given £20,000,000 as compensation.
85 William Pitt (1759–1806) was an English politician who became the youngest British Prime Minister in 1783 at the age of 24. In the wake of the failed 1798 uprising, he believed that a union between Britain and Ireland was necessary. He had hoped to accompany this with Catholic Emancipation, but this was opposed by King George III, leading Pitt to resign as PM in February 1801.
86 The London Stock Exchange. The government had used it to raise large amounts of money for the war against Napoleon.
87 The 1846 Act of Removal, which was part of the English Poor Law legislation, redefined what constituted a 'settlement', that is, a right to relief. Newly-arrived Famine immigrants could be deported if they applied for relief.
88 The *Eclaire* ship of war was infected in July 1845 with yellow fever.
89 Part of an oration by Cicero, a Roman philosopher.
90 Latin: 'together with the state'.
91 Extract from speech by Cicero.
92 Queen Victoria, prompted by the Prime Minister, called for a day of 'fast and humiliation' for Ireland. The day chosen was 24 March 1847. Her appeal was made through Anglican churches in the United Kingdom.

# 12

## CHARLES E. TREVELYAN, *THE IRISH CRISIS: BEING A NARRATIVE OF THE MEASURES FOR THE RELIEF OF THE DISTRESS CAUSED BY THE GREAT IRISH FAMINE OF 1846–7* (JANUARY 1848)

Charles Edward Trevelyan remains a contested and controversial figure within the historiography of the Great Famine.[1] Born in 1807 to a middle-class family in Cornwall, he was the fourth son of George Trevelyan, Archdeacon of Taunton from 1817 until his death in October 1827.

Trevelyan attended the prestigious Charterhouse School, followed by Haileybury, the training college which had been founded in 1806 and was owned by the East India Company.[2] Thomas Malthus, author of *An Essay on the Principle of Population* (1798), was a lecturer in the college from its opening until his death in 1834. A standard text used in teaching was Adam Smith's *A Wealth of Nations* (1776).[3] The views of Smith and Malthus, together with his own evangelical leanings, helped to shape the young Trevelyan's ideological viewpoints.

Trevelyan left Haileybury in 1826, having spent two years there. He had been a diligent student and proved to be a gifted linguist. Shortly after, he travelled to India where he initially studied at the College of Fort William in Calcutta, which had been established by Lord Wellesley in 1800 to train British officials in India in the native languages. There, he mastered Persian and Hindi, which prepared him for his career as a civil servant in India.

An incident that occurred early in his career offers an insight into Trevelyan's sense of public duty. After only two years of working in India, he accused a senior civil servant, Sir Edward Colebrook, of taking bribes from natives. Following an enquiry, Colebrook was sent home in disgrace, while Trevelyan received a commendation.[4]

In 1831, Trevelyan was promoted to deputy secretary of the Political Department of the government, which was located in Calcutta. Before leaving Delhi, he paid for the creation of a new suburb in Delhi, known as Trevelyanpur. It was planned on a grid pattern with wide streets and a public garden. The colonnaded market place was named Bentinckganj.[5] The latter was a reference to Lord William Bentinck, the Governor General of India from 1828 to 1835, and so Trevelyan's superior. When Trevelyan returned to India in 1859 as Governor of Madras, this action was recalled and praised.[6] Regardless of being a civil servant, Trevelyan felt compelled to publish his experiences and opinions on a number of occasions. His publications included, 'A report upon the inland customs and town duties of the Bengal presidency',[7] and 'On the education of the people of India' (1838).[8] In 1834, while in India, Trevelyan met and married Hannah Macaulay. She was a sister of Thomas Babington Macaulay, a member of the Supreme Council of India from 1834 to 1838.[9]

In January 1840, while on leave from India, Trevelyan was appointed assistant secretary of the British Treasury – the most senior official position. He was 32 years old. It was a massive promotion and seems to have been done as a favour to Macaulay, who had also returned to England and had been elected MP for Edinburgh. Macaulay's rationale had been personal rather than professional—he wanted to keep his sister and her children close to him. Macaulay, a devoted brother and uncle, never married.[10] His decision to relocate Trevelyan was to have momentous consequences for Ireland as, for the whole of the Famine period, the Treasury was in charge of overseeing the expenditure of public money on relief. Consequently, Trevelyan was able to place his imprint on events in Ireland between 1845 and 1852.

Trevelyan was no stranger to Irish affairs. In late 1843, he had spent six weeks in the Ireland, his trip coinciding with the climax of O'Connell's repeal movement. His observations on Irish poverty, priests and politics led him to pen his thoughts in two lengthy letter to the *Morning Chronicle*. His prognosis was alarmist: Ireland was ripe for revolution, largely due to the insubordinate actions of the Catholic priests.[11] Although Trevelyan used the pen-name *Philalethes* ('lover of truth'), it was an indiscreet action for a leading civil servant. However, the fact that the letters were reprinted in the London *Times* only two days later, suggested that Trevelyan's words had fallen on receptive ears.

As head of the British Treasury, Trevelyan was involved in Famine relief from the end of 1845, remaining in place when the government changed in summer 1846. Despite being based in London, he was at the centre of a network of officials that included the Dublin Castle Administration, the Relief Commission, the Commissariat, the Poor Law Commission, the Home Office and the Board of Works. He quickly established himself as the most important person within this nexus. Overall, his approach was shaped by his evangelicalism and by his fear of providing relief too liberally, and thus creating a culture of dependency. Sir Randolph Routh who was head of the Commissariat,[12] shared Trevelyan's reforming outlook, as did the Chancellor of the Exchequer, Sir Charles Wood.[13]

*The Irish Crisis* first appeared anonymously in the January 1848 edition of the *Edinburgh Review* and it was published in book form a few months later, with the author's name included. In it, Trevelyan provides a comprehensive defence of the government's actions, together with an assurance that Ireland would benefit from all the changes. If not surreptitiously commissioned by leading members of the Cabinet and the Prime Minister (Lord John Russell may even have written part of it), the article was published with their full approval.[14] *The Irish Crisis* was reprinted in 1880, which coincided with a period of localized famine in Ireland.[15]

Trevelyan was knighted in 1848 in recognition of his services during the Famine, thus becoming Sir Charles Trevelyan.[16] In addition, he was given a 'famine-bonus' of £2,500.[17]

## C. E. TREVELYAN, ESQ., *THE IRISH CRISIS*, REPRINTED FROM THE 'EDINBURGH REVIEW', NO. CLXXV, JANUARY, 1848 (LONDON: LONGMAN, BROWN, GREEN & LONGMANS, 1848).

THE IRISH CRISIS.

The time has not yet arrived at which any man can with confidence say, that he fully appreciates the nature and the bearings of that great event which will long be inseparably associated with the year just departed. Yet we think that we may render some service to the public by attempting thus early to review, with the calm temper of a future generation, the history of the great Irish famine of 1847*.[18] Unless we are much deceived, posterity will trace up to that famine the commencement of a salutary revolution in the habits of a nation long singularly unfortunate, and will acknowledge that on this, as on many other occasions, Supreme Wisdom has educed permanent good out of transient evil.

If, a few months ago, an enlightened man had been asked what he thought the most discouraging circumstance in the state of Ireland, we do not imagine that he would have pitched upon Absenteeism, or Protestant bigotry, or Roman Catholic bigotry, or Orangeism, or Ribbandism, or the Repeal cry, or even the system of threatening notices and midday assassinations.[19] These things, he would have said, are evils; but some of them are curable; and others are merely symptomatic. They do not make the case desperate. But what hope is there for a nation which lives on potatoes?

The consequences of depending upon the potato as the principal article of popular food, had long been foreseen by thinking persons; and the following observations extracted from a paper on the native country of the wild potato*,[20] published in the *Transactions of the Horticultural Society of London* for the year 1822, are a fair specimen of the opinions which prevailed on the subject previously to the great failure of 1845.

> "The increased growth of the potato, not only in these kingdoms, but almost in every civilised part of the globe, has so added to its importance, that any information respecting it has become valuable. With the exception of wheat and rice, it is now certainly the vegetable most employed as the food of man; and it is probable that the period is at no great distance, when its extensive use will even place it before those which

have hitherto been considered the chief staples of life. The effect of the unlimited extent to which its cultivation may be carried, on the human race, must be a subject of deep interest to the political economist. The extension of population will be as unbounded as the production of food, which is capable of being produced in very small space, and with great facility; and the increased number of inhabitants of the earth will necessarily induce changes, not only in the political systems, but in all the artificial relations of civilised life. How far such changes may conduce to or increase the happiness of mankind, is very problematical, more especially when it is considered, that since the potato, when in cultivation, is very liable to injury from casualties of season, and that it is not at present known how to keep it in store for use beyond a few months, a general failure of the year's crop, whenever it shall have become the chief or sole support of a country, must inevitably lead to all the misery of famine, more dreadful in proportion to the numbers exposed to its ravages."

The important influence which has been exercised by this root over the destinies of the human race, arises from the fact that it yields an unusually abundant produce as compared with the extent of ground cultivated, and with the labour, capital, and skill bestowed upon its cultivation. The same land, which when laid down to corn, will maintain a given number of persons, will support three times that number when used for raising potatoes. "A family in the West of Ireland, once located on from one to three or four acres of land, was provided for; a cabin could be raised in a few days without the expense of a sixpence;[21] the potatoes, at the cost of a very little labour, supplied them with a sufficiency of food, with which, from habit, they were perfectly content; and a pig, or with some, a cow, or donkey, or pony, and occasional labour at a very low rate of wages, gave them what was necessary to pay a rent, and for such clothing and other articles as were absolutely necessary, and which, with a great proportion, were on the lowest scale of human existence. The foundation of the whole, however, was the possession of the bit of land; it was the one, and the only one thing absolutely necessary; the rent consequently was high, and generally well paid, being the first demand on all money received, in order to secure that essential tenure; and only what remained became applicable to other objects. Although of the lowest grade, it was an easy mode of subsistence, and led to the encouragement of early marriages, large families, and a rapidly-increasing population, and at the same time afforded the proprietor very good return of profit for his land*."[22]

The relations of employer and employed, which knit together the framework of society, and establish a mutual dependence and good-will, have no existence in the potato system. The Irish small holder lives in a state of isolation, the type of which is to be sought for in the islands of the South Sea, rather than in the great civilized communities of the ancient world. A fortnight for planting, a week or ten days for digging, and another fortnight for turf-cutting, suffice for his subsistence; and during the rest of the year, he is at leisure to follow his own inclinations, without even the safeguard of those intellectual tastes and legitimate objects of ambition which only imperfectly obviate the evils of leisure in the higher ranks of society.

The excessive competition for land maintained rents at a level which left the Irish peasant the bare means of subsistence; and poverty, discontent, and idleness, acting on his excitable nature, produced that state of popular feeling which furnishes the material for every description of illegal association and misdirected political agitation. That agrarian code which is at perpetual war with the laws of God and man, is more especially the offspring of this state of society, the primary object being to secure the possession of the plots of land, which, in the absence of wages, are the sole means of subsistence.

There is a gradation even in potatoes. Those generally used by the people of Ireland were of the coarsest and most prolific kind, called "Lumpers,' or "Horse Potatoes," from their size, and they were, for the most part, cultivated, not in furrows, but in the slovenly mode popularly known as "lazy beds;" so that the principle of seeking the cheapest description of food at the smallest expense of labour, was maintained in all its force. To the universal dependence on the potato, and to the absence of farmers of a superior class, it was owing that agriculture of every description was carried on in a negligent, imperfect manner*.[23] The domestic habits arising out of this mode of subsistence were of the lowest and most degrading kind. The pigs and poultry, which share the food of the peasant's family, became, in course, inmates of the cabin also. The habit of exclusively living on this root produced an entire ignorance of every other food and of the means of preparing it; and there is scarcely a woman of the peasant class in the West of Ireland, whose culinary art exceeds the boiling of a potato. Bread is scarcely ever seen, and an oven is unknown.

The first step to improvement was wanting to this state of things. The people had no incitement to be industrious to procure comforts which were utterly beyond their reach, and which many of them perhaps had never seen. Their ordinary food being of the cheapest and commonest description, and having no value in the market, it gave them no command of butcher's meat, manufactures, colonial produce, or any other article of comfort or enjoyment. To those who subsist chiefly on corn, other articles of equal value are available, which can be substituted for it at their discretion; or if they please, they can, by the adoption of a less expensive diet, accumulate a small capital by which their future condition may be improved and secured; but the only hope for those who lived upon potatoes was in some great intervention of Providence to bring back the potato to its original use and intention as an adjunct, and not as a principal article of national food; and by compelling the people of Ireland to recur to other more nutritious means of aliment, to restore the energy and the vast industrial capabilities of that country.

A population, whose ordinary food is wheat and beef, and whose ordinary drink is porter and ale, can retrench in periods of scarcity, and resort to cheaper kinds of food, such as barley, oats, rice, and potatoes. But those who are habitually and entirely fed on potatoes, live upon the extreme verge of human subsistence, and when they are deprived of their accustomed food, there is nothing cheaper to which they can resort. They have already reached the lowest point in the descending scale, and there is nothing beyond but starvation or beggary. Several circumstances aggravate the hazard of this position. The produce of the potato is more precarious than that of wheat or any other grain. Besides many other proofs of the uncertainty of this crop, there is no instance on record of any such failure of the crops of corn, as occurred in the case of potatoes in 1821, 1845, 1846, and 1847; showing that this root can no longer be depended upon as a staple article of human food. The potato cannot be stored so that the scarcity of one year may be alleviated by bringing forward the reserves of former years, as is always done in corn-feeding countries. Every year is thus left to provide subsistence for itself. When the crop is luxuriant, the surplus must be given to the pigs; and when it is deficient, famine and disease necessarily prevail. Lastly, the bulk of potatoes is such, that they can with difficulty be conveyed from place to place to supply local deficiencies, and it has often happened that severe scarcity has prevailed in districts within fifty miles of which potatoes were to be had in abundance. If a man use two pounds of meal a-day (which is twice the amount of the ration found to be sufficient during the late relief operations), a hundredweight of meal will last him for fifty-six days; whereas a hundredweight of potatoes will not last more than eight days; and when it was proposed to provide seed-potatoes for those who had lost their stock in the failure of 1845–6, the plan was found impracticable, because nearly a ton an acre would have been required for the purpose.

The potato does not, in fact, last even a single year. The old crop becomes unfit for use in July, and the new crop, as raised by the inferior husbandry of the poor, does not come into consumption until September. Hence, July and August are called the "meal months," from the necessity the people are under of living upon meal at that period.[24] This is always a season of great distress and trial for the poorer peasants; and in the districts in which the potato system has been carried to the greatest extent, as, for instance, in the barony of Erris in the county of Mayo, there has been an annual dearth in the summer months for many years past. Every now and then a "meal year" occurs, and then masses of the population become a prey to famine and fever, except so far as they may be relieved by charity.

In 1739 an early and severe frost destroyed the potatoes in the ground, and the helplessness and despair of the people having led to a great falling off of tillage in 1740, the calamity was prolonged to the ensuing year, 1741, which was long known as the *bliadhain an air*, or year of slaughter.[25] The ordinary burial-grounds were not large enough to contain those who died by the roadside, or who were taken from the deserted cabins. The "bloody flux" and "malignant fever,"[26] having begun among the poor, spread to the rich, and numerous individuals occupying prominent positions in society, including one of the judges (Mr. Baron Wainwright), and the Mayor of Limerick (Joseph Roche, Esq.), and many others of the corporation, fell victims. Measures were adopted at Dublin on the principle of the English Poor Law, some of the most essential provisions of which appear to have been well understood in the great towns of Ireland in that day; and it was "hoped, since such provision is made for the poor, the inhabitants of the city will discourage all vagrant beggars, and give their assistance that they may be sent to Bridewell to hard labour,[27] and thereby free themselves from a set of idlers who are a scandal and a reproach to the nation." Soup-kitchens and other modes of relief were established in different parts of the country, in which Primate Boulter and the Society of Friends took the lead;[28] and numerous cargoes of corn were procured on mercantile account from the North American Colonies, the arrival of which was looked for with great anxiety. In only one point is there any decided difference between what then took place in Ireland and the painful events which have just occurred, after the lapse of upwards of a century. The famine of 1741 was not regarded with any active interest either in England or in any foreign country, and the subject is scarcely alluded to in the literature of the day. No measures were adopted either by the Executive or the Legislature for the purpose of relieving the distress caused by this famine.[29] There is no mention of grants or loans; but an Act was passed by the Irish Parliament in 1741 (15 Geo. II, cap. 8), "For the more effectual securing the payment of Rents, and preventing frauds by Tenants*."[30]

The failure of 1822, in the provinces of Munster and Connaught, was owing to a continued and excessive humidity, which caused the potatoes to rot after they had been stored in the pits, so that the deficiency of food was not discovered till late in the season. On the 7th May, 1822, a public meeting was held in London which was attended by the Archbishop of Canterbury and the most eminent persons of the day, when a committee of no less than 109 of the nobility and gentry was formed, and a subscription was entered into, amounting, with the aid of a king's letter, to 311,081*l*. 5s. 7d., of which 44,177*l*. 9s. was raised in Ireland.[31] Many excellent principles were laid down for the distribution of this large sum and after reserving what was required for immediate relief, the balance, amounting to 87,667*l*. was granted to various societies which had been established for the future and permanent benefit of the Irish peasantry*.[32] A committee also sat at the Mansion House at Dublin, which collected 31,260*l*. from various quarters, independently of the grants it received from the London Committee.[33] Central Committees were established in each county town in the distressed districts, and Sub-Committees in each parish. The western portion of Ireland was also divided into three districts, to each of which a civil engineer was appointed for the purpose of employing the destitute in making roads and the following sums were voted by Parliament for carrying on these and other Public Works set on foot with the same object of relieving the distress†:[34]

> On 24 June, 1822, £100,000,
> "for the employment of the poor in Ireland, and other purposes relating thereto as the exigency of affairs may require."
>
> On 23 July, 1822, £200,000;
> "to enable His Majesty to take such measures as the exigency of affairs may require."

And on the 24 June, 1823, £15,000 was voted,

"to facilitate emigration from the south of Ireland to the Cape of Good Hope."[35] In 1831 another failure of the potato crop occurred in the counties of Galway, Mayo, and Donegal, upon which, another meeting was held in the City of London, and one committee was established at the Mansion House, and another at the West End. Great exertions were made to raise subscriptions; a bazaar was held at the Hanover Square Rooms by many of the ladies of the nobility, presided over by the Queen in person; and there was a ball at Drury Lane Theatre, which was honoured by the presence of the King and Queen. The whole amount collected was 74,410*l*.; and besides this 40,000*l*. was granted by Parliament, part of which was expended on relief works, and part in the actual distribution of food. Besides these London Committees, two other Committees were formed at Dublin, through one of which (the Mansion House Committee*)[36] 8,569*l*. was collected, and through the other (the Sackville Street Committee) 21,526*l*.[37]

In each of the years 1835, 1836, and 1837, the potato crop failed in one or other of the districts in the West of Ireland, and sums amounting in the aggregate to 7,572*l*. were expended from Civil Contingencies in relieving the distress thereby occasioned, to which was added the sum of 4,306*l*. remaining from the English and Irish subscriptions of 1831.

In 1839 another failure occurred; and in all the Western and Midland Counties, the average price of potatoes in July and August was 7d. a stone and of oatmeal 18s. or 19s. a cwt.; the former double, and the latter one-third more than the usual price at that time of the year. On this occasion, Captain Chads, R.N.[38] was deputed by the Government to assist the landlords in employing the destitute in constructing roads and other useful public works; and it appears from a report addressed by him to the Chancellor of the Exchequer, dated the 22nd of August, 1839, that 5,441*l*. was expended in this way, of which 1840*l*. was contributed by the Government, besides 1478*l*. disbursed through other channels. Towards the conclusion of his report Captain Chads made the following remarks:—"A recurrence of these seasons of distress, which have been almost periodical hitherto, must, I fear, be necessarily expected, so long as the present condition of the poor continues, and whilst they subsist on that species of food, which in a year of plenty cannot be stored up for the next, which may be one of scarcity. A very great alleviation, however, of this evil is most confidently expected from the Poor Law now being established. I have conversed on this subject with persons of every class of society, from one end of the country to the other, and it is universally regarded as the promise of a great blessing:—to the poor by inducing more provident and industrious habits; and by making it the interest of the landlords to give them employment; and to all other classes, comfort and contentment, from the knowledge that the really distressed are provided for, and that the country is generally improving by the extension of employment."

After this, urgent representations of distress were made in each year to the Irish Government and to the Poor Law Commissioners, until the summer of 1842, which was more than usually wet and unfavourable to vegetation, and it therefore again became necessary to have recourse to extensive measures of relief. On this occasion 3,448*l.* was distributed in aid of local subscriptions, in 121 separate districts; the aggregate sums raised in each case being expended, partly in public works on Captain Chads' plan, and partly in giving gratuitous relief*.[39]

Besides the grants above enumerated, made for the immediate relief of the Irish poor, when failures of the potato crop caused unusual distress, large sums of money have been advanced or granted from the Imperial Treasury from time to time since the Union, for various purposes supposed to be conducive to the tranquility and improvement of the country, and to the removal of the causes of permanent distress, as will be seen from the following specimens taken principally from a return to an order of the House of Commons of the 12th February, 1847, made on the motion of Mr. John O'Connell*.[40]

| | |
|---|---:|
| Works for Special Purposes under the Act 57 Geo. III., cap. 34 | 496,000 |
| Do.[41] for the Employment and Relief of the Poor, under the 1 & 2 Wm. IV., cap. 33, and previous Acts | 1,339,146 |
| Grants in aid of Public Works under various Acts of Parliament | 125,000 |
| Advanced by the London Loan Commissioners for sundry Works between 1826 and 1833 | 322,500 |
| Do. do. for Poor-Law Union Workhouses | 1,145,800 |
| Kingstown Harbour | 1,124,586 |
| Improvement of the River Shannon | 533,359 |
| Wide Street Commissioners, Dublin | 267,778 |
| Improving Post Roads | 515,541 |
| Gaols and Bridewells | 713,005 |
| Asylums for Lunatic Poor | 710,850 |
| Valuation of Lands and Tenements | 172,774 |
| Royal Dublin Society | 285,438 |
| Farming Society, Dublin | 87,132 |
| Linen Board, Dublin | 537,656 |
| Tithe (Relief of Clergy who did not receive Tithes of 1831) | 50,916 |
| Tithe Relief (Million Act) | 918,863 |
| Tithe Relief Commissioners (establishing Composition for Tithes) | 279,217 |
| Relief of Trade | 178,070 |
| Boards and Officers of Health (Cholera) | 196,575 |
| Police Purposes (Proclaimed Districts) | 4,693,871 |
| Police Purposes (Constabulary Police) | 1,748,712 |

Other causes concurred with the natural tendency of every people to have recourse to the cheapest description of food in encouraging the growth of a large population depending for its subsistence on the potato. Ireland was essentially a grazing country until the artificial enhancement of prices caused by the Acts of the Irish

Parliament passed in 1783 and 1784, for granting a bounty on the exportation, and restricting the importation of corn, occasioned an immediate and extraordinary increase of cultivation;[42] and as, owing to the general want of capital, it was impossible to find tenants for large tillage farms, the stimulus intended to act exclusively on agriculture, had a still more powerful effect in causing the subdivision of farms. The new occupiers also, being, for the most part, exceedingly poor, instead of paying their labourers in money, allowed them the use of small pieces of ground whereon they might erect cabins and raise potatoes, and their labour was set off, at so much a-day, against the annual rent. The plan of dividing and subdividing for the purpose of making freeholders, was carried to a great extent after 1792, when the elective franchise was restored to the Roman Catholics; and although the practice was far from being general, yet in some parts of the country, where particular families made it their object to contest or secure the county, it was carried to a very pernicious extent. Another powerful cause is that the emoluments of the Roman Catholic priesthood, including the bishops, depend not only on the extent of the population, but also on its continual increase; and if the parish priests object to emigration and the consolidation of small holdings, and look with favour on early marriages, it is only what any other body of men, in their circumstances, would equally do. Lastly, the small holding and potato system offered the inducement of large rents, obtained at the smallest possible amount of cost and trouble. The embarrassed and improvident landlord, and the leaseholder whose only object it was to make the most of his short tenure, equally found their account in this state of things, and the result in both cases was, that the farms were covered with hovels and miserable cottiers, in order, through them, to create profit-rents. When the failure of the potato forced all the "squatters" and "mock tenants" into notice, the owner of many a neglected estate was surprised by the apparition of hundreds of miserable beings, who had grown up on his property without his knowledge, and now claimed the means of support at his hands. The subsistence of the tenant was at the minimum; the rent was at the maximum; and the interval between the ignorant excitable peasantry and the proprietor in chief, was filled only by the middleman, whose business it was to exact rents and not to employ labourers. The base and the capital of the column were there, but the shaft was almost entirely wanting. The extent to which the welfare of the agricultural population, and through them of the rest of the community, is affected by the conditions upon which landed property is held, has become fearfully apparent during the present social crisis. The dependence for good and evil of workman on master manufacturer, of subject on Government, of child on father, is less absolute than that of the Irish peasant upon the lord of the soil from which he derives his subsistence. This is a subject to which, if we would save ourselves and our country, it behoves us to give our most earnest and careful attention at the present time. We cannot give landed proprietors the will and disposition (where it is wanting) to fulfil the important part they have to perform in the scheme of society, but we have it in our power to strike off the fetters which at present impede every step of their progress in the performance of the duty they owe to themselves and to those dependent on them.

One half of the surface of Ireland is said to be let off in perpetuity leases, with derivative and sub-derivative interests in an endless chain, so as to obtain profit-rents at each stage; and these leases are often open to the additional objection that they are unnecessarily burthensome or uncertain from the particular mode in which they are made; such as "leases for lives renewable for ever by the insertion of other lives when the first-named are dead," "for three lives or thirty-one years," and "for three lives and thirty-one years." Many proposals have at different times been made for the redemption of these various interests; but an arbitrary interference with the rights of property is to be avoided, and our object should rather be to give every prudent facility for the voluntary transfer of land and of the various interests connected with it, which must lead, by a safe but certain gradation, to that degree of improvement of the existing tenures which is necessary for the encouragement of agriculture. In the flourishing islands of Guernsey and Jersey, corn-rents of fixed amount are charged upon the same farm one after another, like the coats of an onion; but the lowest holder, who is the party really interested in the improvement of the property, has every requisite security that he will enjoy the whole profit of any outlay he may make, and the most essential part of the benefit of ownership is thus obtained. In Mayo and other western counties the old barbarous Irish tenure called Rundale (Scotch runrigg), still prevails,[43] which stops short of the institution of individual property, and by making the industrious and thriving responsible for the short-comings of the idle and improvident, effectually destroys the spring of all improvement. The cessation of this antiquated system is an indispensable preliminary to any progress being made in the localities where it exists; but this improvement may be effected by the landlords without any change in the law.

The master evil of the agricultural system of Ireland, however, is the law of Entail, and the Incumbrances which seldom fail to accumulate upon entailed estates.[44] "Proprietors of estates," observes the author of an excellent pamphlet which has recently appeared on this subject*,[45] "are too often but mere nominal owners, without influence or power over the persons holding under them. Their real condition is often pitiable, nor is it possible, in the great majority of cases, to retrieve the estates. The burthen of debt, or the evils of improvident leases, are fastened upon the land in such a manner as to convert the owner into a mere annuitant, often glad to obtain from a good estate a scanty annuity (after payment of the incumbrances thereon and the public burthens) for his own subsistence. Proprietor and tenant are equally powerless for good; and the whole kingdom suffers from the disorders which have resulted from this state of real property in Ireland." And the author of another valuable publication on the same subject*[46] observes as follows: "The evils resulting from settlements and entails may be regarded as arising from insecurity or uncertainty of tenure; because the possessor of the property is not in reality the owner; he cannot deal with it as an owner; he is merely a trustee for others; he has no interest in its future thorough permanent improvement, except so far as he may wish to benefit his successors; he can never reap the benefit himself; he cannot sell; he cannot dispose of a part, even though the alienation of a part might greatly enhance the value of the remainder; he holds it during his lifetime, as his predecessor held it, unaltered, unimproved, to transmit it to his heir clogged with the same restrictions alike injurious to him and to his country. This is the case of an unembarrassed landlord*.[47] But let us suppose, as is unfortunately too often the case, that he has received the estate incumbered under a settlement, with a jointure to the widow of the late possessor, and a provision for daughters and younger sons. In what difficulties is he at once involved! this owner for life of a large tract of country with a long rent-roll, but in fact a small property! He cannot maintain his position in society without spending more than his income; debts accumulate; he mortgages his estate, and insures his life for the security of the mortgagee. Of course he cannot afford to lay out anything on improvements; on the contrary, though perhaps naturally kind-hearted and just, his necessities force him to resort to every means of increasing his present rental. He looks for the utmost amount; he lets to the highest bidder, without regard to character or means of payment. If his tenants are without leases, he raises their rents. If leases fall in, he cannot afford to give the preference to the last occupier. Perhaps, with all his exertions, he is unable to pay the interest or put off his creditors. Proceedings are commenced against him, and the estate passes during his lifetime under the care of the worst possible landlord, a Receiver under the Court of Chancery*."[48]

The remedy for this state of things is simply the sale of the encumbered estate, or of a sufficient portion of it to enable the owner to discharge his encumbrances and to place him in a position to do his duty towards the remainder. This is the master-key to unlock the field of industry in Ireland. The seller, in all such cases, is incapable of making a proper use of the land. The purchaser, on the other hand, may safely be assumed to be an improver. It is a natural feeling in which almost all men indulge, and purchases of land are seldom made without a distinct view to further profitable investments in improvements. "To give every prudent facility for the transfer by sale of real property from man to man, by the adoption of a simple, cheap, and secure system of transfer, in lieu of the present barbarous, unsafe, and expensive system, so that real property could be bought and sold in Ireland with as much freedom and security as other property*,"[49] is, therefore, the object at which we ought to aim, and especially to encourage the investment of small capitals in the land, it being through the instrumentality of small capitalists chiefly that the country can be civilized and improved. "The purchasers would give extensive and permanent employment to numbers of people around them in carrying out that natural desire of man, the improvement of newly-acquired landed property; they would promote industry everywhere; they would greatly increase the value of land generally. By their number, all property in land would be rendered secure against revolutionary violence. The habits and example of men who had made money by industry, and who might invest their savings in land, would place the social system of Ireland on a solid basis. The best of the Protestants and Roman Catholics, those who had been careful and industrious, would be purchasers of land, and all would have a common interest in peace and order. That surplus population beyond the means of present employment, which now oppresses and embarrasses the country, might gradually be absorbed, and become a source of wealth and strength. Towns would everywhere improve, and new ones might arise by the extension of the railway system, spreading industry and civilization among men now sunk in indolence and almost barbarism."*50

All the parties concerned in these transfers would be benefited by them. Lands are comparatively valueless to those who have no capital to improve them, and they are often justly felt to be a burthen and a disgrace, because they entail duties which the nominal owners have no means of performing. The effect on the character and prospects of the whole body of landed proprietors would be as described in the following passage from the author to whom we are already so much indebted: "When men, however young, act under responsibility, they usually proceed with caution; if others will think and act for them, and provide for their wants, and secure them from poverty and danger, their own prudential faculties may become dormant; and a man or any class of men so protected, are likely to exhibit deficiency in the qualities of prudence and good management of their affairs. But owners of land would not evince any such deficiency, if once they felt that they would be ruined, and their families also, if they were not governed by the same rules of prudence which other men must observe, and which necessarily enter into the proper management of all other descriptions of property. The present difficulties of sale of land, and the consequent protection afforded to entailed properties, are the chief reasons why so many persons of the class of proprietors are in difficulties. With more liberty, there would be more prudence and more attention to estates on the part of owners, from which they and the country would be great gainers."*51

The manner in which the interests of the public at large are affected, is correctly described in the following passage from the other pamphlet: "If these premises be correct; if employment with regular wages must be found for the peasantry: if capital be necessary, and the parties holding the land do not possess sufficient for this purpose; it follows, either that Government must continue to supply the capital required, not merely by a loan on an emergency, but as part of its regular system of action; or else that the land must pass into the hands of those who do possess the means of employing the people—of men who will carry on agriculture as a business, and will bring to their occupation the capital, the habits of business, and the energy and intelligence which have raised the commerce and manufactures of this nation to their present pre-eminence."*52

Her Majesty's Government being deeply impressed with the importance of these views, introduced a bill into Parliament in the session of 1847, the object of which was to enable the owners of encumbered estates in Ireland to sell the whole or a portion of them, after the circumstances of each estate had been investigated by a Master in Chancery with a view to secure the due liquidation of every claim upon it. The sale was not to take place without the consent of the first incumbrancer, unless the Court of Chancery should consider the produce sufficient to pay the principal and all arrears of interest, or unless the owner or some subsequent incumbrancer should undertake to pay to the first incumbrancer any deficiency which might exist, and give such security for the performance of his undertaking as the court might direct. This bill passed the House of Lords, but was withdrawn in the Commons, owing to the opposition of some of the Irish proprietors, and to objections entertained by the great Insurance Companies, who are the principal lenders on Irish mortgages, to having their investments disturbed. The failure of the bill was a national misfortune which cannot be too soon remedied.

The Government, however, did what was in its power. A system has existed in Ireland since the time of Queen Anne for the registration of all deeds affecting landed property;[53] and of late years a similar registration has been established of all judgments relating to that description of property. The attention of the Lord Lieutenant has been called to the practicability of diminishing the delay and expense attending transfers of landed property, by the adoption of two simple practical measures, viz., that when searches have been made in the office of the Registrar of Deeds, copies should be recorded in the office, as well as given to the parties on whose behalf they are made; and that when judgments, &c, recorded in the office of the Registrar of Judgments have been satisfied, notice should be immediately sent to the Registrar, in order that such satisfaction may be recorded in the books of his office*.[54] The consequence of the neglect of the first of these obvious precautions was, that, after expensive searches had been made in the Registry Office, the same searches often had to be made again and again, at the same expense, at the instance of other parties, however limited the transactions might be for the security of which these inquiries into past transfers and incumbrances were made; and the consequence of the neglect of the other precaution was, that if, after a search had been made through the records deposited in the office of the Registrar of Judgments, to ascertain whether any judgment had been passed against the estate, it appeared that any such judgment had been given, another search had to be made in the courts of law, involving fresh loss of time and fresh expense, to ascertain whether it had been satisfied†.[55]

But it is time that we should resume our narrative.

The potato disease, which had manifested itself in North America in 1844*,[56] first appeared in these islands late in the autumn of 1845. The early crop of potatoes, which is generally about one-sixth of the whole, and is dug in September and October, escaped;[57] but the late, or what is commonly called the "people's crop" and is taken up in December and January, was tainted after it arrived at an advanced stage of maturity. When the disease had once commenced, it made steady progress, and it was often found, on opening the pits, that the potatoes had become a mass of rottenness. Nevertheless, this year the attack was partial; and although few parts of the country entirely escaped, and the destruction of human food was, on the whole, very great, a considerable portion of the crop, which had been a more than usually large one, was saved. The wheat crop was a full average; oats and barley were abundant; and of turnips, carrots, and green crops, including a plentiful hay harvest, there was a more than sufficient supply. On the Continent, the rye crops failed partially, and the potato disease was very destructive in Holland, Belgium, France, and the west of Germany.

In the following year (1846) the blight in the potatoes took place earlier, and was of a much more sweeping and decisive kind. "On the 27th of last month (July), I passed," Father Mathew writes in a letter published in the Parliamentary Papers,[58] "from Cork to Dublin, and this doomed plant bloomed in all the luxuriance of an abundant harvest. Returning on the 3rd instant (August), I beheld with sorrow one wide waste of putrefying vegetation. In many places the wretched people were seated on the fences of their decaying gardens, wringing their hands, and wailing bitterly the destruction that had left them foodless." The first symptom of the disease was a little brown spot on the leaf, and these spots gradually increased in number and size, until the foliage withered and the stem became brittle, and snapped off immediately when touched. In less than a week the whole process was accomplished*.[59] The fields assumed a blackened appearance, as if they had been burnt up, and the growth of the potatoes was arrested when they were not larger than a marble or a pigeon's egg. No potatoes were pitted this year. In many districts where they had been most abundant, full-grown wholesome potatoes were not to be procured; and even in London and other large towns, they were sold at fancy prices, and were consumed as a luxury by the wealthy, rice and other substitutes being had recourse to by the body of the people. The crop of wheat this year was barely an average one, while barley and oats, and particularly the former, were decidedly deficient. On the Continent, the rye and potato crops again failed, and prices rose early in the season above those ruling in England, which caused the shipments from the Black Sea, Turkey and Egypt, to be sent to France, Italy, and Belgium; and it was not till late in the season, that our prices rose to a point which turned the current of supplies towards England and Ireland. The Indian corn crop in the United States this year was very abundant, and it became a resource of the utmost value to this country.[60]

In the third year (1847) the disease had nearly exhausted itself. It appeared in different parts of the country, but the plants generally exerted fresh vigour and outgrew it. The result, perhaps, could not have been better. The wholesome distrust in the potato was maintained, while time was allowed for making the alterations which the new state of things required. Although the potatoes sown in Ireland in the year 1847 were estimated only at 1-5th or 1-6th of the usual quantity, it would have been a serious aggravation of the difficulties and discouragements under which that portion of the empire was suffering, if the disease had reappeared in its unmitigated form. The crops of wheat, barley, and oats, in almost every part of the United Kingdom, and in most of the neighbouring countries on the Continent, were this year, to use the epithet generally applied to them, magnificent; and it became more and more apparent on the brink of what a precipice we had been standing, as the unusually small remaining stock of old corn came to light, and the exhausted and embarrassed state to which every description of business had been reduced, notwithstanding the advantage of a good harvest, gradually declared itself.

Among the numerous causes which enhanced the difficulty of obtaining adequate foreign supplies at moderate rates during the most exigent period of the winter of

1846–7, one of the most embarrassing, was the sudden and extraordinary advance in freights, which occurred simultaneously in the ports of the United States of America, the Mediterranean, and the Black Sea. Vessels were not obtainable in the Black Sea and the Danube at less than 18s. and 22s. per quarter for corn, whereas the usual rates are 9s. and 11s.; while in the United States, where large shipments of grain, flour, and Indian corn, were going forward to Europe, the comparatively limited number of vessels caused the rates to run up to 9s. per barrel for flour, and 16s. and 18s. per quarter for Indian corn to British ports, the rates usually given being 2s. 6d. to 3s. 6d. per barrel of flour, and 8s. and 9s. per quarter for Indian corn.

On the 27th January, 1846, Sir Robert Peel proposed his measure for the relaxation of the duties on the importation of foreign corn, by which the scale of duties payable on wheat was to range from 4s. to 10s. per quarter, and Indian corn, which had previously been charged with the same duty as barley, was to pay only 1s. a-quarter. This was to last till February 1849, when an uniform duty of 1s. a-quarter was to be charged on every description of grain. The bill passed the House of Lords on the 29th June, 1846; and Sir R. Peel announced his resignation in the House of Commons on the same day.[61]

Immediately on the meeting of Parliament in January, 1847, Lord J. Russell introduced bills to suspend until the 1st September, 1847, the duties on foreign corn, and the restrictions imposed by the Navigation Laws on the importation of corn in foreign vessels; and he at the same time moved a resolution permitting the use of sugar in breweries; all which measures received the sanction of the Legislature. At the close of the same session, the suspension of the Corn and Navigation Laws was extended to the 1st March, 1848.[62]

On the first appearance of the blight in the autumn of 1845, Professors Kane, Lindley, and Playfair, were appointed by Sir Robert Peel to inquire into the nature of it, and to suggest the best means of preserving the stock of potatoes from its ravages. The result showed that the mischief lay beyond the knowledge and power of man. Every remedy which science or experience could dictate was had recourse to, but the potato equally melted away under the most opposite modes of treatment.

The next step was to order from the United States of America 100,000*l.* worth of Indian corn. It was considered that the void caused by the failure of the potato crop might be filled, with the least disturbance of private trade and market prices, by the introduction of a new description of popular food. Owing to the prohibitory duty, Indian corn was unknown as an article of consumption in the United Kingdom*.[63] Private merchants, therefore, could not complain of interference with a trade which did not exist, nor could prices be raised against the home consumer on an article of which no stock was to be found in the home market. Nevertheless, with a view to avoid as long as possible, the doubts and apprehensions which must have arisen if the Government had appeared as a purchaser in a new class of operations, pains were taken to keep the transaction secret, and the first cargoes from America had been more than a fortnight in Cork harbour before it became generally known that such a measure was in progress.

In order to distribute the food so obtained, central depots were established in various parts of Ireland, under the direction of officers of the Commissariat, with sub-depôts under the charge of the Constabulary and Coast Guard; and, when the supplies in the local markets were deficient, meal was sold from these depots at reasonable prices to Relief Committees, where any existed; and where they did not, to the labourers themselves. In the time of the heaviest pressure (June and July 1846); one sub-depôt retailed 20 tons of meal daily, and the issues from a single main depot to its dependencies amounted to 233 tons in one week.

The Relief Committees were formed, under the superintendence of a Central Commission at Dublin; for the purpose of selling food in detail to those who could buy it; and of giving it to those who could not; the requisite funds being derived from private subscriptions, added to, in certain proportions, by Government donations. The Relief Committees also selected the persons to be employed on the Relief Works carried on under the superintendence of the Board of Works. If the Irish poor had been in the habit of buying their food, as is the case in England, the object would have been attained when a cheap substitute had been provided for the potato; but as the labouring class in Ireland had hitherto subsisted on potatoes grown by themselves, and money-wages were almost unknown, it was necessary to adopt some means of giving the people a command over the new description of food. This was done by establishing a system of public works, in accordance with the previous practice on similar occasions, both in Ireland and in other countries.

These works, which consisted principally of roads, were undertaken on the application of the magistrates and principal cess-payers, under the Act 9 & 10 Vic., c. 1,[64] which was passed for the purpose, and the expense of executing them was defrayed by advances of public money, half of which was a grant, and half a loan to be repaid by the barony. The largest number of persons employed in this first season of relief was 97,000, in August, 1846.

The first symptoms of neglected tillage appeared in the Spring of 1846, and they were worst in those districts in which the Relief Works were carried on to the greatest extent. The improvements in progress on the Shannon and the arterial drainages were also impeded by the preference which the labourers showed for the Relief Works.

The measures of which we have been speaking were brought to a close on the 15th August, 1846, and they may be considered to have answered their end. The scarcity being partial and local, the deficiency of one part of the country was supplied from the superabundance of others,[65] and the pains taken to prevent the people from suffering want, led to their being better off than in ordinary years. Above all, Ireland was prepared by the course adopted during this probationary season of distress, as it may be called, to bear better the heavy affliction of the succeeding season. No misapplication of the funds deserving of notice took place, except in the instance of the Relief Works, the cause of which was as follows:—The landed proprietors of Ireland had long been accustomed to rely upon Government loans and grants for making improvements of various kinds, and the terms on which the Relief Works were to be executed being more advantageous than any which had been open to them for many years before, a rush took place from all quarters upon this fund, and the special object of relieving the people from the consequences of the failure of their accustomed food, was to a great extent lost sight of in the general fear, which in many cases was not attempted to be concealed, of being deprived of what the persons interested called "their share of the grant." This description of relief, therefore, instead of acting as a test of real distress, operated as a bounty on applications for public works from a class of persons who were at once charged with the administration of the relief and were interested in the execution of the works. The result was that, while the applications amounted to 1,289,816*l*., the sum actually sanctioned and expended was only 476,000*l*., and great part even of this was merely yielded to the distressing appeals pressed on the Lord Lieutenant on the plea of urgent local destitution, and of the lamentable consequences to be expected from allowing it to remain unrelieved. The other expenses connected with this season of relief were as follows:— Loans on grand jury presentments, 130,000*l*. loss on the purchase and sale of grain, 50,000*l*. given in aid of Relief Committees, 69,845*l*. extra staff of the Board of Works, 7,527*l*. thus making the whole sum expended in relief to Ireland, up to the 15th August, 1846, 733.372*l*., of which 368,000*l*. was in loans, and 365,372*l*. in grants. The sum raised by voluntary subscription through the Relief Committees was 98,000*l*.

The new and more decisive failure of the potato crop called for great exertions from Lord John Russell's recently formed Government, and the plan resolved upon was explained in the Treasury Minute dated the 31st August, 1846, which was published for general information*.[66]

The system of public works was renewed by the Act 9 & 10 Vic., c. 107,[67] which was passed without any opposition in either House of Parliament. In order to check the exorbitant demands which had been made during the preceding season, the whole of the expense was made a local charge, and the advances were directed to be repaid by a rate levied according to the Poor Law valuation, which makes the landlords liable for the whole rate on tenements under 4*l*. yearly value, and for a proportion, generally amounting to one-half, on tenements above that value, instead of according to the grand jury cess (the basis of the repayments under the preceding Act), which lays the whole burden upon the occupier.[68] It was also determined that the wages given on the Relief Works should be somewhat below the average rate of wages in the district; that the persons employed, should, as far as possible, be paid by task or in proportion to the work actually done by them; and that the Relief Committees, instead of giving tickets entitling persons to employment on the public works, should furnish lists of persons requiring relief, which should be carefully revised by the officers of the Board of Works; the experience of the preceding season having shown that these precautions were necessary to confine the Relief Works to the destitute, and to enforce a reasonable quantum of work.[69]

The question which the Government had to decide, in regard to the renewal of the Commissariat operations, was of the most momentous kind. After all that had taken place during the last few months, it could not be expected that private trade would return, as a matter of course, to its accustomed channels. Neither the wholesale dealers in towns, nor the retail dealers in the rural districts, would lay in even their usual stocks of food; still less would they make the extraordinary provision required to meet the coming emergency, while they had before them the prospect of the Government throwing into the market supplies of food of unknown extent, which might make their outlay so much loss to them. The Government could not, therefore, calculate, as it did on the former occasion, on finding the private trade, by means of which the people are ordinarily supplied with food, proceeding as usual, and on being able to add more or less, at its discretion, to the resources which that trade afforded. Mercantile confidence in this branch of business was, for the time, destroyed. The trade was paralysed; and if this state of things had been suffered to continue, the general expectation of the Government again interfering would inevitably have created a necessity for that interference, on a scale which it would have been quite beyond the power of the Government to support. Under these circumstances it was announced,—1st. That no orders for supplies of food would be sent by the Government to foreign countries. 2ndly. That the interference of the Government would be confined to those western districts of Ireland in which, owing to the former prevalence of potato cultivation, no trade in corn for local consumption existed. And 3rdly. That even in these districts, the Government depots would not be opened for the sale of food, while it could be obtained from private dealers at reasonable prices, with reference to those which prevailed at the nearest large marts. It was also determined to adhere to the rule acted upon during the preceding season, not to make any purchases in the local markets of Ireland, where the appearance of the Government as a buyer must have had the effect of keeping up prices and encouraging interested representations; and a promise was given that every practicable effort would be made to protect the supplies of food introduced by private traders, both while they were in transit and when they were stored for future consumption.[70]

The Relief Committees of the preceding season were re-organised; the rules under which they had acted were carefully revised; and inspecting officers were appointed to superintend their proceedings, and keep the Government informed of the progress of events. A large proportion of the people of Ireland had been accustomed to grow the food they required, each for himself, on his own little plot of ground; and the social machinery by which, in other countries, the necessary supplies of food are collected, stored, and distributed, had no existence there. Suddenly, without any preparation, the people passed from a potato food, which they raised themselves, to a grain food, which they had to purchase from others, and which, in great part, had to be imported from abroad; and the country was so entirely destitute of the resources applicable to this new state of things, that often, even in large villages, neither bread nor flour was to be procured; and in country districts, the people had sometimes to walk twenty miles before they could obtain a single stone of meal. The main object for which the Relief Committees were established, therefore, was to provide a temporary substitute for the operations of the corn-factor, miller, baker, and provision-dealer, and to allow time and furnish the example for a sounder and more permanent state of things; but they were not precluded from giving gratuitous relief in cases of more than ordinary destitution. The agency of Relief Committees was this season almost universally substituted for the coast guard and constabulary depots with the object of drawing out the resources of the country before the Government depots were had recourse to, of inducing the upper and middle classes to exert themselves, and of preventing a direct pressure of the mass of the people upon the Government depots, which in a time of real famine it would have been very difficult to resist.

Such was the plan resolved upon for the campaign of 1846–7 against the approaching famine, and we shall now show the result of the struggle.

It was hoped that a breathing-time would have been allowed at the season of harvest, to enable the Board of Works to reorganize their establishments on a scale proportioned to the magnitude of the task about to devolve on them, and to prepare, through their district officers, plans and estimates of suitable works for the assistance of the baronial sessions. This interval was not obtained. The general failure of the potato crop spread despondency and alarm from one end of Ireland to the other, and induced every class of persons to throw themselves upon the Government for aid. On the 6th of September, the Lord Lieutenant ordered all the discontinued works under the 9 & 10 Vic., c. 1, to be recommenced, and sessions were rapidly held in all the southern and western counties of Ireland, at which roads were presented in the mass, under the 9 & 10 Vic., c. 107, the cost of which, in some cases, much exceeded the annual rental of the barony.[71] The resident gentry and rate-payers, whose duty it was to ascertain, as far as possible, the probable amount of destitution in their neighbourhood, the sum required to relieve it, and the works upon which that sum could best be expended, and who had the necessary local knowledge, in almost every case devolved these functions upon the Board of Works, who could only act on such information as they could obtain from naval and military officers and engineers, most of whom were selected from among strangers to the district, in order to prevent undue influence being used. After that, to advance the funds; to select the labourers; to superintend the work; to pay the people weekly; to enforce proper performance of the labour; if the farm works were interrupted, to ascertain the quantity of labour required for them; to select and draft off the proper persons to perform it; to settle the wages to be paid to them by the farmers, and see that they were paid; to furnish food, not only for all the destitute out of doors, but in some measure for the paupers in the workhouses, were the duties which the Government and its officers were called upon to perform. The proprietors and associated rate-payers having presented *indefinitely*, said it was the fault of the Government and its officers if the people were not instantly employed, and these officers were blamed, even by persons of character

and understanding, if they were not at once equal to execute the duties which in this country are performed in their respective districts by thousands of country gentlemen, magistrates, guardians, overseers, surveyors, &c, resident throughout the country, and trained by the experience of years to the performance of their various functions. The Board of Works became the centre of a colossal organization; 5,000 separate works had to be reported upon; 12,000 subordinate officers had to be superintended. Their letters averaged upwards of 800 a-day, and the number received on each of the following days was—
January 4th,-3,104
February 15th,-4,900
April 19th,-4,340
May 17th,-6,033*[72]

The strain on the springs of society from this monstrous system of centralisation was fearful in the extreme. The Government, which ought only to mediate between the different classes of society, had now to bear the immediate pressure of the millions, on the sensitive points of wages and food. The opposition to taskwork was general, and the enforcement of it became a trial of strength between the Government and the multitude. The officers of the Board were in numerous instances the objects of murderous attacks, and it became necessary for the preservation of the whole community, to have recourse to the painful expedient of stopping the works whenever cases of insubordination or outrage occurred.[73]

Meanwhile, the number of persons employed on the works was rapidly on the increase. The utmost exertions of two sets of inspecting officers, one under the Board of Works, and the other under Sir R. Routh, were insufficient to revise the lists; and the Lord Lieutenant in vain directed that no person rated above 6*l*. for the Poor Law cess, should, except under very special circumstances, be eligible for employment. Thousands upon thousands were pressed upon the officers of the Board of Works in every part of Ireland, and it was impossible for those officers to test the accuracy of the urgent representations which were made to them. The attraction of money wages regularly paid from the public purse, or the "Queen's pay," as it was popularly called, led to a general abandonment of other descriptions of industry, in order to participate in the advantages of the Relief Works. Landlords competed with each other in getting the names of their tenants placed on the lists; farmers dismissed their labourers and sent them to the works; the clergy insisted on the claims of the members of their respective congregations; the fisheries were deserted; and it was often-difficult even to get a coat patched or a pair of shoes mended, to such an extent had the population of the south and west of Ireland turned out upon the roads. The average number employed in October was 114,000; in November, 285,000; in December, 440,000; and in January, 1847, 570,000. It was impossible to exact from such multitudes a degree of labour which would act as a test of destitution. Huddled together in masses, they contributed to each other's idleness, and there were no means of knowing who did a fair proportion of work and who did not. The general enforcement of the system of task work had justly been considered necessary to stimulate the industry of the labourers on the Relief Works, but when this point had been carried, after a hard struggle, the old abuse reappeared in the aggravated form of an habitual collusion between the labourers and the overseers who were appointed to measure their work; so that the labourers, if they could be so called, were not only as idle as ever, but were enabled withal to enjoy a rate of wages which ought only to have been the reward of superior industry.

The plan of the Labour Rate Act (9 & 10 Vic. c. 107) was based on the supposition that the great majority of the landlords and farmers would make those exertions and submit to those sacrifices which the magnitude of the crisis demanded, leaving only a manageable proportion of the population to be supported by the Board of Works; and the Act would probably have answered its object, if a larger, instead of a smaller number of persons than usual had been employed in the cultivation and improvement of the land, and the Relief Committees had put only those who were really destitute upon the lists. Including the families of the persons employed, upwards of two millions of people were maintained by the Relief Works, but there were other multitudes behind, including often the most helpless portion of the community, for whom no work could be found. The Relief Works did not always furnish a subsistence even for those who were employed on them. The wages, paid regularly in money, were higher than any which had ever been given for agricultural labour in Ireland, but at the existing prices of food they were insufcient [sic] for the support of a family, melancholy proof of which was afforded by daily instances of starvation in connexion with the Relief Works*.[74] The fearful extent to which the rural population had been thrown for support upon the Board of Works also threatened a disastrous neglect of the ordinary tillage. If the people were retained on the works, their lands must remain uncultivated; if they were put off the works, they must starve. A change of system had become inevitable, and when Parliament met in the end of January, it was announced that the Government intended to put an end to the Public Works, and to substitute for them another mode of relief, which will be hereafter described.[75]

Meanwhile, the pressure on the Relief Works was continually on the increase, and the persons daily employed, who in January had been 570,000, became in February 708,000, and in March amounted to the enormous number of 734,000*,[76] representing, at a moderate estimate of the average extent of each family, upwards of three millions of persons. At last, the Government, seeing that the time suited for agricultural operations was rapidly passing away, and that the utmost exertions made on the spot had failed in keeping the numbers in check, took the matter into its own hands, and directed that on the 20th March, 20 per cent of the persons employed should be struck off the lists; after which, successive reductions were ordered, proportioned to the progress made in bringing the new system of relief into operation in each district.[77] These orders were obeyed, and the crisis passed without any disturbance of the public peace or any perceptible aggravation of the distress. The necessary labour was returned to agriculture, and the foundation was laid of the late abundant harvest in Ireland, by which the downward progress of that country has been mercifully stayed, and new strength and spirits have been given for working out her regeneration. In the first week in April, the persons employed on the Relief Works were reduced to 525,000; in the first week in May to 419,000; in the first week in June to 101,000; and in the week ending the 26th June to 28,000. The remaining expenditure was limited to a sum of 200,000*l*. for the month of May, and to the rate of 100,000*l*. a-month for June, July, and the first fifteen days of August, when the Act expired. These sums were afterwards permitted to be exceeded to a certain extent, but the object was attained of putting a curb on this monstrous system and of bringing it gradually and quietly to a close. Great exertions were made, and a heavy expense was incurred, to leave the roads and other works in progress in a safe and passable state as far as they had gone; but their completion must depend upon the parties locally interested in them. From the first commencement of the Relief Works in February 1846, repeated warnings were given that the object was not the works themselves, but the relief of the prevailing destitution through the employment afforded by them; that the works would be closed as soon as they were no longer required for that purpose; and that if the proprietors desired to complete them, they might do so under the ordinary system of Government loans made on the security of county presentments*.[78]

This system threw off a shoot, the history of which it is necessary to trace. In order to impose some limits on what threatened to become a gigantic system of permanently supporting one portion of the community at the expense of the remainder, and of making provision out of the taxes for classes of undertakings which properly belong to the economy of private life, the application of the public money under the Labour Rate Acts was strictly limited to works of a public character, which were not likely to be undertaken except for the purpose of giving relief. This condition was generally objected to in Ireland; and although no disposition was evinced to take advantage of the loans which the Government was ready to make under the General Improvement and Drainage Acts, a great desire was expressed that the funds advanced under the Labour Rate Act should be employed on what were called reproductive works. The Lord Lieutenant, having obtained the sanction of the Government, yielded to this general feeling, and authorized presentments to be made for the drainage and subsoiling of the estates of individuals, provided they consented to their estates being charged with the repayment of the sums advanced. This was the arrangement which acquired so much notoriety under the name of "Labouchere's Letter" owing to its having been announced by the publication of a letter from Mr. Labouchere, who then held the office of Secretary for Ireland, to the Board of Works, dated 5th October, 1846; but the result did not answer the expectations which had been formed. The aggregate amount presented "under the Letter" was 380,607*l*., of which presentments were acted on to the gross amount of 239,476*l*.[79] The sum actually expended was about 180,000*l*.; and the largest number of persons at any one time employed was 26,961 in the month of May, 1847. Some incidental good was done by the example of the advantages of thorough draining, and of the proper mode of executing it; but, as a remedy for the wide-spread calamity, the plan totally failed.

Upon this, a two-fold agitation sprang up. Some landed proprietors required that their liability should be confined to the relief of the destitute on their own estates; while others demanded that, instead of being employed on the roads, the people should be paid for working on their own farms. Both these movements were steadily resisted by the Government. The objection to the first was, that if the inhabitants of the pauperised districts had been separated from the rest in the administration of the measures of relief, they must either have starved or have become entirely dependent on the Consolidated Fund;[80] while, if the other plan had been adopted, the entire cost of carrying on the agriculture of the country would have been transferred to the Government, without its being possible either to test the applications for assistance, or to enforce a proper amount of exertion. This last scheme was most clamorously urged in the county of Clare, and it may be considered as the masterpiece of that system of social economy according to which the machine of society should be worked backwards, and the Government should be made to support the people, instead of the people the Government. The Government was also to provide tools and seed as well as wages, but the rent was to be received by the same parties as before.

Baronial presentments were authorized for the construction of railway earthworks, as relief works under the 9 & 10 Vic., c. 107, subject to the conditions required for the fulfilment of the object of the Act*;[81] but advantage was taken of this permission only in two baronies of the county of Cork, where the Waterford and Limerick Railway was aided from this source.[82]

The silver currency which had previously sufficed for a people who lived upon potatoes grown by themselves, and paid their rent by so many days' labour, fell short of what was required to pay the labourers employed on the numerous Relief Works carried on simultaneously in different parts of the country, and a large supply was therefore distributed, by means of a Government steamer, among the principal towns on the coast of Ireland.[83] On the cessation of the Relief Works, the greater part of this coin accumulated in the banks, which were relieved by the transmission of the surplus to the Cape of Good Hope to aid in carrying on the Caffre war.[84]

In the Commissariat branch of the operations, every pledge which had been given was strictly adhered to, and confidence having been re-established, prodigious efforts were made by the mercantile community to provide against the approaching scarcity. The whole world was ransacked for supplies. Indian corn, the taste for which had by this time taken root in Ireland, rose to a higher price than wheat; and the London and Liverpool markets were again and again swept by the enterprising operations of the Irish dealers, who, from an early period, appreciated the full extent of the calamity, and acted upon the principle that the gulf which had opened in Ireland would swallow all that could be thrown into it, and remain still unsatisfied. In February 1847, the beneficial effect of these measures began to be apparent.[85] On the 24th of that month, Mr. N. Cummins, a respectable merchant of Cork, wrote as follows to Mr. Trevelyan:

> "From this gloomy picture I turn to the supply of food, and am happy to say that in this quarter the importations, both direct and from England, during the past month, have been very large; heavy cargoes of maize continue almost daily to arrive, and I feel persuaded that the stocks of bread stuffs generally are accumulating here to a much larger amount than some of our dealers would have it believed. Prices cannot, however, be quoted at more than a turn below the extreme point yet; they stand as follows,—say Indian corn, by retail, 17*l*. 15s. and 18*l*. per ton; Indian meal to 19*l*.; oatmeal, 25*l*.; wheaten meal, 19*l*. to 20*l*. per ton.

On the 12th March, the same gentleman wrote, —

> "Our market for Indian corn seems at length quite glutted, the arrivals within the last few days having been so extremely numerous, that the trade is unable to take off the supply, or indeed to find sufficient stowage in the city. Several cargoes for discharge here are at this moment lying under demurrage, and I may quote the article 15s. to 20s. per ton cheaper than a fortnight since."

And on the 19th, —

> "There are at present over 100 sail, containing an aggregate amount of bread stuffs not short of 20,000 tons, afloat in our harbour; and maize, which a month since brought freely 18*l*. per ton, is this day offered in small parcels at 15*l*.

And on the same day Father Matthew [sic] wrote to Mr. Trevelyan as follows : —

> "For the first time since the Lord visited this unhappy land with famine, I address you with delight. The markets are rapidly falling; Indian corn from 16*l*. to 15*l*. per ton. The vast importations, and the still more vast exportations from America, have produced this blessed effect."

On the 26th March, Mr. Cummins states —

> "I have now to report the continuance each day of numerous arrivals of food cargoes here; the additional number during the present week (mostly maize laden) considerably exceeds 100 sail, several being American ships of large burthen; and although many have proceeded to other ports, the number afloat, waiting orders or sale, has been fully doubled. I cannot estimate the fleet this day in our harbours at less than 250 sail, nor the contents at much under 50,000 tons. Indian corn may be purchased at 14*l*. by the cargo, and retailed at 15*l*. per ton."[86]

It now began to be perceived that more was to be expected from the collective exertions of the merchants of the United Kingdom, than from the Admiralty or the Commissariat. The whole quantity of corn imported into Ireland in the first six months of 1847 was 2,849,508 qrs., which was worth, at the then current prices, 8,764,943*l*.; and the Irish market was, to use the words of the present Lord Lieutenant,[87] "freer, cheaper, and better supplied, than that of any country in Europe where distress prevailed, and where those measures of interference and restriction had been unwisely adopted which were successfully resisted here." The price of Indian corn, which in the middle of February had been 19*l*. a-ton, was reduced at the end of March to 13*l*., and at the end of August to 7*l*. 10s., a-ton; and such was the quantity of shipping which flocked to the United States on the first intelligence of the unusual demand for freight, that the rate for the conveyance of corn to the United Kingdom, which had been as high as 9s. per barrel during the winter months, was as low as 4s. 6d. in May, and has since fallen to 1s. 9d. It may safely be asserted that these results would not have been obtained, if the great body of our English and Irish merchants and ship-owners, instead of having free scope given to their exertions, had been left under the discouraging impression that all their calculations might be upset by the sudden appearance in the foreign market, of Government vessels and Government orders for supplies. The noble harbour of Cork was established as the house of call and entrepôt for the grain ships bound to every part of Western Europe; and the merchant being now free either to sell on the spot or to re-export, Ireland began to enjoy the benefit of her admirable commercial position, by getting the first, and largest, and cheapest supply.

Nevertheless, the public establishments were not idle. Upwards of 300,000 quarters of corn were purchased from time to time to supply the Government depôts on the western coast of Ireland*,[88] and large stores of biscuit and salt meat, which had been laid up at the different military stations in the year 1843, in anticipation of popular disturbances arising out of the repeal movement, were now applied to the relief of the people.[89] One of the consequences of the sudden change from a potato to a corn diet, was, that the means of grinding were seriously deficient. The powerful Admiralty mills at Deptford, Portsmouth, Plymouth, and Malta, besides two large hired mills, were therefore constantly employed in grinding the corn bought by the Commissariat, leaving the mill-power of Ireland to the private importers of grain into that country; and hand-mills, on the principle of the old Irish Quern,[90] were made for distribution in the most distressed districts; while others, constructed on an improved principle, were procured from France. Thirty-four large depôts were established on the western side of Ireland, from Dunfanaghy, in the most northern part of Donegal, to Skibbereen, in the south-west of the county of Cork: and the sales were made, as far as possible, to the Relief Committees, with the double object of drawing forth the resources and activity of the upper classes, and of preventing an indiscriminate pressure upon the depôts, which it would have been difficult to resist. Several ships of war were moored in convenient situations and used as store-ships. The largest and most powerful war-steamers, reinforced, when the occasion required it, by sailing vessels, were appropriated to the conveyance of the meal from the mills in England to the depôts in Ireland, and every other available steamer, not excepting the Admiralty yacht, was employed in making the necessary transfers between the depôts, and in conveying the supplies which the Relief Committees had purchased.

The highest praise to which these great operations are entitled, is that they were carried through without any sensible disturbance of the ordinary course of trade, and that in some important respects they even gave new life and development to it. The purchases were all made in the home market, and care was taken never to give the highest current price. The sales were made at the wholesale price of the nearest large mart, with a reasonable addition for the cost of carriage, &c. When supplies of food could be obtained elsewhere, the depôts were closed. Private merchants, therefore, imported largely in the face of the Government depôts; while, in the remote western districts, the Commissariat acted as pioneers to the ordinary trade, and led the way to habits of commercial enterprise where before they had no existence.

There was the same general pressure for the premature opening of the depôts as for the early commencement of Relief Works, but in this case it was successfully resisted. It was explained that the Government depôts were intended to be a last resource to supply the deficiencies of the trade, and not to take the place of that trade; and that if the depôts were opened while the country was still full of the produce of the late harvest, that produce would be exported before the spring supplies arrived from America and the Black Sea, and the population would become entirely dependent upon the depôts, which must, in that case, soon come to a discreditable and disastrous stop. Meanwhile, great exertions were made to protect the provision trade, and the troops and constabulary were harassed by continual escorts. The plunder of bakers' shops and bread-carts, and the shooting of horses and breaking up of roads, to prevent the removal of provisions, were matters of daily occurrence; and at Limerick, Galway, and elsewhere, mobs prevented any articles of food from leaving the towns, while the country people resisted there being carried in. Convoys under military protection proceeded at stated intervals from place to place, without which nothing in the shape of food could be sent with safety.[91]

As many as 1097 Relief Committees were established under the superintendence of the Commissariat; while 199,470*l*.*[92] was subscribed by private individuals, and 189,914*l*. was granted by the Government (making together 389,384*l*.) in support of their operations.

One of the functions of these committees was to provide supplies of food for sale at the current market price; and when the rise of prices began to be seriously felt, the Government was called upon from every part of Ireland to permit the grants of public money made to the committees to be employed in reducing the price of provisions to that of ordinary years. To this demand it was impossible for the Government to accede. In 1845–6 the scarcity was confined to a few districts of Ireland, while there was abundance everywhere else. The question, therefore, at that time, was a money one; and all that was required to relieve the distress, was to purchase a sufficient quantity of food elsewhere and to send it into the distressed districts. In 1846–7, on the contrary, the scarcity was general, extending over all Western Europe, and threatening a famine in other quarters besides Ireland. The present question, therefore, was not a money, but a food question. The entire stock of food for the whole United Kingdom was insufficient, and it was only by carefully husbanding it, that it could be made to last till harvest. If provisions had been cheapened out of the public purse, consumption would have proceeded in a time of severe scarcity, at the same rate as in a time of moderate plenty; the already insufficient stock of food would have been expended with a frightful rapidity, and in order to obtain a few weeks of ease, we should have had to endure a desolating famine. Those Relief Committees which attempted to follow this plan speedily exhausted their capital; and private dealers (who necessarily lay in their stock at the current market price, whatever that may be) retired from the competition with public bodies selling food at prices artificially reduced by charitable subscriptions and grants out of national funds.

The other function of the Relief Committees was to give gratuitous aid in cases of extreme destitution, and this was well performed by them to the extent of their means. As the distress increased, the distribution of cooked food by the establishment of soup-kitchens was found the most effectual means of alleviating it. The attention of the committees was therefore generally directed to this object by the Inspecting Officers. Boilers were manufactured and sent to Ireland in great numbers,[93] and Government donations were now in every case made equal in amount to the private subscriptions ("pound for pound"), and in cases of more than usual pressure, twice or three times that amount was given. This mode of giving relief was not found to be attended with any serious abuse. The committees expended in a great measure their own money, which made them more careful in seeing that it was laid out with the greatest possible advantage and economy; and as the ration of cooked food distributed by them was not an object of desire to persons in comfortable circumstances, as money wages were, it acted in a great degree as a test of destitution. The defect of this system of relief was, that being voluntary, it could not be relied on to meet the necessities of a numerous population in a period of great emergency, and the difficulty of obtaining private subscriptions was often greatest in the most distressed districts.[94]

The point at which we had arrived, therefore, at the commencement of the year 1847, was, that the system of Public Works, although recommended by the example of all former occasions on which relief had been afforded to the people of Ireland in seasons of distress, had completely broken down under the pressure of this wide-spread calamity; while the other concurrent system, which, on the principle of the Poor Law, aimed at giving relief, in the most direct form, out of funds locally raised, had succeeded to the extent to which it had been tried. The works were therefore brought to a close in the manner which has been already described: and it was determined to complete the system of relief by the distribution of food, to give it legal validity, and to place it more decidedly on the basis of the Poor

Law. This was done by the passing of the Act 10 Vic., c. 7. A Relief Committee, composed of the magistrates, one clergyman of each persuasion, the Poor Law guardian, and the three highest rate-payers, was constituted in each electoral division*,[95] the unit of Irish Poor Law statistics. A Finance Committee, consisting of four gentlemen, carefully selected for their weight of character and knowledge of business, was formed to control the expenditure in each union. Inspecting Officers were appointed, most of whom had been trained under the Board of Works and Sir R. Routh; and a Commission sitting in Dublin, of which Sir J. Burgoyne was the head,[96] and the Poor Law Commissioner was one of the members, superintended the whole system.[97] The expense was to be defrayed by payments made by the guardians out of the produce of the rates; and when this fund was insufficient, as it always proved to be, it was reinforced by Government loans, to be repaid by rates subsequently levied. Free grants were also made in aid of the rates in those unions in which the number of destitute poor was largest, compared with the means of relieving them, and when private subscriptions were raised, donations were made to an equal amount.

The check principally relied on, therefore, was, that the expenditure should be conducted, either immediately or proximately, out of the produce of the rates. No loan was to be made to any Board of Guardians until the Inspecting Officer had certified that they had passed a resolution to make the rate upon which it was to be secured, and that, to the best of his belief, they were proceeding with all possible dispatch to make and levy such rate. This principle, although still imperfectly applied, and consequently irregular in its action, exercised a pervading influence over the working of this system of relief. In forming the lists of persons to be relieved, and making their demands upon the Commissioners, few committees altogether rejected the idea that it was their own money which they were spending; and in some districts the farmer rate-payers assembled, and insisted on large numbers of persons being struck off the lists, who they knew were not entitled to relief. The tests applied to the actual recipients of relief were, that the personal attendance of all parties requiring relief was insisted on, exceptions being made in favour of the sick, impotent, and children under nine years of age, and that the relief was directed to be given only in the shape of cooked food, distributed in portions declared by the best medical authorities to be sufficient to maintain health and strength. The "cooked food test *"[98] was found particularly efficacious in preventing abuse; and the enforcement of it in some parts of the country cost a severe struggle. Undressed meal might be converted into cash by those who did not require it as food; and even the most destitute often disposed of it for tea, tobacco, or spirits; but stir-about, which becomes sour by keeping, has no value in the market, and persons were therefore not likely to apply for it, who did not want it for their own consumption. Attempts were made to apply the labour test to this system of relief; but, besides the practical difficulty of want of tools and proper superintendence, the Commissioners considered that, owing to the absence of any adequate motive, it would "lead to a want of exertion on the part of the men which would perhaps be more demoralising than relief without any work." It was therefore left to the Relief Committees in large towns and other situations favourable to such a mode of proceeding, to take their own course upon it; and the result was, that some light kinds of labour, such as cleaning the streets and whitewashing the cabins, were exacted by a few of the more zealous and active committees. Relief in aid of wages was strenuously insisted on by many of the Relief Committees, and was steadily and successfully resisted by the Commission; but it was not considered right, in the administration of a temporary measure, to require the surrender of the land held by applicants, provided they were proved to be at the time in a state of destitution.

This system reached its highest point in the month of July, 1847, when out of 2,049 electoral divisions, into which Ireland is divided, 1,826 had been brought under the operation of the Act, and 3,020,712 persons received separate rations, of whom 2,265,534 were adults, and 755,178 were children. This multitude was again gradually and peaceably thrown on its own resources at the season of harvest, when new and abundant supplies of food became available,[99] and the demand for labour was at its highest amount. Relief was discontinued to fifty-five unions on the 15th August, and the issues to the remaining unions entirely ceased on the 12th September. The latest date allowed by the Act for advances to be made, was the 1st October.

This was the second occasion on which upwards of three millions of people had been fed "out of the hands of the magistrate," but this time it was effectual. The Relief Works had been crowded with persons who had other means of subsistence, to the exclusion of the really destitute; but a ration of cooked food proved less attractive than full money wages, and room was thus made for the helpless portion of the community. The famine was stayed. The "affecting and heart-rending crowds of destitutes*"[100] disappeared from the streets; the cadaverous, hunger-stricken countenances of the people gave place to looks of health; deaths from starvation ceased; and cattle-stealing, plundering provisions, and other crimes prompted by want of food, were diminished by half in the course of a single month.[101] The Commission closed amidst general applause, and "Resolutions were received from many hundreds of the committees, praising the conduct of the inspecting officers, and frankly and honourably expressing their gratitude to Government and the Legislature for the effective means afforded them for carrying out this benevolent operation*."[102] This enterprise was in truth the "grandest attempt ever made to grapple with famine over a whole country†."[103] Organised armies, amounting altogether to some hundreds of thousands, had been rationed before; but neither ancient nor modern history can furnish a parallel to the fact that upwards of three millions of persons were fed every day in the neighbourhood of their own homes, by administrative arrangements emanating from and controlled by one central office.

The expense was moderate compared with the magnitude of the object. The amount at which it was originally estimated by the Commissioners was 3,000,000*l.*; the sum for which Parliament was asked to provide was 2,200,000*l.*, and the sum actually expended was 1,557,212*l*., of which 146,631*l*. was paid to the Commissariat for meal supplied to the Relief Committees from the Government depôts. The price of meal fortunately fell more than one-fifth during the progress of these operations, or from 2½d. a ration, to less than 2d., including all expenses of establishment.

The Finance Committees, which were selected bodies, consisting of from two to four gentlemen in each union, "with rare exceptions acted with zeal and intelligence*."[104] The Relief Committees, a miscellaneous body composed of the foremost persons in each petty district, whoever they might be, showed, as was to be expected, every variety of good and bad conduct. In some cases the three highest rate-payers could not read, and even themselves established claims to be placed on the list of destitute for daily rations. It is a fact very honourable to Ireland, that among upwards of 2000 local bodies to whom advances were made under this Act, there is not one to which, so far as the Government is informed, any suspicion of embezzlement attaches.

In order to check the progress of the fever, which, as usual, followed in the train of famine, the Act 10 Vic., c. 22 was passed,[105] by which the Relief Committees were empowered to attend to the proper burial of the dead, to provide temporary hospitals, to clear away nuisances, and to ventilate and cleanse cabins, the necessary funds being advanced by the Government in the same manner as the advances for providing food.[106] These sanitary arrangements were extensively acted upon and at moderate expense. On the 17th August 326 hospitals and dispensaries had been authorized, with accommodation for more than 23,000 patients, with medical officers, nurses, ward-maids, &c. The additional expense incurred under this Act, was 119,055*l*., the whole of which was made a free grant to the unions, in aid of rates.

The state of the finances of some of the unions was a source of deep anxiety through the winter and spring of 1846–7. Rates were not collected sufficient to defray the current expenses of the workhouses of these unions, and the guardians threatened to turn the inmates into the street, if assistance were not given from the public purse.[107] The dilemma was a painful and perplexing one. There was no reason to doubt the readiness of some of the persons who held this language to put their threat into execution; while, to admit the claim, might bring upon the Government the greater number of the workhouses, in addition to the whole of the outdoor relief; in other words, would transfer to national funds a burden intended by law to be local, and not likely to be administered with economy on any other footing. Important aid was, however, given. Large supplies of clothing were collected from the stores of the army and navy, and sent to Ireland for the use of the workhouses. Small sums of money, amounting in the aggregate to 23,503*l*. were lent from time to time with a sparing hand to assist the guardians in providing food and clothing in the most pressing and necessitous cases; 4,479*l*. was expended in providing proper medical inspection and superintendence in localities in which great sickness prevailed; and 60,000*l*. was advanced for the enlargement of the workhouses, principally by the erection of fever-wards.

The improvement of the Fisheries on the western coast of Ireland has always been an object much pressed upon the Government. In order to give the fishermen a motive for exertion, and to set them an example of improved modes of preparing the fish for sale, experienced curers were obtained from the Fishery Board in Scotland; six stations were formed, at which fish are purchased at a fair market-price, cured, and sold again for consumption to the highest bidder; and supplies of salt and tackle were provided for sale to the fishermen.[108] This was done without any expense to the public, by means of a sum of 5000*l.* placed at the disposal of the Government out of the balance of the subscription for the relief of Irish distress in 1822.

The plan of making small loans to fishermen to enable them to equip themselves for their trade, was not resorted to, because experience had proved that the fishermen are induced by it to rely upon others, instead of themselves, and that they acquire habits of chicanery and bad faith in their prolonged struggle to evade the payment of the loans. Sir J. Burgoyne had authority given him by the British Relief Association, to apply 500*l* to this object, and he induced the Relief Committee of the Society of Friends to take up the same cause. "I have made," he states, "many inquiries for the purpose, but I have always made it a point that there should be a decided prospect of any advances being repaid, and here the matter hangs. The officers all report that they doubt being able to get the money back; and I think it so necessary to be firm on this point, that I have not made use of a penny of the 500*l.*, and have recommended the Friends to reserve their funds also for a better mode of expending them." Since then, the Society of Friends, who are able to give a more particular attention to such subjects than it is possible for the Government to do, have done much good by assisting poor fishermen to redeem their nets and other implements of their trade, which they had pawned during the season of extreme distress; and these excellent people have also adopted an admirable plan of providing good boats and all requisite gear, with a competent person to instruct the native fishermen, who are formed into companies or partnerships and work out the value of the boats, &c, of which they may then become the owners. A large supply of seamen's jackets and trousers, obtained from the Admiralty, was delivered to the Society of Friends, for distribution among the poor fishermen on the west of Ireland.

From the first failure of the potato crop in 1845, the subject of providing seed was repeatedly considered, and the conclusion invariably arrived at was, that the moment it came to be understood that the Government had taken upon itself the responsibility of this delicate and peculiar branch of rural economy, the painful exertions made by private individuals in every part of Ireland to reserve a stock of seed would be relaxed, and the quantity consumed as food in consequence of the interference of the Government, would greatly exceed the quantity supplied by means of that interference.[109] The Government therefore never undertook to supply any kind of seed already in extensive use; but Holland was had recourse to for flax and rye seed, Scotland for the hardy description of barley called bere, and England and the neighbouring Continental countries furnished turnip, carrot, beet-root, and other vegetable and green-crop seeds; all of which were sent to Ireland for sale at low prices, and latterly for gratuitous distribution. More than thirteen tons of turnip seed belonging to the Government and the British Relief Association were distributed in the county of Mayo alone*,[110] besides 125 hogsheads of flax seed; by which means, in addition to the present supply of food obtained, a foundation was laid for an improved system of agriculture by a rotation of crops. One of the remedial measures proposed by the Government at the commencement of the parliamentary session of 1847, was to make loans to landed proprietors to the aggregate amount of 50,000*l*. to enable them to provide their tenants with seed, which loans were to have been repaid out of the produce of the crops raised from the seed; but nobody availed himself of this boon. The objections which exist to the Government leaving its province to interfere in the ordinary business of private life, were in nothing more clearly demonstrated than in what took place in reference to this subject. The accidental detention, by contrary winds, of a vessel laden with rye and bere seed, called forth expressions of anger and disappointment from various parts of the west and south of Ireland which had depended upon this supply; and the unfounded belief that the Government had entered upon a general undertaking to provide seed corn, largely contributed to that criminal apathy which was one of the causes of large tracts of land being left waste in 1846–47. On the other hand, it was found, when inquiries were made for vegetable seeds in the spring of 1847, that every ounce of parsnip seed in the London market had been already bought up and sent to Ireland; which is only one instance among many that might be adduced, of the reliance which may be placed on private interest and enterprise on occasions of this sort*.[111]

There is still another measure which does not the less deserve to be mentioned, because it ended in failure. The Act 9 & 10 Vic. c. 109, passed at the close of the session of 1846, had appropriated a sum of 50,000*l*. to be granted in aid of public works of acknowledged utility, one-half of the expense of which was to be provided for by a loan, and another portion was to be contributed in cash by the persons principally interested in the works. No application was made to participate in the advantage of this arrangement, and the 50,000*l*. was therefore transferred in the next session of Parliament to the erection of Fishery Piers and other useful objects.

The qualities displayed by the officers intrusted with the conduct of these great operations, will always be regarded as a bright spot in the cloud which hangs over this disastrous period. The nation had never been better served. The administrative ability which enabled Sir R. Routh to dispose, without hurry or confusion, of masses of business which to most persons would have been overwhelming; the stoutness of heart with which Colonel Jones commanded, and ultimately disbanded his army of 740,000 able-bodied Irishmen;[112] the admirable sagacity displayed by Sir J. Burgoyne in coming to a safe practical decision upon perplexed social questions, then perhaps for the first time presented to him; the remarkable financial ability of Mr. Bromley, the accountant to the Relief Commission; the cordial co-operation of Admiral Sir Hugh Pigot and his able secretary,

Mr. Nicholls,[113] and the valuable assistance rendered in many different ways by Colonel MacGregor, the head of the Constabulary Force,[114] proved that, however great the crisis might be, the persons in chief trust were equal to it*.[115] But the most gratifying feature of all, was the zeal and unanimity with which the large body of Officers employed devoted themselves to this labour of love†,[116] although they had been suddenly brought together for this particular occasion from many different branches of the public service, or from the retirement of private life. It may truly be said of them, that they "offered themselves willingly among the people;" and several painful casualties from the prevailing fever, and the failing health of others, showed that the risks and hardships attending this service were of no ordinary kind. The officers and men belonging to the numerous ships of war employed in the "Relief Service," entered with characteristic spirit upon duties which indicated in a more direct manner than ever before, that the real object of their noble profession, is, not to destroy men's lives, but to save them; and it was creditable to their seamanship, as well as their humanity, that the dangers and hardships attending their incessant employment on the exposed western coasts of Ireland and Scotland during the stormy months of winter, did not lead to the loss of a single vessel*.[117]

A slight reference to the exertions which had to be made for the single object of conducting and checking the expenditure, will give some idea of the magnitude and difficulty of the task which was imposed on the officers of the Crown.

In establishing a system of Relief Works, intended to bring employment to every man's door, it was impossible to avoid creating an extensive staff for the superintendence and payment of the labouring poor. Very voluminous accounts suddenly poured into the Office of Works from all parts of Ireland; and as the lives of thousands depended upon the supply of funds, is became a duty of the first importance to insure their immediate distribution over the whole surface of the country. Remittances were made to about 600 pay clerks weekly, and it was often found necessary to transfer from one to the other sums of money upon the authority of local officers, whereby an intermixture of accounts of a very intricate description took place. The weekly accounts sent to the office at Dublin exceeded 20,000, and the pay lists were more than a quarter of a million in number, the expenditure being at one time at the rate of a million a-month. To watch the distribution of such large sums would have been a gigantic task, even for a long-established and well-organized department, but for a temporary establishment, composed, for the most part, of persons with little, if any, previous knowledge of business, the duty was one of unprecedented difficulty, and it is a matter of surprise that greater irregularity was not the consequence.

In the books of the temporary Relief Commission, it was found necessary to open accounts with more than 2000 bodies intrusted with the expenditure of public money; and such was the rapidity of the service, that within a period of five months, more than 19,000 estimates were received in the accountant's office, and acted upon, with a like number of accounts, which were registered for examination, and more than 17,000 letters were received and answered. The pecuniary transactions of this Commission were not with public officers, but with ephemeral bodies composed of persons generally unused to business, and almost irresponsible; but the utmost good faith prevailed; and by requiring an immediate account, with vouchers, every fortnight, of the disbursement of the previous amount remitted, with the balance remaining on hand, before a further supply was sent down, the best control upon the expenditure was established, and the result has been the great saving (more than half a million) effected, while scarcely an instance of misappropriation has occurred. It has also been admitted in many parts of Ireland, that these accounts, and the instructions for their preparation, have induced habits of business that never before existed, while at the same time they have urged the Stamp Laws into more active operation.[118]

The prompt examination and audit of the accounts of the Board of Works, the Commissariat, and the Relief Commission, was provided for by the deputation of experienced persons from the offices in London, under whose superintendence the whole of the expenditure has been subjected to a searching local revision, and wherever any symptom of malversation has appeared, the matter has been probed to the bottom.

It has been a popular argument in Ireland, that as the calamity was an imperial one, the whole amount expended in relieving it ought to be defrayed out of the Public Revenue.[119] There can be no doubt that the deplorable consequences of this great calamity extended to the empire at large, but the disease was strictly local, and the cure was to be obtained only by the application of local remedies. If England and Scotland, and great part of the north and east of Ireland had stood alone, the pressure would have been severe, but there would have been no call for assistance from national funds. The west and south of Ireland was the peccant part. The owners and holders of land in those districts had permitted or encouraged the growth of the excessive population which depended upon the precarious potato, and they alone had it in their power to restore society to a safe and healthy state. If all were interested in saving the starving people, they were far more so, because it included their own salvation from the desperate struggles of surrounding multitudes phrenzied[120] with hunger. The economical administration of the relief could only be provided for by making it, in part at least, a local charge. In the invariable contemplation of the law, the classes represented by the rate payers have to bear the whole burden of their own poor; the majority of the British community did so bear it throughout this year of distress; and, besides fulfilling their own duties, they placed in the hands of the minority the means of performing theirs, requiring them to repay only one half.

A special objection has been raised to the repayment of the advances for the Relief Works, on the ground that their cost exceeds that for which they could now be constructed. The answer to this is, that these works were undertaken solely for the purpose of giving employment in a great and pressing emergency, when it was impossible for them to be executed with the same care and economy as in ordinary times\*;[121] that the counties are therefore chargeable with them, not as works, but as relief; and that if they had cost either half as much, or twice as much as they did, the liability would have been the same. But when it is remembered that the expensive character of the works was in a great degree owing to the Board of Works not having received from the Presentment Sessions and the Relief Committees that assistance in keeping down the expenditure, which it was the duty of those bodies to have rendered, both by making a proper selection of the works to be undertaken, and by confining their recommendations for employment on them to those persons who were really destitute, it is a matter of surprise that any answer has been rendered necessary.

We should probably have heard less of these repayments if it had been generally known what their real amount is. The sum expended under the first Relief Works Act (9 & 10 Vic. c. 1) was 476,000*l.*, one half of which was grant, and the other half is to be repaid*[122] by twenty half-yearly instalments amounting on an average, including interest, to about 12,500*l.* each. The expenditure under the second Act (9 & 10 Vic. c. 107) was about 4,850,000*l.*, half of which was remitted, and the other half is repayable by twenty half-yearly instalments of 145,500*l.* each, including interest. The annual addition made to the Rates by the repayments under the two Acts relating to the Relief Works is therefore about 316,000*l.*\*;[123] while by an Act passed on the 28th August, 1846, the Rates were relieved from an annual payment of 192,000*l.*, being the remaining half of the expense of the Constabulary, the other half of which was already defrayed out of national funds. The additional charge upon the Rates, therefore, amounts only to 124,000*l.* a-year for ten years, or 1,240,000*l.* in all. The sum advanced under the 9 & 10 Vic. c. 2, on the security of grand jury presentments was 130,000*l.*, which will have to be repaid in various periods extending from three to ten years; but the expenditure under this Act was merely in anticipation of the usual repairs of the public roads, the cost of which is in ordinary years raised within the year without any advance. Lastly, the sum expended in the distribution of food under the 10 Vic. c. 7, and in medical relief under the 10 Vic. c. 22, was 1,676,268*l.*, of which 961,739*l.* is to be repaid, and the remaining 714,529*l.* is a free grant. The first-mentioned Act included a fund for making grants as well as loans, and the demands for repayment have been adjusted as nearly as possible according to the circumstances of each district. In some of the western unions, where the amount of destitution bears the largest proportion to the means of the rate-payers, and, owing to the extent to which the potato was formerly cultivated, a painful period of transition has yet to be endured, only a small part of the sum expended is required to be repaid*;[124] while in other unions where the return of low prices has restored society to its ordinary state, grants have been confined to those cases in which the expenditure has exceeded a rating of three shillings in the pound on the valuation.

All the claims of the Exchequer, arising out of the Relief operations of 1846 and 1847 have now been described, and it must be borne in mind that the several localities received full value for what they have to pay. They were saved from a prolonged and horrible state of famine, pestilence, and anarchy, which was the main consideration; and they had, besides, the incidental advantage of the labour bestowed upon the Roads and other public works, especially in the poor and wild districts of the West, where lines of road have been opened with the aid of the relief grants and loans, which, although much wanted, could not have been undertaken for years to come without such assistance.[125] The rest of the expenditure, including the large donations made to Relief Committees previously to the passing of the Act 10 Vic. c. 7, the cost of the staff of the Board of Works and of the Relief Commission, the Commissariat staff, and the heavy naval expenditure, has been defrayed out of the public purse; without any demand for repayment.

Hitherto our narrative has been confined to what was done by the Government, but the voluntary exertions of private individuals contributed their full share towards this unprecedented act of public charity.

It is highly to the honour of our countrymen in India, that the first combined movement in any part of the British empire was made by them. On the arrival of the news of the first failure of the potato crop in the Autumn of 1845, a meeting, presided over by Sir John Peter Grant,[126] was held at Calcutta, on the 2nd of January, 1846, for the purpose of concerting measures to raise a fund for the relief of the expected distress; and a committee, consisting of the Duke of Leinster, the Protestant and Roman Catholic Archbishops of Dublin, and six other persons, was solicited to act in Ireland as Trustees for the distribution of such sums as might be subscribed. This example was followed at Madras and Bombay, and the result was that a sum of 13,920*l*., contributed as follows, was placed at the disposal of the committee:

| | |
|---|---|
| Bengal | 8,200 |
| Bombay | 2,976 |
| Madras | 1,150 |
| Ceylon | 718 |
| Hong Kong, 18th Royal Irish | 82 |
| Mobile, U. S. | 192 |
| Toronto, C. W. | 300 |
| England, including 200*l*. from Lord John Russell | 302 |
| | £13,920 |

The whole of this sum was distributed between the 24th of April and the 21st of December, 1846, and was entirely independent of the large subscriptions from different parts of British India subsequently added to the funds of other societies.[127] More than 2000 letters were received by the Trustees of the Indian Relief Fund; and by a strict attention to economy, they were enabled to distribute 13,920*l*. at an expense of 180*l*.

In the United Kingdom, the Society of Friends were, as usual, first in the field of benevolent action. When the renewed and more alarming failure of the potato crop in the autumn of 1846 showed the necessity for serious exertion, a subscription was opened by them in London in the month of November in that year; members of the Society were sent on a deputation to Ireland, and those who resided there aided by their personal exertions and local knowledge.[128] On the 6th January,

1847, a committee, of which Mr. Jones Loyd was chairman, and Mr. Thomas Baring and Baron Rothschild were members, invited contributions under the designation of the "British Association for the Relief of extreme Distress in Ireland and the Highlands and Islands of Scotland."[129] On the 13th of January, 1847, a Queen's Letter was issued with the same object, and the 24th of March was appointed by proclamation, for a General Fast and Humiliation before Almighty God, "in behalf of ourselves and of our brethren, who in many parts of this United Kingdom are suffering extreme famine and sickness."[130] A painful and tender sympathy pervaded every class of society. From the Queen on her throne to the convicts in the hulks,[131] expenses were curtailed, and privations were endured, in order to swell the Irish subscription. The fast was observed with unusual solemnity, and the London season of this year was remarkable for the absence of gaiety and expensive entertainments. The vibration was felt through every nerve of the British Empire. The remotest stations in India, the most recent settlements in the backwoods of Canada, contributed their quota, and 652*l.* was subscribed by the British residing in the city of Mexico, at a time when their trade was cut off, and their personal safety compromised by the war with the United States. The sum collected under the Queen's letter was 171,533*l.* The amount separately contributed through the British Association was 263,251*l.*\*;[132] and this aggregate amount of 434,784*l.*, was divided in the proportion of five-sixths to Ireland and one-sixth to Scotland.[133] But besides this great stream of charity, there were a thousand other channels which it is impossible to trace, and of the aggregate result of which no estimate can be formed. There were separate committees which raised and sent over large sums of money. There were ladies' associations without end to collect small weekly subscriptions and make up clothes to send to Ireland. The opera, the fancy bazaar, the fashionable ball rendered tribute; and, above all, there were the private efforts of numberless individuals, each acting for himself and choosing his own almoners, of which no record exists except on High. Upon application being made to the managers of the Provincial Bank of Ireland to permit English charitable remittances to pass without the usual charge, it turned out that they had been in the habit of doing so for a considerable time, and that the amount sent through that one channel, in the six months ending on the 4th March, 1847, exceeded 20,000*l.* In the contemplation of this great calamity, the people of the United States of America forgot their separate nationality, and remembered only that they were sprung from the same origin as ourselves. The sympathy there was earnest and universal, and the manifestations of it most generous and munificent. The contributions from this land of plenty consisted principally of Indian corn and other kinds of provisions, and the cargoes were, for the most part, consigned to the Society of Friends, whose quiet, patient, practical exertions, commanded universal confidence. The freight and charges on the supplies of food and clothing sent to Ireland by charitable societies and individuals, as well from the United States and Canada on the one side, as from England on the other, were paid by the Government, to an amount exceeding 50,000*l.*\*;[134] all customs dues were remitted, and the meal and other articles were to a great extent taken charge of by the officers of the Commissariat, and held by them at the disposal of the parties to whom they had been consigned for distribution; by which means the necessary harmony was preserved between the operations of the Government and those of the private associations, and the bounty of the subscribers reached the destitute persons for whom it was intended, with as small a deduction as possible for incidental expenses. Thus, when the British Association was desirous of giving the cultivators on the Western Coast of Ireland an opportunity of purchasing seed at a low market price at the close of the sowing season of 1847, five large steamers were collected by the Government, which were loaded in a remarkably short space of time, with oats and other seed provided by the Association, and were sent forth, each to its appointed section of the Western Coast; so that every harbour accessible to a steamer, from Kinsale to Londonderry, was looked into, and what remained unsold was left in the Government depots for subsequent sale or gratuitous distribution. On the other hand, the Government received much assistance and support from the operations of these benevolent societies, and they were especially useful in bridging over the fearful interval between the system of relief by work and relief by food. Several gentlemen, with a noble self-devotion, volunteered their services to the British Association, among whom Lord Robert Clinton, Lord James Butler, Count Strzelecki, and Mr. Higgins, were distinguished by their zeal and ability, and by the fortitude with which, for months together, they endured the pain and risk attending the immediate contact with hunger and disease.[135]

A large committee, with the Marquis of Kildare at its head, was formed in Dublin under the name of the "General Central Relief Committee for all Ireland," the contributions received by which amounted to upwards of 50,000*l*., independently of 10,000*l*. in cash and an equal value in food, entrusted to this committee from the sum raised by the Queen's Letter.[136] British North America contributed through this medium the munificent sum of 12,463*l*., including 5,873*l*. from Montreal; 1571*l*. from Quebec; and 3,472*l*. from Toronto. The United States gave 5,852*l*., of which 3,199*l*. was from New Orleans. British India 5,674*l*.; the Cape of Good Hope 2,900*l*.; Australia 2,282*l*.; South America 772*l*.; the Military 386*l*.; Scotland, France, Germany, Italy, Belgium, Gibraltar, the Channel Islands, West Indies, the Ionian Islands, &c., 2,168*l*.; Ireland, independently of local subscriptions, which were very considerable, 9,888*l*.; and England, over and above the 20,000*l*. remitted from the produce of the Queen's Letter, 8,886*l*.

Subscriptions were received to a smaller amount, but from an earlier period of the distress, by another committee established in Dublin under the name of the "Irish Relief Association for the Destitute Peasantry," which was announced to be a reorganization of the Association formed during the period of famine in the West of Ireland in 1831.[137] The list of patrons commenced with the names of the Archbishop of Dublin and the Duke of Manchester; and, independently of some cargoes of corn, flour, &c, from Canada and the United States, the funds placed at their disposal amounted to nearly 42,000*l*., among the contributions to which, the following were conspicuous:—England, 17,782*l*.; Ireland, 6,151*l* ; France, 1,390*l*.; Italy, including 1,481*l*. from Rome, 2,708*l*.; British North America,

2,821*l*. (1,165*l*. of this being from Quebec); United States, 847*l*.; India, 5,947*l*., of which the large proportion of 4,981*l*. was from Madras; West Indies, 1,043*l*.; Australia, 2,314*l*. ; and from the officers and men of various regiments, and the pensioners and constabulary, 508*l*.

But the most considerable of the Dublin Charitable Committees was that composed of members of the Society of Friends, of which Mr. Joseph Bewley and Mr. Jonathan Pim were the Secretaries.[138] The contributions placed at their disposal since the 3rd of December, 1846, in money and provisions, have been to the amount of upwards of 168,000*l*., of which no less than 108,651*l*. is the estimated value of provisions (7,935 tons) consigned to them from the United States of America. Of the subscriptions in money, 35,393*l*. was remitted by the London Committee of the Society of Friends; 8,494*l*. by members of the Society and others in Dublin; and the large sum of 15,567*l*. by persons residing in the United States. The provisions received from America were as follows: —

|  | Tons | Estimated Value. £ | s. | d. |
|---|---|---|---|---|
| From New York | 4,496 | 58,299 | 15 | 0 |
| " Philadelphia | 1,870¼ | 24,948 | 18 | 0 |
| " New Orleans | 349 | 7,538 | 5 | 0 |
| From Newark, N. J. | 316 ¾ | 5,141 | 0 | 0 |
| " Baltimore | 262 ½ | 3,913 | 10 | 0 |
| " Richmond, V. | 252 ½ | 3486 | 15 | 0 |
| " Charleston | 169 | 2,362 | 0 | 0 |
| " Alexandria, V. | 102 | 1,422 | 10 | 0 |
| From Sundry other Ports, United States, America | 117 | 1,518 | 7 | 10 |

And in addition to these large donations of money and food, consignments of clothing were received from England and America, to the estimated value of from 5,000*l*. to 10,000*l*.

The ladies of Ireland exerted themselves with characteristic zeal and benevolence, to alleviate the sufferings of their country-people, and to promote their moral advancement, by awakening and encouraging a spirit of independent exertion, and fostering habits of industry and self-reliance.[139] The "Ladies' Relief Association for Ireland" in the management of which the Honourable Mrs. Newcombe takes the principal part,[140] and the objects of which are "to encourage industry among the female peasantry of Ireland, to contribute towards providing nourishment for the sick, and to procure clothing for the destitute," raised 11,465*l*. previously to the 1st of August, 1847, of which 3,043*l*. was derived from the proceeds of a Fancy Bazaar in London, and of this sum 2,500*l*. was appropriated to the relief of families whose husbands or fathers "have been removed while performing their painfully laborious duties." The "Ladies' Industrial Society for the Encouragement of Remunerative Labour among the Peasantry of Ireland," of which Mrs. Lloyd is the active promoter, more particularly aims at encouraging the manufacture of those articles which are likely to find a ready sale in the trade; for which purpose, instruction is given in the best and most practicable descriptions of remunerative labour; patterns, models, and implements are furnished, and a sale is provided for the produce, through the intervention of a mercantile agency in Dublin.[141] Numerous benevolent persons adopted the same course in various parts of Ireland, sometimes in connection with these societies, and sometimes using their own means, with such aid as was sent to them by their private friends. Mr. Gildea, the Rector of Newport,[142] and the ladies of his family, revived the manufacture of coarse linen at that place, and they have employed between 500 and 600 females since the beginning of January, in the execution of orders sent them by charitable persons*.[143] The ladies of the Presentation Convent at Galway gave every day a good meal of porridge to upwards of 600 starving children who attended their schools.[144] The ladies of the Owenmore Relief Committee raised and expended in various works of charity, 2,427*l.*, exclusive of grants of the British Association and of the Government, to five parochial kitchens superintended by them. Want of space alone prevents us from alluding to many other similar instances.

In the autumn and winter of 1846 efforts were made to induce the Government to take an active part in assisting emigration by an apportionment of the expense of passage and outfit between the public, the landlords, and the emigrants themselves; but, on a full consideration of the subject, it appeared that the emigration about to take place in the ensuing season to Canada and the United States, without any assistance from the public, was likely to be quite as large as those countries could properly absorb, and that the consequence of the interference of the Government would be that the movement would be carried beyond those limits which were consistent with safety, and that a burthen would be transferred to the taxpayers of the United Kingdom, which would otherwise be borne by those to whom it properly belonged, owing to their interests being more immediately concerned. It is also a point of primary importance, that those persons should emigrate, who, from age, health, character, and circumstances, are best able to contend with the hardships and difficulties of a settler's life, and it was considered that this object would be most fully attained if the emigration were entirely voluntary. The true test of fitness in this case is the possession, on the part of each individual concerned, of the will and ability to emigrate; and the probability of helpless multitudes being sent forth, who, both for their own sakes and for that of the colony, ought to have remained at home, is increased in proportion as other motives and other interests besides those of the emigrant himself influence his act of expatriation. For these reasons Her Majesty's Ministers determined to confine themselves to taking increased securities for the safety of the emigrants during their voyage, and their early and satisfactory settlement after their arrival abroad. Additional emigration agents were appointed to Liverpool and to different Irish ports; the annual vote in aid of colonial funds for the relief of sick and destitute emigrants from the United Kingdom, was increased from 1000*l*. to 10,000*l*.; provision was made for giving assistance in the case of emigrant ships being driven back by stress of weather, and the Governor-General of Canada was informed that Her Majesty's Government would be prepared to defray its fair share of any further expense that might have to be incurred in giving the Emigrants necessary relief, in forwarding them to places where they might obtain employment*.[145]

Early in the year 1847 the roads to the Irish sea-ports were thronged with families hastening to escape the evils which impended over their native land. The complaint in Ireland, at the time, was, that those who went belonged to the best and most substantial class of the agricultural population. The complaint afterwards in Canada was that those who came were the helpless and destitute. The fact was, that the emigrants generally belonged to that class of small holders, who, being somewhat above the level of the prevailing destitution, had sufficient resources left to enable them to make the effort required to affect their removal to a foreign land; and the steps taken by them to convert their property into an available form, had for months before been the subject of observation. Large remittances, estimated to amount to 200,000*l*. in the year ending on the 30th March, 1847, were also made by the Irish emigrants settled in the United States and the British North American provinces, to enable their relations in Ireland to follow them*.[146] The emigration of 1846 from the United Kingdom, which was the largest ever known up to that time, amounted to 129,851 persons; the emigration of the first three quarters of 1847 was 240,461; and almost the whole of it was from Ireland to Canada and the United States*.[147]

Even this does not represent the full extent of the outpouring of the population of Ireland which took place in this eventful year. From the 13th January to the 1st November, 278,005*[148] immigrants arrived at Liverpool from Ireland, of whom only 122,981 sailed from that port to foreign countries. The conflux of this mixed multitude was formidable both to the health and resources of the inhabitants of Liverpool; but they nobly faced the danger, and exerted themselves to meet the emergency with the vigour it required. The portion of the town occupied by the Irish was divided into thirteen districts, in each of which a relief station was opened, and twenty-four additional relieving officers were appointed, under the superintendence of two inspectors. The number of persons relieved daily amounted for some time to upwards of 10,000. The district medical officers were increased from six to twenty-one, and extensive premises were hired or constructed for the purpose of being used as temporary fever hospitals. All this was done at the expense of the inhabitants, and the only assistance given by the Government was, that when the fever increased to an alarming extent, quarantine ships were stationed in the Mersey to receive the infected.[149] Nineteen relieving officers died at Liverpool alone of fever caught in the execution of their duties. The influx of poor Irish by way of Glasgow, Ardrossan, Port Patrick, Fleetwood, the Welsh ports, Bristol, Plymouth, Southampton, and London itself, was also very large; and quarantine arrangements had to be made in the Clyde similar to those at Liverpool.

Some relief was obtained by the passing of the Act 10 & 11 Vic. c. 33, "to amend the Laws relating to the Removal of Poor Persons from England and Scotland;" and 4,583 paupers who had become chargeable to the Liverpool parochial funds, or who applied to be removed, were sent back to their own districts in Ireland, at a cost of 1,322*l*., between the 19th July, when the Act came into operation, and the 31st October.[150] Previously to this, there was very little crime among these poor people, not even in petty thefts; but it soon appeared that they preferred being sent to prison to being sent back to Ireland. In the year ending 30th September, 1846, 398 natives of Ireland were committed to the borough prison at Liverpool for begging, pilfering about the docks, &c. In the year ending 30th September, 1847, 888 were so committed. In the month of October 1846, 80 were committed; in the same month of 1847, 142. This pauper immigration passed inland to all the large towns of this island, as far as London and Edinburgh; and the following statement of the number of Roman Catholic clergymen who died of the Irish fever caught in attending the sick since March 1847, may be taken as an index of the relative pressure*:[151]—

Lancashire.

> Rev. Peter Nightingale, resident priest of St. Anthony's, Great Homer Street, | Liverpool.
> William Parker, senior resident priest of St. Patrick's, Park Lane, Liverpool.
> Richard Grayston, resident priest of St. Patrick's, Park Lane, Liverpool,
> James Haggar, resident priest of St. Patrick's, Park Lane, Liverpool.
> Thomas Kelly, D.D., resident priest of St. Joseph's, Grosvenor Street, Liverpool.
> John F. Whitaker, removed from Manchester to succeed Dr. Kelly at St. Joseph's, where he died.
> J. F. Appleton, D.D., senior resident priest of St. Peter's, Seel Street, Liverpool.
> John A. Gilbert, resident priest of St. Mary's, Edmund Street, Liverpool.
> William V. Dale, resident priest of St. Mary's, Edmund Street, Liverpool.
> Robert Gillow, resident priest of St. Nicholas's, Copperas Hill, Liverpool.
> John Hearne, senior priest of St. John's, Wigan.
> Robert Johnson, resident priest of St. John', Wigan.
> John Dowdall, resident priest in Bolton.

Cheshire.

> Michael Power, resident priest of St. Mary's, Duckinfield.

Yorkshire.

> Thomas Billington, Vicar-General of Yorkshire district, and senior resident priest of St. Mary's, York.
> Henry Walmsley, senior resident priest of St. Ann's [sic], Leeds.

Richard Wilson, resident priest of St. Anne's, Leeds.

Edward Metcalfe, successor to Rev. R. Wilson at St. Anne's, Leeds.

Joseph Curr, Secretary to Bishop Briggs, with whom he resided at Fulford House near York. He volunteered his services after the death of Mr. Metcalfe, and in the course of a few weeks died at St. Anne's, Leeds.

J. Coppinger. Removed from Hull to supply the vacancies caused by the above deaths, and very shortly after his removal died at St. Anne's, Leeds.

Durham.

Joseph Dugdale, resident priest of St. Mary's, Stockton.

Northumberland.

James Standen, senior resident priest of St. Andrew's, Newcastle-on-Tyne.

Right Rev. Dr. Riddell, Vicar Apostolic of the Northern District and Bishop of Longo. After the death of Mr. Standen, Bishop Riddell undertook to attend to the visitation of the sick in person. He very soon caught the fever and died at Newcastle.

Staffordshire.

Rev. James Kennedy, resident priest at Newcastle-under-Lyne.

Gloucestershire.

P. Hartley, resident priest of St. Peter's, Gloucester.

Wales.

Edward Mulcahy, resident priest of St. Mary's, Bangor, North Wales.

M. Carroll, resident priest at Merthyr Tydvil, South Wales.

Scotland.

Richard Sinnott, Stranraer, Greenock.

J. Bremner, Abbey Parish, Paisley.

W. Walsh, Old Monkland.

The pestilence, which all the precautions practicable on land could not overcome, broke out, as was to be expected, with increased virulence on board the emigrant ships. A new law was passed at Boston in Massachusetts, empowering the local authorities to demand a bond of 1000 dollars from the masters of emigrant ships for each passenger apparently indigent, that he should not become chargeable to the State or to the city for ten years, the effect of which was to divert the stream of emigration to a greater extent than usual to Canada and New Brunswick. The deaths on the voyage to Canada increased from 5 in every 1000 persons embarked, to about 60, or to twelve times their previous rate; and so many more arrived sick, that the proportion of deaths in quarantine to the numbers embarked, increased from 1⅓ to about 40 in the 1000, besides still larger numbers who died at Quebec, Montreal, and elsewhere in the interior*.[152] A Medical Board was appointed; large supplies of provisions were dispatched to the quarantine station; tents sufficient for the reception of 10,000 persons were issued from the Ordnance stores, and the labours of the Commissariat in this war against famine and pestilence, were carried on at the same time on both sides of the Atlantic; but the utmost exertions and the most liberal expenditure could not prevent a fearful amount of suffering amongst the emigrants, and a painful spread of disease to the resident population.

We are well aware that among men of talents and of benevolent dispositions, there is a wide difference on the important question of emigration; and in what follows on this subject, we wish to be understood, not as committing ourselves to particular opinions, but merely as making a statement, in pursuance of the historical character of this review, of what we believe to have been the views which guided the resolutions of the Government.

There is no subject of which a merely one-sided view is more commonly taken than that of Emigration. The evils arising from the crowded state of the population, and the facility with which large numbers of persons may be transferred to other countries, are naturally uppermost in the minds of landlords and ratepayers; but Her Majesty's Government, to which the well-being of the British population in every quarter of the globe is confided, must have an equal regard to the interests of the emigrant and of the colonial community of which he may become a member. It is a great mistake to suppose that even Canada and the United States have an unlimited capacity of absorbing a new population. The labour market in the settled districts is always so nearly full, that a small addition to the persons in search of employment makes a sensible difference; while the clearing of new land requires the possession of resources*,[153] and a power of sustained exertion not ordinarily belonging to the newly-arrived Irish emigrant. In this, as well as in the other operations by which society is formed or sustained, there is a natural process which cannot with impunity be departed from. A movement is continually going on towards the backwoods on the part of the young and enterprising portion of the settled population, and of such of the former emigrants as have acquired means and experience; and the room thus made is occupied by persons recently arrived from Europe, who have only their labour to depend upon. The, conquest of the wilderness requires more than the ordinary share of energy and perseverance, and every attempt that has yet been made to turn Paupers into Backwoodsmen by administrative measures, has ended in signal failure. As long as they were rationed, they held together in a feeble, helpless state; and when the issue of rations ceased, they generally returned to the settled parts of the country. Our recent experience of the effects of a similar state of dependence in Ireland, offers no encouragement to renew the experiment in a distant country, where the difficulties are so much greater, and a disastrous result would be so much less capable of being retrieved. It must also be observed, that from an early period of the present distress, two modes of meeting the calamity presented themselves, which have since acquired greater distinctness in people's minds, and have been acted upon in a more and more systematic manner. The first of these was to stimulate the industry of the people, to augment the productive powers of the soil, and to promote the establishment of new industrial occupations, so as to cause the land once more to support its population, and to substitute a higher standard of subsistence, and a higher tone of popular character, for those which prevailed before. This plan aimed at accomplishing the object without the pain or risk of wholesale expatriation; and the result proposed by it was to increase the strength and prosperity of the country and the happiness of the people, by enabling the present population to maintain itself comfortably at home by the exercise of its industry. The Government adopted this plan from the first, and has since promoted its success by every means in its power. The other plan was to relieve the mother-country by transferring large masses of people to the Colonies; and great efforts were made to obtain the command of public funds to assist in paying the expense of this emigration.

The main point, therefore, is, that by taking an active part in assisting emigration, the Government would throw their weight into the scale with the last of these two plans. They would assist it by their means; and, what is of far more consequence, they would countenance it by their authority: and in the same degree, they would discourage and relax the efforts of those who are exerting themselves to carry out the opposite plan. In order to appreciate the full ultimate effect of such an interposition, it must be remembered that the solution of the great difficulty by means of emigration carried out on the scale and in the manner proposed, offers to the promoters of it the attraction of accomplishing their object by a cheap and summary process; while the other remedy, of enabling the population to live comfortably at home, can be arrived at only by an expensive, laborious, and protracted course of exertion: and it therefore behoves the Government, which holds the balance between contending parties, to take care to which side it lends its influence on a social question of this description. Those who have purchased or inherited estates in which a redundant population has been permitted or encouraged to grow up, may with propriety assist some of their people to emigrate, provided they take care to prevent there being left destitute on their arrival in their new country. The expense of assisting emigration under such circumstances properly falls on the proprietor. A surplus population, whether it be owing to the fault or to the misfortune of the proprietor or his predecessors, must, like barrenness, or the absence of improvements, be regarded as one of the disadvantages contingent on the possession of the estate; and he who enjoys the profits and advantages of the estate, must also submit to the less desirable conditions connected with it. So long as emigration is conducted only at the expense of the proprietor, it is not likely to be carried to an injurious or dangerous extent, and it will press so heavily on his resources, as to leave the motives to exertion of a different kind unimpaired. Emigration is open to objection only when the natural checks and correctives have been neutralized by the interposition of the Government, or other public bodies. It then becomes the interest and policy of the landed proprietor to make no exertion to maintain his people at home, to produce a general impression that no such exertion could be successfully made, and to increase by every possible means the pressure upon those parties who, having the command of public funds, are expected to give their assistance; and the responsibility of the consequences, whatever they may be, becomes transferred from the individual proprietors, to the Government or public body which countenances and promotes their proceedings.

Three things had become apparent before the close of the year 1846: the first was, that if these gigantic efforts were much longer continued, they must exhaust and disorganize society throughout the United Kingdom, and reduce all classes of people in Ireland to a state of helpless dependence; the second was, that provision ought to be made for the relief of extreme destitution in some less objectionable mode than that which had been adopted, for want of a better, under the pressure of an alarming emergency; and the third was, that great efforts and great sacrifices were required to provide another and a better subsistence for the large population which had hitherto depended upon the potato. Upon these principles the plan of the Government for the season of 1847–8, and for all after time, was based.

Much the larger portion of the machinery of a good Poor Law had been set up in Ireland by the Irish Poor Relief Act (1 & 2 Vic. c. 56), which was passed in the year 1838. The island had been divided into Unions, which were generally so arranged as to secure easy communication with the central station; and these had been subdivided into electoral districts, each of which appointed its own guardian, and was chargeable only with its own poor, like our parishes.[154] A commodious workhouse had also been built in each union by advances from the Exchequer*,[155] and rates had been established for its support. No relief could, however, be given outside the workhouses, and when these buildings once became filled with widows and children, aged and sick, and others who might with equal safety and more humanity have been supported at their own homes, they ceased to be either a medium of relief or a test of destitution to the other destitute poor of the union.[156] To remedy this and other defects of the existing system, three Acts of Parliament were passed in the Session of 1847†[157] the principal provisions of which were as follows: Destitute persons who are either permanently or temporarily disabled from labour, and destitute widows having two or more legitimate children dependent upon them, may be relieved either in or out of the workhouse, at the discretion of the guardians. If, owing to want of room, or to the prevalence of fever or any infectious disorder, adequate relief cannot be afforded in a workhouse to persons not belonging to either of the above-mentioned classes, the Poor Law Commissioners may authorize the guardians to give them outdoor relief in food only; the Commissioners' order for which purpose can only be made for a period of two months, but, if necessary, it can be renewed from time to time. Relieving officers and medical officers for affording medical relief out of the workhouse are to be appointed; and in cases of sudden and urgent necessity, the relieving officers are to give "immediate and temporary relief in food, lodging, medicine, or medical attendance," until the next meeting of the guardians. After the 1st November, 1847, no person is to be relieved either in or out of a workhouse, who is in the occupation of more than a quarter of an acre of land.[158] No person is to be deemed to have been resident in an electoral division so as to make it chargeable with the expense of relieving him, who shall not during the three years before his application for relief have occupied some tenement within it, or have usually slept within it for thirty calendar months. All magistrates residing in the union are to be ex-officio guardians, provided their number does not exceed that of elected guardians. Greater facilities are given for dissolving Boards of Guardians, in case they do not duly and effectually discharge their duty according to the intention of the several Acts in force.[159] Public beggars and persons going from one district to another for the purpose, of obtaining relief are rendered liable to one month's imprisonment with hard labour; and an independent Poor Law establishment is constituted for Ireland, consisting of three Commissioners (two of whom are to be the Secretary and Under-Secretary for Ireland for the time being), an Assistant Commissioner and Secretary, and as many Inspectors as may be required.[160]

The principle of a comprehensive Poor Law and of the abolition of mendicancy, having thus been established, the efforts of the Government were earnestly directed to the removal of the difficulties likely to impede its satisfactory working. The repayment of the first instalment due on account of the advances for the Relief Works of the winter and spring of 1846–7 (9 & 10 Vic. c. 107), was postponed until after the Spring Assizes of 1848, and it was announced that no demand would be made until after the 1st January, 1848, for the repayment of the advances under the Temporary Relief Act, when the rates levied previously to that date for the current expenses of the permanent Poor Law equalled or exceeded 3s. in the pound, and that even when rates had been struck for the purpose of repaying the advances, they might, if necessary, be applied to defraying those current expenses. By these arrangements the demands for repayment between the Summer Assizes of 1847 and the Spring Assizes of 1848 were limited to the second instalment for the Relief Works and repairs of Grand Jury Roads of 1846 (9 Vic. c. 1 and 2), amounting only to 27,000*l.* for the whole of Ireland; and after providing for this and for the expense of the gaols and other ordinary local demands, all the rates levied from the produce of the abundant harvest of 1847 became applicable to the relief of the people under the Poor Law, then for the first time coming into full operation. The Guardians were at the same time earnestly recommended by the Poor Law Commissioners to strike rates sufficient to meet the exigencies of the coming winter, and to be strict in the levy of them. They were advised to guard against the necessity of giving out-door relief to the able-bodied, by providing for disabled persons, widows, school-children, and fever patients out of the workhouse; and five Boards of Guardians which had obstinately persisted in not doing their duty, were dissolved, and paid Guardians were appointed in their place. Ireland had now had a year and a half's experience of the administration of relief on a great scale and in different ways, and the objects to be aimed at and the abuses to be avoided had become generally known. "The very evil itself," the Relief Commissioners observe in their Sixth Monthly Report, "has been attended with a salutary reaction, and the whole country seems, by this experience, to have been made sensible that it is only by the most rigid and thoroughly controlled principles of affording relief by any public arrangement, that society can be protected from a state of almost universal pauperisation, and that the charge of a more benevolent alleviation of distress than what is absolutely necessary for the bare support of the thoroughly destitute, must and ought to be left to the exertions and voluntary distribution of the charitable and humane, which it is hoped will always be largely afforded." During the week ended Saturday the 14th August, 1847, there were above 20,000 persons on the relief lists of the electoral division which comprises the northern half of the city of Dublin; and as the operations under the Temporary Relief Act terminated in that union on the 15th, the guardians, on the 16th, had to deal with the apparent necessity of having to provide relief for above 20,000 persons. On the morning of that day, however, owing to previous arrangements, they had room in the workhouse of their union for 400 individuals; and by offering workhouse relief to applicants, aided by some assistance from the Mendicity Institution,[161] the guardians were enabled in the course of six days to reduce the number on the relief lists to about 3000 persons. This is only one instance among many that might be adduced, of the practical value of the experience that has been acquired in Ireland of the true principles of Poor Law management.

A principle of great power has thus been introduced into the social system of Ireland, which must be productive of many important consequences, besides those which directly flow from it. Mr. Drummond's apophthegm [sic],[162] that "property has its duties as well as its rights," having now received the sanction of law, it can never hereafter be a matter of indifference to a landed proprietor, what the condition of the people on his estate is.[163] The day has gone by for letting things take their course, and landlords and farmers have the plain alternative placed before them of supporting the people in idleness or in profitable labour. Hitherto the duties of Irish landlords had been, as jurists would say, of imperfect obligation. In other words, their performance depended upon conscience, benevolence, and a more enlightened and far-seeing view of personal interest than belongs to the generality of men; the consequence of which has been a remarkable difference in the conduct of Irish landlords: and while some have made all the sacrifices and exertions which their position required, others have been guilty of that entire abandonment of duty which has brought reproach upon their order. For the future this cannot be. The necessity of self-preservation, and the knowledge that rents can be saved from the encroachments of poor-rates, only in proportion as the poor are cared for and profitably employed, will secure a fair average good conduct on the part of landed proprietors, as in England, and more favourable circumstances will induce improved habits. The poor-rate is an absentee tax of the best description; because, besides bringing non-resident proprietors under contribution, it gives them powerful motives either to reside on their estates or to take care that they are managed, in their absence, with a proper regard to the welfare of the poor*.[164] Lastly, the performance of duty supposes the enjoyment of equivalent rights. When rich and poor are at one again, the repudiating farmer will find the position of his landlord too strong to allow of his taking his present license, and it will then be fearlessly asserted that the converse of Mr. Drummond's maxim is also true, and that "Property has its rights as well as its duties." For the first time in the history of Ireland, the poor man has become sensibly alive to the idea that the law is his friend, and the exhortation of the parish priest of Dingle to his flock in September 1847 indicates an epoch in the progress of society in Ireland:— "Heretofore landlords have had agents who collected their rents, and they supported them. The grand jury had agents to collect the county-cess, and they supported them. Now, for the first time, the poor man has an agent to collect his rent. That agent is the poor-rate collector, and he should be supported by the poor." Time must, however, be allowed for the gradual working of this feeling, before its full effects can be seen.

Those who object to the existing Poor Law are bound to point out a more certain and less objectionable mode of relieving the destitute and securing the regular employment of the poor. The principle of the Poor Law is, that rate after rate should be levied for the *preservation of life*, until the landowners and farmers either enable the people to support themselves by honest industry, or dispose of their property to those who can and will perform this indispensable duty.

The fearful problem to be solved in Ireland, stated in its simplest form, is this. A large population subsisting on potatoes which they raised for themselves, has been deprived of that resource, and how are they now to be supported? The obvious answer is, by growing something else. But that cannot be, because the small patches of land which maintained a family when laid down to potatoes, are insufficient for the purpose when laid down to corn or any other kind of produce; and corn cultivation requires capital and skill, and combined labour, which the cotter and conacre tenants do not possess. The position occupied by these classes is no longer tenable, and it is necessary for them either to become substantial farmers, or to live by the wages of their labour. They must still depend for their subsistence upon agriculture, but upon agriculture conducted according to new and very improved conditions. Both the kind of food and the means of procuring it have changed. The people will henceforth principally live upon grain, either imported from abroad or grown in the country, which they will purchase out of their wages; and corn and cattle will be exported, as the piece-goods of Manchester are, to provide the fund out of which the community will be maintained under the several heads of wages, profits, and rents. It is in vain that the granary of the merchant and the homestead of the farmer are filled to overflowing, if the mass of the people have not the means of purchasing, and it has therefore become of the highest consequence that the resources which are most available for the payment of wages should be cultivated to the utmost. The Poor Law cannot alone bear the whole weight of the existing pauperism of Ireland; and its unproductive expenditure, however indispensable, must be supported by adequate industrial efforts, in order to prevent all classes of society from being involved in one common ruin. Before this crisis occurred, Sir Robert Kane had proved in theory, and many good farmers in practice, that a much larger produce might be raised, and a much larger population might be supported from the soil of Ireland than heretofore; and this view has since been confirmed by numerous surveys conducted under the superintendence of the Board of Works, which have disclosed an extensive and varied field for the investment of capital, upon which the whole unemployed population of Ireland might be employed with much advantage to all parties concerned. The great resource of Ireland consists in the cultivation of her soil, the improvement of her cattle, the extension of her fisheries; and while there are large tracts of flooded land to be reclaimed, and still larger tracts of half-cultivated land to be brought to a higher state of productiveness, it would be a misdirection of capital to employ it in the less profitable manufactures of cotton and wool. Ireland is benefited to a greater extent than many parts of Scotland and England are, by the markets and the means of employment which Manchester and Glasgow afford; but her own staple manufacture is corn.

The Treasury was authorized by the 1 & 2 Wm. IV, c. 33, passed in 1831,[165] to lend money to private individuals for the improvement of their estates, provided the value of the estate was increased 10 per cent, and repayment was made in three years; and by the first Act of the Session of 1846 the period of repayment was extended to twenty years. This power was however very sparingly acted on. Grave objections existed to the State becoming a general creditor throughout the country, and the operations of private capitalists were likely to be deranged and suspended by the interference of such a competitor. A rate of interest (5 per cent.) higher than the market rate for money lent on mortgage, was therefore charged, and the result was, that only three persons took out loans under this arrangement, one of whom was the late Lord Bessborough.[166] At the close of the Session of 1846, the Act 9 & 10 Vic. c. 101, was passed, which 1,000,000*l*. was authorized to be lent for drainage in Ireland, and repayment was to be made in equal half-yearly installments, spread over twenty-two years, including interest at $3\frac{1}{2}$ per cent.; but this Act could not be worked, so far as Ireland was concerned, partly owing to a legal opinion that tenants for life were not eligible for loans under it, and partly because the works must be executed to a certain extent before the money could be advanced. Upon this the Treasury issued a Minute dated the 1st, and a letter dated the 15th December, 1846*,[167] offering to lend money for the general improvement of estates, including drainage, on a footing which combined the advantages of the previous Acts with the indulgent mode of repayment introduced by the last; and in the following session the Act 10 & 11 Vic. c. 32 was passed, by which all the existing legislation on the subject was consolidated, and loans†[168] were authorized to be made in Ireland to the extent of 1,500,000*l*, on the principle that the improvements on each estate are to be executed by the proprietor, and that the interference of the officers of the Government is to be confined to ascertaining, in the first instance, that the proposed improvements are likely to be of such a permanent and productive character as would justify the cost of them being made a charge upon the estate, with priority over other incumbrances, and, afterwards, to inspecting the works from time to time, so as to secure the proper application of the sums advanced to the purposes for which they were intended. No advance can be made under this Act unless the increased annual value to be given to the land by the proposed improvement shall equal the amount to be charged on it; and a difficulty having arisen from the circumstance that the full benefit to be derived from draining is attained in different soils at different periods after the completion of the drains, it was declared by a Treasury Minute dated the 15th June, 1847 that it is not necessary that each portion of land improved should yield, in the first and in every subsequent year, an additional rent equal to 6½ per cent, per annum on the outlay beyond the present rent; but that the general result of the improvement of the lands on which the rent-charge is to be secured, will, one year with another, from the period when the full benefit of the improvement may be supposed to have accrued, be such as to produce an increased annual value to the above extent; taking care, of course, that the rent-charge is fixed upon lands amply sufficient to secure the repayment to the Government of the sums so charged. These directions had particular reference to the circumstances of the poverty-stricken districts in the West of Ireland, where it is peculiarly desirable to increase the food grown on the spot, and to provide the means of employment for the people in the productive avocations of agriculture; and every practicable facility and preference is therefore given to the landed proprietors in those districts, which is not inconsistent with justice to other parties. It was determined by the same Minute, in pursuance of the course taken by Parliament with respect to the loans for drainage in England and Scotland, that the loans to be made to any one landed proprietor should not, under ordinary circumstances, exceed, in the aggregate, the sum of 12,000*l.*; but if, in any particular case, owing to the extent of the property to be improved, or other causes, it should be advisable to enlarge this limit, the Lords of the Treasury will be prepared to authorize such additional sum as may appear to be proper, not exceeding, however, an aggregate amount to the same proprietor, of 20,000*l.*

In taking its line on this subject, the Government had to choose between employing the agency of the landed proprietors and that of public officers; and after much consideration and some experience, the final decision was in favour of the former alternative, as above described.

By following this course, all the existing relations of society were preserved and strengthened; the landed proprietors were held to their responsibility for the well-being of the people residing on their estates, and they were assisted to the extent of the loan fund placed by Parliament at the disposal of the Government. The proprietor or his agent has the strongest interest in seeing that the work is well done, and can exercise the most effectual superintendence over it; and as the people are invited to exert themselves under the eye of their natural employers, the healthy relation of master and labourer becomes established throughout the country. It has not, as yet, been usual in Ireland, for the landlord to undertake to make the more expensive and permanent improvements, as is the case in England, but it may be hoped that an impulse will be given to this wholesome practice by the loans to proprietors under the Land Improvement Act. The landlord will be encouraged to proceed in a course of improvement which he finds by experience to be profitable to him; he will be likely to make further investments on land which has been reclaimed or improved by him, and he will be especially careful to prevent it from being subdivided into small holdings*.[169]

The other plan of reclaiming waste lands by the direct agency of the Government, did not survive the objections made to it on the score of its interference with the rights of private property. The land must be obtained before it could be improved, and was it to be left to the discretion of Commissioners to take any bog-land they pleased at a valuation; to single out, for instance, a tract of unreclaimed land in the centre of an estate? Some firm land also must be annexed to each allotment for the erection of the farm buildings, and to obtain soil for the improvement of the bog, and this would have given a still wider and more arbitrary discretion to the Commissioners. The compulsory powers had therefore to be given up; and without them the plan could not be worked.

But there are other objections to this plan which have a much deeper root. The first result of the Government undertaking to reclaim the waste lands of Ireland would be that the mass of the people would throw themselves on these works, as they did upon the roads, taking it for granted that the means of payment were inexhaustible, and that less labour would be exacted than in employment offered with a view to private profit. The landlords and farmers would consider that, as the Government had undertaken to employ the people and improve the soil, they were themselves absolved from responsibility, and they would refer all the persons who applied to them for employment, to the Government works, as has been so often done on former occasions. The single agency of the Government would be substituted for the exertions of the whole body of the landowners acting in concert with their tenants and dependents; and instead of landed proprietors and farmers laying out their own money for their own benefit, with all the care and economy which this supposes, we should have hundreds of public officers, of various grades and characters, expending public money, for the supposed benefit of the public, in a business totally foreign to the proper functions of Government, and without a possibility of effectual superintendence; the inevitable consequence of which would be, bad work, idle habits, and profuse and wasteful expenditure. Lastly, when the land had been reclaimed, whatever care might be taken to dispose of it in farms of reasonable size, however durable might be the interest granted, or whatever legal restrictions might be attempted to be imposed, the old process of the subdivision of the land, and the multiplication of the persons subsisting upon it, would run its course. Nothing can supply the place of the watchful supervision exercised by a proprietor, for the protection of his own interests, in such a case.

A peasant proprietary may succeed to a certain extent*,[170] where there is a foundation of steadiness of character, and a habit of prudence, and a spring of pride, and a value for independence and comfort; but we fear that all these words merely show the vain nature of schemes of peasant proprietorship for Ireland. The small holders of Belgium†[171] with all their industry and frugality, have, during this calamitous period, been the most distressed population in Europe next to Ireland. Their own resources were too small to carry them through a season of dearth, and they had no employers to assist them. In India, society is based on a system of small holdings, and there is no country in which destructive famines have been so common.[172] In Ireland itself, the greatest over-population, and consequently the greatest distress, prevailed in those districts in which, owing to the existence of long leases, the landlords had no power to prevent the subdivision of the land. Mere security of tenure is of no avail, without the capital, and skill, and habits of life, and, above all, the wholesome moral qualities required to turn this advantage to good account. During the late season of dearth, food was dearer in the long peninsula which stretches to the south-west of England, than it was in Ireland, and the poor had no resource analogous to the farming stock of the Irish small holder; but the Devonshire and Somersetshire labourer lives by wages paid by persons richer than himself; and though severely pinched, he had enough for daily bread, with some assistance from charitable aid, which was generally afforded throughout the west of England, during the late season of distress, either by parochial subscriptions or by allowances from the unions. The south-west of England is the least favourable specimen which Great Britain affords of the system of society based upon wages, because the nourishing manufactures which formerly existed in that quarter have disappeared before the superior natural advantages of the North, and wages are consequently very low*.[173] In every other part of this island the contrast is more decidedly to the disadvantage of the small holdings; and in Northumberland, which is a county of large farms, there may be said to be no poor. Whether the good order, the physical well-being, or the moral and intellectual progress of rural society, be considered, the best model is that in which the educated and enlightened proprietor, the substantial farmer, and the industrious labourer on regular wages, each performs his appropriate part.

The works required for deepening and straightening the course of many of the rivers are of peculiar importance to Ireland; because until the outfalls have been cleared, the landowners cannot enter upon the detailed or thorough drainage of their respective estates. In such cases the necessity of working upon the lands of different proprietors calls for the active interposition of the Board of Works, who make the preliminary survey, execute the work, and afterwards apportion the charge, according to the benefit derived by each person interested. The funds for carrying on these improvements had been chiefly obtained by the issue of debentures under the authority of the Acts of Parliament relating to the subject; but, under existing circumstances, loans were not to be expected from private individuals at a moderate rate of interest; and the ordinary loan fund of the Board of Works amounting to 60,000*l*. a-year, was therefore reinforced with 120,000*l*., transferred to it from the London Loan Commissioners, and 250,000*l*. issued from the Consolidated Fund; making altogether a sum of 430,000*l*. placed at the disposal of the Board of Works, between the 1st April, 1847, and the 1st April, 1848, to be advanced by them for works of utility in Ireland, but principally for drainage of the above-mentioned description.

Next to agricultural improvements, well-selected public works perhaps offer the greatest resource in the present unhappy circumstances of Ireland. It is a mistake to suppose that opening a good road may not be the most reproductive work in many districts; and the construction of railroads on the great lines of communication, does for the whole country what new roads do for particular districts, facilitating and stimulating every description of production, and agriculture more than all, binding society together by a closer intercourse and inter-change of good offices, and rapidly diffusing through the remote provinces the advantages enjoyed by the more favoured parts of the country.

The objection to Lord George Bentinck's plan for assisting Irish railways was, that while it was inadequate as a measure of relief, it was too large and indiscriminate when viewed as a measure for the promotion of public works.[174] Private enterprise would have been overlaid; the bad lines would have been benefited at the expense of the good; the public credit would have been lowered; the available stock of national capital would have suffered an additional drain which it could ill afford; and after all, the object of relieving the existing distress would not have been attained. The famine was then at its height, and it could not be stayed by any measure short of distributing food to the multitude. After allowing for the largest number of persons who could be employed on railways, millions must still have starved, if other more effectual steps had not been taken; and the sums advanced to the Railway Companies, large as they would have been, would not have perceptibly diminished the expense of feeding a whole nation*.[175] When this primary object had been attained, and all the funds had been raised by loan which the state of Ireland required, the Government was then in a position to consider what assistance could be given to railroads in common with other works of public utility; and 620,000$l$. was voted by Parliament to be lent to Railways which were legally able to borrow, owing to their having paid up half their capital, and could undertake to expend within a certain fixed time, another sum of their own equal to that advanced to them. By the aid thus given, the great South-Western Railway of Ireland will be enabled to employ a large number of men throughout the winter, and the important object of opening the communication between Dublin, Cork, and Limerick, will be accomplished at a much earlier period than would otherwise have been the case.

The other works in progress in Ireland with the aid of grants or loans from Parliament, are as follows: the Shannon navigation, which has been in operation for several years; the construction of new floating docks and markets at Limerick; works at Hawlbowline,[176] with a view to render that place more useful as a naval station; four great works of combined navigation and drainage; the construction of three new colleges, and of several prisons and lunatic asylums; and the repair and construction of fishery piers, for which 50,000$l$. was voted in the session of 1846, and a further sum of 40,000$l$. in the session of 1847.

Having thus furnished as clear a sketch as the variety and complexity of the incidents would allow, of this remarkable crisis in our national affairs, when the events of many years were crowded into two short seasons, and a foundation was laid for social changes of the highest importance, it may be asked, what fruits have yet appeared of this portentous seed-time, and what the experience is which we have purchased at so heavy a cost?

First, it has been proved to demonstration, that local distress cannot be relieved out of national funds without great abuses and evils, tending, by a direct and rapid process, to an entire disorganisation of society. This is, in effect, to expose the common stock to a general scramble. All are interested in getting as much as they can. It is nobody's concern to put a check on the expenditure. If the poor man prefers idling on relief works or being rationed with his wife and children, to hard labour; if the farmer discharges his labourers and makes the state of things a plea for not paying rates or rent; if the landed proprietor joins in the common cry, hoping to obtain some present advantage, and trusting to the chance of escaping future repayments, it is not the men, but the system, which is in fault. Ireland is not the only country which would have been thrown off its balance by the attraction of "public money" *à discrétion*. This false principle eats like a canker into the moral health and physical prosperity of the people. All classes "make a poor mouth," as it is expressively called in Ireland.[177] They conceal their advantages, exaggerate their difficulties, and relax their exertions. The cotter does not sow his holding, the proprietor does not employ his poor in improving his estate, because by doing so they would disentitle themselves to their "share of the relief." The common wealth suffers both by the lavish consumption and the diminished production, and the bees of the hive, however they may redouble their exertions, must soon sink under the accumulated burden. The officers of Government, overborne by numbers, and unable to test the interested representations pressed upon them from all quarters, cannot exercise their usual watchful care over the expenditure of the public money. Those persons who have the will to do their duty, have not the power. Those who have the power, have not the will. There is only one way in which the relief of the destitute ever has been, or ever will be, conducted consistently with the general welfare, and that is by *making it a local charge*. Those who know how to discriminate between the different claims for relief, then become actuated by a powerful motive to use that knowledge aright. They are spending *their own money*. At the same time, those who have the means of employing the people in reproductive works, have the strongest inducement given them to do so. The struggle now is to keep the poor off the rates, and if their labour only replaces the cost of their food, it is cheaper than having to maintain them in perfect idleness.

Another point which has been established by the result of these extensive experiments in the science, if it may be so called, of relieving the destitute, is that two things ought to be carefully separated which are often confounded. Improvement is always a good thing, and relief is occasionally a necessary thing, but the mixture of the two is almost always bad; and when it is attempted on a large scale without proper means of keeping it in check, it is likely to affect in a very injurious manner the ordinary motives and processes by which the business of society is carried on. Relief, taken by itself, offers, if it is properly administered, no motive to misrepresent the condition of the people; and being burdensome to the higher, and distasteful to the lower classes, it is capable of being carefully tested and subjected to effectual control [sic]. But when relief is connected with profitable improvements and full wages, the most influential persons in each locality become at once interested in establishing a case in favour of it, and the higher are always ready to join with the lower classes in pressing forward *relief works* on a plea of urgent general distress, which it may be impossible to analyse and difficult to resist. Relief ought to be confined as much as possible to the infirm and helpless. Wages, by means of which improvements are carried on, should be given by preference to the able-bodied and vigorous. Relief ought to be on the lowest scale necessary for subsistence. Wages should be sufficiently liberal to secure the best exertions of the labourer. Relief should be made so unattractive as to furnish no motive to ask for it, except in the absence of every other means of subsistence. Improvements should be encouraged and urged forward by every practicable means, both as regards the parties undertaking them, and those by whom they are executed. If labour is connected with relief, it should only be as a test of the destitution of the applicant, and of his being consequently entitled to a bare subsistence, in the same way as confinement in a workhouse is also a test; and the true way to make relief conducive to improvement, is to give the rich no choice between maintaining the able-bodied labourers as paupers, or employing them on full wages on profitable works, and to take care that the poor have no reason to prefer living on public alms, to the active exercise of their industry in their own behalf.

Among all our discouragements, there are not wanting many and sure grounds of hope for the future. The best sign of all is, that the case of Ireland is at last understood. Irish affairs are no longer a craft and mystery. The abyss has been fathomed. The famine has acted with a force which nothing could resist, and has exposed to view the real state of the country, so that he who runs may read. We have gained, both by what has been unlearned and by what has been learned during the last two years: and the result is, that the great majority of people, both in Ireland and England, are now agreed upon the course which ought to be pursued, in order to arrive at the wished-for end. The attention of the two countries has also been so long directed to the same subject, that a new reciprocity of interest and feeling has been established, and the public opinion of each has begun to act upon the other with a force which was never felt before.

The Irish have been disabused of one of the strangest delusions which ever paralysed the energies of a naturally intelligent and energetic people. Those who knew the country best were aware of the habitual dependence of the upper classes upon the Government; and it was a common saying of former days, that an Irish gentleman could not even marry his daughter without going to the Castle for assistance. The vulgar idea was, that when difficulties occurred, every personal obligation was discharged by "bringing the matter under the consideration of the Government;" and if, in addition to this, "a handsome support" was promised, it seldom meant more than helping to spend any public money that might be forthcoming. But it was reserved for that potent solvent, the Famine, to discover to the full extent, this element of the national character. To pass with safety through this great crisis, required that every man, from the highest nobleman to the meanest peasant, should exert himself to the utmost of his means and ability; instead of which, the entire unassisted burden of employing all the unemployed labourers of Ireland, of improving all the unimproved land of Ireland, and feeding all the destitute persons in Ireland, was heaped upon a Board consisting of five gentlemen, sitting in an office in Dublin. The example of the gentry was followed with customary exaggeration by the lower orders, and throughout extensive districts, the cultivation of the land was suspended in the spring of 1847 until it should be seen what "encouragement" the Government would give, or, as it was sometimes ingenuously expressed, "We expect the Government will till the ground." It is also a fact that the people in some parts of the West of Ireland neglected to a great extent to lay in their usual winter stock of turf in 1847, owing to the prevalence of a popular impression that the Queen would supply them with coals. Ireland has awakened from this dream by the occurrence of the most frightful calamities, and it has at last begun to be understood that the proper business of a Government, is to enable private individuals of every rank and profession in life, to carry on their several occupations with freedom and safety, and not itself to undertake the business of the landowner, merchant, money-lender, or any other function of social life. Reason is now able to make herself heard, and there has not been wanting many a warning and encouraging voice from Ireland herself, declaring—"The prosperity of Ireland is only to be attained by your own strong arms. We are able to help ourselves. We will no longer be dependent on the precarious assistance received from other lands. We will never rest until every sod in Ireland brings forth abundantly—till every inch of ground is in its highest and fullest state of bearing. In a short time we shall have among us more industry and exertion, less politics and more ploughing, less argument and more action, less debating and more doing*."[178]

The uniting power of a common misfortune has also been felt throughout the British Empire. Those who had never before exchanged words or looks of kindness, met to co-operate in this great work of charity, and good men recognised each other's merits under the distinctions by which they had been previously separated. The Protestant and Roman Catholic clergy vied with each other in their exertions for the famishing and fever-stricken people, and in numerous instances their lives became a sacrifice to the discharge of their exhausting, harassing and dangerous duties. To the priests all were indebted for the readiness with which they made their influence over their flocks subservient to the cause of order; and the minister of religion was frequently summoned to the aid of the public officer when all other means of restraining the excited multitude had failed*.[179] The political dissensions which had distracted Ireland for centuries became suddenly allayed. The famine was too strong even for the mighty demagogue, that great mixed character to whom Ireland owes so much good and so much evil. People of every shade of political opinion acted together, not always in an enlightened manner, but always cordially and earnestly, in making the social maladies of Ireland, and the means of healing them, the paramount object. In the hour of her utmost need, Ireland became sensible of an union of feeling and interest with the rest of the empire, which would have moved hearts less susceptible of every generous and grateful emotion than those of her sons and daughters*.[180] Although the public efforts in her behalf were without parallel in ancient and modern history, and the private subscriptions were the largest ever raised for a charitable object, they were less remarkable than the absorbing interest with which her misfortunes were regarded for months together both in Parliament and in society, to the exclusion of almost every other topic. It will also never be forgotten that these efforts and these sacrifices were made at a time when England was herself suffering under a severe scarcity of food, aggravated by the failure of the cotton crop, and by the pecuniary exhaustion consequent upon the vast expenditure for the construction of railways.[181] Even in such a state of things, though serious injury was done to all her interests by the Irish Loan, and though the pressure upon the labouring classes was greatly increased by the wholesale purchase of their food, that it might be given without cost to the starving Irish, yet every sacrifice was submitted to without a murmur by the great body of the people.

Although the process by which long-established habits are changed, and society is reconstructed on a new basis, must necessarily be, slow, there are not wanting signs that we are advancing by sure steps towards the desired end. The cultivation of corn has to a great extent been substituted for that of the potato; the people have become accustomed to a better description of food than the potato*;[182] conacre, and the excessive competition for land, have ceased to exist; the small holdings, which have become deserted, owing to death, or emigration, or the mere inability of the holders to obtain a subsistence from them in the absence of the potato, have, to a considerable extent, been consolidated with the adjoining farms; and the middlemen, whose occupation depends upon the existence of a numerous small tenantry, have begun to disappear. The large quantity of land left uncultivated in some of the western districts is a painful but decisive proof of the extent to which this change is taking place. The class of offences connected with the holding of land, which was the most difficult to deal with, because agrarian crimes were supported by the sympathy and approbation of the body of the people, and were generally the result of secret illegal associations, fell off in a remarkable degree*;[183] and although ofences [sic] against other kinds of property increased, owing to the general distress, the usual difficulty was not experienced in obtaining convictions. The much-desired change in the ownership of land appears also to have commenced; and when great estates are brought to the hammer now, instead of being sold, as formerly, en masse, they are broken up into lots*,[184] which opens the door to a middle class, more likely to become resident and improving proprietors than their predecessors, and better able to maintain the stability of property and of our political institutions, because they are themselves sprung from the people. The most wholesome symptom of all, however, is that a general impression prevails, that the plan of depending on external assistance has been tried to the utmost and has failed; that people have grown worse under it instead of better; and that the experiment ought now to be made of what independent exertion will do. This feeling has been much strengthened by the necessity which has been imposed upon the upper classes through the Poor Law, of caring for the condition of the people; and the attention of the country gentlemen has in many districts been seriously directed to the means of supporting them in a manner which will be alike beneficial to the employer and the employed.

The poet Spenser[185] commences his view of the state of Ireland by these discouraging observations: "Marry, so there have been divers good plots devised, and wise counsels cast already about reformation of that realm, but they say it is the fatal destiny of that land, that no purposes whatsoever which are meant for her good, will prosper or take good effect; which, whether it proceed from the very genius of the soil, or influence of the stars, or that Almighty God hath not yet appointed the time of her reformation, or that he reserveth her in this inquiet state still for some secret scourge, which shall by her come into England, it is hard to be known, but yet much to be feared." Our humble but sincere conviction is, that the appointed time of Ireland's regeneration is at last come. For several centuries we were in a state of open warfare with the native Irish, who were treated as foreign enemies, and were not admitted to the privileges and civilising influences of English law, even when they most desired it. To this succeeded a long period of mixed religious and civil persecution*,[186] when the Irish were treated as the professors of a hostile faith, and had inflicted on them irritating and degrading penalties, of which exclusion from Parliament and from civil and military office was one of the least; the general characteristics of this epoch of Irish management being that the Protestant minority were governed by corruption, and the Roman Catholic majority by intimidation. During all this time England reaped as she sowed: and as she kept the people in a chronic state of exasperation against herself, none of her "good plots and wise counsels" for their benefit succeeded; for there was no want of good intention, and the fault was principally in the mistaken opinions of the age, which led to persecution in other countries besides Ireland. Now, thank God, we are in a different position; and although many waves of disturbance must pass over us before that troubled sea can entirely subside, and time must be allowed for morbid habits to give place to a more healthy action, England and Ireland are, with one great exception, subject to equal laws; and, so far as the maladies of Ireland are traceable to political causes, nearly every practicable remedy has been applied. The deep and inveterate root of social evil remained, and this has been laid bare by a direct stroke of an all-wise and all-merciful Providence, as if this part of the case were beyond the unassisted power of man. Innumerable had been the specifics which the wit of man had devised; but even the idea of the sharp but effectual remedy by which the cure is likely to be effected had never occurred to anyone. God grant that the generation to which this great opportunity has been offered, may rightly perform its part, and that we may not relax our efforts until Ireland fully participates in the social health and physical prosperity of Great Britain, which will be the true consummation of their union.

## Notes

1. For example, in 2006, a leading English newspaper ran an editorial article entitled, 'Was this the most wicked man in Irish history?', *Independent* (London), 30 October 2006.
2. *George Clement Boase,* Trevelyan, Charles Edward, *Dictionary of National Biography*, 1885–1900, vol. 57.
3. 'Explore Haileybury' at: https://www.haileybury.com/explore/haileybury/heritage-archives/notable-haileyburians/three-great-names/thomas-malthus (accessed 10 November 2016).
4. Richard A. Chapman, *Civil Service Commission 1855–1991: A Bureau Biography* (London: Routledge, 2004), p. 13.
5. Ranjana Sengupta, *Delhi Metropolitan. The Making of an Unlikely City* (London: Penguin, 2007), chapter 6.
6. From 'Homeward Mail', The *Spectator*, vol. 32, 22 January 1859, p. 88.
7. Charles E. Trevelyan (Calcutta: pub. not identified, 1835).
8. Charles Trevelyan, *On the education of the people of India* (London: Longman, Orme, Brown, Green and Longmans, 1838).
9. Thomas Babington Macaulay (1800–1859) was a Scottish-born Whig politician and historian. He was an imperialist who believed in the 'civilizing influence of the Protestant religion and of the English language', *The History of England from the Accession of James the Second, 1848*, p. 304.
10. Enda Delaney, *The Curse of Reason, The Great Irish Famine* (Dublin: Gill and Macmillan, 2012), p. 49.
11. *Morning Chronicle*, 14 and 16 October 1843.
12. Sir Randolph Routh (1785–1858) had been appointed Commissary-General in the British army in 1826. From November 1845 until October 1848 he oversaw the distribution of relief in Ireland, for which service he received a KCB in April 1848 (he had also been knighted in 1841).
13. Sir Charles Wood (1800–1885), was an English Whig politician who served as Chancellor of the Exchequer from 1846 to 1852, and thus was in charge of the Treasury. Similarly to Trevelyan, he believed that the Famine provided an opportunity for the moral reform of the Irish.
14. Robin Haines, *Charles Trevelyan and the great Irish Famine* (Dublin: Four Courts Press, 2005), pp. 400–402.
15. Charles E. Trevelyan, *The Irish Crisis* (London: Macmillan, 1880).
16. Traditionally this honour was given to military men but, in 1847, it was extended to civilians.
17. No title, *Morning Chronicle*, 28 November 1848.
18. Author's Note. *We have endeavoured to gather up all the threads of this strange tissue, so that every circumstance of importance connected with the measures of relief may be placed on record; but our narrative does not, except in a few instances, extend beyond September 1847, and the progress of events after that date will form the subject of a separate article.
19. Orangeism is a reference to the Orange Order, and exclusively Protestant (and, at times, vehemently anti-Catholic) organisation that had been founded in 1795; Ribbonism was a generic term for an underground, secret Catholic society that emerged in the early nineteenth century and was most active in rural areas; the Repeal Society had been founded by Daniel O'Connell in 1840 and was dedicated to achieving a repeal of the 1800 Acts of Union by peaceful means.
20. Author's Note. *The author of this paper was the late Mr. Joseph Sabine, the Secretary to the Horticultural Society.
21. Six pennies – or half a shilling. There were 20 shilling in each pound.

22 Author's Note. *Sir John Burgoyne's letter to the "Times", dated th [sic] October, 1847.
23 Author's Note. *The following description of the state of agriculture in "West Clare, previously to the failure in the potato crop in 1845, is taken from a narrative by Captain Mann of the Royal Navy, who had for some time previously been stationed in that district, in charge of the Coast Guard, and when the distress commenced, he took an active and very useful part in assisting in the measures of relief: 'Agriculture at that period was in a very neglected state; wheat, barley, and oats, with potatoes as the food of the poor, being the produce. Of the first very little was produced, and that not good in quality; barley, a larger proportion and good; oats, much greater, but inferior for milling purposes. Various reasons were given for this inferiority in produce, the quality of the land and deteriorated seed being the cause generally assigned; but I would say that the population being content with, and relying on, the produce of the potato as food — which had with very few exceptions hitherto proved abundant — there was a general neglect and want of any attempt at improvement. Green crops were all but unknown, except here and there a little turnip or mangel wurzel in the garden or field of the better class — the former scarcely to be purchased. Even the potatoes were tilled in the easiest way, (in beds called 'lazy beds'), not in drills, so that the hoe might in a very short time clear the weeds and lighten the soil.'"
24 The 'meal months' was the gap between the old potato crop being exhausted and the new one becoming available. During this time, usually oats or oatmeal was eaten. Oats were extensively grown in Ireland, especially in the north-east. Cabbage was also eaten, leading to the phrase *'July an chabdiste'* (July of the cabbage).
25 The Famine of 1739 to 1741 was caused by a mini ice-age in Europe that was particularly severe in Ireland. Historian, David Dickson, in *Artic Ireland* (1997) suggests that proportionately as many people might have died as in the more famous Irish famine a century later.
26 The Bloody Flux was a form of dysentery, so-called because it led to diarrhea with blood.
27 Bridewell was another name for prison. In eighteenth-century Ireland, each county was required to have its own prison located in the chief town. Newgate, in Dublin, was the country's largest prison.
28 Primate Boulter (1672–1742), who was born in London, served as Primate of all Ireland from 1724 until his death. He was generally unsympathetic to Irish Catholics. During the famine of 1739 to 1741, however, he fed the poor in Dublin out of his own expense.
29 This statement is inaccurate. In 1740, the Lord Lieutenant banned grain exports to anywhere except Britain. See Dickson, p. 78.
30 Author's Note. *We are indebted for these particulars to Mr. McCullagh, who has lately collected the contemporary accounts of this famine. It appears that the farmers at this period did not dig their potatoes until about Christmas, and that few stored them at all for use.
31 During the 1822 famine, London was a major source of fund-raising for Ireland, with both men and women being actively involved. The British monarch at the time was King George IV (1762–1830) who had undertaken a state visit to Ireland in August 1821. He opposed Catholic Emancipation. The King's Letter in 1822 was addressed to the clergy.
32 Author's note. * An interesting account by Mr. Bertolacci, of the manner in which this fund and that collected in 1831 were distributed, will be found in the 'Morning Chronicle' of the 25th November, 1847.
33 The Mansion House was the home of the Mayor of Dublin. Relief committees were formed on many occasions in the 19th century on behalf of the Irish poor. The 1822 committee consisted of 'nobility, gentry, clergy, bankers and merchants of the city,'
34 Author's note. † For the details of these operations see the following Parliamentary papers: —

"Copies of the Reports of Messrs. Griffith, Nimmo, and Killaly, the civil engineers employed during the late scarcity, in superintending the Public Works in Ireland; 16 April, 1823 (249)."

"Report from the Select Committee on the employment "of the poor in Ireland; 16 July, 1823 (561)." It is a remarkable testimony to the improvement effected by such works in the social habits of the people, that the district between the Shannon and the Blackwater, which was opened in four directions by the roads executed by Mr. Griffith, although formerly the seat of the Desmond Rebellion, and subsequently, in the year 1821, the asylum for Whiteboys and the focus of the Whiteboy warfare, during which time four regiments were required to repress outrage, became perfectly tranquil, and continued so up to the commencement of the late calamity.

35 In 1823, the British parliament voted a small amount of money for emigration to the Cape of Good Hope (South Africa) and to Upper Canada. Between 300 and 400 artisans and labourers emigrated to the Cape.

36 Author's Note. *The following remarkable passage is extracted from the Report of the Dublin Mansion House Committee, dated the 22nd October, 1831:- "But while the Mansion House Committee thus congratulate themselves and the subscribers upon the success of their efforts to avert famine and disease for a season from so considerable a portion of the island, they owe it also to themselves and the subscribers to avow their honest conviction that similar calls will be periodically made on public benevolence, unless a total change be effected in the condition of the Irish peasant. What means should be adopted to remedy these evils it is not the province of this Committee to suggest; but they deem it their duty to call the attention of the subscribers particularly to this state of things, in the hope of some remedy being discovered and applied before public benevolence is quite exhausted by repeated drains on its sympathy."

On the 21st May, 1838, the Duke of Wellington made the following observations in the debate on the introduction of the Irish Poor Law: — "There never was a country in which poverty existed to so great a degree as it exists in Ireland. I held a high situation in that country thirty years ago, and I must say, that, from that time to this, there has scarcely elapsed a single year, in which the Government has not at certain periods of it entertained the most serious apprehension of actual famine. I am firmly convinced that from the year 1806, down to the present time, a year has not passed in which the Government have not been called on to give assistance to relieve the poverty and distress which prevailed in Ireland."

37 The Sackville Street Committee, more formerly known as the Irish Relief Association for the Destitute Peasants, had offices on 16 Sackville Street (now O'Connell Street) in Dublin. The Duke of Manchester and the Earl of Roden were patrons, both of whom were known for their Protestant evangelical views.

38 In 1839, Captain Henry Ducie Chads, R.N. (1788–1868) was deployed by the British government to investigate the amount of distress in Ireland. The government desired that the extraordinary distress should be kept distinct from the newly introduced Poor Law. During the Great Famine, he was again sent to Ireland to distribute relief.

39 Author's Note. *The particulars of what took place on this occasion will be found in a letter from the Poor Law Commissioners to Sir J. Graham, dated the 9th June, 1842, and in a statement dated 18th August, 1842, prepared under the directions of the Irish Government, showing "the sums issued for the relief of distress in Ireland from the 17th June to the 17th August, 1842," &c.

40 John O'Connell (1810–1858) was one of Daniel O'Connell's four sons. In 1832, he became an MP in the British Parliament. Although not the eldest son, he most closely followed in his father's footsteps, taking over the running of the Repeal Association during his father's illness and following his death in 1847.

Author's Note. * This Return is for sums "advanced on loan since the Union," but in some cases the advances have not been repaid, and in others large grants were made in addition to loans.

41 Shorthand for 'Ditto', meaning same as above.
42 These acts were sponsored by Henry Flood and John Foster respectively. They tied the Irish corn trade to the availability, and thus the price, of corn in Ireland.
43 Rundale was most prevalent in the west of Ireland. It was a system of collective farming, with a group of people cultivating land and leasing it jointly.
44 Entail was a means of limiting the way in which property could be distributed, largely in order to ensure that the estate remain intact. The British government abolished entails in England in 1833. In Ireland, the crisis of the Famine resulted in two Encumbered Estates Acts being passed (1848 and 1849) to facilitate sale of these estates.
45 Author's Note. *"Observations upon certain evils arising out of the present state of the Laws of Real Property in Ireland, and Suggestions for remedying the same." — Dublin: Alex. Thom, 1847. The author of this pamphlet is Mr. Booth, who has for many years past held the responsible office of Clerk of the Survey in Ireland, under the Master-General and Board of Ordnance. It will be seen by a perusal of the pamphlet, that this able and deserving officer has fully availed himself of the opportunities which his situation afforded, for making himself acquainted with the social state of Ireland; and that he has successfully applied to the consideration of the subject, that practical ability from which the public service has derived so much benefit.
46 Author's Note. * "Observations on the evils resulting to Ireland from the insecurity of Title and the existing Laws of Real Property, with some Suggestions towards a remedy." — Dublin: Hodges and Smith. London: Ridgway; 1847. The author of this pamphlet is Mr. Jonathan Pim, who, in the capacity of joint secretary, with Mr. Joseph Bewley, of the Dublin Friends' Relief Committee, took the lead in the admirably benevolent and practical measures adopted by that excellent society for the relief of the distress, and the re-establishment of the industry of Ireland on a more secure and satisfactory footing than before. Mr. Pim is also the author of a more extended work, entitled "The Condition and Prospects of Ireland," which has just been published, and which, if we mistake not, will prove one of the most useful publications which have yet appeared on this deeply interesting subject.
47 Author's Note. * It is perfectly true that the unembarrassed holder of an entailed estate is often not sufficiently owner of it to be able to do justice to it. He cannot sell a portion to improve the remainder, however much both the part sold and the part retained would be benefited by it. He can burden the estate to provide for younger children's portions, but not to carry on improvements which would increase its annual produce. Improvements are generally made out of capital, and not out of income. Owners of entailed estates, for the most part, live up to their means; and when they do not, their savings are seldom sufficient to carry on works of any importance. Over the capital sum representing the aggregate value of the estate, they have no command, except for purposes which make them poorer, and consequently still less able to execute any useful design. At the present crisis of our national affairs, it behoves us to consider what course will be the best both for the landowners and for the community at large. There is a fearful surplus population in Ireland and the north-western part of Scotland which must be provided for; while in England itself thousands of railway labourers and Irish paupers roam unemployed about the country; and the question is, whether, by removing the obstacles which at present oppose the profitable employment of the enormous capital invested in land, we might not obtain new resources which would enrich the owners of land, diffuse comfort and enjoyment in each locality, and help to provide for the unemployed population which is sitting like an incubus upon all the three kingdoms.

48 Author's Note. * The following Table gives the leading particulars relating to the estates under the management of the Courts in Ireland during the years 1841-2 and 3:

### Court of Chancery.

|  | No. of Causes | Rental of Estates. | Arrears of Rent. ||
|  |  |  | When Receiver was appointed. | When Receiver last accounted. |
| --- | --- | --- | --- | --- |
|  |  | £ s. d. | £ s. d. | £ s. d. |
| 1841. | 698 | 598,635 13 10¾ | 39,358 16 4½ | 347,226 14 10 |
| 1842. | 595 | 548,783 12 9 | 3,105 0 10 | 299,554 10 8 |
| 1843. | 764 | 563,022 2 4 | 39,265 13 1 | 290,292 4 10 |
| Average of three years | 686 | 570,147 2 11¾ | 27,243 3 5 | 312,357 16 10 |
| From 1836 to 1843 inclusive. | \multicolumn{4}{c}{Court of Exchequer.} |
|  | 316 | 132,675 2 3 | 56,163 6 6 | 87,849 0 11¼ |

The arrears of rent have since greatly increased, although the object of the Courts is confined to getting in the Rents, improvements being seldom attempted. The condition of the people on these neglected, and with reference to their present state of cultivation, overpopulated estates, is melancholy in the extreme.

49 Author's Note. * "Observations upon certain evils," &c.
50 Author's Note. * "Observations upon certain evils," &c.
51 Author's Note. * "Observations upon certain evils," &c.
52 Author's Note. * "Observations upon certain evils," &c.
53 The Act was 6 Anne C. 2, An Act for the Public Registering of all Deeds, Conveyances and Wills etc.
54 Author's note. *Treasury Minute, October 15, 1847.
55 Author's note. † These useful reforms were suggested by Mr. Pierce Mahony, who is entitled to the gratitude of the public, for the perseverance and ability with which he has, for many years past, with little encouragement either from the public or from those who have administered the Government of the country, advocated these and other measures directed to the extremely important object of simplifying, facilitating, and rendering more secure the transfer and tenure of land.
56 Author's note. * The year 1845 was the second and worst in America; and in 1846, although it still extensively prevailed, the disease was of a milder type and only partially affected the crop.
57 The potato disease appeared in Dublin and other parts of Ireland as early as September 1845. He was one of the first people to warn the government about the seriousness of the potato failure in Ireland.
58 Father Theobald Mathew (1790–1856) was a Cork-based leader of the Irish temperance movement.
59 Captain Mann was part of the Irish Coast Guard who assisted in the distribution of relief in 1845 and 1846.
  Author's note. * The following extract from Captain Mann's Narrative, descriptive of what took place at this period in the county of Clare, will be read with interest: "The early culture of 1846 was in no way improved; a great proportion of the land was again tilled with potatoes, under the expectation that, as in former years, the late scarcity

would be followed by a bountiful supply. The first alarm was in the latter part of July, when the potatoes showed symptoms of the previous year's disease; but I shall never forget the change in one week in August. On the first occasion, on an official visit of inspection, I had passed over thirty-two miles thickly studded with potato fields in full bloom. The next time the face of the whole country was changed; the stalk remained bright green, but the leaves were all scorched black. It was the work of a night. Distress and fear was pictured in every countenance, and there was a general rush to dig and sell, or consume the crop by feeding pigs and cattle, fearing in a short time they would prove unfit for any use. Consequently, there was a very wasteful expenditure, and distress showed itself much earlier than in the preceding season."

60 Indian corn, or maize, was a low nutrition and low cost crop, so called because it was a staple food for the Native people of North America.
61 The repeal of the Corn Laws in early summer 1846 lost Peel the support of the Protectionist wing of the Tory Party. Throughout the Famine, the party remained split, and not about to offer real opposition to the Whig Party.
62 The Navigations Laws were a protectionist body of legislation that aimed to use trade to benefit the empire, as only British-registered ships could convey foreign goods to the UK. This cumbersome body of legislation was repealed in 1849.
63 John Kenny (1792–1879) was parish priest in Kilrush, Co. Clare. Born in Limerick, he was ordained in Maynooth College in 1814. He was a supporter of O'Connell and Repeal of the Union. His work in providing Famine relief was mentioned in many contemporary sources. Kenny was moved to Ennis in 1848 where he was promoted to Dean. His obituary appeared in the *Freeman's Journal* on 14 January 1879.

Author's note. * The following extract from Captain Mann's Narrative will give some idea of the difficulty of prevailing on the people to have recourse to the new food; — "The first issue of Indian corn meal was in March, 1846. It is impossible to conceive the strong prejudice against it; and I may here bear testimony to the benevolent and right feeling of the Rev. J. Kenny, PP. Previously to the sale of the meal being commenced, a small portion was sent to me by Commissary-General (now Sir Edward) Coffin, which I placed in the hands of the reverend gentleman. He tried and approved of it, and in order to overcome any feeling against it, subsequently, with his two curates, all but entirely lived on the meal made into bread and stirabout, for nearly a fortnight using all his influence to convince the people that the pernicious effects ascribed to it were untrue. Such conduct is above any praise of mine. The success attending this measure, it is quite unnecessary for me to allude to; and the merchants profiting by the example, commenced a trade new to them by importing the article." The use of Indian corn meal was adopted in hundreds of households of the higher classes, both Protestant and Roman Catholic, besides that of Father Kenny, for the purpose of over-coming the popular prejudice by the force of example. The Society of Arts awarded a gold medal to Mr. O'Brien, baker, of Leinster Street, Dublin, for the attention paid by him to the introduction of cheap popular modes of preparing Indian corn for use; and tens of thousands of pamphlets and printed sheets were distributed through the Commissariat containing instructions for cooking the Indian corn, and showing the people what other cheap descriptions of food were available to them. Those who know how difficult it is to induce a large population to adopt new habits, will be surprised at the success which attended these efforts. The "yellow meal," as it is called, was first known as "Peel's brimstone," and it was remembered that the attempt to introduce it in a former season of distress occasioned a popular commotion, arising from the absurd notion that it had the effect of turning those who ate it black.
64 Public Works (Ireland) (No. 1) Act 1846 c. 1.
65 The devastating effects of the potato blight, combined with a poor oats' harvest and the onset of an industrial recession throughout the UK meant that Trevelyan's reference to a 'superabundance' of supplies in some parts of Ireland was illusory, rather than real.
66 Author's Note. * This minute will be found from pages 67 to 71 of the first Board of Works Series of Parliamentary Papers for 1847.

## OFFICIAL RESPONSE AND REACTION

67   Poor Employment (Ireland) Act 1846 c. 107.
68   As the Famine progressed, an increased amount of the financial burden for relief was placed on local landowners, especially those in the poorest areas. This inverse relationship whereby the poorest areas had to pay the highest taxes proved to be unsustainable.
69   The policy of keeping wages deliberately low, in a period of famine food prices, placed the food out of reach of the poor, thus creating a starvation gap.
70   These measures were announced by the British government in January 1847. For Isaac Butt and a number of other commentators, they were too little, too late.
71   A barony was a historical division of a county in Ireland. This administrative unit was also used for taxation purposes until replaced by the Local Government Act of 1898.
72   Author's note. *A member of the Board of Works, writing to a friend, observed as follows: — "I hope never to see such a winter and spring again. I can truly say, in looking back upon it, even now, that it appears to me, not a succession of weeks and days, but one long continuous day, with occasional intervals of nightmare sleep. Rest one could never have, night nor day, when one felt that in every minute lost a score of men might die."
73   If an act of resistance took place, the public works were suspended, thus punishing the not only the instigator, but also those poor people who had had no direct involvement.
74   Author's note. *An officer of the Board of Works, observing the emaciated condition of the labourers, reported that, as an engineer, he was ashamed of allotting so little task-work for a day's wages, while, as a man, he was ashamed of requiring so much. In some districts proof of attendance was obliged to be considered sufficient to entitle the labourer to his wages. The exhausted state of the workmen was one main cause of the small quantity of work done compared with the money expended. The Irish peasant had been accustomed to remain at home, cowering over his turf fire, during the inclement season of the year, and exposure to the cold and rain on the roads, without sufficient food or clothing, greatly contributed to the prevailing sickness. In order to obviate this as far as possible, a Circular Letter was issued by the Board of Works (1st series of 1847, page 499) directing that, in case of snow or heavy rain, the labourers should merely attend roll call in the morning, and be entered on the pay list for half a day's pay; and if it afterwards became fine, they were to come to work, which would entitle them to a further allowance.
75   The tardiness in ending the public works was widely criticized in Ireland, including by Isaac Butt. The works were replaced by the Temporary Relief Act, or soup kitchens. This was the first and only time that 'gratuitous' relief was provided during the Famine. As its name suggested, it was a short-term measure only.
76   Author's note. *In this month (March) the expenditure upon the Relief Works was heaviest, viz.: —

| | | |
|---|---|---|
| Labour and Plant | £1,024,518 | |
| Extra Staff | £26,254 | |
| Per Month | £1,050,772 | |
| In the Week ending 13 March, 1847, the expenditure for all the above services was | | £259,105 |
| which gives a Daily average for that week | | £43,184 |
| On the 5th March, there was remitted into the interior for carrying on Relief Works | | £68,000 |
| On the 30th March, only | | £16,000 |
| These two are the extremes during the month. The mean (for the month) of daily remittance | | £38,920 |

77   The arbitrary closing of the public works, in a period that was unseasonably cold and snowy, added considerably to the suffering of the poor. This interim period of

dislocation was alleviated by the intervention of private charities, notably the Society of Friends and the British Relief Association.

78 Author's note. *The proceedings of the Government, in reference to this point, are fully explained in a letter from Mr. Trevelyan to Colonel Jones, and in the accompanying Treasury Minute, printed in the first Board of Works Series for 1847, page 97 to 100.

79 Significantly, Labouchere's Letter of 5 October 1846 provide for relief works to be a charge on the electoral divisions, thus standardizing them into the Poor Law taxation system. Henry Labouchere (1798–1869) was an English politician who served as Chief Secretary for Ireland from 1846 to 1847.

80 The Consolidated Fund is the British Government's general bank account, which is held by the Bank of England. Payments from this account must be authorised in advance by the House of Commons.

81 Author's note. * See page 44 of the first Board of Works Series of 1847.

82 A railway line between Waterford and Limerick was authorised as early as 1826, but it was not until 1834 that the first line was opened between Dublin and Kingstown. The Waterford/Limerick route was commenced in 1848 by the Waterford and Limerick Railway Company. It was completed in 1854.

83 A further problem for those employed on the Public Works was the lack of small currency for wages, which delayed payment and caused considerable hardship.

84 A war between the British colonists and the natives of South Africa commenced at the end of 1845. In February 1848, the British government voted a sum of 1,100,000*l.* to be granted for 'the for Army and Ordnance services occasioned by the Caffre war.' See *Hansard,* 25 February 1848, vol. 96.

85 Regardless of Trevelyan's positive interpretation, by February 1847 thousands of people were dead, or enervated to such an extent that they were vulnerable to the lethal diseases that accompany famine.

86 The arrival of large supplies of Indian corn coincided with the closing of the Public works and the opening of government soup kitchens. During the period of transfer, there was considerable hardship. Eventually, the soup kitchens benefitted due to the availability of cheap food in Ireland.

87 Lord Clarendon, replaced Lord Bessborough, who had died in May 1847.

88 *The following shows the extent of the Government interference in the supply of food in the two seasons of 1845— 46 and 1846— 47:

|   | Reduced to general denomination of quarters. | Cost, £ |
|---|---|---|
| Total quantity of Indian Corn and Oatmeal provided for the Relief Service during the first season of distress, up to August 1846 . | 98,810 | 163,240 |
| Of this quantity there remained in store at the close of the first season of the operations | 14,575 | 24,073 |
| Total quantity of provisions of all kinds (Indian Corn, Wheat, Barley, the meal of those grains, Ryemeal, Biscuit, Peas, Beans, and Rice) provided for the Relief Service, during the second season of distress up to September 1847 . . . | 289,335 | 672,767 |
|   | 303,910 | 696,840 |
| There remained in store at the close of the second season of the operations, about . | 108,960 | 249,836 |

89 Daniel O'Connell had declared 1843 to be Repeal Year. However, when the authorities banned a meeting to be held in Clontarf in October, O'Connell complied, which weakened the movement considerably. The government's apprehensions of follow-up insubordination did not materialize.
90 Querns are stone tools, used in pairs, for grinding. They were used in Ireland during the Celtic period to grind cereals into flour and, in various other forms, throughout the world.
91 In fact, crime rates during the later years of the Famine remained relatively low. See, Kinealy, *Great Irish Famine,*
92 Author's Note: *This was the amount of the private subscriptions upon which Government donations were made; but other large sums were raised by local Irish subscriptions, through the medium of some of the Relief Committees, of which no account was furnished to the Government, because the Committees concerned would not submit to the rule of selling at cost price except in cases of extreme destitution. Large funds were also administered by private individuals, quite independently of the Local Relief Committees; of which class of operations the following account of the expenditure of a Protestant clergyman in the south-west of Ireland, with a parish of 10,000 inhabitants, no resident gentry, not a single town in the whole of it, nor a road through the greater part of it, may be taken as a specimen: —

|  | £ | s. | d. |
|---|---|---|---|
| Gratuitous aid of every sort | 306 | 6 | 0 |
| Loss by sale of food under market price when exorbitant | 208 | 9 | 0 |
| Payment of labour — making road to the bog, and other public works | 150 | 10 | 0 |
| Seed — corn, wheat, oats, and barley | 300 | 0 | 0 |
| Turnip seed | 15 | 0 | 0 |
| Fishing materials | 150 | 10 | 6 |
|  | £1,130 | 15 | 6 |

Funds of this sort administered by benevolent and public-spirited individuals in Ireland, were generally supplied by the exertions of their relations and friends, or by grants from societies in England and elsewhere. It was a common practice for ladies in England to have parishes assigned to them in Ireland, and each lady raised all she could, and made periodical remittances to the clergyman of her adopted parish, receiving accounts from him in return, of the manner in which the money was expended. The self-denial necessary to support this charitable drain was carried to such an extent at Brighton and elsewhere, that the confectioners and other tradespeople suffered severely in their business.
93 The Society of Friends had opened a large number of soup kitchens in the wake of the second potato failure, and it was they who purchased many of the boilers (almost 300) used in the government soup kitchens.
94 Regardless of the problem of surviving on soup over a protracted period of time, the soup kitchens were the most successful and economical of all of the measures introduced by the government. At its height, in July 1847, over three million people a day were being fed in this way, which was a considerable logistical feat.
95 Author's note. *Two electoral divisions were sometimes united under one Relief Committee, but the accounts of each electoral divisions were kept separate.
96 Sir John Fox Burgoyne (1782–1871) was a British Army officer who had fought successfully during the Peninsular War (1807–14). Although he was considered to have done a good job at the Commission, he received no public acknowledgement, apart from the payment of his expenses by the Treasury.

97 Between 1847 and 1849, Sir Edward Twisleton (1809–1874), sometimes rendered as Twistleton, headed the Irish Poor Law. He often clashed with Trevelyan.
98 Author's note. *The ration consisted of one pound of biscuit, meal, or flour; or one quart of soup thickened with meal, with a quarter ration of bread, biscuit or meal. When bread was issued, one pound and a-half was allowed. It was found by experience that the best form in which cooked food could be given, was "stirabout," made of Indian meal and rice steamed, which was sufficiently solid to be easily carried away by the recipients. The pound ration thus prepared, swelled by the absorption of water to three or four pounds.
99 Although there was relatively little blight in the harvest of 1847, the potato crop was far below average.
100 Author's note. *Report from Count Strzelecki to the British Relief Association.
101 This overly optimistic view of the immediate improvement of the people is clearly not borne out by facts; in 1848, over one-and-a-half million people were dependent on the Poor Law for relief, and excess mortality in 1849 may have been higher than it had been in 1847.
102 Author's note. *Seventh and last Monthly Report of the Relief Commissioners.
103 Author's note. † Letter from Sir John Burgoyne, quoted by the Chancellor of the Exchequer in the House of Commons.
104 Author's note. *Third Report of the Relief Commission.
105 The Fever Act was passed in April 1847. It was the second fever act passed during the famine and thought to be more practical than the first one.
106 Like the government soup kitchens, finance for the fever act came from an initial advance from the Treasury, which was then to be repaid out of the poor rates. Both measures considerably added to the financial burdens on the local Poor Law unions.
107 The amended Poor Law of 1847 provided for elected Boards of Poor Law Guardians to be dismissed and replaced by paid officials.
108 As with the soup kitchens, the Society of Friends had also been active in assisting the fishing industry.
109 Also, see section on William Bennett for attitudes and involvement of the Society of Friends.
110 Author's note. *The small holders in the Barony of Erris, in this county, declined at first to accept the seed which was offered them, saying that if they sowed it, the crops would be seized by their landlords. This was not believed at the time in England, but it has nevertheless turned out perfectly true. This barony, of which Belmullet is the principal place, is the darkest corner of Ireland. In some instances broken Landowners and their families were receiving rations, while their Tenants were starving.
111 Author's note. *The following interesting account of what took place in the county of Clare on the subject of seed, is extracted from Captain Mann's Narrative: "The first supply of seed sent for distribution by sale, was received on the 13th March last, up to which period the prospect of the tillage of the land being neglected was very alarming. The seed-grain had been in most cases either partially or wholly consumed for food. Bad advice had been given, that the Government or the landlords would be forced into assisting — the former to pay wages for the time while the work was going on, and the latter to provide seed, if the Government would not. The supply alluded to was bere and rye. By dint of persuasion, and having it published by the Roman Catholic clergy, the quantity sent was taken and planted; and here let me add, that the most sanguine could not have anticipated the great benefit of this importation. The value of the bere as an early crop and produce exceeded every expectation. It was reaped and in the market the latter part of July; and as compared with other barley, it is stated to me, thrashed out five stone to the barb, of twenty hand-sheafs, while the other only yielded three stone from the same quantity. The rye grew on bog merely burnt, and that even slightly; in some cases the heather being in bloom where the rye

in the same ground was ripe. Thus hundreds of acres were cultivated that might have lain waste; and as the rye-meal brought by the 'Sisters' from St. Petersburgh to this depôt, and issued as rations, became, after some opposition, popular with the poor, it does not require any remark to show the value and importance of this article, when considered as an auxiliary substitute for the potato food, and the more so because it can be grown on inferior land here, and not like the Indian corn-meal, which we are forced to look to other countries for. "The supply of green crop and oat-seed by Her Majesty's ship 'Dragon' was received here the 12th of April last. Some few landlords purchased of the first, and supplied their tenantry, but of the latter but little was purchased at that time. The feeling still existed that the Government or the landlords would be forced into providing seed and assisting the tillage; but when that vessel sailed, and they became convinced to the contrary, the most pressing and even distressing applications were made to me by the people to procure a supply of any seed; the fact being clear that grain seed (oats and barley) was not to be procured. Most fortunately, in a few days after, the hired steamer 'Doris' arrived with her cargo of oat-seed, the greater part of which was freely purchased, and a vast quantity of land immediately tilled. A sudden and favourable reaction took place, all appearing anxious to raise something, and not let the land run to waste. Turnip-seed was imported by dealers to a very large amount; and those who could, bought and sowed it. Subsequently a small quantity was sent to me for gratuitous distribution. Lists of the parties who received it, and the quantities allotted, are herewith annexed; and to this were added some small pamphlets given to me by Lord Robert Clinton, my object being to assist the poor, and spread the benefit over the greatest possible extent. 'I have now the pleasure to state, that instead of this part of the country being as described in the first series, with respect to green crops, the turnip particularly has become a general produce with even the poorest. Quantities are daily exposed for sale in the markets, and with a mixture of Indian-corn meal, rice, or flour, it is used as a substitute for bread. Emulation has been excited; and a few days since I was invited to view an exhibition at Colonel Vandeleur's, of the following:

|  | stone. | lbs. |  | lbs. |
|---|---|---|---|---|
| 3 Swedish turnips | 4 | 0 weight. | Heaviest of the 3 | 20 |
| 3 white ditto | 3 11 | "Ditto | 20 |  |
| 3 mangle wurzel | 3 | 8 | "Ditto | 18 |

Beside white carrots, &c. Experiments have been tried with the potato set in drills very successfully; and I do trust that improvement will make further progress under the system of instruction which it is said will be adopted.'"

112 Colonel Harry Jones (1791–1866) was a British Army officer who served in the Royal Engineers. From 1845 to 1850 he was Chairman of the Board of Public Works in Ireland, after which he reverted to military duties. Jones was immortalized in the poem 'The Famine Road 'by Eavan Boland.
113 Admiral Sir Hugh Pigot (1775–1857) was a Royal Navy Officer who was knighted for his services in 1831, 1834 and 1847. From 1844 to July 1847, Pigot was Commander-in-Chief on the Cork Station, from where he oversaw the transport of Indian corn into the country and the protection of all vessels carrying food supplies.
114 Colonel Duncan MacGregor (c. 1786–1881), had been appointed the head of the Constabulary Force in Ireland in 1838, a position that he held for 20 years. He had previously been a military officer, serving in Egypt.

115 Author's note. * The readiness with which the Bank of Ireland, and the Provincial, National and other banks, undertook the office of Treasurer to the Finance Committees, and entered into every proposed detail and accommodation, in support of the operations of the Commissariat, the Relief Commission, and the Board of Works, is very creditable to the managers, and deserves the thanks of the public.
116 Author's note. †All the letters and proceedings of these officers showed that their predominant feeling was an anxious desire to fulfil the benevolent mission on which they had been sent. One observed that he could bear anything but the 'careless misery of the children;' another that his heart was broken by the sobs of the women returning to their homes with a smaller quantity of food than was sufficient for the support of their families.
117 Author's note. * The Four Commissions employed on these operations were composed as follows: —

    The Board of Works.
    Lieut.-Col. H. D. Jones, R.E., Chairman.
    Richard Griffith, Esq., Deputy Chairman.
    John Radcliff, Esq.
    Wm. Thos. Mulvany, Esq.    ... Commissioners.
    Captain Larcom, R.E.    ... Commissioners
The First Relief Commission, appointed by Sir Robert Peel's Government
    Rt. Hon. E. Lucas, Chairman (afterwards retired).
    Com.-Gen. Sir R. I. Routh (afterwards Chairman).
    Colonel D. Mc Gregor.
    Lieut.-Col. H. D. Jones, R.E.
    Sir James Dombrain.
    Professor Sir Robert Kane.
    E. T. B. Twisleton, Esq.
    Theobald Mc Kenna, Esq.
The Second Relief Commission, appointed by Lord John Russell's Government.
    Major-Gen. Sir J. F. Burgoyne, K.C.B., Chairman.
    T. N. Redington, Esq.
    E. T. B. Twisleton, Esq.
    Com.-Gen. Sir R. I. Routh:
    Lieut.-Col. H. D. Jones, R.E.
    Colonel D. Mc Gregor.
The Poor Law Commissioners in Ireland.
    E. T. B. Twisleton, Esq.
    Rt. Hon. Sir W. M. Somerville, Bart.
    T. N. Redington, Esq.
Sir Randolph Routh was in charge of the Commissariat from the commencement to the end of the measures of relief. It is due to Mr. Redington to state that his intimate acquaintance with Ireland, and excellent judgment, were a never-failing ground of reliance in the most difficult emergencies.
118 A Stamp Act had first been introduced in Ireland in March 1774. It was a duty on printed documents, mostly newspapers and was a way of raising revenue.
119 The argument that the Famine was an imperial responsibility was made by people as diverse as Isaac Butt and Edward Twisleton.
120 Archaic form of frenzied.
121 Author's note: * One of the principal causes of the expense incurred, was the necessity of finding work for every person in the neighbourhood of his own home, which added greatly to the number of the works, and to the proportion of them left unfinished.

122 Author's note. * The first instalments due under the 9 & 10 Vic. c. 1 and 2 have been already paid.
123 Author's note: *Viz., 5,000l., being the aggregate of the two half-yearly instalments under the 9 & 10 Vic. c. 1; and 291,000l., the same under the 9 & 10 Vic. c. 107. Total 316,000l.
124 Author's note: * The proportions in which the expenditure was made a local or general charge in the following unions, were —

|  |  | Loan to be repaid. | Grant in aid of rates. |
|---|---|---|---|
| Co. Mayo | Ballina | £13,716 | £43,610 |
| " | Ballinrobe | 12,183 | 27,997 |
| " | Castlebar | 7,282 | 19,813 |
| " | Swineford | 6,620 | 31,797 |
| " | Westport | 5,624 | 37,993 |
| Galway | Clifden | 3,228 | 8,868 |
|  | Gort | 7,663 | 18,475 |
| Clare | Scariff | 6,406 | 10,943 |
| Cork | Bantry | 6,079 | 12,294 |
|  | Skibbereen | 13,451 | 21,627 |
| Kerry | Kenmare | 3,359 | 10,956 |

125 Not all public works were of such utility, leading to the phrase, 'Roads that lead nowhere and walls that surround nothing'.
126 Sir John Peter Grant (1807–1893) was a colonial administrator. He presided over the Indian Relief Fund for Ireland, which was formed at the end of 1845, thus making it one of the first philanthropic interventions during the Famine.
127 By the mid-nineteenth century, Britain controlled most of India, primarily through directly-ruled British presidencies and provinces. The East India Company (which was non-government) governed large areas. The system was changed in 1858 when the rule of the East India Company was transferred to the Crown, that is, Queen Victoria, heralding a period referred to as the British Raj.
128 Trevelyan fails to note the role of the Society of Friends in Ireland who, at the end of 1846, formed their own committee in Dublin, followed by the establishment of other auxiliary committees. They too organized fact-finding missions and personally provided relief. They also worked closely with the committees in London and New York.
129 The British Relief Association was the largest relief body active during the Famine. Its chief agent in Ireland was a Polish explorer, Count Strzelecki, who had offered his services gratuitously. Strzelecki was also knighted in 1848, but some months after Trevelyan.
130 Queen Victoria was privately cynical about the value of such days, but was persuaded to do so by the Prime Minister, Russell. A second Queen's Letter was issued in October 1847, which raised a far lower amount than the first one.
131 Convicts on a prison ship (hulk) in Woolwich, near London, raised 17 shillings in pennies and half-pennies. The convicts were all dead within the following year, having died of ship fever. For more on private philanthropy, see Kinealy, *Kindness of Strangers*.

132 Author's note: * The following are some of the most remarkable contributions: —

| | £ | s. | d. |
|---|---|---|---|
| Her Most Gracious Majesty the Queen | *2,000 | 0 | 0 |
| * Her Majesty also contributed £500 to the Ladies' Clothing Fund, which was established in connection with the British Relief Association. | | | |
| H. R. H. Prince Albert | 500 | 0 | 0 |
| Her Majesty the Queen Dowager | 1,000 | 0 | 0 |
| His Majesty the King of Hanover, as Duke of Cumberland and Chancellor of the University of Dublin | 1,000 | 0 | 0 |
| His Imperial Highness the Sultan | 1,000 | 0 | 0 |
| The East India Company | 1,000 | 0 | 0 |
| The Corporation of the City of London | 1,000 | 0 | 0 |
| The Bank of England | 1,000 | 0 | 0 |
| The Duke of Devonshire | 1,000 | 0 | 0 |
| The Worshipful Company of Grocers | 1,000 | 0 | 0 |
| Messrs. Jones Loyd and Co. | 1,000 | 0 | 0 |
| Rothschild and Co. | 1,000 | 0 | 0 |
| Baring Brothers and Co. | 1,000 | 0 | 0 |
| Truman, Hanbury, and Co. (including 50l. from their clerks, and 8l. 10s. from their workmen) | 1,163 | 10 | 0 |
| Smith, Payne, and Smiths | 1,000 | 0 | 0 |
| Overend, Gurney, & Co. | 1,000 | 0 | 0 |
| An English Friend, two Donations | 1,004 | 0 | 0 |
| An Irish Landlord, for Skibbereen | 1,000 | 0 | 0 |
| Manchester and Salford Relief Committee | 7,785 | 0 | 0 |
| Newcastle and Gateshead ditto | 3,902 | 0 | 0 |
| Hull ditto | 3,800 | 0 | 0 |
| Leeds ditto | 2,500 | 0 | 0 |
| Huddersfield ditto | 2,103 | 0 | 0 |
| Wolverhampton ditto | 1,838 | 0 | 0 |
| York ditto | 1,700 | 0 | 0 |
| Cambridge University and Town, including 617l. 10s. from Trinity College, and 500l. collected at the Baptist Chapel in St. Andrew Street | 2,706 | 0 | 0 |
| Oxford University and City | 1,770 | 0 | 0 |
| Proceeds of a Ball at Florence given by the Prince de Demidoff at San Donato, besides 500l. from the Florence Relief Committee, and 9l. 13s. 9d. from the English servants at Florence | 891 | 17 | 2 |
| St. Petersburgh | 2,644 | 0 | 0 |
| Constantinople | 62 | | |
| Amsterdam; collections in the English Church | 561 | 0 | 0 |
| Denmark; partly collected by Parish Priests in the provinces | 504 | 0 | 0 |
| Malta and Gozo | 720 | 0 | 0 |
| Remittances from British Guiana, the result of public subscription | 3,000 | 0 | 0 |
| Nova Scotia, including a vote of 2,250l. by the House of Assembly | 2,915 | 0 | 0 |
| Barbados Relief Committee | 2,575 | 0 | 0 |
| South Australia £1,000 in money, and an equal value in Wheat | 2,000 | 0 | 0 |
| Jamaica, including a vote of 525l. by the House of Assembly | 1,537 | 0 | 0 |
| Trinidad | 1,350 | 0 | 0 |
| Newfoundland | 868 | 0 | 0 |
| St. Lucia | 614 | 0 | 0 |
| Grenada | 564 | 0 | 0 |
| St. Christopher; vote of the Legislature of the Island | 505 | 0 | 0 |
| Bermuda; vote of the House of Assembly | 500 | 0 | 0 |

OFFICIAL RESPONSE AND REACTION

|  | £ | s. | d. |
|---|---:|---:|---:|
| Hobart Town | 500 | 0 | 0 |
| Bombay | 9,000 | 0 | 0 |
| Madras | 2,150 | 0 | 0 |
| Remittance from the Mauritius, including 111*l.* 16s. 11d. from the Seychelles Islands, and 16*l.* 7s. from Rodrigues, and in addition to 2,211*l.* 13s. collected by the Vicar Apostolic and sent direct to Ireland. (The amount subscribed at the Seychelles Islands, and at Rodrigues, is very remarkable, when the poverty of their inhabitants is considered.) | | | |
|  | 3,020 | 0 | 0 |
| Collection at Basseterre, St. Kitts, from Negroes belonging to the Congregation under the charge of the Moravian Missionaries, per Rev. G. W. Westerley | | | |
|  | 15 | 17 | 10 |
| Officers and crew of Her Majesty's ship "Hibernia" | 167 | 17 | 11 |
| Contribution by the Governor, Commissioner, Lieutenant-Governor, and officers of Greenwich Hospital, being the sum allowed them for a festival dinner in commemoration of the battle off Cape St. Vincent | | | |
|  | 40 | 0 | 0 |
| The 2nd Regiment of Life Guards | 156 | 4 | 6 |
| A diamond cross from a lady (realized) | 42 | 0 | 0 |
| Workmen employed by Sir John Guest at the Dowlas Iron Works | 176 | 17 | 10 |
| Metropolitan Police | 161 | 0 | 0 |
| Proceeds of two amateur performances at the St. James's Theatre | 1,413 | 0 | 0 |
| Collected on board the British and North American Royal Mail steamer "Hibernia" for Ireland | 51 | 12 | 8 |
| Wesleyan Methodists; part of the first distribution of collections in various chapels | 5,000 | 0 | 0 |
| Members of the London Daily Press, chiefly Reporters and Compositors, in addition to other Contributions | 88 | 18 | 0 |
| Proprietors of the "Morning Herald" and "Daily News," each | 100 | 0 | 0 |
| "Punch" | 50 | 0 | 0 |

Many of the smaller subscriptions, such as 800*l.* from the Town of Bridgewater, and 747l. from the Bahamas, are more remarkable in proportion to the means of the contributors, than many of those which have been mentioned.

The officers and men of the Coast Guard raised a fund amounting to 429*l.* which was expended by the members of the force in Ireland in giving relief in the neighbourhood of their respective stations. From the commencement of the distress, the Coast Guard has been distinguished for its active benevolence.

The National Club in London collected a sum of 17,930*l.*, 1000*l.* of which was from various congregations at Brighton, 500*l.* from an anonymous contributor, and 500*l.* from the Wesleyan Irish and Scotch Relief Committee. This fund was intrusted for distribution to the clergy of the Established Church in Ireland, acting under a committee appointed for each diocese, headed by the bishop.

The amount collected by the London Committee of the Society of Friends was 43,026*l.*, nearly the whole of which was disbursed through the Dublin Friends' Committee.

133 The Highlands of Scotland were also undergoing a famine in 1845–47, largely due to the potato failure. Trevelyan was far more sympathetic to the Scottish poor, than he was to the Irish poor. Although referred to as a 'famine', excess mortality was relatively low in Scotland. See, T.M. Devine, *The Great Highland Famine* (1991).

134 Author's note: * Two United States ships of war, the "Jamestown" and "Macedonian," were manned by volunteers, and sent to Ireland and Scotland with the following

charitable supplies, for which no claim for freight was made. These two cargoes will serve as a specimen of the rest: —

"Jamestown."

| Corn and Grain: — | cwt. | qrs. | bshl |
|---|---|---|---|
| Wheat |  | 4 | 0 |
| Barley |  | 3 | 4 |
| Oats |  | 2 | 4 |
| Rye |  | 9 | 2 |
| Peas |  | 30 | 0 |
| Beans |  | 279 | 3 |
| Indian Corn or Maize |  | 339 | 2 |
| Meal and Flour: — |  |  |  |
| Wheatmeal or Flour | 96 | 1 | 0 |
| Barleymeal | 19 | 2 | 16 |
| Oatmeal |  |  |  |
| Indian Corn Meal | 4,229 | 3 | 0 |
| Rice | 154 | 1 | 4 |
| Bread and Biscuit | 1,048 | 3 | 21 |
| Potatoes | 61 | 1 | 1 |
| Apples, dried |  | 6 |  |
| Pork | 707 | 0 | 16 |
| Hams | 291 | 3 | 4 |
| Fish | 4 | 0 | 0 |
| Clothing |  | 10 cases, | 18 barrels. |

"Macedonian."
Landed in Ireland.

| Indian Corn Meal, 5,324 barrels at 196 lbs each | 1,043,504 pounds. |
|---|---|
| Rice, equal to 217 tierces at 6 cwt. each | 145,824 " |
| Beans, 6 tierces of 4 cwt., 66 bbls. of 196 lbs., 38 bags of 100 lbs. | 19,424 " |
| Peas, 53 bbls. of 196 lbs., 100 bags of 100 lbs. each | 11,388 " |
| Indian Corn, 38 bags of 100 lbs | 3,800 " |
| Wheat, 1 bag | 100 " |
| Salt Pork, 1 barrel | 200 " |
| Pounds | 1,224,240 = 546 1200/2240 tons. |

Besides 100 barrels Indian Corn Meal and 3 packages of Clothing, landed as a "private consignment to the Rev. Mr. Taylor."
Clothing, 13 boxes, 3 bales, 3 barrels . . . 19 packages.

Landed in Scotland.

| 1 package clothing, | 133 bags oats, |
|---|---|
| 1 barrel beef, | 2 barrels beans, and |
| 143 barrels meal, | 8 chests of tea. |

Of which the Glasgow Section received —

| 1 package clothing, | 133 bags oats, and |
|---|---|
| 1 barrel beef, | 8 chests tea. |
| 37 barrels meal, |  |

The Edinburgh Section received —
100 barrels meal; and 6 barrels meal and 2 barrels beans were delivered to Mr. Mathieson, of Stirling, as instructed by the manifest.

135 These men were all volunteers for the British Relief Association, but Strzelecki was the most important and devoted. Lord Robert Renebald Pelham-Clinton and Lord James Butler were jointly in charge of counties Clare, Galway, Kerry and Limerick. Clinton (1820–1867), who was aged 27, had no direct connections with Ireland. Butler (1815–93) was part of the Butler family of Kilkenny Castle. Matthew James Higgins (1810–1868) had been born in Co. Meath, but made his living in London as a writer, using the nom-de-plume *Jacob Omnium*. He was sent to Belmullet in Co. Mayo. Count Pawel de Strzelecki (1797–1873) oversaw the work of the BRA in Ireland. He also did so in a volunteer capacity. Strzelecki, formerly an explorer, was initially based in Westport in Co. Mayo, and in 1848, in Dublin. Although he refused to accept any payment, he was knighted at the end of 1848.

136 The General Central Relief Committee was formed at the end of 1846 and worked out of an office in College Green. Its distinguished 31-man committee included Daniel O'Connell.

137 The Irish Relief Association had offices in Upper Sackville Street in Dublin. Regardless of the evangelical leanings of many of the committee, it was effective in providing relief to all denominations.

138 Joseph Bewley (1795–1851) was a Dublin-based Quaker and tea and coffee merchant, who was a founder of the Central Relief Committee in November 1846. Jonathan Pim (1806–1885) and his brother were owners of Dublin firm Pim Brothers & Co., who were drapers and textile manufacturers. In 1865, he became the first Irish Quaker to sit in the British Parliament. During the time of the Famine, there were only about 3,000 Quakers in the whole of Ireland.

139 Ladies' Relief Associations were formed all over the country. The Quakers often worked with local women to set up soup kitchens.

140 Hon. Mrs. Newcombe and Mrs. Humphrey Lloyd were leading members of the 'Dublin Ladies' Reproductive and Industrial Society'. Asenath Nicholson, an American visitor to Ireland during the Famine, and a forthright observer, was critical of the motives of the Dublin women, believing that the women's committee in Belfast was more hard-working and sincere.

141 Dorothea Lloyd (neé Bulwer) was wife of the Trinity College physicist, Humphrey Lloyd. They had married in 1840.

142 Rev. George Robert Gildea (1803–1887). He married Esther (neé Greene) in 1826. She was aged 22. Rev. Gildea later became the Provost of the Cathedral of Tuam.

143 Author's note. * Nearly 3000l. was remitted to Mr. Gildea in advance, in sums of from 10s. to 20l., for linens to be afterwards furnished. He might have received much larger sums, and he found great difficulty in stopping the outpouring of sympathy and support that came upon him; and until it became generally known that he had returned large sums of money, the influx did not cease. It is an interesting fact that of 30,000 yards of linen made up to the end of October, there is only one piece that was not duly returned to him by the workwomen, and Mr. Gildea thinks he shall still get the missing piece.

144 The Presentation Convent was established in October 1815, primarily for the education of poor females.

145 Author's note. * Upwards of 100,000l. has been expended by the Home and Provincial Governments, in giving relief to the sick and destitute emigrants landed in Canada in 1847, and in forwarding them to their destinations.

146 Author's note. * The following extract from a letter from Mr. Jacob Harvey of New York, to Mr. Jonathan Pim, one of the Secretaries of the Dublin Relief Committee of

the Society of Friends, contains many interesting particulars relating to these remittances, which are highly honourable to the Irish character:—

"New York, January 5, 1847.

"The destitution of our poor at this season will certainly curtail the amount for Ireland, and it is used as an excuse by those who feel called upon to assist them at their own doors first. But I am happy to say that the poor labouring Irish themselves are doing their duty fully. Without any public meetings or addresses, they have been silently remitting their little savings to their relations at home; and these remittances, be it remembered, go to every parish in Ireland, and by every packet. These drafts are from 1*l.* and upwards; they probably average from 4*l.* to 5*l.* In my letter to J. H. Todhunter I told him I had ascertained from five houses here, that within the past sixty days, they have received and remitted from the poor Irish 80,000 dollars. I had not time to send round to the other houses that day; but since the steamer sailed, I have collected further returns, although not yet all; and to my no small delight, the sum total remitted since November the 1st amounts to 150,000 dollars or 30,000*l.* sterling. I am now collecting an account of the sums remitted through the same houses by the poor Irish for the year 1846, and I have received returns from the five principal houses, and the sum total is 650,000 dollars, or 130,000*l.* There are yet four houses to hear from, which will swell the amount. This, however, is enough to astonish everybody who has not been aware of the facts; and it is but right that credit should be given to the poor abused Irish for having done their duty. Recollect that the donors are working men and women, and depend upon their daily labour for their daily food; that they have no settled income to rely upon; but with that charming reliance upon Divine Providence which characterizes the Irish peasant, they freely send their first earnings home to father, mother, sister, or brother. I requested J. H. Todhunter to have the facts I gave him published, and I make a similar request to thee, as they are still more cheering. A publication of the kind may stimulate the rich to do their duty, where they have hitherto neglected it; and it will give evidence to those who have no faith in Irishmen, that whenever they are able to get good wages, they never forget their relatives and friends who are in want."

147 Author's note. * The emigration for each division of the United Kingdom during the first three quarters of 1847 was as follows; but it must be remembered that those who embarked at Liverpool consisted almost wholly of Irish. There can also be no doubt that the Irish helped to swell the tide from several other ports of Great Britain, and especially in the west of Scotland.

148 Author's note. * These Irish labourers who annually come to England, by way of Liverpool, to help to gather in the harvest, and return to Ireland after it is over, are included in this number. They are variously estimated at from 10,000 to 30,000.

| From Liverpool | From other English Ports | Total from England |
|---|---|---|
| 114,303 | 20,942 | 136,395 |
| From Scotland | From Ireland | Total |
| 8,155 | 95,911 | 240,461 |

149 As many as 16 quarantine ships were located in the River Mersey in 1847. They were generally regarded as ineffective, as evidenced by the number of diseased emigrants who arrived in North America during the Famine.

150 The Removal Laws only made the removing union responsible for removing the person back to Ireland, not to their home. This resulted in hundreds of people being 'dumped' in the ports of Belfast and Dublin.

151 Author's note. *5000 Irish paupers were relieved in Manchester in the last week in February, and for several weeks following there were more than 4000 on an average receiving outdoor, and from 600 to 700 in-door, relief. This was independent of the adjoining districts of Salford and Chorlton, where great numbers of Irish were also relieved. Nearly 90,000 destitute and disabled Irish, including women and children, were reported to have received parochial relief in Scotland at a total expense of about 34,000l.; but as the same persons were frequently relieved in more than one parish, and were therefore returned by more than one Inspector, the number of persons of this description newly arrived in Scotland is not so great as that above stated.

152 Author's note. *The details of the frightful mortality connected with the great emigration of 1847 from Ireland to Canada, are as follows: —

| Whole number of British emigrants embarked 89,738 | |
|---|---|
| Died on the passage | 5,293 |
| at the quarantine station | 3,452 |
| at the Quebec Emigrant Hospital | 1,041 |
| at the Montreal ditto | 3,579 |
| at Kingston and Toronto | 1,965 |
| | 15,330 |

showing a mortality of rather more than 17 per cent, on the number embarked. One-third of those who arrived in Canada were received into hospital.

The people of Canada deserve great praise for the spirited and benevolent exertions made by them to meet the exigencies of this disastrous emigration, which is described as having "left traces of death and misery along its course, from the Quarantine Establishment at Grosse Isle to the most distant parts of Upper Canada, cutting down in its progress numbers of estimable citizens." Besides the larger hospital establishments, twenty-four Boards of Health were formed in Upper Canada. Numerous deaths also took place among the emigrants to New Brunswick. The ships containing the German emigrants, and two ships fitted out by the Duke of Sutherland from Sutherlandshire, arrived in Canada in a perfectly healthy state.

153 Author's note. * Settlers in the backwoods must have the means of support from twelve to fifteen months after their arrival, and this cannot be accomplished for less than 60l., at the lowest estimate, for each family consisting of a man, his wife, and three children, or equal to 3½ adults on an average.

154 The 1838 Poor Law legislation provided for the country to be divided into 130 Unions, each with its own workhouse. In 1847, it was decided to increase the number of unions to 163. Each union was to be self-financing, with money raised through a new unit of taxations known as poor rates.

155 Author's note. * The repayment of these advances, which amount altogether to £1,145,800, has not yet been pressed, out of consideration for the circumstances of the country.

156 Unlike the poor in the rest of the United Kingdom, the Irish poor were not given a right to relief under the Poor Law legislation.

157 Author's note. † An Act to make further provision for the Relief of the Destitute Poor in Ireland, 10 Vic. cap. 31 — [Passed 8th June, 1847.]

An Act to provide for the Execution of the Laws for the Relief of the Poor in Ireland, 10 & 11 Vic. cap. 90— [Passed 22nd July, 1847.]

An Act to make provision for the Punishment of Vagrants and Persons offending against the Laws in force for the Relief of the Destitute Poor in Ireland, 10 & 11 Vic. cap. 84— [Passed 22nd July, 1847.]

158 The Quarter Acre Clause, or Gregory Clause, was introduced by Irish landowner, Sir William Gregory. It forced small-holders who had survived two years of privations to now choose between giving up their small holdings or receiving poor relief.

159 In total, 39 Boards of Guardians were dissolved between 1847 and 1849, mostly for failing to collect sufficient poor rates. The paid Guardians who replaced them found this task just as difficult.
160 Edward Twisleton was the Poor Law Commissioner until his resignation in 1849, disagreeing with a new tax for the financing of the Poor Law.
161 The Mendicity Institution was an early attempt to relieve poverty, it being established in Dublin in 1818. It was located at Moira House, Usher's Island.
162 An aphorism.
163 Thomas Drummond (1797–1840), who was born in Scotland, was a skilled engineer and administrator. In 1835, he was appointed under-secretary at Dublin Castle, and was widely regarded as being effective and fair. When he died prematurely in 1840, his request was to be buried in his adopted home of Ireland.
164 Author's note. * "I would sincerely regret that anything I have said should appear to be written as if I sought occasion to point out errors and hold them up; far from it; I mention them with sorrow and a kindly wish that they may be corrected. The position of the respectable classes at this moment in many instances is surely pitiable. There is but one course by which this country can rise and take her proper position, and that is by a hearty and sincere determination to work for the public good, at the same time throwing aside all selfish and party feeling. In that case, there is no reason why we should despair; but otherwise, no mortal can either pass laws or propose any other thing which would be attended with success. In this I particularly allude to the Poor Law now about to be administered. I look upon it as an indirect absentee tax, drawing from those who did not contribute before, or in a very slight degree. It assures the poor man that from the land he must have support, and that what he labours on will one day sustain him when he can no longer toil. It will also compel others to consider that unless employment is provided, they must support him without a remunerative return, — and if this is rightly considered, then the heavy affliction which the Almighty has been pleased to lay on them will prove a lesson for good.

"On the subject of relief being given without having a corresponding return for it in labour, I feel very apprehensive that, owing to the habits of the lower orders, the present repugnance to entering the union-house may give way, and that for the sake of an idle life, they may accept the terms. To prevent this and rescue both landlord and peasant from certain ruin, there must be employment given fairly remunerative to both, not by Government, but by the owners of the soil. Until lately, what was the condition of the peasant? Work as he would, till and rear what he might, he could never hope to benefit. His portion was the potato only, shared, it may be said, with his pig. He dare not use anything else. Let misfortune come on him, or disease render him unable to work, he had no claim on the land. One a little less poor than himself might help him, but who else? The charity I have seen has been from the poor to the poor. Is it any wonder that they became spiritless, idle, and even worse?

"A townland near here, owned by a landlord who resides constantly away, islet to a middleman at 10s. an acre. That middleman resides away also, and he relets it to a person who lives in the county of Cork, and only occasionally comes there. It is sublet again, until the price received for a quarter of an acre is £1. 10s. per annum. Can that place be otherwise than full of distress? "Near it is another townland. The owner resides here, but he has never attended to it. In the late calamity he applied to me for seed and assistance, declaring his intention to provide seed at his own expense; and to insure its being sown, he said he should employ a person to superintend the sowing, as the land was prepared. His tenants were without food; but to encourage and assist in this case, an application was made by me to the Society of Friends for a supply to sustain the people while working, which was granted. The party supposed he had about sixty to provide for, but was frightened at over 600 applications for food; and it then [note cont. from pg. 161] came out that his land was underlet to an enormous degree. He had never paid proper attention by inspecting his farms, &c. The result is, that now he can neither get rent, nor the repayment of the value of the seed. What has been grown will not suffice to feed those who are located on the land. They cannot pay rent, and they will not give up their holdings. The population has been increased in such cases, and others, to an extent beyond what the land can bear. Another cause is, that the Roman Catholic clergy derive their income mainly from fees and contributions at marriages and christenings; and though there are some who see the disastrous result of encouraging the increase of the population, and are scrupulous on that head, still, as their subsistence depends on it, it cannot be expected that they mil exert themselves in a way likely to deprive themselves of daily bread by discouraging thoughtless rushing into improvident marriages." — *Captain Mann's Narrative.*

165  A previously passed Act, 1 & 2 Wm. IV, c. 24, had provided £4,700,00 in loans for public works in the UK (Ireland received only £200,000 of this). This Act provided for £500,000 to be loaned to Ireland for public works, sanctioned by the Treasury. The board was comprised of Colonel Burgoyne, the chairman, and two commissioners, Brooke Taylor Ottley and John Ratcliffe. In 1834, a further act was passed to allow £100,000 of this grant to be used by the church temporalities commissioners – which had nothing to do with public works.

166  John William Ponsonby, 4th Earl of Bessborough (1781 – 1847), was a British Whig politician. He served as Lord Lieutenant of Ireland in 1846 and 1847, until his death in May of that year. The family owned Bessborough House in Co. Kilkenny, designed by Francis Bindon around 1744.

167  Author note: * *First Board of Works Series of 1846–7, page 338 to 341.*

168  Author's note. †The purposes to which these loans are applicable are as follows;

   1. The drainage of lands by any means which may be approved by the Commissioners.
   2. The subsoiling, trenching, or otherwise deepening and improving the soil of lands.
   3. The irrigation or warping of lands.
   4. The embankment of lands from the sea or tidal waters, or rivers.
   5. The inclosing or fencing, or improving the fences, drains, streams, or watercourses of land.
   6. The reclamation of waste or other land.
   7. The making of farm roads.
   8. The clearing land of rocks and stones.

169  Author's note: * By neglecting their estates, and omitting to construct proper farm buildings, and to make other necessary improvements, Irish landlords relinquish their position in rural society, and give free scope to the agrarian revolutionary plans which, under the disguise of 'fixity of tenure' and 'tenant right,' would dispossess the landlord, without conferring any permanent benefit on the tenant. In the smaller class of holdings, the entire gross produce is insufficient to support a family, without allowing for either rent, seed, or taxes; and even supposing that, with the dangerous help of the potato, eked out by harvest-work and begging, a rent is paid, the tendency to multiply and subdivide is so strong, that if the whole rent were given up, the holders would become in a generation or two much more numerous and equally poor. The fact is, that the main hope of extrication from the slough of despond in which the small holders in the centre and west of Ireland are at present sunk, is from the enterprise and capital and improved husbandry of the class of owners commonly known by the name of landlords.

170  Author's note. * In what follows we must be understood as giving expression to the practical conclusions of those who, having been charged with the unenviable task of super-intending the measures of relief, and assisting to replace society on a permanent

171 Author's note: † The same results appeared in those parts of France, Switzerland, Germany, and Sweden, in which the subdivision of the land has been carried to the greatest extent. The following extract from a letter received in January last from Brest, contains a correct description of the manner in which that part of France was affected by the dearth: 'All the petty farmers are in the greatest distress, having been obliged to sell their wheat and most of their other grain in October, to pay their rents due on Michaelmas-day. The overplus in the crop of buck-wheat is not sufficient to compensate for the deficiency in their stock of potatoes, and they are now living on cabbages, carrots, and a very small proportion of buckwheat. Unless some stringent measures be adopted to prevent the progressive subdivision of land in France, the country must eventually be reduced to the present state of Ireland.' It has been justly observed, that 'in agriculture, as in every other industrial process, prosperity must depend upon the application of capital to production; and equal injury is done when such application of capital is prevented, either by landlords refusing to give tenants a beneficial interest in their improvements, or by a combination of pauper occupants to prevent capitalists from obtaining possession of land.' Those who take an interest in this important subject will do well to read Mr. M'Culloch's excellent chapter on compulsory partition, in his recently-published work 'On the Succession to Property vacant by Death.'

172 Localised, but deadly, famines were a feature of British rule in India. Major famines had occurred in 1769–70, 1782–83, 1783–84, 1791–92 and 1837–38. Ironically, in the decade after the Irish Famine, Trevelyan returned to India, where he drew up Famine Codes, based on his experiences with Ireland.

173 Author's note. * The inferior condition of the peasantry in the West of England is in a great degree owing to the increased use of the potato, the cultivation of which by the poor was much encouraged by the gentry and clergy as a cheap means of subsistence during the high prices of corn in the last war. Somersetshire and Devonshire were, in fact, fast becoming potato countries; and if the blight of that vegetable had occurred twenty years later, their sufferings might have approached to those of Ireland.

174 Lord William George Bentinck (1802–1848) was a flamboyant Troy politician who rose to political prominence when he opposed Peel's repeal of the Corn Laws. His call for the government to invest in railway development in Ireland, both as a means of providing employment and improving the infra-structure, was widely praised in Ireland, but rejected by the government and Trevelyan

175 Author's note: * Lord George Bentinck stated that 1500 miles of railroad would give constant employment, either on the line or in the various occupations connected with it, to 110,000 able-bodied labourers and artificers, representing, with their families, 550,000 persons; but even supposing that all these had been set to work at once, they would have been selected from the classes of persons least likely to require charitable assistance, while the weak and infirm would have been systematically excluded. The number of persons for whom the Government had to provide the means of subsistence at this crisis, was upwards of three millions; and this had to be done in the neighbourhood of their own homes, which could not be accomplished by means of railroads, employment on which is confined to particular localities. The number of persons stated in the House of Commons as likely to be employed on railroads in Ireland was greatly overrated; the general surface of the country requires scarcely any deep cuttings or embankments, and the eskars [sic – more usually esker], through which the cuttings are made, offer the finest possible material for ballasting.

176 An island in Cork Harbour that contained a small military garrison and a British naval base. During the Famine, provisioning ships frequently docked there.

177 In Irish, *An Béal Bocht*, suggests the deliberate exaggeration of poverty.

178 Author's note. * Speech of Mr. Richard Bourke, M.P. for Kildare, to his father's tenantry, September 1847.
179 Author's note. * Although both did their best, it is fair to state that the Protestant clergy had some advantages which the Roman Catholic clergy did not possess. The Protestant clergy were assisted by liberal subscriptions from England; and as their stipends are primary charges on the rent, they were regularly paid even during the period of the greatest distress. The Roman Catholic clergy, on the contrary, depend, both for their own subsistence, and for the means of helping their poor and ignorant people, upon the voluntary contributions of the people themselves; and when these had nothing to give, owing to the failure of their crops and the want of employment, the clergy were reduced to great straits, which they bore with exemplary patience. The fees on marriages and baptisms which are the principal source of the income of the Roman Catholic clergy, almost entirely ceased in some parts of the country. It is much to the credit of the poor Irish, that now that they have been deprived of the potatoes on which they had been accustomed to bring up their families, marriages have become much less frequent.
180 Author's note. * "A great deal has been written, and many an account given, of the dreadful sufferings endured by the poor, but the reality in most cases far exceeded description. Indeed, none can conceive what it was but those who were in it. For my part, I frequently look back on it as a fearful and horrid dream, scarcely knowing how sufficiently to express gratitude to the Almighty for having brought this country through it, even as it is. If the first measures which prepared us to meet the second and severest calamity had been neglected, it is frightful to suppose what would have been the state of this afflicted country. My opinion is, that there are but very few who will not gratefully remember the generous and prompt relief afforded in this time of trouble; such sufferings, and such help, cannot be easily forgotten."— Captain Mann's Narrative.
181 'The Panic of 1847' refers to a banking crisis in Britain that largely resulted from over extending credit for the building of railways. It coincided with an industrial depression.
182 Author's note. * The Irish peasant made up for the deficiency of nutritive qualities in the potato, by the quantity he ate, amounting generally to as much as fourteen pounds in a single day; and it was therefore a general complaint at first, that the Indian corn left an uneasy sensation, arising from the absence of the habitual distension of the organs of digestion. The half raw state in which it was often eaten, arising partly from ignorance of the proper mode of cooking it, and partly from impatience to satisfy the cravings of hunger, also concurred with the previous debilitated state of the people, to produce sickness when it was first introduced. All this, however, has been got over, and the people have now not only become accustomed to the use of a grain food, but they prefer it, and declare that they feel stronger and more equal to hard work under the influence of a meal of stirabout, than of potatoes; and their improved appearance fully bears out this conclusion. One main cause of the fact which has been so often remarked, that the Irishman works better out of Ireland than in it, is, that when he leaves his native country and obtains regular employment elsewhere he commences at the same time a more strengthening diet than the potato. It is commonly observed in Canada, that the Irish emigrants, although a much larger race of men than the French Canadians, are, for some time after their arrival, inferior to them as farm labourers; and this difference is attributed to their food. The Canadian labourer, who receives his food as part of his hire, has an ample breakfast on bread and milk. He dines at midday on soupe aux pois, with a full quantity of salt pork and bread à discrétion. At four o'clock he is allowed a luncheon of bread and onions, and at night he has a ragout of meat and vegetables for his supper. He however works laboriously, and generally from sunrise to sunset, and is scarcely ever absent a day from his work. An Irishman cannot endure this continuous labour without better food than the potato;

and in every way it is desirable to teach him the use of a more substantial diet, both to enable him to give a proper amount of labour for his hire, and in order to raise him to a higher standard as a social being. We shall not consider the object finally accomplished until the people of Ireland live upon a bread and meat diet, like those of the best parts of England and Scotland.

183 Author's note. * The following is the proportion of agrarian crimes [note cont. from pg. 196] in each quarter from January 1845, to November 1847:

In the Quarter ending
Jan. 31, 1845, the proportion is one in 4¼
| | | |
|---|---|---|
| April 30, 1845 | ,, ,, | 3½/12 |
| July 31, 1845 | ,, ,, | 4⅔ |
| Oct. 31, 1845 | ,, ,, | 5⅓ |
| Jan. 31, 1846 | ,, ,, | 4 |
| April 30, 1846 | ,, ,, | 3 1/3 |
| July 31, 1846 | ,, ,, | 8 |
| Oct. 31, 1846 | ,, ,, | 19 |
| Jan. 31, 1847 | ,, ,, | 54 |
| April 30, 1847 | ,, ,, | 64 |
| July 31, 1847 | ,, ,, | 42 |
| Oct. 31, 1847 | ,, ,, | 12 |

184 Author's note. * The manner in which the Clanmorris and Blessington properties, and a portion of that belonging to the Cunningham family, have been disposed of, are instances in point.

185 Edmund Spenser (1552–1599) was an English poet who wrote during the reign of Elizabeth 1. Despite having an Irish wife, his writings were vehemently anti-Irish, including *A Veue of the Present State of Irelande* (1596). Spenser recommended hunger and famine as a way of subjugating the Irish: '. . . yett sure in all that warr, there perished not manye by the sworde, but all by the extreamytie of famine . . .'

186 Author's note. * Although we do not intend to excuse the system of the Penal Laws, it is fair to mention, that these measures of restraint were considered at the time to be necessary for the protection of the liberty and religion of the country, and that they were imposed at the conclusion of a desperate struggle, the renewal of which was for a long time a source of serious apprehension. The battles of the Boyne, Enniskillen, and Aughrim, the sieges of Londonderry and Limerick, and the critical operations at Athlone, ushered in the Penal Laws, the real object of which was to keep in check the great political party which had arrayed itself on the side of the Stuarts and of their principles of Government; and as the danger diminished, these Laws were gradually relaxed until they were finally abolished by the Catholic Emancipation Act in 1829. It will also be remembered that the Penal Laws were passed by the Irish Parliament and repealed by that of the United Kingdom.

# Part VI

# REFLECTIONS AND REGRETS

# 13

# W. R. WILDE, *IRISH POPULAR SUPERSTITIONS* (1852)

William Robert Wills Wilde (1815–1876) was a renaissance man in terms of his interests, abilities and achievements. His main occupation was as an eye and ear surgeon, but he also published extensively on medicine, archaeology, antiquities and folklore. He worked as Medical Commissioner on the Irish Census Reports of 1841, 1851 and 1861, and, through his involvement with various committees and associations, he was a public intellectual before the phrase was used. Moreover, through his marriage to the acclaimed nationalist poet, Speranza, he was part of a celebrity couple, who were cheered when they appeared in public in Dublin. Retrospectively, he gained a different type of celebrity as the father of the brilliant writer, Oscar Wilde.

Born in Kilkeevin in Roscommon in the west of Ireland, to a Protestant family of English origin, Wilde was unusual in absorbing the culture and traditions of the local people.[1] His pioneering and life-long fascination with folklore, fairy lore and superstitions was particularly unusual for a man of his religion and education, such beliefs being, in the eyes of Protestant evangelicals, equated with ignorance and Catholicism. For him though, such practices, rituals and stories constituted 'the poetry of the people'. Prior to writing *Irish Popular Superstitions*, Wilde had published *The Narrative of a Voyage to Madeira, Teneriffe, and Along the Shores of the Mediterranean* (1840), *Austria and Its Literary, Scientific, and Medical Institutions* (1845) and *The beauties of the Boyne and the Blackwater* (1849), all of which had established his reputation as a gifted travel writer. The first was written when he was on board a yacht, he acting as medical superintendent to an invalid patient. *Superstitions* was less well-known than his previous works,[2] but it was an early example of the recovery and preservation of Ireland's folk traditions, a movement more commonly associated with W. B. Yeats and Lady Gregory, later in the century.[3] Wilde planned to publish two more volumes of *Irish Superstitions*, but the material for them was amongst his unfinished papers at his death.[4]

*Irish Popular Superstitions* was dedicated 'To Speranza', the pen-name of his wife, Jane Elgee, a noted poet and nationalist.[5] They had married in November 1851 in St Peter's Church, the ceremony being performed by William's brother, Rev. John M. Wilde.[6] Together they had three children, William (1852–1899), Oscar (1854–1900) and Isola (1857–1867). It was a close and affectionate family, who were devastated by the premature death of Isola.[7] William also had a number of children out of marriage, to whom he was devoted.[8]

William had qualified as a surgeon at Dr Steevens' Hospital in Dublin in 1837. Shortly afterwards, he established Molesworth St. Hospital (1841) and later, St Mark's Ophthalmic Hospital (1844). The latter became one of the leading eye hospitals in the world, its standing largely based on the brilliance of its founder.[9] Even more remarkably, as soon its reputation was secured, Wilde reassigned its purpose, 'for the use and advantage of the afflicted poor of Ireland'.[10] The building was paid for by public subscription and, in a notice published by the Governors in 1861, the list of donors included: 'Master William Wilde, 1*l*; Master Oscar Wilde, 10s; Miss Isola Wilde, 10s'.[11]

In January 1864, William was conferred with a knighthood. At the ceremony, the Lord Lieutenant, Lord Carlisle, pointed out that the honour was 'not so much in recognition of your high professional reputation—which is European, and has been recognised by many countries in Europe—but to mark my sense of the service you have rendered to Statistical Science, especially in connection with the Irish Census'. Within Ireland, this was welcomed, the *Freeman's Journal* averring, 'A more popular exercise of the viceregal prerogative, nor one more acceptable to all classes in Ireland, could not possibly have been made'.[12] Later that year, Trinity College in Dublin conferred William with the degree of M.D.[13] However, scandal, isolation, declining health and increasing penury marked the final years of his life.[14] Following his death in 1876, the prestigious family home in Merrion Square was sold to pay off debts, following which Speranza moved to London to be close to her sons. William was buried in Mount Jerome Cemetery while Speranza, who survived him by twenty years, was buried in an unmarked grave in Kensal Green in London.[15]

*Irish Popular Superstitions* was based on William's tour of Ireland in 1849, when the Famine was still raging in the western counties. He had not been in those parts of the west since 1837, so he was fully aware of the impact of the potato failures. Moreover, as a Census Commissioner in 1841, 1851 and 1861, William was uniquely placed to understand the consequences of the devastation caused by the Famine.[16] William's publication also provided a romanticized insight into a pre-Famine society that, while simple and superstitious, was happy and unified, until torn asunder by death and emigration.

## W. R. WILDE, *IRISH POPULAR SUPERSTITIONS*: PREFACE AND PAGES 9–12, 72–75 (DUBLIN: JAMES MCGLASHAN, 1852)

PREFACE.

Had Shakespeare[17] not embalmed in the 'Midsummer's Night Dream'[18] the popular superstitions and fairy lore current in England at the time of Elizabeth, the present generations could form but a very faint idea of the ancient belief of our fore-fathers of the witcheries of their sylvan deities and household gods. In this utilitarian age, it would be superfluous to discuss, or even to enumerate, the causes which have combined to obliterate this poetry of the people in England; suffice it to say that it has gradually vanished before the spread of education, and the rapid growth of towns and manufactories.

A wild and daring spirit of adventure—a love of legendary romance—a deep-rooted belief in the supernatural—an unconquerable reverence for ancient customs, and an extensive superstitious creed has, from the earliest times, belonged to the Celtic race. We cannot, therefore, wonder that among the but partially civilized, because neglected and uneducated, yet withal chivalrous inhabitants of a large portion of Ireland, a belief in the marvelous shall linger even to the present day. It is, however—and chiefly for the reasons enumerated in the first chapter of this little work—rapidly becoming obliterated; never to return. When now I enquire after the old farmer who conducted me, in former years, to the ruined Castle or Abbey, and told me the story of its early history or inhabitants, I hear that he died during the famine. On asking for the peasant who used to sit with me in the ancient Rath,[19] and recite the Fairy legends of the locality, the answer is, 'He is gone to America'; and the old woman who took me to the Blessed Well,[20] and gave me an account of its wonderous cures and charms—'Where is she?'—'Living in the Workhouse'.[21]

These legendary tales and Popular Superstitions have now become the history of the past—a portion of the traits and characteristics of other days. Will their recital revive their practice? No! Nothing contributes more to uproot superstitions' rites and forms than to print them; to make them known to the many instead of leaving them among, and secretly practiced by, the few.

These tales form part of a large collection made for my amusement many years ago, or which were remembered since my boyhood, and they have been written as a relaxation from severer toil. Some of them have already appeared in the 'Dublin University Magazine'.[22] They are now collected and presented to the public in their present form, chiefly in the hope of eliciting information from those who may be acquainted with such matters; for which purpose I have here subjoined a list of Queries, from which I should like to have answers from my country readers. I have also added a copious index of names and subjects which will, I trust, likewise assist in bringing forth new matter. Should this little volume be acceptable, it will be followed by another when time permits.

...

The great convulsion which Irish society of all grades here has lately experienced, the failure of the potato crop, pestilence, famine, and a most unparalleled extent of emigration, together with bankrupt landlords, pauperizing poor-laws, grinding officials, and decimating work-houses, have broken up the very foundations of social intercourse, have swept away the established theories of political economists, and uprooted many of our long-cherished opinions. In some places, all the domestic usages of life have been outraged; the tenderest bonds of kindred have been severed; some of the noblest and holiest feelings of human nature have been blotted from the heart, and many of the finest, yet firmest links which united the various classes in the community have been rudely burst asunder. Even the ceremonial of religion has been neglected, and the very rights of sepulture, the most sacred and enduring of all of the tributes of affection or respect, have been neglected or forgotten; the dead body has rotted where it fell, or formed a scanty meal for the famished dogs of the vicinity, or has been thrown, without prayer or mourning, into the adjoining ditch. The hum of the spinning wheel has long since ceased to form an accompaniment to the colleen's song; and that song itself, so sweet and fresh in the cabin, field, or byre, has scarcely left an echo in our glens, or among the hamlets of our land. The Shannaghie[23] and the Callegh in the chimney corner,[24] tell no more the tales and legends of other days. Unwaked, *unkeened*,[25] the dead are buried, where Christian burial has at all been observed; and the ear no longer catches the mournful cadence of the wild Irish cry, wailing on the blast, rising up to us from the valleys, or floating along the winding river when

The skies, the fountains, every region near,
Seemed all one mutual cry.

The fire on the peasant's hearth was quenched, and its comforts banished, even before his roof-tree fell, while the remnant of the hardiest and most stalwart of the people crawl about, listless spectres, unwilling or unable to rise out of their despair. In this state of things, with depopulation the most terrific that any country has ever experienced, on the one hand, and the spread of education, and the introduction of railroads, colleges, industrial and other educational schools, on the other—together with the rapid decay of the Irish vernacular, in which most of our legends, romantic tales, ballads and bardic annals, the vestiges of pagan rites, and the relics of fairy charms were preserved—can superstition, or if superstitious belief, can superstitious practices continue to exist?

But these matters of popular belief and folk's-lore, these rites and legends, and superstitions, were after all, *the poetry of the people*, the bond that knit the peasant to the soil, and cheered and solaced many a cottier's fireside. Without these, on the one side, and without proper education and well-directed means of partaking of and enjoying its blessings, on the other, and without rational amusement besides, he will, and must, and has already in a number of instances, become a perfect brute. The Rath which he revered has been, to our knowledge, ploughed up, the ancient thorn which he referenced has been cut down,[26] and the sacred well polluted, merely in order to uproot his prejudices, and efface his superstition. Has he been improved by such desecration of the landmarks of the past, objects which, independent of their natural beauty, are often the surest footprints of history? We fear not.

'Troth Sir', said Darby Doolin, an old Connaughtman of our acquaintance, when lately conversing upon the subject, 'what betune them national boords, and godless colleges, and other sorts of larnin', and the loss of the pratey,[27] and the sickness, and the all the people that's goin' to 'Merica, and the crathurs that's forced to go into the workhouse, or is dyin' off in the ditches, and the clergy settin' their faes agin them, and tellin' the people not to give *in* to the likes, sarra wan of the *Gintry* (cross about us!) 'ill be found in the country, not a word about them or their doin's in no time'.

The reader must not suppose from this that Darby in any way commiserated or sympathized with the bankrupt landed gentry, or felt 'sore or sorry' that the landlord and the noble were, *en masse*, reduced to the same condition that the merchant, the trader, or the professional man, are, from day to day. Oh no! these were not the people honest Darby alluded to. Small blame to him if he had but little personal acquaintance with such gentry; for 'few of them every stood in the street or darkened the doors' of the cottages of his native village of Kilmucafaudeen'. Darby Doolin's gentry were, a short time ago at least, *resident*, and transacted their own business without either attorney, money-broker, agent, keeper, driver, or pound-keeper;[28] they seldom visited London, and much more rarely Paris, or the Brunnens of Nassau;[29] and though reputedly *lucky* were rarely ever known to frequent the gambling-table or the horse-race, but lived in 'pace and quietness at home, in the ould ancient habitations of the country, riding by night up and down on the moonbeams, changing their residences or localities with the whirlwind; creeping into the russet acorn shells; sleeping in the summer in the purple pendent bells of the foxglove or the wild campanula; quaffing the Maydew from the gossamer threads of the early morning, and living a merry, social life, singing, dancing, and playing, with wild Eolian music,[30] by the streamlet's bank, upon the green hill side, or round the grassy fort'. And though they neither canted nor dispossessed, never took nor demanded 'male nor malt',[31] head-rent, quit-rent, crown-rent, dues or duties, county-cess, parish-cess, tithes, priests' dues, poor rates, rates in aid, driverage, poundage,[32] nor murder-money;*[33] employed neither sheriffs, magistrates, barony constables, bailiffs, keepers, drivers, auctioneers, tax-collectors, process-servers, guagers [sic],[34] spies, poteen-hussars,[35] police, nor standing army; passed no promissory notes, and served neither notices to quit, ejectments, nor civil bills, they exacted from the people a reverence and a respect such as few potentates, civil, military, or ecclesiastical, could ever boast of.

. . .

But what's the use in going over the same story, and ringing the famine and fever, and poor-law desolation in your ears, good Christians, again;—Sure I told how it was with all Ireland when I discoursed you before on the same subject as the present; and if you want to know how Connaught is now, I can tell you it is ten times worse—only that the people (and more is the wonder) are honester, more peaceable, and although given a trifle to lying, bear starvation with less grumbling than in any other part of the world where human beings are subject to like misery, and have so long suffered from the same demoralizing influences.
No one will buy in Connaught now;—it is said they cannot. Why? Certainly English capitalists, some of them of great name, who have lately visited this country, have assured us that it was not the ill-conditioned state of the peasantry—nor the desolate appearance of the country—not the debts due by the landlords, no—nor the want of title, or the defect of drainage—nor of the means of access—nor even the low price of corn—nor the danger to life or property:—all these could be calculated upon; their probably losses and profits summed up; and when a 'view' was

made of the whole, it would be found to be just worth, like any other property, so many years' purchase, and would bring its proper price in the market, but it was the taxation which they dreaded, the poor-law taxation of which they could form no estimate, even for the next couple of years—a taxation which, it is feared, may soon increase to such an extent as to exceed the fee-simple of the land.[36] Well, this is all very true; but this taxation is to feed the people,—will it not increase as the population increases? Yes, but the population *will not, cannot increase under the present circumstances*. Already it has been thinned to an extent almost unparalleled under any condition of the country, as will be proved when the next census is taken.*[37] We now speak of the West, with which we have been long familiar, and we venture to assert that, within two years from the present, the numbers which will have taken advantage of poor-law relief, and must consequently be a burden upon the land, will have reached, if not passed, the maximum; and as the numbers requiring relief, either within door or without, shall be thinned and decreased, so ought the taxation to lessen also.

We lately made a tour of the West, after an absence of twelve years. What we have seen—what was the impression made upon us in passing through the districts with which we have been long familiar? This—that until the late potato failure and consequent famine, there must have been immense agricultural improvement going forward even in Connaught; for, although we passed over miles of country without meeting the face of a human being, and seldom that of a four-footed beast, and though we came, in some places, hot upon the smoking ruins of a recently unroofed village,[38] with the late miserable inmates huddled together and burrowing for shelter among the crushed rafters of their cabins; and although there were large tracts of land untilled and untenanted—still, with the traces of cultivation, far beyond what we remember in former times, passing under our eyes; with improved drainage—in many places rendering the former swamp a meadow; with the dark patches of green crops creeping up the sides of the valleys; with the turnip, the cabbage and the parsnip surrounding the cottage, where alone the potato had a footing previously; and, with large tracts of bogs reclaimed wherever there was an improving, and, consequently, a wise and humane as well as thriving landlord,*[39]—we could not but feel that the appearance of the country, generally, had improved since 1837. But to the subject of the depopulation,—

Thousands of the population have died annually since 1846, over and above the usual standard of mortality, which, in Ireland, according to the only data yet available, did not, upon an average, exceed two per cent at the utmost. Thousands upon thousands of the best and most productive of the population have emigrated; and among those who remain, and who have eked out a most miserable existence without the walls of the poor-house, the births, as a natural consequence of the condition in which the country has been, have been lessened to an extent scarcely credible; and marriages—as the priests know to their cost—have fallen off beyond the remembrance of any former time.[40] The few still standing out among the peasantry, clinging with delusive hope to the potato, and still hanging on, in chronic starvation, to two acres and a-half of ill-tilled land, with that longing for liberty—but alas! not for independence—which made the Irish peasant rather die than quit his native hearth; those supported on public works, where such exist, or who have been receiving from the, as yet, unpauperized landlord five-pence a day, 'without mate or drink',[41] for the few months of spring or harvest, will all have been driven into the poor-house before the beginning of 1853; while those who can muster the price of their package to New York, either by honest accumulation or by robbing their landlords of the crops, will likewise have emigrated.

Let us go into the poor-houses, and walk through the day-wards, and yards, and workshops. We see there two classes: the worn down peasantry, with broken constitutions, spectres of men and women. Listlessly stalking about—moody, unoccupied, brooding over miseries past, without hope for the future; fit recipients, mentally and corporeally, for all the contagious influences necessarily attendant upon the accumulation of such a crowd of human beings; we feel assured, upon looking at them, that the great majority will never number another year. For the other section of this class—the boys and girls, and young men and women— many of them intelligent and with good constitutions, now growing up in the workhouses, and acclimatized to them; we feel that something must be done by legislative enactment, either to provide for them in the colonies, or to transplant them again through the unpopulated districts, or to hire them out as farm servants— their legitimate and proper calling—before two years elapse; or the land must be taken by the poor-law authorities on which to employ them. And the day will come, and it is not far distant, when, unless Ireland be converted into one great grass-farm, the farmer must go to the workhouse to seek labourers for his harvest.

\*—in the text, denotes 'Author's note'.

## Notes

1 Denis Coakley, 'William Wilde in the West of Ireland', in *Irish Journal of Medical Science* vol. 185, issue 2 (May 2016), pp. 277–280.
2 'Reviews', *Belfast News-Letter*, 14 May 1852.
3 W.B. Yeats, for example, published *Fairy and Folk Tales of the Irish Peasantry* (1888) and *The Celtic Twilight* (1893). Lady Gregory published *A Book of Saints and Wonders* (1906). Speranza also published on this topic: *Ancient legends, mystic charms, and superstitions of Ireland* (1887) and *Ancient Cures, Charms and Usages of Ireland* (1890), both made use of William's unpublished material. Collectively, they were an important contribution to the Literary Revival.
4 'Sir William Wilde', *Nation*, 6 May 1876.
5 Jane Elgee (1821?-1896), despite the Protestant and conservative leanings of her family, had commenced writing poetry and prose for the nationalist paper, the *Nation*, in 1845. In January 1847, she published her most famous poem, 'The Famine Year', which was a searing indictment of the relief policies of the British government.
6 Many newspapers carried a notice of the marriage, including, 'Marriages', *Leinster Express*, 15 November 1851—the marriage notice read: 'In Dublin, William R. Wilde, Esq., F.R.C.S, to Jane Francesca, youngest daughter of the late Charles Elgee Esq.' It was a small wedding as Jane was still in mourning for her mother.

7 'Oscar Wilde and the sister's death that haunted his life and work', *Irish Times*, 15 February 2017.
8 William had one illegitimate son, Henry Wilson (1838–1877) who followed him into medicine and also worked in St Mark's Hospital, and two daughters, Emily and Mary Wilde, who tragically burned to death. Sean Ryder, 'Son and Parents: Speranza and William Wilde' in Kerry Powell, Peter Raby (eds), *Oscar Wilde in Context* (Cambridge University Press, 2013), p. 13; 'Secret of Wilde sisters' bizarre death', *Irish Independent*, 21 December 2003.
9 L. B. Somerville-Large, 'Dublin's Eye Hospitals in the 19th Century Dublin' in *Historical Record*, vol. 20, No. 1 (December 1964), pp 19–28, p. 25.
10 Ibid., p. 26.
11 'No title', *Freeman's Journal*, 29 October 1861.
12 'Sir William Wilde', *Freeman's Journal*, 29 January 1864.
13 'Death of Sir William Wilde', *Freeman's Journal*, 20 April 1876.
14 In 1864, William and Jane were involved in a highly public court case, in which Mary Travers accused William of seducing her, 'The Late Libel Action', *Freeman's Journal* (from the *Daily News*), 24 December 1864. Although Travers only received one farthing in damages, the trial damaged the reputation of the Wildes—the *Daily News* referring to it as a 'nauseating scandal'.
15 It was not until 1996 that a plaque was unveiled at William's burial spot, paying tribute to Speranza and their three children, thus reuniting the family again. 'Oscar's mother is honoured at last', *Independent* (London), 28 January 1996.
16 He was first appointed by Lord Elliot, then Chief Secretary, to work on the 1841 Census; in late 1850, the Lord Lieutenant invited Wilde, along with Dr Donnolly, the Registrar General of Marriages in Ireland, to work on the 1851 Census – 'The Census of 1851', *Tuam Herald*, 19 October 1850.
17 William Shakespeare (1564–1616) was an English poet and playwright who is widely regarded as the greatest writer in the English language.
18 *Midsummer's Night Dream* is a comedy play written by Shakespeare in the mid-1590s. It draws heavily from English folklore and popular beliefs, the depiction of fairies being representative of the otherworld.
19 Raths are round earthen fortifications that date back to Celtic times. They were traditionally associated with fairies and the otherworld.
20 There are an estimated 3,000 Blessed or Holy Wells in Ireland that predate Christianity. They were believed to have special or curative powers associated with drinking or bathing in the water. Often, they were situated close to a sacred tree. Early Christian churches were frequently situated close to these pagan wells.
21 Workhouses – 130 in total – were created as part of the Poor Law legislation of 1838. They were an embodiment of the harsh, deterrent principle that under-pinned the giving of relief.
22 The 'Dublin University Magazine' was a literary and cultural journal that was published between 1833 to 1882. Although its perspective was Protestant and Unionist, it also celebrated Irish culture.
23 In Irish, a *seanchaí,* or story teller. Traditionally, they would have been the keepers of the history and legends of their clan.
24 Possibly *cèilidh*, a social visit that usually involved music and dancing.
25 Keening was a traditional practice whereby women would gather and wail in grief at a funeral as a way to vocally lament the passing of the dead. As early as 1833, the *Dublin Penny Journal* described the practice as being of 'the most remote antiquity'.
26 The thorn, or hawthorn, tree was traditionally believed to be the meeting places of the fairies. It brought good luck to the owner. In contrast, the blackthorn tree was associated with the dark, or negative, side of Irish folklore.

27 Potato.
28 A person in charge of a public pound where stray animals, such cattle, horses, pigs and sheep would be rounded up. The owners would have to pay the Pound-Keeper a fee to retrieve their animals.
29 The Brunnens of Nassau were famous for their bubbling spa waters, which made them a favoured destination for the wealthy in Europe.
30 Refers to Aeolus, the Greek God of wind.
31 'Meal nor malt'.
32 Various charges and taxes imposed on the people. Head-rent was the rent payable to a freeholder (who possessed the land free of charges). Quit-rent was a tax paid by tenants to release them from performing services that might otherwise be required of them. The Crown-rent were charges paid to the Crown, they generally originated in the confiscations by the British Crown in earlier centuries, predominantly the 17th century. 'Cess' (from Assess) was a tax levied on land owners and occupiers in the county, which was abolished in 1898. Tithes were tax on those who worked the land to pay ten per cent of the value of their agricultural output, in cash or in kind, for the upkeep of the State Church, that is, the Anglican Church. Widespread resistance to their payment between 1831 and 1836, referred to as 'the tithe war', led to tithes being abolished. Poor rates had first been introduced in 1838 in order to support the newly established Poor Law. They were paid by all occupiers of land, except those whose property was less than £4 in annual value. The Rate-in-Aid tax had been introduced in the latter part of the Famine. It was a levy on all Poor Law unions in Ireland that was then repurposed to the most distressed unions. Poundage was the payment of a particular amount per pound sterling to complete a transaction.
33 Author's note: It is but too fully established that in most instances of agrarian murder, the whole townland was compelled to contribute to the price paid for the bloody deed, or heavily taxed to support the murderer, or pay his passage to America.
34 More likely 'gauger' - an excise man who inspected dutiable bulky goods.
35 'Poteen—Hussars' was a derisive term for men employed in remote districts to prevent illicit distillation, usually of poteen. Their duties were eventually absorbed by the Constabulary.
36 Fee-simple was a form of freehold ownership that gave the owner of the property the right to use or to dispose of it at will.
37 *Author's note: The results of the late census have fully verified this opinion. The loss in Connemara has been 16,493; in the barony of Ballynahinch, 9119; and 7374 in that of Moycullen.
38 Traditionally, when a family were ejected from their home, their thatched roof was set alight to prevent their return.
39 *Author's note: No better proof of this could be adduced than the present condition of the tongue of the land—part of the Barnah property, in Connemara, running in from Ballinakille bay to the shores of Kylemore Lake, and now in the possession of Mr. Graham; on one side of it is the Ballynahinch estate, and on the other the Renville—both worse off than they were ten years ago—while this tract, which we remember red bog and heathy moor, is now growing corn and green crops, and has several snug homesteads upon it.
40 The income of Catholic clergy was largely drawn from performing various ceremonial duties, such as baptisms, burials and marriages.
41 'Meat or drink'.

# 14

# S. REYNOLDS HOLE, *A LITTLE TOUR IN IRELAND BY AN OXONIAN*, CHAPTER V (1859)

Samuel Reynolds Hole (1819–1904) was an English-born author, horticulturist, avid rose-grower, noted horseman, and Anglican priest. He was educated at Brasenose College in Oxford, hence the reference to Oxonian, under which pseudonym the book was originally published. Hole had been ordained in 1844 and, at the time of his tour of Ireland, he was serving as vicar of the parish of St. Andrew's Church in Caunton. He was subsequently appointed Dean of Rochester. *A Little Tour of Ireland* is based on a two week visit to the country in the summer of 1858. Like many travelogue authors, Samuel Hole was charmed by the beauty of the countryside. Less typically, he was also entranced by the people who inhabited it. He was particularly full of praise for the women of Ireland, especially the women of the Claddagh, describing them as 'a tableau not to be forgotten'. Unlike many visitors, he saw beyond their poverty:

> Though their garments are torn, and patched, and discoloured, there is a graceful simple dignity about them which might teach a lesson to Parisian milliners; and to my fancy the most becoming dress in all the world is that of a peasant girl of Connamara [sic].[1]

Throughout, the text is enlivened by illustrations by the well-known artist and caricaturist, John Leech (1817–1864), who, it appears, is referred to as 'Frank' throughout. Leech had started working for *Punch* magazine in 1841, and had popularized the concept of the political cartoon. In 1843, he had provided four much-praised images for Charles Dickens's *A Christmas Carol*. Although Leech had been born in London, his father was from Ireland. Regardless of this, some of his depictions of the Irish conformed to the existing unfavourable stereotypes of the period.[2] The woodcuts that appeared in Hole's book are far more sympathetic. In addition to the many pen sketches, the book included a folding colour drawing of the Claddagh in Galway as a frontispiece. Leech and Hole had only met in 1858, but they became lifelong friends. The idea to travel to Ireland for a period of two weeks was Leech's. Their travel route was chosen by Irish-born John Deane, who had been a member of the Royal Commission at the time of the Great Famine.[3] Hole and Leech sailed from Holyhead to Kingstown (Dún Laoghaire) and, following a brief tour of Dublin, they travelled on the Midland Great Western Railway to Galway, a distance of approximately 130 miles.[4] Their tour also included Connemara, Clifden, Kylemore, Limerick, Killarney, Glengarriff, Cork and Blarney.

The book was published in New York in 1891. It was favourably received in America with one reviewer praising the subtle interplay between the text and the artwork, while describing both men as being genial and Hole having 'an international reputation for being agreeable'.[5] *A Little Tour* was republished in London in 1892. Whereas the original publication had been dedicated to Hole's father, the new edition was dedicated to 'THE MEMORY OF JOHN LEECH, A TRUE ARTIST, A TRUE FRIEND AND A TRUE GENTLEMAN, THIS BOOK WHICH HE MADE A SUCCESS'. It also contained a new author's Preface in which he asked that, 'the failings of the author may be condoned by the talent of the artist.'

Hole's other publications include *Hints to Freshmen* (1847); *A Book about Roses* (1869); *The Memories of Dean Hole* (1893), *A Book about the Garden and the Gardener* (1899), which also contained a frontispiece by Leech.

Hole's style of writing is warm and whimsical. The chapter on the Famine inserts an unusually somber note into the book, and it is one of the few sections that does not contain any of Leech's images. Clearly, his two-week sojourn in Ireland made a lasting impression. In his memoirs published in 1892, when recalling his visit to Ireland, he wrote, 'these are memories to make an old man young'.[6] In his private manuscript, he repeated this sentiment, saying that Leech and he had not behaved like traditional tourists but had gone, 'leisurely like large butterflies from flower to flower. . . . In fact you cannot hurry in Ireland, there is something in the humid atmosphere and in the habits and demeanour of the people which ignores haste. Ah me! how happy we were'.[7]

Today, Hole is largely remembered as a rosarian, whose influence continues in the international horticultural world.[8]

SAMUEL HOLE, *A LITTLE TOUR IN IRELAND. BEING A VISIT TO DUBLIN, GALWAY, CONNAMARA, ATHLONE, LIMERICK, KILLARNEY, GLENGARRIFF, CORK, ETC. ETC, BY AN OXONIAN. WITH ILLUSTRATIONS BY JOHN LEECH* (LONDON: BRADBURY AND EVANS, 1859)

CHAPTER V. THE FAMINE.

As schoolboys, to whom "next half" begins to-morrow—sailors on the eve of a voyage—invalids, expecting a physician, who, they know, will prescribe an unwelcome diet,—yea, even as criminals before execution,—amplify their meals, and, from their dreary expectations, educe a keener relish,—so we, awfully anticipating the *cuisine* of Connamara [sic], made a mighty dinner at Galway. It was brought to us, moreover, by a dear old waiter, who evidently had a proud delight in feeding us, as though he were some affectionate sparrow, and we his callow young, taking off the covers with a triumphant air, like a conjuror sure of his trick, and pouring out our Drogheda ale,[9] with quite as much respect and care as Ganymede could have shown for the Gods.[10]

"Was the salmon caught this morning, waiter?"

"It was, sir. Faith, it's not two hours since that fish was walking round his estates, wid his hands in his pockets, never draming what a pretty invitashun he'd have to jine you gintlemen at dinner."

This was followed by a small saddle of "Arran mutton, y'r onner;" and "what can mortals wish for more," except a soupçon of cheese?

Ah, but we felt almost ashamed of being so full and comfortable, when our conversational attendant began to talk to us about the Great Famine. "That's right, good gintlemen," he said, "niver forget, when ye've had yer males, to thank the Lord as sends them. May ye niver know what it is to crave for food, and may ye niver see what I have seen, here in the town o' Galway. I mind the time when I lived yonder" (and he pointed to Kilroy's Hotel),[11] "and the poor craturs come crawling in from the country with their faces swollen, and grane, and yaller, along of the arbs they'd been ating. We gave them bits and scraps, good gintlemen, and did what we could (the Lord be praised!), but they was mostly too far gone out o' life to want more than the priest and pity. I've gone out of a morning, gintlemen," (his lip quivered as he spoke), "and seen them lying dead in the square, with the green grass in their mouths." And he turned away, (God bless his kind heart!), to hide the tears, which did him so much honour.

Can history or imagination suggest a scene more awfully impressive than that which Ireland presented in the times of the Great Famine? The sorrows of that visitation have been recorded by eloquent, earnest men; but they come home to us with a new and startling influence, when we hear of them upon Irish ground. Most vividly can we realise the wreck, when he, who hardly swam ashore and escaped, points to the scene of peril; and while the storm-clouds still drift in the far horizon, and the broken timbers float upon the seething wave, describes, with an exactness horrible to himself, that last amazement and despair.

In the beautiful land of the merry-hearted, "all joy was darkened,—the mirth of the land was gone." In the country of song, and dance, and laughter, there was not heard, wherever that Famine came, one note of music, nor one cheerful sound,—only the gasp of dying men, and the mourners' melancholy wail. The green grass of the Emerald Isle grew over a nation's grave. The crowning plague of Egypt was transcended here, for not only in some districts, was there in every house "one dead," but there were homes in which there was but one living—homes, in which one little child was found, calling upon father, mother, brothers, and sisters, to wake from their last, long sleep,—homes, from which the last survivor fled away, in wild alarm, from those whom living he had loved so well. Fathers were seen vainly endeavouring (such was their weakness) to dig a grave for their children, reeling and staggering with the useless spade in their hands. The poor widow, who had left her home to beg a coffin for her last, lost child, fell beneath her burden upon the road and died.[12] The mendicant had now no power to beg. The drivers of the public cars went into cottages, and found all dead, or Rachel weeping for her children, and praying that die she might.[13] By the seaside, men seeking shell-fish, fell down upon the sands, and, impotent to rise, were drowned. First they began to bury corpses, coffinless, then could not bury them at all. Of indignities and mutilations, which then befell, I will not, for I cannot, speak.

Indeed, it may be asked, wherefore should we repeat at all these sad, heart-rending details? Because, the oftener they are had in painful remembrance, the less likely they are to recur in terrible reality; because—

> "Never did any public misery
> Rise of itself; God's plagues still grounded are
> On common stains of our humanity;
> And to the flame which ruineth mankind
> Man gives the matter, or at least the wind;"[14]

and because, when we know the cause and the symptoms, we can the more readily prevent and prescribe.

Everyone knows, of course, the origin of the Irish Famine.

"The blight which fell upon the potato produced a deadly famine, because the people had cultivated it so exclusively, that when it failed, millions became as utterly destitute, as if the island were incapable of producing any other species of sustenance."[15] They, "who are habitually and entirely fed on potatoes, live upon the extreme verge of human subsistence, and when they are deprived of their accustomed food, there is nothing cheaper to which they can resort. They have already reached the lowest point in the descending scale, and here is nothing beyond but starvation or beggary."[16]

The remedy is just as clear,—to induce the peasantry of Ireland no longer to *depend* upon an article of food, which is difficult to procure, cumbrous to convey, possesses so little nourishment that it must be consumed in large quantities,[17] creates a strange, unhealthy distaste for other food,[18] is subject to so many diseases from humidity and frost, and which has wrought such grievous desolation through the length and breadth of the land.[19]

*How* that remedy is to be applied, let legislators and landlords tell; meanwhile, my friend, and I, having sorrowfully sipped our pint of sherry, shall essay to cheer ourselves with a mild cigar, and a farewell walk to the Claddagh.

The shades of eve were falling fast, as we set forth, and we were just in time to see the last haul of the nets, and the silver salmon lying on the bank. Then we revived our spirits by a little conversation with young Claddagh, (merry and mischievous urchins), and by a distribution of copper, every halfpenny of which raised such a tumulus of rags as would have kept a paper mill at work for weeks. Then—

> "the sun set,
> And all the land was dark."

## Notes

1 *A Little Tour*, Chapter IV, p. 39.
2 Examples of this included 'The British Lion and the Irish Monkey', *Punch*, 8 April 1848, and 'The English Labourer's Burden', ibid., 2 February 1849.
3 John Connellan Deane (1816–1887) was born in Cork city. Although he was called to both the Dublin and London Bars, he rarely practiced as a Barrister. During the Famine, he was employed as a Temporary Inspecting Officer under the Relief Commission for Ireland overseeing the distribution of food at Inishowen in Co. Donegal, in 1846, and Clifden in Co. Galway in 1847. In the mid-1850s, he moved to England where, amongst other things, he was responsible for the successful 'Art Treasures Exhibition' in Manchester. Regardless of his considerable talents, the colourful Deane was frequently penniless.
4 The Midland Great Western Railway Act was passed in 1845 and construction of the line began the following year. By 1851, the line had been extended to Galway, passing through Athlone. The line commenced in the Broadstone Station in the north of Dublin and stretched to Eyre Square in Galway. The railway followed the route of the Royal Canal. As early as 1847, the Directors of the MGWR had proposed that people in receipt of outdoor relief be employed in clearing the land.
5 Gerald, Stanley Lee, 'Review of *A Little Tour*', in *The Book Buyer* (Charles Scribner's Sons, 1897), p. 648.
6 S. Reynolds Hole, *The Memories of Dean Hole* (London: Edward Arnold, 1893), p. 31.
7 George A. B. Dewar, *The letters of Samuel Reynolds Hole, Dean of Rochester edited, with a memoir* (London: George Allen & Sons, 1907), p. 11.
8 See, www.rirs.org/reynoldshole.htm, accessed 4 March 2017.
9 In 1825 William Cairnes (1787–1863) founded Cairnes Brewery in Drogheda. For the next 150 years, the brewery gave employment to almost 200 workers, achieving praise for its ales and stout. William was father of John Elliot Cairnes (1823–1875), the Irish economist.
10 In Greek mythology, Ganymede was a hero, noted for his beauty. According to one legend, he was abducted to serve as cup-bearer in Olympus, the home of the Greek Gods.
11 The Clanricarde Arms, later Kilroy's Hotel, was opened in 1810 and located at the top of Eyre Square in Galway.
12 Author's note: See a most interesting article on the "Famine in the South of Ireland," in Fraser's Magazine, for April, 1847, p. 499.
13 This is a Biblical reference, the full quote being: 'A voice is heard in Ramah, mourning and great weeping, Rachel weeping for her children and refusing to be comforted, because they are no more.'
14 Author's note. Fulke Greville, Lord Brooke.
   Fulke Greville, 1st Baron Brooke (1554–1628) was an Elizabethan poet and politician. His approach to the world was Calvinistic. This extract is from 'Treatise of Warres', a poem in 68 stanzas, in which he takes a critical view of war-fare and its outcome.
15 Author's note. Report of Census Commissioners for Ireland.
16 Author's note. Edinburgh Review, No. 175, p. 233.
17 Author's note. The evidence taken before the Poor Law Commissioners, previously to the establishment of the New Poor Law in Ireland, proves that "ten pounds, twelve pounds, and even fourteen pounds of potatoes are usually consumed by an Irish peasant each day."—Letters on the Condition of the People of Ireland, by J. Campbell Forster, Esq., the Times' Commissioner.
18 Author's note. "When this famine was at the worst in Connamara, the sea off the coast there teemed with turbot, to such an extent that the laziest of fishermen could not help

catching them in thousands; but the common people would not touch them."—Quarterly Review, vol. lxxxi., p. 435.

This interpretation of why the starving Irish did not eat fish is too simplistic. During the first year of shortages, many fishermen had pawned their boats and nets. Although fish was not part of the traditional diet of the poor, during the Famine they ate any product of the sea that they could find, including limpets, seaweed etc.

19 Author's note. Cobbett called the potato, that "root of poverty."

# 15

# JOHN MITCHEL, *THE LAST CONQUEST OF IRELAND, PERHAPS*. CHAPTER XXIV (1861)

Like that of Charles Trevelyan, John Mitchel's name is indelibly associated with the Great Famine, although for very different reasons. Both wrote about the tragedy, but from opposite perspectives. Their divergent viewpoints about British government culpability set the tone for later explanations associated with the revisionist and nationalist interpretations, respectively. As one historian writing in 2014 explained, 'They may be considered as representative to some extent, albeit in an extreme form, of two dominant trends within its historiography as far as London's role during the Famine is concerned'.[1]

John Mitchel had been born near to Dungiven in County Derry in 1815, the son of a Presbyterian Minister. The family moved to Newry, where he worked in a law office and met Jenny Verner whom he married (some accounts suggest he eloped with) in 1837. Despite being Protestant, both John and his father rejected the sectarianism associated with the anti-Catholic Orange Order. In 1843, he joined the Repeal Association and started to contribute to the newspaper, the *Nation*. Following the premature death of Thomas Davis in 1845, Mitchel was asked to join the staff of the *Nation*, which he agreed to do. As a result, he and his young family moved to Dublin.[2] Mitchel's involvement with the Nation and the emergence within the Repeal movement of a group known as Young Ireland, also coincided with the onset of famine in Ireland. The inadequate relief policies introduced by the British government in response to the food shortages radicalized many nationalists and contributed to a split in the Repeal Association in the summer of 1846. The Famine was also a contributing factor in the doomed Rising in 1848.

In early 1848, when Trevelyan's apologia for the British government, *The Irish Crisis* was first published, Mitchel was involved in a very public dispute with Lord Clarendon, the Viceroy, taunting him through the columns of the radical *United Irishman* with the deaths of thousands of Irish people. Mitchel's actions were part of a wider political agitation that had resulted in the creations of two nationalist groups—Old Ireland (led by Daniel O'Connell) and Young Ireland (led by William Smith O'Brien). By the end of 1847, Mitchel, further radicalized by the Famine, and influenced by James Fintan Lalor,[3] argued that a political revolution needed to be accompanied by a social revolution—an idea abhorrent to the government, Irish landowners, and many of Mitchel's former colleagues.[4] The British government's response was swift and draconian. In April 1848, a Treason-Felony Act was passed, making it illegal to 'compass, imagine, invent, devise, or intend' to overthrow the Queen.[5] The act was used to arrest the outspoken Mitchel, who was found guilty of treason-felony and transported to Bermuda.[6] Consequently, Mitchel did not witness the final years of the Famine, nor did he take part in the short-lived Young Ireland Rising that took place in Ballingarry in County Tipperary in July 1848. From Bermuda, Mitchel was eventually transported to Van Diemen's Land, where a number of the leaders of the Rising had been sent,[7] escaping from there in 1853, and from that point living as an exile in America. He remains restless and frustrated, and angry with the British government, whom he regarded as a personal enemy. The public face of Mitchel, however, belies a man who was loving and loyal to his friends and family, tolerant of all religions (two of his daughters became Catholic nuns) and regardless of his overt support for slavery,[8] refused to actually 'own' another person.[9] He was also a man who inspired loyalty in return, most evidently from his colleagues and the people of Ireland.

Following his conviction and deportation from Ireland, Mitchel chronicled his adventures as a felon in his forthright *Jail Journal*. Following his escape from Van Diemen's Land and eventual arrival in New York, Mitchel started his own newspaper, the *Citizen*, dedicated to Irish affairs. In this, as with all of his writings, he showed himself to be an unrepentant critic of the British government's policies in Ireland. The *Citizen*, as with his subsequent newspapers, was disparaging about the anti-Catholic, anti-immigrant 'Know-Nothing Party'.[10] They were also critical of the authoritarianism of the Catholic Church, which lost him some Catholic support, notably that of Archbishop Hughes who accused Mitchel of having 'red republican' sympathies.[11]

Mitchel took the side of the Confederacy in American Civil War. He paid a high personal price for his stance as two of his sons were killed in the conflict, and his third son, lost an arm. Willie Mitchel was killed at Gettysburg, and 'on learning that a son of John Mitchel was among the Confederate dead, Irish soldiers on the Union side made a special effort to find his body, but it seems that his remains were never identified'.[12] Despite his advancing years, Mitchel had offered his own services to the Confederacy, saying that he was willing to run the blockade, but he was turned down on account of his age and short-sightedness.[13] Moreover, in 1865, Mitchel was imprisoned by the Federal authorities for his outspoken defence of the Confederacy, his release coming when Irish American Fenians based in Philadelphia made a direct appeal to President Johnson. During the course of the appeal, they described Mitchel as 'a man whom they love and venerate for his self-sacrificing devotion to his native land'.[14] Johnson, with an eye on the Irish vote, agreed.[15]

In 1874, Mitchel visited Ireland after an absence of twenty-six years. Regardless of his chequered career, his controversial support for slavery, and his long absence from his native land, he had not been forgotten and he was feted as a hero.[16] In February 1875, Mitchel was elected unopposed as Member of Parliament for County Tipperary, the location of the 1848 uprising. The result was invalidated by the British government on the grounds that he was a felon, but when a second election was held, he was re-elected with an even larger majority. Mitchel died in March 1875, fittingly, while still in Ireland. He was buried in Newry, where he was mourned by all religions equally, and was buried with his father and mother.[17] Notwithstanding Mitchel's final triumphant visit to Ireland, he was a divisive figure both during his lifetime and subsequently amongst those who opposed the national struggle. The contents of *Last Conquest of Ireland, Perhaps* had first appeared as a series of articles in Mitchel's newspaper in 1858, and they were published in book form around 1861.[18] Its reception in Ireland was polarized. In a lengthy review, the *Belfast News-Letter*, no friend to Mitchel, described the *Last Conquest* as:

> ... a dismal panorama of famine and slaughter; in which gaunt semblances of humanity cross the stage in hideous processions, men and women— the *men* with drooping flaccid arms, incapable of labour; the *women* with shrunken breasts, no longer able to yield a drop of nutriment to the babes who lie upon them, expiring of inanition; the dead cover the ground on all sides; and legions of yelling demons scream in chorus from all sides— "England his done this! Accursed England has done this!" ... It would be paying too much respect to a pernicious demagogue to review in detail all his absurd and vindictive statements; but if it be only to declare more fully and widely the character of the man who, a short time since, exercised no inconsiderable influence over the ignorant and disaffected of his countrymen, we will give a few specimens of his temper and worth ... All the worst sufferings of the Irish famine, indeed we might say all the causes or the famine, save the immediate one of the potato blight—are attributed to the blunders or diabolical contrivances of the Government—which, by the way, is always spoken of by Mr. Mitchel as the English Government, without any regard being paid to the Irish in both Houses of Parliament, and in every important department of the public service.[19]

Other reviews were more sympathetic. The *Nation* suggested that the author should abandon the 'perhaps' in the title.[20] The *Munster Express*, while referring to Mitchel's whole body of work, averred:

> Upon whatever subject he may choose to write, John Mitchell [sic], by the force of his wide experience, not less than of his singular genius, will always command respect from many, and attention, we may say, from all ... He has brought to the study of our native chronicles an intensely Irish nature, a splendid intellect, an intolerance of wrong, and a burning love of liberty.[21]

Irrespective of negative reviews, the book sold well in Ireland, with both it and the *Jail Journal* being sold out in the Dublin bookshops, and only being available in second hand book stores.[22] This was not Mitchel's only published work. By the mid-1860s, four of his books were on sale in Ireland, *Life of Hugh O'Neill* (1845), *Jail Journal* (1854), *Last Conquest, Perhaps* (1860) and *History of Ireland* (1868).[23] In the longer-term, it was Mitchel, rather than the other leaders of Young Ireland or the Fenians who influenced the next generation of Irish republicans, with both constitutionalists and 'advanced nationalists' borrowing from his writings. Arthur Griffiths regarded Mitchel as 'the greatest figure in Irish history', while Patrick Pearse ranked him as one of 'the four apostles' of Irish nationalism.[24] In the chapter below—the final chapter of the book—Mitchel takes up the story where Trevelyan ends his. Surprisingly, Mitchel makes few references to Trevelyan in the *Last Conquest*, but did describe him as 'the grand commissioner and factotum of the pauper-system, [who] wove his webs of red tape around them from afar'.[25] Shortly before his deportation, Mitchel had visited the west of Ireland where—unlike Trevelyan—he witnessed the impact of the government's policies first-hand and which he incorporated into the *Last Conquest*.[26]

## JOHN MITCHEL, *THE LAST CONQUEST OF IRELAND*. CHAPTER XXIV (DUBLIN: IRISHMAN OFFICE, 1861)

THE Conquest was now consummated—England, great, populous, and wealthy, with all the resources and vast patronage of an existing government in her hands—with a magnificent army and navy—with the established course and current of commerce steadily flowing in the precise direction that suited her interests—with a powerful party on her side in Ireland itself, bound to her by lineage and by interest—and, above all, with her vast brute mass lying between us and the rest of Europe, enabling her to intercept the natural sympathies of other struggling nations, to interpret between us and the rest of mankind, and represent the troublesome sister island, exactly in the light that she wished us to be regarded—England prosperous, potent, and at peace with all the earth besides—had succeeded (to her immortal honour and glory) in anticipating and crushing out of sight the last agonies of resistance in a small, poor, and divided island, which she had herself made poor and divided, carefully disarmed, almost totally defranchised, and totally deprived of the benefits of that very British "law" against which we revolted with such loathing and horror. England had done this; and whatsoever credit and prestige, whatsoever profit and power could be gained by such a feat, she has them all. "Now, for the first time these six hundred years," said the London *Times*, "England has Ireland at her mercy, and can deal with her as she pleases."[27]

It was an opportunity not to be lost for the interests of British civilization. Parliament met late in January, 1849. The Queen, in her "speech,"[28] lamented that "another failure of the potato crop had caused severe distress in Ireland:" and there-upon asked Parliament to continue, "for a limited period," the extraordinary power; that is, the power of proclaiming any district under martial law, and of throwing suspected persons into prison, without any charge against them.[29] The Act was passed, of course.

Then, as the famine of 1848 was fully as grievous and destructive as any of the previous famines;—as the rate-payers were impoverished, and in most of the "unions," could not pay the rates already due—and were thus rapidly sinking into the condition of paupers; giving up the hopeless effort to maintain themselves by honest industry, and throwing themselves on the earnings of others; as the poor-houses were all filled to overflowing, and the exterminated people were either lying down to die or crowding into the emigrant-ships;—as, in short, the Poor Law, and the New Poor Law, and the Improved Poor Law, and the Supplementary Poor Law, had all manifestly proved a "failure," Lord John Russell's next step was to give Ireland *more* Poor Law.[30]

When I say that the whole code of poor laws was a *failure*, I must qualify that expression, as before. They were a failure for their professed purpose—that of relieving the famine; but were a complete success for their real purpose—that of uprooting the people from the land, and casting them forth to perish. I have not much faith in the "government" statistics of that country, but as some may wish to see how much our enemies were willing to admit, I shall give some details from a report furnished in '48 by Captain Larcom,[31] under the orders of the government, and founded on local reports of police inspectors. I find the main facts epitomized thus, for one year :—

" In the number of farms, of from one to five acres, the decrease has been 24,147; from five to fifteen acres, 27,379; from fifteen to thirty acres, 4,274; whilst of farms above thirty acres the increase has been 3,670. Seventy thousand occupiers, with their families, numbering about three hundred thousand, were rooted out of the land.

" In Leinster, the decrease in the number of holdings not exceeding one acre, as compared with the decrease of '47, was 3,749; above one, and not exceeding five, was 4,026; of five, and not exceeding fifteen, was 2,546; of fifteen to thirty, 891; making a total of 10,617.

" In Munster, the decrease in the holdings, under thirty acres, is stated at 18,814; the increase over thirty acres, 1,399.

" In Ulster, the decrease was 1,502; the increase, 1,134.

"In Connaught, where the labour of extermination was least, the clearance has been most extensive. There, in particular, the roots of holders of the soil were never planted deep beneath the surface, and, consequently, were exposed to every exterminator's hand. There were in 1847, 35,634 holders of from one to five acres. In the following year there were less by 9,703; there were 76,707 holders of from five to fifteen acres, less in one year by 12,891; those of from fifteen to thirty acres were reduced by 2,121; a total depopulation of 26,499 holders of land, exclusive of their families, was effected in Connaught in one year."

On this report it may be remarked that it was a list of killed and wounded in one year of carnage only—and of one class of people only. It takes no account of the dead in that multitudinous class thinned the most by famine, who had no land at all, but lived by the labour of their hands, and who were exposed before others, as having nothing but life to lose. As for the landlords, already encumbered by debt, the pressure of the poor-rates was fast breaking them down. In most cases, they were not so much as the receivers of their own rents, and had no more control over the bailiffs, sheriffs, and police, who plundered and chased away the people, than one of the pillars of their own grand entrance gates.

Take one paragraph now from amongst the commercial reports of the Irish papers, which will suggest more than any laboured narrative could inculcate:—
"Upwards of 150 ass hides have been delivered in Dublin from the county Mayo, for exportation to Liverpool. *The carcasses, owing to the scarcity of provisions, had been used as food!*".

But those who could afford to dine upon famished jackasses were few, indeed. During this winter of '48–9, hundreds of thousands perished of hunger. During this same winter the herds and harvests raised on Irish ground were floating off to England on every tide: and, during this same winter, almost every steam-ship from England daily carried Irish paupers, men, women, and children, away from Liverpool and Bristol, to share the good cheer of their kinsmen at home.
It was in this state of things that Lord John Russell, having first secured a continued suspension of the Habeas Corpus Act, proposed an additional and novel sort of poor-rate for Ireland. It was called the "Rate-in-aid."[32] That is to say, poor-law unions, which were still solvent, and could still in some measure maintain their own local poor, were to be rated for relief of such unions as had, sunk under the pressure. Assuming that Ireland and England are two integral parts of an "United Kingdom," (as we are assured they are), it seems hard to understand why a district in Leinster should be rated to relieve a pauper territory in Mayo—and a district in Yorkshire not.[33] Or to comprehend why old and spent Irish labourers, who had given the best of their health and strength to the service of England, should be shipped off to Ireland to increase and intensify the pauperism and despair.[34] But so it was: the maxim was that "the property of Ireland must support the poverty of Ireland;" without the least consideration of the fact that the property of Ireland was all this time supporting the luxury of England.

The next measure passed in the same session of Parliament was the "Incumbered Estates Act:" the Act of 12th and 13th Victoria, c. 77. Under this, a royal commission was issued, constituting a new court "for the sale of Incumbered Estates," and the scope and intent of it were to give a short and summary method of bringing such estates to sale, on petition either of creditors or of owners.[35] Before that time the only mode of doing this was through the slow and expensive proceedings of the Court of Chancery; and the number of incumbered landlords had grown so very large since the famine began, their debts so overwhelming, and their rental so curtailed, that the London Jews, money-brokers, and insurance offices, required a speedier and cheaper method of bringing their property to the hammer. What I wish to be fully understood is, that this Act was not intended to relieve, and did not relieve, anybody in Ireland; but that, under pretence of facilitating legal proceedings, it contemplated a sweeping confiscation and new "Plantation" of the island. The English press was already complacently anticipating a peaceable transfer of Irish land to English and Scotch capitalists; and took pains to encourage them to invest their money under the new Act. Ireland, it was now declared, had become tranquil: "the Celts were gone:" and if any trouble should arise, there was the Habeas Corpus Suspension Act;[36] and the horse, foot, and artillery, and the juries. Singular to relate, however, the new Act did not operate satisfactorily in that direction. English capitalists had a wholesome terror of Tipperary, and of the precarious tenure by which an Irish landlord holds his life; insomuch that the great bulk of the sales made by the Commissioners were made to Irishmen:—and in the official return of the operations of the court, up to Oct., 1851, I find that while the gross amount produced by the sales had been more than three and a half millions sterling, there had been only fifty-two English and Scottish purchasers, to the amount of £319,486.

Down to the 25th May, 1857, there had been given orders for sale to the number of 3,197: the property had been sold to 7,216 purchasers, of whom 6,902 were Irish—the rest English, Scotch, or other foreigners. The estates already sold brought upwards of twenty millions sterling, which was almost all distributed to creditors and other parties interested. The result to Ireland is simply this—about one-fifteenth part of the island has changed hands; has gone from one landlord and come to another landlord: the result to the great tenant class is simply nil. The new landlord comes over to them armed with the power of life and death, like his predecessor: but he has no local or personal attachment which in some cases used to mitigate the severity of landlord rule;—and he is bound to make interest on his investment. The estates have been broken up, on an average, into one-half their former size: and this has been much dwelt upon as an "amelioration:" but I have yet to learn that small landlords are more mild and merciful than great ones. On the whole, I maintain that the "Incumbered Estates Act" has benefited only the money-lenders of England.

As to "Tenant-Right," the salutary custom which I explained before, and which did once practically secure to the tenantry in some portions of Ulster a permanency of tenure on payment of their rent,[37] our Parliamentary patriots have been agitating for it, begging for it, conferring with Ministers about it, eating public dinners, making speeches and soliciting votes on account of it; but they have never made, and never will make, an approach by one hair's-breadth to its attainment.*[38] It is absolutely essential to the existence of the British Empire, that the Irish peasant class be kept in a condition which will make them entirely manageable—easy to be thinned out when they grow too numerous, and an available *matériel* for armies. This, I say, is necessary to the British commercial and social governmental system—but I do not say it by way of complaint. Those who are of opinion that British civilization is a blessing and a light to lighten the World, will easily reconcile themselves to the needful condition. Those who deem it the most base and horrible tyranny that has ever scandalized the earth, will probably wish that its indispensable prop—Ireland—were knocked from under it.

In the meantime, neither the Incumbered Estates Act, nor any other Act, made or to be made by an English Parliament, has done or aimed to do anything towards giving the Irish tenant-at-will the smallest interest in the land he tills; but, on the contrary, the whole course of the famine legislation was directed to the one end of shaking small lease-holders loose from the soil, and converting them into tenants-at-will, or into "independent labourers," or able-bodied paupers, or lean corpses. Let it be understood further, that the condition of an Irish "Tenant-at-will" is unique on the face of the globe,*[39] is utterly unintelligible to most civilized Europeans, and is only to be found within the sway of that Constitution which is the envy of surrounding nations. The German, Von Raumer,[40] making a tour in Ireland, thus tries to explain the thing:—

"How shall I translate *tenants-at-will*? *Wegjagbare*? Expellable? Serfs? But in the ancient days of vassalage, it consisted rather in keeping the vassals attached to the soil, and by no means in driving them away. An ancient vassal is a lord compared with the present tenant-at-will, to whom the law affords no defence. Why not call them *Jagdbare* (*chaseable*)? But this difference lessens the analogy—that for hares, stags, and deer there is a season during which no one is allowed to hunt them; whereas tenants-at-will are hunted all the year round. And if anyone would defend his farm (as badgers and foxes are allowed to do), it is here denominated *rebellion*."

In 1849, it was still believed that the depopulation had not proceeded far enough; and the English Government was fully determined, having so gracious an opportunity, to make a clean sweep. One of the provisions of Lord John Russell's *Rate-in-Aid* Bill was for imposing an additional rate of two shillings and six-pence in the pound, to promote *emigration*. During the two years, 1848–9, the Government Census Commissioners admit 9,395 deaths by famine alone; a number which would be about true if multiplied by twenty-five. In the year 1850 there were nearly 7,000, as admitted by the same authorities; and in the first quarter of 1851, 652 deaths by hunger, they say, "are recorded." In the very midst of all this havoc, in August, 1849, her Majesty's Ministers thought the coast was clear for a Royal Visit.[41] The Queen had long wished, it was said, to visit her people of Ireland; and the great army of persons, who, in Ireland, are paid to be loyal, were expected to get up the appearance of rejoicing. Of course there were crowds in the streets; and the natural courtesy of the people prevented almost everything which could grate upon the lady's ear or offend her eye. One Mr O'Reilly, indeed, of South Great George's Street, hoisted on the top of his house a large black banner, displaying the crownless Harp; and draped his windows with black curtains, showing the words Famine and Pestilence: but the police burst into his house, viciously tore down the flag and the curtains, and, rudely thrust the proprietor into gaol.[42] One other incident of the royal visit will be enough :—

"The *Freeman* says, that on passing through Parkgate Street, Mr James Nugent, one of the Guardians of the North Union, approached the royal carriage,[43] which was moving rather slowly, and, addressing the Queen, said: 'Mighty Monarch, pardon Smith O'Brien.'[44] Before, however, he had time to get an answer, or even to see how her Majesty received the application, Lord Clarendon rode up and put him aside;[45] and the *cortége* again set out at a dashing pace, which it maintained until it drew up opposite the Vice-Regal Lodge in the Park."[46]

On the whole, however, the Viceroy's precautions against any show of disaffection, were, I take shame to say it, complete and successful. Nine out of ten citizens of Dublin eagerly hoped that her Majesty would make this visit the occasion of a "pardon" to O'Brien and his comrades. Lord Clarendon's organs, therefore, and his thousand, placemen and agents of every grade, diligently whispered into the public ear that the Queen would certainly pardon the State prisoners, if she were not insulted by Repeal demonstrations—in short, if there was not one word said about those prisoners. The consequence was, that no whisper was heard, about Repeal, nor about the State prisoners—except only the exclamation of silly Mr Nugent to his "Mighty Monarch."

Although there was no chance of Tenant-Right, no chance of Ireland being allowed to manage its own affairs—yet towards Catholics of the educated classes there was much liberality. Mr Wyse was sent ambassador to Greece:[47] Mr More O'Ferrall was made Governor of Malta:[48] many barristers, once loud in their patriotic devotion at Conciliation Hall, were appointed to Commissionerships and other minor offices,- and Ireland became "tranquil," enough. For result of the whole long struggle, England was left for a time, more securely in, possession than ever of the property, lives, and industry of the Irish nation. She had not parted with a single atom of her plunder, nor in the slightest degree weakened any of her garrisons, either military, civil, or ecclesiastical. Her "Established Church" remained in full; force—the wealthiest church in the World, quartered upon the poorest people, who abhor its doctrine, and regard its pastors as ravening wolves. It had, indeed, often been denounced in, the London Parliament, by Whigs out of place: Mr Roebuck had called it "the greatest ecclesiastical enormity in Europe;"[49] Mr Macaulay has termed it "the most utterly absurd and indefensible of all the institutions now existing in the civilised world."[50] But everyone knows what value there is in the liberal declarations of Whigs out of place. Once in place and power, they felt that the "enormity" of the Established Church, absurd and indefensible as it was, constituted one of their greatest and surest holds upon the Irish aristocracy, to whose younger sons and dependents it afforded a handsome and not too laborious livelihood. The Archbishop of Armagh alone continued yearly to receive his £14,664—almost thrice the salary of the President of the United States; and the Bishop of Derry nearly double as much as the President—and ten other bishops, emoluments varying from £7,600 down to the lowest, £2,310. Then every parish must have its "rector," though in a great many parishes there are no congregations; and the poor Catholic people, over and above rents, rates, and taxes, must pay these sinecure pastors out of their poor stackyards—the remedy for non-payment being distress by the landlord.*[51] The Orangemen, also, have been maintained in full force. They are all armed: for no bench of magistrates will refuse a good Protestant the liberty of keeping a gun; and lest they might not have enough, the Government sometimes supplies arms for distribution among the lodges. The police and detective system is more highly organized than ever; and the Government Board of "National" Education, more diligently than ever inculcates the folly and vice of national aspirations.[52]

Yet Ireland, we are told, is "improving" and "prosperous." Yes; it cannot be denied that three millions of the people have been slain or driven to seek safety by flight, the survivors begin to live better for the present. There is a smaller supply of labour, with the same demand for it—therefore wages are higher. There is more cattle and grain for export to England, because there are fewer mouths to be fed; and England (in whose hands are the issues of life and death for Ireland) can afford to let *so many* live. Upper classes, and lower classes, merchants, lawyers, state officials, civil and military, are indebted for all that they have, for all that they are or hope for, to the sufferance and forbearance of a foreign and hostile nation. This being the case, everyone must see that the prosperity of Ireland, even such ignominious prosperity as it is, has no guarantee or security. Whenever Irishmen grow numerous again (as they surely will), and whenever "that ancient swelling and desire of liberty," as Lord Mountjoy expressed it,[53] shall once more stir their souls (as once more it certainly will), why, the British Government can crush them again, with greater ease than ever; for the small farmers are destroyed; the middle classes are extensively corrupted; and neither stipendiary officials nor able-bodied paupers ever make revolutions.

This very dismal and humiliating narrative draws to a close. It is the story of an ancient nation stricken down by a war more ruthless and sanguinary than any seven years' war, or thirty years' war, that Europe ever saw. No sack of Magdeburg,[54] or ravage of the Palatinate,[55] ever approached in horror and desolation to the slaughters done in Ireland by mere official red tape and stationery, and the principles of political economy. A few statistics may fitly conclude this dreary subject.

The Census of Ireland, in 1841, gave a population of 8,175,125. At the usual rate of increase, there must have been, in 1846, when the famine commenced, at least eight and a half millions; at the same rate of increase, there ought to have been, in 1851 (according to the estimate of the Census Commissioners), 9,018,799. But in that year, after five seasons of artificial famine, there were found alive only 6,552,385—a deficit of about two millions and a half. Now, what became of those two million and a half?

The "government" Census Commissioners, and compilers of returns of all sorts, whose principal duty it has been, since that fatal time, to conceal the amount of the havoc, attempt to account for nearly the whole deficiency by emigration. In Thom's Official Almanac,[56] I find set down on one side the actual decrease from 1841 to 1851 (that is, without taking into account the increase by births in that period), 1,623,154. Against this, they place their own estimate of the emigration during those same ten years, which they put down at 1,589,133. But, in the first place, the decrease did not *begin* till 1846—there had been till then a rapid increase in the population: the government returns, then, not only ignore the increase, but set the emigration of *ten* years against the do population of *five*. This will not do: we must reduce their emigrants by one-half, say to six hundred thousand—and add to the depopulation the estimated increase *up* to 1846, say half a million. This will give upwards of two millions whose disappearance is to be accounted for—and six hundred thousand emigrants in the other column. Balance unaccounted for, *a million and a half.*

This is without computing those who were born in the five famine years, whom we may leave to be balanced by the deaths from *natural* causes in the same period.

Now, that million and a half of men, women, and children, were carefully, prudently, and peacefully slain by the English government. They died of hunger in the midst of abundance, which their own hands created; and it is quite immaterial to distinguish those who perish in the agonies of famine itself from those who died of typhus fever, which in Ireland is always caused by famine.

Further, I have called it an artificial famine: that is to say, it was a famine which desolated a rich and fertile island, that produced every year abundance and super-abundance to sustain all her people and many more. The English, indeed, call that famine a "dispensation of Providence;" and ascribe it entirely to the blight of the potatoes. But potatoes failed in like manner all over Europe; yet there was no famine save in Ireland. The British account of the matter, then, is first, a fraud—second, a blasphemy. The Almighty, indeed, sent the potato blight, but the English created the famine.

And lastly, I have shown, in the course of this narrative, that the depopulation of the country was not only encouraged by artificial means, namely, the Out-door Relief Act, the Labour-Rate Act, and the emigration schemes, but that extreme care and diligence were used to prevent relief coming to the doomed island from abroad; and that the benevolent contributions of Americans and other foreigners were turned aside from their destined objects—not, let us say, in order that none should be saved alive, but that no interference should be made with the principles of political economy.

The Census Commissioners close their last Report with these words :—

"In conclusion, we feel it will be gratifying to your Excellency, to find, that, although the population has been diminished in so remarkable a manner, by famine, disease, and emigration, and has been since decreasing, the results of the Irish census are, on the whole, satisfactory."[57]

The Commissioners mean that the Census exhibits an increase in sheep and cattle for the English market—and that while men are lean, hogs are fat. "The good of this," said Dean Swift[58]—more than a century ago—"the good of this is, that the more sheep we have, the fewer human creatures are left to wear the wool or eat the flesh. Ajax was mad when he mistook a flock of sheep for his enemies;[59] but we shall never be sober until we have the same way of thinking."

The subjection of Ireland is now probably assured until some external shock shall break up that monstrous commercial firm, the British Empire, which, indeed, is a bankrupt firm, and trading on false credit, and embezzling the goods of others, or robbing on the highway, from Pole to Pole, but its doors are not yet shut; its cup of abomination is not yet running over. If any American has read this narrative, however, he will never wonder hereafter when he hears an Irishman in America fervently curse the British Empire. So long as this hatred and horror shall last—so long as our island refuses to become, like Scotland, a contented province of her enemy, Ireland is not finally subdued. The passionate aspiration for Irish nationhood will out-live the British Empire.

THE END

## Notes

1 Christophe Gillissen, 'Charles Trevelyan, John Mitchel et l'historiographie de la Grande Famine/ Charles Trevelyan, John Mitchel and the historiography of the Great Famine' in 'La grande famine en irlande, 1845–1851, *French Journal of British Studies*, XIX-2 (2014), p. 195.
2 William Dillon, *Life of John Mitchel* (London: Kegan Paul, Trench and Co., 1888, 2 vols), chapter four.
3 James Fintan Lalor (1807–1849) was a radical nationalist and journalist who contributed both to the *Nation* and to the *Felon*. He believed that simply demanding a repeal of the Union was too limited and would ultimately change little. Instead, he suggested

4 For more on the politics of this period, and Mitchel's role within them, see, Christine Kinealy *1848 in Ireland. Repeal and Revolution* (Manchester University Press, 2009).
5 The Treason Felony Act 1848 (11 & 12 Vict. c. 12) by which it was an offence to 'compass, imagine, invent, devise, or intend' any act that would damage the monarch.
6 Mitchel was tried under the newly introduced Treason Felony Act. The fact that all Catholics had been excluded from Mitchel's jury was noted in the Irish press and discussed in the British House of Commons. See *Nation*, 2 June 1848.
7 Mitchel had been moved from Bermuda because of his asthma. He initially was sent to the Cape of Good Hope but internal trouble there meant that he was moved on to Van Diemen's land. The government did not believe that he would survive the long journey at sea. Although he was sick during the voyage, he survived. John Mitchel, *Jail Journal, or Five Years in British Prisons* (New York: office of the *Citizen*, 1854), pp 110–1, 121.
7 Ibid., p. 157.
8 Mitchel's support of slavery has been attributed to a number of reasons, including simple racism, see David T. Gleeson, 'Failing to 'unite with the abolitionists': the Irish Nationalist Press and U.S. emancipation', *Geographies of Race,* vol. 37, issue 3 , *Ireland, Slavery, Anti-Slavery and Empire*, vol. 37 (2016): http://www.tandfonline.com/doi/full/10.1080/0144039X.2016.1208911, accessed 3 March 2017.
9 Insights into Mitchel, the private man, can be gleaned from the letters of his loving wife, Jenny Mitchel: Jenny Mitchel Letters, Manuscripts and Archives Division, The New York Public Library, MSS Col, 2021.
10 The *Citizen*, 9 September 1854.
11 *New York Times*, 19 October 1861.
12 James Quinn, 'Southern Citizen: John Mitchel, the Confederacy and slavery' in *History Ireland,* vol. 15, issue 3 (May/June 2007).
13 John Martin to Eva, 25 September 1862, National Library of Ireland, MS 10,520.
14 'Release of John Mitchel' (from *New York Daily News*), *Freeman's Journal*, 13 November 1865.
15 Bryan P. McGovern, *John Mitchel: Irish Nationalist, Southern Secessionist* (University of Tennessee Press, 2009), p. 152.
16 P. A. Sillard, *The Life of John Mitchel. With an Historical Sketch of the '48 Movement in Ireland* (Dublin: J. Duffy, 1908), pp 258–60.
17 *New York Times*, 5 April 1875.
18 John Mitchel, *The Last Conquest of Ireland, Perhaps* (Dublin: Irishman Office, 1861).
19 'Reviews', *Belfast News-Letter*, 14 February 1861.
20 'Correspondence', *Nation*, 12 November 1864.
21 *Munster Express*, 6 March 1869.
22 'A E N', *Nation*, 15 September 1866.
23 'National Works', *Nation*, 28 December 1867.
24 W. J. McCormack, 'Pádraig Pearse: Preparing for the "end times"', *Irish Times*, 18 November 2015. Mitchel was one of the ghosts of Irish separatism that Pearse alluded to in his 1915 pamphlet, 'Ghosts'.
25 *Last Conquest*, p. 148.
26 Dillon, *Life of John Mitchel*, vol. 1, p. 147.
27 The English (Angevin) invasion of Ireland is generally dated to 1169.
28 The Queen's Speech (or King's) was part of the State opening of the U.K. Parliament, marking the beginning of a parliamentary session. It was attended with many traditional ceremonies including the monarch wearing the Imperial State Crown.
29 During the course of the Queen's Speech, these topics were not linked directly. The political unrest in Ireland was placed in the context of the European-wide unrest in

1848, she saying: 'I observe with satisfaction that this portion of the United Kingdom has remained tranquil amidst the convulsions which have disturbed so many parts of Europe. The insurrection in Ireland has not been renewed, but a spirit of disaffection still exists; and I am compelled, to my great regret, to ask for a continuance, for a limited time, of those powers which in the last session you deemed necessary for the preservation of the public tranquility', 'Opening of the Session', the *Spectator*, 3 February 1849.

30  Lord John Russell (1792–1878) served as Prime Minister from 1846 to 1852. During this time, responsibility for both 'ordinary' and famine relief was transferred to the Irish Poor Law (and thus Irish rate payers), the main legislative change being introduced in 1847.
31  Captain Thomas Larcom (1801–1879) was a prominent member of the Irish Ordnance Survey that had commenced in 1824. He was involved in the 1841 census of Ireland, it being at his initiative that occupations and agricultural statistics were included. During the Famine, he oversaw the operation of the Public Works and, in 1848, Larcom was placed at the head of a commission of inquiry into the operation of the Poor Laws.
32  The Rate-in-Aid Act, which was introduced at the beginning of 1849, levied a new rate (tax) on every Poor Law Union, for redistribution to the 22 poorest ones. A second Rate-in-Aid was introduced in 1850. The tax confirmed the principle that poor relief, including the cost of the Famine, should be a charge on local Irish taxes. They were the final special relief measure introduced for Ireland.
33  A number of politicians and relief officials made this same point. Edward Twisleton, the chief administrator of the Irish Poor Law, resigned in 1849, arguing that the Rate should be an imperial charge, and that he could not implement the tax 'with honour'.
34  Unlike the Irish Poor Law, the English Poor Law included a 'Law of Settlement', which made residency a condition of receiving poor relief in an area. The already complicated law was amended in 1846, to now require five years' residency. Famine emigrants, therefore, were not eligible to receive relief in Britain, but could be returned to Ireland.
35  The first Encumbered Estates legislation was introduced in 1848, but proved to be ineffective, leading to the 1849 Act, which established an Encumbered Estates' Court to facilitate the sale of indebted property. Between 1849 and 1857, approximately 3,000 estates, totalling 5,000,000 acres, were disposed of under these acts
36  Habeas Corpus was suspended in Ireland on 22 July 1848 as a way of forcing Young Ireland into a premature rebellion—they had wanted to wait until following the harvest period. In 1849, its suspension was extended.
37  Tenant Right, also known as the Ulster Custom, had been introduced as part of the Plantation of Ulster as a way of giving some protection to the new tenants.
38  Author's note: * Mr Gladstone's Law, pretending to secure something like a Tenant-right, is, in fact, only an example and a confirmation of the judgment given in the text.
39  Author's note: * Unparalleled in some sort only by the *ryots* of India—another people privileged to enjoy the blessings of British rule. [a *ryot* was a peasant cultivator in India, who worked as a hired labour].
40  Friedrich Ludwig Georg von Raumer (1781–1873) was a German historian who visited Ireland, England and Scotland in the 1820s.
41  Queen Victoria's first visit took place from 2 to 12 August 1849. Both the monarch and her Lord Lieutenant, Lord Clarendon, were pleased with her reception. She spent only five hours in Belfast, the most royalist of all the places that she visited.
42  The *Dublin Directory* for 1850 lists a Michael O'Reilly living at 37 South Great George's street in Dublin.
43  This incident is also reported in the *Freeman's Journal*, 8 August 1849.
44  William Smith O'Brien (1803–1864), a Protestant landowner and Member of the British Parliament, had been the leader of the Young Ireland movement. Reluctantly,

he had headed the Rising in July 1848 and, with the other leaders, had been found guilty of treason and sentenced to death. This sentence was transmuted in 1849 to transportation.
45 George William Frederick Villiers (1800–1870) was the fourth Earl of Clarendon. He served as Viceroy from 1847 to 1852 (being appointed on the death of Lord Bessborough). He admitted privately that he was overwhelmed by the extent of the distress in Ireland.
46 The Vice-Regal Lodge, the home of the Lord Lieutenant, was located in the Phoenix Park. It is now the home of the President of Ireland (*Áras an Uachtaráin*).
47 Thomas Wyse (1791–1862) was a Roman Catholic who, following Emancipation in 1829, was elected to Parliament as a Whig. In 1849, the well-travelled Wyse was appointed British minister to Greece, where he still lived at the time of his death.
48 Richard More O'Ferrall (1797–1880) was an Irish Catholic who was first elected to the British House of Commons in 1832. In 1847, he was appointed the Governor of Malta (the first Catholic to hold this position), but resigned in 1851 in protest at Lord John Russell's anti-Catholic Ecclesiastical Titles Act.
49 John Arthur Roebuck (1802–1879) was a radical politician, who was opposed to the use of coercion in Ireland.
50 Thomas Babington Macaulay (1800–1859) was a Whig politician, imperialist and historian. In 1847, he had supported the increasing of the government's grant to the seminary in Maynooth. He was related through marriage to Charles Trevelyan.
51 Author's note: * In the matter of the Established Church, also, the late Gladstone law ("Disestablishment and Disendowment") is a mere subterfuge and imposture. It has diminished the emoluments of some of the bishops, but has not relieved the people of any part of this burden on account of that church: no, not to the amount of a single farthing.
52 National Schools had been established in Ireland in 1831. They were initially multi-denominational. Attendance was voluntary. The pupils were taught through the medium of the English language.
53 Charles Blount, Lord Mountjoy (1563–1606), was Lord Deputy in 1603 and oversaw the surrender of Hugh O'Neill at the end of the Nine Years' War. To bring the war to an end, he had adopted a scorched earth policy, although the terms of the surrender were relatively liberal.
54 The Sack of Magdeburg took place in 1631 and resulted in the destruction of the largely Protestant city of Magdeburg by Catholic forces.
55 The destruction of the Palatinate was carried out by French troops in 1688–1689, during the reign of Louis XIV. It was one of a number of ruthless attacks on Huguenots.
56 *Thom's Official Almanac* was founded by Scottish publisher Alexander Thom (1801–1879) in 1844, its official title being the *Irish Almanac and Official Directory*.
57 These comments appeared in the 1851 Census for Ireland, which was published in 1854.
58 Jonathan Swift (1667–1745), in addition to his writings and philanthropic works, was Dean of St Patrick's Cathedral, Dublin.
59 Ajax was a mythological Greek hero who appeared in epic poems about the Trojan War. In Sophocles' play about him, Ajax was drugged and mistakenly slaughtered sheep—an act which led him to take his own life.

# Part VII

# A POETIC ENDING

# 16

# GEORGE FRANCIS TRAIN, *THREE CHEERS FOR THE FAMINE* (1872)

Visionary, conman, entrepreneur, poet, travel magnate, braggart, feminist, explorer, eccentric, inventor, Irish nationalist and Presidential candidate, George Francis Train, who was all of the above, defies simple definition.

Train was born in 1829 in Boston to a Methodist family. He was orphaned when aged only 4, his parents dying of yellow fever. Although his grandparents wanted him to train as a Minister, he preferred to utilize his entrepreneurial skills, especially in regard to transport – trams, trains and shipping. In 1860, he visited Cork to establish a horse-tramway. It was not totally successful, but paved the way for a second attempt in 1871 by Clifton Robinson, a protégé of Train's.[1] Around this time, Train came to support an Irish republic, publishing *Irish Independency* in 1865. In the same year, he delivered a speech on Irish independence and English neutrality before the Fenian Congress held in Philadelphia, in front of 6,000 persons.[2] When returning to Ireland in January 1868, he was arrested on board a steamer, off the port of Queenstown.[3] Some reports suggesting that he had been arrested for carrying pro-Fenian literature into the country.[4] In fact, Train was carrying copies of speeches that he had made in America, including a number on Irish independence. Following an appearance before a magistrate, he was released, having promised that his purpose in Ireland had nothing to do with politics.[5] Train was arrested a second time in the same year in Ireland, this time for having outstanding debts. He spent a number of months in Marshalsea prison in Dublin.[6] However, as with much of Train's flamboyant life, the truth was never plain nor simple. Whatever the reality, Train claimed that while in prison in Dublin he made the decision to run for President.[7]

In 1872, Train ran for the highest office in the U.S. under the epithet 'The People's Candidate for President'. He appealed to Irish immigrants, his campaign promising:

> He will not be purchased with gold or silver, like some of his predecessors in office. He will be the right man in the right place. It will be the imperative duty of every Irishman in America to rally round and have him triumphantly returned their President in 1872.[8]

Train went on to promise:

> Then Ireland may rejoice for the day of her deliverance from British tyranny will be at hand, and the cause of Republicanism will deliver new life and vitality, and will spread like wild fire over the whole surface of Continental Europe. And America may boast that she has at length found an honest man who will guide her destinies to a glorious and successful issue.[9]

It was at this time that he penned 'Three Cheers for the Famine'. It was not the only poem that Train wrote about Ireland, he composing one praising the Rising in 1848 and other national struggles:

> Another Kingdom's dying groan,
> Would rouse Fitzgerald, Emmett [sic], Tone
> Go shake the tomb where courage lies
> With eternal cheers for the next that dies.[10]

Inevitably, Train's campaign was noticed in Ireland, including by the conservative *Irish Times* that condemned him and his political aspirations.[11] Train's Presidential bid was unsuccessful.

The three cheers referred to in Train's poem recall a notorious episode in November 1868 when, during an election campaign, Prime Minister Benjamin Disraeli was speaking in Aylesbury in Buckinghamshire, where he had served as MP from 1847 to 1876. Referring to the condition of Ireland twenty-five years earlier, he stated that since then there had been a general improvement in the country, saying, 'The people are now no longer in the condition in which they were; they have better raiment, better residences, and they have much better food'.[12] At this point, a voice shouted out, 'three cheers for the famine', to which Disraeli responded, 'Well you have given three cheers before this for things that have not done so much good to man as that famine'.[13] The incident was widely reported and was recalled long after it had occurred. It was debated as far away as in the Legislative Council in New Zealand, where the Prime Minister, Lord George Grey,[14] was asked for an explanation of its meaning, he responding by quoting reports from the Skibbereen area in the 1840s.[15] Within the British House of Commons, Irish MPs challenged the characterization of the Famine as having been 'a blessing'.[16]

Towards the end of his life, Train was increasingly volatile and his sanity was doubted.[17] Regardless, in 1902, then in his 70s, he wrote his engaging autobiography, *My Life in Many States and in Foreign Lands*. He died, however, in 1904 of smallpox. His passing was noted in Ireland, the *Drogheda Argus and Leinster Journal* claiming that he had 'died of heart failure, at Mills Hotel, a cheap lodging house in New York'. They also pointed out that his publications had included 'Irish Independence'.[18] The notice in the *Freeman's Journal* simply noted that he was 'the pioneer of tramways in this country'.[19] The following day, however, they published an addendum stating:

> The obituary notices of Mr. George Francis Train contain, so far as we are aware, no reference to a chapter in his career in Dublin, where he was for a considerable time in the 'sixties of the last century, a prisoner for debt in the Four Courts, in Marshalsea.[20]

Although not remembered for his poetry, Train was immortalized in literature, he being the model for the character of Phileas Fogg in Jules Verne's *Around the World in Eighty Days*. Train, an intrepid circumnavigator of the globe, had already completed this journey in 1870 in only 72 days.[21]

## GEORGE FRANCIS TRAIN, EPIGRAM ON *THREE CHEERS FOR THE FAMINE* IN GEORGE FRANCIS TRAIN, *THE PEOPLE'S CANDIDATE FOR PRESIDENT, 1872* (NEW YORK: S.N., 1872)

A Voice—'Three cheers for the Famine'
Mr Disraeli—'Well you have given three cheers *for things before this* THAT HAVE NOT DONE SO MUCH GOOD AS THE FAMINE'.
Disraeli at Aylesbury.

> It makes the blood of manhood boil,
> To see the Saxon serpent coil,
> Around these children of the soil,
>    *Three cheers for the Famine!*
> Two millions perished for want of bread,
> No Irish *Green* round their bed,
> The very clay was draped in *Red*,
>    *Three cheers for the Famine!*
> We live as slaves, but die as braves,
> In exile or beneath the waves,
> Or drop down into Pauper's graves,
>    *Three cheers for the Famine!*
> Not dogs in kennel or hog in pens,
> But Irish children, women and men,
> Starved to death in bog and fen,
>    *Three cheers for the Famine!*
> See that young girl with fading eye,
> Goodbye Mother, Please don't cry,
> Goodbye Father, let me die,
>    *Three cheers for the Famine!*
> God in heaven will give you cheer,

Death will dry starvation's tear,
Goodbye, brothers and sisters dear.

## Notes

1 Walter McGrath, *Tram Tracks Through Cork* (Cork: Tower Books, 1981); 'Sir Clifton Robinson', Frank Moore Colby et al, *The New International Year Book* (New York: Dodd, Mead and Company, 1911), p. 632.
2 Speech of George Francis Train on Irish independence and English neutrality: delivered before the Fenian Congress and Fenian chiefs, at the Philadelphia Academy of Music, 18 October 1865, in the presence of 6,000 persons (Philadelphia: T.B. Peterson and Bros, 1865).
3 'Arrest of George Francis Train', *Sydney Morning Herald*, 21 March 1868.
4 Patricia G. Holland, 'George Francis Train and the Woman Suffrage Movement, 1867–70', *Books at Iowa* 46 (April 1987), 8–29, at www./ir.uiowa.edu/bai/vol46/iss1/3/, accessed 2 March 2017.
5 'Arrest of George Francis Train', *Sydney Morning Herald*, 21 March 1868.
6 'Train's Second Arrest. He is conveyed to a debtors' Prison', *Daily Alta California*, vol. 20, 18 April 1868.
7 George Francis Train, *My Life in Many States and in Foreign Lands* (D. Appleton, 1902), p. 314.
8 George Francis Train and John Wesley Nichols, *The People's Candidate for President, 1872* (New York?: s.n., 1872), p. 80.
9 Ibid.
10 Ibid., Train, 'Dedicated to the Irish Republic', p. 78.
11 Ibid., p. 79.
12 *Times*, 20 November 1868.
13 The *Spectator*, 21 November 1868.
14 George Grey (1812–1898) had an Irish mother. As a young soldier, he served in Ireland where he was appalled by the poverty of the people, seeing emigration, and the breakup of large estates as a solution
15 Debate in House of Representatives, *Parliamentary Debates: Legislative Council and House of Representatives*, vol. 32 (New Zealand: W.A.G. Skinner, Government Printer, 1879), 7 October 1879, pp. 165–166.
16 This wording was used by James Delahunty (1808–1885), the Liberal (later Home Rule) MP for Waterford City during a debate on the Land Bill on 5 April 1870, Thomas Curson Hansard, *Hansard's Parliamentary Debates for March and April 1870* (London: Cornelius Buck, 1870), pp 1305–1306.
17 Clark Bell, *Speech . . . upon the Inquiry as to the Sanity or Insanity of George Francis Train* (New York: Russell Bros., 1873); 'George Francis Train Not to be Sent to an Insane Asylum', *New York Times*, 27 March 1873.
18 'Death of George Francis Train', *Drogheda Argus and Leinster Journal*, 23 January 1904.
19 *Freeman's Journal*, 20 January 1904.
20 Ibid., 21 January 1904.
21 'Death of George Francis Train. Eccentric Author Passes away in New York', *Los Angeles Herald*, 19 January 1904.

# BIBLIOGRAPHY

Angel-Perez, E., and A. Poulain (eds), *Hunger on the Stage* (Newcastle: Cambridge Scholars, 2009).
Austin Bourke, P. M., *The Visitation of God? The Potato and the Great Irish Famine* (Dublin: Lilliput Press, 1993).
Benson, A. C., and R. B. B. Esher (eds), *The Letters of Queen Victoria: A Selection From Her Majesty's Correspondence Between the Years 1837 and 1862*, 3 vols (London: John Murray, 1907).
Bradshaw, B., 'Nationalism and historical scholarship in Ireland', *Irish Historical Studies*, xxvi (November 1989), pp. 329–351.
Brady, C. (ed.), *Worsted in the Game: Losers in Irish History* (Dublin: Lilliput Press, 1989).
Broderick, E., 'The Famine and religious controversy in waterford, 1847–1850', *Decies*, 51 (1995), pp. 11–24.
Campbell, P., *Death in Templecrone – an Account of the Famine Years in Northwest Donegal, 1845–1850* (Jersey City, NY: Princeton Academic Press, 1995).
Clarkson, L. A., P. S. Ell, and L. Kennedy, *Mapping the Great Irish Famine: An Atlas of the Famine Years* (Dublin: Four Courts Press, 1999).
Coogan, T. P., *The Famine Plot, England's Role in Ireland's Greatest Tragedy* (London: Palgrave Macmillan, 2012).
Corporaal, M., 'Memories of the Great Famine and ethnic identity in novels by Victorian Irish women writers', *English Studies*, 90.2 (2009), pp. 142–156.
——, *Relocated Memories: The Great Famine in Irish and Diaspora Fiction, 1846–1870* (Syracuse, NY: Syracuse University Press, 2017).
Crawford, M. (ed.), *Famine. The Irish Experience 900 to 1900. Subsistence Crises and Famines in Ireland* (Edinburgh: John MacDonald, 1989).
Crowley, J., W. J. Smyth, and M. Murphy (eds), *The Atlas of the Great Irish Famine, 1845–52* (Cork: Cork University Press, 2011).
Cusack, G., and S. Goss (eds), *Hungry Words: Images of Famine in the Irish Canon* (Dublin: Irish Academic Press, 2006).
Daly, M. E., *The Famine in Ireland* (Dundalk: Dublin Historical Association, 1986).
Deane, S., *Strange Country: Modernity and Nationhood in Irish Writing Since 1790* (Oxford: Clarendon Press, 1997).
—— (ed.), *The Field Day Anthology of Irish Writing* (Derry: Field Day, 1991).
Devereux, S., *Theories of Famine* (New York: Harvester Wheatsheaf, 1994).
Dickson, D., *Artic Ireland: The Extraordinary Story of the Great Frost and Forgotten Famine of 1740–41* (Belfast: White Row Press, 1997).

## BIBLIOGRAPHY

Dillon, W., *Life of John Mitchel*, 2 vols (London: Kegan Paul, Trench and Co., 1888).

Donnelly, Jr., J. S., 'The Great Famine and its interpreters, old and new', *History Ireland*, 1.3 (Autumn 1993), pp. 27–33.

———, *The Great Irish Potato Famine* (Gloucestershire: Sutton, 2002).

Dorian, H., B. Mac Suibhne, and D. Dickson, *The Outer Edge of Ulster: A Memoir of Social Life in Nineteenth-Century Donegal* (Notre Dame, IN: University of Notre Dame Press, 2001).

Eagleton, T., *Heathcliff and the Great Hunger* (London: Verso, 1995).

———, 'The ideology of Irish studies', *Bullán: An Irish Studies Journal*, 3.1 (Spring 1997), pp. 5–14.

Edwards, R. D., and T. D. Williams (eds), *The Great Famine: Studies in Irish History 1845–52* (Dublin: Browne and Nolan, 1956).

Esse, J. S., *Hunger* (Dublin: The Candle Press, 1918).

Fegan, M., 'The traveller's experience of Famine Ireland', *Irish Studies Review*, 9.3 (2001), pp. 361–371.

———, *Literature and the Irish Famine, 1845–1919* (Oxford: Clarendon Press, 2002).

Foster, R., 'We are all revisionists now', *The Irish Review*, 1 (1986), pp. 1–5.

Fry, E., *James Hack Tuke: A Memoir* (London: Palgrave Macmillan, 1899).

Geary, L. M., *Medicine and Charity in Ireland, 1718–1851* (Dublin: University College Dublin Press, 2005).

Geber, J., *Victims of Ireland's Great Famine: The Bioarchaeology of Mass Burials at Kilkenny Union Workhouse* (Gainesville, FL: University Press of Florida, 2015).

Gillissen, C., 'Charles Trevelyan, John Mitchel et l'historiographie de la Grande Famine [Charles Trevelyan, John Mitchel and the historiography of the Great Famine]', *La grande famine en irlande, 1845–1851*, XIX-2 (2014), pp. 195–212.

Gleeson, D. T., 'Failing to "unite with the abolitionists": The Irish Nationalist Press and U.S. emancipation', *Geographies of Race*, 37.3; *Ireland, Slavery, Anti-Slavery and Empire*, 37 (2016), pp. 622–637.

Gooch, G. P., *The Later Correspondence of Lord John Russell 1840–1878*, Vol. 1 (London: Longmans, Green & Co., 1925).

Goodbody, R., *A Suitable Channel: Quaker Relief in the Great Famine* (Dublin: Pale Publishing, 1995).

Gray, P., 'National humiliation and the Great Hunger: Fast and Famine in 1847', *Irish Historical Studies*, 21.126 (November 2000), pp. 193–216.

———, *Famine, Land and Politics: British Government and Irish Society, 1843–50* (Dublin: Irish Academic Press, 2001).

Gribben, A. (ed.), *The Great Famine and the Irish Diaspora* (Amherst, MA: University of Massachusetts, 1999).

Haines, R., *Charles Trevelyan and the Great Irish Famine* (Dublin: Four Courts Press, 2004).

Hart, J., 'Sir Charles Trevelyan at the treasury', *English Historical Review*, LXXXV (1960), pp. 92–110.

Hassard, J. R. G., *Life of the Most Reverend John Hughes, D.D.: First Archbishop of New York*, Part 4 (New York: D. Appleton & Co., 1866).

Hayden, T., *Irish Hunger: Personal Reflections on the Legacy of the Famine* (Colorado: Roberts Rinehart, 1997).

Healy, G., *The Black Stranger: A Play in Three Acts* (Dublin: James Duffy, 1950).

Hickey, P., *The Famine in West Cork: The Mizen Peninsula, Land and People* (Cork: Mercier Press, 2002).

Kelly, J., 'Scarcity and poor relief in eighteenth-century Ireland: The subsistence crisis of 1782–4', *Irish Historical Studies*, 28.109 (May 1992), pp. 38–62.

Kerr, D., *A Nation of Beggars: Priests, People and Politics in Famine Ireland* (Oxford: Clarendon Press, 1994).

Killen, W. D., *Memoir of Dr John Edgar* (Belfast: C. Aitchison, 1867).

Kinealy, C., *A Death-Dealing Famine: The Great Hunger* (London: Pluto Press, 1997).

———, *The Great Irish Famine: Impact, Ideology and Rebellion* (London: Palgrave Macmillan, 2002).

———, *This Great Calamity: The Irish Famine 1845–52* (Dublin: Gill and Macmillan, 1994; Repub. 2006).

———, *Repeal and Revolution. 1848 in Ireland* (Manchester: Manchester University Press, 2009).

Kinealy, C., Jason King, and Ciarán Reilly (eds), *Women and the Great Hunger* (Hamden, CT and Cork: Quinnipiac University Press and Cork University Press, 2017).

Kinealy, C., and G. MacAtasney, *The Hidden Famine: Hunger, Poverty and Sectarianism in Belfast* (London: Pluto Press, 2000).

Kinealy, C., and J. Walsh, *The Bad Times: An Droch Shaol* (Hamden, CT: Quinnipiac University Press, 2015; Dublin: Coiscéim, 2016).

Lawless, V., *Personal Recollections of the Life and Times, With Extracts From the Correspondence of Valentine Lord Cloncurry* (Dublin: James McGlashan; London: W.S. Orr, 1849).

MacAtasney, G., *The Famine in Lurgan/Portadown* (Belfast: Beyond the Pale, 1997).

———, *The Other Famine: The 1822 Crisis in County Leitrim* (Stroud: History Press, 2011).

MacDonough, T., *Was Ireland a Colony? Economy, Politics, Ideology and Culture in Nineteenth-Century Ireland* (Dublin: Irish Academic Press, 2005).

MacHale, T., *Correspondence Between the Most Rev. Dr MacHale, Archbishop of Tuam and the Most Rev. Dr Murray, Archbishop of Dublin, Relative to an Address to Be Presented to Her Majesty Queen Victoria, on the Occasion of Her Visit to Ireland in 1849* (Dublin: M.H. Gill, 1885).Mahon Lord, and E. Cardwell, *Memoirs of the Right Honorable Sir Robert Peel* (London: John Murray, 1857).

Malcolm, E., 'On fire: The Great Hunger: Ireland 1845–1849', *New Hibernian Review*, 12.4 (Winter 2008), pp. 143–148.

Mark-FitzGerald, E., *Commemorating the Irish Famine: Memory and the Monument* (Oxford: Oxford University Press, 2015).

McDowell, R. B., *McDowell on McDowell: A Memoir* (Dublin: Lilliput Press, 2012).

McGovern, B. P., *John Mitchel: Irish Nationalist, Southern Secessionist* (Knoxville, TN: University of Tennessee Press, 2009).

McLean, S. J., *The Event and Its Terrors: Ireland, Famine, Modernity* (Palo Alto, CA: Stanford University Press, 2004).

Moody, T. W., 'Irish history and Irish mythology', *Hermathena*, University of Dublin, 124 (1978), pp. 1–24.

Moran, G., and N. O Muraile (eds), *Mayo: History and Society* (Dublin: Geography Publications, 2015).

Morris, H., *Portrait of a Chef: The Life of Alexis Soyer, Sometime Chef to the Reform Club* (Cambridge: Cambridge University Press, 1938).

Murphy, M. O., *Compassionate Stranger: Asenath Nicholson and the Great Irish Famine* (Syracuse, NY: Syracuse University Press, 2015).

Nally, D. P., *Human Encumbrances: Political Violence and the Great Irish Famine* (Notre Dame, IN: University of Notre Dame Press, 2011).

Nicholls, *A History of the Irish Poor Law: In Connexion With the Condition of the People* (London: John Murray, 1856).

Noack, C., L. Janssen, and V. Comerford (eds), *Holodomor and Gorta Mór: Histories, Memories and Representations of Famine in Ukraine and Ireland* (London: Anthem Press, 2012).

Northend, C. (ed.), *Elihu Burritt: A Memorial Volume Containing a Sketch of His Life and Labors With Selections From His Writings and Lectures, and Extracts From His Private Journals in Europe and America* (New York: D. Appleton & Co., 1879).

O'Brien, G., *An Economic History of Ireland From the Union to the Famine* (London: Longmans, Green & Co., 1921).

O'Brien, W. B., *The Great Famine in Ireland and a Retrospect of the Fifty Years 1845–95, With a Sketch of the Present Condition and Future Prospects of the Congested Districts* (London: Downey, 1896).

O Cioséin, N., 'Was there "silence" about the Famine?', *Irish Studies Review*, 13 (Winter 1995–96), pp. 7–10.

Odling, E. M. S., *Memoir of the Late Alfred Smee, F.R.S. by His Daughter, With a Selection From His Miscellaneous Writings* (London: George Bell and Sons, 1878).

Ó Gráda, C., 'Making history in the Ireland of the 1940s and 1950s: The saga of the Great Famine', *The Irish Review*, 12 (Spring/Summer 1992), pp. 87–107.

———, *An Drochshaol: Béaloideas agus Amhráin* (Baile Atha Cliath: Coiscéim, 1994).

———, *Black '47 and Beyond: The Great Irish Famine in History, Economy, and Memory* (Princeton, NJ: Princeton University Press, 2000).

———, *Famine: A Short History* (Princeton, NJ: Princeton University Press, 2010).

O'Herlihy, T., *The Famine, 1845–47: A Survey of Its Ravages and Causes* (Dublin: St Peter's Phibsboro, 1947).

Ó Murchadha, C., *The Great Famine: Ireland's Agony 1845–1852* (London: Hambledon Continuum, 2011).

———, *Figures in a Famine Landscape* (London: Bloomsbury Press, 2016).

O'Rourke, J., *The Great Irish Famine* (Dublin: Veritas Publications, 1989; First pub. in 1874).

Póirtéir, C. (ed.), *Famine Echoes* (Dublin: Gill and Macmillan, 1995).

———, *The Great Irish Famine* (Cork: Mercier Press, 1997).

Reilly, C., *Strokestown and the Great Irish Famine* (Dublin: Irish Academic Press, 2014).

Schultz, M., *Haunted Histories: The Rhetoric of Ideology in Postcolonial Irish Fiction* (Manchester: Manchester University Press, 2014).

Sen, A., *Poverty and Famines: An Essay on Entitlement and Deprivation* (Oxford: Oxford University Press, 1981).

Smart, R., *Black Roads: The Famine in Irish Literature* (Hamden, CT and Cork: Quinnipiac University Press and Cork University Press, 2015).

Somerville, A., *Letters From Ireland During the Famine of 1847* (Dublin: Irish Academic Press, 1995).

Somerville-Large, L. B., 'Dublin's eye hospitals in the 19th century', *Dublin Historical Record*, 20.1 (December 1964), pp. 19–28.

Tóibín, C., and D. Ferriter, *The Irish Famine: A Documentary* (London: Profile Books, 1999).

Thompson, S., 'Famine travel: Irish tourism from the Great Famine to decolonization', in Benjamin Colbert (ed.), *Travel Writing and Tourism in Britain and Ireland* (London: Palgrave Macmillan, 2011), pp. 164–180.

Valone, D. (ed.), *Ireland's Great Hunger: Relief, Representation, and Remembrance* (Lanham, MD: University Press of America, 2009).

Valone, D., and C. Kinealy (eds), *Memory, Silence and Commemoration: Ireland's Great Hunger* (Lanham, MD: University Press of America, 2002).

Various authors, *Famine Folios* (Hamden, CT and Cork: Quinnipiac University Press and Cork University Press, 2015).

Williamson, P., 'State prayers, fasts and thanksgivings: Public worship in Britain 1830–1897', *Past and Present*, 200.1 (2008), pp. 121–174.

Woodham-Smith, C., *The Great Hunger, 1845–49* (London: Hamish Hamilton, 1962).

## Primary Sources

Bennett, W., *Narrative of a Recent Journey of Six Weeks in Ireland: In Connexion With the Subject of Supplying Small Seed to Some of the Remoter Districts* (Dublin: Charles Gilpin, 1847).

### British Parliamentary Papers

*British Relief Association for the Relief of Extreme Distress in Ireland and Scotland* (London: Richard Clay, 1849).

Butt, I., *A Voice for Ireland, the Famine in the Land: What Has Been Done and What Is to Be Done* (Dublin: James McGlashan, 21 D'Olier-Street; London: William S. Ore and Co., 147; Edinburgh: Fraser and Co., 1847).

### Dublin Medical Press

Dufferin, F. T. B., and G. F. Boyle, *Narrative of a Journey From Oxford to Skibbereen During the Year of the Irish Famine* (Oxford: John Henry Parker, 1847).

Edgar, J., *An Appeal on Behalf of the Home Mission of the General Assembly of the Presbyterian Church in Ireland, Respectfully Addressed to Their Christian Brethren of All Evangelical Denominations in America* (Belfast, 1847).

———, *The Women of the West: Ireland Helped to Help Herself* (Belfast: Banner of Ulster Office, 1849).

Edgeworth, M., *Tour in Connemara and the Martins of Ballinahinch* (London: Constable, 1950).

Elihu Burritt Papers, New Britain Library, New Britain, CT.

Fisher, L. J. L., *Letters From the Kingdom of Kerry in the Year 1845* (Dublin: Webb and Chapman, 1847).

Hughes, J., *A Lecture on the Antecedent Causes of the Irish Famine in 1847: Delivered Under the Auspices of the General Committee for the Relief of the Suffering Poor of Ireland By the Right Rev. John Hughes, D.D., Bishop of New York, at the Broadway Tabernacle, March 20th, 1847* (New York: Edward Dunigan, 1847).

### Hansard

Hole, S., *A Little Tour in Ireland: Being a Visit to Dublin, Galway, Connamara, Athlone, Limerick, Killarney, Glengarriff, Cork, etc. etc, by an Oxonian. With Illustrations by John Leech* (London: Bradbury and Evans, 1859).

## BIBLIOGRAPHY

Irish Almanac and Official Directory

Irish Relief Association for the Destitute Peasantry, *Distress in Ireland* (Dublin: P. D. Hardy, 1847).

Letter Books of the Earl of Clarendon, Bodleian Library, Oxford.

Letters of 'Eva' of the *Nation*, National Library of Ireland, MS. 10,498.

Letters of Jenny Mitchel, Manuscripts and Archives Division, The New York Public Library, New York.

Malthus, T. R., *An Essay on the Principle of Population as It Affects the Future Improvement of Society: With Remarks on the Speculations of Mr. Godwin, M. Condorcet and Other Writers* (London: J. Johnson, 1798).

Mansion House Committee, *Report of the Mansion House Committee on the Potato Disease* (Dublin: J. Browne, 1846).

Martineau, H., *Letters From Ireland* (London: John Chapman, 1852).

Minutes of British Relief Association, National Library of Ireland, Dublin.

Mitchel, J., *Jail Journal, or Five Years in British Prisons* (New York: Office of the Citizen, 1854).

―――, *The Last Conquest of Ireland, Perhaps* (Dublin: Irishman Office, 1861).

National College of Art, *Thomas Davis and the Young Ireland Movement Centenary: Exhibition of Pictures of Irish Historical Interest* (Dublin: Alexander Thom, 1946).

New England Relief Committee Papers, Special Archives and Collections, Liverpool University, Liverpool.

Newspaper – various, both hard copy and digital.

Nicholls, G., *Eight Letters on the Management of Our Poor, and the General Administration of the Poor Laws: In Which Is Shewn the System That Has Been Adopted, and the Saving in the Poor Rates, Which Has Recently Been Affected in the Two Parishes of Southwell and Bingham, in the County of Nottingham, Respectfully Offered to the Consideration of Magistrates, and Earnestly Recommended to the Attention of all Parish Officers* (Newark: S. and J. Ridge, 1822).

Nicholson, A., *Annals of the Famine in Ireland, in 1847, 1848, and 1849* (New York: French, 1851).

*Parliamentary Debates: Legislative Council and House of Representatives*, Vol. 32 (New Zealand: W.A.G. Skinner, Government Printer, 1879).

Papers of Lord John Russell, National Archives of England, Richmond.

Papers of Queen Victoria, Windsor Castle, Windsor.

Smee, A., *The Potatoe Plant, Its Uses and Properties: Together With the Cause of the Present Malady* (London: Longmans, Green & Co., 1846).

Society of Friends, *Transactions of the Central Relief Committee During the Famine in Ireland in 1846 and 1847* (Dublin: Hodges and Figgis, 1852).

Train, G. F., and J. W. Nichols, *The People's Candidate for President, 1872* (New York?: s.n., 1872).

Trevelyan, C., 'The Irish crisis', *Edinburgh Review* (1848).

Wilde, W. R., *Irish Popular Superstitions* (Dublin: James McGlashan, 1852).

# KEYWORDS

alcohol
Anglican Church
art
averted births
Belfast
Belfast Ladies' Committee for Connaught
Bennett, William
Bentinck, Lord George
Bessborough, Lord John
blight
British army
British government
British Relief Association
Burritt, Elihu
Butt, Isaac
cannibalism
Carton Estate
census returns
Clarendon, Earl of
Cork City
County Clare
County Cork
County Kerry
County Mayo
Crawford, William Sharman
cultural impact of famine
de Valera, Éamon
Deane, Seamus
Devon Commission
disease
Disraeli, Benjamin

distressed unions
Dufferin, Lord
Edgar, Dr John
emigration
Encumbered Estates Acts
epigenetics
evangelicalism
evictions
export of food
famine of 1741
famines prior to 1845
Fisher, Lydia Jane
folklore
Forster, William
historians
historiography
Hole, Samuel
Hughes, Bishop John
*Illustrated London News*
India
Indian Corn
Kilrush
Ladies' Relief Committees
landlords
Literary Revival
literature
McHale, Bishop John
Mahon, Major
Mahony, James
Mansion House Committee
Mathew, Father Theobald
Maynooth College

medical doctors
memorialization
Mitchel, John
Monteagle, Lord
monuments
mortality
National Famine Commemoration Day
nationalism
navigation laws
Nicholls, George
Nicholson, Asenath
O'Brien, William Patrick
O'Brien, William Smith
O'Connell, Daniel
O'Herlihy, Father Timothy
O'Rourke, Canon John
parliament
Peel, Sir Robert
philanthropy
Playfair, Dr Lyon
Poor Enquiry, 1833–1836
Poor Laws
poor rates
Pope Pius IX
population
potatoes
Power, Alfred
prayer
proselytism
Protestantism
public works
Quarter-Acre Clause
Queen Victoria
questionnaires
Railway Bill
Rate in Aid
relief measures
religion
repeal

revisionism
Rothschild, Lionel de
Routh, Sir Randolph
Russell, Lord John
Scientific Commissioners
Scotland
Scrope, George Poulett
Second World War
seeds
sesquicentenary of Famine
Skibbereen
Sligo, Marquess of
Smee, Alfred
Society of Friends
soup kitchens
Soyer, Alexis
Speranza
starvation
Strokestown Estate
Strzelecki, Pawel (Paul)
Temporary Relief Act
theatre
Tóibín, Colm
Train, George Francis
Treasury
Trevelyan, Charles
Tuke, James Hack
Twisleton, Edward
United Kingdom
Vandeleur, Colonel
weather
Westport
Whately, Archbishop Richard
Wilde, William
women
Woodham-Smith, Cecil
workhouses
'Year of Slaughter'
Young Ireland